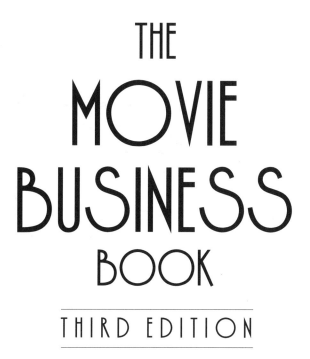

THE
MOVIE
BUSINESS
BOOK

THIRD EDITION

EDITED BY
JASON E. SQUIRE

Open University Press
McGraw-Hill Education
McGraw-Hill House
Shoppenhangers Road
Maidenhead
Berkshire
England
SL6 2QL

email: enquiries@openup.co.uk
world wide web: www.openup.co.uk

This edition first published in the USA by Simon & Schuster
First published 2006

A catalogue record of this book is available from the British Library

ISBN-10: 0 335 22002 9 (pb) 0 335 22003 7 (hb)
ISBN-13: 978 0 335 22002 1 (pb) 978 0 335 22003 8 (hb)

Library of Congress Cataloging-in-Publication Data
CIP data applied for

Typeset by Fakenham Photosetting Limited, Fakenham, Norfolk
Printed in Great Britain by Bell & Bain Ltd, Glasgow

For Tari, my love

CONTENTS

I. THE CREATORS

II. THE PROPERTY

VI. PRODUCTION

VII. MARKETING

VIII. THE REVENUE STREAMS

IX. THEATRICAL DISTRIBUTION

X. THEATRICAL EXHIBITION

XI. HOME VIDEO

XII. CONSUMER PRODUCTS

XIII. INTERNATIONAL

XIV. THE FUTURE

For moviegoers and movie makers,
and to everyone who has two businesses—
their own and the movie business.

THANK-YOUS

Movies are collaborative and so is this book.

First and foremost, my deepest gratitude goes to the contributors. These extraordinary professionals took considerable time out of their business lives to make their articles as empowering as possible for the readers. It was joyous to spend time with those returning to revise their articles, and also to work with new participants.

Every article was created exclusively for this book. In this third edition, more than half are new, and the others have been meticulously updated. That's the technical side; on the personal side, these collaborations have fostered friendships and admiration.

None of this would have worked as smoothly as it did without the care and kindness of these good people:

Bill Anderson, Rosie Arnold, Maryanne Benane, Tom Campanella, Lillian Cano, Carole Cosgrove, Michele Cournoyer, David Davis, Ronna Dolin, Elyse Eisenberg, Steve Elzer, Kim Gilligan, Flo Grace, Michael Hagemeyer, Jeff Hall, Keizo Kabata, Richard Lorber, Justin Manask, Michael Mand, Eric Marti, Martin Meyers, Armando Nunez, Claire Ollstein, Rick Olshansky, Donna Ostroff, D. Barry Reardon, Joyce Rome, Jon Shaughnessy, Donna Smith, Ray Strache, Don Tannenbaum, Neil Watson and Jennifer Yale.

Others who know how helpful they were during the process are Walter C. Squire, Beverly Taylor and Hal Vogel; Doris Cooper of Simon & Schuster / Fireside; Gary Hiller of Movie Magic Technologies, Inc.; Mary Ann Grasso, Executive Director of the National Association of Theatre Owners, whose support of the book has been unwavering over the years;

and those students who prove each semester why it's been wonderful serving on the adjunct faculty at the USC School of Cinema-Television.

For their insights and suggestions about new contributors, deep thanks go to Josef Adalian, Benjamin S. Feingold, Dr. Raymond Fielding, Joe Flint, Dr. Sam Grogg, Nancy Juvonen, Warren Lieberfarb and Van Wallach.

For the production paperwork article on *Charlie's Angels* by Christina Fong, all materials furnished are courtesy of Columbia Pictures, which was gracious in granting permission to reprint the samples, as were the *Charlie's Angels* creative team of Drew Barrymore, Nancy Juvonen and McG. This all stemmed from their appearing as guest speakers in my case study class (CTPR 386) on *Charlie's Angels* at the USC School of Cinema-Television.

It's a pleasure to thank John Schulman of Warner Bros. for allowing samples of distribution illustrations in Dan Fellman's article.

Deep bows to John Trevor Wolff for his computer expertise; and to *Leonard Maltin's Movie & Video Guide,* Box Office Mojo (boxofficemojo. com), Internet Movie Database (IMDb.com) and of course the powerful Google search engine, all for answers to research questions at a moment's notice. Visit the official *Movie Business Book* Web site at www.movie businessbook.com.

Special appreciation goes to Thomas D. Selz of the law firm of Frankfurt, Kurnit, Klein & Selz, New York, who years ago rescued the ambition of this book by organizing an effort to allow me to pursue a broader, more thorough approach to the subject. Richard B. Heller of the same firm was a wonderful advocate as well. Joan Brandt of the Sterling Lord Agency in New York was instrumental in finding a publisher.

For her love and understanding throughout, a big hug goes to my dear, sweet wife, Tari Susan Hartman.

See you at the movies. . . .

JES
West Los Angeles, California

PREFACE TO THE INTERNATIONAL EDITION

BY JASON E. SQUIRE

Warm greetings to the global reader. Your interest in this field reflects a new, international movie and media business taking hold as boundaries and barriers are falling and more venues for different kinds of visual expression are emerging.

It's an exciting time for the entrepreneurial person working in or planning to work in media: a time of transition from analogue to digital; a time when types of media are morphing; a time when traditional business models are changing, removing the intermediary by placing buyer and seller in direct contact via the Internet; a time when boundaries are fading, making product highly transportable in a world hungry for visual expression. This harks back to the origins of movies when, in silent form, they were highly exportable, with no language barrier.

Although this book was created in the United States, it was intended to be used around the world. Full credit for recognizing and achieving this intention goes to Christopher Cudmore, senior commissioning editor for media, film and cultural studies at Open University Press McGraw-Hill.

The entertainment business is global, in spite of efforts to protect local product. The descriptions of business practices, deal points, relationships and strategic decisions herein will be similar to the ones you will encounter wherever you are based, since many agreements and concepts can be traced back to their origins in American models. Financial examples are expressed in US dollars, so to apply things to your own experience, simply convert the dollar examples in this book to local currency.

THE GLOBAL VIEW

With the US movie industry now mature, the markets outside the US, dynamic and fascinating, represent the growth part of the global industry. Some countries are bypassing cable, with its labour-intensive infrastructure, and moving to satellite, computer and mobile phone for communication and entertainment. Any list of the most popular movies or TV shows in a given country show that an increasing number are home-grown (although studio products still tend to dominate).

Entrepreneurial talents are making more movies and other visual entertainment than ever before. Some examples of this local product, with a power to engage, happen to possess intangible elements of universal appeal. At this point, business kicks in. Ideally, this product is identified via word-of-mouth by scouts for international distributors whose job is to seek out examples that are exportable, that can easily travel. In this process, a most fascinating, timeless entertainment judgment is being applied: the simple, vulnerable, subjective human instinct as to whether a given product can, through business transactions, transform this intangible entertainment value into revenue.

A map of this process is at the heart of this book.

Because a growing number of centres of culture are contributing their movies or other product to the global business system, curious viewers in many countries have the advantage of enjoying such movies, and, happily, the process slowly chips away whatever cultural or social barriers that might have existed. After all, the visual language of movies has always been universal.

At the same time, the process benefits customers and practitioners. Customers become more energetic in seeking out obscure product, in theatres, on video or on the Web, and then those titles can become mainstream. As a result, talented practitioners are inspired to stretch their creativity to make projects in an increasingly vibrant system. Based on commercial or aesthetic success, such talented people are invited to their next job, wherever in the world it is shooting, thereby joining the itinerant global community of media artists. They, too, simply apply their subjective, creative instincts and time will tell whether their product will travel. (This is confirmed every semester, as more international students take my classes at the USC School of Cinema-Television, representing the next generation of global media practitioners whose work will have an enormous impact on screens large and small, and on the World Wide Web.)

THE WORLD WIDE WEB

WWW: A vast, thriving, borderless, virtual society. In commerce and communication, the Internet eliminates an intermediary. Everything is direct. This acts as a template for future media transactions (and future societies, as well). In media, the traditional intermediary is the distribution entity that extracts a small percentage or fee from each transaction for linking the seller to buyer. The Web allows for sellers and buyers to be easily connected. When applied to media, any creator can initiate direct-to-customer transactions on the Web, reducing costs considerably.

This is arguably the best time in the history of visual media for anyone to enter or further one's career because the barriers to entry have nearly disappeared. You can shoot and edit a movie digitally in your home, then distribute it to the world on the Web. This allows for an open commerce of creators, dabblers and experimenters connecting with watchers, enhancers and customers, involving types of creative product as limitless as the imagination. It is the best of times for anyone willing to experiment with content and formats, and profitable cottage industries will develop from that. Video blogs and other expressions that become popular will lead to business models allowing for a return on investment, and profits as well. The tools and concepts needed to harness this are contained in this book.

THE PERSONAL SCREEN

A revolution is taking place in the way we see movies and the kind of movies we see. Certainly advanced digital projection and the social pleasure of community will keep people going to theatres in the time-honored search for a compelling story in the dark. Beyond that, a sweeping change will expand the way we see movies with the advent of the personal screen, or portable screen. Wireless, on-demand delivery will be directly to mobile phones, PDAs, video iPods, Playstations, video game screens, or other platforms that haven't yet emerged. As a result, consumer behaviour and habits will be changing and that takes time, perhaps another generation. Ultimately, this will mean new revenue streams for traditional movies or movie hybrids.

HYBRIDS

Entrepreneurs are working on new forms of entertainment for the Web; at the USC School of Cinema-Television, we have an entire division of students studying interactive media. New forms will have new names, expanding the universe of popular culture. For example, the manipulation of images and characters from a video game that exist outside the game with new dialogue performed by the at-home artist, goes by the hybrid name "machinima," marrying machine with cinema and using disciplines of theatre, music, radio and movies.

On the horizon is nothing less than the creative expansion and morphing of cinematic expression into new forms and experiences. There will be hybrid movies, whether experimental, memoir, subjective, objective, interactive, episodic, or styles which have not been invented yet, for entirely new niche markets.

What could be more exciting than that? The business challenge becomes whether or how to organize a subscription or other payment system so that new artists can produce and thrive in the Internet economy. Where will studios be in the face of these advances? If a measure is their reaction to the introduction of earlier technologies, such as television and home video, they will remain on the sidelines until a hungry, outsider entrepreneur scores a financial success. In addition, there will be competition from global Web-based players such as Google and Yahoo entering this new arena.

If the reader is as excited by all of this as the writer, you are ready for the journey offered by this book which will empower you to follow your instincts and take your place in the growing media marketplace.

PREFACE

This third edition is a major overhaul of *The Movie Business Book*, taking into account the vast changes in the business since the 1992 second edition.

A little history: Published by Prentice-Hall in 1983, *The Movie Business Book* was republished by Simon & Schuster's Touchstone imprint in 1986 and Fireside imprint in 1988. Its lineage traces back to the pioneering text *The Movie Business: American Film Industry Practice,* published by Hastings House in 1972; it was my privilege to work with Professor A. William Bluem as his coeditor on that book.

We began in 1970 and it was pretty discouraging at first. Early efforts to enlist industry experts were unsuccessful. One famous lawyer explained he was unwilling to share "industry secrets" and suggested that was the reason why no book on the movie business had been done. But there were enough worthy professionals who understood the need for such a work, and their expertise made *The Movie Business: American Film Industry Practice* the primary text in the field, adopted at universities all over the country.

The warm reception of that first book coincided with the growth of film study on campuses. Universities offering courses in movie production, history and aesthetics began to broaden their curricula to introduce the business of motion pictures as an interdisciplinary study often coordinated with law and business schools as part of a well-rounded treatment of mass communications and popular culture.

When Prof. Bluem died in 1974, I lost my mentor and good friend. A few years later, I rededicated myself to the work we started together. The result was the first edition of *The Movie Business Book* (1983), which came out in a favorable climate as well. Curiosity about the behind-the-scenes money dealings of the business was on the rise. TV viewers watching *Entertainment Tonight* and other programs became familiar with the latest weekend grosses and wanted to know more. The book was adopted as a text by professors who recognized its structure as a one-semester survey course. A growing international readership of students and professionals began inquiring about a second edition, which was published in 1992. By now, the work was translated into Japanese, Korean and German.

Readers have asked how this book is put together. It takes about three years. The pathway to a new edition proceeds on two parallel tracks: working with returning contributors and seeking out new ones. First, the decisions are made as to who should return in the new edition. Since the book's success is due to the contributors, they are locked in again as early as possible. Those who have retired have been gracious enough to recommend successors. The returning contributors revisit their articles with me, and we work hard to make them as current as possible. Sometimes, returning people want to do an entirely new article, and we work together on that.

Deciding on new topics and searching for new experts is the most challenging part of the process. It's a matter of instinct as to what new subjects to present and what voids to fill. After all, much has changed since the last edition. Finding a new expert is only half the battle; the ideal person must know how to clearly explain the subject and be comfortable with the back-and-forth inherent in the process. Most newcomers worked from my outlines, after deciding whether to write an essay or be interviewed for the core material. Then the results are debated and brooded over, honed and structured, rewritten and rewritten, as we engage in an exciting and delightful process, working closely and even obsessively, via e-mail and over the phone, to get the article right. I deeply appreciate each contributor's cooperation as additional material was added for teaching purposes.

A note on style: The contributors will often use terms that are interchangeable in industry jargon. A movie is a picture or a film, and a studio is a financier-distributor or a major. *Italics* are used to flag a definition; the term is usually defined in the same sentence. Any area of specialty develops its own sets of initials, separating the initiated from newcomers, and the entertainment industry is not immune to this; it's a world of acronyms. Every effort has been made to define and demystify acronyms as they appear.

Another big change is that there are hardly any statistics in this edition. That's due to the power of the Internet. Since any statistic is old upon publication, the reader is invited to surf the Web for the very latest numbers, data and other time-sensitive material.

The sequence of chapters covers the life span of a movie, with every section building upon the preceding one. After an orientation in Section One, chapters follow the outlay of money spent on the creative process of writing, financing, management, dealmaking, production and marketing. Then the study turns to money returning through revenue streams from theatres, home video, consumer products and international markets.

The format breaks down as follows:

I. *The Creators.* An orientation, this section focuses on the most visible of moviemakers. The producer, represented by David Puttnam, often chooses the story, does the hiring, is responsible for the money spent and is the chief executive on a picture, staying with it longer than anyone. The director, personified by Sydney Pollack, is the captain on the set, working closely with the producer on creative and business decisions. The director is usually the single artist most closely identified with the finished picture. The range of creators includes a comic genius, Mel Brooks, and a filmmaker who does it all himself, Henry Jaglom.

II. *The Property.* This section returns to the source of a movie's life. The work of the writer, discussed by William Goldman, is represented in the marketplace by a literary agent, such as Lee G. Rosenberg (one of the founders of Triad Artists), whose job is to sell the work so that it becomes property, in a process involving submission to a buyer often supported by a story editor such as Romy Kaufman of Universal. A movie deal might increase the property's value in published form, as outlined by literary consultant Roberta Kent and Joel Gotler of Joel Gotler & Associates.

III. *The Money.* Money spent for services rendered is the basis for almost all activity in the business. In this section, the practices of movie financing are examined. Trends in protecting investments and issues of increasing costs are examined by management consultant/lawyer Peter J. Dekom. Different types of financing, detailed by Norman H. Garey, include venture-capital strategies, delineated by AFI Conservatory Dean Sam L Grogg based on his experience as a principal of FilmDallas, and widen to an overview from entertainment industry analyst Harold L. Vogel of Vogel Capital Management in New York.

IV. *The Management.* The collective expertise responsible for decision-making is covered next. Movie executive philosophy is described from the unique vantage point of Tom Rothman, chairman of Fox Filmed Entertainment, interpreted by industry consultant Richard Lederer, and reflected upon by producer David V. Picker, president of worldwide production for Hallmark Entertainment, who has also served as president of United Artists, Paramount and Columbia Pictures. The independent tradition is outlined by UCLA Film, Television and Digital Media chair Barbara Boyle, based on her executive career.

V. *The Deal.* All major transactions are structured and set down in written agreements. The basic elements of every deal are: What is the property or service; who is providing it to whom; what is the time frame; and what is the compensation. A chief architect for many deals is the entertainment lawyer, personified by Norman H. Garey, who negotiates the picture deal on behalf of a producer-client with the financier-distributor's business affairs chief executive. Talent also is represented by agents and business affairs departments, exemplified by Stephen M. Kravit, executive vice president of the Gersh Agency. The producer would probably have to secure over-budget protection, as explained by Norman G. Rudman, Of Counsel at Stein & Flugge, LLP, and Lionel A. Ephraim, senior vice president, Cinema Completions International, and, in pursuit of specific talent, will have countless dealings with agents, as related by Jessica Tuchinsky of Creative Artists Agency.

VI. *Production.* All of the complex preparation and military-style logistical planning is played out in principal photography. Coordinating all the details is the daily responsibility of production management, recounted by Michael Grillo, head of feature film production at DreamWorks SKG. This includes the nuts-and-bolts paperwork generated by the director's unit, and specifically by second assistant directors such as Christina Fong (*Charlie's Angels*), which frees the director to create the necessary illusions with the other artists under constant pressures of time and money. Each year, hundreds of movies for television follow the same disciplines as theatrical film production, as revealed by former NBC executive Lindy DeKoven of DeKoven Entertainment.

VII. *Marketing.* Completing the movie is only half the battle. The entire enterprise is in financial peril unless the audience can be seduced to pay for experiencing it. Positioning the worldwide paying audience at the first point of sale—theatrical release—is the role of motion picture marketing, highlighted by Robert G. Friedman, vice chairman of the Motion Picture Group and chief operating officer of Paramount Pictures. Market research, a little-known world with great influence, is illuminated by Kevin Yoder, cochief operating officer of Nielsen NRG. Film festivals and markets are especially important to the positioning and selling of independent films, and the process is presented by festival consultant Steve Montal.

VIII. *The Revenue Streams.* This is the critical shift in the movie business model from money going out to money coming in. To understand the orderly "windows" of timed releases that comprise the exploitable life of a movie, the complete system is detailed and examined by Steven E. Blume, chief financial officer of Brillstein-Grey Entertainment.

IX. *Theatrical Distribution.* Distributors are the vital first link to the paying public. Part salesmen and part magicians, theatrical distribution executives carry on a love-hate relationship with exhibitors to get the product into theatres, while weighing, with marketing executives, the spending of advertising dollars against box-office revenue. Distribution companies range from studio financier-distributors such as Daniel R. Fellman, president of Warner Bros. Pictures Domestic Distribution in Burbank, to independents such as Bob Berney, president of Newmarket Films in New York. (On a personal note, it's a special pleasure to welcome Dan because his father, Nat D. Fellman, contributed to the first edition *Movie Business Book*, as founder of Exhibitor Relations Company and former president of National General Theatres, Inc., now Mann Theatres).

X. *Theatrical Exhibition.* Theatre owners are the first retailers in the movie business, with the earliest direct contact with customers. They are bound together with distributors by their need for each other. Similar business issues are shared by large theatre chains, as represented by Shari E. Redstone, president of National Amusements in Dedham, Massachusetts, and independent exhibitors such as Robert Laemmle of Laemmle Theatres in Los Angeles.

XI. *Home Video.* The most lucrative revenue stream is home video, detailed by Benjamin S. Feingold, president, business & operations, Columbia TriStar Motion Picture Group. The home-video retailer has undergone upheaval, and the process is delineated by Paul Sweeting, Washington, D.C.–based reporter and columnist for *Video Business* magazine. Made-for-video movies are a growing market, as described by Louis A. Feola, president of Universal Worldwide Home Entertainment.

XII. *Consumer Products.* The licensing and merchandising of titles or characters, especially from franchise movies, have become highly profitable forms of brand extension. But these deals are as speculative as any movie, since the products must be designed, made, shipped and stocked in thousands of retail stores well before the movie's release date. The relationship between the distributor-licensor and the manufacturer-licensee is described by Al Ovadia, executive vice president, Sony Pictures Consumer Products.

XIII. *International.* Movies are a global business, with more than half of a popular movie's money made outside the United States. The growing worldwide market is analyzed country-by-country in a detailed overview covering delivery systems and sources of revenue by international distribution consultant Rob Aft. Anyone becoming involved in coproductions or overseas picturemaking will come across overseas tax incentives and government subsidies, as outlined, market-by-market, by Steven Gerse, vice president, business and legal affairs, Walt Disney Pictures.

XIV. *The Future.* In a world where technological advances occur at breakneck speed, it's important to understand the origins and development of entertainment machinery to fully appreciate where they are heading. A comprehensive review of media technology past, present and future links the related pathways of movies, television, home video, music, the Internet and other media as analyzed by futurist and *Millimeter* magazine senior editor Dan Ochiva in New York.

This book sets out to shed light on the entire spectrum of feature moviemaking and related businesses. The idea is to cover this territory from the first-hand vantage points of specialists on the industry front lines, as a service to moviegoers and moviemakers. From this flow other purposes: to reveal the pressures and priorities of business decisions that affect the final product shown in local theatres and at home; to acquaint people working in any one part of the business with how their jobs relate to the wider industry; to remove misconceptions or resistance about the money side of movies; and to act as a record of current industry attitudes and practices that may take on new interest with the passage of time.

If the reader gains a basic understanding of how the movie business works and enjoys the journey along the way, these goals will have been fulfilled.

THE
MOVIE
BUSINESS
BOOK

INTRODUCTION

BY JASON E. SQUIRE

This book is all about the business side of movies. Spawned over a century ago, motion pictures matured in one generation into a complex mixture of art and commerce, capturing the imaginations of worldwide audiences and having a profound impact on behavior, culture, politics and economics.

At its simplest, the feature film is the arranging of light images to win hearts in dark rooms. At its most complex, it is a massive venture of global commerce, a vast creative enterprise requiring the logistical discipline of the military, the financial forecasting of the Federal Reserve, and the gambling instinct of wildcat oil drillers, all harnessed in private hands on behalf of the telling of a story. The profit motive is at work here, but the formula that attracts audiences is as speculative, uncertain and elusive as can be.

MOVIES AS PRODUCT

To the new reader, a warm welcome.

To the returning reader, there have been profound changes in the movie business since our last time together.

The theatrical market has shifted from a profit center to a loss leader.

The industry is in transition from analog to digital. This changeover is complete in postproduction. A growing number of movies are also being shot digitally, and digital projection can be found in major cities while distributors and theatre owners continue to debate its value.

The biggest change since our last visit is that movies are no longer stand-alone amusements. Rather, they are an important piece in a complex mosaic of marketing and reincarnations into a variety of products, each using the movie's title or brand. The ideal product mix based on one project would flow through various divisions of one of the global entertainment companies that today control the studios: through movies, home video, television, books, music, video games, toys and other consumer products. On a more realistic basis, every movie is a prototype that of course does not lend itself to such crossover. But that won't stop efforts at synergy, which will succeed or fail due to the whims of the marketplace. At its core, any movie investment is speculative, high risk, and at the mercy of customers.

The simple choice of going to the movies in theatres faces more competition than ever, because it involves leaving home. Think about all the alternative recreational choices out of the house: sports (playing or watching), exercise, concerts, shopping, dining, museums, sightseeing or just plain lounging, among others. Now consider all the choices that keep customers at home: the Internet (for surfing, chatting or commerce), video games, studying (for business or school), eating, watching TV or DVDs, reading, listening to music or just "a quiet evening at home." With these competing pressures in place when targeted audience members decide what to do some evening, it's no wonder that movie marketing costs— spent to induce one specific choice out of a cluttered marketplace—are growing exponentially.

A related issue is time. Time is finite, but the alternatives to fill it are infinite. A movie usually takes two hours of one's time. With competing recreational choices inside or outside the home often delivering similar value in less time (or in smaller, more controllable portions), movies are under more pressure than ever before.

A motion picture is an extremely perishable commodity. It lives and has value as long as it is on people's minds or in their frame of reference. The public's perception of an average movie's value decreases as access to it increases and as it ages. A successful movie can remain in theatrical release for six months or more, while a failure can be gone from theatre screens in two weekends, as an impatient audience goes on to the "next big thing." After the theatrical run, movies are sold as home videos, producing revenue that can meet or exceed their box office grosses. Later, movies enjoy rejuvenated value each time they are sold in libraries of product, reaching new audiences in other countries.

There is worldwide interest in opening weekend box office grosses, much like the tracking of a weekly horse race. (What product outside popular culture trumpets weekly sales figures to the press?) But now and then, savvy reporters claim some numbers are bogus. Moviegoers enjoy following these races because of their emotional investment in movies they've seen and because of the high stakes involved. Industry trackers pay special attention to the second weekend's percent change and to ultimate box office performance because those numbers might foreshadow the accumulated commercial value of each title. In addition, some after-theatrical deals, such as for television licensing, are often pegged at a percentage of box office gross.

The life cycle of a motion picture consists of orderly revenue streams built into calculated time frames or "windows." Theatrical exhibition is first, but not necessarily the most lucrative; home video has that honor for the most popular titles. The theatrical marketing campaign is expensive because it conveys a movie's image, which becomes linked to the product throughout its exploitable life around the world. In the United States, early weeks of a theatrical run will call for an after-overhead formula of some 90% of box office gross returned to the distributor, while later weeks, if the picture has staying power ("legs"), will find the exhibitor receiving a growing share of revenue as the product ages.

The next major revenue stream, some four to six months after theatrical, is home video, once the movie has disappeared from neighborhood theatres. The distributor's share can be substantial in this market, and the product can enjoy a long shelf life, having made the leap from theatres into the home, from being licensed by distributors and *experienced* by customers to being sold by distributors and *owned* by customers.

The picture ages further before it is available to the millions of subscribers of home pay-cable or satellite services, the next big revenue stream. Revenue to the distributor from this market is based on a formula geared to subscriber fees.

Another contractual time frame generally passes before the movie can be shown on network broadcast television; or on a basic cable network; or on an ad hoc broadcast network of TV stations created to show a library of, say, one studio's recent films; or in a group of films sold in a TV syndication package to a syndicate of local stations for a certain number of runs over a period of years. The picture has decreased in value because of its exposure, and revenue is turned over to the copyright owners based on negotiated payments triggered by each run.

Pictures originating as made-for-network (broadcast, cable or pay) television movies are subsequently licensed via domestic television syndication as further product for local TV station libraries, and are also sold, usually in packages, to different countries. Movies originating as made-for-video product premiere in video stores and can enjoy lucrative life spans in subsequent revenue streams all over the world.

Markets outside the United States follow this same general pattern; the global entertainment business is based on the American model. Each country's rollout is dictated by territorial owners of distribution rights and the sophistication of home technology. Naturally, some pictures will experiment with the pattern, shifting sequence because of specific deals, or perhaps returning to certain formats as revivals because of their uniqueness, depending on what the market will bear. For instance, in the U.S., *The Rocky Horror Picture Show* pioneered the concept of weekend midnight showings and still enjoys a cult following; and a version of *A Christmas Carol* can always be found on a local TV station around that holiday.

THE MOVIE BUSINESS

Like any business, the motion picture business exists to make money. Comparisons can be loosely made to other industries: production encompasses research, development and manufacturing; while distribution can be compared to wholesaling and exhibition to retailing. But there the comparisons end, because the public's demand and use of entertainment products such as motion pictures are unlike the demand and use of any other product. In no other business is a single product fully created at an investment of tens of millions of dollars, with no real assurance that the public will buy it. In no other business does the public "use" the product and then take away with them (as Samuel Marx observed in his book *Mayer and Thalberg*) merely the memory of it. In the truest sense, it's an industry based on dreams, and the service that is rendered is entertainment, leaving—at its best—an afterglow of warm emotions and recollections.

A note about "business." The very word puts some people off. When applied to movies, it once conjured up conflicts pitting West Coast against East Coast, the creative community against the business community, art against commerce. That's all changed. The motion picture professional learns early to mix the creative and business sense out of self-defense.

There continues to be no magic formula for a commercial movie, but patterns emerge, emulating prior successes. Buzzwords come and go. When franchises are in vogue, an increasing number of branded sequels results, all containing a form of insurance that audiences will want to return to the familiar. Branding is relatively new to the movie business, derived from the consumer products industry, and box office results encourage the trend. But there are still edgy movies being made, especially in the independent arena: *The Blair Witch Project, Memento.* And in the studio arena: *Three Kings, Adaptation.*

In earlier days, as the industry grew, studios were vertically integrated production/distribution/exhibition factories. By the late 1940s, the U.S. Department of Justice concluded that this structure was a monopolistic restraint of trade, and forced divorcement of exhibition in order to enhance competition. This landmark divestiture of theatres by studios encouraged the growth of independent exhibitors. Forty years later, legal overseers deemed that the climate had changed, and permitted certain studios to buy or invest in theatre chains.

The movie industry defies strict analysis from a traditional business point of view because of the uncertainties involved in making and marketing the product. What are the hallmarks of the movie *business*? That movies are a collaborative medium; every picturemaking experience is different; there are no hard and fast rules; financing is an enormous crapshoot; an entire investment is made before anyone knows if the product is marketable; many essential choices spring from intuitive leaps; most successful practitioners possess a personal mix of creative and business sense; judgments frequently rely on relationships and personalities; decisions are often made with a long lead time, making it harder to anticipate audience trends; and as far as profits are concerned, the sky's the limit.

It is a cyclical industry, difficult to chart, rooted in creativity and intuition, involving narcissism and greed, capable of dismal losses and euphoric profits, engaged in an ongoing seduction of the paying audience. The single universally acknowledged marketing tool—favorable audience word of mouth—cannot be controlled. As distribution executive Peter Myers once noted, it is a supremely democratic form of entertainment, where customers vote for one movie over another by simply putting down hard cash.

The high risk inherent in the movie business points to why conservative capital has historically shied away from investing, although control of motion picture companies has always been attractive to a broad spectrum of players. Industry observers insist that "It's not a business," as a shorthand for explaining its unpredictable elements, while movies continue to attract creative entrepreneurs and artists who are devoted to this most valuable and influential national resource and export.

At its core, the industry can be reduced to competing for the work of creators in a limited talent pool that shifts based on audience acceptance. The list of producers, directors, writers, actors and others who have earned an industry following is very exclusive. Energies are intensely spent daily to compete for this limited talent pool and to create new entries into it.

Movies struggle in a cluttered marketplace for the attention of targeted, youthful audience members whose own attention spans are contracting. And the stakes are higher than ever.

Some history: The 1970s witnessed a shift from regional television advertising to national network buys, ushering in the national release pattern. That decade also witnessed a redefining of box office potential, with breakout successes such as *Jaws* and *Star Wars* underscoring the newly discovered value of branded merchandising, book publishing and recorded music sales.

The 1980s were the boom years of home video and cable, and their increasing revenue streams were used as cushions for higher budgets. Studio distributors built divisions devoted to home video to organize something they had never done before: selling movies directly to customers who could actually take them home. Those distributors that had music divisions used them as a model, since both home video and music involve selling packaged goods via retailers. The decade also witnessed continual escalations in costs for movie production and marketing.

The 1990s saw movie companies absorbed by vast media conglomerates taking a global view. *Titanic* became the highest-grossing picture worldwide while serving as a poor business model, going so far over budget that the initiating studio was forced to take on a rival studio partner. International export markets generated increasing revenue, and the most popular English-language movies were making more money outside the United States than inside. At the same time, a surge of acquisitions resulted in half of American studio ownership resting in overseas hands.

After the turn of the century, a new era of uncertainty emerged. Entrenched entertainment companies were staring into the future represented by the Internet, a nirvana promising direct-to-customer commerce. But the movie industry's exploration of this new, interactive pipeline into the home was slowed by the serious threat of piracy. As of this writing, it's too early to tell whether piracy can be circumvented when people pay for movies on the Web, or to what extent a new revenue stream can securely develop, but it sure is exciting to follow the progress of this new frontier.

The most influential of these changes can be broken down in chronological order: network TV advertising, *Star Wars*, home video, the continuing cost spirals, globalization and the Internet.

NETWORK TV ADVERTISING

Through the 1960s, motion pictures were released regionally and advertised with a mixture of local newspaper and local television campaigns.

Then, a distribution company named Sunn Classics began experimenting with national network television advertising for the regional release of family pictures. That move to saturation-level national TV advertising indirectly led to the escalating costs of today's movies.

When studios recognized the cost-efficiency of network television buys, that expenditure forced the simultaneous blanket national release of certain pictures. Over the years, with the advent of theatre multiplexes, print runs escalated from 500 to 8,000 or more for the most commercial product to maximize audience access, generate heat, make the most money in the shortest period of time (reducing interest costs on capital needed for the production and marketing of the product) and discourage piracy. With more wide releases, the die was cast, and advertising and print costs would continue to rise.

Massive studio releases leave less room for independent distributors, whose aggressive, niche-marketing approach to specialized films are the last link to the kind of grassroots, hands-on distribution that can be traced back to the beginnings of the industry. In today's movie business, these independents compete with studio-owned indie-style distribution labels, making it even more difficult to secure and maintain screens, and their story is also represented in the pages of this book.

STAR WARS

Star Wars rewrote the economics of the movie business. This landmark picture, released by Twentieth Century Fox in 1977, not only broke through the upper limits of grossing potential via repeat business, but also redefined worldwide income in book, music and merchandising sales. When the dust cleared, brand-new businesses had been established that changed the profile of movie economics by generating substantial revenue in other media. With *Star Wars*, product merchandising went through the roof. The success of a variety of movie-related books solidified the publishing offshoot of movie tie-ins; and soundtrack albums sales came into their own, proving that an orchestral score could shoot to the top of the charts. Other well-known franchises would follow, but at the time there was nothing—nothing—like the economic impact of *Star Wars*.

HOME VIDEO

Once upon a time, you couldn't own movies, and if you were lucky enough to see them on TV, you couldn't decide when. This stemmed from the long-held industry sensitivity over product ownership. Movies were licensed, never sold, until "the home-video revolution." That term has become a cliché, but the impact of home video on the movie business was nothing short of revolutionary. It has expanded the movie-watching aesthetic, added new household appliances—the VCR and the DVD player, among others—to popular culture, and changed in-home viewing from passive to active. In less than ten years, home video grew from an infant market to a serious revenue stream. Studios at first resisted this new technology, much as they had resisted television. They waited on the sidelines as young upstart companies begin reaping enormous sums before testing the waters themselves.

Today, every studio has a home-video division, and every household with a video camera and computer is an instant studio. Since filmmaking is a natural form of expression, anyone can learn its aesthetics by simply shooting and viewing the results. When instinctive corrections are made in the next try, the language of film is being adopted. On household screens, personal home movies have become interchangeable with major motion pictures. Relatives and friends are seen on the same screen as movie stars.

Feature films have never been more accessible. Home video has changed people's moviegoing habits and increased the numbers of movies we see. The question is no longer whether to see a movie, but whether to leave the house to see one.

For distributors, the home-video numbers are enormous. A turning point occurred in 2000 when Universal's hit *The Mummy* grossed more in its first week of U.S. home-video release than in its first week in theatrical. This pattern continues for the most popular movies, with home video outgrossing theatrical.

THE CONTINUING COST SPIRALS

Since the 1980s, a dual cost spiral has evolved—the upward trajectory of production budgets and marketing costs. Increased production costs were being rationalized to allow for the shooting time needed for the kind of complicated visual effects audiences were responding to. Another reason was to pay the higher salaries negotiated for certain key artists by their agents, who had taken on a proprietary role in dealmaking. Increased marketing costs were being rationalized as benefiting markets that followed theatrical release, especially home video.

The other, more seductive culprit was home video itself, with ever-increasing revenue promising to offset a significant percentage of negative cost. This gave a false sense of security to movie executives who were approving higher budgets in light of a seemingly ever-expanding cushion. But by the end of the 1980s, home video values had stopped growing, having stabilized into a mature market. In contrast, studio picture budgets continued to rise at alarming rates. The press would report annual market-share statistics, accompanied by studio bragging rights, with little regard to the true measure of financial success, which is profitability. Tension between market share and profitability continues to this day.

By 1990, high-risk, high-reward picturemaking was supposedly warranted in light of the potential global return from theatrical, home video and other revenue streams. Meanwhile, agents continued to achieve more money for their clients, while the audience hungered for ever more impressive filmmaking. Once certain levels of artist compensation were reached (gross multiples instead of net, for example), there was no turning back.

Today, outlays for mainstream studio product, whose mass audience expects "tentpoles" of entertainment during the summer and winter holidays, continue to escalate. Shooting days are more costly; advertising is more costly; mistakes are more costly. It's more of a crapshoot than ever, at a table restricted to high rollers. Strategies to reduce expenditures inevitably follow (some are expressed within the pages of this book), but short-term solutions have found movie companies either restructuring, merging or being purchased by larger international parents to achieve financial security. Costs simply can't continue to rise at their current rate. It's a continual spiral, with management hoping that no implosion occurs on its watch.

GLOBALIZATION

By the beginning of the new century, vast media empires, intent on delivering content in any new method that technology and customer convenience would allow, had bought studio distributors and their valuable movie libraries. Entertainment, like most industries, had gone global. For their part, the studios were looking for deeper-pocketed parents to help them survive lean periods. News Corporation had bought Fox; Sony had bought Columbia; Viacom had bought Paramount (and later CBS); AOL was merging with Time Warner; Ted Turner had bought New Line, which became part of AOL Time Warner; and soon Vivendi would take over Universal. Then, Time Warner dropped "AOL" from its name, and General Electric's NBC merged with Vivendi Universal to become NBC Universal. Only Disney remained its own master, while buying Miramax and ABC. And these relationships will no doubt shift in the near term.

Most parent companies came from successes in other businesses. For example, Sony was known for its primacy in consumer electronics, News Corporation for newspaper and magazine publishing. A visit to the corporate Web sites of Walt Disney, Viacom or Time Warner shows how active they are in nonmovie, entertainment-related businesses. This is increasingly essential for any player to offset cash-flow uncertainty, the between-hits periods that are the downside of the movie business. But with each conglomerate takeover, motion pictures play a smaller and smaller role in relation to other sources of revenue. Top movie executives, who would have been company owners a generation ago, are middle managers of global media empires today.

Actually, the movie business has always been an international business. The pantomime of silent films was a universal vocabulary easily exported with title cards conforming to the local language. But the coming of sound created dialogue barriers that, along with issues of politics and economics, curtailed the growing film industries until after World War II. Then, a flourishing of artistic expression in countries including those in western Europe and Japan—coupled with tourism and the natural curiosity that goes with it—created a cultural appetite that led to the vibrant business of importing and exporting motion pictures and later television programming.

In the United States, the studios were fully financing pictures and distributing them worldwide. But in the 1960s and 1970s, in a new global approach, entrepreneurs such as Joseph E. Levine and Dino De Laurentiis raised money by combining financing from different countries, in exchange for distribution rights divided among those countries. Today, American studios have taken on partners to share increasing risk. These partners are often entrepreneurs who have bargained with territorial distributors to bring equity financing to the table, offsetting half of a studio's risk on selected movies in exchange for distribution rights in those same territories.

Around the world, countries support movie industries whose product roughly divide into three types. The first is domestic, which simply doesn't travel. The second, suitable for export because of its content and style, is made available through sales organizations to a global market in a variety of formats. The third is the high-priced, mass-market English-language movie often laden with stars, crafted as a global entertainment.

The system of buying and selling movies for import and export is based on supply and demand. Variables such as currency fluctuation, government regulation, frozen funds, local taste, censorship and piracy come into play. The highlights of this commerce are film festivals and selling markets worldwide.

The global industry will expand as countries stabilize politically. A popular entertainment industry can develop and thrive only within a democratic society with a large middle class. After all, leisure-time purchases are made from discretionary income—not money used to pay for essentials—by members of a solid middle class who have embraced entertainment as part of their recreational lifestyle.

Although issues of market potential, investment regulation, film content and audience taste vary around the world, the basic business skills applied to commercial moviemaking remain the same. In developing a screenplay, action may be rewritten to conform to budget; in dealmaking, all parties must be protected; in securing funds, ingenuity prevails; in production, creativity is influenced by pressures of time and money; in distribution, imaginative selling is required; and in exhibition, the anxiety of anticipating public response is universal. Because the product requires the spending of huge amounts of money, it is up to lawyers, accountants and agents to apply formulas and intuition to reduce odds and construct frameworks of responsibility and recourse on behalf of financiers and creators.

THE INTERNET

The World Wide Web represents the gold ring of commerce, the ability to reach customers directly in their homes on a global basis. In a single decade, people have moved from computer novices to sophisticated Web surfers and online purchasers. Most computer owners can recall an information epiphany, when a fact or outcome could be learned immediately on the Web, or an e-commerce epiphany, whereby a hard-to-find product was easily purchased without leaving home.

The movie industry is on the verge of translating this ease of access and use to movies. But the music industry's experience of customers downloading music in what amounted to piracy was such a financial disaster for the music business that it forced change in its business model. How will the Internet affect movies? Stay tuned.

NEW CHALLENGES

We are in an era of media transition, with business models transforming.

In music, the traditional business model is being replaced by a Web-driven consumer revolution of downloading and file sharing. The industry response has been slow but encouraging, with the creation of value-added CDs, for example, offering the customer perks unavailable through file sharing.

In television, broadcast networks are on the decline, with cable networks emerging and growing in ratings, shifting emphasis from broadcasting to narrowcasting.

Advertising, that great machine that feeds on media, is also in transition. For example, television advertising no longer delivers reliable consumer impressions due to time-shifting on home video systems.

And in motion pictures, costs simply can't continue to rise as they have been.

Out of these challenging times can come innovative relationships between media and customers. With the Internet as the wild west, it will be exciting to watch players gamble with new concepts in the ongoing adventure that is mass entertainment.

ENTERTAINMENT STUDIES

In the time between the last edition and this one, as I continued teaching movie business at the USC School of Cinema-Television, it became clear that there was a broader way to teach the field, because movies were no longer stand-alone enterprises. Rather, movies as product are linked to other entertainment products, from music to theme parks, consistent with the expansion of media companies.

My goal is to use this edition as a platform to encourage academic colleagues to group their instruction of consumer media together under a horizon of "entertainment studies." Movies, TV, home video and interactive games should be studied together with recorded music, publishing, toys, radio, theatre, theme parks, concerts and sports. This will equip undergraduates with the background and tools to compete in an evolving industry where the lines between these products increasingly blur. After all, it's likely that their careers will span a full spectrum of products, and they must be prepared for the crossover. Examples of this expanded horizon can be found sprinkled throughout the book.

This idea was crystallized in my article for *The New York Times* Sunday Money & Business section on April 19, 1998, entitled "What's Your Major? Entertainment Studies." How pleasant it was to hear from students, professors and industry executives around the country who either hoped for such a curriculum, or were planning a class to reflect this approach or were already offering one.

Using the movie business as a template to study how money is arranged for, spent, protected, and returned in a creative industry is at the heart of this third edition *Movie Business Book*. With the same enthusiasm as anyone discovering this material for the first time, it is a pleasure to present it to the reader.

I

THE CREATORS

THE PRODUCER

by **DAVID PUTTNAM,** the Oscar-winning producer of *Chariots of Fire, The Killing Fields, Midnight Express, Local Hero* and *The Mission.* He was chairman of Columbia Pictures from 1986 to 1988 and now works principally in the field of education and the creative industries, serving in England as chairman of the General Teaching Council (GTC), as chairman of the National Endowment for Science, Technology and the Arts (NESTA), and as chancellor of the University of Sunderland. In 1995 he received a knighthood for his services to the British film industry, and in 1997 he was appointed to the House of Lords. He divides his time between England and a home in Ireland.

> The producer has one absolutely crucial week on a movie; it may even come down to three days: the Wednesday, Thursday and Friday of the second week [of shooting].

The actual job of putting a film together has barely changed since the days when the Lumière brothers created the very first moving images more than one hundred years ago. It involves the same disappointments, the same problems and similar triumphs. What has changed, and changed dramatically, is the sheer complexity of it all, particularly in the legal, contract and copyright areas. So one of the basic skills that producers must develop is the ability to work across a range of very different activities, managing very different types of people in sometimes very different circumstances.

There are almost as many ways of functioning as a producer as there are producers. Sensible producers devise a working system that maximizes their personal strengths—personality, knowledge, talent—and minimizes their weaknesses, bringing in people to compensate for those weaknesses. It's dangerous, in fact (and not particularly helpful), to mandate a way of producing pictures or to try to be someone else's type of producer. I admonish the reader to take the following observations as mere advice and to strike out on one's own to develop a personal style of producing.

In many respects I am something of a throwback. I started out working in an advertising agency where, as an account executive, I was discouraged from having very much input into the creative process. Luckily I was able to reconstruct the job in such a way as to give myself a fair amount of say as to who wrote and designed the ads I worked on. Coming to movies from this experience, I had the confidence to apply the same skepticism and reconstruct the role of the producer in a way that offered the type of creative satisfaction that I was seeking.

The first film I produced, *Melody,* fell together more by luck than by judgment. Although I was more of a passenger, I made sure to pay close attention to the process, and didn't make too much of a fool of myself. The second film (*The Pied Piper*) was just the opposite, a catastrophe. I learned a great deal from my mistakes and completely revised my thinking. In those days a producer's job was simply packaging. I decided that if I was going to have ghastly experiences like this second picture, I'd like them to be my fault, instead of trying to ride herd on a situation over which I had no real control. As a result, on the third film, *That'll Be the Day,* I set the parameters around which I've worked ever since: very hands-on, very involved, with semiautobiographical story elements that I can specifically relate to. Now let me tour through the picture-making process and explain how I applied these parameters to the job of producing.

With few exceptions I would generally either conceive of my stories or find them in newspapers. *Chariots of Fire, Local Hero* and *The Killing Fields* all had their origins in this type of research. It's impossible to explain why one story intuitively imposes itself on your imagination rather than another—a bit like trying to justify falling in love with one woman in a room in which many would seem equally attractive. This is organic and should stay that way!

The casting of screenwriters to fit material stems from reading vast numbers of screenplays, becoming familiar with writers and their craft and knowing the tone and content you want. Monte Merrick was chosen for *Memphis Belle,* a movie with ten major roles, because I had read a screenplay of his wherein he juggled several characters, giving them all quite specific identities.

In my development process I would normally pay for an option to buy the chosen material, say an original screenplay, making sure to have the right to extend the option period for a smaller additional sum of money, whether or not the extension money is applied against the purchase price. Because I'd work slowly, my option period would be longer than most, normally covering two years, extendable for a third.

In terms of cutoffs in a screenplay deal I would be quite singular; I'd normally stay with a writer over many, many drafts. Over the years I've observed that the batting average of writers coming in and rewriting is low. This puzzled me until I went to Columbia. There it was clear that a studio executive has an average of forty minutes for a script conference and is under great pressure to report progress at weekly production meetings. The easy way to apparent "action" is to decide to replace a writer in the course of that script conference rather than taking the time necessary for the complex, tedious, difficult task of properly developing a screenplay from one draft to the next. Unless a writer feels "written out," I would try to stick with the same one, since that person probably understands the story problems and solutions better than anyone and, I would hope, remains eager to implement them; it's the devil you know as opposed to the devil you don't know—and probably can't afford!

A fundamental task of a producer is to make the project as risk-averse as possible. My advice is to bring in bargains, relatively inexpensive pictures on or under budget, since you can't mandate the success of a movie. Here is where the American system is forgiving and the European system is not. In the American system, if you deliver a *good* movie in a timely and responsible manner but the picture fails at the box office, you are not regarded as a failure. With the next project you are remembered as the person who delivered the last picture properly. In Europe, no matter how well you produce a film, if it's not a critical or commercial success, there is the smell of failure about *you,* and the next project may suffer.

The key to remaining stable is being prepared to think the unthinkable, being prepared to "walk away from this picture," which can be an expression of either power or sacrifice. I've done it a few times and saved myself an awful lot of grief, most notably on *Greystoke.* During preproduction I suddenly realized I didn't know *how* to produce the film; it was too complex. I didn't believe it could be done for the amount that Warner Bros. wanted to spend, and I didn't want to be on the sharp end of their disappointment. I walked away and saved myself a year or more of deep pain.

Once a project is green-lighted, there are certain dangers to watch for. One is being pushed into a fixed release date, which is lethal for a producer. This got to be known as "shooting a release date" and doesn't happen very often (though there are well-publicized examples). Once a producer is trapped into this, all of the normal controls that exist in the making of a movie can go out the window. Another danger is building the film's existence around one important cast name. Once this occurs, you are to a very great extent at that person's mercy. There are several films that never got beyond the development stage because of the rewriting demands of major actors who were attached too early on.

Another danger is the pressure to deliver a budget before locations have been adequately scouted. This is always counterproductive, since a cheaper way of making the movie results from a full assessment of all the possible locations with the production designer and director. Money wisely spent in preproduction is an *investment.* Spending an extra $100,000 in preproduction can save $1 million during shooting. Sometimes it's difficult for studios to understand this, since preproduction expenses seem like high-risk money (in that there's still a chance the picture can be canceled), but their attitude and their professionalism in this respect is steadily improving.

My advice in budgeting is: Don't lie to yourself. The temptation is there, especially if a picture won't go forward if it's budgeted over a certain figure. When you begin to trim a budget to reach a financier's rigid number, you start questioning items, which *can* lead to disaster. Do we really need a unit doctor? Do we need a standby ambulance? No, until something goes wrong, just as with insurance. On location for *Memphis Belle* there was a plane crash, and three fire engines raced to the scene in seconds. At that moment I realized that if anyone had asked during preproduction whether we needed three fire engines standing by, the answer probably would have been to cut back and save money. After that I wrote to Warners suggesting a firm corporate policy that, notwithstanding budgetary pressures, certain areas should *never* be cut, including medical, security and fire. In this way if someone is irresponsible enough to cut back in those areas and there is an accident, a company can honestly point to this rule in their terms of business and protect themselves.

In scheduling the same rule applies: Don't lie to yourself. Also, keep aside some sequences that you know you could complete the movie without and place them at the end of the schedule. In other words, don't find yourself shooting sequences in week 2 that, if push came to shove, you could drop. Keep them tucked into the end of the schedule so that they can be deleted if need be. They can also act as a valuable spur to a tired director!

On *Chariots of Fire* I made a scheduling decision that turned out wonderfully well in hindsight. There was a rather tenuous financing arrangement involving two companies who were funding it not out of any particular enthusiasm but because of other, more complex commitments. I wanted to impress them, so I scheduled a rather big production sequence for the first week. Sure enough, in week 2, when problems began to arise, I had something wonderful to show them. There was a sense of relief on the part of the financiers, who later generously agreed to invest additional money.

This leads to another bit of advice: While it can be important to shoot a complicated production sequence in the first week to get it behind you, tuck it into Thursday or Friday. It takes at least seventy-two hours for a crew to get to know each other. It may appear as if everyone is functioning properly that first Monday morning, but the real work won't emerge until Wednesday. You've got to be emotionally and, if possible, financially prepared literally to throw away the first two days of shooting.

The producer has one absolutely crucial week on a movie; it may even come down to three days: the Wednesday, Thursday and Friday of the second week. All the most fundamental decisions will have to be made within that time. Whatever is going wrong must either be changed then or you will be stuck with those problems for the duration of the production.

Two examples involve the relationship with the director and the working rhythm of the film, both of which become established very quickly. As producer you should already have done your homework and learned about the director's style and the other artists' abilities by asking those who have worked with them in the past. Your choices should have been based on this *and* on intuitive judgment. Certainly problems during that precious first week of shooting will ring alarm bells in your head, since they may well be contrary to those early assumptions. If need be, this is the time to have a confrontation with the director. There is a week's rushes to look at, enough material to judge the competency of the director as expressed through the visual style and the performances. If changes are required, there is this narrow window of opportunity; now's the time. If the working rhythm indicates, when charted out through the schedule, that you will be two weeks over, it must be adjusted, with the director's cooperation, by the end of that second week, or you *are* destined to go over.

Once a film has started shooting, the pivotal relationship is between the producer and the director. The best "in-production" relationship I ever had was with Roland Joffe on *The Killing Fields*. Because it was an enormously complicated film, we would dine together almost every night, talking over that day's problems and the next day's challenges, and that was very productive. There was never any equivocation. When we had crises, he totally understood them; when things were working well, he knew why. The key is trust. If the director suspects the producer is likely to lie about having more money (or less resources) available than there actually is, the basis of the relationship will be undermined quickly. It is demoralizing for a director to think the producer has a hidden agenda, just as it is demoralizing for a producer to believe the studio has another agenda altogether.

Let me emphasize that once a film is green-lighted, the key is absolute trust. A producer must have the confidence to be able to say to the director, "This is not working," and the director must have the confidence to respond, "How am I going to dig my way out of this?" Then you work together to dig your way out. There *will* be crises; there's never been a movie made without crises. It's the ability to deal with those crises that is the making of a good or a bad producer. Once a film starts, producing is, for the most part, crisis management; you have no other real function. In most other respects you're in the way!

During shooting I would try to time my appearances so that they would have some relevance. I'd try to be there at the beginning of the day (if you're there, why isn't everyone else?), during lunch and at the end of the day. It is very good for the crew to see the producer lunching with the director and other artists, for it communicates a sense of continuity, of family. I would always reserve the right to decide what time the movie wraps, rather than hand that over to the director. If that is lost, you have effectively lost budgetary control of the film. If the director decides how long to shoot, the director controls the budget. There are exceptions. On a shoot in Hungary we took out a completion bond with a local studio, so I didn't have to look at my watch once. Whether we wanted to wrap at six or at nine, we had a fixed cost; any overage was their problem.

The core working group from the producer's perspective during shooting is the production manager, first assistant director and production accountant. They're your SWAT team, who help sort out your problems. With their input you bring a series of sensibly thought-out options to the director, and the director decides among those options. As an example, on *The Duellists* we were behind from day 1 due to weather. I would meet with Ridley Scott every night and discuss options to get back on schedule, such as condensing a sequence and moving on after lunch or cutting the size of a crowd, and he would decide.

Let's consider the issue of going over budget. As noted earlier, the first line of defense is to recognize the pattern early (again, by the beginning of week 2) and confer with the director in order to correct it by reworking the schedule or your shooting system in order to catch up. But what if the picture is clearly better off for going over one week? In that case, instead of trying to hold to the schedule, you must pay for the overage by imposing savings from other below-the-line categories. Either decision is made by working closely with your SWAT team and presenting the alternatives to the director. It's important not to become ideological about it, not to see it as a war between producer and director, because like it or not, you're in it together.

In the unlikely event that the director does not respond constructively in the face of such an overage, you have a battle on your hands. It also means you've made a flawed judgment in selecting that director. One of the things I would try to do in preproduction is to feel out that type of issue, to create one or two minicrises to see how the director reacts. During the location reconnaissance ("reccie"), if option A is closed down, how flexible is the director in exploring option B? What you don't want is a "pussycat" director—"Everything is fine, whatever you say"—because that kind of lack of conviction will end up on the screen. The ideal director is someone who is decisive and flexible: firm in what he or she wants; flexible in understanding the nature of the producer's problems and in helping solve or at least address them.

The value of choosing to work on location is realism. Another important element, especially in exotic locations, is the ability to photograph indigenous people rather than shipping in extras. Since travel time is wasted time, another concern is how close the crew lives to the location. If travel time is an hour and a half, that means three hours are wasted each day, and that's both expensive and stupid; every fourth day is effectively wasted.

Currency is another issue on distant locations, and my advice is to buy currency forward. Once you *know* what the picture is going to cost, buy the currency for the entire location schedule; don't be a victim of fluctuation. As an example, assume the pound moves against the dollar from $1.40 to $1.61 over several weeks. If the movie is budgeted in dollars but you are spending pounds, the cost of your dollars has escalated by some 15%, a heavy unforeseen overage. To avoid this, convert your financing into the local currency as soon as possible. (If a studio balks, reach agreement with them such that they can keep any benefit from fluctuation but that they protect you from any losses.) Don't play the currency market—it's not your job, and you've got a movie to produce.

Logistics are extremely important, since shooting on location is parallel to a military operation, calling for moving great numbers of people and equipment, keeping lines of communication open, seeing that everyone is well fed and maintaining flexibility so that plans can be changed at short notice.

As producer you have the absolute obligation to keep the crew happy, well fed and not exploited in terms of working ridiculous hours, which may become counterproductive, making them tired and irritable. At the end of week 2 it's a good idea to throw a little unit party, which brings people together and consolidates relationships. One should be reasonably quick to criticize but even faster to praise. I would advocate a "slush fund" in a budget of perhaps 1% of the budget from which you can buy small things such as birthday presents or a round of drinks or award bonuses where deserved, all of which, in addition to a couple of unit parties, generate good morale and a sense of well-being.

Outsiders wonder why so many people are needed on location. In my experience there are in reality seldom more people than are necessary, especially in support staff, who can always fill in where needed. The most expensive element in shooting a film is *time*. The addition of an extra person can often fill a gap so that every given hour in the day is properly used. Don't scrimp with your key personnel. Beware of bargains. If proper planning with an experienced director of photography avoids *one* day's error, he has paid for himself. ~

During production it's important to prepare a weekly progress report reflecting the budget changes, specifying over- and under-budget shifts from the previous week. I would force myself to spend half a day a week on this. In every area where the change is significant I'd write a detailed explanation. This is not only for the record; I have found that writing about these problems would make me address them head-on and search for solutions in the coming week. I'm a great believer in putting thoughts on paper.

If you've prepared properly and done your numbers right, the relationship with the financier during production should be amiable. Stay in contact through phone calls every week or so, reporting progress. I would adamantly resist sending rushes back to the studio; they have every chance of being misinterpreted. The *only* people who can really understand the rushes are the director and the editor and, to a limited degree, the producer. Rather, after a few weeks I'd send them a series of selected takes, to offer a flavor of the movie. On *Midnight Express* the rushes for two out of the first three days were unusable. Had Columbia seen that material, they might have panicked. Luckily we were on location in Malta and were able to cover by rescheduling and get back on track. Crews are great at covering for each other!

Editing normally begins *during* shooting, and your relationship with the editor is most important. I've done three-quarters of my films with the same two editors and would trust them implicitly. The director must come to trust the editor's judgment as well. But let me emphasize that the director-editor rapport must be such that the editor tells the director the *truth*. If the rushes aren't working, the editor is the first person who knows it and must be comfortable enough in the relationship to convey that to the director. Bluntly, the editor must not be someone who looks to the director to remain employed. On location we would see rushes on video, so the daily call to the editor at home base to assess the quality of the rushes would be vital. On *Mahler* I asked Ken Russell if he wanted to look at the rushes. He asked if we had any room in the schedule to reshoot, and I said no. Then he said, "What's the point in looking at the rushes?"

I would try to bring the composer on very early, if possible at the screenplay level. The three essential creative contributions on a movie exist on two tiers. On the first tier is the director, writer and composer, followed by the trio of production designer, editor and cameraman. What you see on the screen is an amalgam of their work, and the producer's job is to ride herd on them. In the case of *Chariots of Fire* it's hard to say what the movie would have been like without Vangelis's brilliant score. Since I happen to enjoy music, my research into finding composers was a constant delight. On *The Killing Fields* we decided that, visually, many sequences would end with machinery wiping the human element off screen. We sought a cacophony of sound, and I thought of Mike Oldfield's *Tubular Bells*. He was keen to do the film and came on board before shooting started.

Now let us assume we have completed principal photography on schedule and we turn to the final phase, postproduction. It's important to do postproduction close to home, which in my case is in England. This way you are familiar with all the elements and can maintain control. I'd worked with the same dubbing mixer for twenty years, and there was a mutual trust and a shorthand that developed.

During the latter stage of postproduction there is the question of when to preview. We would do a rough, four-day mix to give a sense of the sound track, including some music, for the previews. Only after the previews would we do the full-blown sound mix, finely detailed.

Previews are immensely valuable. It's the first time you learn how your preconceptions fit with those of the actual audience. First, the film will *feel* long. Individual cuts, scenes, moments and rhythms you've grown to like will have to be adjusted, because you can feel the audience wanting the film to move on. Next, you forget how smart the audience is, and find that the opening reel is far too expository; you just don't need that body of exposition. I would always try to leave some money in the budget for reshooting a couple of days of odds and ends, useful inserts learned about in the previews. This "shooting to the cut" is remarkably economical (with an almost 1:1 shooting ratio) and can solve enormous problems. Not every studio will agree to this, but it's extremely valuable and often comes down to a measure of their enthusiasm for the picture.

What's the ideal preview audience? It depends on the picture. We previewed *Memphis Belle* to very broad audiences and took our chances. On *Meeting Venus* we previewed to preselected audiences of people who had seen films like *Dangerous Liaisons* or *Reversal of Fortune*. Before I would preview for the studio in Los Angeles, I would pre-preview in the U.K. to discover obvious problems and make adjustments in advance.

There are two types of preview: for production and for distribution. The production preview would point up the strengths and weaknesses of the movie and allows us to make improvements before the final mix. Then you lock the film and move to the marketing and distribution issues. For distribution previews we would show essentially a finished movie and would be addressing marketing decisions and market positioning.

Conferring with marketing executives is an ongoing process. After the film is locked in, the key relationships for me would become the head of marketing, the person who cuts the trailers and does the print ads, and the head of distribution, who handles the release pattern and theatre dates. I would trust these executives totally and prefer to bow to their expertise. If we disagree, I would on balance rather have them misjudge a movie and remain confident in me as a colleague than win some hysterical disagreement over a specific movie and destroy the relationships. Also, since I would not be prepared to accept interference in *my* area, I would in fairness take a similar view and respect what they do.

Approaching the release date, marketing expenses are committed, theatres are committed and tension is enormous. You die a little, because there's not much you can do to affect the outcome! If a picture opens stronger than expected, rejoice and chase it with resources to maximize it. At this point significant sums of money must be available to drive it over the top. If a picture opens poorly and it is in broad release, there's *nothing* you can do. If it is in platform release, there may be ways to rescue it if reviews are good and exit surveys are positive. Perhaps the movie can be repositioned through recutting the trailer and rethinking the advertising campaign.

Once a picture is released, it takes on a life of its own as it proceeds through the varied release patterns and viewing formats to the increasing movie audience around the world, making, one sincerely hopes, some kind of positive impact.

THE DIRECTOR

by **SYDNEY POLLACK,** who has earned distinction as a director with such theatrical feature credits as *Random Hearts, Sabrina, The Firm, Havana, Out of Africa* (winner of seven Oscars, including Best Picture, Best Director and Best Screenplay), *Tootsie* (New York Film Critics Award), *Absence of Malice, The Electric Horseman, Bobby Deerfield, Three Days of the Condor, The Yakuza, The Way We Were, Jeremiah Johnson, They Shoot Horses, Don't They?, Castle Keep, The Scalphunters, This Property Is Condemned* and *The Slender Thread.* His eighteen pictures have received 46 Academy Award nominations (four for Best Picture), and eight appear on *Variety's* list of "All Time Rental Champs." Mr. Pollack has also received the Golden Globe, the National Society of Film Critics' Award, the NATO Director of the Year Award and prizes at the Moscow, Taormina, Brussels, Belgrade and San Sebastian film festivals. In addition, he has produced many of the pictures he directed. Beyond those, Mr. Pollack was executive producer of features including *Honeysuckle Rose, The Fabulous Baker Boys, White Palace, Leaving Normal, Searching for Bobby Fischer, Sense and Sensibility, The Talented Mr. Ripley, Iris* and *The Quiet American,* as well as producer of *Songwriter, Bright Lights, Big City, Presumed Innocent, Sliding Doors* and *Cold Mountain.*

Every time the director says, "Let's *try* it this way," and not "Let's *do* it this way," money is being spent at enormous rates.

For me the first stage in developing a film is, obviously, finding and working on the story. Source material can be in almost any form, from pre-publication galleys of a novel to a treatment (or a long synopsis of a story), to firsthand discussions with writers on original ideas, to magazine or newspaper articles. Development is simply bringing the project from a raw, nonproduceable state to a produceable state. In practice, what it means to me is "kneading" the material like dough, through plain hard work with the screenwriter, until it has characters and a "world" that I feel enthusiastic about and comfortable with.

Some writers like to have lots of meetings, get the director's input, then go off alone to complete an entire draft screenplay. This is a gamble that sometimes leads to success and sometimes doesn't. If the writer is off on an unwanted story tangent, the problem will usually be compounded throughout the screenplay. Other writers like to give a director four to five pages at a time, discuss them, and rewrite as necessary. A middle ground might have the director and writer meeting several times before the writer goes off and completes half a screenplay, fifty to sixty pages. Then they might meet again and discuss any problems or new ideas growing out of those pages. Another method might find the writer and director writing together in a room, arguing about characters and dialogue. This is the closest form of collaboration and depends on a strong relationship between the two. Naturally, whatever choice is made originates with the personalities and work habits of those involved. Since I am not a writer, I selfishly look for a kind of alter ego who can come closest to creating a work that accurately depicts what I visualize or care about. In the best of circumstances a shorthand is developed, a mutual intuition.

All creative work is some form of a controlled free-association process, which doesn't evolve 100% consciously. For me, working with the writer means page-by-page analysis (sometimes to the exasperation of the writer), covering details ranging from something as specific as dialogue rhythm to something as general as the central idea—a theme, spine, arma-ture—to be used as a guide. It is useful to identify and state problems through the posing of questions. Sometimes you just talk, or "hang out." Nothing is ever really wasted. It may appear to be wasteful to go for a walk and have some coffee together, but it is all part of the process. If you can clearly articulate a story problem, for example, then it remains on your mind, consciously or unconsciously, always percolating. That evolves into specific work when the writer turns to rewriting. A final technique for me is to sit with the writer as I type through the screenplay myself. This way I absorb it and also begin staging the scenes in my head. Sometimes I find holes or story problems during typing that are not otherwise apparent.

As far as reading material, I sometimes use readers for the initial screening because of the sheer bulk of submissions. Often I've chosen ma-terial that has no objective merit, only subjective merit. In those cases the value of the project becomes clear only after it is developed to conform to a subjective vision. On the other hand, there have been many projects that I have turned down but that other directors have made into wonderful movies.

It is impossible to end any discussion of material selection today with-out referring to agency packaging. Although I frankly don't like the idea of being part of a package, I would not have made *Tootsie* otherwise. The script came to me with Dustin Hoffman attached from our then mutual agent, Michael Ovitz of Creative Artists. Although I responded to the idea of the story, there were problems with the screenplay, so I initially passed. Michael persuaded me to develop the script to see if I might find an ap-proach that was satisfying. This worked, happily, but I would never have been involved without his perseverance.

Agents have become very powerful. In order to be competitive, they have had to invent new ways of agenting. In earlier times most agents functioned as dealmakers and morale boosters, and it became a matter of choosing a compatible personality. But agents began to define new tests of their agentry. One way is to involve a director earlier than someone else, even though he or she has not been offered that script. This is sometimes an uncomfortable situation to be put in: agents sometimes submit photo-copies of scripts that they are not actually supposed to be reading. The triumph for the agent may be to boast of access to the director. Another "emblem" of agenting can involve information, whereby one agent demonstrates better connections than another. The newer, tougher breed of agents define their merit by a new set of standards, having to do with being packagers, politicians, intelligence gatherers and information traders, to ingratiate themselves and be viewed as distinctive in order to compete. Whether or not some of this behavior is arguably unprincipled, it represents a change in the function of agents and how they are perceived in the business.

A result of their new power is that agencies today share with studios much of the decision-making process as to what movies get made. That process was once exclusively studio-driven. The question is, Has this resulted in better films? I don't think so. Do these pictures make more money? Without question, yes. Is that the primary reason for the existence of Hollywood? Unequivocally, yes. In this way the agencies are helping accomplish what the system is designed to do.

Today studios are small divisions of multinational conglomerates, and this has an impact on the spectrum of films they are willing to gamble on. There is a mentality bred by big business that once a recipe is found, stick with it and put your effort into marketing it; expand the base of people who are exposed to it, rather than experiment with the recipe. The discussion becomes "What's the poster? What's the trailer? Can I sell it in ten seconds?" Some films are too complicated for this. But despite the fact that big money is pushing toward a kind of conformity, motion picture audiences still reassert their appetite for pushing the envelope, and redefine the business every time a picture is released.

Economics is the most inhibiting factor for a mainstream director making a film. Increments of over-budget twenty years ago were minuscule compared with those of today. When you start moving in fractional increments of $40 million, it's a lot different than $10 million. Most creative people, with the exception of actors and directors, create alone and in silence. With actors and directors it's a little like taking your clothes off in public. There are hundreds of technicians; if we are on a street, there are horns honking and the clock is ticking away. Every time the director says, "Let's *try* it this way," and not "Let's *do* it this way," money is being spent at enormous rates. The average Hollywood studio out on location spends between $150,000 and $200,000 a day. The high range often applies to period pictures, calling for rentals of vintage cars and wardrobe for extras whose costumes must be fitted and sewn. Because the numbers are so high, one is far more conscious of dollar pressure when making choices during shooting. Is take 7 really better than take 1? How much better? $5,000 better? $10,000 better? No one can decide that except the director, who must try to be intransigent while hoping that every decision is making the picture better and therefore is not wasteful.

Once the studio green-lights the picture, preproduction begins. On *Tootsie,* this ran three and a half months; on *The Firm,* nine months; on *Out of Africa* it was a year. What accounts for this spread? *Tootsie* was a modern-dress picture shot in the studio and on location in New York. For *Out of Africa* farmland had to be planted, locations had to be scouted, a period reproduction of a town had to be built, clothes designed for 1913 had to be made, extras had to be found.

In preproduction the main focus is on finalizing the script, budgeting, scheduling, casting and location scouting. As a director who also produces, I use a line producer to help me make economically sound decisions, with an eye to what the creative consequences will be. That person signs the checks, advises on union rules and negotiates the deals with most of the below-the-line personnel, such as location managers, production designers, prop manufacturers and costume designers, among others.

The person functioning as line producer for me does the same job that is known variously as production manager, unit production manager or associate producer, and the actual credit designation has to do with experience as well as the hierarchy and division of labor on a specific picture. There are directors who turn all of the producing decisions over to one person, who is justifiably termed the producer. My own feeling is that the person who is designated "producer" should be the person who also has a direct say in creative areas, including selecting the director, the cast and heads of departments.

The first thing usually asked a director is, "How much do you think it will cost?" Sometimes it is difficult to know in the beginning, but I make an educated guess. Then I work with the production manager/line producer to make a *breakdown,* a scene-by-scene itemization of what will be required: How many days will it take? Should a set be rented or built? Will we be on location or in a studio? How many extras? How much will living expenses be? How large a crew? How much action will there be? Where will we need multiple cameras? (For a specimen of a breakdown sheet and other production paperwork, see article by Christina Fong, p. 250.) Sometimes, in trying to be conscientious, you might decide to shoot a complex sequence in one night. The production manager might say no, it involves 800 extras, and after they are dressed, you won't be able to start shooting until three hours after their call; it needs two nights. For every segment of location shooting it is important to save interior sequences as cover sets, to turn to in case of bad weather. It's just common sense.

Casting impacts budget. If a high-end star is committed, the production is saddled with special charges on top of the star salary, such as hiring the star's hairdressers, makeup artist, secretary and security. Each requires another hotel room on location, another airplane ticket, another per diem, another driver (at teamster driver rates), another car rental, plus fringes.

The *shooting schedule* is derived from the breakdown pages, the scheduling of production days in a certain order. Scheduling is a compromise between the aesthetic advantage of shooting in sequence versus the practical, economic needs dictated by shooting out of sequence. Pictures are rarely shot in continuity. The goal is to strike a balance. Obviously in a relationship story one tries not to shoot the emotional breakup scene before the characters have met. For *The Way We Were* we shot act 1 first, which was the college sequence, but within the act, we shot out of order. Then we had to mix act 2 (New York) and act 3 (California) together, because we built the New York interiors in Burbank. When we moved to New York after shooting the college scenes, we shot only exteriors, including the end of the picture, and then had to skip the emotional interior sequences pending our return to the West Coast.

Let's assume we have gone through the entire script in such detail and come down to sixty days of shooting. Since we have discussed the amount of personnel and equipment needed in front of and behind the camera for each shooting segment, we can arrive at a rough budget figure covering per-day costs. Add to that items that are fixed costs, such as site rentals, set building and insurance, along with postproduction costs, for a below-the-line budget. This would not include the above-the-line costs, which cover the salaries of the creative people: writers, producers, director and actors. The studio may then say, "We can't spend that much money." So we start to cut. Instead of carrying a crane and the additional men required to operate it for ten weeks, one might agree to group all the crane shots into a two-week period. We forget the 400 extras in scene 24 and do it with 200 well-spaced extras. But nothing saves money on a film as much as cutting days off the schedule; other changes become relatively minor. Eventually, with more discussion back and forth with the financing studio, there is a shooting schedule and matching budget that is approved by everyone.

The choice of crew is next and is obviously extremely important. Not only do their various creative and mechanical abilities contribute to the final film, but every moment they save is an extra moment that can be spent creatively. Every director researches the background of proposed crew members religiously. What pictures have they done? What are their personalities? How fast are they? Do they get on well with other crew members?

The early stages of production depend upon the nature of the individual picture. If it requires an enormous amount of set construction, for example, the production designer is one of the first people hired. He may have a practical problem: to build a town that will take two months to construct and we are three months away from shooting.

I start thinking about a cinematographer from the first day I come on a picture. We may sit down together two months before shooting, just to talk. He may be finishing another picture, but we will get together for a couple of evenings, run some pictures together, talk about an effect, a concept, a way of working, f-stops, light level, color level, focus. These aspects of photography are all part of any filmmaker's vocabulary. It's possible to shoot the same scene twice, doing the same thing with the same actors; yet if they are photographed differently, the mood and emotional effect will obviously change. *Random Hearts* posed a common problem. Since color film tends to glamorize and enrich, the challenge was how to make it look unglamorous. Philippe Rousselot, the cinematographer, found a way to use diffused lighting to get around that.

Location scouting starts with the creative and ends up with the practical—the terrible compromise that characterizes filmmaking. First you look for the physical requirements, and for a certain kind of light and positioning in relation to the sun. If the plan calls for filming all day, you usually try to avoid shooting in the direction of sunrise or sunset. Otherwise, every couple of hours the location will be lit differently, and it will be difficult to match shots. This is an economic issue. Instead shoot against the light, or with the light behind you, for the minimum amount of change. Shooting toward south or north, shots can be matched over a longer period of time than shooting east or west. One would consult weather charts for the area for the specific time the shooting is planned, as opposed to when the scouting is done. You would also look for enough area for the crew to park. It's often misleading to scout on holidays. The idea is to anticipate the exact conditions of shooting. Inquire as to possible distractions. Will there be planes overhead? Traffic nearby? A different season? Again, common sense. I try to minimize looping, so it's important to make sure the location will be as quiet as possible. There is a world of difference between the immediacy of the emotional sound of a live performance and the artificial sound duplicated months later in a looping studio.

During principal photography I take great pains with performances. I try to rehearse only the day of shooting, to find a certain freshness. Other directors spend detailed rehearsal time prior to shooting. Sometimes I imagine a role differently from the way the actor sees it. If interpretations differ, there are only three options: Be persuasive and articulate enough to convince the actor; be open to modifying your approach if the actor is persuasive; or fire the actor. I've had to make the third choice only once.

While shooting, the director is closest (in no order of importance) to the cinematographer, the production designer, the first assistant director, the editor and often the costume designer. Then, on a more technical level, the sound people, script supervisor, prop people and others. Every director works differently. I look to the script supervisor for thorough notes for the editor, not for shot coverage. Generally I don't storyboard, except on a large-scale sequence involving lots of extras and expensive equipment. Sometimes I will draw stick figures for the crew, including a shot list, to visualize where we are going. Much of this is like diet: Moderation is the answer. A shot list can help organize thoughts but should never blind a director to spontaneous opportunities; on the set you always try to see what's unfolding before your eyes.

There are two philosophies about production, and both work. The one I subscribe to involves making the film at the very moment you are making it. In the other, the shooting is the photographic record of something that has been preplanned and rehearsed; Hitchcock worked that way. For me the film gets made at the moment it is happening. I try to be very alert to what is in front of me at that moment that isn't planned, that is new, but I don't hold that out as a preferable way to work for anyone else.

During production weather is often the most unpredictable factor. On *Out of Africa* there was an evening call for 5,000 extras and it began to rain. The water soaked and ruined the handmade costumes, and everyone had to be sent home. If it had been an intimate scene, we could have rewritten it for the rain. But in this case we had to take the loss on the costumes and shoot an alternate sequence while they were made again. This is an example of the kind of crisis situation a director sometimes faces in managing the financial impact of location emergencies. The bigger the production gets, the greater the potential for catastrophe. And problems can come from the most unexpected sources. On *Havana* a cargo container with all our wardrobe was stolen at the airport by someone who thought it would be valuable to them. Even governments can take advantage. In Kenya during *Out of Africa* the government imposed a customs duty on every roll of film coming into the country, even though the film was obviously not remaining there. The film didn't qualify as a duty item under their customs rules, but that didn't stop them. On *Havana* we were careful to complete shooting in the Dominican Republic two weeks before elections, for fear of violence.

There's no magic to running a set. It is a matter of choosing professional craftsmen with compatible personalities. (Nobody likes a screamer or a hysteric.) You try to strike a balance between being relatively comfortable and relatively tense. That edge of tension is helpful, but it has to be balanced with a kind of confidence and relaxation so that people trust you, want to listen to you and believe you know what you're doing (even though it may not always be true). One mistake a new director can make out of insecurity is to "show them who's boss." Crew members see through that right away.

Surprisingly, one of the most important aspects of making a movie is staying in shape, keeping your stamina up for the sheer physical rigors of shooting. People underestimate the workload: up at 5:30 A.M., in bed at 11:30 P.M. six days a week, over forty to seventy days. (*Out of Africa* shot for over 100 days.) Everyone has his or her own technique to stay fit. I try to exercise every morning, follow a diet during the week loaded with carbohydrates and vegetables, very little protein. On the weekends this can loosen up.

There are all kinds of problems that lead to falling behind schedule, and solutions involve common sense and ingenuity. If it starts to rain, you might try to include that in the scene; if an actor is sick, try to place his material in another scene; if there is a stop date with an actor, try to shoot all his scenes first. Sometimes a complicated sequence scheduled for two days may be redesigned as one shot, perhaps an elaborate camera move completed in half a day. Another way might be to shoot with very long lenses, too far away to see the actors' lips move. Shoot the scene, record the dialogue five minutes later, and two pages can sometimes be shot in an hour. These are extremes, but they work. Sometimes they're even preferable to your first ideas.

This business has its own etiquette for problems. A new director will surely get calls and visits from management. I got them every day when I was starting out. With an established director, management may be worried, but they communicate it in a more subtle way. Perhaps they make suggestions, in a spirit of cooperation, such as asking you to reduce the size of a sequence, or to change locations in the interest of speed, or to move a driving scene to a walking scene. In looking for cost-saving changes, I would usually call the writer, who might come up with solutions as well.

I view the dailies each night and discuss with the editor the takes I like best. We might use a piece of take 1 and another piece from take 2 and so on. The editor starts assembling the film from these designated takes as soon as possible. I view this *rough assembly* about two or three weeks after filming. This is always demoralizing for me because it never looks like what

I've imagined. Then the fine cutting begins. Working on the Avid, I usually put the edited version on one screen and the outtakes of the same scene on another screen, to compare them. Then, with the editor, I begin to redis-cuss each scene. We work through the film scene by scene in this way, which takes about six weeks to two months. I don't try to shape the movie at this point, but try to get each scene to play as well as possible. This con-cerns details like who to favor in a scene, whose face to be on for a given line, how much time to allow between reactions, whether to start a scene on a close-up of an actor, on an object, on a two-shot or on a master. Each decision has its aesthetic consequences.

Once I am satisfied that this is the best version I can achieve for each scene, we start considering the shape and rhythm of the overall movie: This scene is too slow; that scene should be cut in half; that one's not needed; this should be moved up front; we need a new scene here that we don't have; some voice-over is necessary; *that* point is never going to be clear; the audience won't understand what we meant in scene 6 when it was set up in scene 2, so we have to do some looping to put a line offscreen to set up scene 6 in scene 2. At the same time I usually start laying tempo-rary music to the cut picture, which helps me test the emotional result.

Then postsynchronization (or *looping*) occurs, which involves bring-ing the actors back to an audio studio, perhaps to add certain dialogue for clarity or rewrite purposes, or maybe for voice-overs. This process is speeded up with ADR, computer-assisted automatic dialogue replacement.

Next is a *spotting session* with the composer, who was probably chosen before shooting. We watch the movie, discussing in great detail the texture of the music and where it should be placed. What sort of emotion is needed? Should there be a solo instrument with a lot of air around it? In tempo or not? With rhythm? A thick sound? A transparent one? Wistful? It gets very specific. We might decide, "Start the music when she turns her head there and continue to the point where he walks out the door." That calls for a musical cue that is exactly 130 feet 6 frames in length. The music editor creates a master log of all these choices and times. Then the com-poser goes off to write the score. Sometimes the composer might play some key melodies early on for me, before they are fully orchestrated.

Then several things are happening at once: The titles are being laid out and opticals (such as dissolves, fades and superimpositions) are being or-dered; the mixers are choosing sound effects and processing and cleaning up dialogue for the final mixing of the picture; and the theatre trailer is probably being prepared, along with approaches for the print advertising campaign.

All of the postproduction elements require close attention, and most point up the importance of sound. The sound editors and I discuss such things as street sounds; sounds offstage; background ambience in any given scene; the atmosphere of a night at the campfire; the echo of the animals on the plains. These details infuse scenes with reality and mood—a kind of emotional underpinning. There is a premix period of about two weeks, for the primary sound engineer (the dialogue engineer) to conform the dialogue tracks electronically and equalize them. Microphones are not like human ears; they hear things in "patterns." Depending on the angle of the microphone during shooting, the equalization and sound of a voice might be completely different from shot to shot. If part of a scene was shot in the morning and part was shot in the afternoon, and the mike was not in precisely the same position, the sound will be different and must be conformed. There can be different background noise on a track in the third line of a speech than on the first line of the speech. If a close-up was shot later than the master, the cut-in from the master to the close-up might be jarring aurally when this background noise changes. The background can be "cleaned out." But when a sound frequency is cleaned out in the background, the same frequency is also cleaned out in the voice. To avoid this, there are devices, filters, that shut off automatically when the voice starts and turn on when the voice ends.

Around the same time there are the *scoring sessions,* which I always find very exciting. Days are spent with the composer and often with a full symphony orchestra, who perform the musical cues to picture on a soundstage. Assisting the composer, who usually conducts, there might be an orchestrator. Some composers do their own orchestrations, some don't. There is also the contractor, who handles the business aspects of the sessions. Issues of performance are discussed, and evaluations are made that sometimes lead to instantaneous rewrites of a particular cue.

At the final mix the three sound sources—dialogue, music and effects—are carefully blended with the picture in stereo (left, middle, right) and interwoven to fill out the emotional content of each reel, a process that moves at about a reel a day (a two-hour picture runs twelve reels). In this process there are decisions on equalization and balances: At what level of consciousness should we hear the wind, versus the music, versus the dialogue, versus the seagulls, versus the soldiers marching in the distance, versus a woman singing, drunk, in an alleyway? The musical mix from scoring can also be modified in the final mix. And since the picture is usually in stereo, one is also conscious about assigning information to the left, middle, right and/or surround channels.

It's possible radically to alter what an audience feels by tiny variations from literal reality in the soundtrack: when a sound starts and when it fades; whether it cuts off or overlaps slightly into the next scene; whether it previews the coming scene by beginning just a touch before the cut. Quite often I'll make a straight cut visually but soften it by cross-fading the sound behind it rather than cutting from one sound to another.

Reverb can be a valuable tool to make a sound dissolve. It can be thin and transparent; you can hear through it, much the way you see through an image dissolve. On a mixing board, where one knob controls the source and one controls reverb, pushing the reverb and pulling back on the source at the same time can create a sound that is increasingly transparent and less opaque, becoming ethereal. This can be a useful effect. There was a section in *Out of Africa*, for instance, where I needed Karen (Meryl Streep) to realize that Denys (Robert Redford) was dead. He was hundreds of miles away, but she needed suddenly to *sense* it while she's just standing there. We communicated this with sound, suddenly chopping off the source sound and pushing the reverb all the way so that there was an odd, eerie echo. The soundtrack can guide the audience often as much as the visual.

Sometimes, in reaction to an artificial emptiness in the background sound of a scene, I wonder how to fill it. A woman's laugh? Two people whispering? Would construction sounds add to the scene? One of my favorite background tracks is the sound of someone practicing a piano, scales in the distance. It's a very evocative sound—moody.

Next is working with the cinematographer at the laboratory in timing the print, correcting the density and the color-balance. Density refers to lightness and darkness, and color-balance is concerned with choosing the warmer (toward red) and/or colder (toward blue) tones. Does the scene require a warm or a cold feeling? More red? More blue? Balancing is a subjective art. Often flesh tones in a given scene are the best guide. Since everybody sees differently, this is also subjective. What's too warm to my eye may be cold to someone else's. We look at a *mute answer print*. It has no sound because until now we have been working with magnetic sound on strips of film separate from the picture. The merger of sound and picture will happen in the printing process.

Meanwhile the sound has been transferred to an optical negative and sent to the lab. A bunch of squiggly black lines become squiggly white lines on the positive, which will be "read" by a projector and translated into sound. The laboratory takes all of the technical data from viewing the mute answer print, joins the sound negative with it and strikes the first final-viewing answer print. The response to all of the postproduction questions should be found in the answer print. From there all the other prints are made.

Next is the film's transfer to video. This can be done in two ways:

either from an approved positive color print or from the cut negative. Tests are made from each to decide which should be the source. In the video transfer it's possible to make up for all kinds of imaging mistakes that cannot be corrected on film.

Marketing, which accelerates with a completed film, is a mysterious process. (See article by Robert G. Friedman, p. 282.) The tension in marketing is often found between the need for the marketing team to persuade as large an audience as possible to attend on opening weekend and the wish the director has for the marketing campaign to be honest as to what they are going to see. Marketing executives are always straddling this conundrum. Since many pictures are either made or broken on their opening weekend, there is enormous pressure to bring people into theatres that weekend at all costs. A primary tool is the trailer, which isolates the dramatic high points while perhaps slightly misrepresenting the film as a result. This forces a film into a category—love story, action, suspense, mystery—which may not be a proper fit. If the picture is misrepresented in its campaign and the wrong audience shows up, they will not like the movie, generating bad word of mouth. How does marketing represent a picture truthfully and still get the maximum number of people to attend? That can be a dilemma.

Sometimes I travel around the United States and sometimes other countries to help sell the picture. The major publicity tours can be divided into sectors. Heading east, the major markets are England, Belgium, France, Germany, Italy, Spain, Sweden, Holland and Hungary. To the west there are Australia and Japan. In the south there are Mexico, Brazil and Argentina.

As far as preparing for the overseas markets, it is nice to see that most European countries are leaning toward subtitles instead of dubbing. This is a relief for directors, since a dubbed picture can sound dreadful. In dubbing, different actors are used, and this loses subtleties of performance and ambience. I try to minimize this by working with translators and subtitlers, using dialogue transcriptions, and by approving the voices of actors for other languages. For a measure of how potent the global market has become, *Out of Africa* did 65 percent of its business outside the United States. It was thought of as an American picture since it was made by an American company, with two American stars (even though one of them plays a Dane), and is about English characters. Yet it made most of its money overseas.

No discussion of directing can be complete without reference to technical advances that can be helpful to new filmmakers such as digital video and the Internet. Years ago, there was no way for a director to demonstrate talent without getting a job as a director, and no one would hire an untested director; it was a catch-22. Today, because it costs so little to make a film on digital video, people come out of college with twenty-minute or longer movies that help launch their careers. Also, the Internet has become a showcase for short films, allowing new filmmakers to show their work to a growing online audience, and I think that's great.

MY MOVIES: THE COLLISION OF ART AND MONEY

by **MEL BROOKS,** who was one of the writers on Sid Caesar's classic television program *Your Show of Shows*. Then he turned to movies, where he won an Oscar for writing and directing a short subject, *The Critic*. He won another Oscar for writing *The Producers*, which was also the first feature he directed, and went on to write and direct *The Twelve Chairs* and cowrite and direct *Blazing Saddles* and *Young Frankenstein*. Brooks managed to add more hyphens to his credits for subsequent pictures *Silent Movie* (actor-director-cowriter), *High Anxiety, History of the World, Part I, Spaceballs, Life Stinks, Robin Hood: Men in Tights* and *Dracula: Dead and Loving It* (producer-actor-director-writer). His production company, Brooksfilms, has produced such pictures as *The Elephant Man, My Favorite Year, Frances, To Be or Not to Be, 84 Charing Cross Road, The Fly, The Fly II* and *The Vagrant*. Later, he won three Tony Awards (best original score, best book of a musical and best musical) for converting *The Producers* into a hit Broadway show that won a record-setting twelve Tonys. In addition to industry awards, he has received France's Legion of Honor, Order of Arts and Letters.

> What is the toughest thing about making film? Putting in the little holes.

'm primarily an observer of life who formalizes his observations by writing them down. Some of us have no need to tell anybody else about those observations. I happen to have a need to pronounce myself. I started my career as a drummer; I'm sorry I stopped because it is still the best and the loudest way of calling attention to myself.

I began as a writer and I'm still basically a writer. I directed a summer stock company when I was a little boy in Red Bank, New Jersey; I also directed some theatre in the borscht belt and was a drummer-comic there. I'd been writing *Your Show of Shows* and then *Caesar's Hour* on television for years when I decided that it was time for me to leave and do something else with my life. Maybe become a housewife.

When I moved away from Sid Caesar and went into the real world of writing television specials, it was very difficult when the director or producer would say "Thank you" and that was it; I had no control over the material. When I wrote my first movie, *The Producers*, I decided that I would also direct it to protect my vision.

The Producers was first written as a novel. It talked too much, so I made it into a play, which ended up with too many locations, so I turned it into a film. It was right out of my own life experience; I once worked with a man who did make serious love to very old ladies late at night on an old leather office couch. They would give him blank checks, and he would produce phony plays. I can't mention his name because he would go to jail. Just for the old ladies alone he would go to jail. I wrote my heart out, and the movie, I think, is one of my best, though it was not very commercial.

I directed *The Producers* because I didn't want anybody interfering with my words. It was a very difficult course for me to chart because I didn't realize that movies are so expensive.

The story of *The Producers* is a very interesting one. I wrote the script with help from my assistant, Alfa-Betty Olsen, and every studio said, "Please, no. Try not to come back here." An agent, Barry Levinson (no relation to the filmmaker), knew producer Sidney Glazier. Barry set a meeting (in those days you didn't "take" a meeting) with me, and Sidney, who read it, shook my hand and said, "It's the funniest thing I've ever heard. We're going to make a movie out of this." He went to Joseph E. Levine (Embassy Pictures at that time) and said to Joe, "I will raise half a million dollars if you put up half a million dollars. You distribute the film; it will cost a million dollars to make." Joe Levine said yes but "Brooks can't direct." I said no.

Levine wanted a real director. At a luncheon meeting, I ate very nicely; I didn't want to make any mistakes, nothing dropped out of my mouth. I didn't eat bread and butter because I didn't know whether you should cut the bread or break it. Meanwhile Joe ate everything; I had nothing to worry about. At the end of the meal, Levine turned to me casually and said, "Hey, kid, you think you can direct a picture?" I said, "Sure." He said, "Swear to God?" I said, "Yes." He said, "OK. Go ahead," and shook my hand. He was impressed with me; he thought I was nice and cute and funny. He hadn't read the script, but he liked the idea. Like the old Hollywood producers who never read anything, he liked to hear things. "Tell it to me," they'd say. "He goes to this place called Shangri-La." "Yeah?" "And there are these people, they look young, but they're really old." "Sounds good, sounds good."

Sidney Glazier raised half a million dollars from a company called Universal Marion Corporation, and Joe Levine and Embassy put up half a million. I cast the picture with Zero Mostel and Gene Wilder, and we shot it in eight weeks; the budget was $946,000.

When we finished the picture, we took it to the Lane Theatre in Philadelphia for a sneak preview around Christmas 1967. Nobody came. Twelve hundred seats. Eleven people showed up. The movie was over, and I got on a slow train back to New York. Then, since we had shown the picture to some critics earlier in Philadelphia, the reviews came out. They were horrible. Joe Levine was going to shelve it but Sidney Glazier prevailed upon him to wait and to start a little campaign of sneak previews in New York. We opened at the Fine Arts Theatre in Manhattan. Word of mouth had spread; there was a line around the block; you couldn't get in. Levine opened the picture slowly elsewhere, handling it carefully. Eventually it became a moneymaker, though it took four years to get its money back. Levine had risked almost a million dollars. He put up $500,000 for the negative and about $400,000 for prints, advertising and openings. It took a lot of perseverance and work to make that picture become profitable.

I learned a little about movie financing from *The Producers* because I had a participation in the movie, and it was important for me to learn why I wasn't getting any money for my participation. It's impossible for a profit participant to make any money on a movie unless it's a gigantic hit because overhead and interest are always being charged to the film.

My second picture was *The Twelve Chairs*. For it, I actually went to Yugoslavia and learned there are two basic costs in a movie: *below-the-line,* which refers to materials and the technical aspects of the film, such as personnel, set construction, wires, lights, cameras, and transportation; and *above-the-line,* the more creative aspects of the film, such as the property itself, writers, producer, director, stars, and principals. Extras are (no offense) below-the-line.

When I finished my next picture, *Blazing Saddles,* I screened it for the Warner Bros. executives. It was quiet. Not even the world-famous bean scene got a laugh. I turned very pale. Thank God it was dark. John Calley, who was in charge of production at the time, and Ted Ashley, who was running Warner Bros., were very nice to me and said, "It's crazy. We like it. Forgive the fact that there was no laughter. These people are studying their various jobs in connection with the picture, and they don't know what to make of it." I said to myself, "It's a failure."

Mike Hertzberg, the producer, was alone with me after they had all cleared out of that screening room, and suddenly he's on the telephone saying, "Yes, yes, screening room twelve, eight o'clock. Be there; invite people." I said, "What are you doing?" He said, "We're having a screening of the same movie. Tonight. All the secretaries at Warner Bros. I'm getting 200 people to see it." Eight o'clock comes, 200 plain humans are packed into this room. They're very quiet and polite. Frankie Laine sings the title song. The whip cracks start; laughter begins. We go to the railroad segment. Lyle, the cruel overseer, says to Cleavon Little, "How about a little good old nigger work song?" The audience gets a little chilled. Cleavon Little and the other guys working on the railroad begin to sing "I Get No Kick From Champagne." People leave their chairs in ecstasy, float upside down, and the laughter never stops from that moment on.

We next had a sneak preview in Westwood, and that, too, was successful. It was then that the studio executives screened *Blazing Saddles* again and changed their minds. The picture opened to mixed reviews. My films have never gotten unanimously good reviews; I hope they never will.

"Everything Mel Brooks has learned about films," said *The New York Times,* "seems to have been forgotten in this mess called *Blazing Saddles.*" When my next picture, *Young Frankenstein,* was released, one critic said, "Where was the great anarchic beauty of *Blazing Saddles?*" It takes them a while to like my films.

When *Blazing Saddles* opened, it got fairly bad reviews and was an instant hit in New York. But Warner Bros. opened it in about 500 theatres in one day across the country. It did well only in 15 big cities. In every other place, like Lubbock, Amarillo, Pittsfield and Des Moines, it died. The picture didn't get the word of mouth it needed, so it closed. The Warners advertising executive, Dick Lederer, was my guardian angel. (For an article by Mr. Lederer, see p. 148.) He said, "I think we should spend $3 million to advertise it. Pull it out of all these little cities, open it in the summer when it's gained a reputation, and spend $3 million to support it." There was a mixed vote in the room; the deciding votes belonged to Ted Ashley and John Calley. They said, "OK, we go with you. Let's spend $3 million, and we'll try and see what we can do." To their credit, *Blazing Saddles* opened wide in June to tremendous business around the country. It's done over $80 million in rentals worldwide in 1974 dollars.

In my experience directing comedies, I've found that timing for laughs is critical. How much space should you leave on screen for laughter before you go on to the next sound on the soundtrack? Once you've shown the picture to an audience, you and the editor decide. You say, "Look, they're laughing pretty heavily here. Can I have some more frames before we cut from that shot?" That helps. There are ways to find the proper rhythm of jokes and laughter. The Marx Brothers actually went on the road with some of the comedy sequences from their films to test the timing on live audiences.

After a while, I can judge within a few seconds either way just how much laughter we can get. Sometimes I'm dead wrong. In *Silent Movie,* there was a sequence that no one will ever see; it's on the cutting-room floor. The sequence is called "Lobsters in New York." It starts with a shot of a neon sign that reads "Chez Lobster." The camera drops down to restaurant doors and pulls back. The doors open, the camera goes inside, and we see greeting us a huge well-dressed lobster with claws and tails; around the camera come two other very well-dressed lobsters in evening clothes. The maitre d' lobster leads them to a waiter lobster in a white jacket, who leads them to a table. They order, then follow the waiter lobster to a huge tank. In the tank, little people are swimming around. We thought this was hysterical. The lobsters choose some people, pick them up squirming around, and the sequence ends. Every time we saw this sequence, we were on the floor laughing. When we showed it to an audience of secretaries—the first audience to see any of my films—they did not laugh at all at "Lobsters in New York." They stared at each other. Not one snicker. Finally, we got some embarrassed sounds and yawns. We threw out the entire sequence as a result. That was one of the surprises that comedy screenwriters get from time to time.

When I did *Silent Movie,* I used a Sony videotape camera that showed us exactly what we'd just shot when we played it back. I also consulted on the set with the three writers who had written the picture with me. The same team later wrote *High Anxiety* with me, and I wanted them around to be harsh critics. Film is such a collaborative process that unless you're writing a very personal story, it's helpful to write with another person. You become a mini-audience right there and then; multiple judgments enter into what you're doing, and that's important early on.

Writers! Do not discuss embryonic ideas. Incipient ideas are your own and nobody else's. When you have coffee, don't talk to other people in the business about your ideas until they are fully written and registered with the Writers Guild. You will not get help; you'll get envy and you'll get stealing. Your ideas are private. Not only will an idea get stolen, but you will let the vapor of creation escape when you tell it. Talk to yourself through the paper; write it down. It's a good exercise, and sometimes it makes money for you.

Comedy is a rough form to sell to studios and independent producers. It's the most mercurial cinematic item. Every once in a while a good comedy comes along. *Sibling Rivalry,* Carl Reiner's film, is a terrific comedy, but nobody saw it because the studio didn't support it enough. Then there is the "Friday-night phenomenon." If it doesn't do terrific business on opening night, marketing monies are soon scarce. Studios rarely take a chance on comedy. When I made my studio deal at Twentieth Century Fox, I didn't know *Blazing Saddles* was going to go through the roof. I just wanted security, a place to work and an assurance that I would make at least three movies. I still respect Fox for taking a chance on me when I was relatively unknown and for giving me the opportunity to make my three movies for them. I don't need studio front money now; all I really need is a studio's distribution expertise and muscle.

When I presented the idea of *Silent Movie* to Fox, their mouths dropped open. They were very shocked, but they didn't want to turn me down because of my track record. That's "The Green Awning Syndrome." After Mike Nichols made *The Graduate,* I said, "If Mike Nichols went to Joe Levine and said, 'I want to do *The Green Awning,*' the answer would be, 'The what?' '*The Green Awning.*' 'What is it?' 'It's a movie about a green awning.'

'Does any famous star walk under the green awning?' 'No, all unknowns.' 'Are there any naked women near the green awning?' 'No, no naked women.' 'Are people talking and eating sandwiches and scrambled eggs on outdoor tables under the green awning?' 'No, it's just a green awning.' 'Panavision?' 'No, just a green awning. It doesn't move.' 'How long would it be?' 'Two hours.' 'For two hours nothing but a green awning on the screen? No talking, no dialogue, nothing? All right, we'll do it.' " That's the Green Awning Syndrome. When I said, "Silent Movie," in 1976, they said, "Sounds interesting." I knew in their hearts they were saying, "Oh, God! How can we say no without hurting his feelings, without losing him?" I explained later that there might be some great movie stars in it.

As it happened, I worked with five stars in *Silent Movie:* Liza Minnelli, Paul Newman, Anne Bancroft, Jimmy Caan, and Burt Reynolds. I chose them because I knew they were pleasures to work with. Fox was more amenable to the idea of *Silent Movie* when I told them there would be stars in it. "No dialogue in 1976? That's a toughie." They were very brave to make that picture. I wasn't frightened at all until the first dailies. I said, "What the hell are we doing? I can't hear anybody! This is crazy. You've done it, Brooks, this is it. Sanity has finally caught up with you." But it all worked out, and the picture was a huge success.

I wanted to keep the writing team on *Silent Movie* together, but they were ready to go off in different directions when the picture was over. Casually at lunch one day, I said, "What about a movie called *High Anxiety?*" "What's that?" "It's Hitchcock." "Oh, yeah?" We discussed it and then wrote it in sixteen weeks. We knew that we had to have the Psychoneurotic Institute for the Very, Very Nervous, and I knew that I would be Professor Richard Harpo Thorndyke. Six years I was in analysis, and I wanted to get even with them. *High Anxiety* is a tribute to Alfred Hitchcock; there were many scenes from his films in it, and stylistically it's very much like him. Through that picture I could talk about psychoanalysis and psychiatry, which I care about a lot. I can't make fun of anything I don't care about. The budget of *High Anxiety* was $4.3 million; I brought it in for $3.4 million.

In order to direct comedy, the first step is to understand the script thoroughly: how it translates into sound and action and how the characters relate to each other. Once it is understood, you get a picture in your mind that is always altered by the specific gifts of the actors and actresses. My secret is very simple. Early on, I have three or four casual readings of the entire movie script around a big table with all the principal players. Questions come up. I will say things like, "Gee, that's a strange approach to that line; I heard it differently. But I like it." An actor will invariably say,

"What do you mean? How did you hear it?" I'll say, "Well, forget it." He'll say, "No, no, please." In that way, I sneak in a line reading and he thinks he discovered it himself.

I try to keep the atmosphere on the set buoyant and relaxed because there's a lot of tension in making a movie. The cinematographer is always worried about the lights. If he's outdoors, he's a maniac because a cloud might go by. The actors are always worried about getting the scene right, and often when they've done it perfectly, they will ask for one more take because they're not sure. First, there is the artistic pressure of capturing life itself through that one-eyed monster; second, there is the budget, in which every dollar is a second that is ticking away. The pressure is especially great when you're doing a big scene with a lot of extras.

For the writer-director, there is often a conflict when you'd like to do something lavish in a scene, but you're not sure whether it's worth the cost. For example, at the same time that I'm writing a big grand salon scene in *History of the World, Part I* for the French Revolution sequence, I think of the budget and how much it will cost to reconstruct the Palace of Versailles. How am I going to get those verisimilitudinous qualities . . . which is very difficult to say and to get. In this case, I spoke to my friend Albert Whitlock, who paints the greatest mattes in the world. He can paint on glass and take a few live characters and paint Versailles around them. If I were to try to construct Versailles, the picture would cost $100 million.

On my pictures since *History of the World, Part I,* Brooksfilms has managed to retain all or most of the overseas rights. Emile Buyse, who ran Fox's international operation for years, was stolen by me to run Brooksfilms' overseas sales, and he was the architect behind this. Generally, a domestic distributor puts up roughly 60% to 70% of the negative cost, and the balance is financed through overseas sales. (I take a reduced fee for my multiple services so that the picture is not saddled with huge above-the-line costs.)

I direct a film to protect the writing. I produce a film to have total business control as well as creative control over the film's future. Little by little, in defense of the initial vision, I've learned to put on other hats. In the movie business, it's important to understand the nature of money and how to sail through those terrible white waters with reefs and sharks, where art and money meet. For example, there are little nuances to watch for in contracts with a domestic distributor. They might throw in a clause that is easily overlooked, stating that revenue from airline play on any and all airlines serviced in the United States is the property of the domestic distributor. Seems innocuous, but it can be dangerous, costing hundreds of thousands of dollars. All monies derived from airlines that are based abroad and fly foreign flags should be constituted as *international revenue* to keep them from falling into the domestic distributor's pocket.

Another business issue is whether to go union or nonunion. The answer is, sometimes it's cheaper to go union. Mistakes that nonunion crews can make can be incredibly costly: loading the film incorrectly, not checking the gate for scratches or dirt and focusing improperly can all be disastrous. Here are some guidelines on keeping costs down: Rehearse as many days as possible before shooting, never rehearse on shooting days and curtail the number of shooting days.

Transportation is costly. Don't move your cast and crew from a studio to location more than once. Schedule all your location shooting together. On *Life Stinks,* we shot on location for the first seven weeks and finished up the last five weeks in the studio. In writing the film, I was very conscious of trying to keep most of the action shot on location happening during the day. Night shooting is very difficult, very tiring and in the end, very costly. God is very nice, giving the filmmaker a lovely sun to light the world with. Use it in good health.

Generally, in production, I take as much time as each film needs. Now, I take even more time in the distribution of the picture. What does the one-sheet look like? Where is the picture opening? Is there a good sound system? Is the theatre equipped with Dolby? Newspaper advertising is archaic and very costly; I would rather spend money on a good television campaign.

Since I'm very proud of my image abroad as a filmmaker, I'll travel to help sell my films. It's possible to get a lot of coverage in European newspapers simply by going there and doing interviews. I won't do that in the States because I don't want the same high level of exposure here. My pictures do very well in Sweden, Germany, Italy and France; in England, they do pretty well, but not as well as I'd like because of the high cost of advertising there. China is an exciting market. If everybody in China went to see my movies and paid one penny to get in, I'd be rich. Besides, I love Chinese food.

My advice as to the best way to break into the business is to write. Or be a big movie star. If Tom Cruise wants to direct a picture, they'll let him. Very few of us are going to become big movie stars, but we can write if we apply ourselves. To me, the vapor of human existence is best captured in film; it's a great molding of all the primary creative arts. If a writer is talented, his talent can open the door to directing. The director, in the end, is the real author of a movie.

It's very important for a creative personality—writer, director or actor—to have good advisors. I have a lawyer, Alan U. Schwartz (May The

Schwartz Be With You), who has been a friend since the beginning. I also have a good business manager–accountant, Robert Goldberg, who protects me from studio accounting. Studio accounting should be a Busby Berkeley musical. When do they stop taking money? They take overhead on interest and interest on overhead. If a picture costs a million dollars to make, it's a third more just because of studio accounting procedures. If it's $15 million to honestly and actually produce, it will cost $26 million for the same picture to be done at a major studio. For their part, they're risking a lot of money, which is how they justify it.

As for the future of the business, I see bigger profits on fewer pictures. The home-entertainment technology scares me more than anything because I want an audience to laugh at my movies. I want people to sit in a dark theatre, let the silver screen bathe them with images and have them laugh as a group. It's thrilling to hear a lot of people laughing together. But with the direction of current technology, it seems we'll have tiny little groups at home, or sometimes even one skinny person watching a big fat Mel Brooks movie. You can't get a lot of laughs that way. I wasn't born to make one thin person laugh; I was born to make a lot of fat and skinny people sit in the dark and laugh together.

What is the toughest thing about making film? Putting in the little holes. The sprocket holes are the hardest thing to make. Everything else is easy, but all night you have to sit with that little puncher and make the holes on the side of the film. You could faint from that work. The rest is easy: the script is easy, the acting is easy, the directing is a breeze . . . but the sprockets will tear your heart out.

THE INDEPENDENT FILMMAKER

by **HENRY JAGLOM,** whose films as writer-director include *A Safe Place, Tracks, Sitting Ducks, Can She Bake a Cherry Pie?, Always, Someone to Love, New Year's Day, Eating, Venice/Venice, Babyfever, Last Summer in the Hamptons, Déjà Vu* and *Festival in Cannes*. He began his career as an actor and appeared in films directed by Jack Nicholson, Dennis Hopper and Orson Welles (each of whom he subsequently directed in return). Mr. Jaglom is unusual among filmmakers in that he produces his pictures often financed through foreign presales and frequently distributes them domestically through his own company, Rainbow Releasing, a subsidiary of his Los Angeles–based Rainbow Film Company.

I had come upon a formula that has lasted to this day: If I could make a picture inexpensively enough, say for 5% to 10% of what an average studio film would cost, I could have the luxury of aiming at only 5% to 10% of the audience to show a profit.

While it has been said that I "do it all myself" and this is rare in American filmmaking, I see it simply as the businessperson part of me taking care of the artist. A creative person can't just stop with the creative work. You have to learn how to get your work seen, how to force your vision out to the public against all the pressures that try to stop you. I've seen many wonderful, creative people trampled on because they have not known how to take care of the business aspects of themselves. Orson Welles was the prime example of this, and it was very sad for me to watch him be unable to get his films made.

Early in my career it was clear that there was no established economic mechanism to support the kind of films I wanted to make. I came out to Los Angeles in the late 1960s as an actor, was put under contract to Screen Gems and began peddling my own scripts. After the success of *Easy Rider*, Columbia wanted to reward the people who had been involved in that movie (I had worked on the editing), which allowed producer Bert Schneider to let Jack Nicholson direct *Drive, He Said*, Bob Rafelson direct *Five Easy Pieces* and me adapt and direct the screen version of my play *A Safe Place* (1971), starring Tuesday Weld, Orson Welles and Jack Nicholson. Schneider gave me creative control and ultimately final cut on that first film, which spoiled me for life. Columbia could not be bothered with it; they had *Nicholas and Alexandra*. My picture was a small poetic art film, made for a big company, and didn't do any business. Although I was offered other studio pictures based on a gift they thought I had for directing actors and creating screen reality, I would no longer be given creative control. They wouldn't give me final cut, no matter what else they offered. And without final cut I couldn't imagine making my kind of films.

I had to find another way to make the kind of intimate, small-scale human picture that appealed to me. It took me five years to finance my second film, *Tracks*, starring Dennis Hopper. I had wanted to make a film about the Vietnam War, but at the time, the war was still going on, and the only thing less popular than making a film about the war was wanting Dennis Hopper to star in it. It would never have been made had it not been for an economically corrupt system that existed at that time involving tax shelters.

Tracks was originally financed in 1973–74. My partner at the time, Howard Zuker, raised $1 million through dentists and doctors investing $25,000 to $50,000 apiece, each of whom could write off seven or eight times that amount under the tax shelter laws then in place. The investors were not interested in picture content; they were only interested in the write-off. In fact, when Columbia refused to release Bert Schneider and Peter Davis's brilliant documentary about the Vietnam War, *Hearts and Minds*, we took that initial $1 million raised by Zuker and used it to get *Hearts and Minds* away from Columbia and released by Warner Bros., and started raising money all over again for *Tracks*, which is why the film didn't come out until 1976.

At the time, another roadblock was that there were no small distribution companies of the sort that were later to proliferate. There were only majors, and none of them wanted to release *Tracks;* it remains the only picture of mine that never had a real theatrical release. After playing a couple of weeks in a few cities, it was gone.

Luckily, since *A Safe Place* was an extraordinary success in Europe (playing for years in Paris) and *Tracks* performed strongly as well (sharing Italy's Donatello award with Woody Allen's *Manhattan*), I was able to finance my third film in Europe, as tax shelter financing was ending in the United States. It was slowly dawning on the major distributors that there was money to be made releasing smaller, artistic pictures, so they launched specialty divisions: Triumph at Columbia, Orion Classics at Orion, Universal Classics. Other companies began emerging to release independent pictures just in time for my third film, *Sitting Ducks* (1980), which happened to be quite commercially successful for an independent. It had taken ten years since my first picture to get my third picture released. *Sitting Ducks* was distributed by United Film Distribution, an arm of United Artists Theatres.

By this time I had come upon a formula that has lasted to this day: If I could make a picture inexpensively enough, say for 5% to 10% of what an average studio film would cost, I could have the luxury of aiming at only 5% to 10% of the audience to show a profit. At the same time, video-cassettes and cable technologies offered new sources of income for films. And there were these new independent distributors, including at the time New Line, Goldwyn, Atlantic, Island, Alive, Castle Hill, Skouras and, later and most successfully, Fine Line and Miramax, who realized that if a picture cost $1 million and made $5 million, everyone would be very happy. If that same picture were made by a studio for $10 to $12 million and made the same $5 million, it would, of course, be a disaster. These smaller distributors were doing well handling smaller-scale quality pictures such as mine with lower advertising costs than the majors, films aimed at intelligent, adult audiences who wanted to see serious work about human relationships.

The question became how do I, from an economic standpoint, devise a system to finance films for that minority audience? First, I found that Europe was an ideal source of financing. For example, a German distributor comes to me with a contract offering $200,000 for their territory for each film I make. They don't ask for titles or casting, but only that each film be in the English language, 35mm, color, no less than eighty minutes, no longer than two and a half hours, and "signed by Jaglom," as they put it. With another $150,000 from England, $100,000 from Italy, $75,000 from Scandinavia, for example, and similar amounts from other European territories, I could easily achieve my budget, still retain all rights in the United States and, most importantly, keep my ownership of the negative. Since then, happily, my pictures have increased in value, and new formats such as home video, DVD, video-on-demand, cable and satellite have added to the size and source of advances, and even created many markets where formerly there were none.

Since I owned the negative in the United States, I could then find the most sympathetic small distributor to release my pictures properly, aimed at that 5% to 10% of the movie audience who would positively respond to my films. *Can She Bake a Cherry Pie?* (1983) was released by Castle Hill; *Always* (1985) was released by the Samuel Goldwyn Company (for an advance of $1 million); and *Someone to Love* (1987) was codistributed by Castle Hill and my own company. That's how I got into distribution.

When I saw how it all worked, I decided I could actually release my own pictures, so I began Rainbow Releasing as a subsidiary of our production company, the Rainbow Film Company, and starting with *New Year's Day* (1989) and *Eating* (1990), we did so. There is really no mystery as to how it works. For a small, artistic "quality" picture in America, there are perhaps two or three theatres in each city to choose from to begin with. You show them the picture; they make an offer; you discuss advances and terms and how many weeks for the length of the run, and do this for each city. Once a theatre is chosen, we allocate a print, trailers, posters and press kits, all self-generated. This way we control the quality of the print, what photos are sent, the advertising campaign and the one-sheets. I am so hands-on that I even draw the artwork title for most of my movies, which has become a kind of signature, I guess.

My release strategy is often to have the first opening in Los Angeles, where I have had a strong following, usually in a Laemmle theatre. (See article by Robert Laemmle, p. 401.) In the tenth week in Los Angeles I may very well do better than in the fourth week, thanks to word of mouth. In Boston or San Francisco, my pictures may run for close to a year. In each city my audiences tend to build through word of mouth, so the picture must be able to hold in the theatre for this to occur. Obviously I must find sympathetic exhibitors willing to allow the time. On *Eating* I found a small New York theatre in a wonderful location in Greenwich Village that was willing to hold the picture for many months. Once word of mouth catches on, I can spend less on advertising, which in any case can never compete with the big companies' full-page ads and TV campaigns. To my delight my audience is growing with each picture. The result is I now play most films in over 300 cities theatrically. *Déjà Vu* played in over 350.

Let me underscore the importance of finding theatres willing to have my pictures settle in for a period of time. After all, I make movies for an audience that I hope will feel less isolated, less crazy, because they see something that touches upon some truths about their own lives. A film of mine is not for everybody, but those people who want it should be able to find it. My job is to find ways to make it available to them.

Overseas this is equally important. After *Eating* was shown at the Deauville festival, for example, I was able to make a deal with a top French distributor, MK2, which greatly improved my position in that territory, and of course I made sure to visit Paris to do press to support the release of the film there. It became a smash hit! Finding that ideal distributor in each overseas territory is an important step, just as finding a proper theatre in each American city is. With each move I build relationships with distributors and exhibitors, supportive journalists and growing audiences to position my next film and also to benefit my prior pictures in cassette/DVD sales and on TV. As new technologies emerge in growing territories, this means more revenue. Since I own the negatives, I continually make new deals for old films as opportunities arise. For example, I sold *Tracks* to an

Asian country for a satellite delivery system that of course didn't exist when the picture first came out. *Sitting Ducks* has even played Mozambique! All my films have played on Polish TV! Who would have thought this possible just a few years ago?

My system is working well. Part of the reason is that I don't have an ego about spending a lot of money. It's the other way around; my ego is in striving for quality for *little* money. I am often juggling a couple of movies, planning one, editing another and working on the release of a third.

Orson Welles once said to me at lunch, "The enemy of art is the absence of limitations." Economically and creatively that's the most important advice you can be given. You have limitations; you don't have $1 million to blow up that bridge, so you have to create something else on film to produce the same effect which heightens the originality. Instead of having money to hire hundreds of extras, you have to sneak a cameraman in a wheelchair through the streets of New York City and steal the shot, which gives you a look of much greater reality. With economic limitations you are forced to create art. As an example, on *Can She Bake a Cherry Pie?* I could not afford to rent a restaurant. So I asked the owner if I could put a few chairs *outside,* as if it were an outdoor café. The scene was shot, and there was all this wonderful, natural background activity *inside* the restaurant. Afterward the owner kept the outside area as a new feature of his restaurant. "The absence of limitations is the enemy of art." For those of us who have the pretension to claim to try to be artists in this business so many love to call their "industry," money limitations or time limitations are not a problem, they are a spur to be creative.

To give you a sense of my working process, I often get my actors together and work with them in creating their characters and *encourage* the dialogue out of them, rather than predetermining it, using *their* language, *their* memories, *their* personalities to fit into *my* overview. Movies, to me (as opposed to plays or novels), exist when they are *shot,* so you cannot predetermine what the look, nuance or emotion of a scene will ultimately be. You create it, and *then* it exists, not the other way around.

Afterward I go into my editing room and "write" the movie with what the actors have given me on film. My most scripted movie was my first, *A Safe Place,* which was also the most poetic and difficult to make. Every movie since has had less of a conventionally written script and been developed more in my head and on my feet. I always go into a project with a strange sense of knowing, in my mind, what the whole movie is supposed to feel like. Orson Welles said the difference between me and other filmmakers is that others first write their story and try to find their theme *in* that story; I start with my theme—the end of a marriage, the loneliness of a generation, trying to move on in life, eating disorders, the biological clock, the insanity of show business, soul mates—and *then* work at that, figuring that my story will emerge. I don't think of myself as writing and directing a movie so much as *creating* a movie, and I love the process of trying to take these pieces, like a jigsaw puzzle in my brain that keeps changing shape, and putting them together. I thought this was a very original way to work until I started reading about the great filmmakers of the silent period and found it's how most of them made pictures. Chaplin made up a lot of his work as he went along.

I will generally shoot for a few weeks, then edit for many, many months, then go back to shoot an extra day or two, if necessary. It is like working on a painting; how do I know I'm finished until I finish? I don't want to predetermine it; I want it to become real, authentic, alive, and follow its own needs. Because of this fluidity, shooting can sometimes overlap. One day I found myself shooting sequences for *three* movies: I had been editing *New Year's Day* and *Eating* while shooting *Venice/Venice,* when I decided to pick up some bathroom scenes for *Eating* and also needed an opening and closing shot for *New Year's Day.* I had my crew intact for *Venice/Venice,* so all I had to do was gather together a few of the actors from the other two movies and change the furniture around a bit. "The enemy of art is the absence of limitations." When you're forced to create, you create. And it frees you.

Dividing my energies among four movies at a time can be exhilarating. Returning to the editing of one movie after concentrating on another sheds new light on the first one. It's all part of the same organic process. And if I happen to take a year to edit a movie, there is no economic pressure, no money on loan from banks, nobody worrying, as long as I turn in a picture each year or so to my exhibitors around the United States and my distributors in Europe. And each year the audience continues to grow, which is very exciting.

Videocassettes, cable and DVDs have been a great boon to independent filmmakers. Not only do they provide a source of revenue, but they are a great leveler. In stores my pictures are next to multimillion-dollar studio pictures, for rent at exactly the same price. Since my economics are so low, I exert my energies upon reaching the literate movie audience, without regard to demographics or popular opinion, giving me the freedom to make films exactly the way I want to. I'm enormously lucky in that regard.

For home video I used to sell to the highest bidder, taking the best economic deal I could get. Then I found that certain companies handled films with greater care and sensitivity than others. Warner Home Video has done a terrific job on *Déjà Vu* (1999), reaching new audiences (for me) at every Blockbuster video store in the country and in many other outlets where my earlier films weren't available or were hard to find.

The amazing thing about all this is that everyone ends up making quite a bit of money, although that was never the driving force. With a budget of, say, $3 million and another half-million or so in prints and advertising, $8 to $10 million in revenue worldwide means we make $4.5 to $6.5 million profit, far more than I ever thought a movie of mine could pull in. So the irony of this modest filmmaking formula is that it can be surprisingly profitable, and yet gives me complete control over my pictures, with none of the bureaucratic, creative or financial headaches that my counterparts who work for studios seem always to be complaining about.

Lately I've been working in partnership with a British company, Revere Entertainment, and a producer, John Goldstone, with long experience making independent films. He produced all the Monty Python films, for example. Revere puts up the money and we supply the creative elements. This has worked particularly well on my two recent films *Déjà Vu* and *Festival in Cannes* (2001), both of which were entirely shot in Europe, with European crews.

When making films at this level, ways must be found to create attention, to make up for the lack of millions of dollars in advertising. For example, we are now involved in book publishing and merchandising; on our Web site, we even have a store, the Rainbow Film Company Store, where we sell the videos of some of the older films that have come back to us, T-shirts, caps, autographed scripts, and books of the screenplays with photos and actors' comments in the back. Anything to help expand our audience.

To sell my films in overseas territories I often attend the Cannes Film Festival, the Venice Film Festival, Toronto, wherever I can go. I screen my movie, discuss terms with interested distributors and make my deals. My main market is Western Europe, Australia, South Africa; I have no audience to speak of so far in Asia but a growing one in South America. Recently Eastern European countries from the former Soviet bloc have become interested. Because my movies are very verbal, dubbing them doesn't work that well; my audience has to be literate and comfortable reading subtitles. I do believe, though, that it's just a matter of time before that same 5% to 10% audience share that is mine in the United States (and higher in Western Europe) will slowly find my movies in Asia as well.

My advice to new filmmakers is quite simple: *Do not accept anyone's word that something is impossible;* it's the limitation of the person telling you that that makes them say it can't be done. Do not acknowledge that there's a wrong way to do something just because somebody else says so;

they just don't know how to do it yet. To make a movie, you need as much money as you've got, not a penny more. If it's just $20,000 you can raise, take a video or digital camera and go make a movie. Someone will see it and you'll be on your way. Don't talk about it; *do it*. This is a *great* time for independent filmmakers because of all the new formats that need to be fed as well as the new technologies that keep making the actual production of a film easier and less expensive. The business today is analogous to book publishing, with studios releasing the equivalent of mass-market paper-backs and independents making the "hardcovers" for a smaller audience. Thanks to home video and DVD, they are all side by side on the store shelf, all equally accessible to the public. There are no rules to any of this; any-one following rules is falling into traps laid by people with limited imagi-nations. Just trust yourself and don't take "no" for an answer.

II

THE PROPERTY

THE SCREENWRITER

by **WILLIAM GOLDMAN,** a distinguished novelist and also a screenwriter who has won Academy Awards for his original screenplay *Butch Cassidy and the Sundance Kid* and for his adaptation of *All the President's Men*. He has adapted his novels *Marathon Man, Magic, Heat* and *The Princess Bride* for the screen and has written the screenplays for *Harper, The Hot Rock, A Bridge Too Far, Misery, Maverick, The Chamber, The Ghost and the Darkness, Absolute Power* and *Hearts in Atlantis*. Among his other novels are *The Temple of Gold, Soldier in the Rain, Boys and Girls Together, Tinsel, Control* and *The Color of Light*. His nonfiction books include *Adventures in the Screen Trade: A Personal View of Hollywood and Screenwriting, Which Lie Did I Tell? More Adventures in the Screen Trade* and *Hype and Glory*, which deals with his experiences as a judge at the Cannes Film Festival and the Miss America contest.

> What movies get made reflect the executive mentality; what movies are successful reflect the audience.

Writers have always been secondary in Hollywood. But ask *any* director and he will tell you he is only as good as his screenplay. There is no picture without a script. When you read that a producer announces a new $75 million picture from a novel he has bought, that's nonsense. No one knows what a film will cost until there is a screenplay. There is no film; there is no anything at all in this world until there is a screenplay. A screenplay is gold.

Hollywood is constantly shifting. It's a whole new and unpredictable ball game. Now one can write anything. Since no one knows anymore what will or won't go, almost anything has a chance of getting made. Now it seems possible for a writer to say what he wants through film and make a living at it.

One of the things that no one tells an eager author in college is that if he writes a novel, the chances are that he won't get it published. And if he does get it published, he might make five thousand dollars or maybe even ten. It takes years and years to become an established fiction writer, and one can hardly support a family that way. There aren't more than a handful of writers who can actually make a living out of hardcover fiction writing. Film writing, on the other hand, not only pays, it overpays. And it is a way for one to exercise his craft and still feed his children—both critical aspects of a writer's life.

There is more interest in screenwriters today than ever before because of money. People are beginning to wonder why screenwriters get so much money, since the star makes up his part and the director has all the visual concepts. The answer is that it all starts with the word: the screenplay. The reason that the director gets all the publicity is because he's the most visible person during shooting, which is the only time the press is allowed around a picture. They are not present during preshooting, when the writer, producer and director are working on the script or are assembling the cast with the help of the casting director. No one is present postshooting, when the editors and composer are working their magic. And though the press may be on the set during a day's shooting, they're not around the night before, when that day's schedule is mapped out. At this critical session, the production designer will say, "We must have the door here," and the cinematographer will say, "Well, if you move the door here, I can give you this shot coming in, which will scare everybody," and the director will agree or disagree, or he won't know. He's just one of many people going down the river on this boat, hoping they get past the rapids.

Movies are a group endeavor. There is a group of six or eight technicians who are essential to the collaborative process: the writer, director, cinematographer, editor, production designer, producer, production manager and sometimes the composer. As for writers, we are more essential than the public gives us credit for, but no more essential than the other technicians. But our visibility is low because few of us go out on publicity junkets. Basically we are very dull people.

Some authors start out, no doubt, knowing they want to write screenplays. I am basically a novelist, and I fell into screenplay writing rather by misinterpretation. It happened at a time when I was in the middle of a monstrous novel called *Boys and Girls Together*. I was hung up in the thing, and to try to unstick myself, I wrote a ten-day book called *No Way to Treat a Lady*, which was published under another name. It is a short book with fifty or sixty chapters. Cliff Robertson got hold of it and thought it was a screen treatment rather than a novel. At the time he had a short story called *Flowers for Algernon*, which eventually became *Charly*. He asked me to do the screenplay, but when he saw the results, he promptly fired me, hired a new writer and went on to win the Oscar for Best Actor.

The whole sequence of events did prompt me to learn more about screenwriting. I bought the only book available—called *How to Write a Screenplay*, or some such title—and discovered that screenplays are unreadable. The style is impossible and must be dispensed with. It always has those big capital-letter things that say, "EXT. JOHN'S HOUSE DAY." I realized that I cannot write this way. Instead I use run-on sentences. I use the phrase *cut to* the way I use *said* in a novel—strictly for rhythm. And I am perfectly willing to let one sentence fill a whole page. Here's an example from the ending of *Butch Cassidy and the Sundance Kid:*

CUT TO:

BUTCH

streaking, diving again, then up, and the bullets
landing around him aren't even close as--

CUT TO:

SUNDANCE

whirling and spinning, continuing to fire and--

CUT TO:

SEVERAL POLICEMEN

dropping for safety behind the wall and--

CUT TO:

BUTCH

really moving now, dodging, diving, up again and--

CUT TO:

SUNDANCE

flinging away one gun, grabbing another from his
holster, continuing to turn and fire and--

CUT TO:

TWO POLICEMEN

falling wounded to the ground and--

CUT TO:

BUTCH

letting out a notch, then launching into another dive
forward and--

                                        CUT TO:

SUNDANCE

whirling, but you never know which way he's going to
spin and--

                                        CUT TO:

THE HEAD POLICEMAN

cursing, forced to drop for safety behind the wall and--

                                        CUT TO:

BUTCH

racing to the mules, and then he is there, grabbing at
the near mule for ammunition and--

                                        CUT TO:

SUNDANCE

throwing the second gun away, reaching into his holster
for another, continuing to spin and fire and--

                                        CUT TO:

BUTCH

who has the ammunition now and--

                                        CUT TO:

ANOTHER POLICEMAN

screaming as he falls and--

                                        CUT TO:

BUTCH

his arms loaded, tearing away from the mules and
they're still not even coming close to him as they

fire and the mules are behind him now as he runs and
cuts and cuts again, going full out and--

                                                    CUT TO:

THE HEAD POLICEMAN

cursing incoherently at what is happening and--

                                                    CUT TO:

SUNDANCE

whirling faster than ever and--

                                                    CUT TO:

BUTCH

dodging and cutting and as a pattern of bullets rips
into his body he somersaults and lies there, pouring
blood and--

                                                    CUT TO:

SUNDANCE

running toward him and--

                                                    CUT TO:

ALL THE POLICEMEN

rising up behind the wall now, firing, and--

                                                    CUT TO:

SUNDANCE

as he falls.

In this sequence I've used the proper form, but I never want to let the reader's eye go—it's all one sentence.

A writer needs to find his own style, something he is comfortable with. For example, I use tons of camera directions, all for rhythm. It often upsets the directors, who shoot the scenes the way they want them anyway. But it *looks* like a screenplay, and yet it is *readable*. The standard form cannot be read by man or beast.

Anyone wanting to be a screenwriter should write a screenplay—not an outline or a screen treatment or a novel that then has to be adapted. A studio can have over a million dollars tied up in a property between the time it is purchased as a novel and the time a script is ready. And this is aside from subsequent production costs. If an author writes a screenplay, it is already there to be seen and judged. The company can say right off, "Yeah, we'll shoot it," or "No, we won't." If it sells, it pays the bills. And besides this essential aspect, it is a legitimate and honorable kind of piece to write.

Background reading and research can be important for a writer. For one thing, sometimes he just stumbles upon something that really grabs him and that he knows he wants to do something with. It was way back in 1958 or '59 that I first came across the material about Butch Cassidy and was moved by it and knew I wanted someday to write a movie about it. I continued researching the subject off and on for ten years, finding things to read that added background and depth. There is a lot available on Cassidy but almost nothing on Longbaugh (Sundance). Larry Turman, a good friend, who produced *The Graduate,* was very important in helping me to structure it.

Since I am basically a novelist, it never occurred to me to ask for advance money on "spec" based on an outline that I might sell to someone. I just wrote as if I were writing a novel. This is an unusual occurrence, at least for a Class A picture. The professional screenwriter doesn't usually just write an original screenplay and then look for a market. If he makes his living as a screenwriter, what he probably does is "buckshot" it. That is, he writes ten outlines and circulates them, hoping that one of the ten clicks and someone gives him money for it. He then writes the full screenplay with financial backing.

I wrote the first draft of *Butch Cassidy and the Sundance Kid* in 1965 and showed it to a few people, none of whom was interested. I rewrote it, really changing very little, and suddenly, for whatever reason, everyone went mad for it. Five out of the seven sources in Hollywood who could buy a screenplay were after it. It was this unexpected competition—not my particular skill with the rewrite—that sent the price so high.

Authors who write in various other forms of fiction and nonfiction besides screenplays often have two agents, one on each coast. The one on the West Coast handles the film material, while the New York agent handles all of the other manuscripts. My Hollywood agent at the time, the marvelous Evarts Ziegler, handled all negotiations for *Butch Cassidy.* My only contact with the deal was that he called me in New York every day to keep me posted on the bidding and warned me to stand by the phone to get his call when the bidding was over. It was up to me to give the final okay. The screenplay was finally bought by Fox.

No doubt many authors write a film imagining a certain actor in a specific role. Right from the beginning I had Paul Newman in mind. Actually as I wrote the picture originally, I saw Paul Newman and Jack Lemmon in the main roles. Jack Lemmon had just done a movie called *Cowboy,* and I thought he would do a fine Butch Cassidy. Paul Newman had done a movie about Billy the Kid, and I saw him as the Sundance Kid. As the years went on, Lemmon disappeared from my mind, but Newman agreed that he would play the Sundance Kid. Then, when George Hill (who was eventually signed as director) read the script, he mistakenly assumed that Newman was going to play Butch. When that happened, Newman, who wasn't really eager to play Sundance, was delighted to change roles. Then the long search began for the actor who would play the Sundance Kid. Every star in Hollywood was up for it. There were arguments about certain choices. Under such circumstances an author doesn't have very much power. Long ago Hollywood decided that the way to keep people quiet is to overpay them. An author paid all that money should go home and count it and be content. I was in there arguing, and so were others who had more influence, notably Newman and Hill. We finally won the battle, and Robert Redford, who in those days was not nearly so well known as some of the other candidates, got the part.

I was really fortunate. Overall I happened to be delighted with *Butch Cassidy.* In many ways it is better than what I wrote; in many ways it isn't; and in many ways it's different. My script was much darker and, I think, would not have been so successful. And most of the credit for its coming off so well I give to George Roy Hill, the director.

Butch Cassidy is an example of an original screenplay. I've also adapted my own novels (*Marathon Man, Magic, The Princess Bride*) and books written by others (*Misery, All the President's Men, A Bridge Too Far*). The hardest thing to write is an original because it's creative; the easiest thing is an adaptation of somebody else's. On a straight adaptation, I don't have to deal with the anguish of the original writer. But when I'm adapting my own work, I think, "That was so hard to write, I'd like to keep it." I'm not as ruthless as I should be. The Faulkner phrase "You must kill all your darlings" is basically true.

For example, one scene in *Marathon Man* that I cared about was the run. The hero runs along and fantasizes that legendary runners come alongside him and get him out of a scrape. In the first draft screenplay, I wrote it as a fantasy, as in the book. John Schlesinger, the director, said, "I can't shoot this; it's a literary conceit and it won't play." When a director says, "I don't know how to make that play," it's best to change it, rather than risking that his uncertainty will show through in the film.

The assignment on *A Bridge Too Far* was unique because it was financed not by a studio but by one man, Joseph E. Levine. In order for the story to be told properly and for it to be faithful to Cornelius Ryan's book, one had to have a lot of stars. The use of stars would help the audience organize the several parallel stories to be told. This affected the writing of the screenplay since, in a scene of two characters talking, if the scene legitimately belonged to character A but character B was cast with a star, I would flip the scene so that it would favor character B.

Films that become successful tend to reinforce our expectations; films that are not as successful but are equally competent tell audiences things they don't want to know. For example, everyone in this country thinks of *A Bridge Too Far* as being a commercial failure. In fact, it was a giant success in Japan and Great Britain and did very well all over the world, except for the United States. It told Americans something they didn't want to know: Battles and wars can be lost. All over the world people have lost wars and know that kind of suffering and agony firsthand; we don't.

On *All the President's Men,* if there was a contribution in the screenplay that was valid, it was deciding to end the film in the middle of the book, on a less-than-triumphant note for Woodward and Bernstein. Instead of having them get saved by the cavalry at the end, the idea was to have the audience apply what they knew and fill in the ultimate victory. No one knew at the time that *President's Men* would become a very successful film. People were saying, "Haven't we had enough of Watergate?" Nobody knows what's going to work. Hollywood is based on a search for past magic. "Redford and Newman worked twice (*Butch Cassidy* and *The Sting*); if we could only get Redford and Newman in a picture we'd all be rich." The reality is that nobody knows. One can guess that a movie about some robots in the future will work, and that George Lucas will handle it well, but Universal didn't think so. They passed on *Star Wars* when they had *American Graffiti.*

How close is a writer allowed to the actual production? To a degree the answer lies in how big a writer he is. The bigger the name, the more likely he is to have a say about the details of production. Generally, the answer is that the writer gets as close to the production as his director allows. The production is really the director's baby. If he has faith in the author's judgment, the director will be more willing to tolerate his presence during filming. If the director doesn't want him, there is nothing the writer can do about it.

An author is blessed if he has a director who is interested in working closely with him as he prepares for production. The time when the author is most essential is in the story conferences with the director prior to filming. It is during these very crucial days that he tells the director over and over again exactly what he meant. Talking it all out in minute detail with the director can clarify the content and ensure the director's chance of a clean and accurate interpretation. It is during these conferences that scenes are cut, added or otherwise modified. In *Butch Cassidy*, for example, the screenplay was changed, but never basically. Certain scenes were cut; the musical numbers were added, but the thing that makes the movie work—the basic relationship established between the two men—was left essentially unchanged.

In one specific instance I had written an atrocious scene, the opening scene of Robert Redford and the card game. Everyone said, "Get rid of it! It stinks!" And I kept saying, "I know it stinks, but it's the best I can do." And all the time I was going through that pressure, George Hill kept saying, "You're not going to change it!" George knew how to make it play. He took the scene and put it in sepia, which gave it an old look. And he had what is probably the longest close-up in modern film history on Bob Redford. It's about ninety seconds of solid Redford, and the scene really plays. He gets a tremendous tension out of it. This is a striking example of how a good director can take even a rotten scene and make it work.

I went out to Hollywood in June 1968. George Hill was already there. For about ninety days, he and I met every day, spending most of each day talking about every aspect of the script and coming up with ideas for it. These meetings lasted until mid-September and included a two-week rehearsal period prior to actual filming. Until the filming began, I was involved in many decisions that were made, but the final work necessarily was that of the director. I returned in the middle of production for one week of shooting at the studio between location work in Utah and Colorado and in Mexico. On this visit I saw four or five hours of rushes that George had shot in Utah and Colorado and gave him my reactions. That basically was my contact with the production of the film.

My own feeling is that I don't want to be around on a film I have written. There are times when an author can be helpful. In *Butch Cassidy*, for example, there were a couple of scenes misdone. Had I been around, I could have said, "Oh, no, no, no, no—I meant this." You see, they were actually miswritten, and I didn't realize it until I saw them on film. They are not, incidentally, in the final film. Had I been around, I could have said, "I miswrote that. Don't play what I wrote; play it this way."

Generally, however, I don't like to be around for two reasons. First of all, because I am the screenwriter, nobody really wants me around. If a line is misspoken with the proper emotion or spoken properly without the proper emotion, there can be problems. The writer thinks the actors are ruining his lines, and the actors resent the author's presence. And similar tensions can arise between director and author over interpretation. Second, although there is nothing more exciting than your first day on a movie-star-laden set seeing all your dreams come true, by the second day you are bored with it. By the third day everything is so technical that you are ready to scream, "Let me out of here!" The idea of standing around for seventy-two days of shooting, bothering people and saying such insignificant things as "The line is 'There's the fireplace,' not 'Where's the fireplace,' " is madness. Since the author just doesn't know when he might be really helpful, he might as well stay away and avoid the agony for himself and everyone else.

In *Adventures in the Screen Trade* I wrote that nobody knows anything in the movie business because no one can predict popular taste. In 1999, *The Blair Witch Project* was one of the most profitable movies. The distributor was an independent company, Artisan. Studio executives were scratching their heads, wondering "How did we miss on that one?" The fact is they don't know, since they're in this blizzard, and the snow won't ever stop coming down on them. It's a fascinating business to watch from a distance, and I'm glad I never had to be a studio executive.

What movies get made reflect the executive mentality; what movies are successful reflect the audience. I have no idea what they will like; I try to write a screenplay that I will like, and I pray. If I want to continue working in pictures, it's essential first that my screenplay gets made and second that it gets made properly. After all, the business pays attention only to writers who write movies that are commercially viable. But, beyond it all, nobody really knows which films will be big. There are no sure-fire commercial ideas anymore. And there are no unbreakable rules. Classically, westerns have villains. *Butch Cassidy,* however, the most successful western ever made, has no tangible villain, no confrontation in the usual sense. Perhaps the success for the movie with kids is in the concept of the "super posse," a force that follows them and makes them do terrible things that they cannot control.

My advice to screenwriters starting out is hustle, pester, embarrass yourselves to get to any contact in the business you can, and move to Los Angeles, because that's where the business is. Also, you must be able to handle rejection.

Over the years, my writing habits haven't changed. I go to the office every day, if only to check out sports scores. When I am working on a screenplay, it's seven days a week. I start at three pages a day and won't stop until I've done the three pages. This is after months of working out the story structure which I place on my wall in the form of twenty-five or thirty connective phrases. Gradually, once the characters become more familiar and I gain more confidence, I'll write four or five pages a day, and then have half a script. Although I don't like my writing, alas, I do like to finish, so I tend to generate more pages per day as I'm heading for the ending.

If screenwriting were the only kind of writing I did, however, I think I would find it desperately frustrating. When I write a novel, I take it to my editor. He says, "This stinks and I want you to change it." If I agree with him, I say, "Okay," and I change it. If I don't agree with him, I can say, "Good-bye." It is my baby and I can fight to the death. I can either not get it published at all or get it published as I want elsewhere. At least it is *my* fight to make if I choose. In films an author doesn't have that right. In films he must assume the director or producer will be ultimately responsible for what the finished product is and whether it works or not. And, of course, there is no guarantee that he will get a director or producer who will listen to him.

One thing that really pleases me about movies today is that advertising and publicity and critical reviews don't mean anything anymore. *Butch Cassidy* opened in New York to pretty bad notices but tremendous business. Happily, the reviews are totally unimportant on a film. No one except maybe the critic's mother is going to go to a film or stay away from a film because the critic says it's good or bad. Movie audiences will not be lectured to. It is a golden time.

THE LITERARY AGENT

by **LEE G. ROSENBERG,** one of the founders of Triad Artists, Inc., a full-service talent agency that was based in Los Angeles. Educated at the Choate School and Harvard College, Mr. Rosenberg held production positions in films and television before cofounding the literary agency Adams, Ray & Rosenberg, which thrived from 1963 to 1984. In 1984 Mr. Rosenberg founded Triad Artists, one of the largest talent agencies, which served a wide range of clients in entertainment markets around the world. Triad was sold to the William Morris Agency in 1993; Mr. Rosenberg retired in 2000 and became a senior executive at Comsense, Ltd., a global high-tech company.

> In the negotiation of subsequent covering documentation there is a give-and-take that usually takes from the writer.

Writers are born, not trained. Talent is genetic. A writer may have talent, but what one learns from instruction or by examining screenplays or movies is craft, the form in which talent expresses itself. Durable success is dependent upon this duality.

In the entertainment industry a writer's career combines creativity and business. The business life of a writer is protected by the literary agent. Literary agents are employed by writers to seek out and formalize employment within the context of wider career guidance.

To begin a study of the agent-client symbiosis, let us examine a writer's initial problem: finding and engaging an agent.

This is often difficult for the unknown writer. First, simply saying one is a writer doesn't make it so. Second, once a writer has something to offer—perhaps a completed screenplay—he must attempt to interest an agent. Consider the direct phone call, for example. While most agents won't accept a "cold call," the impression of personality and intellect the writer might make on an agent willing to take the call is possibly more important than coming to the office and saying, "Here's my script." Motivating an agent to take calls like these depends upon whether there has been prior contact about the writer from someone the agent knows and trusts. In rare cases, an agent might read a letter from a writer that sounds reasonable and intelligent and perhaps reflects the writer's ability to communicate an original point of view. The inventive applicant may attract the interest of even a busy agent, who might then agree to listen to him. Compounding the issue is that many agencies do not accept unsolicited material unless it comes from a source whose judgment is respected.

However the writer manages it, after the initial connection he then must put a screenplay on the agent's desk. Sitting and conversing accomplishes little; the agent must read the script. And this points up the greatest problem of all: finding time for reading. If an agent is conscientious and successful, there is a prodigious amount of reading to do, from at least three sources: his own coterie of clients; submissions from the marketplace presented to his clients for assignment; and writing samples from potential new clients. Following the submission of a writing sample the writer must be very patient.

If the agent is impressed, he may call the writer to discuss the work and arrange a meeting to talk things over. Considering this meeting a first date that may lead to marriage, the agent projects his own personal chemistry while seeking to get acquainted with the author as a person. As in any marriage, a couple never knows whether they have made the right choice until they have lived together for a few years. At this first encounter the parties begin to assess each other. The agent will react to the material as a sample of the writer's work and as an index of his ability to handle the visual medium. The writer will be seeking a sense of confidence that this agent is the person to guide his career.

If it's good, the writer's work will be circulated among other agents within the agency. In an enterprise calling for so subjective a judgment on the part of the reader, there is added insurance of success if the agents ultimately shouldering the work of representation are all enthusiastic about the writer. For the alliance to succeed, there must be mutual trust and genuine enthusiasm between agency and client.

There is usually a signing committee at large agencies that analyzes how the potential newcomer fits into the overall client mix. A talented beginner will require infinitely more time than an established writer, so the signing decision is also evaluated in terms of time versus the point in the career at which the agency is entering the life of a client. Periodically agents gather at retreats to consider whether the balance of a client list is appropriate. In the end they all understand that the lifeblood of the agency—and of the industry—is new talent.

I would keep an eye on new clients to make sure they were being placed in the marketplace with early assignments in proportion to their talent. For example, a junior agent came across a writer who had just graduated from an eastern college and had written a spec (speculative) script for a television series, and then was hired on to that series as a sort of intern. The writing, as a measure of promise, was excellent, but promise implies a period of time before its value is realized. So there was considerable internal debate as to whether the agency should make the investment in time to nurture this talent. The debate was intricate, subjective and abstract. Discussion ranged over various components as well as qualities of the writing: dialogue, structure, characterization, craft, and so on. Finally the agents decided to take on the responsibility.

This writer was then signed to standard agency agreements of two years' duration. The Writers Guild of America provides that the first-term writer, one who signs with an agency for the first time, may terminate the agreement after eighteen months upon written notice.

Agents do not employ writers; writers employ agents. If the agency loses enthusiasm and therefore effectiveness for a client in the marketplace, the agent must so advise the client. This can be a terrible dilemma, which must be resolved with candor and courage.

If the client seeks to terminate but has an unexpired contract, that creates an issue. Usually a substantial amount of time, effort and overhead has been invested in behalf of that client. The agent's inclination is to resist giving up the client's contractual future without recouping that investment.

However, poor conditions may exist in the agency-client relationship that can be improved. Perhaps there has been inadequate communication between the writer and the agent, causing the writer to feel his interests have been neglected. His complaint may clarify things and initiate satisfactory correction. In this case the contract allows the agency legally to hold the client while the parties have an opportunity to reassess their attitudes, creating an involuntary cooling-off period. If the parties still can't resolve their differences, the client has the right to dismiss the agency and hire another, with the understanding that his present agent may not wish to work out a commission settlement arrangement with the new agent. Of course the agency may release the client completely from any continuing obligations.

The agency commission is 10% of all gross monies received by the writer, whether from profit participation or from payment made for rights and/or services. All monies go directly to the agency. The commission is usually deducted and the client's check issued within three to five days.

Once the agency contract is signed, the agent begins the process of seeking work for the client. Generally the writer has either written a spec script that may lend itself to packaging or auction or is seeking employment as a writer-for-hire. The acquisition of rights and services is governed by the Writers Guild of America Theatrical and Television Basic Agreement. (Inquiries as to content should be addressed to the Writers Guild of

America West, 7000 West Third Street, Los Angeles, CA 90048; phone 323-951-4000; or Writers Guild of America East, 555 West 57th Street, New York, NY 10019, phone 212-767-7800.) Some contractual terms covering sale of a spec script, as well as contractual terms of a script written for hire (including performance of specific services such as drafts, rewrites, polishes), will enjoy a congruency, since they both fall under the WGA Basic Agreement. In the case of a writer making his first sale, I strongly recommend that terms of the WGA Basic Agreement be "included by reference" in the deal.

Let's examine selling strategy for a spec script. First we determine whether there is a duplication in the marketplace. If another project exists that is similar, it reduces the value of ours. When three competing studios each developed Robin Hood screenplays with directors, the first to attract a major star—Kevin Costner—knocked the others out of competition. Another went on to be made for television, and the third dissipated.

Second we determine whether there is a studio with a special relationship with a producer, director or star who is particularly suitable for the screenplay. This judgment is often intuitive, based on the joint experience of agents covering the tastes of potential buyers.

As the market plan falls into place, it includes a list of buyers targeted for submission, when to submit the project, predisposing elements of the project, and how the chess game is likely to unfold. Perhaps a marketing device will be added. With one screenplay, which concerned a hidden ticking bomb, alarm clocks were sent out with the script, set to go off at a particular hour. This created a stir among buyers, who got themselves mutually excited about the script.

As the agent moves in to close a deal, he must nail down as many specific details as possible. If he is dealing with people he knows who are knowledgeable and have studio bureaucracies backing them, he is usually safe in making verbal commitments. With anyone else, however, he will be wise, before proceeding, to insist that a memorandum agreement be drawn up and, in extreme cases, that funds be put in escrow. Proving damages in a broken verbal agreement is excessively difficult and costly. An agency generally executes a seven-page *deal letter* outlining substantive points including price, general rights acquired, and certain other stipulations that may be unique in a given case. Details are set down so that a lawyer can actually draft a contract from the letter. Once the deal letter has been initialed by the parties concerned, agents record it in synopsis form in an internal *deal memo*, including the client's name, commission, the buyer's corporate designation, the starting date of services, and many other items distilled from the deal letter. After agreeing upon the deal, there is an administrative period while contracts are drawn up and payments are made. The agent can help to keep lines of communication open between writer and buyer and to work out problems that might arise from misunderstandings or differences of opinion.

In a typical deal the following points are discussed between the agent representing the writer-seller and, say, the business affairs executive representing a producer-buyer.

First is the duration of the initial option period, and of subsequent option periods, which could be of any length and of any number.

As to monies paid for the option, one would negotiate a sum for the initial option period (which may or may not be applicable against the purchase price) and for the second, third and other optional periods. There is a standard of one year for an initial option period and extensions of six months or a year for the second and subsequent optional periods. There are no standards as to price, which depends upon what the market is willing to pay.

Second, one would specify what is required to exercise the option, in other words, notice and payment of the purchase price only; or commencement of principal photography plus payment of the purchase price; or a third-party commitment (from a director or star, perhaps) plus payment of the purchase price or other conditions.

If the work is "written for hire" instead of a speculative screenplay, other questions arise. Does the purchaser have the right to hire an additional writer (other than the writer of the screenplay) to perform writing services during the option period? Is any portion of the option money applicable against money payable to the initial writer for his services? If the initial writer performs services during the option period, is any portion of that money paid to him applicable against the purchase price?

The full purchase price is then negotiated, which may include a deferred amount, payable upon an event that may occur in the future, such as the start of principal photography of the picture.

Next, one must determine if the writer is entitled to participate in revenues generated by the film. The purchase price and profit participation must be negotiated with great care at the outset of the transaction, when the buyer's appetite is at its zenith.

Participation usually ranges from 5% to 15% of something. That "something" may be net profits, gross, gross after breakeven (or earlier), or some other formula. Each of these positions within the revenue stream must be carefully negotiated with the help of an accountant and legal counsel. (See "Elements of Feature Financing" by Norman H. Garey, p. 117.) Otherwise, a great deal of leverage is lost, and in the negotiation of subsequent covering documentation there is a give-and-take that usually takes from the writer.

One key issue is whether the participation is levied on 100% of revenue—gross, net or otherwise—or on that portion of revenue that is retained by the producer. In the former there is a "wholeness" to the participation; in the latter there is a "halfness" because the producer rarely receives more than 50% of 100% of the net profits (or some commensurate amount of gross). Therefore 10% of the producer's net may be 5% of 100% of the net of the picture. The magnitude of profit participation is usually tied to the screenplay credit determined by the Writers Guild. A shared credit generally reduces the writer's participation by half.

Other niceties regarding the participation include a definition no less favorable than that of the producer or other person with leverage, auditing rights and other concerns.

In a transaction for a spec screenplay there are additional questions about reserved rights (covered below); payments from possible theatrical remakes or sequels; payments from possible television remakes or sequels; additional compensation for release of a television film in theatres in the United States and/or overseas; payments for a miniseries or television series or spin-offs. For example, if characters from a successful television series (such as *M*A*S*H*) are spun off into a second series (like *Trapper John, M.D.*), what is the compensation?

It might be helpful at this point to explain the concept of *reserved rights* or *separation of rights* as it affects the writer client. The Writers Guild, through negotiation with management, has established, among other minimums, that certain rights are the property of the writer or writers who receive story credit in motion pictures and television. The precise definition of these rights and the conditions that surround them are available in the Writers Guild Basic Agreement. The rights *separated* out and *reserved* for such a writer include dramatic stage, radio, live TV, merchandising and publishing. (For details on exploiting book-publishing rights, see the article by Roberta Kent and Joel Gotler, p. 91.)

When making development arrangements for a theatrical feature, a two-hour movie for television or a television miniseries, publication rights are treated as a valuable point. Naturally the agent wants to make a publication deal as early as possible in order to have the necessary lead time to get the book published well in advance of film production.

Since the financing studio contributes millions to the development and production of the film, they insist upon a sizable chunk when a publication deal is made. The agent resolves this in many instances by giving the studio 20% of net publication revenue after agency commissions have been deducted. In a typical transaction, the client retains 80% of net publication revenue and the studio retains 20%. It was fortunate that the studio allowed a commission off the top rather than simply off the client's share. (Sometimes commissions can go as high as 25% in foreign publication deals. Since the base agent has to share with the agent abroad—to motivate that overseas agent—half of the usual 10% commission is not enough. Occasionally the overseas agent receives as much as 12½% while the U.S. agent receives a like amount, for a total of 25% of commissions.)

Publication revenue includes the publisher's advances as well as royalties earned after recoupment of advances. An advance is simply a royalty paid in advance. If a client has received a $300,000 advance from a publisher for writing a book after a studio deal has been made, the studio gets 20% and the client gets 80%; the payments generally will be $100,000 upon signing the contract, $100,000 when the manuscript is delivered and $100,000 upon publication. From the $300,000 the agent takes his 10% commission, and the balance is divided between the author and the studio in the 80/20 relationship.

For the writer who has not yet determined whether to write exclusively for motion pictures or for publication, it's useful to be aware of the economics of both industries and some of the attendant selling problems. In the case of a first novelist, less money is available for a book than for a screenplay written for hire and based upon an original idea. If the novel is enormously successful, the economics even out. Also, writing a book produces certain collateral economic problems that relate to the producer-buyer's attitude toward the risk involved in acquiring the book rights and then investing even more risk capital in the development of a screenplay. When a development deal is made exclusively for a screenplay, there is only one investment and one assessable risk. As an example, if a book seems desirable for film purposes, it must be either optioned or acquired outright, depending on conditions imposed by the author. The producer knows that in addition to the money spent for the option or outright purchase, he still has to arrange a substantial additional investment for development of the screenplay. The same story might have been developed for somewhat less money as a screenplay. Obviously it's not unwise to write a book; it simply adds a dimension of time and risk for the entire process, which might diminish marketability of the property.

Returning to our hypothetical negotiation, one additional issue to be resolved is whether the writer has the right of *turnaround*. This would be triggered if the producer or studio fails to produce a film after a certain period of time, whereupon all rights revert to the writer, allowing for resale of the property, contingent upon repayment of invested costs by the subsequent purchaser.

When writers were called upon to write material years ago, frequently they weren't paid if a producer didn't like the result. Further, there was no machinery to guarantee the writer credit on the screen for what he had written. The Guild has now established that no writer may speculate his writing for an employer or potential employer; he must be paid for what he writes. Also, every writer must receive credit for what he has written. Because it's a highly subjective business, one writer's work may be combined with that of another in the course of a rewrite or an adaptation of a story. In such a case, the Writers Guild, not the studio or employer, is the final arbiter as to who receives credit.

If arbitration seems necessary, the Guild will submit proposed credits to selected member writers, who will read the material and recommend who gets what credit. In this arbitration procedure, the writer is given an opportunity to examine the list of potential arbitrators and eliminate a reasonable number of those who might have some bias.

No discussion of the literary agent can be complete without references to packaging, auctioning and managing.

Packaging is the process of assembling several creative elements—director or producer or star, or any combination—with a screenplay and offering them to a financing source in order to enhance the transaction. To achieve this, the larger agencies are at an advantage because they have a wider talent pool from which to choose. Because it places a certain pressure on potential buyers, packaging is sometimes maligned. After all, a producer-buyer of a screenplay alone would then proceed to "package" it, in effect, by assembling creative elements from a pool wider than that of a single agency. But from the writer-client's perspective the process can be constructive. For example, a screenplay was recently sold that, in my estimation, would not have sold had it not been coupled with a star of some magnitude. The film went on to be successful. But there are other instances where agents have put clients together in packages that have ultimately failed at the box office. The executives who bought these packages had the ability to "pass" at the time of the offering, but the failure of the films led to criticism of the agency packaging process. It all comes down to imaginative coupling, subjective judgment and the courage to pass or proceed.

Before discussing auctions, I want readers to realize that far more screenplays are sold without auctions. These are screenplay transactions in which the agent believes there is only one correct buyer, especially suited to the material—perhaps a producer or a director with a specific track record who is willing to pay a fair and competitive price. These may be viewed as common-sense deals or preemptive buys.

Before an auction, the first decision is whether the property is worthy, since auctioning can have a reverse impact. As quickly as the market can heat up for a property, it can cool down. Assuming a screenplay is auction-able, strategy is then drawn up, including a list of targeted buyers; ele-ments that might be added, as in packaging; and how marketplace response will be communicated from buyer to buyer. The idea of the auc-tion process is to create an atmosphere of insecurity among the buyers. If there is more than one bidder, it reassures the others that their judgment is sound.

If the agent is confident, perhaps a deadline for bids is stated. A set of rules may call for the highest bid to win; or the author will determine among all bids so that the highest bid will not necessarily win; or if there are ties, the author will consult with the offerors and determine among them. A price doesn't have to be stated; the market sets its own price in most cases. If a plateau is bid, there may be a "topping procedure," whereby each potential purchaser is advised of the figure and has an op-portunity to bid more, and an escalation occurs. At some point the buyers will sift themselves out. The auction process has been around for years, but is being used more recently because the literary marketplace has become very aggressive. Million-dollar deals for screenplays are occurring more often.

The agency business today is expansive, and there has been an expan-sion in the market calling for services of writers, directors and actors, since more films are being made. In features the essential market is composed of the major studios. In television, buyers for two-hour movies are the three domestic broadcast networks—ABC, CBS, NBC—the Fox Network, and cable channels TNT (Turner Network Television), the USA Network, HBO (Home Box Office), Lifetime, the Family Channel, the Disney Channel and others.

Finally, as to managing: The fundamental differences between agents and managers have to do with securing employment for a client and the commission charged to that client. Agents can solicit employment and make deals, but managers cannot. This right is reserved for agents, and they are regulated by a state licensing authority and by the guilds that fran-chise agents covering performers, writers and directors. An agent's com-mission, also regulated by the state, is 10% of a client's gross income. Managers, *who are unregulated,* have taken between 15% and 50%, depend-ing on the industry in which the client is employed.

This is a hotly contested arena among agents and managers. Managers often generate employment by, for example, having lunch with a buyer and discussing the virtues of a client. When it comes down to the actual making of a deal, a lawyer instead of an agent might be employed to do that. Also, certain law firms perform the agent's function of securing employment during their usual barrage of lunches and phone calls with buyers. Here a law firm is arguably practicing agency business as much as practicing law, but any agent objecting to this would run the risk of being cut off from that law firm's stream of clients. Securing employment is a very subtle mechanism, very hard to discipline.

What is the theoretical function of a manager? Everything but securing employment. A manager must keep track of a client's business, embracing employment, law, publicity, and accounting. In theory, a manager spends a lot of time building a client's career. But many agents would argue, "That's what I do for a living, I build careers."

Is there tension and resentment? Yes, because of overlapping efforts and the disparity in commissions. There are managers who have taken 15% for their basic service, then partnered in productions where they have received producing fees and percentages of the profits for their producing services. In success, the client earns a lot of money and doesn't question such a system. In failure, it makes no difference, since nothing has been paid and nothing has been earned.

The most successful agent-manager-client flow features a high degree of mutual trust. The agent knows there are many phone calls that can best be fielded by the manager; the manager recognizes the value of the agent to mobilize marketplace data about available work opportunities for the client. All of the client's support people—agent, manager, lawyer, accountant, public relations—try to contribute to the matrix of services that enhance a client's career.

THE STORY EDITOR

by **ROMY KAUFMAN,** vice president of the story department at Universal Pictures. After graduating from UCLA with a degree in English literature, Ms. Kaufman entered the entertainment business as an assistant to theatrical producer Carol Shorenstein-Hays, later moved to Guber Peters Entertainment, then became story editor at TriStar Pictures. She joined Universal in 1997 as executive story editor and was appointed vice president, story department, one year later.

> Coverage is merely a tool, not the extent of the development process itself, and the story analyst is one voice in that process.

The phrase "information is power" is true in many contexts, and it accurately defines a story department. Often the busiest intersection at any studio or production company, the story department, or "story," is usually the first stop for literary material on its way to becoming a feature film, going on to track and support the material's progress from inception to theatrical release. The department is comprised of story analysts who read and evaluate submitted material. Other staffers do research for executives, such as compiling writer or director lists and offering a kind of full-service "story.com," tracking down hard-to-find books and videos. As a result, the story editor job demands strong written and organizational skills and an ability to prioritize and manage a fast-paced, detail-oriented, volatile flow of information. Story is often both the 411 and 911 to the executives it supports in production, marketing, business affairs, legal, distribution, home video and theme parks.

A story department has its own three-act structure, much like any screenplay: Act I is the submission, Act II is the coverage, Act III is the response.

ACT I

Material is usually submitted to a production executive by an agent or producer who has an established relationship or a deal with the studio. Most of this literary material is routed to the story department, which performs a kind of triage depending on urgency, then generates a synopsis, or *cover-*

age, of the work, which is forwarded to the executive, who must respond to the submission. (More about coverage in Act II.) In the hierarchy of a motion picture group, the story department interacts with production executives, who then make buying decisions and oversee the development and production of projects, including decisions on hiring writers, directors and other talent.

A writer who wishes to make an unsolicited submission (that is, without agency representation) will usually be required to sign a *release form,* releasing the studio of any liability in connection with the project. Writers are cautioned that an unsolicited submission is not a productive way to get a screenplay read, since it lacks both legitimacy and the marketplace guidance a good agent can provide. The Writers Guild of America publishes a list of agency signatories; other listings of agencies are available through the *Hollywood Creative Directory.* As discouraging as it can be for a new writer to find an agent, representation is essential for anyone serious about being a screenwriter. A word to the wise: Find an agent who not only likes your work, but who believes in your potential over the long haul. Also, as the agency playing field has changed dramatically over the past few years, so has the opportunity for "boutique" or midsized agencies to compete more effectively against the larger agency powerhouses.

The most common submission is a screenplay, either an original screenplay such as *Gladiator* or an adaptation of something preexisting, such as *A Beautiful Mind,* which was adapted from a nonfiction book. Typical screenplay length is approximately 120 pages. In any screenplay, it is important to adhere to proper formatting and structure. While the story is of foremost importance, a writer who turns in a clean, typo-free and properly formatted script demonstrates the kind of professionalism expected in this marketplace. Readers can't help but be skeptical about a screenplay submitted in faulty format or with proofreading errors. Also, try to avoid elaborate binders, color-coordinated folders with tabs, illustrations or other extras; they do little to enhance a script and actually wind up detracting from it.

In addition to a completed screenplay, a movie can originate from a true-life story *(Erin Brockovich),* a novel *(Don't Say a Word),* a short story *(The Palace Thief),* another movie (*The Truth About Charlie,* a remake of *Charade*), a magazine article (*The Fast and the Furious* came from a *Vibe* magazine piece), a comic book *(The Hulk)* or a video game *(Lara Croft: Tomb Raider).* Other sources include a *pitch* (an idea perhaps presented at a studio meeting with the writer and/or producer), a *book proposal* (often consisting of sample chapters or book outline presented by the author), a *treatment* (a sort of short-story version of a screenplay, written in prose form and detailed enough to become the basis of a screenplay) and an *outline* (of a screen story, less detailed than a treatment). Screenwriters are discouraged from submitting anything other than a complete screenplay, since that's the only way their screenwriting talent can be judged.

Most books are seen in the prepublished formats of *manuscripts* (the author's version, as submitted to the publisher) or *galleys* (bound pages which have gone through the publishing production process). This early look is usually through a studio or producer's New York office covering the publishing world or, increasingly, a scouting service. Producers often compete for an agent or editor to slip them a highly anticipated manuscript confidentially, so as to be first to bring it to the studio. New York–based offices and scouts also help a studio cover theatre and periodicals. Some basic resources that the story departments use include *Publishers Weekly, Kirkus Reviews, The New York Times Book Review, Theatrical Index* and *TheatreScope*.

The ideal form for any submission is a screenplay, rather than a treatment or an outline, for several reasons: It is the best and most reliable way to judge the cinematic viability of a storyline or central idea; it provides a clear view of the writer's ability and command of dramatic structure; and it is the source material most production-ready. While a studio is always willing to invest in a project that originates in another form and go through the labor-intensive development of screenplay adaptations, it is the screenplay version that gets the movie made. Therefore, a project that starts as a screenplay has a competitive edge over other types of submissions.

ACT II

The executive who receives the submission will "put it in for coverage." This is where the story analysts, or readers, get involved. Most story departments have staffs of twelve to sixteen story analysts; some work at the studio, others work at home. Studios must employ only union story analysts who belong to the Story Analysts Guild (Local 700 of IATSE). They are paid on an hourly basis, whereas freelance readers generally are paid by the piece (averaging $50 per script and more for books, depending on the page count). *Coverage* consists of a summary topsheet, a synopsis, (or streamlined narrative of the story line) and comments, which make the case for or against the material. The heart of a reader's coverage lies in the clear, concise presentation of the story, intended to also answer the following questions: Is the story commercial? What is the overall level of execution? Who's the audience? Is it castable? What budget challenges does it pose? The reader is also helping answer the submission executive's unspoken time-management questions: Do I need to take the time to read this? What can you tell me about this material I don't already know?

In addition to assisting executives with time management, coverage serves other purposes. On an administrative level, it provides a valuable historic and legal record of the submission to the studio, and assists executives in prioritizing and managing what otherwise would be a veritable avalanche of reading. A studio can receive up to 400 submissions a month. Divide that among the six to ten creative executives, who already are developing up to forty of their own projects, and it's easy to recognize the necessity of relying on coverage, since the overwhelming majority of projects are rejected. But for those projects that spark interest, coverage is the beginning of a critical internal dialogue, the conversation starter for motion picture group executives as they evaluate and build consensus on key buying decisions.

Readers occupy positions of little power in the industry hierarchy, and yet, paradoxically, they can wield considerable influence in determining which scripts reach the right people and which ones don't. That said, let me dispel an urban legend—that most readers are embittered would-be writers who take evil pleasure in writing withering, dismissive coverage and rendering a pass, or rejection, whenever they get the chance. While this idea might make for entertaining anecdotes among screenwriters, I can assure you that, among the majority of readers, nothing could be further from the truth. Story analysts are some of the brightest people working in the movie business and are integral to the development process. Well-read and movie-literate, they are eager to read a script that engages, entertains and offers an original idea in a well-told story with characters they can root for and stakes they care about. Under relentless deadlines, they have to render a decision, either a "pass" or a "consider," with no room for fence-sitting or maybes. But for every script that may never make an executive's weekend read due to negative coverage, there are just as many that get read, bought, and eventually produced in spite of such coverage. Put simply, coverage is merely a tool, not the extent of the development process itself, and the story analyst is one voice in that process. While his or her role serves a critical function in development, it is by no means the last word.

ACT III

Once the coverage is completed and returned to the executive, what happens? Under a fast-track scenario, when the submitting agent makes it clear that the material is being read simultaneously by rival producers or studios, the receiving executive will read it in conjunction with the analyst. In other cases, where there is more time and if the coverage is favorable, the script will go on the *weekend read.* This is an agenda consisting of scripts, books and other material that require executive attention over the weekend, compiled and assigned by the story department and usually divided between submissions and projects. (In this case, *projects* refer to material the studio has already invested in, that is, material that has been optioned or is otherwise under active development.) Included with the submission or project might be a list of *elements,* referring to attached talent such as an actor eager to star, a writer set to adapt or a director who is interested. It's a judgment game as to whether an attached element can help or hurt a project. For example, what might otherwise be a fairly generic romantic comedy suddenly takes on new cachet when Julia Roberts comes attached to star; however, a thriller might lose luster if the attached director is out of favor.

In the Monday morning *weekend read meeting,* each executive weighs in on what they read; decisions are reached on whether to proceed or pass on submissions, as well as how to proceed on existing projects in development. If the material is a pass, the receiving executive is responsible for responding directly to whoever submitted it, usually that same day or within that week. Depending on the relationship, an executive will usually pass in a phone call. If there is more time or if the circumstances require a more formal response, a pass letter briefly detailing the creative response will be sent back along with the material.

In addition to their impact on submissions and projects, story analysts are involved in the development process, contributing notes on each *draft,* or version, of a project. Development *notes* represent a more intensive, hands-on version of coverage. Coverage is designed to identify problems, weigh them against the material's strengths and make a recommendation. Notes, on the other hand, are prepared after a property has been optioned and the studio has spent money on its development. They should provide a blueprint for rewriting a script into the version the studio wishes to make. While many writers often object to studio notes, charging that they are contradictory or vague, there are just as many who welcome them as useful and instructive. Notes work best when they offer a clear, unifying vision for the movie and how to get there. It is up to the production executive, working with the producer, to articulate this vision. A story department with strong reader talent can greatly enhance this development process so that story problems can be fixed and screenplays can move forward in the system.

The evolution of a project takes the screenplay through drafts. The first draft usually requires a standard twelve-week writing period. Each subsequent draft can be a step in the writer's deal, consisting of a series of contractual rewrites or polishes. A *rewrite* usually requires up to eight weeks and represents a more substantial set of changes than a polish, reflecting larger shifts in tone, structure or character beats. A *polish* is a shorter step, usually taking four weeks or less and generally reserved for clean-up work or dialogue fixes.

Certain high-end writers particularly adept at specific genres, types of dialogue or character work are often brought in for dialogue or character polishes, or to punch up the action in a screenplay. Sometimes referred to as *script doctors* or *closers,* these writers, while often uncredited for their work, are some of the highest-paid and most in-demand in the business. It is often their finesse that achieves the commitment of a movie star for an important role or the studio management's *green light* to proceed to production.

Throughout the life of a project, the story department maintains a complete creative and business profile of the material. For example, the department oversees the writer getting paid for each step by generating notices detailing the official step achieved, the contractual dollar amount due the writer, and the next step going forward. This profile also might include *option notices* generated by a studio's legal department since material is not purchased outright but optioned for a specified term. An *option* calls for the studio to pay a portion of a negotiated purchase price for exclusive rights to a project during a specific period of time. Before an option expires, a notice goes out from legal as a reminder of the date and pertinent details of the acquisition deal for the project. At this point, the production executive has three choices: extend the option, let it lapse or exercise the option and purchase the material. To help make this decision, the executive will rely on story's project profile, including creative notes, committed costs and any outstanding writing steps under the deal.

A story editor's typical day begins with assigning material for coverage. When a creative executive's office receives a submission, it logs it in to story. Once we confirm that the submission information is accurate and complete, the material is given to a story analyst in an effort to match material to reader. Generally, however, studio analysts are expected to be versatile across all genres and able to handle submissions ranging from dense spy thrillers to romantic comedy and classic literature. Material is often reassigned or "bumped" to insure that the most time-sensitive material is covered first. These rush requests are most common in a potential bidding situation, when a *spec screenplay* (written on speculation, rather than for hire) is being submitted by an agency simultaneously to competing studios and producers. The story editor must anticipate fluctuations in reading deadlines in a kind of juggling act of priorities.

The rest of the day is spent fielding inquiries, updating and adding new records to the story library and handling a variety of research requests, both legal and creative. These can be answered by consulting online information systems or our customized in-house database designed to generate searches and reports. Maintaining and updating this data is an important part of the story editor's job, as costly decisions are made based on the accuracy of the information. Inquiries run the gamut from requests for *log lines* (thumbnail plot summaries) to questions about whether the motion picture rights to a certain novel are available. For this, a handy reference is the *LMP* or *Literary Market Place,* updated annually, which includes comprehensive lists of literary agents, publishing houses and their imprints. A story editor must know the best Internet resources and online librarians such as LexisNexis (for periodicals), Baseline (film credits and talent directory), Bibliofind (hard-to-find or out-of-print books) and IMDb (the Internet Movie Database, a popular Web site particularly useful for credits and other film/video research). Rights inquiries on older produced and unproduced properties are becoming more common and often have the same urgency as current coverage requests.

Much of a story department's library resources can still be found the old-fashioned way: on the shelves. These include sample scripts, videos, director reels and/or supporting materials for projects; subscriptions to and archived issues of major newspapers and magazines; *The Motion Picture Guide,* a multivolume encyclopedia of movie titles going back to the silent era, offering detailed synopses, credits and awards; and literary resources such as *Masterplots,* another excellent collection of volumes that breaks down plots and includes critical essays surveying world literature.

A fair percentage of industry hopefuls regard the story department as a useful stop on the way to an executive or producing career. Indeed, the story department does provide a rigorous boot camp and finishing school rolled into one for those interested in the development side of the business. Also, it represents a great opportunity for those with screenwriting aspirations to learn about dramatic structure through the disciplined writing and problem-solving inherent in story analysis.

EXPLOITING
BOOK-PUBLISHING RIGHTS

by **ROBERTA KENT,** who was a literary agent for twenty-five years, working first as a publishing agent in New York, then as a literary agent in Los Angeles representing novelists, screenwriters, directors and producers. She is currently a literary consultant based in Ashland, Oregon.

and **JOEL GOTLER,** president, Intellectual Property Group, a literary management company based in Los Angeles, where his film clients include James Ellroy, Michael Connelly, Richard Russo, James Lee Burke, Harlan Coben, Alice McDermott and Andre Dubus. Mr. Gotler began his career at the William Morris Agency in New York, then moved to Hollywood to work with the legendary agent H. N. Swanson. In 1987 he created Los Angeles Literary Associates, a full-service agency for novelists, and later became a partner in the literary agency Renaissance. Renaissance was sold to Michael Ovitz's Artists Management Group in 1999, and Mr. Gotler was named president and CEO of AMG/Renaissance. When AMG changed ownership in 2002, Mr. Gotler established his own company, Joel Gotler & Associates, which became part of IPG a year later.

An important lesson is that the prices usually quoted as sales to paperback houses for movie tie-in rights are guaranteed advances
against royalties to be earned by sales.

The value of book-publishing rights in connection with motion pictures
can be traced from one of three sources: manuscript, original screenplay
or existing novel.

With an author's manuscript the agent will either auction or nurture.
An auction is a calculated risk, applied to a presumably hot book, in order
to avoid alienating the deep-pocketed movie buyers expected to bid. To
auction movie rights (one of the subsidiary rights) of a novel, manuscripts
are sent to competing parties (production companies or financier-
distributors), a deadline is set and bids come in. This rarely used process
can raise prices into the millions. Michael Crichton's novel *Jurassic Park*
was sold in 1990 for $2 million plus points to Universal in a deal that in-
cluded the author's commitment to write the screenplay and anticipated
Steven Spielberg to direct for his Amblin Entertainment. The landmark
deal in this area at the time was made in 1979 when United Artists bought
motion picture rights for the novel *Thy Neighbor's Wife* by Gay Talese for
$2.5 million plus points. The book went on to become a major bestseller,
but no movie was ever made. More recently, a typical Tom Clancy book has
sold for $6 to $8 million and Michael Crichton will earn about $18 million
for *Timeline.*

The strategy of nurturing a movie sale is far more usual. When a writer-
client completes a manuscript, the agent must decide when to offer movie
rights to prospective buyers. Rights can be offered to a movie source at the
same time the manuscript is offered to publishers; or, more typically, after

the publishing deal is made; or closer to publication, in galley form, to take advantage of favorable reviews. Timing and strategies vary depending upon instinct, intuition and an assessment of buyers and the marketplace.

If an original screenplay is commissioned by a producer, or written on spec by a writer and then purchased by a producer, there may be an effort to make a book deal before a financier-distributor gets involved. In this case the screenplay will be submitted to publishers (hardcover or softcover) for evaluation. If the publishers feel that the property will not succeed on its own as a book, they may want to review it when a movie deal is set (involving commitment of financing, a director and stars). This is most common. But if the producer must wait, the issue of lead time becomes a factor.

It's appropriate to review the mechanics of publishing at this point because as a movie project gets farther along, time pressure becomes more acute. A novel can take anywhere from three to eighteen months to write. The manuscript is turned in to the publisher, who starts the editing and then the printing process. It takes a minimum of six to nine months to get that hardcover book into print and another month to distribute it to bookstores. This pattern also applies to books on tape. A paperback generally comes out nine months to a year following the publication of the hardcover edition. Usually timing calls for a hardcover novel to be in bookstores at the time the picture is shooting, while the paperback tie-in will be published just about the time the motion picture is released. A paperback original requires about as much lead time for publication as does a hardcover, to allow for design, typesetting and printing.

To return to the hypothetical screenplay example, assume the producer is having no success in preselling hardcover or softcover publication rights to the original screenplay. When he makes a deal with a financier-distributor, however, it's a new ball game. Now the mass-market paperback houses (Bantam Dell, Avon, New American Library, etc.) become interested because the screenplay will be a movie and therefore has new value. The financier-distributor usually takes over from here and makes a novelization deal with a paperback house that involves the screenwriter and producer. Essential to the movie tie-in deal is the acquisition of the movie logo (called *artwork*) and stills, which must be obtained from the distributor.

Before the elements of such a deal between financier-distributor and paperback publisher are described, the issue of who writes the movie tie-in for an original screenplay must be covered. Under the Writers Guild of America Basic Agreement, the Guild can tentatively name who will receive "story by" or "written by" credit prior to formal designation of screen credit, and that writer benefits from separated rights (including publication rights) and thereby has first chance to make the novelization deal. This would require her dealing with the producer for permission to use the artwork and stills from the movie as well as with an interested publisher. If the Guild-named writer does not make a novelization deal within a stipulated period of time, it falls to the producer to do so with another writer and then pay the Guild-named writer a percentage of the adjusted gross receipts from such a novelization deal. For example, a paperback publisher could pay a $100,000 advance to a studio for the novelization of an original screenplay that the screenwriter declines to novelize. (The Guild requires the studio to pay $3,500 separately to the Guild-named screenwriter in that event.) Then the studio may pay a novelization specialist a flat fee of, say, $15,000 to do the job. The Guild permits a deduction of $7,000 from the studio's share covering a use fee for the artwork, which the studio pays to itself before reaching "adjusted gross receipts" of $78,000 (subtracting novelizer's fee and the fee for the artwork from $100,000 publisher's nonrefundable advance). Under the Guild rules, the Guild-named writer will receive 35% of the adjusted gross receipts, minus the $3,500 advance, or $23,800 in this example, a sum higher than the novelizer receives.

The elements to be negotiated in a novelization deal with a softcover house include the *advance,* which averages $50,000 to $60,000 but can be as high as six figures or as low as $5,000. Usually everyone involved in the project receives a slice of the advance: producer, financing entity, screenwriter and writer of the novelization. Next there is a *royalty,* which is generally 6% to 10% of the cover price for the first 150,000 copies sold, 8% for the next 150,000 and 10% thereafter. The royalty is also divided between the entities, but only a novelizer with strong bargaining power will share in this amount. The *territory* usually covers the United States and Canada only, but sometimes worldwide rights are sold, and the advance reflects that. Ideally *timing* is planned so that one month before the picture's release the book is on the stands and the public can become familiar with it. Other negotiated points include completion of the manuscript and coordination of the artwork. Obviously, as soon as there is a logo design and production stills, the distributor should send them to the publisher in an effort to reduce the necessary lead time. If a publisher has paid a substantial sum to a financing entity for novelization rights, the contract will usually state that the financing entity will supply artwork at no extra charge.

There had been movie tie-ins for years, but when David Seltzer's 1973 book version of *The Omen* (written after his original screenplay) sold more than 3 million copies, yielding royalties in six figures, the book-publishing world and moviemakers recognized the increasing value of coordinating book sales with movie sales to their mutual benefit.

After the huge success of *The Omen* novelization (a made-up word that offends many novel writers), there followed years of escalating sales to paperback houses that wanted to publish book versions of screenplays projected to be successful films. Movie tie-ins that once brought in $3,500 as a total advance from a publisher began attracting prices of $100,000 and more. The market became as cutthroat as the paperback competition for a hardback bestseller. Agents held auction sales, and every few months new price records were set. If *The Omen* heralded the market boom in 1973, *F.I.S.T.* was the turning point in 1978. The $400,000 sales for Joe Eszterhas's powerful novelization of his original screenplay was associated with an unsuccessful film in the marketplace. Just as the movie company was shocked when it did not do well on the film, the book company was appalled when book sales were low. This taught the publishing industry that the only reliable value of a movie tie-in was as an adjunct to the picture. The result has been that guaranteed advances have leveled off to an average of $50,000 to $60,000 for novelization rights and remain there because the market is not as potent as it used to be. What has become more popular is publishing a movie's screenplay along with photographs from the film, also timed to the picture's release. A tech-driven success such as *The Matrix* can produce a book featuring the artwork behind the production design, a format made popular by the first *Star Wars* movie.

An important lesson is that the prices usually quoted as sales to paperback houses for movie tie-in rights are guaranteed advances against royalties to be earned by sales. High advances anticipate high sales. The paperback house pays this amount, which is nonrefundable, to the holder of the novelization rights. But whether the advance is $7,500 or $75,000, the money earned on a book (the royalty) will be the same if it sells two million copies. The only difference is the spread of the initial advances spent. On a strong sale of two million copies the advance, whether large or small, will be earned back, and the extra earnings will be converted to royalties. Today publishers have decided to rely more on the strength of the movie tie-in to attract sales (and therefore royalties) on its own, with decreased advances paid, rather than hoping that royalties from high sales will equal a strong advance.

One other factor that bottomed out the movie tie-in market was that publishers were buying novelization rights to television movies, but people were not buying these books. The only television program that can usually succeed in selling tie-in books is the long-form miniseries.

If the first is the novelization, the original screenplay is the second type of source material that can be exploited in book publishing. A third type is the existing novel, which can be issued in paperback as a tie-in, timed with the release of the motion picture.

A publisher generally makes comparatively little money publishing and selling a hardcover book. The primary source of income for a hardcover house is the sale of subsidiary rights, such as book-club and paperback rights. Revenues from these sources are usually divided by giving 50% to the author and 50% to the hardcover publisher. Movie rights are generally held by the author. Paperback rights are sold by competitive auction, which accounts for the huge sums often involved. Each year several sales are made in the million-dollar area. However, a book must earn back that advance in sales before a dime of royalty is collected. It was estimated that for Bantam Books to earn back the $3.2 million advance to Judith Krantz on *Princess Daisy,* 9 million paperback copies had to be sold. Usually a bestseller in hardcover is one that has sold 50,000 or more copies; a moderate-sized first printing in paperback is 100,000; if a paperback has sold a million copies, it is selling phenomenally.

On a prestige book, subsidiary rights deals are generally made when the book is in galley form, any time from two months to two weeks before publication. The paperback house, movie producer and studio will work very closely on the timing of the book. If the film will be a long time in the making, the paperback house will publish one edition and then reissue it at the time of the movie's release. The difference is that the reissue will contain the artwork and stills that coincide with the marketing of the film.

There is a symbiosis that can take place among the sales of the various subsidiary rights. A book that is a book-club selection with large paperback sales will certainly be offered as an attractive and expensive movie sale. Conversely, if a book has been sold as a movie, the amount paid for the book by a book club or paperback house increases; the pressure goes both ways. The publisher pressures the agent to sell the movie rights to enhance the subsidiary value of the book, and the movie buyer pressures the agent or publisher to sell the rights to enhance the value of his screen property.

One issue that arises involves advertising costs. If a hardback publisher has benefited from a large paperback sale made on the heels of a major movie sale, the producer can ask the hardback publisher to share those benefits with the movie by committing sufficient money to successfully promote the book, "creating a bestseller." The hardcover publisher can argue that the big movie sale was made on the strength of the literary material alone and can suggest that the producer contribute to the book's advertising budget to boost sales potential. This issue is unresolved.

Another wrinkle is that the studios have gone into the book business.

Disney owns Hyperion Books; Viacom's Paramount owns Simon & Schuster; Time Warner owns Warner Books. But the studios and their book-publishing subsidiaries don't cross-pollinate as much as one would expect.

To review, if a movie's source material is an original screenplay, it can be sold as a hardcover or softcover book before the movie becomes a reality. If the source material is an existing novel, a subsequent paperback edition can become a movie tie-in timed with the release of the picture. If a project originates as a magazine article, either the author of the article will expand it into a book or a book will be derived from the eventual screenplay. *Saturday Night Fever,* which originated as a *New York* magazine article, became a novelization based on the screenplay. *The Insider* began as a *Vanity Fair* article by Marie Brenner. Other movies with origins as articles were *Testament* and *Funny About Love.*

Yet another way a studio can exploit book-publishing rights is to finance the writing of a novel. This way the studio gets a screen property for a relatively small investment, is involved in its earliest development, can help in obtaining publishing deals and participates in the revenue from all deals made. This strategy was in vogue in the late 1970s and early 1980s, but fell out of favor when certain deals resulted in disappointing novel sales, usually canceling the film version.

Book-publishing rights can be further exploited in the form of photo novels, "The Making of . . ." books, large-sized art books and calendars. *Star Wars, Godzilla* and *Toy Story* offer examples of the possibilities.

The future of publishing will find more paperback originals being developed, either from original screenplays or from novelists. The publishing business is going to become more dependent on nonprint avenues of promotion, such as radio and television. Our society is becoming less a printed-word society and more an image society, and publishers will be more dependent on those images to sell the word. The business is as brisk as ever and is always adapting to change. Books on tape carved out a new niche in the market. Another new arena is electronic publishing, a specific right conveyed to the publisher in its agreement with an author, covering e-books read on computer or other handheld devices. The publishing and consumer electronics industries are poised for this new revenue stream, which will be evolving over the next decade.

III
THE MONEY

MOVIES, MONEY AND MADNESS

by **PETER J. DEKOM,** Of Counsel to the law firm of Weissmann, Wolff, Bergman, Coleman, Grodin & Evall, LLP, in Beverly Hills, specializing in entertainment-related legal and business matters for a diverse client base of actors, directors, producers and executives. Earlier, he was a partner in the Los Angeles law firm of Bloom, Dekom, Hergott and Cook. A graduate of Yale University and the UCLA School of Law (first in his class), Mr. Dekom has served as an adjunct professor in the graduate school of UCLA, teaching legal and business principles to film, business and law students. His numerous articles have appeared in such diverse publications as the *UCLA Law Review* and *Fordham Law Review,* in a series of books issued by the Practicing Law Institute and in *American Premiere* magazine. He is co-author, with Peter Sealey, of *Not On My Watch . . . Hollywood vs. the Future,* published by New Millennium Press. A member of the California bar, Mr. Dekom has lectured extensively all over the world on entertainment issues. He has served on the board of directors of several companies, including Imagine Films and Cinebase Software, as co-chairman of the American Cinematheque and on the advisory board of the Shanghai International Film Festival.

> It is one thing for an executive to ignore the numbers having con-
> sidered them carefully, but it is quite another not to understand their
> meaning and to decide independent of mathematical analysis. . . .

As film libraries and studios continue to change hands, bidding up the asset value of films made in the past, it seems impossible to lose money in the movie business. Yet there are a few facts, connected to a lower profitability for a number of major studios in spite of the reported huge grosses, that bear focusing upon.

As of this writing, the average major studio feature budget is at the $59 million mark. The average cost of opening a film wide in domestic theatrical release hovers around $30 million. When one adds interest and overhead (yes, folks, these are real hard costs), the average film has to generate a vast amount just to break even. That figure must come from theatrical film rental, not box office dollars (rentals are about half of box office), and the net revenues from home video, not the retail selling price of cassettes and DVDs (wholesale on cassette averages around 65% of retail).

With price escalations going through the roof, studios are all saying they want more product, more films to distribute, to fill up their monstrous distribution mechanisms, to fatten their libraries, to build their asset base, to improve their cash flow. One may very well ask, "What's going on here?"

1. The profit margins in the motion picture business are coming down.

The internal rate of return (return on investment), like interest on a checking account, is a measure of profitability for a specific business. In some high-volume companies, the profit margins are very slim. For example, in the retail grocery business, profits range from 1% to 3%, and money is made by sheer volume. In other businesses, such as the soft-drink business, internal rates of return can exceed 40% (as in the case of the Coca-Cola Company). Generally investors who are looking for high-risk opportunities (typical of venture-capital situations) expect rates of return in the 25% to 30% or more category. Everyone knows that the motion picture business is risky; shirts that people have lost in this industry would easily fill the entire Sears retail chain. So, typically, when people are asked how profitable the movie business is, those with a modicum of business understanding will suggest that the rates of return must be well in excess of 30%, given the risks involved and the intense media hype about Hollywood cash flow. But this is not the case.

In the early days of the movie business the rates of return were vastly higher than 30%, sometimes hitting as high as 100%, given that the studios controlled production, distribution and exhibition and held contract players to remarkably "low" salaries relative to the revenues that were coming in.

Talent profit participations were virtually unheard of (the Marx Brothers did some pioneering in obtaining a significant piece of their films), and studio moguls grew rich on incredibly high rates of return. As profit participants began to appear on the horizon, and as residuals began to chip away at the rock pile since the 1960s, the internal rates of return at studios began to drop sharply, but were still in the 30% to 50% range for many years.

Today, looking at the motion picture groups of the various studios (including development, production, distribution and overhead of all kinds, but excluding their television wings and any ancillary nonmovie operations), the motion picture business generates internal rates of return of between -20% and 20% or more, with the average (and mean) over the last five years somewhere in the -5% area (yes, movies are, on the whole, losers). For people generating 8% to 15% on certificates of deposit, mutual funds and other relatively low-risk investments, the fact that a motion picture company—taking the huge risk of making and releasing movies—is generating rates of return well below those numbers must come as quite a shock.

While it is terrific to look at a single successful motion picture, studios also have to take the losers into consideration. Absent an occasional aberration, no consistently active major studio (taking its overhead into account) today experiences higher than 20% internal rates of return on its motion picture group as a whole (and that is an extremely rarified year!). And given current trends in talent cash costs and back-end participations, it is likely these numbers will decrease, especially as studios increase production output, causing them to incur higher production costs because of the higher volume but not seeing the offsetting revenues until sometime in the future. (If we were to focus solely on the cash invested in the individual film slate, as opposed to running the studio as well, we would see that this specific return on investment would of course be higher than these corporate rates that are more reflective of reality.)

As a corollary to the drop in the internal rate of return, the time period needed for most studios to recover the cost of their investment, including interest, has become longer. In the early days of the business 100% of the investment was recovered in just a few months after theatrical release.

Today studios rely on the windows of home video, pay-television and syndication for recoupment and, hopefully, profitability. This can take years. In fact it is these vast libraries of preexisting film and TV product that are generating the cash flow to keep many studios afloat, or at least in a linear and predictable cash-flow position. Thus studios are very anxious to build up the value of these libraries, and their distribution mechanisms are capable of handling many more movies in the ancillary markets than they are currently processing. However, there are some serious questions as to whether the major studio theatrical marketplace can handle the increased volume of product that this foretells. As new markets open up overseas, as new methods of home delivery expand, as new technologies add new potentials to existing libraries, the desire to make product to fill that perpetual hopper increases exponentially. Is the Internet going to create incremental additional new revenues, cannibalize many of the old ones, create a cash-depleting piracy opportunity or represent an entire paradigm shift to a new posttheatrical economy?

Given this, there is one key question with a number of potential responses. With the rates of return dropping and the risks increasing, what are the likely economic solutions to this problem?

A. *The general-store model.* The grocery chain has a very low internal rate of return, but makes up for this through volume. Hence, if a studio were making fewer dollars for every film it produced (based on capital invested), it might simply make more films. This simplistic analysis seems to have captured the imagination of many studio executives and, when coupled with the need to build the ancillary values as described above, creates a veritable feeding frenzy. Volume does have the benefit of amortizing the relatively high cost of maintaining distribution and production operations over more films, but it also forces management to split its time among more projects, allowing a lot more product into the system with a lot less control. Another aspect of this approach dictates that by creating more product, a studio takes up more shelf space and squeezes out its competition, a theory that seems to have been disproven on more than one occasion.

B. *Reduce costs, increase revenues.* This form of solution goes along with the "buy low and sell high" philosophy of doing business. It is great, until you try to figure out how to apply it to motion pictures. In network television this philosophy gave rise to reality-based programming, the revenues from which have been either quite good or at least equal to those of dramatic programming. Is there a parallel development in the movie business? Since the market does not appear to be inclined to an entirely different kind of motion picture, the focus here would be on cost reduction of the existing format. But this is extremely difficult, considering the competitive salaries of desirable writers, directors and performers in a limited talent pool. Further, labor unions and guilds are not about to cooperate in a cost reduction scenario. Perhaps Canada, with a much softer currency, will continue to experience production increases just as Hollywood feels the loss in production.

C. *Sell the beast.* While rates of return have been relatively small, the price-earnings ratios in the motion picture industry have been remarkably good. Companies with huge asset bases (large libraries, real estate holdings, ancillary businesses) cloud the issue somewhat, but on a pure motion picture industry basis, it might well be better to sell the company (assuming solvency and some solidity) and take advantage of the high price-earnings ratio rather than hold on to a losing beast. In fact, in recent years studios have appreciated at an annual rate averaging 17%, and it looks like that trend is here to stay (on a long-term basis with normal market fluctuations), simply because there are very few studios and a lot of people interested in Hollywood whether for strategic reasons (AOL and Sony) or simply the glitz and glamour of a high-profile industry. While Wall Street is beginning to question entertainment stock values, there always seems to be a buyer waiting in the wings.

D. *Diversify.* This area is fraught with risks, particularly in the age of interest uncertainty. However, for extremely well-capitalized companies, the opportunity to take advantage of parallel businesses can be quite lucrative. For example, some traditional broadcast networks are now owned by studios: ABC by Disney, Fox by Fox, CBS by Viacom (which owns Paramount). Both Universal and Disney have demonstrated this philosophy extremely well with their studio tours and theme parks. There, characters created in motion picture divisions are exploited in another extremely heavy positive cash-flow business. While the need for initial capitalization in theme parks/tours is very high, well-placed strategic investments (as opposed to head-to-head competition, which seems to be de rigueur these days) can generate untold future dollars. Likewise, these types of synergies are present in record companies, television and radio stations, and the very profitable basic pay-television networks.

E. *Take greater risks.* This seems to be directly contrary to the theme running above, but in fact every time somebody avoids a future risk by taking a present payment, they have in effect shifted that risk (and some *profits*) to someone else. This happens, for example, when someone presells video or overseas rights. In these instances the person who is taking the risk (the video or overseas-rights buyer) will now have to take a larger piece of the pie, reducing the seller's upside accordingly, in order to justify the risk taken. Since we have already noted that the profit margins in the movie business are slender at best, further diluting the profitability of a motion picture must, necessarily, yield lower revenue streams to the filmmaker. But given the risks, the studios have sought out OPM (other peoples' money) in a big way.

F. *Focus on marketable concepts without big stars.* Where budgets can be contained and the concept is marketable, this is a risky but not unreasonable approach. But a "bad" big movie with stars may well make money, while an unsuccessful concept movie without stars will definitely lose money. This approach takes guts, but usually the record-breaking films offer the audience something new or something they haven't seen in a while. Sometimes you just have to swim upstream.

In the case of major studios, avoiding risks (by taking serious downside protection) is simply not a business plan. If a film is so risky that one wishes to shift that burden to someone else, then the studio in question should simply not make that movie unless it is a joint venture with cheap capital. If the management has insufficient confidence in its own abilities to choose and distribute motion pictures, perhaps they should find solace in another industry. The business of business is risk.

2. Costs, costs, costs!

By looking at the landscape, one must conclude that budgets cannot continue to spiral upward at the same rate as in the past. If anything, there should be a period of contraction and consolidation in film costs, if for no other reason than to accommodate the larger volume of product being produced.

For those who have wondered where the difference between the old and new internal rates of return has gone, just look to individuals: studio executives, directors, writers and, most of all, highly paid megastars. Hollywood is and always has been an industry of millionaires and aspiring millionaires, the latter perhaps severely underpaid and the former among the most highly compensated individuals on earth, exceeding the highest levels of corporate America. The list of $20 million-plus actors (applied against dollar-one gross) would probably appall a newcomer, but salaries have escalated way beyond that point, especially for sequels and presold materials.

Where did this price escalation come from? Why does the average major studio action-adventure piece cost well above $70 million? Certainly, below-the-line costs have increased, but the real cost factors lie in the highly compensated talent pools (the above-the-line personnel), mainly actors and directors. Seven-figure scripts are no longer aberrations, and many directors make at least $1 million per film. (Directors' salaries north of $8 million are not so uncommon these days.)

The recent feeding frenzy in the overseas marketplace has certainly added fuel to the cost-escalation fires. Companies that specialized in financing their motion pictures by looking at presales overseas well understood the value of a big name in terms of hard dollars. It did not take long, however, for the agents and representatives of this special talent to recognize the premium being earned by these foreign-driven production companies, mostly independents distributing through major studios. The awareness of these premiums, and the willingness of foreign-driven independents to pay increasingly high sums for this talent, led to a bidding war that generally moved acting and directing salaries into a new, stratospheric level. Even marginal actors whose recognition was just beginning overseas found wages rising faster than the blood pressure of a number of Hollywood major-studio executives.

As Hollywood studios escalated their budgets, thereby increasing their risk in hard-value terms, they wanted some kind of "insurance" that they could "open" their films. Historically big stars and a few megadirectors were able to draw the audience in for that crucial opening weekend, and from that point on, the film's quality (fueled by word of mouth) would support the remaining run of the movie. Hence, studios purchased "opening insurance" by hiring these megastars for their product, even though their prices had recently been bid up by the foreign-driven production companies. It got more expensive all around.

The higher costs for talent are shifting the internal rates of return away from the studios and into the purses of these creative individuals and, gratifyingly, their representatives. People often ask agents and lawyers how they can continue to extract increasingly high salaries for creative personnel. As one studio executive put it, "Don't you understand what you're doing to this industry?" But the role of the negotiation process is necessarily an adversarial one. The agent or lawyer who decides not to take a higher salary for his or her client because it may be "bad for the industry" is likely to find himself or herself in a different business. As long as there is a willing buyer, representatives will continue to guide clients as best they can and secure the highest prices obtainable. If the studios object to these escalating costs, they should exercise restraint and not require these creative individuals to be involved in their movies.

Pressures are even mounting from net-profit participants, who also want a piece of the pie in spite of extremely lopsided contractual definitions. One such participant, Art Buchwald, has even managed to convince a trial court that such net-profit definitions are unconscionable and represent contracts of "adhesion." Clauses that charged expenses on an accrual basis but included income on a cash basis, included gross participations as negative-cost items that accrued both overhead and interest, and provisions relating to the charging of interest and overhead against each other were rejected by the court.

There are solutions to the price-escalation wars, even though some have long-term fuses. They are painful and risky, but something needs to be done.

A. *Increase the talent pool.* Looking at the supply-and-demand curve, it doesn't take an economic genius to recognize that if studios insist on a limited pool of acceptable directors and actors, and if they are increasing production of movies, then the prices for that limited talent pool must escalate. Thus it is in the studios' interest to increase the supply of actors, writers, producers and directors whom they deem acceptable. (And given the tendency of the under-25 "Generation Y" to reject stars, perhaps there is hope.)

The techniques for this are myriad. The first is a Disney technique, which recognizes that once a person is a star, even if his or her fortunes seem to have changed, he or she is still generally recognized and valued by the public. By uniting an attractive concept, well marketed, with a recognizable name (although perhaps a face from the recent past), Disney has been able to generate considerable grosses. By obtaining options and multiyear agreements with these same actors, Disney has also ensured itself of a talent pool for the future at generally reasonable rates. These performers have now rejoined the acceptable talent pool.

Second, studios need slowly to move directors from the television divisions, in a managed manner, into features. The path is simple: from directing episodic series to long-forms to lower-budget features to higher-budget features.

Third, pairing a skilled and charismatic actor who has low recognizability with a megastar (probably in more than one movie) will eventually bring that skilled actor's abilities to the attention of the public. Although audiences are coming to see the megastar, they cannot help but notice the secondary player, who may eventually become valued as a "star" as well. If the studios' executives have good creative instincts, they can recognize this type of talent and experiment accordingly. Further, they could secure this actor's "loyalty" either as a contract player (as in the old days) or through a series of successive options on more films. Even if the contracts and/or options are renegotiated to higher prices, they will never mirror the prices that could be paid in an open bidding war. There is one fly in this ointment, though, since big stars usually want "names" to play opposite. It may take moving a potential star into third position a few times to make him or her sufficiently acceptable as a second lead to the top-liner on a subsequent film.

B. *Develop screenplays internally.* Studios that wait for packages to materialize at their door are likely to suffer from one of three possible scenarios:

(i) They are vulnerable to an outrageous bidding war in which the package and/or script winds up costing the studio a vast multiple of what it would have cost to develop alone in the first place.

(ii) They receive prepackaged mediocrity that may or may not have been passed on by other studios.

(iii) They learn there are almost no real packages anyway (that is, there are vastly fewer fully cast, ready-to-film projects than the public perceives).

Effective internal development is the key to success of virtually any studio (or production company, for that matter), although this is not the sole route for the acquisition of film product. Strong relationships with proven creative talent are another important facet to studio success. Internal development requires creative executives who, instead of doing favors for their friends, marry hard concepts (many of which are created by the executives themselves) with good workmanlike writers and, potentially, the directors who will be asked to shepherd the productions into existence. At the concept stage, discussions can even be had with marketing people to learn whether the potential movie can be sold. This is not to relieve the creative executives from the responsibility of fighting for quality, even when marketing may disagree. It is simply to encourage a greater level of budgetary and marketing responsibility in the executives who develop such properties.

By developing a script internally, a studio clearly avoids the bidding war that would probably accompany an independent screenplay that was strong enough to be the basis of a green-lighted movie. Also, if a studio happens to own a script that a star insists on doing, there is even more bargaining power in the negotiation of compensation for that performer. Studios that develop an internal stable of competent producers who truly manage development and, ultimately, production also increase the studio's ability to control costs of its product. Unfortunately, history has shown studios to be weak in being able to shepherd quality screenplays from inception to shooting script.

C. *Consider "rent-a-system" distribution deals.* For those studios short on capital or needing additional product, they can focus on a short slate of high-quality movies by opening up their distribution systems to respected creative filmmakers—and their outside financing groups—who are prepared either to cofinance the production/distribution risks with the studio or to put up all the risk dollars involved, including prints and advertising, in a separate slate of studio-type films. Both New Regency and Morgan Creek are examples of companies that take such financial risks and look to the studios principally for distribution only. These "rent-a-system" deals, where the outside financing entity literally "rents" the studio's distribution network (usually only domestically), do not provide high upside dollars for the studio. After all, the studio often negotiates a downscaled distribution fee in such cases (averaging less than 20% as opposed to a 33% average fee applied to studio-financed product) and maintains no net-profit position in these outside-financed films. But this type of deal does offer a studio an easy way to amortize the overhead costs of maintaining production and distribution operations and provides dollar-one gross participations with no cash risks. Any studio relying principally on this form of product would ultimately fail, however, since the cost of maintaining operations cannot be covered solely in this way.

D. *One megastar may be enough.* Many studios will load a motion picture with several megastars plus a very expensive director. But since this is basically "opening day" insurance, having one such actor should be sufficient to get people in the door. Two or more such actors, receiving high cash advances against their dollar-one gross participations, would generally make the motion picture top-heavy, too risky and economically unjustifiable absent extraordinary circumstances. (In some cases a top star asks for great coleads as a form of failure insurance for the insecure megastar.) Or, if Generation Y has its way, maybe the story and the visuals can be the stars.

E. *Creative financing partnerships.* Extremely high-budget motion pictures might be an area for joint ventures between studios and outside equity and/or overseas distribution ventures. If breakeven is being pushed that far back, and if the risks are truly that high, then the studio either should not make the movie at all (probably the better choice), or, if it must, it may want to share the risk with an outside entity. There is enough money "out there" available for this type of coproduction, but unfortunately studios cannot arbitrarily choose the deals in which they wish to include outside money and those they do not. Hence these coproductions frequently involve producers and/or separately funded production companies that have developed these extremely costly films themselves and are more likely to participate with the studio in their production and financing, but the upside to the studio is accordingly reduced.

F. *Know the math.* Creative executives must understand the mathematics behind film production and distribution. People who have the power to make deals and green-light development and/or production must understand the economics involved in their decisions. This encompasses legal and business-affairs personnel too. Unfortunately, too few executives, especially in the creative areas, really understand these economic points. Obviously top executives at successful studios can probably recite mathematical models in their sleep (if they are getting any).

A bit of training might go a long way. Sophisticated computer modeling is available today at all major studios. The projections, giving varying revenue assumptions, are extremely accurate and are getting better all the time. This probably does not give too much solace to those writers and directors who really like "off-the-wall" material, but it does equip a studio executive to make a meaningful decision. It is one thing for an executive to ignore the numbers having considered them carefully, but it is quite another not to understand their meaning and to decide independent of mathematical analysis. Certainly there is a time and place to disagree with the number crunchers, but at least one ought to see their opinions before writing them off. How many times have studio executives green-lighted movies with truly uncertain futures where breakeven required more than $100 million? This should never happen.

3. The negative side of increased product demand.

While each of the major studios is well positioned to market ancillary rights, regardless of volume, it is a very big question as to whether any studio is capable of properly marketing and domestically distributing annually the twenty-four to forty releases theatrically each is claiming it would like to release. This requires the marketing organizations of each company to create an entirely new advertising, promotional and publicity campaign for a theatrical release occurring, on average, every week and a half to two weeks. Decisions as to which films should be supported and at what level become intertwined in a cacophony of excess volume.

In the area of large media advertising buys, for instance, the major studios are forced to escalate their releasing costs to pay for advertising campaigns and saturation media buys in order to distinguish their movies from the flood of other product from the other studios. This is contrary to the economics of scale that usually accompany such large media buys. Competition for magazine covers, critics' reviews and so forth escalates, and the costs of supporting those mechanisms go up accordingly. Publicity and promotion, the much-undervalued stepchildren of the marketing wing, are also flooded with a product flow beyond their ability to handle.

How much of this very complicated marketing strategy can actually be coordinated by a single marketing organization within the studio? And if multiple marketing divisions are established, how does one keep them from competing with each other and reducing the impact of each other's advertising in the general marketplace? The use of independent-contractor ad agencies will surely increase, but in this arena the jury is still out. Can the studios actually handle the theatrical marketing, at least domestically, of this increased volume of product?

4. The trends toward diversification and consolidation.

There are two basic methods by which companies increase in size:

A. *Growing the core business* through success and, perhaps, adding new businesses that are developed totally internally; and

B. *Acquiring preexisting product or businesses* through purchases and/or mergers.

Internal growth in studios appears to be stimulated by bringing together marketing and distribution operations, creating greater interrelating among the development and production executives and their distribution counterparts. As talent moves freely across television and motion picture borders, there is increasing reason to consolidate movie and TV divisions under the helm of a senior executive with an eye for moving television performers into the theatrical arena, and taking movie product and developing it in the TV arena as well.

Growing new businesses is extremely time-consuming (it may take years to catch up to the competition) and may require some kind of a jump start with at least a minor acquisition. Different players approach the problem with different solutions: Sony acquired a record company (CBS), while Disney has so far failed at growing one. Growing businesses requires high amounts of capitalization (without offsetting assets), with significant losses anticipated in the early years. This long development period, requiring the patience to withstand the pressures for instantaneous success, is part of the process. Disney and Universal grew studio tours and/or theme parks; Fox grew Fox Broadcasting; Turner grew TNT; and many new companies are on the drawing boards of other studios. If successful, the payoff is tremendous.

The latter, external method allows companies to carefully examine their targets before acquisition and see (a) how the new company would fit into the existing structure; (b) what savings could be effected by consolidating overlapping functions; and (c) what portions of the new company can be sold off to help pay for the purchase.

The risks in such acquisitions are of course manifold: An adverse change in the marketplace (as in the collapse of many junk-bond deals) could raise interest rates and change inherent values of properties that were going to be spun off for purposes of paying for the acquisition; the government might intervene to prevent anticompetitive mergers (less of a problem these days); insufficient due diligence (in examining the target company before acquisition) could lead to some unpleasant surprises; golden parachutes costing more than originally bargained for might open (again, a fault of inadequate due diligence); shareholders could bring an unexpected, but successful, derivative action; one might find oneself in the middle of a bidding war, having placed the target company "in play" and thus open to other suitors; and the list goes on.

For companies following this route there are a few admonitions. First, the concept of being big for bigness's sake is not enough. Management cannot use the generic argument that to compete in the global marketplace of large conglomerates one must become one. The "world player" argument common today, absent a specific business plan with staged growth, is simply an excuse to spend money and increase personal power. This type of thinking leads to excessive debt and a monolithic bureaucracy that is virtually impossible to govern.

Mergers and acquisitions in the movie business must be driven by a precise strategy as to what will transpire following the consolidation of the entities in question. Executives must determine what the new business plan will be, where they expect the key synergies, and how best to consolidate, eliminating overlap and waste between the two companies. For example, if a company with a strong theme park acquires another company with a lot of well-known comic characters, those characters should be in the theme parks as quickly as can be done under strict quality-control measures.

It is an unfortunate reality that, in many cases of merger and acquisition, jobs are lost. However, the increase in efficiencies should be such that the new entity is even stronger than the previous two and will serve to better protect the jobs that remain.

In the late 1980s it was very much a major studio trend to purchase movie theatres. Each studio believed that once the feeding frenzy commenced, they would be at an extreme disadvantage if all the other major studios owned theatres and they were left out in the cold. This motivation, principally fear (almost always a bad reason, by itself, to act), generated sales of theatres to studios and their affiliates at twelve to fourteen times net positive cash flow, one of the most alarming outlays of cash in recent memory. Paramount (later partnered with Warners) bought Mann Theatres (now spun off); Sony bought Loews Theatres (spun off), and Universal acquired half of Cineplex Odeon (spun off). Today the value of theatres has plummeted, as over 70% of all U.S. exhibitors filed for protection under bankruptcy law. In short, the major studios could have generated vastly higher profits by buying certificates of deposit than engaging in the theatre-buying feeding frenzy. The fear factor was simply never justified.

5. Trends and the ancillaries.

No discussion of movies and money can be complete without a look into the future. In the twenty-first century we are seeing many new technologies (see the article by Dan Ochiva, p. 498) with a lot of interesting initials. Will DBS (direct-broadcast satellite) threaten pay cable? Will HDTV (high-definition television) render obsolete the videotapes and laserdiscs we have accumulated? Will DVDs themselves or another smaller device replace videotape as the medium of choice for rentals and purchase? Will basic pay television become an increasingly necessary substitute for syndication of motion picture product? What will happen to the video marketplace if pay-per-view increases in volume? Will the telephone companies be permitted to compete head-to-head with cable operators, and vice versa? When does the broadband Internet replace them all? The questions go on forever, and any good long-term strategist has to be worried about the answers.

The cable industry has long argued that its franchises are vastly undervalued. Notwithstanding the very real fear of re-regulation (at which point they cry poverty), they argue to the investment community that their products generate huge cash flows from basically captive audiences. They quiver from fear at the thought of new delivery systems, particularly any controlled by the telephone company, which currently has access to virtually every home in the United States. Yet how many cable subscribers are disappointed in the quality of the service (poor reception and many breakdowns) and the outrageously increasing costs of the system as a whole? In Los Angeles, monthly cable bills can easily exceed $100, an extremely high price for the typical family. Thus, the thought of having a hand-size satellite dish receiving over 100 channels from a high-powered satellite transponder for a price significantly less than what is being paid for current cable service is very appealing. The lack of cable competition due to local neighborhood franchises has certainly made the pay services expensive, but what would happen if they faced true competition from a readily accessible direct broadcast satellite? This is a tough market to second-guess.

With the price of DVD players dropping, the DVD, with its superior picture quality, has become the medium of choice for people buying videos, until even smaller, microchip and/or small-disc technology takes over. Discs are easier to store, do not deteriorate nearly as rapidly as tape, produce the highest quality digital audio sound (the same as compact disc) and generate image quality that can be as high as 40% to 60% better than that available on videotape. The only drawback is that one cannot record on a DVD without expensive equipment; hence, it is primarily a playback medium.

The battle between pay-per-view and home video has not really become nasty yet, because pay-per-view systems still only reach about 14 million subscribers, many on antiquated ordering systems. But as pay-per-view systems become more sophisticated and can deliver viewing on demand, complete with the ability to interrupt, one would expect to see a significant if not total erosion of the home-video rental business. Revenues on a per-picture basis (wide-release major studio product) is in the midrange of six figures, with escalations into seven figures for high-performing product.

As the domestic marketplace becomes glutted with TV movies, made-for-cable movies and theatrical films, the domestic after-market for syndication is reaching a saturation point, with per-picture revenues (exclusive of the hot performers) plummeting. As Fox Broadcasting, HBO, TNT, Viacom, the Family Channel, the USA Network and others manufacture more movies for first-run showing in their respective media, likewise, the after-market gets quite crowded, and the supply-and-demand curve will be and is causing a drop in prices.

Enter basic-pay (stations like USA, Lifetime, TNT, etc.) and the superstations (WTBS, WWOR, WGN). In many cases studios are now skipping the initial window of syndication and placing their product directly onto these basic-pay services for significant seven-figure license fees. To companies like Universal and Paramount, the ability to play something on their own basic cable service is reassuring insurance in this era of decreasing free television syndication values. Basic cable has come to the rescue of a number of TV series that were unable to find syndication homes and is now doing the same for new packages of currently produced feature-length motion pictures. The trend is likely to continue and probably will help ensure those who are still in the syndication market that at least there is some outside competition to keep the syndication-level prices from eroding totally.

The battle in pay television, on the premium services, escalated when Universal recently skipped the pay window on a number of successful features and resurrected high-end network (CBS) deals instead. Will this trend continue? Do studios feel intimidated that HBO, one of the two major pay services, is owned by a competitor, Time Warner? Stay tuned.

6. Capital is king.

The 1990s opened with a very strong emphasis on those companies that were adequately capitalized with a reasonable debt service. Undercapitalized companies could not face the challenges of the nineties and survive into the new century.

Growth is now likely to be focused in core and related businesses, and diversification is unlikely to continue into unrelated areas. Acquisitions will be strategic and synergistic rather than reflecting growth for growth's sake. Will companies that are thinly capitalized with heavy debt service be able to limp on, or will they be mercifully taken off the market for friendly mergers or acquisitions involving significant recapitalization? The issues abound.

In the independent world there is a resurgence of a firm and healthy marketplace for smaller companies. But as these companies expand, the temptation to move their product line into direct competition with major studios, capitalized many times more than any independent, is a temptation that has led, in the past, to the demise of a number of companies. Independents must continue to conserve their capital, keep their budgets low and by all means avoid the money-eating ravages of continual and sequential wide releases for their film product. Arguably an independent distributor should release a film wide (400 to 2,000 or more theatres) only under two conditions: (a) if the movie is a sequel to an already successful film; or (b) if there is a built-in marketplace for the product in question. In all other cases, independent product should be nurtured into the market on a platformed basis. Direct head-to-head competition with major studios at major budget levels should be avoided, because it does not take many failures to drag an independent company down.

Is the movie business healthy? On the whole we may be in for some material shake-ups in the near future, but it has and will continue to survive and produce jobs and cash flow.

The trend toward an increasing number of independently financed companies funneling their product (at least domestically theatrically) through the major studios is likely to continue. Where such an independent company is founded upon established talent with an average per-picture performance track record higher than that of the average major studios, the rates of return will be sufficiently high to justify such equity investment. This is further enhanced by the reality that an independent does not have to manufacture product to feed a distribution monster, but can concentrate on making movies in which it completely and totally believes. Careful cost management can also make such companies more profitable.

However, I see many potential companies out for funding that are offering investors noneconomic deals and/or insufficiently proven talent to justify an equity investment. In the high-pressure world of raising private capital, many investment banks and individuals have gotten on the bandwagon in the hopes of getting a good finders fee for setting up deals that, in all likelihood, will find their way to the motion picture graveyard where the corpses of Atlantic Releasing, Orion, New World Pictures and the old Cannon, just to name a few, rest under newly turned soil. And just as has occurred in the past, upon the failure of a few of these independently financed companies, Wall Street and independent equity investors will say that this form of investment, as a whole, could not have worked in the first place, and the well will run dry once again. It will be a little-noted fact that those independently financed companies that were well formulated with good business plans and strong management will continue to manufacture top-quality films and be quite profitable. (For example, New Line and Imagine have long since become part of the larger studio system, representing hope for the next generation of independents; and DreamWorks, with its megastar management and huge capital investment, has become a major player in just a few short years.) Then the investment community will find a new vehicle to apply to motion pictures. And so it goes, as the movie business makes its way into a new century possessing the same enigmatic qualities that make it attractive in the first place.

ELEMENTS OF FEATURE FINANCING

by **NORMAN H. GAREY,** who was a partner in the law firm of Garey, Mason & Sloane, based in the west side of Los Angeles. He represented actors, directors, writers, producers and production companies in the motion picture and television industries. Mr. Garey graduated from Stanford University and Stanford Law School, lectured at Stanford, at the USC Entertainment Law Institute and at the UCLA Entertainment Law Symposium, and was a member of the Los Angeles Copyright Society and the California bar. He died before publication of this book.

> An important lesson is to define at what point one's gross or net-profit position is achieved. . . . Another lesson is not to use phrases like net, *or* gross, *but rather to define net* of what *or gross* after what.

The matter of feature motion picture financing usually begins with the philosophy of the entrepreneurial producer. There are many established producers, for example, who are not particularly interested in buying or optioning a big, bestselling book or a finished original screenplay by a "star" screenwriter because these are very costly items, and many producers don't wish to spend a lot of money out of their own pockets. They would prefer to be original and either create ideas themselves and hire writers to develop them or induce financial sources to hire these writers. Or a producer may want to buy or option a screenplay that comes in from a relatively unknown source, perhaps a young writer who is a graduate student at UCLA or USC. It may be that the writer who is a bit better established, and who has an agent, in the normal professional course of events makes a submission of his material through the agent to the producer, who reads it and decides to buy it.

First, the producer's lawyer will commission the requisite title search to make sure that the material (and hopefully its title as well) can safely be used and that there aren't any conflicting claims, at least as disclosed by the copyright records in Washington. Next, the producer will decide how much to spend in option money and what kind of price to establish with the writer's agent. If it's a finished screenplay that the writer has written on speculation, he or she deserves some reward for it, which is generally reflected in the purchase price due on option exercise. The price would be constructed not only in terms of the cash payment due upon exercise of option and/or commencement of photography, but also (in many cases) in terms of contingent compensation as well.

As an example, suppose that the writer is established and has at least one produced screen credit and that the producer is negotiating for an original screenplay. If the producer is putting up $25,000 for a year's option with the right of a renewal for a second year for another $25,000 (usually the first payment applies against the purchase price, and perhaps the second does as well), the purchase price may easily be $250,000 or more. That second option period for the second $25,000 may be necessary because it takes that long to mount the production, to secure the elements necessary to put the financing in place, and to know that there will in fact be a movie that then warrants exercising the option and paying the $250,000.

On the "back end," this deal may provide that 5% of 100% of the picture's net profits will be payable to the writer. But both the cash payment due on option exercise and the 5% of 100% of net could be made to depend on that writer's having received sole screenplay credit. If another writer has to be brought in, then the first writer arguably hasn't completely delivered the value expected. The Writers Guild, in making its credit determination, may find that there was material in the shooting script that was created by the second writer, who naturally has also been paid. Some flexibility must be allowed in constructing the first writer's deal for the potential necessity of bringing in a second writer and for the economic consequences of that eventuality. Thus both the cash and the contingent compensation of the first writer may be reducible if that writer shares screenplay credit.

Suppose, as another example, that the writer is even more well established than the one just described. Perhaps he or she wants a lot more than $25,000 option money up front. Maybe the writer wants $50,000 to $75,000 up front in option money for a year, or even wants the work purchased outright rather than optioned at all. The producer doesn't want to spend that much out of pocket and doesn't want to go to a studio for it because that will mean giving too much away at the back end of his or her own deal. The producer may then establish a partnership with the writer, whereby the producer's profit points and the writer's profit points (and perhaps even their cash compensation) are pooled and divided in some way. Under such an arrangement, the writer takes a risk along with the producer, but also stands to be rewarded along with the producer if they're successful. This doesn't mean that the pooling and division necessarily result in a 50/50 split. It could be 66/33, 75/25, 60/40 or some other percentage. But the pooling and division partnership has become a rather frequently used device to accomplish a deal between a producer and a writer or the owner of a piece of material when the producer doesn't want to lay out a lot of money and the writer doesn't want to accept short money up front without a commensurate back-end reward for doing so.

A more typical deal is the for-hire development deal, in which a producer creates the idea and will either hire a writer out of his or her own money or go to a studio for development money to hire a writer. In this deal the writer will frequently ask for a large cash fee as well as for participation in the profits of the picture and the proceeds of the subsidiary or "separated" rights. These negotiations are frequently difficult ones. The writer may conceive that he is the originator of the material since he is creating certain of the characters and their inter-relationships, even though usually the story line and the plot premise at least have already been created by the producer. There is often some up-front ego conflict in these cases about who's contributing what. But these matters can be resolved by allowing the writer for hire to participate to some degree, beyond what the Writers Guild Minimum Basic Agreement requires, in the proceeds of the subsidiary or separated rights (such as theatrical and television sequel, print-publishing, and merchandising rights), or by rewarding the writer with a net-profit participation, which the Guild agreement does not require at all. If a significant cash fee is being paid up front, then the writer generally doesn't deserve all that; he's performing an employee's function and taking no risk at all. If, on the other hand, he is taking less than his normal front money and is contributing a great deal, then perhaps he does deserve to participate in these back-end rights and/or in the movie's net profits.

Assuming that the screenplay is of very good quality, the producer will then want to go to the marketplace and seek production financing based on this material. He might approach either a financier-distributor (a major studio) or one of the major independent production financiers. There are certain independent production companies that finance pictures but do not distribute their own product, and therein lies the distinction between them and the so-called majors. If the material is absolutely sensational, the producer may be fortunate enough to be able to sell the "minipackage" consisting of script, rights and producer's services. Knowing what the costs are, the producer should be in a position to construct a price, both in terms of guaranteed cash compensation (part of which may have to be earned out by producer services rendered over a future period) and contingent compensation, whether measured in terms of gross receipts, gross receipts from some future breakeven point, or net profits.

On the other hand, it may be that the material, while very good, is only very good when allied with certain other creative elements. In that case, it may be necessary to do some prepackaging. This may involve negotiating for a certain director, either because his name will help attract financing and/or cast or because the material may need further development. In the latter case it's wiser from a creative standpoint to involve the director who is actually going to make the movie in further developing the screenplay. It may also be desirable to attach some actors and thus complete a major package for delivery to the production financier; a complete package will improve the producer's deal vastly.

The philosophy that one must recognize and observe in making these decisions is that of the risk-reward ratio: The farther a producer has moved the project—that is, the greater the investment he has made in terms of time, effort and money and the more finished the product he is delivering—the more he's going to get for it, both in cash and in back-end contingent interest. If he's in a position to bring in what is nearly a completed movie that just hasn't been shot yet, he's going to be able to make the best deal with the financier. However, there are some risks to this approach, both strategic and financial. That's what makes the game interesting. Perhaps the elements one involves may turn out to be liabilities. The director may be terrific for the material but turn out to be unacceptable to the financier. Or, although everybody may have thought that the actor's last picture did very well and therefore that he should provide a big advantage, a picture that he made a while ago may come out in the meantime and turn out to be a disaster, whereupon no financier wants him anymore. The producer may have to drop one or both of these people from the package, politely and without creating any legal or economic liability in the process.

Sometimes it's necessary, in order to involve a director or an actor, to put up *holding money* or option money, just as one would do to secure rights to a literary property. An actor's time and a director's time are valuable, and they will not always pledge their availability to a certain project without knowing either that there is financing that guarantees their future compensation or that there's some money payable now for which they're willing to give the producer a temporary hold on their services. Naturally the independent producer's lawyer must negotiate separately for the services of each of the creative people in the package before going into the final negotiation with the production financier.

Thus if the producer is in a position to bring a finished script to a studio, and the studio has not taken the development risk (because the producer has done so), he can command a far better deal from the studio. If he's willing to take it a step farther and put down some money to tie up a director and/or actor, then he's entitled to even more from the studio. Perhaps that entrepreneurial producer can also independently raise production financing from private sources, either those who, as in the tax-shelter days, were seeking a write-off but also liked the movie business for its glamour, or from genuine equity financiers. If he can take the project all the way to completed film and then merely seek distribution for it, the producer will make an even better deal.

There are other potential sources of production financing to consider. Assume the producer is beginning to assemble those creative and money elements necessary to physically produce the film. Those sources of money may be *territorial;* that is, he may sell off the distribution rights for all media in certain territories of the world in order to raise money out of those territories with which to produce the movie. These guarantees received from overseas territories can be taken to banks and discounted for cash, which is then used to finance the movie. The producer may wish to sell off or license in advance the right to receive income from certain ancillary rights sources, such as soundtrack album recording and publishing rights to the music used in the movie. It may be that the merchandising rights are extremely valuable; if it's a high-technology picture, there's a lot of gadgetry that can become good toys. The merchandising rights may also be presold for guarantees that can be turned into cash. Book publishing is another possible source. A publishing house may be willing to put up money in advance of the material being secured or written. This investment will come at the earliest possible time if the producer is going to presell the publishing rights.

One technique that has been used to finance many low-budget films is raising money through *limited partnerships* formed by individual investors. Each investor is a "limited partner" (in that his liability for losses is limited to the amount he invests, and he incurs no personal liability beyond the amount) whose contribution, when aggregated with those of his partners, totals some proportion of the total production cost of the film. As a unit, these investors share a percentage of the "money's" share of the film's net profits (usually at least 50%) equal to the percentage that their total investment bears to the total production cost of the picture. The remaining net-profit shares are retained by other "money" (who get the balance of that 50%) and by the producers and other creative elements, who get the other 50% (or less) of the net profits. Broadway shows are traditionally financed in this manner. The individual investor can be attracted to films by means of the limited partnership, which finds doctors, accountants, farmers, realtors and a whole cross-section of society drawn to the glamour of movies.

The financing devices used in the motion picture industry are strongly similar to those used in the real estate development and construction industry. Making a movie is analogous to building a building on a lot. The literary property is the lot, the piece of real property. The movie is analogous to the building. The screenwriter is the architect, the director is the contractor and the producer is theoretically the owner. The major studio (if one is involved) can variously represent a lending institution, equity partner and/or leasing agent for the finished building (in its capacity as distributor).

If the producer is financing the picture privately, without going to a studio, it will be absolutely necessary to secure a completion guarantee from one of the traditional sources (unless his own financial resources are so substantial that he can and will place at risk his own general assets). There are a handful of recognized, professional completion guarantors. (See article by Norman Rudman and Lionel A. Ephraim, p. 207.) A *completion guarantor* is a kind of cost insurer, or insurance company. He agrees (for a premium usually computed as a percentage of the picture's production cost) that out of his resources or financial contacts he will guarantee the money necessary to complete the picture if the money that has been raised from other sources turns out to be inadequate, for example if the picture runs well over the original budget. The producer must satisfy the completion guarantor that he has a good track record for cost responsibility going in and that the director also does, because the director is in a real sense the general contractor in the field. He's responsible for building the building, and if the costs are going to run over, it'll probably be because of him. The completion guarantor will want to put his own supervisor or production manager and location auditor on the picture to watch what's going on, in order to protect his risk. He may insist on the right to take over the picture, to take it out of the producer's and the director's control, if it's going substantially over budget. There may be penalty clauses in the completion guarantee stating that if the completion guarantor is required to come up with money, that is, if his guarantee is actually called upon, he has the right to invade the contingent compensation (or in some cases even the cash compensation) of the producer or director or both. The controls that the completion guarantor will insist upon may be at least as onerous as those that a major studio would impose upon a producer if the studio were putting up the money. The source that's ultimately answerable financially is the one considered entitled to impose those controls. The completion guarantee then has to be approved by the basic financing source(s), because they want to know that there's a real guarantee in place; they don't want to be confronted with the unwelcome choice of either accepting a three-fourths completed film after having put up all of the money or having to put up money beyond their original commitment in order to complete the picture.

Another way to finance a picture is through a *negative pickup*. It may be that the producer hasn't been able to raise all of the production money from nonstudio sources, but only a part of it. If there's a completion guarantor willing to back the ultimate cost of the project, the producer can then go to a studio (or other production financier) where the management believes in the picture enough to take a limited financial risk on it. They will agree to guarantee payment of part or all of the negative cost upon delivery of the negative. The studio is not taking a production risk because if the negative is not delivered, the studio has no obligation. On the other hand, if the negative is delivered but the picture is not very good, the studio is still obligated to pay the "pickup" price. That negative pickup guarantee by the studio can be taken to a bank and turned into cash.

One other way for a producer to proceed is to go directly to a bank and secure a production loan on the strength of all the other guarantees that he has assembled. The bank loan itself can be "taken out" (discharged or paid off) by a negative-pickup guarantee from a studio. That's another little wrinkle in the financing package. Basically the bank's loan is interim financing, and the negative pickup is permanent financing or the "takeout loan," as it would be called in real estate parlance.

If the producer has completed the film entirely from nonstudio sources of financing and is now seeking distribution, he would screen it for a major studio distributor. If it was well received, the producer could possibly command a deal for the film in which the studio would advance all or more than all of the negative cost, thereby perhaps generating an immediate profit as a result of simply making the deal. He might further obtain a guarantee from the studio of a certain number of dollars toward print and advertising expenses. This guarantee is very important because the commitment of exploitation money frequently indicates the seriousness of the distributor's intent. Even the best film is not going to be successful if it's advertised poorly or inadequately promoted.

Next the producer will probably be able to command some kind of gross-receipts participation deal. This is structured so that once the studio has recouped its expenditures (its outlay for prints and advertising and the advance made to the producer to cover the negative cost outlay, enabling the producer in turn to pay off the various loans taken out along the way), the proceeds derived thereafter will be divided between the producer and the distributor on a gross basis, without any further deductions. The division could be 50/50 after recoupment by the studio, or it could be an alternating 60/40 deal. This might call for a 60% split in the studio's favor until the studio has recouped all of its outlay (prints and ads, its advance to the producer, etc.), with the percentage then shifting in the producer's favor up to a further point based on gross receipts before flattening out at 50/50 or some other split. There are varying combinations, depending on bargaining power.

If the producer does not require any advance whatsoever from the studio because money from foreign territorial sales and other sources has financed the picture as well as all print and advertising costs, he can hire the studio as pure distributor on a reduced distribution fee basis. There is conceded to be a variable profit factor in the standard 30% U.S. domestic distribution fee, so that it is possible, when the studio has taken no financial risk, for the producer to hire the studio as salesman only ("leasing agent" in the real estate analogy) and expect the studio to distribute the picture at a less-than-normal fee, for example at 22½% domestically instead of 30%, and at 32½% instead of 40% for any previously unsold foreign territories.

Producers raise production financing themselves to avoid having to go to the domestic distributor earlier than necessary because the farther down the road one can go alone, the better the deal will be with that major studio distributor at the end of the line. The best position for a producer is to be able to walk into a distributor with a completed film and say, "Okay, we'd like to have you as a distributor. What kind of guarantee of prints and advertising are you willing to make, and what kind of reduced distribution fee are you willing to quote?" The more studio money the producer accepts and the earlier he accepts it, the greater the risk he asks the studio to take and the more the studio will expect to be rewarded for it. Again, the risk-reward ratio operates. If the financier-distributor is asked to take the entire production risk, the best the producer can expect—assuming he's assembled all the elements and has paid the entire development cost—is usually a 50/50 net-profit deal. For that much risk the financier-distributor is generally considered to be entitled to at least 50% of the net profits, and perhaps more, and to insist on the standard distribution fee of 30% for the U.S. and Canada.

The producer's profit percentage will be reducible by the profit participations given up along the way to raise the money or to obtain the creative elements. The writer will probably receive 5% to 10%, the director 10% to 15%. Immediately the producer has given away perhaps 25% of 100% of the net profits, half his share, and that's with virtually no cast. If there is major casting, he may be giving away gross participations that, at best, come off the top and significantly reduce what constitutes net profits in the first place and, at worst, may also come to some extent from his end of the net profits. With studio financing, the producer may end up with somewhere between 10% and (if he is relatively fortunate or has been able to negotiate a net-profit "floor" as a protection against further reductions) 20% of the net profits, with some gross participations off the top that reduce the net-profit pie before it can be cut up.

To understand this in practical terms, one should track the money flow briefly. A ticket dollar comes in at the box office to the exhibitor during the first week of the picture's run in a major city. The distributor has been able to negotiate typical terms from the exhibitor, a 90/10 split in favor of the distributor. First, we must deduct from that dollar the exhibitor's house nut (or expenses) of around 10%, so we're down to 90¢. If the 90/10 deal calls for the distributor to receive 90% of the remainder, that's about 80¢ out of the dollar that has come in at the box office; 80¢ of that dollar constitutes the distributor's rentals. In the U.S. and Canada the distributor is entitled to a 30% distribution fee, which is 24¢, so now we're down to 56¢. The 30% distribution fee is to pay the distributor's own nut, or internal expenses, and is conceded to contain a profit factor the amount of which depends on how many pictures the distributor has in exploitation in a given year and thus how easily the fixed costs are covered that year. Advertising and publicity expenses are very high, especially television advertising; let's assume 25% of rentals, and these expenses come next. If our rentals were 80¢, deduct 25% of that for advertising, or 20¢, bringing our 56¢ down to 36¢. We haven't even considered other distribution expenses, such as the cost of striking prints, taxes, dubbing, the MPAA seal, shipping and transportation. With all these the 36¢ will be reduced to less than 30¢. Now the negative cost of the picture must be recovered. If it's supposed that the negative cost was roughly one-third of the total dollar that came in, we've got nothing left. Thus, if we're lucky, we've covered the negative cost of the picture, but we probably haven't. We're probably going to have to wait significantly far into the next dollars that come in to break even and to begin computing net profits, if any.

If we are barely into net profits, the studio is entitled to 50% for putting up the production money. They're the investing partner in this sense, not the salesman, in that they've received their distribution fee earlier. If there were 2¢ left out of that original dollar (let's be generous to ourselves), the studio gets 1¢. But wait—if there was a gross participation out to a major star, then that actor's participation would come off the original 80¢ that we took in at the box office. If he received a 10%-of-gross participation, there would have been another 8¢ gone before we even got this far. So instead of having 2¢ left, we'd be minus 6¢; we'd be unrecouped.

If you take that dollar and multiply it by many millions, it illustrates the difference between that actor's being a gross participant and that same actor's being a net-profit participant. If he was a 10% net-profit participant, that actor would wind up with nothing or with his minor share of 1¢. But because he is a popular actor and has a good enough agent, he commands a 10% gross participation from the first dollar and comes out of that sample dollar with 8¢ (which is far more than anyone else except the distributor) rather than (maybe) a fraction of 1¢.

Only a small number of directors in the world can command first-dollar gross participations of a significant kind, and hardly any writers can. However, there are many actors and directors, and even a few writers, who are given gross participations from breakeven, that is, once breakeven is achieved. So once we got down to that 1¢ and beyond, which is theoretically breakeven, then and only then (on the next dollar) would this hypothetical actor or director or writer participant's gross participation be payable. (See article by Steven E. Blume, p. 332.)

An important lesson is to define at what point one's gross or net-profit position is achieved. If it's gross from first dollar, that's very different from gross after breakeven or some other break point. In our hypothetical example, the gross-from-first-dollar participant would have gotten 8¢. The gross-from-breakeven participant would have gotten nothing or nearly nothing because we barely reached breakeven out of that last cent of the dollar. Another lesson is not to use phrases like *net* or *gross,* but rather to define net *of what* or gross *after what.*

The foregoing has used the producer with a track record as its focus. The new or impoverished producer will be stung when going to a studio because he or she has no leverage. In this case there may be a small cash fee and an even smaller profit participation, certainly not 50% or anything very close to it.

VENTURE-CAPITAL STRATEGY AND THE FILMDALLAS MODEL

by **SAM L GROGG,** dean of the American Film Institute Conservatory in Los Angeles. He holds a Ph.D. in popular culture from Bowling Green University and has executive produced and produced a number of motion pictures and movies for television, including *The Trip to Bountiful, Patti Rocks, Spike of Bensonhurst* and *Da*. Grogg was the managing general partner of FilmDallas Investment Fund, a pioneering venture capital fund supporting independent film production.

> FilmDallas pioneered a concept that many regional production centers might still consider; it remains an excellent model for entrepreneurs interested in developing capital for independent motion picture production.

The past few decades have witnessed a significant geographical shift in the traditional centers of the motion picture industry. Hollywood has not been displaced as the industry's Mecca, but significant production centers have emerged outside Southern California. The industry trade magazines have dubbed this phenomenon "runaway production" and printed story after story on the economic threat that such increasing regionalism represents to Hollywood-based studios and related companies. However, the trend persists and grows in the new millennium as more of the motion picture industry recognizes the potential—both creative and economic—of new production centers in Texas, North Carolina, Florida, Vancouver and Toronto, among others.

As regional production centers strengthen, local financial resources have begun to explore ways to become involved in the activity and its economic potential. In many cases, the regional centers are exploring ways to use not only their interesting locations, strong crew base and other resources to attract production, but also to offer investment capital as an attractive incentive.

The newly developing production centers act as beacons to draw entrepreneurs from across the country to consider involvement in the upswing of a booming film industry—cable has matured, and new digital delivery systems and the expansion of home video/DVD continue to signal a healthy demand for moving-image content. As part of this, investment in independent motion picture production has become a routine consideration for venture capitalists. For the entrepreneur seeking production investment, the challenge has been to create an investment strategy that provides a sense of comfort and understanding that will encourage venture capital support.

This challenge was at the heart of the original FilmDallas Investment Fund. FilmDallas pioneered a concept that many regional production centers might still consider; it remains an excellent model for entrepreneurs interested in developing capital for independent motion picture production.

The original goal was simple—create a venture-capital vehicle, modeled on the mutual-fund concept, to invest in motion picture development, production and distribution. By taking positions in a variety of investments, the fund was designed to generate returns that could be used in a "roll-over" fashion in order to participate in additional opportunities and to generate a meaningful annual rate of return for its investors. The application of this fundamental concept led the FilmDallas Fund to significant investments in several motion pictures, among them Academy Award–nominated *Kiss of the Spider Woman,* for which William Hurt won the Oscar for Best Actor, and *The Trip to Bountiful,* for which Geraldine Page won the Oscar for Best Actress. Eventually the fund, its affiliated entities and successors would participate in the financing of development, production and distribution of fifteen motion pictures over a period of four years in the late 1980s.

Years later, the basic structure of FilmDallas continues to be a viable vehicle for the development of venture capital for independent production. While the industry has certainly evolved in many respects, the expansion of delivery systems and media, along with a pressing need for the continuing replenishment of content, are reasons to revisit the FilmDallas concept.

THE STRUCTURE

The original FilmDallas Investment Fund was structured as a private limited partnership organized under Regulation D of the Securities and Exchange Commission code. The limited partnership structure (or LLC, Limited Liability Company) was chosen in order to limit financial liability on the part of the investors to no more than their individual investment. While limited partnerships for movie investments had, in earlier decades, offered some economic advantages through tax credits, such advantages had long since disappeared and do not exist today. The limited-liability structure is not only attractive to investors for liability reasons, it also addresses concerns of filmmakers about fear of investor involvement in creative decisions.

The partnership consisted of three general partners and thirty-five limited partners. All of the partners qualified as accredited investors meeting SEC "accredited investor requirements" under Regulation D. The general partners offered the investment via a comprehensive disclosure document. Likewise, the general partners were responsible for the management of the partnership while (as with all limited-liability vehicles) the limited partners were not involved in any aspect of the partnership's management in order to afford them limited-liability status.

The original fund was designed as a modest fundraising effort. Limited partnership units were sold in the amount of $50,000 per unit. The minimum number of units offered was fifty (or $2.5 million). The offering was closed at its minimum, but FilmDallas-related entities subsequently raised over $20 million in development, production, acquisition and distribution funds. The seed capital was small, but through its managed investment, it grew dramatically.

The fund's limited partners had a choice of paying cash for their units or financing their purchase through a prearranged loan facility at a reasonable interest rate. Investors choosing the financing facility could elect that their proceeds be distributed directly to the lender in order to pay back the loan.

The strategic decisions of choosing a limited-liability vehicle, setting a minimum investment level and the alternative of purchasing of units by means of a promissory note were consciously designed to keep the investment simple, attainable and attractive to potential investors. Investors were familiar with the limited-partnership vehicle from their participation in other ventures such as real estate and energy. The minimum level of funding was modest and attainable, but it also prevented the venture from compromising its capital needs during the offering. The promissory note alternative allowed the investors to make their purchase without dipping into their liquid capital.

Even more central to the strategy of the venture-capital fund was the realization that most efforts to raise financing for motion picture production and related activities turn on the ability of the investor to analyze the potential likelihood of success of a single motion picture. Hundreds of limited partnerships and other investment opportunities had been presented over the years whereby the prospective investor was asked to make a decision regarding whether or not a particular combination of screen-play, talent and budget level might form the basis of an enterprise that would realize a profit. It was the expectation on the part of investment pro-moters that prospective investors could or even wanted to make such a decision that had been at the heart of most failed efforts to raise private in-vestment capital for movies.

As the strategy for FilmDallas was developed, the general partners monitored the experience of many other film investments that had circu-lated among the investment community to which they were about to offer their plan. The sophisticated investors of Texas had seen all sorts of movie deals from all kinds of promoters. They were used to high risk/high reward venture investments, and the entertainment industry had the type of charisma that the community relished. The Texas investment community had cut its teeth on land and energy speculation and knew the gamble that many of these prospects represented. In many respects, investment in mo-tion pictures seemed just right for such an investment mindset. However, for one reason or another, this risk-taking investment community had not backed any meaningful percentage of investments in motion pictures or related activities.

One basic reason for the wariness of motion picture investments, then and now, is really quite simple: potential private investors do not want to make the decision regarding the potential success of a motion picture. Most of these successful businessmen and women do not have the under-standing or even the intuitive feel of what is a potentially successful in-vestment in motion pictures. And most of their opportunities are limited to one project, one spin of the wheel—a gamble that even the most diehard wildcatter finds difficult to take.

The strategy that was developed for FilmDallas grew out of an ac-knowledgement that sophisticated investors tend to avoid the complete unknown. The fund offered a plan that took the decision regarding a par-ticular investment in either a motion picture or some aspect of develop-ment, production or distribution out of the investors' hands. The "mutual fund" concept presented a structure whereby an investor's capital would be administered, and an informed and experienced manager would make investment decisions. Further, the manager of the fund would invest its capital according to a set of specific criteria that were designed to minimize risk and diversify opportunities for profit. And while the investors did not have to make a decision regarding what movie to back, they did have the opportunity to examine in detail the plan by which their investment capi-tal would be managed.

THE INVESTMENT CRITERIA

The general strategy inherent in a mutual fund—managed capital designed to be allocated among a number of potential opportunities in order to realize an attractive rate of return—was refined into a set of general criteria that ruled the actions of FilmDallas's management. In summary, the criteria were as follows:

1. The fund would not invest more than $500,000 in any one project or endeavor. The plan was to diversify the fund across a number of projects, spreading risk in order to create several opportunities for success and to offset those investments that would fail.

2. The total amount of overall financial commitment per investment could not be more than $2 million, with the FilmDallas contribution representing no less than 25% of any total financial commitment, nor more than 50%. While the maximum investment level might be raised somewhat to adjust for current economics, the essential idea was that a modest total investment obviously required modest returns to recoup. The 25% minimum and 50% maximum allowed the fund's investment a significant enough position to influence the terms of the deal but not so much as to bear complete risk for a project. A major tenet of the fund's overall management philosophy was to identify investments and positions in those investments where the fund's contribution could maintain a certain level of influence yet share risk with others.

3. At least one-half of all funds available in the investment fund were required to be invested in activities that could take advantage of regional production resources. This requirement allowed half of the fund's investments to be monitored close to home rather than in far-flung locations, a problem with most private investments in motion picture production. (More often than not, the filmmakers who raise money for motion picture production want to spend that money as far away from their investors as possible.) The FilmDallas plan sought to keep investments geographically close at hand, to take advantage of the relationships its management had developed in the region, and to pledge that local investment would be spent in the local community.

There were several other internal criteria that the fund used to analyze investments: requiring distribution agreements for motion picture productions; approving all key creative elements of any project in which the fund took a large percentage; and reviewing and evaluating all significant contracts that might influence the individual investment.

Financial judgment was left as uncompromised and as unprejudiced as possible when investment opportunities were analyzed. Many projects were reviewed, and only a few became fund investments. Initially the fund sought to be as passive as possible in its investments after the initial negotiations were consummated. However, as time went on, the fund became more and more active in the management of a particular investment throughout the development, production and distribution process. And in the end, the fund did evolve into a more traditional producer's role, requiring that all of the standard elements and ingredients of the motion picture production process be weighed as decisions were made, in order to protect and enhance the future of the particular project/investment.

THE INVESTORS' "DEAL"

Investors in the original FilmDallas Fund received a very favorable participation in the fund's returns. The allocation of proceeds was divided as follows:

	Investors' Percentage of Proceeds	Managers' Percentage of Proceeds
From $0 until recoupment of original investment	99%	1%
From 100% to 300% of original investment	80%	20%
From 300% to 500% of original investment	60%	40%
Thereafter	50%	50%

A typical split between Managers (Producer) and Investors in a film deal was 100% to the investors until they had recouped all of their original investment and a 50/50 split thereafter. FilmDallas sought to offer a better deal to its investors, one that compensated them for the risk they were taking and the time value of their money. More importantly, weighting the deal in favor of the investors demonstrated the confidence of the fund managers that their plan would produce results benefiting all parties favorably. There have been many deals offered, then and to this day, in which the promoters of the investments take positions in the revenue stream that raise concerns regarding their willingness to stand aside until their investors have had an opportunity to be well compensated.

One of the most often abused relationships between deal promoters and investors is the split of proceeds. Respect for the investors' risk is key to winning their support. Weighting the split in favor of the investor at the front end of the potential-return revenue stream is a clear acknowledgement of their financial risk and a demonstration of the promoter's confidence that the deal will be successful. Deals where the promoter seeks early equal advantage with the investor can raise suspicions as to motive and confidence.

THE INVESTMENTS

The planning of the fund's administration required that diversification of the capital be a primary objective. Also, the roll-over concept, whereby revenues were to be reinvested to expand the fund's portfolio, called for analyzing the timing of potential investments versus their projected revenue return. By projecting the timing of return on each investment, the fund manager could hope to replace invested funds with revenues and thereby extend the life of the active investment pool beyond original capitalization. A program was devised that would involve a combination of short, near and long-term investments which would realize returns within six to nine months, twelve to eighteen months and over twenty-four months respectively.

An understanding of motion picture expenses and revenue cash flows was essential to this planning process. For instance, investing in theatrical distribution costs or film acquisition costs (rather than production) can provide a relatively short-term return, since the period from the time of the investment until the time of revenue generation is fairly short. A typical motion picture distributor recoups money in the following order:

1. The Distributor's Fee (from various formats)

2. Then Distribution Expenses (typically advertising and print-duplication costs)

3. Then Cost of Production (advances and/or negative cost)

4. Then Profits

Investment in distribution garners a return in the recoupment stream ahead of a production investment, which was considered a near- to long-term investment, since it returns at a later time, depending on the quantity of revenues from the various markets. Investment in the development phase was considered a long-term investment because of the lag time until those revenues might be recouped—unless a picture is made quickly and development costs are repaid out of the production budget. The fund sought to take positions in each of these arenas—distribution, production and development.

Some of the investments the fund made included the following:

Choose Me, directed by Alan Rudolph, was the fund's initial investment. The picture had been completed and had just begun its theatrical release. The fund made a deal to invest a total of $500,000 in two positions: $300,000 in distribution costs and $200,000 in the cost of production. For these investments, the fund received a percentage of gross receipts from the theatrical distribution of the picture, before distribution fees and expenses, as well as participation in net revenues from all sources. The distribution investment began returning revenues within six months; the production investment generated returns in approximately a year. Within three years of the original investment, revenues back to the fund had amounted to approximately 60% of the original $500,000. Not a success, but not a complete loss.

Kiss of the Spider Woman, directed by Hector Babenco, was the fund's second major investment. $500,000 was invested in the acquisition of North American distribution rights. The investment terms provided for a sliding percentage participation in "adjusted" gross receipts, defined as those receipts to the distributor after deducting distribution expenses only (no distribution fees). The investment returned approximately 200% of its original contribution within two years.

FilmDallas's financing and production of *The Trip to Bountiful,* directed by Peter Masterson, followed on the heels of *Kiss of the Spider Woman.* Here, the fund invested $500,000 in the development and production of the project. The fund management also produced the picture and served as general partner of a separate limited partnership that financed the entire cost of production. The fund received its pro-rata share of all proceeds resulting from the exploitation of the picture throughout the world. In about three years, the investment had returned approximately 175% of its original contribution.

Overall, these investments represented a variety of financial analyses, structures, expectations and results. Each returned its revenues on relatively different schedules and in different amounts. Together the investments formed a portfolio that spread risk over several opportunities, provided the ability to expand the investment pool beyond its original limitations, and resulted in some significant pictures being made.

As a concept for developing regional independent motion picture production investment, the FilmDallas fund represents a model that can still work. The approach was an attempt to be "smart" in making what are often irrationally influenced decisions. Nothing is more illogical, it seems, than the success or failure of a motion picture. Good movies fail and bad movies become hits on a regular basis. But surrounding these unpredictable events is a strong and continuing industry that has spread its wings across an entire continent. That industry holds tremendous opportunity for those whose aspirations embrace a modestly conceived plan of attack with careful and considered decisions at its heart.

ANALYZING MOVIE COMPANIES

by **HAROLD L. VOGEL,** author of *Entertainment Industry Economics: A Guide for Financial Analysis* (Fifth Edition) and of the companion volume, *Travel Industry Economics: A Guide for Financial Analysis,* both published by Cambridge University Press. He was ranked as top entertainment industry analyst for a record ten years by *Institutional Investor* magazine and was the senior entertainment industry analyst at Merrill Lynch for seventeen years. A chartered financial analyst (C.F.A.), Mr. Vogel served on the New York State Governor's Motion Picture and Television Advisory Board and as an adjunct professor of media economics at Columbia University's Graduate School of Business. Currently a venture capitalist and fund manager based in New York, he is still hoping that his novel, *Short Three Thousand,* will one day make it onto the big screen.

> Standard cookie-cutter accounting and forecasting methods don't seem to work well when applied to this industry.

Once upon a time, movies and movie people were truly at the center of the entertainment industry universe. But now, at least from an economic and financial standpoint, they have to share the entertainment industry spotlight with other products such as music, video games, books and sports, to name a few. This makes analyzing the financial impact of movies more interesting as well as more complicated than ever before.

In contrast to the early days of the feature film business, when movies simply appeared on theater screens and quickly disappeared from sight, movies of both the past and the present are today seen and distributed internationally using a wide variety of systems and devices. Yet each of these distribution vehicles—be it broadcast television, digital video (discs and Internet), cable or something else—operate under substantially different business models and economic assumptions. For instance, broadcast television is advertiser-based, cable is pay-per-view or by subscription, and home video may be through either rental or direct purchase.

The ever-increasing complexity accentuates what I had noted in the previous edition of this compilation, which is that if you really want to see lots of movies, you probably shouldn't become an investment analyst. Over my many years of analyzing the business of making movies, I've not found enough time to see all the films I'd like to see. And my personal reactions are quite irrelevant when it comes to predicting how the public at large and stock market investors in particular might treat the shares of the company that produced or distributed a specific film.

My interests notwithstanding, there are, in fact, many other variables that may affect the profitability performance of most entertainment companies and the value of their shares. What's happening to cable subscriptions? How's theme park attendance? Is advertising, tied as it is to the current and prospective condition of the economy, likely to rise or fall? In today's world of multilayered, multipurpose global entertainment and media companies, the answers to such questions will often far overshadow the earnings-impact significance of a film's opening weekend gross receipts performance at the box office.

What has not changed at all, however, is the uniqueness of investing in movies as opposed to investing in industries that manufacture hard, finished goods, such as cars or computers. Entertainment industries instead produce things you can't hold in your hands, or taste, or smell; they produce things that you *experience* and that you emotionally carry away with you long after a movie's last reel has been metaphorically unspooled or a recording's last note has been sounded. As the history of the movies and of other forms of entertainment has shown, people will pay a lot to have their thoughts and emotions transported.

In the year 2000, for example, people in the United States paid approximately $8 billion for movie tickets, about $10 billion for video rentals, $14 billion for music, $38 billion for cable television services, and nearly $62 billion for gaming and wagering services such as those offered by casinos and state lotteries. Spending on *all* recreation activities, as defined in National Income and Product Account (NIPA) statistics from the U.S. Department of Commerce, amounted in that year to nearly $260 billion, of which spending on entertainment *services* comprised around 45%. It is also probably safe to extrapolate that the rest of the world combined spent at least an equal amount on recreation, which would bring total global spending in this category to around half a trillion dollars.

The most important aspect, though, is that the percentage of total personal consumption expenditures (PCEs) for entertainment services has risen gradually since 1980 from 2.4% to 3.8%, even as the percentages of PCEs earmarked for purchases of clothing (5% in 2000) and food (14%), for instance, have been declining. This suggests that, for most people in the developed world, entertainment is coming to be seen as an essential need once the basics of food, clothing, and shelter have been covered by after-tax earned income.

Of course, at first glance, it is easy for a prospective entertainment-industry analyst to be overwhelmed: Standard cookie-cutter accounting and forecasting methods don't seem to work well when applied to this industry. Each completed film is produced with unique elements and cost structures that will never be identical to those of any other film. Indeed, from its first date of release, each film is in and of itself a marketing experiment, conducted in real time and without recourse to a second chance. Moreover, unlike in marketing for laundry soaps or sodas or cigarettes, a distributor's brand name doesn't much matter (with the possible exception of Disney); no one goes specifically to see a film distributed by Fox instead of, say, Paramount. Instead, certain stars or directors and famous movie titles and series may sometimes evolve into franchises or brands of a sort, but usually with relatively limited shelf lives.

If the top-down forecasting methods that are so useful, perhaps, in estimating future demand for housing or horseradishes don't seem to work well in entertainment, what then? The answer—that there is no single, simple answer—is not very comforting to those who seek decimal-point precision for their projections. The fanciest spreadsheet analysis in the world cannot precisely predict how a film will perform for the company that has produced and distributed it. In reality, entertainment-industry investments have proven over time to be far more sensitive to the deftness of a company's management in the formulation and execution of long-term growth strategies than to changes in broad economic variables that might include measures of things like real disposable incomes, household wealth, and interest rates.

In other words, *only* if a company has demonstrated ability to *profitably* attract and retain creative talent might the analyst then be able to reasonably assume with some confidence that future performance could be extrapolated from the successes of the past. More to the point, proficiency in the care and feeding of many large (if not often irrationally inflated) creative egos is in and of itself a decisive management skill. Still, that alone does not a good investment make. Also needed are a little luck and pluck, and the accumulation of a significant film library and/or other large pool of intellectual property rights.

For the investment decision-making process, it is the expected stream of cash receipts that are to be generated from exploitations of this pool of rights that then becomes most important. Once such cash-flow estimates have been discounted back to net present value through the application of interest-rate mathematics and then further adjusted for a company's debt load and risk profile, the analyst may finally have a basis on which to make a recommendation.

All of this would, of course, be relatively straightforward and simple were it not for the uncertainties in forecasting the size and regularity of such future cash receipts, or income ultimates, as they've come to be called by industry accountants. Any number of things, including fads and fashion styles and shifts of consumer sentiment, can affect the size and probability of receipt of such ultimates. Thus, valuation of entertainment-library assets and earnings remains yet more an art than a science. In fact, statistical research suggests that the success and profitability of any film, no matter what the star, genre, budget, or target demographic, is pretty much a hit-or-miss, best-guess proposition. (See "Bose-Einstein Dynamics and Adaptive Contracting in the Motion Picture Industry" by Arthur De Vany and W. David Walls in *The Economic Journal*, November 1996).

Nowhere does the notion of financial artistry become more evident, it would seem, than in accounting for film-company profits—a subject on which cynicism abounds. Here, though, it might be remembered that the basic purpose of accounting rules is to formulate a method through which revenues and expenses can be properly matched so that readers of financial statements may obtain a reasonably accurate picture of a company's current financial condition.

Unfortunately, however, this is often more easily said than done, because intelligent and honest people can have significant differences of opinion as to how best to account for their incomes and costs. For example, if a studio licenses a television program or a feature film to a television network and receives the promised license fees in cash installments, should such revenues to the studio also be recognized in corresponding installments, or should they all be immediately recognized at one point in time?

And what about accounting treatments for the costs of making programs or features? Should production expenses that may have been incurred a long time ago (and when the buying power of a dollar or the currency exchange rate was different) be somehow charged against the current-period license fees, or should such expenses have been fully charged against revenues that had been previously received? How long, anyhow, should a movie studio wait before it finally recognizes that the production boss's hot picture of the year is really a dud that will never recover its costs?

For the outside investor, and also for the financial analyst, the problem is that the so-called income-forecast method of accounting used by the industry and now codified in Financial Accounting Standards Board (FASB) Statement of Position (SOP) 00-2 relies to a great extent on a *management's* estimates (possibly far into the future) of how much cash income a film or television series might generate. As it happens, there are few if any means through which a management's estimates can be directly challenged or validated by interested third parties.

Although some controversy remains, under the new and somewhat stricter standards of SOP 00-2, there is more uniformity—and thus greater comparability—across a wide spectrum of filmed entertainment companies than there used to be under the previous FASB Statement No. 53, which was rescinded as of the year 2000. The new standards bring previously variable treatments of certain expenses, especially those relating to advertising and marketing costs, into greater conformity while retaining the basic architecture of FASB No. 53. Under the new rules, marketing expenses are written down immediately, and requirements in reporting of television syndication profits have been tightened, thereby reducing the ability of companies to inflate stated profits in a film's (or series's) early years, just after release.

Up to a point, analysts can further circumvent the difficulties caused by varying treatments of income statement items—and adjust their opinions accordingly—by paying careful attention to the balance sheet footnotes, which provide additional clues as to the accounting-treatment policies that a filmed entertainment company's management has adopted. In this regard, it ought to be recognized that the stock market may not always see through film accounting gimmicks over the short run, but it always gets it right over the long run.

Accounting treatments for individual profit participants, however, seem to attract the most attention, and it is important to recognize that such profit participations are structured as contingent compensation subject to the overall success of a project. In this context, the words "net profits" have no intrinsic meaning beyond that which has been decided by the participants' attorneys. (See article by Steven Blume, p. 332.) From the outside analyst's point of view, the essential element is that the expected value of a profit participation will normally be a function of the relative negotiating clout of the parties *before* a project is begun.

No matter what the accounting variances, though, it is the magnitude, availability and predictability of cash flow that is the analyst's most fundamental concern. In this respect, the movie industry as a whole has struggled, even as revenues from new ancillary-market sources have burgeoned. Budgets for production and marketing of features released by the major studio distributors have consistently grown at rates (8% annually since 1980) that are more than double the rate of inflation seen in the overall economy.

Indeed, the decline of film and television profit margins at the major studios, from around 8% in the 1980s to at best 5% by the early 2000s, has occurred in an environment of ever-escalating star salaries, special effects, and marketing pressures. As a result, barriers of entry into the business have risen and the industry has had to seek new sources of financing and support through mergers with larger, overseas players such as Sony of Japan and News Corporation of Australia. Cost pressures have also given birth to the widely held view in both Wall Street and Hollywood that, for corporations, bigger is better and that you have to go global to survive.

The movie business itself has, accordingly, become just another product line (and a relatively low-profit one at that) for the large conglomerates that own studio distributors, often alongside cable systems (multiple-system operators, or MSOs), broadcast television and cable networks, TV stations, theme parks, publishing assets, global Internet service providers and satellite enterprises. Such business-segment relationships, as taken from the perspective of the major Hollywood studios as of 2003, are illustrated in a chart at the end of this article.

Given the much more impressive returns on invested capital—both in size *and* consistency—that are usually derived from the ownership of other entertainment distribution enterprises, it is difficult to blame the large media companies for diverting their attention elsewhere and allowing the business of making and marketing films to be overshadowed. Compare the measly 5% operating margins in movies and television to the 40% operating margins typical in ownership of cable franchise or network assets (and even some broadcast assets) and it is easy to see that there is no contest; movies are not even close. The decline of profit margins, dating from the early 1970s, for an aggregate of the filmed entertainment (including television series production) divisions of the largest distributors is shown in the chart on the next page.

Do movies affect stock prices? In the days when the business was a lot simpler, it sometimes seemed that analysts and investors could decide on whether to buy or sell movie-related stocks just by reading a film's weekly grosses in the trades. The first *Star Wars* in 1977, for instance, led to a more than quintupling of the shares of its distributor, Fox, within a few weeks of the film's opening. Perhaps the only way that such a speculation could be traded on today is in the rare events, once every five or ten years, when a film produces *Titanic*-sized ($1.8 billion worldwide) box office performance. The global home video, DVD, cable, television syndication and merchandising revenues that flow from a hit of this size are of such dimension as to make a visible earnings impact on the bottom lines even of a media-business behemoth.

Still, it seems that anything less than a $100 million box office performance gets lost in the shuffle, becoming the practical equivalent to a rounding error when calculating after-tax earnings per share. That's because the corporations that own the major studios have over the years diversified through acquisitions into many nonfilm segments and have paid

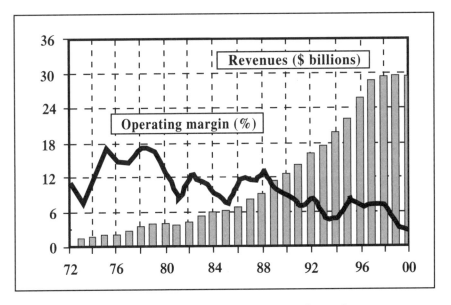

Major filmed entertainment companies, operating margins and revenues, 1972–2000.

for those acquisitions by issuing many new shares. In addition, they have been generous in grants of stock options to top managers and executives. In 2001, for example, the Walt Disney Company had approximately 2.1 *billion* shares outstanding, and Time Warner 4.4 billion; in the 1970s and early 1980s, share counts were typically no more than one-tenth as large.

Because most studios have become parts of much larger corporate entities, and because entertainment has become a truly global, capital-intensive, technology-driven business, the process of investment analysis is more complex and demanding. However, although films have lost relative strength and importance in this sphere of financial economics, they remain the bedrock, or core components, for many of the world's entertainment distribution services. The movie business produces an essential art form, reflecting and transmitting our deepest and most universal emotions, spirits, and cultural values. And, with all the never-ending action, onscreen and off, it's also still fun to analyze.

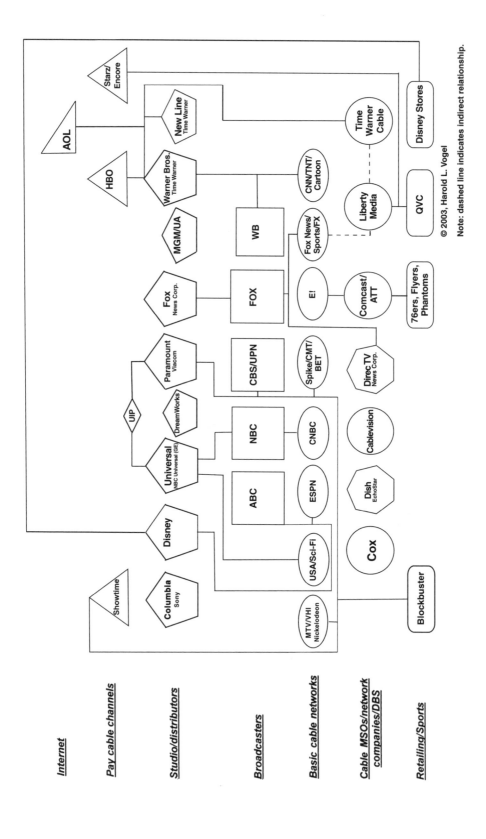

Internet

Pay cable channels

Studio/distributors

Broadcasters

Basic cable networks

Cable MSOs/network companies/DBS

Retailing/Sports

© 2003, Harold L. Vogel

Note: dashed line indicates indirect relationship.

IV
THE MANAGEMENT

A CHAIRMAN'S VIEW

by **TOM ROTHMAN,** chairman of Fox Filmed Entertainment, earlier president of Twentieth Century Fox Film Group, based in West Los Angeles. Among the many signature Fox films made during his production tenure are *Minority Report, Cast Away, X-Men, Moulin Rouge, Antwone Fisher, There's Something About Mary, Ice Age,* and the number-one grossing movie of all time, *Titanic.* Mr. Rothman was the founder and president of Fox Searchlight Pictures; has served as president of worldwide production for the Samuel Goldwyn Company and executive vice president of production for Columbia Pictures; and was a partner at the New York entertainment law firm of Frankfurt, Garbus, Klein & Selz. A magna cum laude, Phi Beta Kappa graduate of Brown University, Mr. Rothman is also a graduate of Columbia Law School, and a two-time James Kent Scholar. He is a member of the board of directors of the Sundance Institute, and recently received the Arthur B. Krim Award from Columbia University for outstanding achievement in entertainment.

> Art and commerce battle back and forth over shifting sands of taste, talent and economics, wrestling with each other for the magical balance that produces enduring popular cinema, the defining modern art form.

"Now, gods, stand up for bastards!"
                Edmund, Act I, Scene 2, *King Lear*

Recently, a new heinous character has entered the popular lexicon. Joining the Craven Politician and the Venal Lawyer in the pantheon of clichéd generalizations is the Philistine Studio Executive, the narrow-minded Hollywood "suit" who exists only to stifle the creative outpourings of the gifted and the bold. Once merely the province of those with inside interest (or readers of Fitzgerald or Schulberg), media coverage about the business of the entertainment business has exploded. The seemingly insatiable appetite for the culture of celebrity has moved this caricature squarely into the public mindset, and the entertainment press, never able to resist an easy oversimplification, perpetuates it with relish.

While there are doubtless some studio executives who fit the stereotype (as with attorneys and politicians), most do not. I, for one, do wear a suit on occasion (and although I admit my disheveledness is legendary, it's not true, as many of my colleagues claim, that it's the *same* suit). Beyond that, little of the public conception is accurate.

Indeed, in the complex, competitive and capital-intensive world of the modern movie business, some of the very brightest, bravest and most boldly creative minds at work are the top tier of studio executives. Name a great, enduring motion picture and chances are that joining a filmmaker or a star or a writer or a producer, or all of those, is a studio executive who sweated blood and, not infrequently, put his or her very livelihood on the line to bring that movie into existence. Peter Jackson knows that without Bob Shaye at New Line, there would be no *The Lord of the Rings*. Ron Howard knows that without Stacey Snider at Universal, there would be no *A Beautiful Mind*. Mel Gibson knows that without Jim Gianopulos's faith, *Braveheart* would not have gotten made. Robert Zemeckis, Tom Hanks and Bill Broyles know, and frequently say in public, that without the determination of my colleague Elizabeth Gabler, who developed *Cast Away* from a blank page and persevered with it for eight years, that picture, which I consider one of the finest I have ever worked on, would not exist. And certainly, in the most legendary example of all, without the courage of my boss, Peter Chernin, and his, Rupert Murdoch, the most difficult and most successful movie of all time, *Titanic,* would never have reached the screen.

When my mother asks me why, given that I work six and a half days a week, week in and week out, neither my name nor any of my colleagues' appear anywhere on our movies, I tell her that when she hears the famous fanfare in the beginning and sees the searchlights swing across the monument, it represents *all* 3,000-plus Twentieth Century Fox employees who helped make that movie happen. I am intensely proud of what I do and consider each day, when I drive onto our historic lot on Pico Boulevard in West Los Angeles, that it's a joy and privilege to be such a "suit."

I am currently the chairman of Fox Filmed Entertainment (FFE), the parent company of Twentieth Century Fox film studio. I share this position with my partner and friend Jim Gianopulos. Together we are responsible for all of the departments involved in the development, production, marketing and distribution of all the movies made or acquired by Fox each year, including those from our specialized division Fox Searchlight (an entity I founded when I first came to Fox some years ago). In addition, Fox's worldwide home video and television distribution businesses, music publishing business, interactive business, our CGI animation operation Blue Sky Studios (*Ice Age*) and our filmmaking studios in Los Angeles, Baja California and Sydney, Australia, also come under our purview.

If this sounds large in scope, note that FFE is itself a division of News Corporation, a global media company based in Adelaide, Australia, at the forefront of content creation and distribution in almost every medium, including books, newspapers, broadcast and satellite television, on every continent on earth. Clearly, doing our job today requires understanding the full complications of the worldwide media revolution, and that challenge is what makes it so constantly stimulating. First and foremost, however, to run a movie studio, you must love movies, truly love movies.

In that regard, we are much the same as the studio executives of old—in the case of Fox, legends like Darryl Zanuck, whose very office I sit in today (rather, a piece of that office, as it now makes ample room for several). Likewise, the daily dichotomy of our lives is the same as that of all studio executives since the beginning of the business, a dichotomy of art and commerce that I will explain presently. But in almost every aspect of the actual execution of our jobs, the similarity ends. I often smile when people speak in reverential tones of the great Irving Thalberg of MGM, said to be the single greatest practitioner of the movie executive art form, who had achieved so much by his early passing at 37. Well, he had everyone under contract! From grips and designers to writers, directors and, most tellingly, stars, in the halcyon days of MGM, they all worked for him. Greta Garbo, Clark Gable, Joan Crawford, Spencer Tracy, Mickey Rooney and Jean Harlow were all under contract to MGM and they worked on what he wanted, when he wanted. If they didn't wish to do a particular project he had in mind, they could stay home.

When the independent spirit of post–World War II America took hold in Hollywood and this "studio system" was snapped, all that changed irrevocably. The current day-to-day process to try to have Tom Hanks do *Cast Away,* a film he actually produced, or Tom Cruise *Minority Report,* as examples, bears almost no relation to the old studio system. It is a far more complex and more challenging process and, I would hazard to say, perhaps more American in character in that the individual, not the institution, makes the fundamental creative choice to participate. Still, the central dichotomy that Thalberg or Zanuck or Goldwyn struggled with every day is the identical one with which we still wrestle.

There are two dangerous fault lines that run through the heart of Los Angeles. One is the San Andreas. The other is the equally tectonic line between Art and Commerce that runs smack down the middle of the movie business. Each day, my colleagues and I stand with one foot on either side of that line, trying to balance. Every single decision we make has both creative and economic implications, for it is the perpetual and unique nature of the motion picture business that every single decision is *both* an economic one and a creative one. Every movie is made up of thousands of such decisions and every movie company rises or falls on the success of that balancing act.

Why is the tug of war between art and commerce so much more intense in the movies than in other creative disciplines? The answer comes in one word: cost. Movies are expensive to create, and now even more expensive to sell. On a comparative economic basis, they have always been so, though things have become far worse in the last decade. Ironically, they remain relatively cheap to experience. For that reason, they have always been counterrecessionary. But the creation and marketing of movies as an ongoing business, as opposed to one-off independent ventures, is enormously capital-intensive. Quite simply, though of course there are exceptions, it costs substantially more to make a mainstream Hollywood film than to create a TV pilot, record an album, or publish a novel.

The stakes are massive. The MPAA, the trade organization for the seven major studios (Fox, Universal, Paramount, Sony, Disney, Warner Bros. and MGM), recently reported that the average negative cost (the cost of developing, filming and finishing the movie itself) has risen to $59 million, while the average domestic marketing costs (making prints of that film to show in theatres, TV plus newspaper advertising and publicity) was $30 million. Add in international marketing costs (about half of all movie revenues come from overseas) plus home entertainment marketing costs, and the average decision to make a single movie puts over $100 million at risk! And that is the average. When a studio commits to large-scale movies with significant production values or big stars, the investment can be substantially more. Of course, the upside can be huge, and indeed, the box office has grown and DVDs have opened a vast new source of revenue, but the downside risk is equally large.

Thus, there is enormous pressure to correctly balance the creative risk with the financial risk. Still, this is not necessarily about playing things safe, as I believe you can fail just as readily by not taking enough risks as by taking too many. Instead, the pressure is to make every single aspect of a project, whether large, small, or in-between, as strong creatively as it can possibly be. When the nattering nabobs complain of "endless development," there is a huge temptation to point to some half-baked scripts that got made that should have spent a lot more time in development, and to remind folks of those cost figures above.

At Fox, our philosophy is to try to match the creative risk to the level of the financial risk, so that we can continue to push the boundaries and still deliver strong returns for our shareholders. My own personal approach to navigating that nasty fault line running down the middle of my office emphasizes the script first and foremost.

In handling the volume of material that comes through, many executives inherit the methodology of those with whom they first worked in the business. For example, I learned well from the late Dawn Steel that it's easier (not to mention more polite) to return all calls, in most cases within 24 hours. Reviewing and responding to all material can be tedious but is, in my view, essential. Some executives allow the passage of time to substitute for articulating a "pass." For me, not only for the relationship's sake but also out of respect, a phone call or short note remains worth the effort.

I am also an executive who reads. In Hollywood, you hear "around the town" of some senior executives who don't read. This doesn't mean, by the way, they are illiterate. It means that after years and years of filling up weekends and nights reading bad screenplay after bad screenplay (the vast majority of submissions we get are indeed quite bad, sad to say), those execs have given up carefully reading and thinking about individual scripts, their structural problems, their inner potential. I am sympathetic and maybe a bit jealous of such execs, because it is wearying week in and week out to read and read and read. But I could not do my job well otherwise. Perhaps it's because in my first career I was an English teacher, or because I spent several years working with Sam Goldwyn, Jr., (who learned to love writers from his father), that I have ultimate respect for great screenwriting. And great concern for how little such writing *craft* exists. I think it is occasionally possible, but very, very unlikely, to have a great movie without a great script.

At Fox, most of our movies begin, in one way or another, with an underlying property that one or more of our executives truly, madly, deeply (a movie I worked on, by the way) loves. Whether you are talking about the genius of the script for *Minority Report,* or the inspired lunacy of *There's Something About Mary,* or even the ridiculousness of *Dude, Where's My Car?,* we believe the old saw: "If it ain't on the page, it ain't on the stage."

Ironically for a visually driven medium, the filmmaking process usually begins with the written word. I will begin there to outline the various key stages along the path from idea to megaplex for a major studio film (the course for independent films is often quite different) and give a sense of the modern film executives' role in those steps. At Fox, we get more than 5,000 submissions of material each year. These run the gamut from complete screenplays offered for sale ("spec" screenplays) to magazine articles, true-life stories, books, treatments and so-called "pitches" (whereby a writer or filmmaker has an idea for a movie and tells it to an executive in the hope that the studio will commission a screenplay for it). In addition, we generate our own ideas for movies and find writers and filmmakers to work on them.

I am notorious for being skeptical of pitches. Our statistics show that they have by far the lowest conversion rate from development to film of any kind of project source. That is because talking is easy and great screenwriting, a vanishing craft, is hard. "It will be really, really funny." "It will be really scarry." "It will be a great part for Tom Cruise." Much of the sense of mockery of the process comes from moments like those. I'd like to "pitch" the Lakers to play guard: "I would play tough D, penetrate off the dribble and hit the 3." Yeah? Let's see it, baby!

Likewise, we try to teach our young executives that solid screenwriting is about structure, not dialogue. I am again notorious for the note on the side of too many script pages that reads: "bla, bla, bla." I learned this from a story Sam Goldwyn, Jr., told me of his father who picked up a typically verbose script one day and flipped quickly through the pages thusly: "Bla, bla, bla, he picked up the gun. Bla, bla, bla, he kissed the girl." I have all our young executives read Bill Broyles's script for *Cast Away*. (Through a dozen or more drafts, he was the *only* writer on the project.) It is a script with little or no dialogue through two-thirds of the film. Yet it demonstrates a mastery of structure and dramatized emotion. It is shocking to me how many in our industry don't understand such essential fundamentals. Numerous Academy members told me they loved the movie but didn't vote for Bill because there was "no dialogue." Great scripts have great drama, not necessarily through spoken words.

Out of those thousands of submissions and ideas, we will put maybe a total of 150 into development in all of our filmmaking divisions combined at any one time. Of those, we will make fifteen to twenty mainstream and another five or so specialized films (the balance of Searchlight's movies come from acquisitions) in total during any one year. Long odds indeed.

Those development decisions are made by a group of production or creative executives, assisted by a story department. (See the article by Romy Kaufman, p. 83.) For these executives, certain traits lend themselves to success in the business. Passion is key, as is a love of reading. But so are tact and the ability to think strategically and articulate a point of view. And let us not forget patience balanced with aggressiveness. Material is out there. Finding *good* material is *the* trick of the trade and no worthy executive just sits and waits for its submission. I have long believed that any studio can only be as good as those frontline decisionmakers. Accordingly, we spend a great deal of time at Fox discussing what makes good films, what the audience is looking for now, what trends are emerging, and who are the dynamic new talents we can bring to work with us.

Fortunately, our creative divisions at Fox are run by a Fab Four of exceedingly talented production executives whom Jim and I have worked with for many years: Hutch Parker, president of TCF; Elizabeth Gabler of Fox 2000; Peter Rice of Searchlight; and Sanford Panitch at our sister company, New Regency. They and their teams, with Jim's and my counsel, make the decisions of what ideas to pursue and which talent to pursue them with, decisions that ultimately drive all the revenues of our *$4 billion* global film business. Still, those are just the first decisions in long lines of choices.

The reason we prize effective development so much is that above all else, I adhere to the maxim taught to me by the late, extravagant, way-ahead-of-her-time executive Dawn Steel: "Talent follows material." A myth about studio execs is that they are buyers, not sellers like producers. Not if you want to excel at it. Not by a mile. An effective studio exec is always "selling up," trying to interest the best writer in working on a project, trying to attract the best director, best actor and on and on. The better your material, the stronger the chance you have to "sell" it to someone great to make it. Have excellent material, perseverance and good judgment of talent and you stand a chance of making an outstanding picture.

Master and Commander: The Far Side of the World is just one example of these principles from my own career. Over a decade ago, when I was at the Goldwyn Company, I happened to take a vacation at my father-in-law's in rural Connecticut. The rain was incessant and I ran out of things to read. One evening, he gave me a tattered copy of a novel by Patrick O'Brian, the first in the so-called Aubrey/Maturin series. All these many years later, a film of that series, starring Russell Crowe as Lucky Jack Aubrey and directed by master filmmaker Peter Weir, has completed principal photography at the Fox studios in Baja. For the decade in between, as I worked my way up and around the production ranks, I persevered and tried to "sell up." Sam Goldwyn, Jr., optioned the material and we first took it to Disney, where it was developed for several years. Then he brought it to Fox and we tried another approach to the adaptation. We knew the screenplay was not yet good enough to interest the level of filmmaker we wanted for a project of this scope. We could, at many times along the way, have settled for lesser directors, but held out.

Finally, Peter Weir, a filmmaker we hold in the pantheon of working directors, came to town looking for his next movie. Every studio met with him and pitched their wares. (How different is this from the old Thalberg days?) At our pitch, we discussed several projects, and then at the end, knowing he had read the books, I brought out a British Navy sword I'd had our props department make. "Peter, these are all good projects, but what you should really do is take command of the *Surprise*." Was I a buyer or a seller? Well, both, of course. Luckily for Fox, he bought, and with his acumen and experience he solved the adaptation riddle we had been unable to lick. Peter and John Collee wrote a script and then, because of the strength of that script and because Peter was directing, Russell Crowe, the only actor alive I could think of who could be Jack Aubrey today, agreed to star. Then Jim Gianopulos and I had to convince ourselves that all of these elements together were worth the financial risk it takes today to make a movie of that size and scope. As of this writing, we can't know if that gamble will pay off, if we have walked the fault line between art and commerce successfully; only the audience can tell us that. But we do know we have a great chance at it, because, ultimately, *talent follows material*.

This part of the process, commonly called "packaging," is probably the point at which the studio has the most influence and control. Depending on the level of the director and his or her contractual rights, a studio may have many legal controls at later points, but it has always been my experience that if it comes to needing to invoke those, the game is usually lost. At the packaging and budgeting stage, the studio can still choose whether to make the film or not. At the production stage, the studio and filmmakers are in it together and have to pull together to make it work. A solid piece of material, matched with filmmakers capable of executing it well, casting it well, with (in today's world of complex technical requirements) ample preparatory time, can all combine for a shot to make the magic happen. Even then, there are no guarantees. Moviemaking is after all an intangible, creative alchemic process—which is what makes it so cool.

Crucial to giving the film the best chance, however, I believe is a common purpose between the studio and the filmmakers. This is often expressed as "are we making the same movie?" In other words, are the ambitions and overall intentions of the filmmakers consistent with the movie the studio is hoping for? If not, hang on for a painful ride. If so, and if the right talent is in place, the anywhere from eight to twenty weeks it can take to shoot a film, and the myriad of things that can and will and always do go wrong, can be a great collective adventure.

Still, before we even contemplate rolling the camera, because of the financial stakes involved, profit and loss scenarios (p&l's, as we call them) are run with a series of critical assumptions that allow us to get a sense of what kind of performance at the box office would be necessary to have the movie make good business sense. These projections also lay out a framework for the negotiations that must take place before the green light. In-demand talent (and, by extension, their representation) holds a certain amount of power up until the breaking point—that point where the economics no longer make sense. Therein lies the studio's bargaining chip: the power to say no. And, difficult though it may be, sometimes the best decision is to decline to move forward.

Talent negotiations function largely on a quote system where, assuming roles sufficiently commercial and comparable (including length of the shoot and overall budget), actors will receive whatever they got for their last picture, plus perhaps a raise. In some cases, actors may agree to take a more creative deal where they forgo some of their up-front money in favor of the back end. With the back end, the talent takes a percentage of the film's proceeds (note that unlike in the past, it's often not profits but a portion of what's called *first-dollar*, or literally every dollar that flows in) to make them whole. It's a complex system of breakevens and gross points that might in the end allow the picture to be made. (See the article on business affairs by Stephen M. Kravit, p. 194.) Once the package is in place, the decisive moment arrives—do we make the movie?

To get here, certain things must happen: A script must be complete and ready to shoot (though the script process is a continual one that yields a rainbow-colored shooting script as changes continue to be made during photography), and a budget must be vetted (which answers all the requisite questions about the length of principal photography, the postproduction period and money for visual effects, among others). Deals must be closed (and in the case of Fox, which—unlike some—is a so-called "signed contracts" company, actually signed) on all important fronts (director, rights, key cast). Then, experience, intuition and analysis all come together to determine whether to pull the trigger to proceed to production.

Once shooting, if a film is proceeding on budget and on schedule, the best value studio execs can be to the people making the film is similar to that of a detached editor to a novelist. Moviemakers must have the freedom and room to reach high, but what if their ambitions are not coming through in the material? The interests of the studio may sometimes conflict with the filmmakers' points of view, but without debate there can be no resolution, only procrastination. Communication between the studio and the filmmakers thus remains essential throughout the entire process. This I find to be the best use of *dailies,* the rushes of each day's work that the director, the crew, the studio and (depending or their individual preferences) the actors view. Although my current job is quite time-consuming, I still find time each week to catch up on dailies. I do this now for a different reason than I used to as a line production executive whose job it was to be sure the work is getting done properly. I do it now to get a "feel" for the film well in advance of its completion. That is because the time frames of making and selling films in the modern marketplace have altered dramatically.

In the old days (just a few years ago), twelve weeks was a fairly standard prep period for a studio film and twenty-four weeks a typical post period. Film marketing started when most of the movie was ready, and release dates were often not chosen until the studio had seen a cut. Ancient history. In the world of digital effects, spectacle cinema and superwide, event-level, saturation releases, the amount of time involved in making big effect pictures has expanded dramatically. The digital revolution has made possible the creation of anything a director can imagine, but it hasn't made the work faster or cheaper. And the competitive nature of marketing and release issues call for choosing dates for movies and beginning their marketing campaigns far in advance—sometimes *years.* Neither of these trends are healthy for the creative juice of moviemaking, nor for the economics of the business, but they are realities and must be dealt with.

A big special effects film like *X2: X-Men United* calls for the studio to actively prepare for shooting for six to eight months or more after the completion of the screenplay. Today, complicated digital effects are planned months in advance and actually laid out in *animatics*—computerized storyboards—to facilitate shooting, significantly lengthening many preproduction periods. All the while, the need to be ahead of the marketing of major films has increased.

In the case of *X2,* we chose its May 3, 2003, release date more than a year and a half earlier. We worked on special teaser trailers to be in theatres in summer 2002 and Christmas 2002, well before the normal eight weeks in advance of release when a traditional trailer is shown in theatres. This kind of marketing effort is necessary now that big event films open on as many as 3,000 to 8,000 screens simultaneously out of some 30,000 screens in America. The studios then spend massive amounts of national television advertising money to motivate the audience to a first weekend urgency.

While we at Fox, like most of the other studios, have become very good at exploiting this trend for commercial success, it is worth considering whether all the Chicken Littles decrying the dearth of imagination and the suffocating effects of the "blockbuster mentality" in modern Hollywood are right. My own answer may surprise both sides of the partisan debate and seems a fitting place to conclude this rumination.

I have perhaps a unique perspective on the constant debate over the state of the American motion picture at the start of its second century, as I believe I may be the only person who has ever been head of film production for a true independent company, a studio specialized division, and a major studio. From this vantage point, I invoke *A Tale of Two Cities* (not LA and NY): "It is the best of times and the worst of times." The box office is growing, filmed entertainment is the second largest export industry in the nation and extraordinary films are being made every year: great blockbuster films, like *The Lord of the Rings, Cast Away* or *Minority Report;* inventive, daring films, like *Moulin Rouge, Boys Don't Cry* or *American Beauty.* Sensational new talents emerge and old lions roar. The best of times. Yet, terrible, empty, noisy films are being made and promoted to a deadened audience. Bad movies do lots of business and the audience attention span, wired up by MTV and dumbed down by repetition and formulaic story telling, gets too short for character development, originality or texture. The worst of times. Both are true. But here is the twist. It has *always* been thus. Scholars will say that 1939, the year of *Gone With the Wind, The Wiz-*

ard of Oz, Mr. Smith Goes to Washington and *Wuthering Heights,* is the greatest year ever for film. Well, in 1939, there was also *Chicken Wagon Family* and *Mesquite Buckaroo.* Is 1974 the year Hollywood was saved? With movies like *The Godfather II, The Conversation, Chinatown* and *Lenny?* Perhaps, yes. But, mercifully, time forgets *The House on Skull Mountain* and *The Bat People.*

It has always been thus, and I believe will always be, because of that nasty fault line. Art and commerce battle back and forth over shifting sands of taste, talent and economics, wrestling with each other for the magical balance that produces enduring popular cinema, the defining modern art form. Smack in the middle of this struggle stands the much-maligned studio executive, trying to move the whole process forward and not let it collapse in on itself. Though constantly embattled on all fronts, true love of movies, the courage of convictions, and a very thick skin can make that duty a noble profession and a fascinating life. I recommend it.

MANAGEMENT: NEW RULES OF THE GAME

by **RICHARD LEDERER,** a marketing consultant in the film industry who has served as vice president of worldwide marketing at Orion Pictures and as a consultant to Francis Coppola's Zoetrope Studios in the areas of film marketing, advertising and publicity. Mr. Lederer was vice president of worldwide advertising and publicity for Warner Bros. from 1960 to 1975, during which period he served for a year as a production executive at the Warner Bros. studio. He produced *The Hollywood Knights* for Columbia Pictures, coproduced with John Boorman *Exorcist II: The Heretic* for Warners and has lectured widely in the field of motion pictures.

> Evaluation of what the audience will accept is difficult at best and impossible at worst. . . . The only business that comes rather close to it . . . is fashion.

The industry is changing, but only to the extent that it always has throughout its history. It has never been static; it has always reacted in one way or another to new conditions. It has never stood still as a communication form or—to a lesser degree—as an art form.

Yet it is too easy to assume that some violent upheaval has taken place, that a new art form, a new audience and a whole new set of business rules are at hand. We must in fact observe that pictures made today—some of which are the most successful films in the history of the industry—are traditional in terms of their dramatic content. What has changed is the filmmakers' technique. New technology has given filmmakers the mobility to shoot a picture more realistically and with more visual excitement than ever before. The audience raised on television, and on music videos in particular, is comfortable with shortcuts in visual storytelling, allowing more information to be imparted in less time. Thus movies move a little faster today and are more "cinematic" than they used to be, but the stories are essentially the same.

It should not detract from the expression of social concern or the aesthetic possibilities of film that major companies who have an economic interest in the business must continue to regard movies primarily as an escapist entertainment form. The management of these publicly owned companies must show a responsibility to shareholders and consequently to profit-and-loss statements. These are the realities a major studio must observe, and it therefore follows that the studios will be making pretty much the same kind of films they have always made. But this hardly implies that a slow evolution is not constantly in progress. Taste is more advanced and technique is more sophisticated than in the past. The nation has matured with regard to what it will accept and what it will tolerate in the arts and literature. Audiences have accepted, for example, a far more candid and explicit screen exploration of sexual relations. Essentially, however, the movies are simply dealing with human problems in a more realistic fashion, and the degree of realism and detail should not suggest a trend away from the basic escapist-entertainment appeals.

We must not confuse, however, *what* is made with *how* it is made. Having said, in effect, that there is a great deal of stability in the fundamental nature of movies, I must now turn to the factors that set motion pictures apart from other businesses.

One of the greatest of these is the uncertainty of the marketplace. Many other industries have accurate indications of their market when they set out each year. The home appliance industry can judge its potential sales and make sound business decisions regarding refrigerator styles, models and the number of units to manufacture. Unfortunately, the movie business has not enjoyed that degree of predictability since before the Consent Decree, when a major company owned its own theatres and consequently knew where its marketplace was. It knew how many films it could make a year and that those films would be exhibited in regular fashion. Today, with studios owned by global companies, uncertainty still prevails in the theatrical marketplace.

A second major factor that distinguishes motion pictures from all other businesses arises from the enormous impact of individual creative talent upon production cost and upon market success. Evaluation of what the audience will accept is difficult at best and impossible at worst. This is a major aspect of the "old game," and new rules are not really changing it. The only business that comes rather close to it, I should think, is fashion, where trying to judge what styles will sell next year—how to tailor an inventory, how much cloth to buy, how much to cut and so forth—is a bit of a guessing game. But movies are the super, number-one guessing game. Making movies, as one old-timer put it, is "not an industry, but a disease."

Let's consider the role of talent in this game. Ultimately movies are products, and the product comes in a package that can be more important than what it contains. The package can be more or less attractive depending on the names that are associated with it. A producer who has a fairly good action script, for example, can make the film for $45 million with a good actor and $75 million with a top actor. That extra cost is something he must think about in terms of actual return. Is it worth the extra millions? Will the film do that much more in business as a result of overinvestment in the top actor? There are, after all, only a few actors who seem capable of delivering a larger audience than the ordinary actor, and a good deal of that happens overseas. Escapist entertainment is still the major attraction around the world, and although the "star system" is in the past in America, many a picture is made only because a certain actor will commit to do it.

To some degree, the contemporary audience dictates the type of film Hollywood will produce. It is sad but true that movies have always been an imitative—not an innovative—industry. Miscalculation abounds. In the 1970s, everyone read the new demographics and learned that we have a young audience. Their immediate reaction was to plan and make films that were geared to the tastes and interests of young people. This in turn resulted in all kinds of unsuccessful films. It has always been that way, and I don't suspect it will ever change.

An extraordinary contribution made by the younger generation of moviegoers in this period is the capacity for repeat business, which derives from TV viewing. Children enjoy this, and it's become part of their experience, like going back to visit a friend. Repeat business is the key to huge successes such as *Titanic* and the *Star Wars* series. Proceeds from these pictures have redefined the higher limits of profit potential, and new pictures are constantly challenging these heights.

By the 1990s we had the phenomenon of the graying of the American movie audience, tracing back to such successes as *Cocoon* and *Parenthood*. The baby boomers in their forties and fifties had grown up receiving most of their information from a screen. Weaned on television, they found a symbiotic relationship between TV and the movies, and going to the movies continues as part of their lifestyle.

Children today continue this screen-based tradition, as computers and televisions merge. A great deal of want-to-see for a movie is generated on the Internet; computer-literate kids are way ahead of their elders who are not so computer-literate. *The Blair Witch Project* demonstrated the power of the Internet to "get the word out." Simply stated, the Internet represents a whole new world of channeling information directly to young opinion-makers via Web sites.

It is a fact that people in the industry, in their frantic efforts to analyze audience desires, deny the history of movie entertainment as well as their own instincts by jumping on the topical bandwagon. Management's alternative, if there is any single approach to planning successful pictures, is to try to make interesting films without regard, necessarily, to whether they really are geared to a certain type of audience. A major studio committed to doing ten to fifteen films a year should be trying to make marvelous stories—films that are interesting, different, special.

The evidence is there. Successful films have always been well-directed, well-written, well-made films about something that a majority of the people can relate to or empathize with. But this does not mean management should avoid taking risks on what is new, fresh and has a specialized appeal.

Miscalculations are possible, of course, under the best of circumstances, but I think they are even more likely to occur because of industry developments such as the controls upon management that conglomerate takeovers introduce. In such cases there are predictable changes, and my guess is that they are usually for the worst. We must remember that until the 1950s the industry was still in the hands of the so-called pioneers. Good, bad, or indifferent, right or wrong, they were a unique breed in American business life. Their backgrounds were dissimilar. None of them came out of film schools. Many were immigrants, barely teenagers when they arrived in this country. With no academic training, they went into various businesses and happened to be around when movies were born. All had an innate sense of showmanship, an instinct about this country and a prescience about the entertainment that movies would become.

These were very special people. When their kind passed on, new management or ownership replaced them, and some significant things happened. In nearly every case where the new management was a conglomerate, the company became overly business-oriented. This new breed, in the best American tradition, was made up of well-trained business-management graduates who were used to systematized and highly structured business organizations. They knew everything on the business side of how to run a company. After one look at a movie company, they found it to be amorphous and seemingly running amok. They were aghast. Their strict sense of business training was offended, and their impulse was to systematize and structure, to make the company, in their terms, "make sense." This often led to near disaster.

The conglomerate takeovers seem to be truly lasting. Examples: Coca-Cola purchased Columbia Pictures in 1982 with much fanfare, only to reduce its position to half a few years later and sell out entirely when Sony bought Columbia in 1989. Under Charles Bluhdorn, the 1966 Gulf + Western purchase of Paramount Pictures was successful, with the movie company taking on such corporate importance that G + W changed its name to Paramount Communications in 1989; in 1994, Viacom bought Paramount. Warner Bros. was acquired by Seven Arts in 1967, and there followed mostly unsuccessful films. It was only when Kinney Services, under

Steve Ross, bought the company from Seven Arts in 1969 and restaffed it that Warners was revitalized. Veteran Kinney executives preferred business with no inventory, and Kinney had been thriving with an office-building-cleaning business, funeral homes and parking lots. But Steve Ross saw the potential in the expanding world of entertainment, mixed movies with music and television to great success, changed the parent company name to Warner Communications, and merged it with Time Inc. in 1989 to form Time Warner Inc. News Corporation bought Twentieth Century Fox in 1985. MCA Universal, a bulwark of stability since its 1962 merger, was acquired by Matsushita in 1991, then by Seagram in 1995, then combined with Vivendi in 2000, then announced a merger with GE's NBC in 2003.

The old-timers were born gamblers; the new people are forced into being gamblers, and they're uncomfortable with it. They're businessmen, and no good businessman likes to gamble; rather, they like to insure their bets whenever possible. But "insurance" such as high-priced stars or high-priced directors can be disastrous, as in *The Postman* and *Battlefield Earth*.

There is an interesting cycle in management that has repeated itself recently in the movie business. It occurs when a new generation of production executives takes over a studio. They are usually somewhat unfamiliar with certain phases of the business, particularly marketing and distribution. They approach their head of sales or marketing and ask how many movies should be made this year. The answer is, "If you made six successful pictures, that's all the playing time I can handle; if you make twenty failures, I haven't got enough." The insecurity that runs through this new generation of studio executive stems not from deciding what pictures to make, but how many. Because of the powerful impulse to make movies, they reach for material a more conservative management might turn down, due either to story content or to the high numbers involved. But they are hungry to make movies, so they make risky, innovative decisions. In the three years it takes from making the decisions to tracking the results at the box office, this generation of studio executives usually has some phenomenal hits on its hands; the gambles have paid off. But they are also watching some of their profits dissipate because hefty participations were built into certain artists' deals on these pictures. This executive team is now rich and successful; they're no longer the gamblers they were three years earlier. They may even begin to think they know what they're doing, which is a terrible mistake in this business. They start making tougher deals, minimizing outside participations in order to protect their profits. They're not hungry anymore.

At this point another group of new production executives takes over another studio, and they are as hungry as the first group was three years ago. An agent approaches the first group with a strong package, asking high fees and participations for his or her clients in the package. The first company refuses to make such a rich deal, so the agent goes across the street to the second studio, makes a deal with the eager executives and the cycle goes on. Interestingly, studios that have been forced to gamble on material out of desperation or need have generally been successful. Intuition and luck play enormous roles in the business.

One more challenge in the management game is to harness the great potential of overseas revenue. As an example, the box office of *Titanic* was as strong outside the United States as inside, with a global theatrical gross of approximately $1.2 billion, $600 million overseas and $600 million domestic. Further, the excitement generated by an American movie-launching spreads quickly around the world via the Internet and the global reach of CNN and MTV. To capitalize on this publicity, studio management has moved up the worldwide release patterns of movies. Today the timing of international release dates is generally identical to that of the American launching.

Unfortunately, movies are not a business in the strict sense of the word. Studios demand unique talent and unique understanding if they are to be run effectively. The successful major motion picture studio of the future will be one that manages the following: (1) bringing inflated above-the-line salaries and production overheads down to reasonable scales; (2) the development within its creative manpower of a "sure nose" for potential motion picture material that will be popular worldwide; (3) the ability and know-how to attract the proper talent in the industry to these various projects; (4) the diplomatic skill needed to cope understandingly with the creative temperaments and excesses of these gifted producers, directors, writers and stars while at the same time imposing upon them realistic and responsible fiscal controls; (5) contending with a new layer of executives who may be unfamiliar with the movie business, brought in after a merger or acquisition, so that corporate cultures do not collide. Utopia? Maybe. Admittedly a nearly impossible set of conditions—but there are clear signs that management is slowly meeting this challenge.

THE FILM COMPANY AS
FINANCIER-DISTRIBUTOR

by **DAVID V. PICKER,** president of worldwide production at Hallmark Entertainment. Based in New York, he has served as president of three financier-distributors: United Artists (1969–72), Paramount's motion picture division (1976–78) and Columbia Pictures (1986–87). A graduate of Dartmouth College, Mr. Picker joined UA in 1956, rose through the ranks and was responsible for such pictures as *Tom Jones,* the James Bond series, the Woody Allen movies and *Midnight Cowboy,* among others. At Paramount his pictures included *Saturday Night Fever, Grease, Days of Heaven* and *Ordinary People.* After a stint as president of feature films at Lorimar *(Being There, An Officer and a Gentleman),* Mr. Picker produced movies independently before joining David Puttnam at Columbia as president and chief operating officer *(Hope and Glory, School Daze, Punchline).* As a producer his credits include *Lenny, Smile, Juggernaut, Bloodline, Oliver's Story, The Jerk, Dead Men Don't Wear Plaid, The Man With Two Brains, Beat Street, The Goodbye People, Stella, Leap of Faith, The Saint of Fort Washington* and *The Crucible.*

> A company cannot remain stable making $40 to $100 million movies every year; the risk is simply too great.

Since 1950, the major studios established in earlier years have had to seek new roles and functions for themselves within a changing industry. United Artists created what may in many ways be regarded as a blueprint for film companies that sought to combine an already-existing enterprise with the skills of successful financing and distributing of motion pictures.

In order to understand how this new identity was established, we need to begin when Arthur Krim and Robert Benjamin bought control of United Artists from Charles Chaplin and Mary Pickford in 1951. The company had been losing money. But by late 1952 United Artists was in the black, and Krim and Benjamin were in a position to consider financing their own productions. Their plan was to finance pictures by dealing directly with the creative forces who make them. Their initial concept involved the extension of creative autonomy and a percentage of profits to the filmmaker. The company's interest was to secure all distribution rights and a share of the profit in the film. This modus operandi was clearly contradictory to the policy of the major studios that owned all their films and—by keeping editing powers to themselves—did not relinquish creative control to individual filmmakers.

This idea could not be given any real test, of course, until United Artists built a strong financial base. But as a result of a succession of good pictures, the concept that Krim and Benjamin had initiated became a way of life for the company. Such early successes as *High Noon*, *The African Queen* and *Moulin Rouge* resulted from deals with filmmakers. By the mid-

1950s they had also initiated production programs with various film companies, one of which was Hecht-Hill-Lancaster, and this resulted in such remarkable films as the Academy Award–winning *Marty, Trapeze* and *Sweet Smell of Success.* Later they established a relationship with the Mirisch Company that lasted some sixty pictures.

Throughout its history the management of United Artists gave creative filmmakers the right—within various approved frameworks of budget, script, cast and director—to make films as they wanted to make them. In exchange for that right, which was revolutionary for Hollywood, UA was able to attract many of the top filmmakers in the world.

Other companies eventually caught on because there was nothing essentially unique in what UA offered, with the exception of its own management techniques. The Krim-Benjamin philosophy of extending creative freedom to the filmmaker in 1952 led to the general industry approach of today.

It may be informative to consider in some detail the way this philosophy has been translated into operational realities for other financier-distributors. We can usefully examine what happens to a dollar that comes in at the theatre box office window, following its course backward from there in order to see how a company makes its money.

Let us assume that half of the average box office dollar is retained by the exhibitor and half is turned over to the distributor of the film. That distributor does not share in the receipts from concessions in the theatre, which are exclusively the exhibitor's (see the article by Shari E. Redstone, p. 386). The 50¢ that comes to the distributor represents 100% of *film rental.* When distribution executives say a picture has "done $40 million," that does not mean its box office gross is $40 million, but that the film rental earned by the distributor is $40 million. The figure in fact represents, depending on various deals in various theatres throughout the world, the sum that comes to the financier-distributor.

A percentage of this money is charged for distributing the film: 30% of the gross for the United States and Canada, more overseas. Out of each dollar of film rental paid to the distributor domestically, 30¢ is generally retained as its distribution fee. In addition, distribution costs are deducted, including prints, advertising and interest as well as other expenses. From the "film rental dollar," then, 30¢ is taken as distribution cost and another amount is taken to cover the cost of prints, advertising, interest, taxes and distribution expenses. (Marketing costs can be enormous, in some cases half or more of a film's negative cost.) What is left is sometimes known as the *net producer's share,* which is used to help pay off the loan secured to fund the negative cost of the picture. If a picture costs $80 million to finance and distribute, then the returns that constitute the net producer's share in this hypothetical must add up to $80 million before the picture approaches breakeven. But that rarely happens from theatrical alone. Studios need the huge revenue streams from home video/DVD, TV and other formats, coupled with strong receipts from overseas, to theoretically reach breakeven.

At this point all profits are split between the financier-distributor and producer on a basis that can vary from 50/50 to 80/20, usually favoring the financier, and depending upon bargaining power. Because of the great delay in reaching profits (if any), many more "gross deals" are being made, wherein gross participants get money "off the top," without any concern for what the actual profits are. Various formulas may find a director or star receiving a percentage of the gross from first dollar, a percentage of the gross after an agreed-upon, fixed breakeven formula is reached (but before profits are divided), or a percentage of the gross after a multiple of the negative cost is reached. In these cases "gross" is the distributor's film rental, not the theatre gross. For example, a certain actor might be given $2 million cash against 10% of the gross. If the film rental on the picture totals $40 million, that actor will have received $2 million in advance against the total $4 million he will earn on the film without regard to distribution costs, prints, advertising or any other costs. A *percentage of the gross* deal, it might well be said, is a favorable deal if a picture does well.

To summarize: If the net producer's share from all sources equals the amount of overall production risk, the company is in good shape. If it falls short, and losses can be recouped from the various distribution fees without threatening a basic financial position strong enough to carry on the organization, then they are also in good shape. Where they can get into trouble is with a motion picture that costs a great deal of money and grosses nothing at all. This is why it is so dangerous for any company to sink an enormous amount of money into one picture. If the picture fails, they not only have lost the distribution fees that keep their establishment going but also have no distribution-fee profit to pay off the loan against the picture. And of course they lose the net producer's share as well.

In 1967 Transamerica Corporation acquired UA in an effort to diversify into the leisure-time field, just as Gulf + Western had acquired Paramount the year before. The move gave United Artists an umbrella of enormous importance, since it was now part of a corporation with over a billion dollars in assets. With the advent of nonmovie corporate management, the gap between executive and filmmaker and between corporation and filmmaker became increasingly wide. In the case of the Krim and Benjamin team, certain policies set down by the parent company were so unsettling that, in 1978, they left United Artists and established Orion Pictures. Transamerica got out of the movie business in 1981; the Coca-Cola Company, which had purchased Columbia Pictures in 1982, left the business by selling to the Sony Corporation in 1989; Matsushita ended its five-year ownership of Universal in 1995 by selling it to Seagram, which sold the studio to Vivendi in 2000. Then Vivendi announced a merger of its studio assets with General Electric's NBC in 2003 to form NBC Universal. Orion declared bankruptcy in 1992; both the Orion and United Artists film libraries are now owned by MGM.

In analyzing how movie companies are run today, conventional wisdom calls for long-term management to establish an operating philosophy and to hold to it. Until such discipline and philosophy on a long-term basis are established, the market is chaotic, because there are always players who are prepared to outspend the others to prove they are in the business or to own what they think is the sure hit.

The result is that costs escalate beyond control. A company cannot remain stable making $40 to $100 million movies every year; the risk is simply too great. And regardless of negative cost, marketing expenses are astronomical. (See the article by Robert G. Friedman, p. 282.) This inhibits pictures of a special or unusual nature, because such risky pictures cost millions to open and play to a global audience. But if a company defines its philosophy, is smart, lucky, disciplined and is prepared to say no to those tempting, high-cost packages, the risk of making movies can be reduced.

In reviewing how the business has changed over the years, agents are at the forefront. They have become stars, and are the key power players, as opposed to the clients they represent. The deal has become more important than the product, the dealmaker more important than the filmmaker. And the movies have become somewhat formularized as a result. An example was the spate of produced sequels (now in decline), since sequels represent a form of insurance rather than creative ingenuity. Management's justification was that the audience was saying, "I like what I know." But making high-priced sequels meant that those dollars were not available for something the audience didn't know, and the risk to pursue that was too great.

The training ground for the business has changed as well. Where do new filmmakers come from? Mostly from film schools, rather than television or the studios, as in the past. Studios look at students' work while they're still wet behind the ears, and pay enormous sums of money. A young writer coming out of film school can be paid $800,000 for a screenplay and is expected to deliver as if he's been making movies all his life. There are very few talents who can survive that kind of pressure.

The way the majors do business hasn't changed in forty years. Any producer who makes a development deal does so with eyes wide open, has more or less muscle depending on the elements brought to the deal and knows that the financier-distributor will own the lion's share of the project. This hasn't changed at all. Anyone who wants a more favorable position must bring substantial financing to the table and make an output deal with a given studio.

Although this is still a relationship business, what has changed is the nature of those relationships. Today they are based on deals, money and power, as opposed to a filmmaker deciding to make a long-term association with a studio to find artistic and commercial expression in the best atmosphere. The Mirisch brothers made sixty-six movies at United Artists, Stanley Kramer made ten. Today it is difficult to find someone who will make two pictures in a row for the same company. Do you want a relationship today? Pay more and you have it.

It's a seller's market, and because of this there are no longer any deal terms that are sacrosanct. If a seller has a project that is in demand, companies such as Columbia, Paramount and Fox can step up to competitive deals. Issues such as overhead, viewing of dailies, final cut, and the net-profits definition can favor the seller if his project is desirable. Bargaining power decreases if the project is something the financier-distributor would be willing to develop on a less-competitive basis. In this case the seller will face tougher terms and definitions.

A producer faces the same basic dilemma that confronts any financier or distributor. What an audience is going to want to see, how they will respond to a given motion picture, and all the variables that take place while a picture is in production—these factors are beyond analysis. One difficulty in this regard is the lag between the time the decision is made to finance a script or go into production and the time the picture is released. In addition, there has been a polarization in taste. In practice this means that the successful picture is more successful than ever, but the unsuccessful picture is more unsuccessful. There used to be a base audience; you knew you could count on certain numbers for almost every picture. That audience simply does not exist anymore. How can we know that the $80 million that is going to be spent is being invested in a product the mass audience will want to see a year hence?

In closing, I might say that we are in a time that is more precarious, but at the same time more exciting, than ever before. Audiences are extremely unpredictable, and their decisions often have nothing to do with a film's merit. When millions are being risked in an effort to choose those few pictures that audiences will decide to see, it can become a pretty scary business. The trouble with our business is that nobody trusts anybody in it. The distributor doesn't trust the exhibitor. The exhibitor doesn't trust the distributor. The producer doesn't trust the creator. The creator is sure the distributor is putting in invalid charges against his picture. The financier is positive that the creator has spent forty-three unnecessary days in shooting the picture. Despite all this, somehow or other we wind up with films that people sometimes go to see.

As to the future of the pictures I've green-lighted over the years, the legacy will always be there on the screen. But it is poignant that the library of United Artists pictures from the late fifties to the early seventies, for instance, is no longer related to anyone who had any involvement in making those movies; it's in the hands of money people who paid for the rights to that library.

The management atmosphere at UA in that period was warm and familial, which sparked a unique allegiance between filmmakers and executives. Today's movie management style is more in line with that of corporate America, which does not engender that kind of warm feeling. Players in the business must find a way to make that work for themselves. This business was run for many years by people who were tough and idiosyncratic, but who grew up in a business that they loved and understood. Today it's really not a motion picture business; it's a product business that happens to be film, which then has multiple financial uses. The focus is not on the filmmaker and the product (except in publicity terms), it's on the results, the money that can be made with it, what deals are required to get it, and how to achieve the best possible deal. That doesn't necessarily bode well for the content of the material on the screen.

THE INDEPENDENT SPIRIT

by **BARBARA BOYLE,** chair of the Department of Film, Television and Digital Media at the UCLA School of Theater, Film and Television in West Los Angeles. Earlier, she was president of Valhalla Motion Pictures, a leading producer of films and television worldwide. As a partner in Boyle-Taylor Productions, she produced features including *Instinct, Phenomenon* and *Bottle Rocket.* Ms. Boyle cofounded and was president of Sovereign Pictures, which cofinanced and distributed 25 films in the global market, including *My Left Foot, Cinema Paradiso,* and *The Commitments.* She also served as executive vice president of production for RKO Pictures *(Plenty, Hamburger Hill);* senior vice president of worldwide production at Orion Pictures *(The Terminator, Desperately Seeking Susan, Platoon);* and chief operating officer and executive vice president for Roger Corman's New World Pictures. A graduate of UCLA School of Law, which honored her with the Alumni of the Year award in 1999, Ms. Boyle began her career as a corporate counsel for independent production and distribution company American International Pictures (AIP), then entered private practice in the entertainment law firm Cohen & Boyle. A charter member of Women In Film, she served as president and was honored in 2000 with its prestigious Crystal Award. Ms. Boyle is a founding member of the UCLA School of Law Entertainment Advisory Council and of the Hollywood Women's Political Committee; she is on the board of Independent Feature Project / Los Angeles and was its president.

"Essentially, the independent spirit comes down to integrity of control and of vision."

The independent spirit is the impulse of talent to create movies outside the studio system, resulting in more risky productions and often more compelling stories than those found in the traditional studio pipeline.

Through the history of movies, there has always been a strong independent spirit, from the founding partners of United Artists in 1919 (Charlie Chaplin, Douglas Fairbanks, D. W. Griffith and Mary Pickford); to producer Samuel Goldwyn; to Orson Welles; to directors (such as Alfred Hitchcock) whose bargaining power by the 1950s allowed them to partner with studios rather than work for them; to Stanley Kramer, a producer turned director with a social conscience; to the partners in the revived United Artists of 1952, Arthur Krim and Robert Benjamin, who created alliances with independent producers including the Mirisch Company, Hecht-Hill-Lancaster and Kramer; to Russ Meyer, who made and distributed his own movies; to John Cassavetes, who also made and distributed his own movies; to Sam Arkoff and James Nicholson's American International Pictures; to Roger Corman's New World; to distributor Samuel Goldwyn, Jr.; to Henry Jaglom today (see his article, p. 49). There are countless others who possess the independent spirit, too many to name here.

The contemporary independent movement can be traced to the 1950s, after studios had signed Justice Department Consent Decrees divesting themselves of their theatres. The 1952 Krim-Benjamin United Artists management attracted independent-spirited filmmakers by developing a hands-off system in the production of their films after approving the director, producer, principal cast, screenplay, budget and rating. (See article by David V. Picker, p. 167.) Their business plan was to function as a financier-distributor, stepping in only if a producer departed from the agreed-upon approvals, such as exceeding a budget or replacing a principal cast member. Otherwise, UA management would await delivery of the completed film, and then work on marketing and distribution.

This article focuses on independent filmmakers, rather than distributors. (See article on independent distribution by Bob Berney, p. 375.) But since distribution is the linchpin that connects independent filmmakers to the audience, any discussion of the independent spirit must credit the two main rivals in American independent distribution from the 1970s to the 1990s, New Line and Miramax. In a period when studios were careful not to brand themselves, audiences began to look to New Line for terrific genre movies (the *Friday the 13th* series, the *Nightmare on Elm Street* series, *Teenage Mutant Ninja Turtles*) and to Miramax for provocative foreign-language films or English-language films made outside the U.S. (*Cinema Paradiso, My Left Foot, The Crying Game*). The reader need only refer to their Web sites for impressive lists of independent films made in the U.S. and overseas. Today, these companies are technically no longer independent; New Line is part of Time Warner and Miramax is part of Disney.

The growth of home-video revenue in the early 1980s had a great and positive impact on independent financing and distribution because a significant percentage of a movie's budget could be secured by an advance from licensing home-video deals, in effect subsidizing independent filmmaking. At that time, an independent producer seeking financing could separate U.S. home video and theatrical distribution rights, since home-video distributors were usually stand-alone, new, start-up companies. It took years for studios to decide to cut out the middleman and build their own home-video divisions, at which point separate advances for home video rights declined as U.S. distributors required all rights in all formats.

The absorption of New Line and Miramax by larger companies, as well as the demise of studio-style independent Orion Pictures (even after distributing back-to-back Oscar winners for best picture *Dances With Wolves* and *Silence of the Lambs*) proved that independent distributors could not easily survive as stand-alone financier-distributors, since both production and marketing costs continued to rise. Today, most studios run independent-style distribution labels, or classics divisions, further eroding truly independent distribution. They are like a department store where, to use Sony as an example, on the first floor is Sony Classics, on the second floor is Screen Gems, and in the penthouse is Columbia, with proportionally increasing budgets. Of the few truly independent distributors remaining, Lions Gate bought Artisan in 2003.

Essentially, the independent spirit comes down to integrity of control and of vision. In 1980, a group of Los Angeles writers, directors, actors and producers joined together to share ideas about the independent filmmaking process. They formed the nonprofit Independent Feature Project, which carries forward the ideals of independent filmmaking.

Today, under the visionary leadership of Dawn Hudson, the IFP has chapters in Los Angeles, New York, Chicago, Miami, Minneapolis–St. Paul and Seattle, representing a membership 9,000 strong. I am proud to be a board member and past president.

The IFP's stated mission is "to champion the cause of independent film and support a community of artists who embody diversity, innovation, and uniqueness of vision." IFP programs and services can be divided roughly into three categories: education, support and building audiences.

To enhance education, IFP's Los Angeles and New York chapters publish *Filmmaker* magazine. IFP/LA organizes a series of screenings and seminars geared not only to introduce members and other filmmakers to compelling new work, but also to foster learning more about the craft of moviemaking.

Examples of yearly educational programs are the Film Financing Conference, the Digital Series, and the Independent Producer Series. Filmmaker laboratories are also supported by IFP/LA, with separate sessions for directors, writers and producers. In a typical year, sample programs have ranged from a masters' class with a legendary cinematographer (with applicants having to have made two films as a director of photography) to a six-week seminar on producing open to everyone, members and nonmembers alike.

IFP/LA also sponsors Project Involve, offering training and mentoring to new filmmakers. This program focuses on diversity, matching new talent with mentors over a period of months. Applicants can apply to separate series in New York or Los Angeles, must be eighteen to twenty-eight years old, have prior filmmaking experience, and be of color or gay or lesbian.

In the area of member support, the IFP provides vendor discounts; free business and legal consultations; casting facilities; equipment (including digital cameras and editing); a resource library of sample contracts and budgets; and production and screenwriting software. The group also actively brokers relationships between members and industry contacts.

Building audiences for independent film is an important part of the

IFP Independent Spirit Awards, a tradition that dates back to 1984. The Santa Monica–based awards show is televised on the Bravo cable network and the Independent Film Channel. The official nominating guidelines for the Spirit Awards offer an excellent, expanded definition of the independent filmmaking sensibility:

- uniqueness of vision;

- original, provocative subject matter;

- economy of means (with particular attention paid to total production cost and individual compensation); and

- percentage of financing from independent sources.

A search of the IFP Web site (www.ifp.org) on a given day finds a wealth of free information for filmmakers. Here's a sample: The home page provides a toolbar with headings. Each heading opens a drag-down menu allowing for deeper research. For example, the heading "News" leads to feature articles, filmmaker interviews, submission deadlines for film festivals or other competitions and also member news briefs. "Programs & Events" brings up links to current events in each of the city chapters. "Make Your Movie" lets the visitor explore forums, expert Q&As and reports specifically addressing preproduction, production, post and distribution. "Networking Center" opens job listings, classifieds, vendor discounts and directories. "Directories" is actually a powerful search engine covering a full spectrum of companies involved in media, including contact information and staff names. In addition, the IFP Web site has details on the IFP Market, a New York–based film market serving buyers and sellers of completed films; *Filmmaker* magazine; and the IFP Gotham Awards, an annual gala that takes place in Manhattan.

If you are a filmmaker or other worker in the media industry, or a student in the field, or if your career is in another area but you are interested in some aspect of filmmaking, I urge you to attend any of the events being held in Seattle, Minneapolis–St. Paul, Miami, Chicago, New York or Los Angeles. Palpable excitement takes place when filmmakers and others meet to exchange ideas and experiences. What begins as a networking experience can build to achieving valuable contacts, employment opportunities and friendships.

The independent spirit can supply creative solutions for business issues. A chapter from my history with Roger Corman and his New World Pictures provides an example of this. The business issue was that distributor New World needed winter pictures. We had succeeded with a series of summer genre movies (*Piranha*, directed by Joe Dante; *Grand Theft Auto*, directed by Ron Howard), which usually played through Labor Day. Since exhibitors would often not pay us until the next April, when our summer pictures began again, we needed pictures that would play during the winter to improve our cash flow. The creative solution was to canvass the marketplace in search of completed independent pictures seeking distribution in the United States. After a thorough search and screenings, I acquired Ingmar Bergman's *Cries and Whispers*, which became such a success that Roger wanted more. We acquired during the next eight years François Truffaut's *The Story of Adele H.* and some twenty additional finished films from some of the world's greatest filmmakers. This enhanced New World's reputation and coincidentally led to United Artists starting the first studio-branded classics division, UA Classics. Interestingly enough, some of the films New World acquired for U.S. distribution were financed by UA or other major U.S. studios which retained only certain international markets, but not the U.S. market.

Independent filmmakers have always flourished. John Sayles is perhaps the best example of a writer-director with a prolific output of vivid, extraordinary films, all financed independently, spanning a 30-year career. Adding examples like Robert Rodriguez, Steven Soderbergh, Kimberly Peirce and Darren Aronofsky, who shift between independent companies and studios, depending on the project, inevitably leaves out a long list of your favorite filmmakers.

In my own view, the independent world is not a farm team that graduates filmmakers into the majors. Instead, to continue the baseball analogy, the independent and studio spheres represent the National and American Leagues, separate entities that coexist in the same industry. As an example of how this can work for producers, in the same year Michael Taylor and I produced *Instinct*, costing $54 million, we also produced *The Hi-Line*, which cost $250,000.

Independent-style filmmaking continues to be fashionable today, with English-language art house films taking their place alongside foreign-language films for audiences seeking quality entertainment. Every now and then, one independent movie breaks out to substantial box office dollars. Examples from my own career include *Breaker Morant, My Left Foot, Cinema Paradiso* and *Impromptu*, and readers of this article have their own lists of favorite independent movies.

Economy of means continues to be an independent hallmark, along with source of money. The truly independent producer today cobbles together budget financing from several sources in exchange for distribution rights defined not by media but by territory. In this way, the producer of an independent film is much more responsible for obtaining financing than the studio-hired producer. But the struggle to achieve financing independent of a studio has become even more difficult. For example, for years German tax-shelter and Neuer Markt monies had been available for movie financing, but today that source is limited. As mentioned earlier, there are fewer stand-alone independent distributors, so if the studio classics divisions pass, there are fewer buyers left. Television licenses are on the decline, and while home video/DVD sales are rising, those rights are folded into overall rights packages.

The reality is that at this moment, the motion picture industry in general is financially challenged, despite spikes in annual ticket sales or box office gross. Publicly held entertainment companies' stocks are down. The ownership changes within the last few decades have been significant. Columbia, once owned by Coca-Cola, is now owned by Sony. MCA/Universal's ownership has shifted from Matsushita to Seagram to Vivendi to GE. Ted Turner acquired New Line, which in turn was bought by Time Warner, which was acquired in turn by America Online. What does this mean for independent financing?

Follow the money to understand the economic pressures on our industry and especially the independents. In an economic upswing, capital markets seem to be accessible for financing movies. Studio management seems resistant to such off-balance-sheet financing because their stock is strong, and their diverse entities (motion picture, television, theme parks and merchandising) seem to be successfully generating cash. But in an economically depressed market, the studios are anxious for off-balance-sheet funding, and quickly seek to exploit whatever capital markets are available. For the independent producer, the competition for capital may become not another independent, but instead a studio that is aggressively competing for that same capital.

What does the future hold? Some say that emerging technologies will enhance creativity, bringing filmmaking to the desktop, making a parallel to the development of garage bands that burn their own CDs and sell them on the Internet. But access to a pencil and a pad does not make a successful writer, so access to technology does not make a successful filmmaker. There is a level of creativity and professionalism that comes from experience and talent and separates gifted filmmakers from others, regardless of equipment. The Internet has obviously had a great impact on new filmmakers, with Web sites showing original short films. It continues to influence worldwide buzz about features through instantaneous word of mouth, and promises to become a new revenue stream by offering feature films to viewers at home.

What does the financial future hold? Finding money for financing independent films has always been difficult. But the independent spirit is alive and well in the hearts of filmmakers and audience members throughout the world. It's a challenging time for independents. The idea is to accept the challenge, and go do your thing.

V
THE DEAL

THE ENTERTAINMENT LAWYER

by **NORMAN H. GAREY.** For a biographical note on Mr. Garey, see page 117.

> A lawyer in the entertainment field must . . . get along with people under difficult circumstances, and sometimes . . . know the client perhaps better than he or she knows himself or herself.

An entertainment lawyer's practice and relationships with clients may differ significantly from those of other practitioners. The emphasis is on servicing an individual and thus on the relationship between an individual lawyer and an individual client. These relationships are often lifelong, or at least careerlong, and go deeper than traditional lawyer-client relationships in other areas of legal practice.

The clients an entertainment practitioner has are typically creative, volatile and quixotic. A lawyer in the entertainment field must have the ability to adjust and adapt to disparate personalities, to get along with people under difficult circumstances, and sometimes to know the client perhaps better than he or she knows himself or herself. Many clients realize this and often ask for or expect advice that is not, strictly speaking, legal advice.

In the feature motion picture business there are several individuals besides the lawyer who typically influence the client's life and career. A performer will usually have a business manager–accountant responsible for financial counseling and planning, an agent, perhaps a public relations counselor and sometimes a personal manager as well. It's interesting how these interpersonal relationships overlap and how they affect one another in the decision-making process that goes on for each issue in the client's life; it often seems that an actor's life is run by committee. A producer will usually have only a lawyer and a business manager or accountant; a director or writer will have a lawyer, business manager and in most cases an agent.

If the *lient* is a performer, a writer for hire or a director for hire—somebody *who* simply renders services for compensation—it is the primary *function* of the *agent* to seek, find and negotiate the basic terms of employ*ment* for that individual; it is not (and should not be) a lawyer's respons*ibility.* The lawyer should be working closely with the agent, and ideally *they* should have a good personal relationship with each other. The law*yer* (and the business manager) should be kept apprised by the agent of th*e* client's career prospects, including what possibilities are being ex*plor*ed and what the status of each of these explorations or negotiations is; *in* other words, it should be very much a team effort.

However, if the client is a producer, an "entrepreneurial" or "promoter" producer, the lawyer's involvement should generally be primary. Frequently the agent doesn't have the formal background in business organization, accounting principles, economic theory or literary rights in the legal sense that a lawyer has. And all of these areas of preparation are necessary for effective representation of a producer or of an entrepreneurial writer or director who also acts in a packaging or producing capacity.

If a client simply renders services for hire, it's not necessary that the lawyer hear from the agent until the agent has struck the basic deal for the employment of the client, whether as writer, director or both. When that is done, the lawyer becomes involved in the negotiation to assist in refining the deal, particularly in developing the formulae that relate to the net-profit or other contingent compensation position and definition. A lawyer generally shouldn't have to get involved in the up-front negotiation, which includes such major terms as cash fee, services to be rendered, time periods involved in the rendition of those services and the basic rights to be granted (if there are rights to be granted). All of the selling and positioning that it takes to get a client a job in the first place, to create the "want to buy" on the part of the buyer, are an agent's function. Upon entry into the negotiation, the lawyer should learn the history of the negotiation from the agent and then generally speak to the business affairs person with whom the agent has been negotiating—the buyer. The business affairs vice president is usually the primary negotiating representative of the buyer, if the buyer is a studio financier-distributor or a major independent production company (see article by Stephen M. Kravit, p. 194). If the buyer is an individual producer, the attorney in question may deal with the buyer-producer's own outside lawyer. In any event, the buyer's representative and the lawyer will then refine the deal further, and the documentation will commence. The lawyer generally ought not to get involved in the negotiation until he has seen something in writing, whether it has come from the buyer's representative in the form of a deal memo or from the agent for his client in the form of a deal letter that informs him rather clearly where things stand at that point. It's part of the agent's task to memorialize in writing the basic terms that he has negotiated.

If the creator-writer client wants to buy the rights, for example, to a magazine article on which to base a story in a script, it is his lawyer who will typically supervise the buying activities, such as acquiring the rights and checking and clearing them. But when it comes to selling the completed screenplay of the writer-creator, that more properly is an agent's role. If the agent is experienced knows the buyers and will listen to a lawyer when it comes to constructing price, he will then perform the primary selling function.

In the case of a screenwriter selling writing services to adapt a novel for a producer-buyer or studio-buyer, the documentation would be generally in the form of an *employment agreement,* in which the writer-client is acting as a writer for hire; or a *loan-out agreement,* in which case he has his own internal corporation formed for various corporate and tax purposes, which loans his services to the buyer. However, if that same writer plans to render writing services in the adaptation of the magazine article he's already bought, the documentation would characteristically take a bifurcated form. There would be an employment agreement prepared with respect to the rendition of his future services, and there would be a rights option and acquisition agreement prepared with respect to the property rights being conveyed, in this case the rights to the existing magazine article.

For any pure creator, whether writer, actor or director, there are employment agreements that focus on the nature of the services to be performed. These agreements include a definition of the responsibility assumed; the period of time during which the client is expected to render services; whether and, if so, to what extent he's to be exclusive during that period of time (i.e., whether he can engage in work on other projects); and the money involved. A myriad of questions can arise within those general categories. If he's not to be exclusive, what is his availability? Does he have to be on first call, giving first priority to this project? Are there options in favor of the employer-buyer for any further services? How much is to be paid for the services? How, and over what period of time, is the guaranteed compensation to be paid? Regarding contingent compensation, is there a *deferment,* meaning a fixed amount of money paid on a contingent basis if a certain time event, profit event or other event comes about? How does the deferment relate in order of priority to any other deferments? Is there a contingent participation (gross receipts or net profit)? If there is a gross-receipts participation, when does it accrue? If it's a net-profit participation, how are net profits defined and determined? Is there a reducibility factor—

that is, is the client's participation reducible by participations granted to others?

Then there's the important area of controls. This isn't quite as important in an actor's or writer's deal, because writers and actors generally are considered under the control of the producer or director for whom they work. The director generally is considered to be under the control of the producer, but not always. The director's control may supersede the producer's in certain areas and under certain circumstances. For example, the director's cutting rights may be superior to anybody else's; he may in fact have final cut. But a "star" writer, for example, may have the equivalent of the Dramatists Guild covenant for his protection: "Thou shalt not touch my work." That's very rare, but there are a number of top writers who have the exclusive right to perform personally whatever changes are requested to be written and to be paid for doing so. In this fashion a writer is able to exert a degree of control over the progress and integrity of his work.

The actor is typically not in a much different position than a writer for hire or a director for hire from the standpoint of controls—he's going to be rendering certain services under the instruction of others. But there are certain rights that arise out of an actor's services that are unique to an actor. Merchandising happens to be one of them. The actor has a face. If it is well known, people will want to put it on box tops, sweatshirts, T-shirts, book jackets and record labels; it's a valuable right that has to be negotiated for an actor client with some attention. If he is an important actor, his image carries with it a certain dignity that must be preserved. This is also a valuable asset, which must not be merchandised in a denigrating fashion; controls must be negotiated and employed. It isn't just a matter of how much money will be paid and whether it will be in the form of a gross piece ("gross" in the merchandising business is generally represented by royalties) or a net-profit piece.

An important issue arises with respect to whether and when an actor may be paid off without his services having been used. What is the talent losing by not being used if he's been paid? The answer is credit and billing. Credit and billing have a value in this business far beyond just seeing a name on a marquee, because credit and billing may get an actor his next job or the opportunity to advance his career in various ways. In the early days of the film business, if an actor was fired and a jury had to assess the damages that arose from the employer's breach of contract, they would often determine that the actor was guaranteed the salary he'd lost and should in fact be paid. But since he also wasn't used in the picture and didn't get the billing or the enhanced reputation that might have resulted, the jury placed another value on that. The sum might be astronomical because the issue is so amorphous. So the producers and financiers, in order to protect themselves, developed what is called the *pay or play clause,* which says in effect, "We can pay you off, we don't have to use you, and if we do that, all we owe you is your guaranteed compensation. Don't look to us for anything else; you don't have the right to." That has become the almost invariable custom of the business. But today the term *pay or play* is frequently used as a shorthand method for saying simply that there is a firm financial commitment under a deal. The distinction, however, is whether that firm financial commitment also requires the financier to use the person's services, which means it's more accurately pay *and* play (in which case the loss of credit may be compensable in damages) or whether it doesn't require the financier actually to use the actor's personal services, in which case it's pay *or* play, based on what has become the custom.

Producers' controls are many, and the negotiation of controls between a producer and a financing entity occupies a great deal of time because not only artistic and creative controls but financial controls as well have to be worked out between financier and producer in great detail. Attention also has to be paid to a producer's credit; he or she will get not only the "produced by" credit but also in most cases some kind of entrepreneurial, proprietary, presentation or production credit. Questions arise: Does it go above the title or below the title? In what kinds of ads must it appear? These are negotiable points. When getting into directors', writers' or actors' credits, the lawyer can refer to the relevant guild contracts on the subject, which stipulate order and size. Beyond that (and this is particularly true of producers, whose credits are not regulated directly by guild contracts) credit is mostly a matter of prestige, stature and precedent, a question of who comes before whom. What is the placement? Must the credit appear in paid advertising? (*Paid advertising* is all advertising, as distinct from screen credit, issued by or under the control of the distributor—in print campaign ads, display ads, television ads, etc.) Most lawyers leave credit negotiations (except for producers) to the agent.

A director differs in one respect from an actor, writer or producer who renders services for hire. The director has an interest in protecting the integrity of his work that goes slightly beyond the interest of the others because the director is generally considered to be responsible for the total creative rendition of the product, and his or her reputation rides on the overall result. The writer, for example, is responsible only for the literary contribution, as opposed to the visual and audio contribution made by the director. The actor is responsible for the performance of his role. The director is held responsible for all of the performances in the picture. Therefore, the director's cutting rights—the right to protect the integrity of his work—have to be negotiated with some care. Who gets to perform the television cut or supervise it? Who gets to do the foreign censorship cutting or supervise it? How many cuts does the director get? How many previews? When do they have to take place? Who has the right to select the preview sites (an important item, since audience reactions may differ widely from site to site)? Does a particularly important director's right to final cut depend on budgetary, marketing or other financial or commercial considerations?

In all of the foregoing matters the agent and lawyer ideally function as a team. But if a client is an entrepreneurial producer, the lawyer, and usually only the lawyer, will be involved from the very beginning, from the very moment the movie idea is conceived. First, there will be a rights question. If the entrepreneurial producer is planning to acquire a piece of published material, a title search is conducted. The lawyer should have one of the major organizations that perform this function do so at the copyright register in Washington, D.C., to find out whether the idea or material has been exploited before and, if so, to what extent and by whom. This has a definite bearing on how much should be paid for it. Second, it must be determined that the rights are indeed owned by the person who is planning to purvey them and, if they aren't, it is important to know who else owns any of them. Third, are there any further title problems? Can the title be used? Can it be used only in connection with this material? Can it be used in adaptations of this material? The lawyer will usually conduct the negotiation for the acquisition of the rights on behalf of the producer or entrepreneurial creator (which would include an entrepreneurial director, writer or, sometimes, actor who acts in a producing capacity).

When the rights have been secured, there is then the necessity (unless the client is also a writer) to have the material developed into screenplay form. A negotiation must take place with a representative of the writer who will develop the material if the producer client is going to finance the development. There may be still another negotiation, this one with a development-financing source, if it is not the producer client who will finance the development of the material.

There is one situation in which no negotiation takes place up front: that is where the client is an entrepreneurial writer who has conceived the idea and is also going to write the screenplay and ultimately sell it for financing or set it up for financing. In this case there won't be any negotiations until sometime later, but the rights-checking process still has to occur. The lawyer may have to learn whether the writer's idea is as original as his client thinks it is or whether he will perhaps be infringing on somebody else's rights if he develops this project in the way he wishes.

An early issue that arises is the establishment of price. From the standpoint of an entrepreneurial creator, what are his cost factors? What's his out-of-pocket expense, what is it for and what commitments have to be assumed by somebody else or discharged by him and then made whole with somebody else's money? That's bedrock. Next, what kind of speculative risk has to be taken? How much of the creator's time, energy and services are at risk for no money? What is the return to the financier likely to be if this project is exploited successfully? All these factors must be taken into account.

The price of services is influenced very greatly by the factor of sales strategy or positioning. How do you make something seem more than it is? How does synergism develop through the uniting of several different elements? These are intangibles. Selling is the function of an entrepreneurial producer or creator or of an agent; it is not a lawyer's function. But sometimes, when the entrepreneurial creator is engaging in packaging and the lawyer is assisting in this effort, the lawyer can usefully participate very directly in the politics necessary to get people together and then to create excitement around them. In this connection, is the entertainment lawyer acting as more than a lawyer? Is he allowed to do this? The California Labor Code and Business and Professions Code lay out the requirements for licensing on the part of those who solicit employment opportunities for people in the entertainment industry and the rules of professional conduct for lawyers. The codes, and the regulations adopted under them, as well as certain bar association rulings and opinions, support the proposition that a lawyer (or an accountant) who performs such services incidental to his professional practice may do so without a separate license. Thus, it is not unethical or inappropriate for a lawyer to engage in the kind of activity that real estate brokers, loan brokers or insurance brokers engage in as long as it is incidental to the performance of services in his or her professional practice. Certainly these functions extend beyond what most lawyers would consider traditional legal practice. On the other hand, there are lawyers practicing in real estate, in the insurance industry and in the financial community who perform functions above and beyond the traditional law practice. Entertainment lawyers are no different from those people, they are just more visible.

In any negotiation it's important to know the psychology of the buyer with whom one is dealing and to have a very real sense of the value of the elements within the package one is representing. Frequently the entrepreneurial creator who is in touch with the marketplace has a better sense of the situation than the negotiating lawyer. Therefore a lawyer negotiator has to stay in very close contact with the entrepreneurial client during negotiations. That may mean from one to twelve phone conversations during the course of any single day, because frequently the lawyer will be negotiating with the business affairs vice president, whose authority is limited to devising mechanical ways of shifting money to accomplish a certain result. This vice president doesn't have the authority to commit more than a certain amount without going back to his creative principal, who is usually the production head of the studio. Frequently that studio head and the entrepreneurial creator (the client) will be talking at the same time; thus the negotiation often proceeds simultaneously on two levels.

Once a transaction has resulted in a signed document, problems may arise in the administration or implementation of the deal. If it's a legal problem, then the lawyer had better become involved promptly. Frequently the problem will not at first be a legal problem, but rather a relationship problem. Perhaps communication has broken down between the creative people involved, and it's simply a battle of egos about whose creative views should prevail. Rather than expressing it in just that way, the creative people will often start looking for business reasons to further the dispute. This kind of problem can often be solved just by counseling and mediating. On the other hand, sometimes it genuinely is a legal problem. Perhaps something has come up that makes performance as originally contemplated more difficult, more expensive or in fact impossible. Circumstances may have changed; expenses may have exceeded what was originally estimated. In these situations lawyers obviously have to step in. Lawsuits are filed in some cases, but most are settled. There is more contention and less completed litigation in the entertainment business than in most other industries. However, there are some problems that cannot be solved by mediation or negotiation; arbitration and litigation are the only way to solve them.

There are a number of matters for the entertainment lawyer who is administering a career that are more financial than strictly legal in nature. For example, there is an important function to be performed in the area of tax planning and general financial planning and implementation. The matter of auditing net-profit participations or gross-receipts participations in connection with motion picture, home video or television product is a very important function. It is imperative that the distributors who are responsible for the payment of these participations be policed, because they do make mistakes, both from an accounting and from a contract-interpretation standpoint. In all of these areas it is important that the lawyer and the business manager or accountant maintain an effective working relationship.

There is also the matter of organizing the personal affairs of a client.

People in the entertainment business engage in politics; get married and divorced; have problems with lovers, spouses and children; pay taxes, buy and sell property and do all the things other people do, but often with more flair and a great deal more visibility. The entertainment lawyer frequently has to serve as a liaison between the client and the other partners or associates in the law firm who are performing the more traditional legal functions for that client, and often must simultaneously monitor publicity (wanted or unwanted) that may be attendant to the legal matter at hand.

Finally, the lawyer in many cases may be asked to perform a kind of psychological, rabbinical or personal-counseling function in addition to the business function. Advice sought is frequently personal advice about how to conduct not only one's career, but one's life. Lawyers in many cases may have neither the formal training nor the temperamental inclination for these kinds of counseling. It is always possible, however, for the lawyer to consult and involve others who do have the requisite background and either to use their advice in counseling the client or to involve them directly when the occasion requires it. One danger of the close working relationship between lawyer and client is the lawyer's temptation to assume the persona of the client. There is sometimes a seductive sense of power to be derived from those acts of guidance and decisionmaking, both personal and professional, that shape a prominent client's life. As exhilarating as this can be, it can also take a toll on the practitioner's own sense of self. If one is sensitive to this danger, the practice of entertainment law can be fascinating, rewarding and satisfying.

The talent receives a large cash payment as part of the negative cost, which is applied against, say, 10% of the gross from first dollar of film rental, escalating at higher levels.

Today's motion picture legal and business affairs practices can be traced to the days, between the twenties and forties, when studios maintained their key creative talent under exclusive contract. Those agreements granted the employer the right to order activity and obligated the employee to perform as directed so as to get paid. Except for compensation, most contracts were standard, long-term and exclusive, and studio lawyers and outside law firms developed forms to speed up documentation.

By the 1950s the economics of the movie industry had changed as a result of government intervention (via antitrust consent decrees), heavy taxation, the growth of television, a decline in theatre attendance and the development of profit-sharing arrangements with talent who used their increased bargaining power to free themselves from long-term exclusive arrangements. As a result, a new form of contract developed that provided creative talent with picture-by-picture, company-by-company relationships, instead of the previous long-term agreements with one studio employer.

Over the years the intricacy of these agreements has led to lawyers in entertainment firms becoming dealmakers as well as legal advisors, applying business, creative, legal and tax expertise in order to make the best possible deal for the client. (See "The Entertainment Lawyer" by Norman Garey, p. 184.) The role of the agent has changed as well. Whereas formerly agents focused on getting clients their next jobs, today they are dealmakers and packagers, in a climate where buyers compete for a limited and unique talent pool. From the buyer's point of view, whether studio or independent producer, dealmaking expertise has evolved into a professional skill performed by business affairs executives who generally possess a legal background. At a studio a business affairs department is normally headed by a senior executive and is supported by administrative personnel and several negotiators.

Within a fully structured company, business affairs (or dealmaking) ranks as one of the five key management-level divisions, along with production, distribution (or sales), marketing and finance, all reporting to the chief operating officer.

Business affairs gets involved as soon as production becomes interested enough in a project to pursue it. For purposes of illustration, let us assume we are describing the work of a studio financier-distributor. If a proposed project involves important creative talent and therefore significant money, the head of production, sometimes the board chairman and sometimes the president, gets involved, along with the head of business affairs, in setting financial parameters with the lawyers and agents representing the project. Deals with less complexity begin on other levels, but all deals involve a business affairs representative as the point person of the company negotiating team, with input from the production, distribution, tax, finance and legal departments.

In making its recommendations on complex deals, business affairs will usually prepare and present to top management various pro forma profit-and-loss calculations based upon expected and hypothetical levels of negative cost, marketing expenses and distribution revenues, factoring in various possible gross and net participations. These calculations, or "numbers," are projection models inputted with the time-tested experience of company experts and will help to determine whether or not to make the deal, or green-light a production. However, since they are based on past performance, they will often not be accurate reflections of newly emerging or future trends, nor could they be, in light of the two-year average lead time between the decision to proceed and the release of a picture. More than one set of numbers has caused embarrassment when the public's response to a movie is unexpected and overwhelming, outperforming the rejecting studio's numbers model. The film business began as a gambler's business where one's "gut" reactions and passion for talent and material were the only guides. Since no one can accurately predict audience taste, this business—even with all of the financial prediction possibilities of a studio—will continue to remain a "gut" business.

The authorization to make a deal comes from the head of production. Then the head of business affairs judges the complexity of the deal and decides to what extent to become personally involved in the negotiation. Since scores of negotiations are going forward at the same time, delegation is important. In the press of daily work, getting the job done is more important than following a rigid command structure.

In dealmaking everything revolves around money. The negotiation between the studio and the talent must culminate in an agreement as to what duties the talent will perform in return for how much compensation (and other benefits). The rights, options or opportunities of each party—and their cost levels—as the project continues to develop, and, if the picture is made, the accounting and division of receipts from distribution, must all be resolved in this negotiation.

Once these basic terms are reached, the studio legal department (not the law firm for the other party) will generally draw up the contractual documentation covering the deal. This can range from an exchange of faxes or e-mails to a formal agreement of 80 to 120 pages. Not all agreements are embodied in formal, signed documents. Oral agreements are not unusual and generally are equally as binding as those in tangible form. Naturally, if oral agreements are questioned, they are more difficult to prove. As an alternative, and especially if there is an impending start date, the business affairs department may prepare and secure the execution of a binding *deal memo,* a short-form agreement covering those essential money elements critical to the deal. In this case long-form formal contracts are not signed, the picture goes into production and any unresolved issues become moot with the passage of time. However, the trend among major studios is to insist on signed long-form agreements before allowing talent to start work or get paid.

The length and complexity of agreements in the movie business reflect a lack of trust between the parties, compounded by corporate instability. New managements, looking to enhance their relationships with talent and quickly build a production slate, often push for shortened agreements that can be signed quickly. Then, when a problem arises that is not specifically covered (inevitable when using shortform documents), management insists on expanding the document to assure protection on that detail in the future. Thus, the short form slowly balloons into the long form and the cycle is complete.

Most desirable talent are involved in developing several projects at once. However, since agreements are generally entered into on a per-project basis, the talent in effect selects the next project by making a deal. And since no one can force someone to make a deal, it can be said that creative freedom begins with this ability to choose.

Deals involving personal services (for directors, stars or writers, as examples) are generally direct employment agreements, though some are treated as loan-out agreements for tax purposes. For example, a star might create a company that has exclusive control over his or her services. That company, as the star's nominal employer, loans out the star's services to the real employer, the studio, and whatever tax advantages there might be would flow to the loan-out company, not the studio.

Writers' agreements can be in a variety of forms: a screenplay written-for-hire to be owned by the employer; or the purchase of an idea; or securing the rights to a play, published book or existing speculative screenplay; or agreements for rewrites or polishes. There are also agreements to be reached with the producer, director, executive producer, lead actors, cast and technical personnel, such as the production manager, cinematographer, editor and composer.

In addition, there are agreements relating to shared financing. Tax-shelter deals were the most prominent of these. Although they have been virtually eliminated in the United States, they can be a spur to movie production elsewhere, as in Canada. A significant replacement for them has been cofinancing, split-hemisphere deals among studios. For example, MGM and Universal cofinanced *Hannibal,* with MGM releasing in the United States and Universal overseas. *Gladiator* combined DreamWorks (domestic) with Universal (overseas); *Cast Away* partnered Fox (domestic) with DreamWorks (overseas). These deals reduce cash flow (which saves on the cost of money) and investment risk for the parties involved. This is significant in an environment where combined studio budget and marketing costs per picture are in the $90 million and above range. (*Titanic,* with Paramount taking domestic rights and Fox overseas, cost well over $200 million for production alone; marketing added another $100 million.) In such deals, studios share costs and risk in a variety of negotiated ways: 50/50, 60/40 or other formulae.

Another concept is joint venturing between an American studio, a producer and overseas distributors. For example, production financing can be fully furnished by the producer and his overseas distributors/venturers, with studio risk limited to guaranteeing a major domestic release and distribution in certain overseas territories, and the balance of territories remaining with the overseas distributors/venturers.

One more basic type of agreement is the *pickup deal,* covering pictures usually financed outside the studio system. Under this type of deal, subject to certain requirements, the studio will agree to pick up the picture for distribution and pay an amount upon delivery of the negative. This is useful to the producer, who uses the contract as the basis on which to obtain production financing, and is attractive to the studio because it precludes the risk of cost overages (since the pickup payment is a fixed amount) and the risk of noncompletion, since that becomes the burden of the completion guarantor. (For the workings of a completion guarantee, see the article by Norman Rudman and Lionel A. Ephraim, p. 207.)

To secure the most desirable talent today, studios have reverted to the long-term, multiple-picture arrangement, known as the *overall deal.* From the studio's point of view this brings a sense of optimism in that their release schedule will be highlighted by the proven talent. Also, there is the hope for a breakout success "locomotive" picture that will carry along their other titles, especially overseas, where entire schedules of product are often sold together in a form of block booking. From the point of view of the talent, that person has a home, with the security, overhead, office, staff and perks that that implies. On the other hand, such talent cannot auction their services for the duration of the deal; they are taken off the market. In such deals the studio generally gives top talent early participation in gross. These gross participations accrue earlier in the revenue stream than traditional net participations and involve a reduced distribution fee to the studio. Typically these format in one of two modes. In the first mode the talent receives a large cash payment as part of the negative cost, which is applied against, say, 10% of the gross from first dollar of film rental, escalating at higher levels of film rental. In the second mode the talent takes a reduced cash payment (less than market price) as part of the negative cost, which is applied against an enhanced percentage (say, 12½% or 15%) of gross from first dollar of film rental. There are numerous permutations—sliding scales, increments of achieved gross, accruals/deferments versus payments as earned—that can be factored into these kinds of deals.

The *PFD agreement,* short for production, financing and distribution agreement, usually contains all the elements of the individual agreements outlined above. What follows is a generalized tour through its basic elements for a sample picture, simplified for the reader being introduced to the area.

The first section of a PFD agreement generally deals with development. It states the current form in which the project exists: as an outline, treatment, screenplay or other form. Then it identifies the role of the talent tied to it. The producer involved is named, along with the terms of the producer's agreement. If there are writers attached, they are named, along with their terms and responsibilities. Are they writing a new screenplay? Are they rewriting? There are other issues. Has the project been budgeted? Is the producer seeking a director? What is the financial commitment of the studio and what payments are required as the project progresses? On what basis is it deemed to be a "go" picture? All of the answers are spelled out in the contract.

Because the development process is based on a series of steps, development deals within the PFD structure are called *step deals*. At each step a financial expenditure is made. For instance, when there's an existing script, the rewrite could be considered step one. Committing to a director before a second rewrite could be step two. Preparing a budget and production schedule could be step three. This is all spelled out in the development section, with each step having a cutoff to give the financing entity various "outs."

During this process the PFD agreement generally requires a producer or director to oversee the rewriting of the script, help in preparing the budget and shooting schedule and offer casting suggestions. *Suggestions* is a word of art that contractually means the producer must assist the studio in securing talent ready, willing and able to perform required services in the proposed picture, usually at a certain price.

Fees for the producer are normally also tied to steps. For responsibility over a rewrite only, that's one fee. For taking a project from an idea through various screenplay drafts and budgets, the producer would be entitled to more money because more services are being performed over an extended period of time. Writers' deals follow a similar pattern. Producers work on different projects at the same time and are considered nonexclusive. Writers may also work on different development projects, but are generally contracted to finish one specific project exclusively before beginning another. This is changing, though, to reflect the reality that writers may spend time setting up their next project while working on another one.

When the development process is completed, the financier-distributor must decide whether the picture will go forward. The time frame of development usually ends when there are in place those elements that would allow for making a decision on whether or not to proceed: generally a developed script, budget, director, producer and major casting. The theory of a time frame gives the producer a trigger to force a yes-or-no decision from the studio.

If the answer is no, *turnaround* usually kicks in. Turnaround is the effort, after abandonment, to set a project up elsewhere, repay prior investments and get the picture made. Many hit pictures have been in turnaround in one form or another. *Star Wars* was abandoned by Universal; *Home Alone* was abandoned by Warners; studios turned down *Forrest Gump*, *Runaway Bride* and *Black Hawk Down*. Turnaround can be affected by the *changed-element* clause. The abandoning studio does so on the basis of a specific screenplay, budget and talent. If an element changes, there is usually an obligation on the part of the producer to return to the abandoning studio and offer it with the revised element. For example, if a project is developed at Columbia without a star, then moves to Paramount with Kevin Costner attached, Columbia should have another chance to commit to the package with Costner on board. In the turnaround area most people act in good faith, because it's a round world; they will have to deal with an abandoning studio on a new project in the future.

If the studio decides to proceed to production, the PFD agreement states how, what and when key talent will be paid. Usually, this means that salaries begin weekly when the cameras turn, upon "the start of principal photography." However, strong directors or stars may have a *pay or play* deal, whereupon total salary is due whether the picture is made or not, as long as the talent is ready, willing and able to perform during a specific period. When a producer, director or other talent receives salary amounts prior to principal photography, that is usually the result of bargaining leverage.

The production section also contains other requirements and obligations. There is language stating a "producer's obligation to produce the picture," which is standard, and states the producer's role. There are paragraphs stipulating the picture must be made on locations approved by the studio; the running time; where the picture is to be delivered; the picture's technical requirements, including the MPAA rating; studio consultation requirements as to music, casting and other matters; and business and creative approvals during production.

Generally the studio will allow the most experienced filmmakers to arrange for their chosen crew to be engaged, subject to budget, union requirements, EEOC hiring and other government regulations. But the studio normally retains the right to approve the production manager and to select the production auditor, because they deal directly with the money.

Since there are a mass of contracts involved in production, legal fees must be negotiated. Some studios allow the producer's own lawyer to handle this, rather than doing it in-house. Among the most prominent entertainment-law firms who handle the bulk of the documentation on major pictures, there have evolved certain mutually agreed-upon standard forms of legal boilerplate for contracts that can apply to different echelons of talent. Often these forms, with their permutations, are easily slotted in during documentation, in the legal back-and-forth.

The MPAA rating is stipulated in the production section, usually as "no more severe than R," or "NC-17." The producer, director and studio generally agree as to the target rating, but can't guarantee the picture will be so rated by the ratings board. The PFD agreement spells out what happens if the ratings board gives a disapproved rating.

Another area is "television coverage," which also applies to airlines and some overseas markets. The filmmakers making the theatrical picture must plan reshooting or redubbing to cover language or visuals unacceptable in these formats. This must be spelled out in terms of scheduling so that the parties know what to expect.

The right of the studio to view dailies can be a touchy area. Some directors object to studio executives watching their dailies; others are happy to show them. This comes down to the players, their sensibilities, relationships and bargaining power.

The contract also generally covers where the film is to be processed and what lab is to be used. A filmmaker may be more comfortable with one laboratory over another. In the old studio days this was a major issue, sometimes because of laboratory ownership by the studio and sometimes because of kickbacks paid by the laboratory to the producers and studio in return for obtaining the business. Today the sole criterion is technical skill, and the studio generally allows the director and producer to go to whichever competent lab they elect, but at rates no higher than what the studio itself would pay.

Pictures financed by studios are required to comply with industry union agreements. Studios are signatories to dozens of union agreements and therefore impose these obligations, as to salary rates, work rules and benefits, upon the picturemakers.

Another area to specify in the production section of the agreement is the rights of the parties. When a producer is producing, a director is directing and a studio is financing, who is ultimately in charge? The contract must spell out whose decision is final. The sensitive area of "final cut" comes into play. In most PFD agreements, the studio's decision is final, since its money is at work, and money speaks loudest. However, in practice a studio will rarely if ever intrude on a director's finished work, since that risks bad publicity and alienating talent.

Determining the start date is another crucial contractual element, especially for those pictures scheduled for summer or Christmas release. Working backward, it's important to allow for enough time in the production schedule to meet the goal. Too often a major production targeted as a big seasonal release can be rushed into production, placing everyone under stress. But all of the personnel agree to the schedule in advance, sometimes unrealistically.

Overhead costs must also be dealt with, and there are two types. One is overhead for purposes of budgeting a picture and represents a cash outlay to financier/investors. The other, which presents no cash risk to financier/investors, is overhead as it relates to recoupment in paying the various talent who are percentage participants. Major studios no longer include overhead in budgets for their own productions; they budget actual cash costs. However, for purposes of payouts to participants, the studios generally charge a 15% overhead fee on the negative cost as an item of recoupment in determining the level of receipts necessary for such payments.

Next there are questions about contract breaches, which can be complicated. What happens if the director gets drunk, doesn't show up, doesn't perform? What if a producer has completed much work before the picture starts shooting, but dies or breaches or does whatever producers do before going farther? The outcome is not necessarily that the picture doesn't get made or that the producer loses everything, but there must be a negotiated counterweight to discourage any breach. Settlements or payment vesting (if someone has breached) should be agreed upon as part of the employment contracts referred to in the PFD agreement.

That's a review of the production section, the P of a sample PFD agreement. The financing section of the PFD agreement is set out in a few paragraphs, describing exactly how production money is to be allocated. This is often stated simply, noting that there will be a production schedule, production board and budget, and whatever costs are based on those items are to be paid.

The question of securing an outside completion guarantee for a studio picture is arguably a great scam, generally used by insecure executives to fool their bosses that their investment is covered. (For independent productions, however, it is often essential insurance that is required by banks to loan production financing using distribution agreements as collateral.) If a studio is financing a picture, it must do so until completion. In the vast majority of cases the outside completion guarantor will never be permitted to make good on that guarantee, since no studio wants a picture completed by bond-company executives or bankers rather than filmmakers. The guarantor will get his fee and do nothing, and the investors end up carrying the over-budget costs for the picture.

In the distribution section of the PFD agreement, the first important area is credit, which can take the longest to negotiate of any topic in dealmaking. The agreement stipulates the precise credit to be given the director, producer, writer (and book author) and actors, both on the screen and in paid advertising. Details involve size, color, type, order and relationship to other credits. When negotiating credits for paid advertising, lawyers and agents spend hours discussing whose name should go first and on which line, if anyone else's name should be placed on their line, or whose name is larger. The result is that half a print ad can be taken up with names, many of which have no meaning at the box office. Advertising space costs money. While distributors do not object to crediting the creators of a movie, or the well-known talent that helps sell a movie, they can object to trying to sell a picture using a newspaper ad wherein, by contract, a name or likeness must be placed in a specific size and location, regardless of how these requirements may reduce the aesthetics or impact of the ad.

We now turn to money in relation to distribution, and this is the heart of the PFD agreement. It is here that *gross receipts* are defined, which is a calculation representing the "picture pot," into which picture revenues flow and out of which percentage participants are paid. For example, cash received from the theatres—not the box office gross, but the amount the theatre turns over to the distributor (or studio financing entity) after making its own deductions—is included in this pot. This amount is also known as *film rental* or *distributor's share of gross receipts.* Also included is income from home video/DVD (see article by Benjamin S. Feingold, p. 408), pay and free television, merchandising (see article by Al Ovadia, p. 446), soundtracks, book publishing (see article by Roberta Kent and Joel Gotler, p. 91), and music publishing. From this pot the distributor takes a distribution fee for each format as his cost of selling the movie in the United States. Generally the fee is territorial, at 30% for U.S. revenues and 40% to 45% for overseas revenues. Sometimes this fee can be negotiated downward if a producing entity brings financing or print and ad expenditures to the table. Certain media and territories have different fees, which relate to the cost of selling in particular fields. Distribution fees are the lifeblood of the production/financing/distribution business.

Some fees may appear unfair to one party or another; competitive factors also exert a ceiling. There may be different fees in different countries for the same format because it may be more difficult to accomplish the sale in one country than another. For example, the theatrical distribution fee for the United Kingdom can be 35% and for the rest of the world 40% because it is easier to distribute in the U.K. than in, say, Germany or France, because the latter require dubbing or subtitling, which are distribution expenses.

Sometimes a studio can make a "profit" on its fees, particularly with a big hit picture. Paramount and Fox each made so much money on *Titanic* that the single picture virtually carried each entire distribution organization for that year. *How the Grinch Stole Christmas* did the same for Universal. However, as others have noted in this book, the feature film game is one of high stakes and much risk. Even for a major studio, if the production and worldwide marketing costs of any given year's slate of films exceeds that studio's worldwide film rentals for the year (and the per-picture average is around $90 million, excluding out-of-pocket development and overhead not appearing on screen), no distribution fee is earned and the studio is in a loss position.

After deducting distribution fees, the remaining money is applied toward recouping advertising expenses, the cost of prints (today a broad domestic release can cost $5 million or more just for prints), shipping, insurance, inspection and delivery. Next in the PFD agreement is the studio's right to market the picture in any reasonable way, in two theatres or two thousand theatres, or anything in between. The studio's ultimate control over advertising follows, often with an obligation to consult with the producer, director and/or stars on the amount of the advertising budget and the conceptual advertising campaigns, which must comply with credit requirements.

Recoupment of negative cost and interest on the negative cost are covered in the next part of the distribution section. *Negative cost* is the cost of physically making the picture, before prints and advertising charges are incurred. The next step in the revenue flow is the recovery of the picture loan or investment, plus interest, from what remains of film rental.

Notice that, up to this point, all of the effort is being applied to simply recoup money that has already been paid out. Once the picture recovers its costs, it reaches the rarefied realm of breakeven or "net profits." Then, using our model, these profits are split, usually 50% to the financing entity (the studio) and 50% to the participants. As previously noted, special talent in a superior bargaining position, such as a top actor or top director, would receive percentages of proceeds at stages defined earlier than others in the revenue stream. For example, major stars like Julia Roberts, Tom Hanks or Tom Cruise are likely to receive money ahead of other participants.

The accounting portion is also included in the distribution section of the PFD agreement, covering such details as when statements are due; who checks accounting statements; how much detail is provided in them; what their frequency is; what the auditing rights are; what effect an audit has; how much time there is to audit; how much time there is to object.

What follows is a series of relatively standard provisions covering the ownership of the picture, the right of the financing entity to copyright it, the right to distribute the picture in all media worldwide (including the Internet), the right to settle or file lawsuits and the right to settle with exhibitors and other licensees. This group of provisions is intended to state that the financing studio, not the filmmakers, is the owner of the picture, although the filmmakers are entitled to certain financial interests. Insurance requirements are also stated, and if there is an insurance loss, how it is applied. For example, a studio would not take a distribution fee on an insurance recovery, but someone could suggest it and the producer could be naive enough to agree.

Another section covers theatrical sequel, remake and television-production rights. Normally people involved in a successful picture should have first refusal to do a remake, sequel or television production based on that picture. If they decline, there is some argument as to whether they are entitled to money from the derivative work for the act of making the original, even though the derivative work has its own creators and filmmakers. This is especially important today, with the multitude of sequels being made. After all, they arguably reduce risk, since the audience has approved of the prior, successful picture. Sequel, remake and TV rights, and the obligations of the studio and picturemakers to one another in these areas, can be intensely fought-over issues.

In reviewing the documentation for a picture, of course, all of the related agreements, such as those for the producer, director, stars and other key creative people, must mesh with the PFD agreement and its details. When the negotiations and documentation are finalized, the work of business affairs is completed. Once the picture is released, we can only hope we've protected the financier-distributor so that, if it's successful, there is enough revenue to satisfy the investors and to make more movies.

THE FINISHING TOUCH:
THE COMPLETION GUARANTEE

by **NORMAN G. RUDMAN,** who is Of Counsel to the law firm of Stein & Flugge, LLP, in Los Angeles. He was educated at UCLA and the Boalt Hall School of Law (UC Berkeley) and has written and lectured on a variety of subjects including constitutional law, bankruptcy, divorce and the development, financing and production of feature films. Involved as counsel in many motion picture productions, he has also served as executive producer of several films.

and **LIONEL A. EPHRAIM,** senior vice president, Cinema Completions International in Studio City, which has provided completion bonds for numerous films, including Academy Award–winners *The English Patient, Crouching Tiger, Hidden Dragon* and *Traffic*. Before joining CCI, he served as president, west coast, of the Motion Picture Bond Company and as president of Percenterprises Completion Bonds. A member of the Directors Guild, Mr. Ephraim began his career as associate producer of *The Mary Tyler Moore Show,* built the production arm of MTM Enterprises and produced many TV and feature films.

> It can fairly be said that the cost of guaranteeing completion is the only cost of producing a movie that has actually shrunk, at least when measured as a percentage of budget, since the last edition of this book.

For producers and their investors, the motion picture business is a risky, highly speculative business. The investors take risks on many factors: on the creative capabilities of the writer, producer, director and actors and on the ability to secure distribution and compete in the marketplace, to name a few of the more obvious. But the single risk that any investor will find intolerable is the risk that a picture will not be completed. In the production of any motion picture, whether a studio project or an independent venture, the need is always present to assure that what is started will be finished. That is where the issue of "completion" enters into the structuring of a motion picture deal.

If a studio-financed picture goes over budget, for whatever cause, there is reasonable certainty that the studio has the financial strength to cover the extra costs. For undertaking the risk of over-budget costs, the studio may add to the budget or retain a contractual right to recoup a cost item in the area of 5% to 6%. Further, the studio may invoke contractual penalties against the producer and/or director for any excess costs unless such costs result from studio-approved enhancement such as content not found in the approved screenplay prior to shooting or a studio-approved increase in the number of shooting days.

Assume a studio picture budgeted at $50 million. In addition to the producer's fee and overhead allowance, the producer's deal with the studio would typically give him or her a share of the net profits of the picture, say

50%, reducible for profits paid to other talent to a floor of perhaps 20% of 100% as defined in the studio's standard PFD (production, financing and distribution) agreement. (For details of a sample PFD agreement, see article by Stephen M. Kravit, p. 194.) Assume this is a generous studio that allows the producer a 10% contingency over the going-in budget so that he or she is not penalized if the picture comes in at a negative cost of up to $55 million. What happens if the cost reaches $56 million? One of the consequences may be that the producer's profits are, by contract, delayed while the studio recoups not only the $56 million (plus, of course, all distribution expenses, interest and distribution fees) but also double the over-budget costs, or an additional $1 million, before profits are deemed to have been reached. Or the producer may be required to agree that part of his or her fee be payable on a deferred basis and that, to the extent the picture goes over budget, such deferment is paid to the studio to cover the excess costs, rather than to the producer.

The specifics will, of course, depend on the producer's bargaining power vis-à-vis the studio, and what has been said with regard to the producer's deal might, in certain cases, apply to the director's as well. The point is that the studio will take the budget seriously; hence, if the costs run over, the studio is likely to believe either that the budget was false to begin with or that the producer did not manage the production competently. In either event it will likely want to spread the burdens of the extra costs to those most directly responsible.

In independent production the need for completion protection can be fulfilled in a variety of ways. A producer may be capable of meeting excess costs out of his or her own pocket; the deal with investors may permit an overcall; a standby commitment may be in place for over-budget financing on certain terms; or a producer may deal with a company whose business it is to provide a completion guarantee. Indeed, of late it has become a familiar practice even for studios to use outside completion guarantees.

A producer who is strong enough financially to sign a personal guarantee of completion is generally strong enough on the line to assure that the picture comes in without invading personal resources. This type of completion assurance can be as simple as the producer informally assuring investors that he or she will complete the picture.

A second form of completion assurance is simply an overcall from investors. For example, if investors are organized into a limited partnership, the partnership agreement may permit going back to the investors for an extra 10% or 20% of their investment in order to meet overbudget costs.

A third approach might be a standby commitment to invest over-budget costs as called for. Assume an independent picture is budgeted at $8

million. The standby investor, for a negotiated cash fee or other consideration, might commit to provide an additional amount up to, say, $2 mil-
lion. If called upon to put up any of that money, he might be entitled to
take over production. (The completion guarantor, the fourth general category of completion assurance, is also likely to reserve the right to take over
control of the production, without interfering with the ownership of the
production.) The principal distinction between the standby investor and
the completion guarantor is that the standby investor will normally obtain
a recoupment position prior to or at least equal to the people who put up
the $8 million for the principal budget, and a profits interest in the picture
besides. The profits interest is likely to be calculated at a better rate (say,
double) than what the original investors would receive. (That profits interest would normally come out of the producer's share rather than the financiers' share of the profits.) If the original investors were receiving 50% of
the profits for their $8 million, each would have one percentage point of
profit for every $160,000 of money invested. If an investor put up
$400,000 he would be entitled to 2½% of the net profits of the picture. But
let's assume that $400,000 of the standby investor's money is used. On the
standby deal hypothesized above, he or she would be entitled to five
points of profit for that $400,000, but out of the producer's end, not that
allocated to the principal financiers.

We distinguish between a standby investment and a completion guarantee because the standby investment dilutes or postpones the recoupment position of the original investors while the completion guarantee
does not. Further, the completion guarantee as it has developed does not
require the producer to give up any profits for the use of the guarantor's
money, although those profits will be delayed or deferred until after the
guarantor recoups its investment. On the other hand, the standby investor
may be willing to pay for the costs of enhancing a picture. The completion
guarantor will not. The standby-investor format might provide acceptable
completion assurance to equity investors. It would not satisfy a bank if a
bank were putting up any of the production money, because the bank
would not accept any position other than first recoupment and would
want to be assured either of successful delivery of the picture or of payback
if the project were to be abandoned. For the same reason, it would not satisfy most distributors putting up production money in the form of negative pickups or distribution licenses.

As another example, assume it actually cost $9 million to make the
picture budgeted at $8 million, and that the standby investor advanced
the $1 million over-budget costs. Assume further that the distributor has
collected film rentals that, after deduction of distribution fees, print and

advertising costs and other distribution expenses, leave $2 million of "pro-ducer's share" to be devoted to recoupment of production costs. If the pic-ture had been brought in on budget or, as is explained below, if the over-budget costs had been paid for under a typical completion guarantee, that $2 million would be divided pro rata among the investors who funded the budget. Each would receive roughly one-fourth of his money at this point. But if a standby investor put up $1 million (because the picture ac-tually cost $9 million to complete), under a deal calling for his recoupment prior to the original investors, the first $1 million plus interest of that $2 million goes to him. That leaves only $1 million to be divided among the original investors of $8 million, who would get back roughly 12½% instead of 25%. Similarly, if the standby investor's deal calls for recoupment pro rata with the principal investors, then the $2 million recoupment is di-vided among $9 million of investors, making a return of roughly 22% of investment. Thus the standby investment commitment is not a comple-tion guarantee, because *the essence of a completion guarantee is that the in-vestors will get a finished picture for the budget amount they have financed.* If their recoupment is subordinated by the prior, or diluted by the concur-rent (even if pro rata), recoupment of a standby investor, they have not had the benefit of their original bargain in that respect.

A fourth category of completion assurance is the only one properly en-titled to be called a completion guarantee. It is common in the industry to refer to such a guarantee as a bond, and indeed, several companies in the completion-guarantee business use the word *bond* as part of their corporate names. This is a specific type of over-budget insurance underwritten by an insurance carrier. For example, the completion guarantees furnished by Cinema Completions International are underwritten by Continental Ca-sualty Company, a division of CNA.

The typical completion guarantee is a three-sided transaction among bank, producer and guarantor. The guarantor guarantees to the bank the producer's performance of the conditions of the loan agreement. It is not uncommon that completion guarantees are issued in two-sided (producer-guarantor) transactions, where the production financing comes not from bank loans but from equity investment or direct studio financing that is circumscribed by direct studio involvement in production. Here the guar-antor may in effect be guaranteeing the performance of the producer to the producer himself, or to a party so closely allied with the producer as to be chargeable with the producer's actions. The differences between three- and two-sided transactions are most clearly seen in the framing of issues in disputes over whether a guarantor is responsible for an over-budget cost.

To illustrate how a three-sided completion guarantee works, let's turn to an example of an independent picture budgeted at $10 million. To raise that money, assume the producer makes a pickup deal with an American distributor for theatrical, pay-TV and free-TV rights in the United States and Canada for $5 million, payable on delivery of the picture. A foreign-sales representative may sell distribution rights in twenty-five territories in the world and come back with as many contracts, some for $5,000, some for $100,000, making a total package of $3 million, all payable on delivery. And a video distributor might commit the remaining $2 million. Ignoring, for ease of illustration, such complicating factors as interest, discounts, fees, commissions, compensating balances and the like, these numbers round out the $10 million budget. With the exception of relatively nominal down payments, these contracts will usually be payable not on signing but only on or after the delivery of the specific picture. The contracts will not be collectible if the delivered picture does not meet specified conditions, such as that it must be based on a specific screenplay, directed by a certain director, have specific stars and running time, meet first-class technical requirements and be delivered by a specific outside date. The producer takes the contracts to a bank that deals in motion picture transactions and "discounts" them, that is, tenders them as security and the source of repayment for the $10 million production loan.

What is the bank going to require in order to make the $10 million loan? It would be an unusual producer whose credit was good enough to support such a loan. All the bank can look to for payment is the fulfillment of the conditions set forth in the various (often numerous) distribution contracts. If it is assured that those conditions will be met, it may make the production loan. Furnishing such assurance is the function of the completion guarantee. Naturally it is the bank's burden to satisfy itself as to the creditworthiness of the paper against which it is lending. Since the producer is the borrower, the completion guarantee enhances the producer's creditworthiness and allows the bank to lend money (via notes, letters of credit or contracts) to the production. And the delivery conditions that must be fulfilled to make notes collectible, letters of credit draftable or contracts enforceable are what the completion guarantor guarantees.

As earlier observed, banks will make loans against distribution contracts only if they, and only they, have recourse to those contracts until their loans are repaid in full. For this reason the completion assurances of a so-called standby investor will not be acceptable to a bank if the investor has a recoupment position ahead of or even equal to the bank's. Professional completion guarantors, such as Cinema Completions International or Film Finances, have accepted this fixed truth. They offer a standard completion guarantee format involving subordinated recoupment that will very likely be acceptable, depending, of course, on the bank's assessment of the specifics of the guarantor's contract and financial responsibility. Professional completion guarantors have learned to live with having recoupments of their advances, if any, subordinated to the bank or distributor recoupments or, if need be, to equity investors.

The producer in search of a completion guarantee has several markets to explore. The guarantors are highly competitive, so much so that it can fairly be said that the cost of guaranteeing completion is the only cost of producing a movie that has actually shrunk, at least when measured as a percentage of budget, since the last edition of this book.

Historically, when the completion-guarantee business began and guarantors were conceived of as standby investors, the typical cost of a bond was 5% of direct-cost budget. When banks began to play a larger role in financing films, as described above, guarantors were compelled to accept the enlarged risks of subordinated recoupment. As a consequence, their fees increased to an average of 6% of budgeted direct costs. Quietly producers began to rebel, especially those producers of demonstrated competence (and good fortune) whose films usually finished on schedule and within budget. Guarantors then devised the "no-claim bonus" as an inducement to keep those producers coming back. Originating as a modest credit for a successful production that the producer could utilize against the cost of the guarantee on the next project, the "no-claim bonus" evolved over time into a refund of 50% of the guarantee fee paid on each successfully produced picture. The refund could be collected immediately upon timely delivery of the picture and release of any right to call on the guarantor for funds.

The current state of affairs is that guarantees are priced in the neighborhood of 5% to 6% of budgeted costs. One half of that amount goes to the guarantor as its fee; the other half is held in reserve by the bank, to be paid to the guarantor only in the event that the guarantor is called upon to put funds into the picture. If that reserved amount is not used, it would customarily be applied to reduce the cost of the picture.

It is also standard for the guarantor to require a 10% contingency in the approved budget, so that it advances no funds until the picture goes 10% over budget, much like a 10% insurance deductible. But that 10% contingency is not free and clear for the producer to use at will; rather, it is defined to cover those events that are unexpected and outside the control of the producer.

Of late, a new permutation of the completion-guarantee pricing formula has arisen. Over the years most, if not all, professional guarantors have relied on financial backing from insurance companies. Of course, every production needs a wide range of insurance coverages. The typical producer's package policy includes such coverages as cast, negative and faulty stock, workers compensation, liability and equipment; extraordinary conditions may suggest such coverages as foreign business interruption or adverse weather conditions; errors and omissions coverage will be a sine qua non for distribution and often for financing. Often this package is offered by the same insurance interests who have backed the guarantors. It is thus a natural development that some completion guarantors have also become markets for the procurement of insurance coverage combined with completion guarantees. Thus far this development has generally been financially beneficial for producers. Combined rates have been less than the total of separately purchased completion guarantees and insurance. So long as the completion-guarantee business remains competitive, that condition should persist.

When a producer approaches a guarantor for a bond, the guarantor will commence an inquiry to satisfy itself that the picture qualifies and to determine the price it will quote. The inquiry begins with an examination of the screenplay, budget, shooting schedule, rights documents, principal employment and facilities agreements, backgrounds of the key personnel and any and all supporting materials that bear upon the budget, production schedule and delivery requirements.

To a completion guarantor a screenplay is a legal document, signed off by the distributor, lender, bonder, producer and director, analogous to what the plans and specifications for a building are to a construction firm. The guarantor regards the screenplay not merely as a story to be told on film but as the definitive description of the qualities and characteristics to be embodied in that film, including specific action, sets, props, locations, costumes and effects, among other elements. Like the screenplay, the budget, schedule, production board and delivery schedule are of vital importance. The guarantor will be concerned with the whole panoply of issues that may affect the bottom-line question of whether the picture can be completed and delivered at the price, on the schedule and to meet the requirements of the distribution agreements being financed. The inquiry may range from the obvious (is the cast budget large enough to pay the prices of the stars promised to the distributors?) to more subtle matters. For example, a guarantor once deemed it necessary to decline to guarantee a picture scheduled for exterior shooting on a school campus during summer vacations because the school refused to allow shooting to continue past opening of the fall term, and weather-service records suggested that rain would probably delay shooting long enough to cast doubt on the producer's ability to finish filming at that location before the stop date. Few problems that emerge from such an inquiry require so drastic a response. Most lend themselves to cure by the negotiation of adjustments in budgeting, scheduling or staffing. If the distribution agreement calls for delivery of an interpositive and internegative, but the budget allowances for film and lab are too small, the solution is to find the extra money somewhere else. If the star has another commitment to follow this film, and therefore a stop date, reboarding to schedule his scenes to be shot with ample cushion for delays may cure the concern that the stop date might arrive before his services are completed. In addition to reviewing the documents, the guarantor in "vetting" the project may well want to meet with the producer, director, cinematographer or production manager to thrash out anticipated production problems and proposed solutions.

The guarantor's objective is to bring the picture in within the budget and on schedule, thereby fulfilling the delivery requirements of the various distribution contracts. Therefore it is the specific proposed picture disclosed by the screenplay and production plan that becomes the subject of the guarantee, just as it is the subject of the distribution contracts and the production loan. The difference between the guarantor's objectives and those of the bank and the distributors in this respect is that the latter normally have no responsibility for costs beyond their loan or pickup commitments. They can hardly be expected to object if the picture's cost zooms far beyond budget. The guarantor, however, has such responsibility if the cost of the specific guaranteed picture escalates and will, therefore, resist being charged for cost escalations that are voluntarily or incompetently incurred by the producer. Changes in script, new locations, unscripted effects—all such things in the nature of enhancement of the picture will be outside the guarantee and will not be permitted by the guarantor. The only additions or enhancement that would be allowed during shooting are those that are budgeted and approved by the guarantor, distributor and producer.

In reviewing a proposed picture to be guaranteed, the guarantor will want, among other requirements, to see the budget proved, will be suspicious of round figures and will find the word "allowance" in a budget intolerable. The budget will be closely analyzed in relation to the screenplay, the shooting schedule and the professionalism of the principal creative, production and business personnel.

The completion guarantor will have to be satisfied with the director, cinematographer, production manager, location manager, production designer and stars, among others. Does the cinematographer have a history of taking too long to light every shot? Does the director show up on the set without a shot list, so that there is downtime between setups? If the same person is going to star in and direct the picture and the director must be replaced during shooting, will the star show up on the set? Is the director married to the star?

Another issue the guarantor is wary of is a "sweetheart deal" whereby the producer is acquiring some essential service (such as postproduction facilities) on a better-than-prevailing-rate basis. If the sweetheart nature of the deal is what brings the budget down, then the picture is almost certain to go over budget if the sweetheart deal falls out. All of these issues and more must be resolved to the satisfaction of the completion guarantor before the guarantee will be issued.

Aside from the fee, what does the producer give up to the guarantor? Guarantors normally require that they be vested with certain powers to police and oversee the course of production in order to keep it to schedule and budget. Included among such powers may be the right to cosign production-account checks; to observe on the set during shooting; to screen all the rushes; to sit in on all production meetings; to review the books; to receive on a timely basis copies of all production reports, such as camera, sound, production manager and script supervisor reports; to demand and receive answers to questions, and to become coinsured under all the production's insurance. This way the completion guarantor can review the financial status of the picture on a daily or weekly basis, in partnership with the production company, to anticipate and correct potential overbudget incidents. In case of trouble, the completion guarantor can exercise the right to take over control of the production and, if need be, to fire personnel whose performance is below par (subject, of course, to the requirements of distribution, collective bargaining and other relevant agreements). Despite the competitiveness of the completion-guarantee business, it has been next to impossible for any producer to convince a prospective guarantor to forgo any of these rights and powers during the negotiation process. Yet, though the guarantee documentation will almost inevitably contain all of these rights and powers, a guarantor once vested with them is unlikely to throw its weight around. It is only in that most rare case of extreme and otherwise unavoidable jeopardy that a guarantor is likely to exercise its takeover right, and so long as the producer, director and their cast and crew are responding to the exigencies of production with diligence and competence, the guarantor will content itself with keeping a watchful eye on things and offering counsel and assistance in solving problems as they arise. Most have ample qualifications and experience to bring to bear in doing so, and most prefer to be regarded as a resource to be called upon in bringing to fruition the picture the producer and director want to make and the distributor wants to distribute rather than as an assassin lurking in the shadows.

The typical completion-guarantee transaction contains many documents, including a complex one between the producer and the completion guarantor that details the completion guarantor's rights. The guarantee itself is likely to be a simple and straightforward document in favor of the bank, whereby the guarantor undertakes to assure completion and delivery of the picture. The guarantee may also provide that, in the event the guarantor is impelled to declare a production hopeless and abandoned, the guarantor will simply repay the bank its production loan. Abandonment is rarely invoked because it is simply too expensive.

Essentially the guarantee has both time and money aspects. Not only does the guarantor undertake to assure delivery of a specifically described film, the guarantor undertakes to deliver it by a prescribed date. Distributors who have committed to take the picture will ordinarily have conditioned their commitments on delivery by a specific date, because they will have begun the process of booking theatres and preparing their advertising and publicity campaigns while production proceeds. Moreover, production is a labor-intensive activity, hence the more time it takes, the more money it costs. It follows that an understanding of completion guarantees requires an understanding of why pictures sometimes run over budget. The reasons may vary:

- *Some budget elements may have been underestimated.* Although guarantors prefer to deal with budgets priced out in concrete terms based on actual deals or on generally prevailing rates, some budget categories are often not contracted until well after the guarantee has been issued. In the interim, prices may rise. This eventuality might affect the costs of services or facilities needed in postproduction or even during shooting. So simple an item as the cost of money may be a variable. Assume a $10 million budget and a picture to be shot on a foreign location. Assume that 40% of the picture's budget is to be expended in the local currency, for local cast, crew, facilities, housing and the like. If the producer has not purchased all of the local currency expected to be used at the exchange rates prevailing when the budget is approved and, later, those rates change 10% to the detriment of the dollar, the cost of the picture may rise several hundred thousand dollars. Yet, buying the foreign currency in advance might cost the producer the ability to save money if the value of the dollar rises. A completion guarantor may be expected to seek protection against such eventualities either by requiring the producer to make protective deals early or, if such exclusion does not cause the bank to object, by excluding such variations from its risk.

- *Unforeseen events may intrude.* Adverse weather or labor difficulties may crop up. Suppose the picture was budgeted to be shot nonunion. Even if the budgeted wage and salary scales were at union minimums or better, the producer did not budget to pay union overtime, fringes, vacation pay or penalties or to hire the full complement of people a union contract might require. Also suppose the producer hired certain key people who happen to be members of the union and, upon learning of the production, the union has told those people they may not work for a nonsignatory employer. The producer may then face a Hobson's choice, between delaying production while trying to hire replacements and negotiating a hasty adherence to the union's collective-bargaining agreement. The latter choice might increase the cost 30% or so in the affected labor categories; the former choice will also be expensive, though it is impossible to predict how much it will cost. If the guarantor had not required a separate contingency to cover this possibility, the guarantor would be responsible for these overages.

- *The pace of shooting may be slower than expected.* It has been said, perhaps apocryphally, that on the first day of principal photography a picture will usually be a week behind schedule. Inevitably, as the time required for shooting increases, so, too, does the negative cost. While some flat deals may be made, or "free" periods negotiated in connection with some engagements, most cast and crew hirings are done on a daily or weekly rate, and most stages, locations, facilities and equipment are rented on a time basis as well. The causes for delay are so many and varied as to be impossible to exhaust or even classify. Temperamental stars, obsessed directors, poky camera crews, feuds between key personnel and a multitude of other such phenomena are all within experience. Although no completion guarantee was involved, one of the most celebrated of the industry's experiences with a production that could not be kept within bounds monetarily or temporally is chronicled in Steven Bach's book *Final Cut.* It details a sobering account of Murphy's law enforced with a vengeance. Other tales of similar woes abound. Perhaps it is human nature to dismiss from mind the overwhelming number of films that have been routinely and economically brought in by application of the competence and professionalism of their makers. Only the catastrophes grow legendary. For example, on a certain picture one scene required forty-five takes. The scene, set in a pool hall over a table, required dialogue between the female and male leads while he made a difficult trick shot. Because the male lead was rather accomplished with a cue stick, the scene was not to be cheated with inserts. In the early takes he made the shot consistently, but she had trouble with her lines, sometimes misspeaking, sometimes stepping on his lines. After a break the dialogue went fine, but he was tired and kept missing the shot. The day's shooting extended to over twelve hours, and at the end of it only a fraction of the day's scheduled pages were in the can. That loss of time in itself posed no insurmountable problem. Had similar losses, for similar or different reasons, occurred again and again, however, the obvious cumulative impact might have been difficult to bear.

- *Illness, accidents and force majeure may intervene.* Cast insurance on most pictures covers only a few people. Unless special provisions are made and extra premiums paid, the cast insurance policy will cover only the top three or four stars and the director and producer. The theory is to cover those people whose performances on the film would be extraordinarily expensive to replicate or whose unavailability would paralyze the production, not merely delay it some. The completion guarantor bears the more comprehensive risk of delays caused by illness or injury to people not covered by cast insurance. Moreover, cast insurers will sometimes exclude from the risks they assume any losses that may result from the age of elderly actors, or known health defects that may afflict a person covered, or known insalubrious habits in such a person's history. If despite the cast insurer's warning the producer hires an actor with a heart condition or one with a history of substance abuse, the cast insurer will not bear or share in the extra cost if the risk posed by that condition becomes reality. Therefore, the completion guarantor will not approve the hiring of this actor unless the producer is able to remove the exclusion on such actor by paying an extra premium.

    Force majeure events, such as war, civil disturbance, labor dispute, fire, flood and the like, are both impossible to predict and costly. Most distribution agreements will allow a modest and limited extension of the delivery date for an event of force majeure, hence it would be possible to collect on the distributor's cash commitment despite some tardiness in delivery if the delay was the result of such an event. But even where this is so, the additional costs incident to an event of force majeure are the guarantor's concern.

- *Enhancement.* It is not uncommon in the production of films that what is scripted is not shot and what is shot was not originally scripted. Although the script, budget, shooting schedule and other documents evidencing the production plan were supposed to be final when the guarantee was issued, subject only to minor variations responsive to the exigencies of production, a screenwriter may be kept on tap during the shoot. Ostensibly, when this happens, the purpose is to keep the dialogue fresh. Dialogue is inexpensive. What often happens, however, is that shooting discloses weaknesses in the plot line or characterizations, and some effort must be made to strengthen the weak spots. Hence one may find new scenes written, new characters introduced, new locations, sets, props and action. These are not inexpensive. The producer may believe them essential to the making of a picture as good as he intended at the outset. In the eyes of the guarantor, however, the producer is welcome to them, but at his own cost, unless the producer can save the equivalent amounts in other areas.

New writing is only illustrative of the ways in which the scope of a production may be enlarged from what was guaranteed. Others include expansion of stunts or special effects, augmentation of the initially conceived music score (what director can resist the lure of a soundtrack crammed full of the sounds of hit records of the period being filmed?) or adding stars in cameo roles to the cast.

There are certain areas of controversy characteristic of completion guarantees. The most common issue in the area of claims is the difference between a legitimate over-budget cost, part of making the picture as contemplated and guaranteed, versus enhancement. In the three-sided transaction the guarantor usually has no choice but to finish the picture. If the guarantor has failed to police the production, and the producer has thereby succeeded in raising the cost of the picture by enhancing it, the guarantor is still obligated to the bank to make delivery notwithstanding over-budget costs. The guarantor may have to advance these costs and then bring an action against the producer to collect that portion of the extra costs occasioned by enhancement rather than by legitimate over-budget contingencies. In a two-sided transaction the issue may also arise in the context of a lawsuit by the producer (or a closely allied financier) against the guarantor, wherein the guarantor raises the defense that the costs in question are enhancement costs rather than legitimate over-budget costs.

Another source of dispute may be diversion of a picture's budgeted production funds to some purpose other than payment of the production's expenses. The possibilities are limitless. They include the charging of travel to the budget where the travel is actually related to another project or a personal frolic of the producer; concealment of personal debt repayment in checks to vendors ostensibly for materials or equipment for the production; and purchase, rather than rental for the limited period of production, of long-term capital assets out of the budget. While the completion guarantor's watchword is always vigilance, such occurrences will have different ramifications in the two-sided as against the three-sided transaction. If, in the two-sided transaction, someone on the production team has succeeded in diverting funds from the production budget to some other purpose, resulting in a need for additional cash for completion, the guarantor may simply refuse to put it up. The guarantor could rely for a defense on the producer's own default by failing to devote the production budget solely and exclusively to the production of the picture. But this wouldn't be so if the guarantor's obligation is owed to a bank. Here the guarantor still must finish and deliver the picture and look to its own devices to attempt to retrieve any diverted funds from the producer.

The remarkable fact, considering the complexity and scope of feature film production, is that there are few such disputes. The guarantees of the established guarantors are rather routinely accepted, relied upon and performed, and guarantors make payment of substantially more money to producers or investors in the form of "no-claim bonuses" or rebates than on over-budget claims.

The completion guarantee, as developed in the industry, is only one of several possible ways of assuring that the picture will be finished. It is probably the most satisfactory approach for independently financed pictures. The concept of the completion guarantee is very much in the minds of bankers considering entrance into motion picture work, securities brokers as they review movie financing through public issues and investment counselors as they give advice on private placements. Since even the most competently prepared budget is at best only an estimate of what it will take to bring a picture in, pictures do go over budget and over schedule, notwithstanding the best intentions and efforts of all involved. For that exigency, the completion guarantee provides a significant measure of protection.

THE TALENT AGENT

by **JESSICA TUCHINSKY,** an agent in the motion picture department at Creative Artists Agency (CAA) in Beverly Hills. Ms. Tuchinsky represents many acclaimed actors, writers and directors, including Bill Murray, Uma Thurman, Andrew Niccol, Scott Silver and Steve Kloves. A graduate of George Washington University with degrees in international politics and economics, Ms. Tuchinsky also studied in France and Japan before joining CAA as an agents' assistant in 1990.

Dealmaking can be learned; the inventiveness, intuition and drive to spot talent, build relationships and know how to combine them cannot be learned; it is inherent.

A gencies have a tradition of starting people in the mail room at very low pay, regardless of background. There they learn the geography of the agency, the hierarchy and atmosphere of a range of people and offices. The entertainment industry is filled with high-level executives who began their work experience in a mail room. The stint can last from one to five years, and also weeds out those who simply have difficulty, for whatever reasons, working at the seemingly menial but important tasks of sorting and delivering mail.

The next rung up is the job of desk assistant to an agent. The desk assistant works extremely long hours, under often stressful conditions, acting as the agent's point person by rolling phone calls and handling the myriad of logistical tasks required by the agent. This position can last from one to five (or more) years. It's a high-pressure, highly detailed job and the best training in the intangibles required to become an agent, since the assistant observes the agent's business life close up and executes all the agent's support work. The agent and the desk assistant work in close proximity; in fact, the desk assistant is being groomed to become an agent. Sometimes the assistant learns from the experience that he or she is not cut out for an agent's life and will move on to another kind of job in the entertainment industry. Whatever the path, the assistant job offers great perspective on the entertainment business and first-hand insights about the players—who you want to work for, and who you want to emulate.

The Creative Artists Agency, founded in 1975, is composed of several departments: motion pictures, television, music, corporate consulting and the CAA Foundation, which is actively engaged in philanthropy. All of the agents share all of the clients, and these departments coexist peacefully in an atmosphere of mutual respect. (For example, a comic-book character represented by the motion picture division can cross over to a video game under technology and spin off into a television show.) The agency is owned by a managing group comprised of agent-partners.

In the traditional sense, an agent's job is to field offers and negotiate deals for clients. As agencies evolved over the years, in some cases the role of the agent added an entrepreneurial component, requiring creative instincts to combine certain literary material with appropriate director and/or acting talent in a package presented to financing sources/studios. As a result, a critical part of an agency's function is to gather the huge amount of project and talent information that travels around on a given day, decipher it, and use it in support of the business lives of its clients. This requires a kind of intuition that cannot be learned in school, which is why the desk assistant experience is so fundamental to the development of an agent's career.

It cannot be emphasized enough how important information is. Agents carry around in their heads an ever-growing database of names, faces, job titles, credits, deal points, rumors, relationships, and business and creative judgments to best service their clients. Outside the extremely hectic business day, it is essential to read books, screenplays and magazine articles; attend stage plays, movies and concerts; and watch videos as soon as possible, all of which is added to one's mental database in order to maintain a business/creative sense of new and established talent and how they might blend with the agency's talent roster. For example, if a name acting client asks a literary agent who the up-and-coming movie directors are, that agent should have already seen the current "hot" directors' work, before the general public has. If not, the client is being placed at a disadvantage.

Within the motion picture department at CAA, there are literary agents who represent literary talent (including authors of books, and screenplays, as well as directors) and talent agents who represent acting talent. (See "The Literary Agent" by Lee G. Rosenberg, p. 72.) More and more, these titles are blending as talent becomes more diversified. I happen to be a crossover agent, working in both the literary and talent areas, and this article focuses on the work of the talent agent.

There are nuances involved in working with acting talent in different stages of their careers. It goes without saying that part of an agent's job is being completely conversant with a client's work, familiar with everything the client has done. With an above-the-title, sought-after movie star, obviously, an agent's job is a matter of evaluating offers rather than finding the star work. What gets complicated is framing the back-end or participation part of the deal. Since a financing studio has only so much gross to give to such high-end talent, the agent must be imaginative as to how to satisfy the client's share in the context of what has already been given to others. If the client has received first-dollar gross in the past, will this deal maintain or improve that position? If not, will this deal establish a precedent for the client that the money (that is, the financing studio) is willing to allow? This can become a threshold issue if the talent is willing to walk away from the project, or if the money is willing to walk away. What other offers does the talent have on the table? What other names is the studio considering? This mutual tension is part of what can make or break a deal.

At this level the heat of negotiations is compelling, since there is so much money at stake. I work very closely with CAA business affairs executives, who are privy to every single deal made around town. This is a very small industry, and in dealmaking especially, most agents know most entertainment lawyers and business affairs executives. There is a high degree of mutual trust and honesty in the community, and most dealmaking is conducted with professionalism even though it often involves differences of opinion and an adversarial environment. Sometimes deals fall apart based on money, sometimes based on inflexibility or lack of imagination.

Another element of representing established talent holds true for all talent: The agent must make the best use of the talent's precious time. For stars, there are usually only one or two windows of time per year available to perform acting services. Since a movie commitment takes a talent's time off the market, how is that time valued? The answer is found in the talent's deal.

In some cases, an established star might want to work in a smaller, independent-style film. How is that time valued? Assuming the budget is far too low to accommodate the talent's going rate, negotiations become inventive in constructing the back-end deal. The result would be a deal wherein the talent forgoes much of the usual up-front cash compensation in exchange for sharing in the success of the movie through an appropriate back-end deal. The talent is willing to risk the up-front cash and take him- or herself off the market for a period of time out of love for the project.

This leads to a recent trend with established talent: They are willing to work with newcomers, either actors, writers or directors, whether in the studio or independent world. Established talent know their presence can enhance the marketplace value of a smaller, independent film that often allows a star to work against type and stretch acting muscles.

The established talent has a support team comprised of the primary agent, often a literary contact at the agency, a business affairs contact, an outside manager, and an outside, personal lawyer. Agents receive a commission of 10% of the talent's gross revenue, managers an additional 15%, lawyers can take an additional 5% or be paid by the hour or some other formula; easily 30% can be deducted in such fees before the talent sees the balance.

Representing someone whose career is in transition is both exciting and challenging. It is an opportunity to guide someone to the next career stage. For example, someone who has enjoyed a career as a star may transition into other roles while still bringing specific charisma to the project. If multimillion-dollar starring roles are no longer being offered, there may be a high-impact role in a movie requiring only two weeks of shooting, with the up-front dollars reduced accordingly; the role may be a cameo and billed as such. If the talent is resistant, honesty is important in presenting career choices in the context of marketplace reality. Usually, the talent welcomes the guidance and becomes a participant in a career move. The reader can probably think of a current example of a movie star recreating a career in television, theatre or in pivotal smaller movie roles. In these as in all cases, the careful selection of material is key.

Another typical transition is when a talent who has made a name in smaller roles is deemed ready to break out into more important opportunities. Just as in the earlier example, this case calls for carefully choosing the roles that would create momentum. When Jude Law appeared in *A.I.: Artificial Intelligence* and then *Road to Perdition,* those two highly contrasting roles had an enormously favorable impact on the creative community, critics and the audience in general. The reader no doubt can think of current examples of an actor or actress who is "discovered" in an independent movie and is then found in important supporting roles in two or three movies over the next year. Over this time the audience discovers the talent, and might even start remembering the name.

Once this kind of talent is in a breakout role, however small the movie might be, the agency circulates the movie among those who are considered tastemakers. This leads to general meetings for the talent with industry executives and creators. The agency would also have the talent attend premieres, social events or other venues where tastemakers congregate. A buzz can develop and suddenly the talent's name appears on casting lists.

After the talent has done the projects that have led to this kind of exposure, it might be useful to hold him or her back and wait for the further buzz that is likely to develop, in order to find the perfect next role. At this point, it's not about the money but about the strategic development of a career; the money will come later. These choices, again, come down to instinct and taste (which can't be taught), based on the access to information that an agency has about projects in development. Since offers come in all the time, it might be wise not to jump on the latest offer, because the ideal project might be slowly being developed elsewhere. It's often best to wait for the project that has more potential to springboard the talent to a higher stature.

Another aspect of representation is finding new talent. Film festivals are venues rich in new acting talent (as are plays), so it's useful to cover movies screening in festivals when seeking new talent. Often, director clients discover new and exciting talent in their own searches and alert agents. Seeking new talent is every agents' specialty; it is the future of the business.

Assume an agent is impressed with an actress in a play. Instinct kicks in, and the agent will pursue the talent for representation; often, rival agents (or managers) are doing the same thing. Casting directors are already aware of the actress, since she was cast by a casting director.

At CAA, an agent can only sign a new client with the consent of the entire department. This is consistent with the idea that each CAA client is represented by the entire agency as a team, not one agent. Everybody shares; it is communal and collaborative. A CAA client may work closely with a primary agent, but every agent in the agency is working on that client's behalf.

If the talent decides to go with CAA, papers are signed so that the agency exclusively represents the talent for a certain agreed-upon time period. At the heart of the agency-talent deal is the standard 10% agency commission on all dollars due to the client. The CAA accounting department tracks all client agreements and makes sure, with the help of CAA business affairs executives, that payments are made when they are due. These payments go directly to CAA; the 10% commission is deducted and the balance is sent to the client or the client's business manager or lawyer on behalf of the client. There are also SAG and WGA residual payments due at certain times, and the CAA residuals department follows up on those. On behalf of clients, audits are periodically conducted to verify participation statements.

Early in new-talent representation, it's important to listen to the client. What does he or she want to do? How do they see themselves? What might follow is a series of introductions to director clients, executives, producers, casting directors and others around town who are in hiring positions, called "a round of meetings," which are time-consuming but valuable.

Launching a newcomer can involve stage work, a movie role or a television commitment; there is no formula. What prevails is whatever is going to get the talent noticed by the most appropriate audience. Good work gets noticed, whatever the outlet. Negotiations at this level are an effort to achieve as much cash and back-end as possible, based on what the market will bear. Sometimes there is increased bargaining power if the director's heart is set on casting the talent; sometimes there is little bargaining power. But with each new commitment, the newcomer deserves a bump in salary.

Another area worthy of mention is the concept of holding talent. Bluntly, the agency business is highly competitive, and agencies work hard at retaining their clients. Actors or actresses are seduceable, and when certain ones are going through a transition, they may be lured away to another agency. Personally, I view every day as an opportunity to prevent this by thinking of new opportunities for a client (or thinking, what would a rival agent be doing for that client?); that's just part of doing a good job as an agent. No agent can take any client for granted. At CAA, we are trained to be thorough in our representation. Should a given acting client be meeting with the books department in order to branch out into developing material? Who else should a new actor be meeting with? The list is endless.

Because of the way CAA functions, with all agents working for all clients, if an agent is somehow not working out with a particular client, another agent can take over representation; this is a sort of fail-safe within the system.

Often agents work closely with a clients' managers. A good manager can complement the agency team, bringing added value to the mix, such as coming up with useful ideas for meetings the client should have. A bad manager calls and asks, "What's going on?" in order to take credit for bringing that information to the client. Needless to say, this can be intrusive. Ideally, the manager should be thinking ahead (much like the agent) and coming up with an inventive approach to help the client's career that might require the CAA arsenal of talent or access.

What's such fun about the agent's job is that there is no typical day. At CAA, there is a schedule of meetings where information is exchanged and strategy is planned. A Monday morning meeting of the motion picture department covers what was read over the weekend, box office performance and the films people saw; later, motion picture talent agents have a luncheon meeting. On Tuesday, motion picture literary has a luncheon meeting. On Wednesday morning, the entire motion picture department and agents representing other departments meet to cover progress on every deal, relationship and nuance involving clients, and how agents will follow through. This is the longest meeting of the week, when all information is exchanged. On Thursday, the talent and literary departments meet separately in the morning, and on Friday is the weekend read meeting, where people share opinions on what they will be reading over the weekend. I want to read every single project that is mentioned, so that on Monday morning there is a renewed sense of purpose. Time between these meetings is spent moving clients' careers forward via phone calls, business lunches and dinners, screenings and breakfast meetings; most working days start at 7:30 or 8:30 A.M. with breakfast meetings and end around 10 P.M. More than a job, it's a lifestyle.

This article began by tracing the traditional training ground for agents, the mail room experience. What cannot be trained is an inherent literary or aesthetic taste and a personality mix capable of dealing with a range of talented clients as well as a range of smart, gifted lawyers and business executives. It goes without saying that reading is central, especially mastering the specific craft of reading screenplays, a form of technical writing. Some say it takes reading hundreds of screenplays before you can really analyze them; some say it takes a thousand. What develops in the business is a series of relationships of mutual respect based on shared taste, something that also can't be trained. Finding people—whether talent, studio executives or other agents—with similar sensibilities saves time and energy, and in a business where time is at a premium, this kind of networking is very useful. At the same time, agents hope they are earning individual credibility as to taste, so that a call to a studio executive, for example, will be answered quickly and a project under discussion will be taken seriously. What also can't be trained is an inherent drive to perform the work of an agent, which requires aggressively going after projects you respond to, or talent you respond to, and servicing them and selling them to people who can benefit from them. There is no secret to the job; no M.B.A. or law degree will guarantee success. In fact, degrees in history or literature, coupled with travel and an inquisitive mind, are good preparation for the agent's job. The more interesting and well-versed in life a person is, the more open to talent he or she is likely to be. Dealmaking can be learned; the inventiveness, intuition and drive to spot talent, build relationships and know how to combine them cannot be learned; it is inherent.

VI
PRODUCTION

PRODUCTION MANAGEMENT

by **MICHAEL GRILLO,** head of feature film production at DreamWorks SKG. Mr. Grillo has worked his way up through the production ranks over many years, starting as a DGA trainee on *Young Frankenstein* and *The Towering Inferno;* then becoming assistant director on *New York, New York, The Deer Hunter, Breaking Away, Heaven's Gate, Body Heat* and *The Big Chill;* and working with director Lawrence Kasdan as executive producer on *Silverado, I Love You to Death* and *Wyatt Earp* and as producer of *Grand Canyon* and *The Accidental Tourist,* for which he received an Academy Award nomination for Best Picture. Later, he produced *Defending Your Life,* directed by Albert Brooks, and *The Trigger Effect,* written and directed by David Koepp. He was executive producer on DreamWorks' first feature film, *The Peacemaker.* Mr. Grillo is a member of the Academy of Motion Pictures Arts and Sciences and the Directors Guild of America.

Some of the responsibilities of the line producer, production manager and production accountant involve monitoring the costs of prep, shoot and wrap, projecting possible overages or savings and generating a weekly cost report that is distributed to the studio.

The job of the head of feature production at DreamWorks is to partner with the creative team on multiple projects to make critically and financially successful feature films. When a project is in development and close to starting prep, I read the screenplay and share my thoughts with Walter Parkes and Laurie MacDonald, the coheads of the motion picture division. We confer on where we should film, how much it will cost, how long it will take to prep, shoot, and post to make a particular release date, along with discussing possible directors, creative producers, cast and line producers who may be right for the project. My work is more involved with the line producer, who reports directly to me during the production process.

The initial reading of the screenplay is a very quick one, as I try to imagine the film we will be attempting to make. During the second reading, I pay closer attention to details that may increase both the time and money needed for the production. Some of the issues considered are whether it is a contemporary or period piece, the number of domestic and distant locations, whether actual locations exist or need to be created, expensive props and set dressing, action sequences, night filming, the number of actors and extras in each scene, minors in lead roles, physical effects, visual effects, music (including licensing), second-unit work and complex postproduction. This early stage involves a series of assumptions and educated guesses that lead to an estimated budget number and a rough calendar representing the proposed prep, shoot, and postproduction period, a preliminary approach until a director and producer come on board and the film is cast. It is not unusual to work more than a year on a film from the start of prep through the scheduled release date, a time frame that can be greatly extended depending on the complexity of a project. On the first *Jurassic Park,* for instance, there was a research and development period before the usual preparation period due to new and complicated effects. Steven Spielberg worked on storyboards, and the resulting combination of Stan Winston's creatures, along with digital dinosaurs and effects added later by Industrial Light & Magic, represented a breakthrough in filmmaking.

Formal prep does not start until a producer and a director are involved in a project. Producers come from two traditions, the creative producer and the line producer. The creative producer, whose credit may be producer or executive producer, is often the person who acquired the underlying literary material, developed the screenplay and packaged the project with talent strong enough to attract DreamWorks. Other times, the creative producer is assigned to the project by the studio, after the material has been developed in-house, to support the creative views of the director and the studio. The line producer, whose credit may be producer, executive producer, co-producer, associate producer, or executive in charge of production, is the one with physical production experience, and is responsible for overseeing the coordination and cost of the production. Sometimes the director or creative producer has his or her own line producer, but it is more common for me to select one who will fit for that particular team and project. I'm not fond of the term "line producer," since the title tends to connote only financial management of the production. The best producers have nuts-and-bolts physical production experience along with the ability to work with the director on the script, casting, scouting, shot lists, performance of actors, and all of the creative aspects of filmmaking. Occasionally we have one individual who is capable of covering all of the areas of producing, both creative and physical. It's best to hire producers you've worked with before, since you develop a shorthand in communication and a trust in their production instincts.

Each movie presents unique challenges in production planning. *Gladiator,* for instance, was one of our more difficult and interesting productions because the world it takes place in no longer exists. How and where do you create Rome? Do you build the whole Roman Colosseum? How much will the film cost and when can we have it ready for a theatrical release? We were fortunate to have very talented and experienced people on this project. Ridley Scott came on as the director, Doug Wick and David

Franzoni as creative producers (David also wrote the original screenplay), Walter Parkes and Laurie MacDonald as executive producers, and Branko Lustig (who had also been the line producer on *Schindler's List* and *The Peacemaker,* DreamWorks' first feature production) as the line producer. Ridley Scott had scouted the island of Malta for a prior film and found a large open area surrounded by period structures made of limestone that could double for Rome. He worked closely with the visual effects company, The Mill, and production designer Arthur Max in laying out the Colosseum in this open area. Measurements of the actual Colosseum in Rome were programmed into computer software, which generated models and camera points of view. The computer imagery created a virtual set that helped Ridley plan camera angles and stage fight scenes within the space of a proposed set, which ultimately ended up being one-quarter the size of the actual Colosseum. Another, smaller section where the emperor sat was built for reverse angles and cutting pieces. The balance of the Colosseum was filled in with computer-generated images (CGI) and models. This research enabled the filmmakers to limit construction and the number of visual effects shots, keeping costs down. There were one or two visual effects "money" shots, such as the overhead establishing shot, similar to a shot from a blimp in a football broadcast, and Russell Crowe's entrance into the Colosseum, which became a 360-degree Steadicam shot. Once those shots worked successfully, the illusion of a complete structure was sold. The production designer Arthur Max was nominated for an Oscar, and *Gladiator* ultimately won the Academy Award for Best Picture.

The production board and shooting schedule of a movie are generated during the initial steps of prep. They are usually completed by the line producer and ultimately taken over by the production manager and first assistant director. The board and schedule are created by breaking down the screenplay into shooting segments. They represent the amount of days needed for filming, the locations, a breakdown of all scenes, actors and extras needed and other key elements. (For examples of production paperwork, see the article by Christina Fong on p. 250.) This information is based on input from the director, whose creative intentions and style, discussed scene by scene, will help define the schedule required to logistically and economically plan production.

There are many issues to factor into scheduling a motion picture. All exterior night filming is generally grouped together, while the weekends are used to return the cast and crew to a day schedule. Since actors are paid based on consecutive employment, there is an attempt to condense their time on a production. The availability dates of the major stars are always an issue. Action scenes take more time, given the possibility of additional cameras and second units. Directors and actors would love to film in continuity, but it is usually not possible due to production and budget constraints. Additional issues to be considered are the amount of daylight or nighttime hours during certain parts of the year, travel time to location, the creation of physical and visual effects, specialty makeup, limitations on filming hours for minors, weather conditions, crowd control on the streets and in the cities, and the level of experience and efficiency of a director, among other things. It takes a very knowledgeable production person to create a practical and efficient shooting schedule. The total production plan and budget are based on it.

A generic budget topsheet, or summary page, is found on p. 237. The typical budget, running twenty to thirty or more pages, depending on how intricate the shooting will be, is divided into two sections: above-the-line and below-the line. The budget covers all of the costs of the film, from development through the release of the production, but does not include the expense of marketing or distribution. *Fringes,* defined as pension, health and welfare payments, are added to the salaries of both above-the-line and below-the-line guild personnel, such as those in DGA (Directors Guild of America), WGA (Writers Guild of America), SAG (Screen Actors Guild), and IATSE (International Alliance of Theatrical Stage Employees). For information regarding current guild minimums or other questions, the reader is invited to contact the DGA at one of these addresses: 7920 Sunset Boulevard, Los Angeles, CA 90046 (phone 310-289-2000); 110 West 57 Street, New York, NY 10019 (212-581-0370); or 520 North Michigan Avenue, Suite 1026, Chicago, IL 60611 (312-644-5050), or visit their Web site at www. dga.org. To contact the WGA, see the information in Lee Rosenberg's article, p. 72, or visit their Web site at www.wga.org. Contact SAG at 7065 Hollywood Boulevard, Hollywood, CA 90028 (213-465-4600) or visit their Web site, www.sag.org.

Above-the-line: Most of these costs are finalized prior to the start of principal photography. They include story rights, the purchase of the screenplay, and all writing fees. The producer and director fees are included here along with their support teams and expenses. All cast and casting expenses are part of the above-the-line costs. All necessary travel and living expenses must be reflected; all labor costs must be fringed.

Below-the-line: This is divided into three areas. The first is known as the *production period,* which refers to the direct costs during the filming of the production. Featured in these accounts are the production team (i.e., production manager and assistant directors), extras, the complete art department (including the production designer), set construction and set dressing, set operations, property, wardrobe, makeup and hair, camera, lighting, sound, transportation, locations, etc. Each account contains all equipment necessary for the making of the movie and all labor expenses, such as salaries, travel and living, and fringes. The second area refers to *postproduction,* which covers the editorial crew, music, post sound, film and lab, and credits. The third area is known as *total other* and refers to categories such as insurance and general expenses.

The cost of a studio production can range from under $10 million for smaller contemporary performance pieces to over $100 million for large visual effects action productions. It is common to give first-time directors

TITLE OF STUDIO or PRODUCTION COMPANY
"TITLE OF PRODUCTION"

DIRECTOR:		START DATE:	09/16/02
PRODUCERS:		FINISH DATE:	11/22/02
SCRIPT DATED:		PRINCIPAL PHOTOGRAPHY:	48 Days
BUDGET DATED:		POST PRODUCTION:	20 Weeks

Acct#	Category Title	Page	Total
1000	STORY RIGHTS	1	$0
1100	WRITING	1	$0
1200	PRODUCER	1	$0
1300	DIRECTOR	2	$0
1400	TALENT	2	$0
1700	TRAVEL & LIVING	3	$0
1900	**ATL FRINGES**		$0
	TOTAL ABOVE THE LINE		$0
2000	PRODUCTION STAFF	3	$0
2100	ART DEPARTMENT	4	$0
2200	CONSTRUCTION	4	$0
2300	SET DRESSING	5	$0
2400	PROPERTY	6	$0
2500	SPECIAL EFFECTS	6	$0
2600	SET OPERATIONS	6	$0
2700	ELECTRICAL	7	$0
2800	CAMERA	8	$0
2900	SOUND	8	$0
3100	WARDROBE	9	$0
3200	MAKEUP/HAIR	9	$0
3300	EXTRAS	10	$0
3400	PIC VEH & ANIMALS	10	$0
3500	TRANSPORTATION	11	$0
3600	LOCATION	11	$0
3700	FILM & LAB	12	$0
3800	2ND UNIT, INSERTS	13	$0
3900	TEST	14	$0
4000	STAGES, FACILITIES	14	$0
4100	VISUAL EFFECTS	15	$0
4200	CREATURE FABRICATION & OPERATION	16	$0
4900	**PRODUCTION FRINGES**		$0
	TOTAL PRODUCTION		$0
6100	EDITORIAL	16	$0
6300	MUSIC	17	$0
6400	POST PROD SOUND	18	$0
6500	POST TAPE, FILM & LAB	18	$0
6600	TITLES & OPTICALS	19	$0
6900	**POST PROD FRINGES**		$0
	TOTAL POST PRODUCTION		$0
7000	INSURANCE	19	$0
7100	PUBLICITY	19	$0
7500	GENERAL EXPENSE	19	$0
7900	**OTHER FRINGES**		$0
	TOTAL OTHER CHARGES		$0
	TOTAL ABOVE-THE-LINE		$0
	TOTAL BELOW-THE-LINE		$0
	TOTAL ABOVE & BELOW-THE-LINE		$0
	GRAND TOTAL		$0

their shot on the lower-budgeted movies. Regardless of the script or the team that is put together, there is always one consistent complaint: They never have enough time or money. Many times financial challenges are good for a film on a creative level, since cost issues force filmmakers to prioritize and put the money into what is most important in telling the story. A larger budget does not necessarily make a better movie. One of our most successful films, *American Beauty,* had one of our smallest budgets and shortest schedules. It ultimately garnered five Academy Awards, including Best Picture and Best Director for Sam Mendes.

While a producer is working on a preliminary budget and schedule, location scouting kicks in, whether domestic or overseas. Film commissions are contacted to supply location information, including visuals. The location manager does initial scouting, bringing back photos and video to show the director. Unions are contacted and issues of labor relations considered. Hotels are selected and rooms reserved, since living accommodations are crucial for such a large group. Group rates are negotiated with airlines or charter flights are put in place. Local weather charts are analyzed, with attention to sunrise and sunset, rainfall, snow, wind and temperature variations during the period of expected filming. On *Gladiator,* experienced crews were hired from the United States, England, Italy, Croatia, Malta and Morocco. On *Cast Away,* we shot in California, Texas, Tennessee, Russia and a remote island in Fiji. We returned to Fiji nine months later, after Tom Hanks lost a considerable amount of weight to show a transition of time. Unusual production issues included transporting people to and from the island locations, living on boats, and of course keeping footprints off the sand. Obviously, the demands of individual productions vary tremendously.

A script based in the past or the future can add millions to the budget. Consider, for example, a shot in which a man walks down a street and enters a store. On a contemporary film, the shot can be grabbed quickly and maybe even done with a small second unit. In a period film, that same action calls for removing parking meters and traffic lights, clearing out all the cars, controlling and diverting traffic, and adding extra police and security. If the camera looks down the end of the street, a visual effects extension may need to be added. Period vehicles must be found and brought in. All actors and extras must be fitted in advance with period costumes, hairstyles, and makeup. Each location, prop, and sign must be dressed to conform to the period, which can be extremely costly. A one-hour shot now can take half a day.

For most of the people employed in feature production, it is a freelance world. Since talent moves from picture to picture, selling yourself and staying employed is a large measure of your success. My production team negotiates most of the key department-head deals, including that of the director of photography, production designer, costume designer and editor. Below-the-line agents are working on getting their clients on these productions. In order to be prepared when needs arise in assembling a crew, we meet with these agents, interview their clients, watch film credits, view director of photography and visual effects supervisor reels and review submitted résumés.

As preparation heats up, department heads are busy reserving camera equipment, film stock, grip and electric equipment, as well as choosing soundstages and putting holds on dubbing and scoring stages. Bank accounts for the specific production are put in place and checks are printed. On location, where soundstages don't exist, a warehouse can double for a stage. Cover sets are built indoors and used if bad weather prevents scheduled exterior filming. The production schedule is constantly revised as more information is collected, locations are found, adjustments are made for actor availability, script revisions and other contingencies. We try to limit, first, the number of countries we need to film in, then the number of cities, and then the number of locations, as company moves are time-consuming and expensive. At this point, the production designer's team is busy choosing and designing sets, leading to set construction and set dressing, while the legal department is finalizing contracts, location agreements and script clearances.

Casting continues throughout the prep period. This leads to screen tests, along with hair, makeup and wardrobe tests. It is not uncommon to have multiple actors test for key roles. A chart known as a "day out of days" tracks each performer's schedule in the movie, listing start, finish, travel and holding days, and is used by casting directors to finalize talent deals. Casting can greatly impact the shooting schedule. For instance, if a major star has agreed to a supporting role contingent on being finished in three weeks because of a prior commitment, all of those scenes must be consolidated. This may call for moving back and forth between locations, shooting out of continuity, weekend work, or extended hours.

Depending on the movie, extended prep may be needed for training actors in special skills such as horseback riding, fencing, ice skating, singing, dancing, fighting or other physical training. For example, the key cast of *Saving Private Ryan* went through the equivalent of Army basic training. Stand-ins for the lead actors must have similar builds and coloring and be approved by the director of photography, since those people take the place of the actors when lighting is set up. Stunt doubles are cast as necessary, with wigs and hair coloring a common necessity. Most directors request at least a one-week rehearsal period to work with their key actors. A full cast read-through will be scheduled to include the director, producers, studio executives, script supervisor and writer. This process of reading through the entire script can be extremely helpful in analyzing character development and reviewing the pacing of the material.

Stunts and physical effects have become major factors in production and require the hiring of experts. It is vital to plan how each stunt will be carried out with the utmost safety. The first assistant director will hold a safety meeting prior to any stunt so that all department heads know what's going on and all questions are answered. Stunt doubles are used in place of the actors whenever possible. Multiple cameras give added coverage and limit the number of takes required. DreamWorks, like most studios, has a head of safety, who supervises all major stunts on our productions.

Although everyone always feels they need more prep, filming finally commences. The actors arrive on the set and rehearse with the director. After their actions have been blocked (that is, their movements have been worked out), a camera setup is finalized and the cast returns to makeup, hair and wardrobe while the crew starts lighting the set. The director usually has a proposed shot list for the director of photography, the first assistant director and the script supervisor. This list helps everyone manage and organize the day's work. Once the set is lit and the actors ready, filming begins.

During the day, the line producer and production manager check in with the studio with a progress report. After working for approximately six hours, the cast and crew break for a meal. The director, producers and assistant director usually meet during lunch and evaluate their progress. If they're not holding to their scheduled day, they discuss the necessary coverage and the possibility of cutting shots. A normal filming day is twelve hours, and everything is done to try to complete the scheduled work during that time frame. Dramatic measures to keep the production on schedule sometimes involve cutting the script (with the studio's approval), making sure all wide shots are addressed (while close-ups are cheated elsewhere on another day) or other considerations to keep from dropping a day. The cost of a day is only part of the issue; availability of actors and locations may make a change in the schedule logistically and financially prohibitive.

During filming, specific paperwork is used to inform the crew and document the day's events. Some of the responsibilities of the line producer, production manager and production accountant involve monitoring the costs of prep, shoot and wrap, projecting possible overages or savings, and generating a weekly cost report that is distributed to the studio. *Call sheets* are handed out, detailing the scenes to be shot the next day and the call times for each cast and crew member. *Production reports* stipulate what actually happened that day, all the people who worked and when, the scenes that were shot, the film used and any unusual events such as injuries or illnesses, all for future reference. (For examples of production paperwork, see the article by Christina Fong, p. 250.)

A good caterer can be essential and an incredible morale booster. Experienced caterers manage to prepare meals for hundreds to thousands of people under extreme weather conditions and extended hours. On *Gladiator*, menus were designed to allow Roman extras wearing white togas to eat fast, stay clean and return quickly to the Colosseum. Throughout the shooting day, snacks are always available at the craft service tables. Night shooting calls for hot soup, chili and other comfort food, heaters to keep people warm and covered holding areas for people to sit during inclement weather. Anticipating such common-sense requirements is extremely important.

While the crew is filming on one location, the production manager and production office are preparing future locations. Subsequent sets must be dressed and approved by the director. Actors, stunt people and additional crew who will be working in the future have their travel booked, get their plane tickets and *per diem* (daily living expenses) in hand, have their contracts signed and are flown to location. Special equipment is brought in as necessary. Film is sent to the lab and dailies prepared by the editor.

For troubleshooting a production, there is nothing like experience. To address a problem, it's useful to get everyone involved in one room, talk through the issues, and be clear about the steps necessary for resolution. Reduce the wasteful games of blame and finger-pointing and cut right to the heart of addressing the problems and finding solutions.

As scenes are completed, construction crews are busy striking those sets that have been shot. After the director views the dailies, editors start to cut the selected takes together in the editing suite, while the production crew continues to make the movie. Others are planning postproduction, such as booking dubbing and scoring stages and licensing music.

Once principal photography is over, all the final bills come in and must be analyzed. Some sets can be folded and held for possible reshoots. Set dressing, props and wardrobe might also be needed for reshoots, or have an afterlife in a sequel. Decisions are made to hold, sell or archive them. The director has ten weeks (per his or her DGA contract) to complete a rough cut, but this may vary depending on factors such as visual effects or release date. This rough cut of the movie with a temporary dub is used for research screenings. (For more on research screenings, see article by Kevin Yoder, p. 300.) Previewing with a recruited audience can be extremely helpful in evaluating what is working and what still needs to be addressed.

At some point, the film is locked. The music scoring and sound dubbing are completed. The titles are set (see title templates at the end of this article). The negative is cut, and the director of photography works with the lab on a color-corrected print of the film. Release prints are manufactured. The marketing executives have been working on the trailer for both theatrical and TV release, along with artwork for one-sheets, billboards and newspapers. Press kits are assembled for print and video journalists, and press junkets are scheduled in advance of the release date. The journey ends for most at the premiere and, we all hope, a successful opening weekend.

What follows is an outline of the key steps in filmmaking, and then generic main- and end-title templates. They represent the varied responsibilities of filmmakers and the diversity of jobs available on a feature film.

THE KEY STEPS OF FILMMAKING

Preproduction

1. Meetings with director, other producers and studio executives

2. Meetings with key studio personnel, including production, business affairs, project attorney, labor relations, and postproduction

3. Schedule the film production (board and shooting schedule)

4. Budget the production

5. Monitor changing script

6. Set up deals with guilds and unions

7. Find office space, set up production office and personnel

8. Hire key crew, including setting up interviews for director (director of photography, production designer, costume designer, editor, etc.)

9. Contact and meet with film commissions

10. Meet with city, state, and government officials

11. Scout locations

12. Study past weather conditions—highs, lows, sunrise, sunset, wind chill, snow, rain, clouds, hurricanes, cyclones, changing of the seasons, etc.

13. Find and hold stages

14. Negotiate crew deals

15. Negotiate equipment deals

16. Negotiate deals with hotels and airlines

17. Lock locations and sign contracts

18. Build and dress sets

19. Cast the film, including actors, stunts, stand-ins, extras, and animals

20. Physicals for the cast

21. Test wardrobe, makeup, hair, and key props

22. Select picture cars, cast trailers, mobile phones

23. Discuss set safety and sexual harassment issues with cast and crew

24. Create call sheets, production reports, start slips

25. Tech location scout for director and department heads

26. Production meeting

27. Cast rehearsal

28. Set up editing room and projection facility for viewing dailies

Production

1. Run the set

2. Daily production meetings

3. Daily and weekly cost reports

4. Communication with studio on creative and financial issues

5. Analyze the past, monitor the present, and prep the future

6. Monitor script changes

7. Adjust shooting schedules

8. View and analyze dailies

9. Deal with lab

10. Electronic press kit

11. Deal with publicity and press

12. Oversee visual effects

13. Handle all cast and crew travel

14. Wrap party

Postproduction

1. Monitor the wrap of principal photography

2. Examine final bills

3. Fold and hold sets, wardrobe, hair, makeup, set dressing, props

4. Return rentals; sell, store, or archive purchases

5. Shut down production office

6. View and analyze director's rough cut

7. Additional photography?

8. Sound effects

9. Visual effects

10. Looping

11. Scoring

12. Temp dub

13. Research screenings

14. Final dub

15. Preview

16. Cut negative

17. Create answer print

18. Cut trailers

19. Design poster and press kits

20. Schedule press junkets

21. Schedule release dates and distribution philosophy

22. Premiere the film

23. Release the film

24. Sell foreign rights, cable, TV, etc.

25. Fulfill all studio delivery requirements

MAIN TITLE CREDITS

Picture (logo)
Pictures presents
"Film by" and Production credits (if contractual)
Principal Cast (if contractual)
Title
Supporting Cast
Casting by
Co-Producers (if applicable)
Music by
Costume Designer
Film Editor
Production Designer
Director of Photography
Executive Producers (if applicable)
Produced by
Written by (Screenplay by)
Directed by

END TITLE CREDITS

Cast Crawl

Unit Production Manager
First Assistant Director
Second Assistant Director

Second Unit Director
Associate Producer
Visual Effects Supervisor/Producer

Crew

Art Director
Assistant Art Director
Set Decorator

Camera Operator
First Assistant Camera
Second Assistant Camera
Steadicam Operator
Still Photographer
Script Supervisor
Production Sound Mixer
Boom Operator
Cableman
Video Operator
Chief Lighting Technician (replaces Gaffer)
Asst. Chief Lighting Technician (replaces Best Boy)
Electricians
Rigging Gaffer
Key Grip
Best Boy Grip
Dolly Grip
Grips
Rigging Grip
Property Master
Assistant Property Master
Special Effects
Costume Supervisor
Women's Costumer
Men's Costumer
Key Makeup Artist
Makeup Artist
Key Hair Stylist
Hair Stylist
Production Coordinator
Assistant Production Coordinator
Production Secretary
Production Controller
Production Accountant
Assistant Accountant
Postproduction Accountant
Location Manager
Second Second Assistant Director
DGA Trainee
Casting Assistants
Extras Casting

Unit Publicist
Art Department Coordinator
Set Designer
Production Illustrator
Storyboard Artist
Leadperson
Swing Gang
Construction Coordinator
Construction Foreman
Labor Foreman
Greens Foreman
Paint Foreman
Standby Painter
Transportation Coordinator
Transportation Captain
Drivers
Craft Service
Caterer
Animal Handlers (if applicable)
Technical Advisors (if applicable)
Teacher (if applicable)
Assistants to the Producers
Assistant to Ms./Ms. _____ (Director)
Assistants to Mr./Ms. _____ (Stars)
Production Assistants
Stand-ins
First Aid
Supervising Sound Editor
Re-Recording Mixers
Postproduction Executive
Postproduction Supervisor
Postproduction Coordinator
Assistant Editor
Sound Editors
ADR Editors
ADR Mixer
ADR Group Coordinator
Foley Editor
Re-Recorded at
Music Editor
Orchestrator

Orchestrations
Executive in Charge of Music
Title Design
Titles & Opticals
Negative Cutter
Color Timer

Second (and other applicable) Units

Effects Vendors

The Producers Wish to Thank:

Filmed at:

Songs

Soundtrack Album

Color by

Prints by

Produced and Distributed on EASTMAN FILM

Camera Credit

If Panavision: FILMED WITH PANAVISION® CAMERAS & LENSES (logo)
(On one half of a title card on which card no other credit shall appear,
n/l/t the larger of the following (i) 33⅓% of the size of type used for the title
(ii) size of type used for the larger of the color, laboratory or sound credit.)

MPAA # _____	I.A.T.S.E.	AVID (if applicable)
(logo)	(bug)	(logo)

		SDDS Sony
Dolby ™ Digital	DTS ™ Sound	Dynamic Digital Sound
In Selected Theatres	In Selected Theatres	In Selected Theatres
(logo)	(logo)	(logo)

Copyright © Year, Studio LLC
All Rights Reserved

Studio LLC is the author and creator of this motion picture for purposes
of the Berne Convention and all national laws giving effect thereto,
and for purposes of copyright law in the United Kingdom.

AHA logo—American Humane Association disclaimer here (if applicable)

THIS MOTION PICTURE IS PROTECTED UNDER THE LAWS OF THE UNITED
STATES AND OTHER COUNTRIES. UNAUTHORIZED DUPLICATION,
DISTRIBUTION OR EXHIBITION MAY RESULT IN CIVIL LIABILITY AND
CRIMINAL PROSECUTION.

Distributed by

Studio

(logo)

If you experienced any conditions that detracted
from the theatrical presentation of this film, please call

1-800-PHONE-THX

or visit http://www.thx.com

Quality assurance services were provided by
the THX Theatre Alignment Program.

(TAP logo)

This film is rated _____ . (8 feet)

CHARLIE'S ANGELS: PRODUCTION PAPERWORK

by **CHRISTINA FONG,** second assistant director on *Charlie's Angels* and *Charlie's Angels: Full Throttle,* who started in the business as a production assistant, then moved up to second second assistant director on such features as *Virtuosity* and *Down Periscope.* Later, Ms. Fong become a second assistant director on features including *The Beautician and the Beast, Fear and Loathing in Las Vegas, Office Space, Whatever It Takes, Swordfish* and *Max Keeble's Big Movie,* as well as the TV series *Silk Stalkings,* the miniseries *The Siege at Ruby Ridge* and the TV movie *Hefner: Unauthorized.* A member of the Directors Guild of America, Ms. Fong has also worked as second assistant director on commercials for Continental Airlines, Foster's Beer, Coca-Cola, Pepsi and Ikea.

> "This report documents all that was accomplished during that day of shooting, including the sets used, locations, scenes completed, film inventory and cast and crew timings."

The director's unit on *Charlie's Angels* was comprised of director McG, who interviewed a number of first assistants and chose first assistant director Mark Cotone, who in turn interviewed several candidates before choosing me to work with him as second assistant director. A second second, Mark Constance, then came on board, as well as a number of production assistants (PAs). As director, McG was the key creative person on the movie, while unit production manager/executive producer Joseph M. Caracciolo was the key financial person on the set. These working relationships are formalized under our union, the Directors Guild of America; for precise details of job descriptions, working rules and more, visit the Directors Guild of America's Web site at www.dga.org.

When first assistant director Mark Cotone receives a final shooting screenplay, he goes through it, noting all the action, personnel and equipment required for each scene, adding lines between scenes and numbering scenes; later, when new pages come in, he adds them (for example, "scene 34A") to the numbering system that appears on all the paperwork discussed in this article.

Mark Cotone downloads all this information into his computer via the Movie Magic Scheduling program and uses it to fill in the breakdown sheets (including cast, props, set dressing, special effects, transportation). This data is then converted into one-line day-breakdown strips for each scene. These strips divide each day into shooting segments that comprise the breakdown board/one-liners, and the same information is integrated into the shooting schedule, which will be changed often during the course of production. Mark sees this process as an intense puzzle, placing all the necessary pieces into the most expedient and efficient schedule in order to shoot the picture. While the first assistant works on scheduling, the unit production manager is working on budget issues relating to shooting scenes. All of this planning is done in consultation with the director, the producers and the financing studio-distributor.

During shooting, the first assistant director (1st AD) is always on the set with the director, always focused, always on target, without a break (except maybe for lunch). While the 1st AD handles the efficiency of the shooting unit (the director working with actors), the 2nd AD handles the next-wider circle of communication (arranging background players, anticipating details of upcoming shots, prepping for the next day's work). The 2nd AD backs up the 1st AD on issues such as crew or cast tardiness, illness, injury; if a set must be changed; and on any conflicts which must be resolved before they intrude upon shooting. During a shot, while McG is working with the actors on performance, Mark is concentrating on that work, while also thinking about which shot is next, which setup is next, will it use a Steadicam or a crane and so forth; my job as 2nd AD is making sure all those advance details are ready, while placing background players.

On a typical shooting day, I carry a walkie-talkie that's attached to my belt and connected to a headset with sixteen channels (a numbering system isolates specific departments), a flashlight, a fanny pack containing pencils and paper, red and black markers (Sharpies), a Swiss army knife, white-out, gum (McG and Mark always like gum), and DGA and SAG representative's cards. I leave my Macintosh Powerbook in a secure trailer, along with all essential paperwork, including cast and crew lists, time cards, insurance paperwork and workers' compensation paperwork in case anyone is injured.

Now let's trace the flow of production paperwork, starting with the screenplay pages, through the breakdown sheets, breakdown board/one-liners, shooting schedule, call sheet and production report. These examples are furnished courtesy of Columbia Pictures, Flower Films producers Nancy Juvonen and Drew Barrymore, first assistant director Mark Cotone and director McG.

SCREENPLAY PAGES

The first day of shooting was planned to be low-key, since crew members and other talent are just getting to know each other and easing into the groove of long production days on an eighty-day schedule. Mark Cotone selected scenes 8, 15 and 11 for day 1. Scene 8 calls for Lucy Liu as Alex to ride a horse and accept a trophy, scene 15 has the three camouflaged angels pushing through bamboo, and scene 11 finds Lucy Liu as Alex winning a fencing match. For the athletics required in scenes 8 and 15, Lucy Liu already knew how to ride a horse, and took fencing lessons before shooting the fencing scene.

The scenes can be found on the following pages 7, 8 and 9 from the *Charlie's Angels* screenplay, written by Ryan Rowe & Ed Solomon and John August. Since this version is from the shooting script, scene numbers have been added in both margins; scene numbers don't appear in screenplays that haven't gone through the scheduling process. Page 7 is shorter than a full page because it is a revised page, dropped into the shooting script as a replacement; the newly omitted scene 5 had filled out the page. Also, the asterisks (*) in the right-hand margin indicate where new material has been added to this draft, compared to the last one.

4   CONTINUED: (2)   4 *

        FREEZE FRAME   *

5   OMIT   5 *

6   AND THE TITLE SEQUENCE BEGINS...   6 *

                          CHARLIE (V.O.)
                    Once upon a time...

        THREE FOURTH GRADE SCHOOL PHOTOS FILL THE FRAME, side by side
        by side. These are three very different girls.

        NATALIE, sports glasses and braces; a bit awkward and gangly,
        even shy.

        ALEX, in a boarding-school uniform with perfect pigtails, is
        sophisticated and self-possessed; a class act, even at ten.

        DYLAN, wild blond hair and a faded T-shirt, has a jaded,
        street-wise smirk; even at this young age, her isolation and
        disillusionment are masked by seeming confidence.

                          CHARLIE (CONT'D) (V.O.)
                    ...there were three very different
                    little girls.

        The triptych remains on screen. Now it shifts into:

7   NATALIE, in a "driver's ed" car, runs the orange cones at   7
        record speed -- and flawlessly. Behind her headgear and the
        Princess Leia buns, there's a mad grin. Her INSTRUCTOR is
        terrified. FREEZE.

8   ALEX, in riding gear, accepting her steeple-chase trophy.   8
        She knows where to look for the camera. FREEZE.

9   DYLAN, smoking with her tough-girl friends in the girls' room   9
     of her reform school. She looks up at the video camera watching
     them from a ceiling corner and flips it off. FREEZE.

                         CHARLIE (CONT'D) (V.O.)
                    Who grew up to be three very different
                    women.

TRIPTYCH CONTINUES

They're all WOMEN now, in their early twenties.

10   NATALIE, ON VIDEO, is a five-time champion on JEOPARDY!   10
     (That's what the titles say.) She's beaming as Alex Trebek
     shakes her hand.

11   ALEX, thrusting and parrying her way through a fencing match.   11
     She pulls off her mask, victorious.

12   DYLAN, one of about 20 POLICE ACADEMY RECRUITS standing at   12
     attention, watches as a FEMALE COP yells in another recruit's
     ear. Finally, Dylan can take no more. She slugs her,
     knocking her out cold.

                         CHARLIE (CONT'D) (V.O.)
                    But they have three things in common...

TRIPTYCH ENDS

13   The three angels meet up, walking together towards camera.   13
     All gorgeous, all self-assured. FREEZE FRAME.

                         CHARLIE (CONT'D) (V.O.)
                    They're brilliant. They're beautiful.
                    And they work for me.

14   Now, FIREBALL EXPLOSIONS completely fill the screen.   14

                         CHARLIE (CONT'D) (V.O.)
                    My name is Charlie.

ANGELS SILHOUETTES appear, in flames. New MUSIC kicks in.

                         "CHARLIE'S ANGELS"

...And a new title sequence takes over:

VARIOUS SHOTS: MONTAGE   (OVER MUSIC)

Credits continue as we watch the angels in action (from,
presumably, previous adventures...)

9.

14A   -- The three angels jump off the roof of an exploding building.   14A

15   -- Glistening from sweat, camouflaged angels push through a   15
       thick grove of bamboo.

16   -- Natalie plays stickball with a couple of kids.   16

17   -- The three angels rock out -- they're a band onstage at a   17
       club. Dylan's on bass, Alex sings and plays guitar. Natalie
       pounds the drums, a complete Tommy Lee.

17A   OMIT   17A

18   -- In prison blues, the angels escape from a female chain-   18
       gang.

19   -- OMIT   19 *

20   -- OMIT   20 *

20A   -- SLOW MOTION. Heat rises off the tarmac. In flight gear,   20A*
       holding helmets at their sides, three ASTRONAUTS stride   *
       shoulder-to-shoulder, straight toward us. Two are hulking   *
       all-American men with buzz cuts. The center astronaut --   *
       Alex.   *

21   -- Dylan, in a monk's outfit, finds a secret switch. She   21
       pushes back a bookcase to reveal secret stairs.

22   -- The three angels push their way through a roller-derby   22
       match. Dylan and Natalie whip-push jammer Alex ahead to
       smash the VILLAINESS.

22A   -- The three angels buy a paper, grin at the headline,   22A*
       "Mystery Women Save Mount Rushmore." As they high-five,   *
       Dylan's cone of gelato drops to the sidewalk. The angels   *
       look at it, look at each other...and just have to laugh.   *

23   OMIT   23

24   OMIT   24

       TITLE SEQUENCE ENDS.

25   INT.   TINY HOUSEBOAT BEDROOM - DAY   25

       CLOSE ON angelic looking Dylan, asleep in a tangle of ugly
       sheets. From another room, a man's voice SINGS along with
       the radio to "Angel of the Morning."

       Dylan stirs. Lifts her head, reveals the other side of her
       face -- lined with pillow creases and smudged make-up.

                                                         (CONTINUED)

BREAKDOWN SHEETS

Of the three scenes shot on day 1, scene 8 is the most complicated. Although the scene description runs only two lines on the screenplay page, the shooting segment is considered ⅛ of a page, the shortest segment in scheduling, which breaks down shooting segments of less than one page into eighths of a page, such as ⅛, ⅖, ⅜ and so on, up to ⅞ of a page.

The breakdown sheets, made by first assistant director Mark Cotone on Movie Magic Scheduling, list the people needed in front of the camera as well as all equipment, by category: cast members, background extras, props, livestock, set dressing, general notes, AD thoughts, a location question, grip and electric requirements, camera and safety. Notice how specifically the background extras are stipulated, down to gender, age and demeanor. One of the jobs of the second assistant director is the hiring of background players and making sure they are properly placed. When Mark determines that we need fifty background for a specific scene, together we'll break down how many riders, photographers, upscale spectators and aristocratic owners, by age range, gender and ethnicity. Other details on the breakdown sheet for this scene call for flash cameras from the 1940s and a "damn cooperative horse for Alex."

Scene 15 is the first scene with all three angels together: Drew Barrymore as Dylan, Lucy Liu as Alex and Cameron Diaz as Natalie. It calls for the three angels to sneak out of surrounding bamboo. Because scene 15 is simpler than scene 8, the breakdown sheet is simpler, calling for mobile bamboo listed under "greenery." Scene 11 finds Lucy Liu as Alex winning a fencing match, and the shot requires a fencing stunt double for Alex as well as an opponent fencer. Notice that, on the breakdown sheets, each cast member is identified with a number for cross-referencing in subsequent paperwork.

CHARLIE'S ANGELS
Breakdown Sheet

Sheet: **13**   I/E: **EXT**   Set: **TS - STEEPLE CHASE COURSE**   D/N: **Day**

Scenes: **8**   Pages: **1/8**

Synopsis: **A mounted Alex searches out the camera as she accepts her trophy.**

Location:

Sequence: Script Day: Script Page: **7**

Cast Members
- 2. Alex
- 2A. Alex Dble

Extras
- 1 Official Scorer
- 1 Real Female Rider (per Sheri)
- 1 Real Male Rider (per Sheri)
- 1 Timekeeper
- 1 Trophy Presenter In Official Ascot (Old Money - Fit - 55)
- 13 Upscale Spectators (7M/6F, 25-40 yrs)
- 3 Owners' Kids (18 to look younger)
- 4 Field Workers In Jumpsuits
- 4 Horsehandlers (3 per Sheri, 1 per Jack)
- 5 Aristocratic Owners (40-60 yrs)
- 5 Aristocratic Owners' Spouses (40-60 yrs)
- 5 Judges (3M/2F)
- 5 Younger Upscale Spectators (3M/2F, 20s)
- 6 Photographers (4M/2F, w/old School cameras)

Props
- 40's Old School Paparazzi Cameras W/flashbars
- Trophy

Livestock
- Damn Cooperative Horse For Alex
- Four Horses

Set Dressing
- Dye grass if needed
- Set Dressed The Day Before

Notes
Generator Near Set - Sound Under Theme
McG - Macro Shot Of Bulb Flashing
Transpo - Golf Carts?
Transpo - Trucks In On Friday

AD Thoughts
8A Shooting Call (Really 815A)

Crane Chassis On Road - Plywood Handy
Falling tree safety meeting
Leave B camera behind for "jump" shot
Macro Flashbulb At End Of Day
Set Up Course On Friday
Vic, Andy, Jon and Steve to join

Locations
How's The Grass Holding Up?

Grip/Electric
ELEC - 2 X 1200 Amp Gen
GRIP & ELEC - Stake Bed To Set
GRIP - 80' Condor
GRIP - Mirrors to help trees in distance
GRIP - Silk and negative fill (12 X 12 Min)
GRIP - Super Techno Crane - Early Call - Chasis On Road

Camera
Additional Body - High Speed

Safety Memos
Animal
Stunt

CHARLIE'S ANGELS
Breakdown Sheet

Sheet: **20A**   I/E: **EXT**   Set: **TS - BAMBOO CURTAIN**   D/N: **Day**

Scenes: **15**   Pages: **1/8**

Synopsis: **The three Angels sneak out of the orange-fogged bamboo.**

Location:

Sequence: Script Day: Script Page: **9**

Cast Members
1. Dylan
2. Alex
3. Natalie

Props
    Machete
    Nam Field Phone

Makeup
    Camo Makeup?
    Dripping Angels

Set Dressing
    Mobile Bamboo

Greenery
    Mobile Bamboo

Special FX
    Fx Fans
    Orange Smoke
    Wet Down/Up - Hose

AD Thoughts
If time a concern, Alex need not be in scene

Grip/Electric
ELEC - 2 X 1200 Amp Gen
GRIP - Dolly on sled wheels

Safety Memos
Smoke

CHARLIE'S ANGELS
Breakdown Sheet

Sheet: **16**   I/E: **EXT**   Set: **TS - MAUSOLEUM FENCING MATCH**   D/N: **Day**

Scenes: **11**   Pages: **1/8**

Synopsis: **Thrusting and parrying, Alex wins the match and removes her mask.**

Location:

Sequence: Script Day: Script Page: **8**

Cast Members
  2. Alex
  2D. Alex Fencing Dble (ST)
  93. Opponent Fencer (ST)
 	
Extras
    1 Butler w/silver pitcher -(Batman's Alfred)
 	
Props
    1 Silver Water Pitcher
    Epees
    Masks
 	
Set Dressing
    How's That Bald Spot - On The Grass
    Mobile Fencing Platform
 	
Greenery
    Foreground Branches
 	
Grip/Electric
ELEC - 2 X 1200 Amp Gen
GRIP - 20 x 20 Overhead
GRIP - 50' Track & Ramp
GRIP - Super Techno	

8	EXT TS - STEEPLE CHASE COURSE	Day	1/8 pgs.	2, 2A
	A mounted Alex searches out the camera as she accepts her trophy.			
15	EXT TS - BAMBOO CURTAIN	Day	1/8 pgs.	1, 2, 3
	The three Angels sneak out of the orange-fogged bamboo.			
11	EXT TS - MAUSOLEUM FENCING MATCH	Day	1/8 pgs.	2, 2D, 93
	Thrusting and parrying, Alex wins the match and removes her mask.			

--- END OF DAY 1 -- Mon, Jan 10, 2000 -- 3/8 pgs.

112	INT RED STAR SYSTEMS/CUBICLE AREA	Day	6/8 pgs.	1, 2, 3, 12, 18, 37
	A crisply dressed Alex and a manly Dylan and Natalie blow past the slightly confused Doris.			
113	INT RED STAR SYSTEMS/CUBICLE AREA	Day	4/8 pgs.	12, 37
	Wrinkly-Shirt Guy and his Friend are SO going to see the hot seminar chick.			

--- END OF DAY 2 -- Tue, Jan 11, 2000 -- 1 2/8 pgs.

| 42Apt | EXT TASTEE FREEZE | Day | 1 3/8 pgs. | 1, 2, 3, 98 |
| | While the girls wait for their order, Natalie gets a kidnapper's composite off her laptop. | | | |

--- END OF DAY 3 -- Wed, Jan 12, 2000 -- 1 3/8 pgs.

26	EXT TINY HOUSEBOAT BEDROOM	Day	4/8 pgs.	1, 13
	Chad thinks it's magic. Dylan thinks it's a mistake. He pleads. She splits.			
25	INT TINY HOUSEBOAT BEDROOM	Day	7/8 pgs.	1, 13
	A skinny shirtless Chad offers a naked Dylan his eggs.			

--- END OF DAY 4 -- Thu, Jan 13, 2000 -- 1 3/8 pgs.

33pt	EXT PARK	Day	1/8 pgs.	6
	PLAYBACK - CNN profile - Eric Knox jogging through a park without his dog.			
16	EXT TS - STICK BALL STREET	Day	1/8 pgs.	3
	Natalie plays stickball with a couple of kids.			
141	I/E HOUSE IN THE HILLS	Night	7/8 pgs.	1, 1A, 26, 27, 153
	Two ten year old boys, joysticks in hand, have their "naked girl" prayers answered.			

--- END OF DAY 5 -- Fri, Jan 14, 2000 -- 1 1/8 pgs.

*** END WEEK #1 ***

7	EXT TS - DRIVER'S ED COURSE	Day	1/8 pgs.	3, 3A, 97, 200
	An icy-calm Natalie runs the cones in record time while her instructor fills his Depends.			
9	INT TS - REFORM SCHOOL GIRLS' ROOM	Day	2/8 pgs.	1, 152, 153
	A smoking Dylan flips off the girls' room video camera.			
12	INT TS - CONTINUING EDUCATION	Day	2/8 pgs.	1, 79
	Dylan punches out her Police Academy Officer/Instructor. The students are impressed.			

--- END OF DAY 6 -- Mon, Jan 17, 2000 -- 5/8 pgs.

| 29C | INT NATALIE'S APARTMENT - FRONT DOOR | Night | 6/8 pgs. | 3, 137 |
| | It's the UPS Man with an early morning delivery. | | | |

** COMPANY MOVE TO STAGE **

29B	INT NATALIE'S APARTMENT - BEDROOM	Night	4/8 pgs.	3
	Natalie's performing the morning ritual when the doorbell rings.			
29D	INT NATALIE'S APARTMENT - FRONT DOOR	Night	7/8 pgs.	3
	Natalie arms herself before heading out into a new world of leisure time enjoyment.			

--- END OF DAY 7 -- Tue, Jan 18, 2000 -- 2 1/8 pgs.

14Apt	EXT TS - ROOFTOP	Day	1/8 pgs.	1, 2, 3, 201
	Hey look, this one's back...The three angels jump off an exploding rooftops.			
142pt	EXT TOWNSEND DETECTIVE AGENCY/SUNSET BOULEVARD	Night	1 1/8 pgs.	1, 2, 3
	The Angels back at the Townsend Agency as we...hand off to second unit.			

--- END OF DAY 8 -- Wed, Jan 19, 2000 -- 1 2/8 pgs.

| 126 | EXT BUSY SIDEWALK CAFE | Night | 1 1/8 pgs. | 14, 45, 96 |
| | Alex is killed eating dinner with Jason. Hey, who's that Director? | | | |

--- END OF DAY 9 -- Thu, Jan 20, 2000 -- 1 1/8 pgs.

BREAKDOWN BOARD/ONE-LINER

The scenes are then converted to one-liners, creating a virtual breakdown board. The breakdown board traditionally was a long board with several attached sides, each measuring about ten inches by fifteen inches, that would open up to a length of six feet or more. One-line cardboard strips of shooting segments would be placed on the board, rearranged and shuffled to create the most practical order of shooting possible.

Today, a virtual breakdown board is used and is known as a one-liner. Each shooting segment can be easily moved around in the computer to propose and compare different orders of scheduling depending on cost, cast availability, and whether set construction or locations are ready. On page 261 is an excerpt from the beginning of the *Charlie's Angels* one-liner that shows the three scenes scheduled for day 1 by screenplay heading (INT., EXT., plus set description), synopsis, whether it is day or night, number of pages and cast members required, designated by assigned number. Each shooting day is divided by a thick black line that indicates the calendar day and total number of pages shot. The complete one-liner can run ten to fifteen pages.

SHOOTING SCHEDULE

The shooting schedule contains the data from the breakdown sheets, this time placed in the proposed order of shooting.

The category "AD Thoughts" is something Mark Cotone added, with specific notes pertaining to shooting each scene: Will there be plywood for the crane to ride on, if needed? What about that unstable tree on location? As second assistant, I will remind Mark about these and other issues during the shooting day.

The next two pages reproduce the first two pages of the shooting schedule, featuring day 1 of shooting, which was Monday, January 10, 2000.

CALL SHEET

The call sheet (page 265–266) is created by the second assistant director and is always handed out the day before (in this case, the Friday before the first Monday of shooting). It is designed to pack all information needed by cast and crew onto one easy-to-read form. The top segment includes the now-familiar one-liners, scene numbers, cast numbers and page count, with the addition of the shooting location. For example, the steeplechase

CHARLIE'S ANGELS

Shooting Schedule

SHOOT DAY #1 -- Mon, Jan 10, 2000

| Scene #8 | EXT - TS - STEEPLE CHASE COURSE - Day | 1/8 Pgs. |

A mounted Alex searches out the camera as she accepts her trophy.

Cast Members
2. Alex
2A. Alex Dble

Extras
1 Official Scorer
1 Real Female Rider (per Sheri)
1 Real Male Rider (per Sheri)
1 Timekeeper
1 Trophy Presenter In Official Ascot (Old Money - Fit - 55)
13 Upscale Spectators (7M/6F, 25-40 yrs)
3 Owners' Kids (18 to look younger)
4 Field Workers In Jumpsuits
4 Horsehandlers (3 per Sheri, 1 per Jack)
5 Aristocratic Owners (40-60 yrs)
5 Aristocratic Owners' Spouses (40-60 yrs)
5 Judges (3M/2F)
5 Younger Upscale Spectators (3M/2F, 20s)
6 Photographers (4M/2F, w/old School cameras)

Locations
How's The Grass Holding Up?

AD Thoughts
8A Shooting Call (Really 815A)
Crane Chassis On Road - Plywood Handy
Falling tree safety meeting
Leave B camera behind for "jump" shot
Macro Flashbulb At End Of Day
Set Up Course On Friday
Vic, Andy, Jon and Steve to join

Props
40's Old School Paparazzi Cameras W/flashbars
Trophy

Grip/Electric
ELEC - 2 X 1200 Amp Gen
GRIP & ELEC - Stake Bed To Set
GRIP - 80' Condor
GRIP - Mirrors to help trees in distance
GRIP - Silk and negative fill (12 X 12 Min)
GRIP - Super Techno Crane - Early Call - Chasis On Road

Set Dressing
Dye grass if needed
Set Dressed The Day Before

Camera
Additional Body - High Speed

Safety Memos
Animal
Stunt

Livestock
Damn Cooperative Horse For Alex
Four Horses

CHARLIE'S ANGELS
Shooting Schedule

Scene #15   **EXT - TS - BAMBOO CURTAIN - Day**   1/8 Pgs.
The three Angels sneak out of the orange-fogged bamboo.

Cast Members
1. Dylan
2. Alex
3. Natalie

AD Thoughts
If time a concern, Alex need not be in scene

Props
Machete
Nam Field Phone

Grip/Electric
ELEC - 2 X 1200 Amp Gen
GRIP - Dolly on sled wheels

Set Dressing
Mobile Bamboo

Makeup
Camo Makeup?
Dripping Angels

Greenery
Mobile Bamboo

Special FX
Fx Fans
Orange Smoke
Wet Down/Up - Hose

Safety Memos
Smoke

Scene #11   **EXT - TS - MAUSOLEUM FENCING MATCH - Day**   1/8 Pgs.
Thrusting and parrying, Alex wins the match and removes her mask.

Cast Members
2. Alex
2D. Alex Fencing Dble (ST)
93. Opponent Fencer (ST)

Extras
1 Butler w/silver pitcher - Batman's Alfred)

Props
1 Silver Water Pitcher
Epees
Masks

Grip/Electric
ELEC - 2 X 1200 Amp Gen
GRIP - 20 x 20 Overhead
GRIP - 50' Track & Ramp
GRIP - Super Techno

Set Dressing
How's That Bald Spot - On The Grass
Mobile Fencing Platform

Greenery
Foreground Branches

END OF DAY #1 - 3/8 Total Pages

SHOOT DAY #2 -- Tue, Jan 11, 2000

Scene #112   **INT - RED STAR SYSTEMS/CUBICLE AREA - Day**   6/8 Pgs.
A crisply dressed Alex and a manly Dylan and Natalieblow past the slightly confused Doris.

Cast Members
1. Dylan
2. Alex
3. Natalie
12. Wrinkle-Shirt Guy
18. Doris
37. WSG's Friend

Extras
80 Computer Geeks (M - under 30 - that wierd hair and braces look)

AD Thoughts
20 Computer Faces
Be ready to add something to this day

Grip/Electric
ELEC - 1200 Amp Gen

Makeup
Girls are guys

"Video" Playback
Screen Displays

CALL SHEET	"CHARLIE'S ANGELS"	DATE: MON. JAN. 10, 2000

Producers: Leonard Goldberg, Drew Barrymore, Nancy Juvonen, Betty Thomas, Jenno Topping — DAY: 1 OF 80

Executive Producer: Joe Caracciolo	Director: MC G	Prod. #: K30303	CREW CALL: 6A

Weather: DAY - MOSTLY SUNNY 75 — NIGHT - CLEAR 55 — Shooting Call: 7:30A

Sunrise: 6:59A   Sunset: 5:02P   CLOSED SET - NO VISITORS WITHOUT PRIOR APPROVAL FROM PRODUCTION OFFICE

SET	SCENES	CAST #'S	D/N	PAGES	LOCATION
EXT. TS STEEPLE CHASE COURSE:	8PT	2, 2C, X, XX, A		1/8	HUNTINGTON LIBRARY
A MOUNTED ALEX SEARCHES OUT THE CAMERA, ACCEPTS TROPHY					1151 OXFORD ROAD
EXT. TS - BAMBOO CURTAIN:	15	1, 2, 3		1/8	SAN MARINO, CA
THE THREE ANGELS SNEAK OUT OF THE ORANGE FOGGED BAMBOO					CONTACT: LEAH
EXT. TS - MAUSOLEUM FENCING MATCH:	11	2, 2B, 93, X, XX, A		1/8	(626)-405-2215
ALEX WINS THE MATCH AND REMOVED HER MASK					CREW PARKING-SEE MAP
WHEN COMPANY MOVES TO FENCING SET A STILL PHOTO WILL BE SHOT BY BAMBOO SET:					PARK AT LOCATION AS
EXT. ARMY CAMP (STILL PHOTO):		A			DIRECTED
YOUNG CHARLIE & YOUNG KNOX FATHER BY ARMY BASECAMP					T.G. PG 566 C-6
B CAMERA TO SHOOT:					A HOT BREAKFAST
EXT. TS HORSE JUMPING:	8PT	2C, X, A		.	WILL BE PROVIDED AT
		TOTAL PGS:		3/8	CREW CALL

#	CAST AND DAY PLAYERS		ROLE	P/U	MAKEUP	SET CALL	REMARKS
1	DREW BARRYMORE	W	DYLAN	6:15A	7A	9A	P/U @ 6:15A PER CHRIS
2	LUCY LIU	W	ALEX		6A	7:30A	RPT TO BASECAMP
3	CAMERON DIAZ	W	NATALIE		6:30A	9A	RPT TO BASECAMP
2B	ROBERTA BROWN	SWF	ALEX FENCING DBL		10:30A	12:45P	RPT TO CREW PARKING
2C	DAWN THOMPSON	SWF	ALEX RIDING DBL		6A	7:30A	RPT TO CREW PARKING
93	MARK RYAN	SWF	FENCING OPPONENT		11A	12:45P	RPT TO CREW PARKING
X	VIC ARMSTRONG	W	STUNT COORDINATOR	.		6A	RPT TO CREW PARKING
XX	ANDY ARMSTRONG	SWF	CO-COORDINATOR	.		6A	RPT TO CREW PARKING
	CASEY, WEISINGER, NISHAWAKI		STUNT DBLS		TRAINING @ PARK PLAZA		
	LIU, HEE, EVANS, WARREN, MARTIN		STUNT DBLS		TRAINING @ PARK PLAZA		

ATMOSPHERE AND STANDINS		SPECIAL INSTRUCTIONS	
ALL BG RPT TO CREW PARKING		PROPS:	SC. 8: OLD SCHOOL CAMERA W/ FLASHES, FLASHBARS, TROPHY
RPT	DESCRIPTION		SC. 15: MESHETTE, FIELD PHONE
	STANDINS		SC. 11: SILVER WATER PITCHER, EPEES, MASKS
6A	AMY		STILL PHOTO: BACKPACKS, ARMY BELTS, DOG TAGS
8A	HEATHER, MELANIE	B CAMERA:	SHOOT HORSE JUMPING WHILE 1ST UNIT MOVES TO BAMBOO CURTAIN SET
	ATMOSPHERE	EFX:	SC. 15: FANS, ORANGE SMOKE, WET DOWN, STILL PHOTO: SMOKE
	SC. 8:	PROD:	TREE SAFETY, 4 MUHAIR STATIONS
6A	3 REAL RIDERS (1M, 2F - SHERRI)	CAMERA:	SC. 8: 2ND CAMERA, HIGH SPEED
6A	3 HORSE HANDLERS (SHERRI)	SET DRESS:	SC. 15: MOBILE BAMBOO, SC. 11: GREENS, MOBILE FENCING PLATFORM
6A	5 OWNERS, 5 OWNERS WIFE		STILL PHOTO: TENT
6A	3 OWNERS KIDS	GRIP/ ELEC:	SC. 8: 2 X 1200 AMP GENNIES, STAKEBEDS TO SET, 80' CONDOR, MIRRORS
6A	13 UPSCALE SPECTATORS		TO HELP TREES IN DISTANCE, SILK AND NEGATIVE FILL (12 X 12 MIN),
6A	5 YOUNGER UPSCALE SPECS		SUPER TECHNO CRANE - CHASIS ON ROAD, PRE-CALL
6A	6 PHOTOGRAPHERS		SC. 11: 20 X 20 OVERHEAD, 50' TRACK & RAMP, SUPER TECHNO CRANE,
6A	4 FIELD WORKERS		2 X 1200 AMP GENNIES
6A	1 TIME KEEPER	MU:	SC. 15: SOME CAMO MU, ANGELS SWEAT, STILL PHOTO: SWEAT
6A	1 TROPHY PRESENTER		RENATA TO VISIT SET @ 4P
6A	1 OFFICIAL SCORER	TRANSPO:	STILL PHOTO: ARMY JEEP
	STILL PHOTO:	NOTE:	ATMOS. SMOKE WILL BE USED ON SET THE MSDS REPORT AVAIL W/ EFX COORD.
8:30A	YOUNG KNOX, YOUNG CHARLIE	WRANGLER:	SC. 8: 3 JUMPING HERO HORSES, STANDING HERO HORSE, 2 BG HORSES
	SC. 11:	NOTE:	ABSOLUTELY NO PERSONAL CARS OR PETS ALLOWED ON SET OR BASECAMP
10:30A	1 BUTLER	WARD:	STILL PHOTO: OLD CAMMIES

ADVANCE SHOOTING NOTES

DATE	SCENE	SET	CAST	D/N	PAGES
DAY 2	112	INT. CUBICLE AREA: ALEX, DYLAN BLOW PAST DORIS	1, 2, 3, 12, 18, 37, A	D-5	7/8
TUE 1/11	113	INT. CUBICLE AREA: THEY'RE ARE GOING TO SEE THE CHICKS	12, 37, A	D-5	4/8
1 3/8 PG					
STAGES					
DAY 3	42A	EXT. TASTEE FREEZE: GIRLS ORDER, NAT PULLS UP KIDNAPPER	1, 2, 3, 98, A	D-1	1 2/8
WED 1/12					
1 2/8 PG					
TORRANCE					
DAY 4	26	EXT. HOUSEBOAT: CHAD THINKS IT'S MAGIC, DYLAN DOESN'T	1, 13	D-1	5/8
THU 1/13		MINI- COMPANY MOVE			
4/8 PG	25	INT. HOUSEBOAT: CHAD OFFERS DYAN HIS EGGS	1, 13	D-1	7/8
SAN PEDRO					

U.P.M.: Joe Caracciolo	First Asst. Dir.: Mark Cotone	2nd Asst. Dir.: Christina Fong
Prod. Office:	(213)534-3020, (213)534-3021 (F)	2nd 2nd Asst. Dir.: Mark Constance
	1201 W. 5th Street #M180, LA, CA 90017	Set Pager # (213)303-3112

Quote of the day   "Nothing, of course, begins at the time you think it did" – Lillian Hellman

Song of the day   "START ME UP"   "HERE WE GO AGAIN"   "AIN'T NO STOPPING US NOW"

"CHARLIE'S ANGELS"
Call Sheet

CREW CALL: 6A
DATE: MON. JAN 10, 2000

No	Title	Name	Call	No	Title	Name	Call	No	Title	Name	Call
	PRODUCTION				SPECIAL EFFECTS				TRANSPORTATION		
1	Director	MC G	6A	1	SFX Coordinator	Paul Lombardi	O/C	1	Trans Captain	John Orlebeck	O/C
1	UPM	Joe Caracciolo	O/C	1	SFX Foreman	Dick Wood	6A	1	Trans Co-Captain	Jeff Couch	O/C
1	Production Supervisor	David Grant	O/C	3	SFX Technicians	per Lombardi	6A	1	Picture Car Driver	Dave Sevenn	O/C
1	1st Assistant Director	Mark Cotone	O/C					1	Camera Trk/ Video Trlr		
1	2nd Assistant Director	Christina Fong	5:30A		MAKE-UP AND HAIR			1	Grip Truck		
1	2nd 2nd Asst. Director	Mark Constance	5:30A	1	Dept. Head Make-Up Artist	Kimberly Greene	5:42A	1	Electric Truck		
1	Set Staff Assistant	Jeff Bilger	5:30A	1	Key Make - Up Artist	Joni Powell	5:42A	1	Prop Trailer		ALL
1	Set Staff Assistant	Shea Varge	5:30A	1	Ms. Lui Make - Up Artist	David C. Forrest	5:42A	1	Craft Service Truck		CALLS
1	Set Staff Assistant	Julie Shack	5:30A	1	Ms. Diaz Make - Up Artist	Cheryl Nick	6:12A	2	Make-Up/Hair Trailers		PER
1	Set Staff Assistant	Kenny Vasquez	5:30A	1	Make Up Artist	Denise Dellevalle	5:42A	2	Wardrobe Trailers		
1	Set Staff Assistant	Matt Byerts	5:30A	1	Make Up Artist	TBD	5:42A	8	Room Honeywagon		O
1	1st A.D. 2nd Unit	Steve Love	6A					4	Single Trailers		R
1	2nd A.D. 2nd Unit	Cindy Potthast	6A	1	Dept. Head Hairstylist	Barbara Olvera	6A	2	Room Trailers		L
2	2nd Unit Set Staff Assistant	O'Banion, Bruning	6A	1	Key Hairstylist	Lori McCoy - Bell	5:42A	3	Room Trailers		E
1	Script Supervisor	Jayne-Anne Tenggren	6A	1	Ms. Lui Hairstylist	Barbara Lorenz	5:42A	1	Fuel Truck / Tow Jenny		B
1	Associate Producer	Amanda Goldberg	O/C	1	Ms. Diaz Hairstylist	Ann Morgan	6:12A	5	Stakebeds/ Crew cabs		E
	CAMERA			1	Hair Stylist	Alisha Trippi	5:42A	6	Golf carts		C
1	Director of Photography	Russell Carpenter	6A	1	Hair Stylist	Audrey Stern	5:42A	4	Maxi vans		K
1	"A" Cam. Operator	Michael St. Hilaire	6A		SFX Makeup						
1	1st Assistant "A" Camera	Dennis Seawright	6A						Add'l Honeywagon		
1	2nd Asst. "A" Camera	Kirk Bloom	6A		WARDROBE			2	Set Dressing Trk		
1	Loader	Scott Ronnow	6A	1	Costume Designer	Joseph G. Aulisi	O/C	2	Special EFX Truck		
1	Operator "B" Camera	Mark Jackson	6A	1	Costume Supervisor	Cheryl Beasley	O/C	2	Elec / Grip Rigging Trks		
1	1st Asst. "B" Camera	Eric Brown	6A	1	Asst. Costume Designer	Florence Megginson	O/C	2	Construction Trk / Trlr		
1	2nd Asst. "B" Camera	Vince Mata	6A	1	Asst. Costume Designer	Randy Gardell	O/C				
1	D. P. 2nd Unit	Jonathan Taylor	6A	1	Key Set Costumer	Lucy Campbell	O/C				
1	Operator "C" Camera			1	Set Costumer	Cynthia Black	5:42A	1	Transpo Office Coord.	Barry Bardsley	O/C
1	1st Assistant "C" Camera			1	Set Costumer	Susan Lichtman	5:42A	X	Picture cars: (see front)		
1	Steadicam Operator	Bob Ulland	-	1	Add'l Set Costumer	Kim Holley	5:42A		LOCATIONS		
1	Steadicam 1st A.C.			1	Add'l Set Costumer	Larrey Velasco	5:42A	1	Location Manager	Marc Strachan	O/C
1	Video Asst	Bryce Shields	6A					1	Asst. Location Manager	Scott Mosher	O/C
2	24 Frame Playback	Dan Dobson + 1	-					1	Location Scout	Baron Miller	O/C
1	Still Photographer	Darren Michaele	7A					8	Security	Per Locations	Per Loc
	GRIP				ART DEPARTMENT			1	Police	Per Locations	Per Loc
1	Key Grip	Lloyd Moriarity	6A	1	Production Designer	J. Michael Riva	O/C	-	Fire Safety Officer	Per Locations	Per Loc
1	Best Boy Grip	Jeffrey (JJ) Johnson	6A	1	Supervising Art Director	David Klassen	O/C		PRODUCTION OFFICE		
1	Dolly Grip	John Murphy	6A	1	Art Director	Richard Mays	O/C	1	Production Coordinator	Tracy Kettler	O/C
1	Grip	Ray Garcia	6A					1	Asst. Production Coord.	Jennifer Webb	O/C
1	Grip	Sid Hajdu	6A	1	Sr. Set Designer	Clare Bosanpulis	O/C	1	Production Secretary	Angela Pritchard	O/C
1	Grip	Randy Smith	6A	1	Set Designer	Dawn Manser	O/C	1	Prod. Receptionist	Judy Biggs	O/C
1	Grip	Ron Bentoyo	6A	1	Set Designer	Noelle King	O/C	1	Office Staff Assistant	VW Scheich	O/C
	Grip			1	Illustrator	Jack Johnson	O/C	1	Office Staff Assistant	Karin Oughourlian	O/C
	Grip			2	Storyboard Artist	A. Martinez, M. Baisi	O/C	1	Mr. MC G's Asst.	Rebecca Penrose	O/C
	Grip							1	Mr. Goldberg's Asst.	Ursula	O/C
								1	Ms. Thomas' Asst.	Jason Behrman	O/C
1	Rigging Key Grip	Charley Gilleran	O/C	2	Staff Assistants	A. Sears, N. Martino	O/C	1	Ms. Barrymore's Asst.	Chris Miller	O/C
1	Rigging Best Boy Grip	Michael McFedden	O/C		SET DECORATING			1	Ms. Juvonen's Asst.	Cate Engel	O/C
X	Rigging Grip	Per Gilleran	O/C	1	Set Decorator	Lauri Gaffin	O/C	1	Ms. Topping's Asst.	Erin Stam	O/C
				1	Leadman	Ben Woolverton	O/C	1	Mr. Caracciolo's Asst.	Rachel Kielborn	O/C
	ELECTRIC			2	Swing Gang	D. McKay, M. Lopez	O/C		ACCOUNTING		
1	Gaffer	John Buckley	6A	2	Swing Gang	T. Little, T. Doherty	O/C	1	Production Accountant	Elizabeth Tompkins	O/C
1	Best Boy Elec.	Michael Yope	6A	3	Swing Gang	Rice, Ladish, Perez	O/C	1	1st Asst. Accountant	Victoria Gregory	O/C
1	Electrician	Bill Fine	6A	1	On Set Dresser	Val Harris	6A	2	2nd Asst. Accountant	T. Dlanda, L. Hernandez	O/C
1	Electrician	Doug Keegan	6A	1	Shopper	Amy Feldman	O/C	1	2nd Asst. Accountant	Bettina Vidaurreta	O/C
1	Electrician	John Fine	6A	1	Drapery Foreman	Steve Baer	O/C	1	Construction Accountant	Dee Homik	O/C
	Electrician	John Zirbel	6A					1	Payroll Accountant	Angela Randazzo	O/C
	Electrician			1	Construction Coordinator	Well Hadfield	O/C	2	Clerks	T. Shapiro, L. Tolan	O/C
	Electrician			1	General Foreman	James Walker	O/C		CASTING		
				1	Loc. Foreman	Jan Young	O/C	1	Casting Director	Kim Davis	O/C
				1	Toolman	Kelly Birrer	O/C	1	Casting Director	Justine Baddeley	O/C
				1	Paint Foreman	David Goldstein	O/C	1	Casting Associate	Jennifer Ricchiazzi	O/C
1	Rigging Gaffer	Mike Amorelli	O/C	1	Plaster Foreman	Luke Adkins	O/C	1	Background Casting	Tony Hobbs	O/C
1	Rigging Best Boy Elec.	Mark Marino	O/C	1	Greensman	Dennis Butterworth	6A	1	Background Casting Asst.	Lisa Gabaldon	O/C
X	Rigging Electric	Per Ammo	O/C	1	Stand By Painter	Billy Hoyt	6A		EDITORIAL		
	SOUND							1	Editor	Jim Miller	O/C
1	Sound Mixer	Willie Burton	6A		THE LEG ACTION			1	1st Asst. Editor	Ken Terry	O/C
1	Boom Operator	Marvin Lewis	6A	1	Galahad	Tony Masnardi	9A	1	2nd Asst. Editor	Lisa Dannenbaum	O/C
1	Cable Person	Bob Harris	6A	1	Publicist	Guy Adan	O/C	1	Asst. Editor	Adam Hernandez	O/C
				5	Paws for Effect	Sheri + 4	6A	1	Avid	Michael Koz	O/C
				1	Medic	Hal Fowler	6A		CRAFT SERVICE/ CATERING		
86	Radios		Truck	1	Medic Training	Henry Humphreys	9A	1	Craft Service	Mike Randolph - RDY	6A
	PROPS			1	Martial Arts Specialist	Cheung-Yan Yuen	9A	1	Craft Service	John Randolph - RDY	6A
1	Property Master	Russell Bobbitt	6A	2	Wire Technician	Hu Chen, Qiao Tan	9A	X	Tony's Catering		
1	Asst. Property Master	David Seltzman	6A	2	Wire Technician	Kim Wong, Tin Yick	9A	135	Breakfasts	Served	6A
1	Assistant Props	Mike Suhy	6A	2	Wire Technician	Fong Tai Chan	9A	135	Lunches	Served	12P
1	Assistant Props			1	Liaison	Daxing Zhang	9A	60	Extras Breakfast	Served	6A
				1	Training Assistant	Mark Carter	9A	60	Extras Lunches	Served	12P

HOSPITAL: ST. LUKES MEDICAL CENTER (626)797-1411
2632 E. WASHINGTON BLVD.
PASADENA, CA 91107, T.G. PG 566 E-1

SAFETY IS OF PRIMARY IMPORTANCE, PLEASE REPORT ANY UNSAFE OR POTENTIALLY HAZARDOUS CONDITIONS TO THE FIRST ASSISTANT DIRECTOR

"CHARLIE'S ANGELS"

course used for the horse-riding scene was shot at the beautiful Huntington Library in San Marino, not far from Los Angeles.

The next segment focuses on the cast and day players, with their pickup times, time to report to makeup, and set call. For instance, Lucy Liu had to be in makeup by 6 A.M. (same time as the crew call) and be on set by 7:30, the shooting call. Stunt coordinators Vic and Andy Armstrong (designated as cast numbers X and XX) must also be on set at 6 A.M. SWF indicates whether someone will start, work or finish on that day.

Next is atmosphere and stand-ins, and their report times, so that makeup and wardrobe know when the different character types will arrive. The section "special instructions" contains notes for specific departments. For example, under MU, or makeup, facial camouflage and sweat are needed for scene 15. Because scene 8 uses horses, a wrangler is required, along with a representative from the Humane Society.

The section "advance shooting notes" is derived from the one-liner, covering two or three days so that personnel can anticipate upcoming needs and locations.

The back of the call sheet (page 266) lists the entire crew by name and job title and their call, or starting times. Further down is the address and phone number of the nearest hospital, as a safety precaution. Notice that my own call for the next day is 5:30 A.M. People with O/C next to their names are "on call" and on a separate schedule. They are not involved in the day's shooting but are working, perhaps on a set for the next day.

The call sheet is usually given to cast and crew late in the shooting day, since it covers the following day's work. On a project as complex as *Charlie's Angels,* I would pass around a "pre-pre" call sheet to crew members early in the morning so that any equipment orders, scheduling issues or shooting details are handled as soon as possible.

PRODUCTION REPORT

The daily production report is based on a form endorsed by Columbia Pictures that I give to the 2nd 2nd AD, who fills it out by hand before it goes to the UPM (unit production manager) for approval. Then the figures are typed in for the style that is reproduced here. This report documents all that was accomplished during that day of shooting, including the sets used, locations, scenes completed, film inventory and cast and crew timings. Notice how detailed the film inventory is, broken down by footage loaded, good, no good, wasted, and total footage used, along with summaries.

Next is the cast and character list, with the actual clock readings in

"CHARLIE'S ANGELS"
DAILY PRODUCTION REPORT

Producer Leonard Goldberg, Drew Barrymore, Nancy Juvonen, Betty Thomas, Jenno Topping	Day/Date:	MONDAY, 1/10/00
Exec. Producer/UPM: Joe Caracciolo	Start Date:	January 10, 2000
Director McG	Scheduled Finish Date:	May 9, 2000
Prod. No. K30303	Estimated Finish Date:	May 9, 2000
Weather		

	SHOOT	TEST	HOLIDAYS	IDLE	REHEARSAL	2ND UNIT	TOTAL	AHEAD	BEHIND
SCHEDULED	86	4	5		64		159		
ACTUAL	1	4	3		64		72		

SET (S): Ext. TS steeple chase course Sc. 8pt., Ext. TS Bamboo Curtain Sc. 15, Ext. TS Mausoleum Sc. 11,
Ext. Army Camp (still photo)

LOCATION (S): Huntington Library
1151 Oxford Rd.
San Manno, CA

CREW CALL:	6A	SHOOTING CALL:	7:30A	1ST SHOT:	(AM)	8:55A	(PM)	2:43P	CAMERA WRAP:	4:05P
LAST MAN OUT:				1ST MEAL:	12:30-1P		2ND MEAL:			

SCRIPT	PAGES	SCENES	MINUTES	SETUPS	ADDED SCS	RETAKES	SCENES COMPLETED TODAY
Script Total	80 1/8	137					8, 11, 15
Taken Previously							
Taken Today	3/8	3	38	16			
Taken To Date	3/8	3	38	16			
Total To Be Taken	79 6/8	134					

Film Use 5245	LOADED	GOOD	N.G.	WASTE	TOTAL	S.E.	SOUND	DAT	¼"
Previous							Previous		
Today	5600	1820	2720	460	5000	600	Today	1	
To Date	5600	1820	2720	460	5000	600	To Date	1	
Film Use 5274	LOADED	GOOD	N.G.	WASTE	TOTAL	S.E.			
Previous									
Today	1600	1120	320	160	1600				
To Date	1600	1120	320	160	1600				
Film Use 5279	LOADED	GOOD	N.G.	WASTE	TOTAL	S.E.			
Previous									
Today									
To Date									

PRINCIPAL FILM SUMMARY						TEST FILM SUMMARY						
FILM INVENTORY	5245	5274	5279				5245	5246	5248	5274	5277	5279
Raw Stock to date	23000	23000	23000				2800	2000	3600	11600	400	8000
Additional stock												
Raw Stock Total												
Previously shot							2660	1600		11600	130	5260
Shot today	5000	1600										
Total to date	5000	1600					2800	1700	400	11600	400	7000
On hand	18000	21400	23000				0	300	3200	0	0	1000

CAST	CHARACTER	W H S F R TR	M/U WDRB	On Set	Dismiss Set	1ST Meal Out	1ST Meal In	Leave for Loc	Arrive Loc	Leave Loc	Arrive Studio
• NDM											
1 Drew Barrymore	Dylan	W	7A	1135A	445P	1230P	1P				
2 Lucy Liu* •	Alex	W	545A	750A	445P	1230P	1P				
3 Cameron Diaz	Natalie	W	630A	1135A	445P	1230P	1P				
2B Roberta Brown	Alex Fencing Dbl.	SW	1030A	145P	415P	12P	1230P				
2C Dawn Thompson	Alex Riding Dbl.	SWF	6A	920A	3P	12P	1230P				
93 Mark Ryan	Fencing Opponent	SW	11A	145P	415P	12P	1230P				
X Vic Armstrong	Stunt Coord.	W		6A	430P	12P	1230P				
XX Andy Armstrong	Co. Stunt Coord.	SWF		6A	430P	12P	1230P				
Daxing Zhang^	Martial Arts Int.	SW		9A	6P	1P	2P				
Eileen Weisinger*	Stunts	R		9A	3P						
Maria Casey	Stunts	R		9A	3P						
Mishiko Nishawaki	Stunts	R		9A	3P						
Ming Lui	Stunts	H									
Donna Evans	Stunts	H									
Dana Hee	Stunts	R		9A	3P						
Garreth Warren	Stunts	R		9A	3P						
Brad Martin	Stunts	R		9A	3P						
• = 1MPV											
* = Not Photographed											
^ = NDB 5.45a-6a											

NO.	RATE	IN	OUT	MEAL	ADJ	NO.	RATE	IN	OUT	MEAL	ADJ
2	200	830A	12P		26M						
1	115	6A	130P	1230-1P	26M/SMOKE/1MPV						
1	95	6A	1230P	12-1230P	26M						
1	115	830A	430P	1230-1P	26M/SMOKE/1MPV						
1	115	6A	430P	1230-1P	26M/SMOKE/1MPV						
1	95	1030A	430P	12-1230P	26M/FITTING						
9	95	6A	430P	12-1230P	26M						
32	95	6A	412P	12-1230P	26M						
6	46	6A	4P	12-1230P							

Unit Production Manager

Assistant Directors

Day/Date: Monday, Jan. 10, 2000

PRODUCTION

#		Name	IN	OUT
	Director	McG	O/C	O/C
	PM	J Caracciolo	O/C	O/C
	1st AD	M Colone/S Love	O/C/6.0	O/C/16.1
	2nd AD	C Fong/C Pndhast	5.2/6.0	17.5/16.4
	2nd 2nd AD	M Constance	5.2	17.5
	Key Set PA	J Bilger	5.2	19.5
	Set PA	S. Varge	5.2	19.5
	Set PA	J Shack	5.2	19.0
2	Set PA	O'Banion, Vasquez	6.0/5.2	16.0/19.0
2	Set PA	Bruning/M. Byerts	6.0/5.2	16.0/16.7

SCRIPT/STILLS

#		Name	IN	OUT
	Script Supervisor	J.A. Tenggren	6.0	17.2
	Stills	D Michaels	7.0	17.3

CAMERA

#		Name	IN	OUT
	Dir of Photography	R. Carpenter	6.0	16.1
	Cam Oper	M. St. Hillaire	6.0	17.0
	1st AC	D. Seawright	6.0	17.7
	2nd AC	K. Bloom	6.0	17.7
	Loader	S. Ronnow	6.0	17.7
	"B" Camera Oper	M. Jackson	6.0	17.0
	"B" 1st AC	E. Brown	6.0	17.7
	"B" 2nd AC	V. Mata	6.0	17.7
	2nd Unit DP	J. Taylor	6.0	17.7
	Video Asst	B Shields	6.0	17.3
	24 Frame	M. Swann		
1	2nd Unit Video Asst	D. Presley	6.0	17.5

SOUND

#		Name	IN	OUT
	Sound Mixer	W Burton	6.0	16.5
	Boom Operator	M. Lewis	6.0	16.5
	Cableman	B Harris	6.0	16.5
63	Walkies			

ELECTRIC

#		Name	IN	OUT
	Gaffer	J. Buckley	6.0	18.2
	Best Boy	M. Yope	6.0	18.2
2	Electrican	B. Fine, J. Fine	6.0	18.2
2	Electrican	D. Keegan, J. Zirbel	6.0	18.2
	Rigging Gaffer	M. Amorelli	6.0	18.2
	Rigging BB	M. Marino	6.0	18.2
2	Riggers	R. Redner, L. Gonzales	6.0	18.2
2	Riggers	C. Lama, A. Eismont	6.0	18.2

GRIP

#		Name	IN	OUT
	Key Grip	L. Moriarity	6.0	18.0
	Best B	JJ Johnson	6.0	18.0
	Dolly	J. Murphy	6.0	18.0
	Grip	R. Garcia, S. Hadju	6.0	18.0
	Grip	R. Smith, R. Santoyo	6.0	18.0
	Key Grip	C. Gilleran	6.0	17.5
	Rig BB	M. McFadden	6.0	17.5
3	Riggers	McCarron, Fahey, Gilleran	6.5	18.5
2	Riggers	Hughes, Early	6.5	18.5
3	Riggers	M Fahey, Martinez, Andres	6.0	17.5

CASTING

#		Name	IN	OUT
1	Casting/L.A.	Davis, Baddeley	O/C	O/C
	Central Casting	Tony Hobbs	O/C	O/C
	Central Casting	L. Gabaldon	O/C	O/C

OFFICE

#		Name	IN	OUT
	Prod. Supervisor	D. Grant	O/C	O/C
	Prod Coordinator	T. Kettler	O/C	O/C
	Asst Prod. Coord.	J. Webb	O/C	O/C
	Prod. Secretary	A. Prichard	O/C	O/C
	Office PA	Scheich/Biggs	O/C	O/C
5	Pers. Assts	Engel,Miller,Penrose,Starr,Keilhorn	O/C	O/C
6	Add'l PA	Per Departments	O/C	O/C

ACCOUNTING

#		Name	IN	OUT
	Accountant	E. Tompkins	O/C	O/C
2	Asst. Accountant	Gregory, Apana-Dianda	O/C	O/C
2	Pa	Randazzo, Shapiro	O/C	O/C
	AC	Herrera, Vidaurreta	O/C	O/C
	C	D. Hornik	O/C	O/C
	Clerk	Tolan	O/C	O/C

PROPERTY

#		Name	IN	OUT
	Prop Master	R. Bobbit	6.0	17.5
	Asst Props	D. Saltzman	6.0	17.5
	Asst Props	M. Suhy	6.0	17.5

SPECIAL EFFECTS

#		Name	IN	OUT
	SPFX Coordinator	P. Lombardi	O/C	O/C
	Foreman	D. Woods	6.0	17.3
	SPFX	Blackwell, Willard, Rand	6.0	17.3
20	SPFX	Per Lombardi		

MEDIC

#		Name	IN	OUT
	Set Medic	H. Fowler	6.0	18.2
	Construction Medic	J. Baxier	O/C	O/C
	Training Medic	H. Humphreys	O/C	O/C

PUBLICITY

#		Name	IN	OUT
	Publicist	G. Adam	O/C	O/C

EDITING

#		Name	IN	OUT
	Editor	J. Miller	O/C	O/C
	Asst Editor	Terry Dannenbaum, Hernanadez	O/C	O/C
		M. Koz	O/C	O/C

ART DEPARTMENT

#		Name	IN	OUT
1	Prod. Designer	J. M. Riva	O/C	O/C
2	Art Director	Klassen, Mays	O/C	O/C
2	Art Dept.	A. Sears, N. Martinez	O/C	O/C
	Draftsman	Scarpulla/Brown/King	O/C	O/C
	Set Decorator	L. Gaffin	O/C	O/C
	Leadman	B. Woolverton	O/C	O/C
	Buyer	A. Feldman	O/C	O/C
	Drapery	S. Baer	O/C	O/C
9	Dressers	Per B. Woolverton	O/C	O/C
	On Set Dresser	V. Harris	6.0	17.5

CONSTRUCTION

#		Name	IN	OUT
1	Const. Coord.	W. Hadfield	O/C	O/C
2	Const. Foreman	Walker/Young	O/C	O/C
17	Carpenters		Per WH	Per WH
4	Laborers		Per WH	Per WH
1	Lead Scenic	D. Goldstein	O/C	O/C
2	Greensman	F. Caprillo, D. Butterworth	6.0	16.0
1	Standby Painter	B. Hoyt	6.0	17.5
5	Painters		Per DG	Per DG

MAKE-UP/HAIR

#		Name	IN	OUT
1	MU Dept Head	K. Green	5.7	16.7
1	Key MU	J. Powell	5.7	16.7
1	Liu MU	D.C. Forrest	5.5	17.8
1	Diaz MU	C. Nick	6.2	17.3
2	Make-up	M. Delprete, D.Dellevalle	5.7	16.7
1	Hair Dept. Head	B. Olvers	6.0	18.0
1	Key Hair	L.McCoy	5.7	18.0
2	Liu Hair/Diaz Hair	B. Lorenz/A. Morgan	5.5/6.2	17.8/18.0
2	Hair	Tripp, Partner	5.7	17.0/14.2

WARDROBE

#		Name	IN	OUT
1	Costume Designer	J. Aulisi	O/C	O/C
1	Ward. Supervisor	C. Beasley	O/C	O/C
2	Asst. Cost. Des.	Megginson, Gardell	O/C	O/C
1	Key Costumer	L. Campbell	O/C	O/C
2	Set Costumer	Black, Lichtman	5.5	17.9/17.0
2	Set Costumer	Hollgy, Velasco	5.5	17.0
	Seamstress			

LOCATIONS

#		Name	IN	OUT
1	Loc. Manager	M. Strachan	O/C	O/C
2	Loc. Asst.	Mosher/Miller	O/C	O/C
	Police	Per M.S.		
6	Security	Per M.S.		
1	Personal Security	T. Mainardi		

CATERING

#				
	Breakfast & Lunches Served	CREW	243	EXTRAS
	Dinners Served	CREW		EXTRAS

CRAFT SERVICE

#		Name	IN	OUT
1	Craft Service	M. Randolph	4.5	19.0
1	Helper	J. Randolph	4.5	19.0
1	Chef	T. Karem	1.5	18.0
2	Asst. Cook	Garcia, Torrs	1.5	18.0
1	Asst. Cook	Muntz, Karem, Holmes	1.5	18.0
4	Asst. Cook	Topic, Aparicio, Ochs, Fernandez	1.5	18.0

TRANSPORTATION

#		Name	IN	OUT
1	Transpo Captain	J. Orlebeck	O/C	O/C
1	Transpo Co-Captain	J. Couch	PER J.O.	
1	Picture Car Captain	D. Severin	PER J.O.	
1	Camera/Video Truck		PER J.O.	
1	Grip Truck		PER J.O.	
1	Electric Truck		PER J.O.	
1	Prop Truck		PER J.O.	
1	Craft Svc.		PER J.O.	
2	MU/Hair Trlr.		PER J.O.	
2	Wardrobe		PER J.O.	
3/1	3AX/2AX Tractors		PER J.O.	
1	8 Room Honeywagon		PER J.O.	
3/2	10 tons/Gen Tractors		PER J.O.	
5	Single Trailers		PER J.O.	
2	2 Room Trailers		PER J.O.	
3	Generators		PER J.O.	
1	Fuel Truck/Tow Jenny		PER J.O.	
24	Stakebeds/Crew Cabs		PER J.O.	
6	Golf Carts		PER J.O.	
7	Maxi Vans		PER J.O.	
2	Set Dressing Truck		PER J.O.	
2	SPFX Truck		PER J.O.	
2	Elec/Grip Truck		PER J.O.	
2	Construction		PER J.O.	
3/1	Lifts/Condor		PER J.O.	
1	Sound/Video Truck		PER J.O.	

MISC. EQUIPMENT

#		Name	IN	OUT
1	Supertechno crane	Hurley, Folk	5.0/6.0	16.5/17.0

MISC. SET OPERATIONS

#		Name	IN	OUT
7	Wire Spec.	Yuen,Ling,Chen,Tan,Wong,Chan,Yick	O/C	O/C
1	Storyboards	Martinez	O/C	O/C
2	Illustrators	Johnson/Baird	O/C	O/C
1	Training Assts.	M. Carter	O/C	O/C
9	Paws for Effect	Sherm + 8	4.0	17.5

COMMENTS, ABSENCES, DELAYS \ SPECIAL EQUIPMENT, STAFF, CREW

CONDUCTED A SAFETY MEETING. Regarding general set safety, location/permit restrictions, safety while working with stunts, safety while working with horses. Horses where working around a cleaning tree. 3) Horses were wrapped at 3:20p. 4) DGA Meal Money: C. Fong M. Constance. Graham transpo reported being stung on Friday 1/7 by an unknown insect on the forehead while parking truck on set. Seen by medic, returned to work. Company moved to Bamboo curtain @ 10a. 7) Company move to the mausoleum @ 12:30p. 8) Company went into 1MPV at lunch to complete the filming of Sc. 15. Camera/Grip/Electric went into 2 MPV at lunch in order to move to the mausoleum. 10) Re-rates: V. Mata 1st AC B camera - S. Ronnow 2nd AC B camera.

makeup and wardrobe, on the set and at meals; this list includes the actors, stunt doubles, stunt coordinators and other stunt people.

The back of the production report features all of the crew members, much like the back of the call sheet, but times in and out are actual times instead of scheduled times. The bottom comments are always interesting to read; this sample refers to a safety meeting, meal penalties and a crew member who was stung by an insect, seen by the medic and returned to work. The production report acts as an accounting record of the day, especially useful for payroll, and it memorializes business information for future reference by the studio or producers.

Production calls for long, physically demanding days over many months, often on distant locations. Anyone interested in the work must enjoy such difficult conditions. The work of the second assistant director is stressful and intense, and you have to be able to thrive in such an exciting, arduous environment. Those of us who worked on *Charlie's Angels* were lucky because, although the shooting days were demanding, the producers and director created an atmosphere that was joyous as well as challenging, and the kind of high-energy fun that existed on the set was transferred to the screen.

MOVIES FOR TELEVISION

by **LINDY DEKOVEN,** president of DeKoven Entertainment, an independent production company with projects in both film and television, based in Los Angeles. Ms. DeKoven served as executive vice president, miniseries and motion pictures for television, for NBC Entertainment and NBC Studios. She organized, built and led the NBC Entertainment Longform Division to eight straight season wins as the top-rated broadcast network in longform programming among adults 18–49 from 1993 to 2001. Among the movies made in that period were the Emmy Award winners *Merlin, Gulliver's Travels,* and *Serving in Silence: The Margarethe Cammermeyer Story, The Odyssey, Alice in Wonderland, The '60s, Asteroid* and *Noah's Ark.* Previously, DeKoven was senior vice president, miniseries and motion pictures for NBC Television; vice president, movies and miniseries, Lorimar Television; vice president of creative affairs for the Landsburg Company; and director, network television development for Walt Disney Television. A graduate of the University of Arizona, Ms. DeKoven is on the board of trustees of the Los Angeles Zoo, the AFI Directing Workshop for Women and the Koreh L.A. literacy program.

Ratings are the barometer of television programming, and are responsible for setting the lifeblood of the broadcast business, the values of advertising time.

The history of movies for television can be traced back to the launching of the Hallmark Hall of Fame, sponsored by Hallmark Cards, on NBC in 1951 with *Amahl and the Night Visitors*. This was a simpler time in the television industry, before cable and before home video. There were only three networks (CBS, NBC, ABC), and the bulk of their programming was original series. By the 1960s, feature films had been added to the schedules, the networks having licensed them for television airings in their first after-theatrical exposure. As audiences began leveling off, network executives realized that viewers were perceiving these movies as used goods, since they had already been shown in theatres. Also, for the money these licenses were costing, original movies could be produced and a library of original movies-for-television could be built, premiering on the network and garnering subsequent revenue in overseas TV and domestic postnetwork TV syndication. Barry Diller is the ABC Television network executive credited with launching the "movie of the week" format in 1969, which each week premiered original movies costing under $1 million.

By the 1970s, all three networks were making original movies of the week (MOWs) at a good pace. A turning point was the Sunday night when an original MOW beat a rerun of *Gone With the Wind* in the ratings. The movie for television had come of age. Highlights along the way include *Brian's Song* and *That Certain Summer* in the 1970s and *Something About Amelia, An Early Frost* and *Adam* in the 1980s.

During the same period, networks were experimenting in *long-form*, defined as a movie or miniseries running more than two hours. The landmark, multinight *Roots* miniseries on ABC in 1977 became a cultural phenomenon, with high ratings posted every night. *Roots: The Next Generation* followed two years later. Long-form programming required appointment viewing on the part of the audience. Classic examples were *Centennial* and *Rich Man, Poor Man*. The miniseries reached a peak with *The Winds of War*, which successfully ran for eighteen hours over seven nights in 1983, then began a downtrend, as viewers were less inclined to return to the same TV appointment night after night and more inclined to use their VCRs.

The 1990s began a network era of belt-tightening and reduced ratings, with fewer dollars spent on original programming and more on newsmagazines (*20/20, Dateline NBC*). By 2000, reality-based shows (*Fear Factor, Survivor*) represented a new creative cycle; these shows cost networks some $400,000 an hour and often delivered more viewers than an original movie costing $2 million per hour.

Another trend leading to the decline of original broadcast movies was the discovery that networks could effectively counterprogram against movies taken from recent headlines with the same story on a newsmagazine show. The magazine show would tell the same story in condensed form, with a more up-to-date outcome, and the original movie's ratings declined as a result. For example, NBC's miniseries *The Ira Einhorn Story*, airing over two nights, suffered when a rival network broadcast a newsmagazine show on the same subject in an hour.

Also, advertisers began shying away from paying for commercials on original movies with what they perceived as controversial subject matter. *Serving in Silence: The Margarethe Cammermeyer Story*, about a courageous lesbian serving in the armed forces, lost some advertising support. This was in sharp contrast to airings of important movies in the 1980s such as *Something About Amelia* (about child molestation) or *An Early Frost* (about AIDS).

At the same time, the overseas values of original movies were decreasing, part of an overall downturn in the international-sales side of the business. But as original movie output on broadcast networks declined, cable networks began investing in original movies, as a form of branding and—in a repeat of broadcast network reasoning—to attract viewers to cable premieres and build film libraries for after-cable revenue streams.

In a given year, there are over 100 movies for television being made by broadcast and cable networks in the two-hour format (actually around ninety-three minutes of running time) and hundreds of hours of long-form programming, defined as running longer than two hours.

This vast production output is divided among broadcast and cable networks, which function under different rules with different business plans that impact upon their content. Broadcast networks survive on advertising revenue, which is based on ratings. Their programming aims to achieve the broadest possible national audience, represented by ratings which generate proportional advertising dollars. During "sweeps weeks," every February, May, and November, these ratings are used to calculate costs of advertising time for the following year, which accounts for the upswing in programming in those periods. Broadcast networks are beholden to advertisers and work under content restrictions overseen by the Federal Communications Commission.

Cable networks offer niche programming to attract their specific audiences. (Lifetime targets women, Nickelodeon kids.) The cable universe is divided between advertiser-based networks, such as USA and TNT, and subscriber-based networks, such as HBO and Showtime. Advertiser-based cable channels select programming to attract advertisers to their delivery of a specific niche market—the History Channel, for instance, attracts older males—and also as a means of branding ("This Week in History"). Subscriber-based networks, unregulated by the FCC, create programming without constraints on subject matter or dialogue, and produce programs dedicated to increasing their number of subscribers.

As a result, management objectives are different. For instance, at ABC, the mandate might be "How do we program movies that will increase ratings?" while at HBO it might be "How do we program movies to attract new subscribers?"

Movie budgets are also different, which influences quality. A typical broadcast network might make forty-five movies a year, with license fees ranging from $3 million to $4 million (and budgets somewhat higher) for two-hour movies, while HBO might make sixteen movies budgeted at $6 to $7 million. A typical four-hour miniseries might be budgeted at $15 million, with a network's license fee of $9 million.

Another purpose of original movies or miniseries on TV is to publicize programming on the rest of the week. For example, a highly rated NBC Sunday night movie would include promotions for the following week's series.

Now let's pause and review some basics of the broadcast television business: deficit financing and ratings. Broadcast networks airing original movies do not fully finance them. Instead, they pay a license fee to the production company in exchange for two network runs of the movie. The subsequent exploitable life of the movie is owned by the production company. The balance of the budget is typically financed by the production company, often via *deficit financing,* whereby they expect to make up the budget deficit from future revenue as the movie plays in postnetwork markets such as home video/DVD, domestic TV syndication and overseas TV and home video/DVD.

Ratings are the barometer of television programming, and are responsible for setting the lifeblood of the broadcast business, the values of advertising time. Ratings are determined by selected households whose viewing habits are entered into diaries monitored by ratings services such as Neilsen Media Research. As mentioned earlier, during sweeps weeks, these ratings are used to calculate the costs of advertising time for the following year. The ratings service then reports diary results to advertisers and the industry, and rate cards of future advertising time are created.

Ratings are expressed as two numbers, *rating points* and percentage *share*. A strong series rating as of this writing is "11.4/29." According to Neilsen, a single rating point today represents 1% of all American households, or 1,055,000 households. A rating of 11.4 indicates the delivery of just over 12 million households to the program. The second number, 29, represents the share, or the percentage of active TV sets that are tuned to the specific program. (Surf the Web for trade press or other sites like Yahoo! that report Neilsen ratings.) These figures are substantially down since the 1970s, when there was little competition for home entertainment and a winning share could be over 50.

Today, networks have shifted their ratings emphasis from the race for total households to pleasing advertisers by achieving specific demographics, such as adults aged 18–49, whose purchasing power is highly valued. During a given season, all three broadcast networks can trumpet victories. CBS might report delivering the most households, likely putting them ahead in total viewers; NBC might focus on demographics and report winning the 18–49 age group, the most important victory for them; ABC might report the most gains, increasing ratings across the boards. There is a lot of jockeying for position, and the reader is invited to read the trade papers or magazines and visit their Web sites to track and become more familiar with ratings.

At the networks, ratings are known very early the next morning, and fortunes rise or fall based on this report card. For network movies, the objective is to win by increasing viewership over the two-hour duration. The job of the network promotion department is to attract viewers to the movie's time slot; the job of the programming department is to keep the audience interested throughout the movie. If the audience is building, the movie is often a success. TV movies that open with strong numbers then drop may be victims of the fragmented attention span of the viewer, or to channel surfing because of the multiple choices available on the home TV screen. Therefore, it's important to grab the audience emotionally at the outset.

How does a network or a TV station make money on a TV movie? From their share of minutes of advertising time, either network or local, paid for by advertising sponsors during the show. The value of advertising time for two network runs of a given movie easily exceeds the license fee paid by the network. How does a production company make money on a TV movie? The production company (not the network) owns the movie, and makes money from the postnetwork life of the movie, depending on its success. The lifeblood of a production company is building a film library of exploitable titles and licensing them in all formats, country by country, around the world. (See the article on international distribution by Rob Aft, p. 458).

A typical, successful television movie will have its premiere on the originating network, followed by a home-video release, then be sold in a package of the production company's movies to overseas distributors, who show it on TV, home video or, perhaps, initially theatrically in their respective territories. Back in the United States, the movie may be included in a domestic package sold to the syndication market, where it will be aired by local television stations over a negotiated period of years and number of times. Other exploitation might include soundtrack albums, as with the successful miniseries *The '60s*.

On the network side, a hypothetical original two-hour TV movie might cost $4 million for two runs, which would generate perhaps forty-five to forty-eight national network thirty-second spots for each run, costing advertisers between $65,000 and $105,000 per thirty-second spot. At the high end, a two-hour movie pays for itself during the first network run, with advertising exceeding the license fee.

On the production company side, the same movie might cost as much as $1 million in excess of the network license fee to produce, and the company does not share in ad revenue. Instead, they would own the movie beyond its network television exposure, licensing it throughout the world. A successful two-hour TV movie, packaged with others from a major supplier, could have worldwide sales for overseas TV and home video, plus U.S. after-network TV and home video, from $500,000 to $1.5 million—a broad range, since local taste varies widely.

A hypothetical four-hour TV miniseries might cost $8 million for two network runs, and generate perhaps ninety to ninety-six national network thirty-second spots for each run, costing advertisers the same $65,000 to $105,000 per thirty-second spot. Again, at the high end of these rates, the four-hour miniseries pays for itself during the first network run, with advertising exceeding the license fee.

A major change in broadcast television business models occurred in 1995 when the FCC ended its Financial Interest and Syndication Rules. Under these *"Fin-Syn Rules,"* established in 1970, broadcast networks were prohibited from either having a financial interest in or syndicating their programming. These rules were put in place to ease network power and to encourage new, independent companies to become part of the TV landscape. In 1995, after fierce lobbying by networks and production companies, the FCC ended the rules, believing they had done their job. This delighted the networks, which moved to increase their ownership of programming, and severely hurt production companies, which suffered serious decline. The deficit financing model for original movies continued, but this time networks, not independent production companies, were often the producing entities. Without a healthy mix of companies producing broadcast movies, some feel that originality suffered.

Producing original TV movies is much like producing independent feature films in that budgets and time are limited (typically $4 million over eighteen shooting days), challenging filmmakers to do their best within constraints. Another difference is aesthetics. Since the dynamics of watching the home screen lends itself to close-ups, and television often involves family members gathered in a familiar setting, many original TV movies are intimate stories about people, relationships and challenges.

As for final cut, the network always has approval over every part of the process. Also, television is a producer's medium. When feature producers turn to TV, they are impressed with the amount of influence they have in the process.

It's always useful for a network executive to imagine the home viewer using the remote control to change channels at a rapid pace. The creative question becomes how to keep them watching your movie. One technique is to begin with a stunning emotional hook to capture the viewer; another is to encourage act breaks with cliff-hangers (a two-hour television movie contains seven acts). The rest has to do with unique visual imagery (as in *Gulliver's Travels*) and a strong emotional core (*Serving in Silence*).

At NBC, the development process was also similar to that of independent features, with a highly disciplined 1.5:1 ratio of developed screenplays to completed films. The decision to proceed to production is made working closely with a number of network executives; for example, the network scheduler is involved because that executive schedules out the entire year, matching movies to air dates. Often, these movies are on the schedule even before they're made. An example of what might alter the schedule would be a delivered rewrite requiring more work. In such a case, the project would simply be replaced by another one.

Movies were divided among two staffs of executives, one on the NBC Entertainment (network) side and one on the NBC Studios side. (NBC Studios is a production company that supplies programming, including movies, to NBC Entertainment, as well as to other broadcast and cable networks.) Each staff would monitor development, production and postproduction. Typical production emergencies would involve falling behind schedule, disappointing performances, dailies not delivering the intended impact or weather problems—again, just as in feature production. In some cases, well-known feature directors had to adjust their style to the accelerated pace of a TV movie's schedule, and to the intimate, close-up expectations of the TV audience.

Original movies on broadcast networks would often feature a series star, who would make the movie during the series's hiatus. Often a network would include a commitment to an actor in his or her series negotiation to star in an original movie. However, some cast members (*Friends*) crossed over to theatrical features rather than original TV movies. At the same time, feature stars were following the material over to television; in 1995, for example, when Sally Field starred in *A Woman of Independent Means*, the ratings were very strong. Today there is a lot of crossover, with TV stars and feature stars going back and forth wherever excellent writing is found.

The goal of the broadcast network is to reach the largest audience. Whether the network programs a movie that is a thriller, an action-based drama, or a female-based true story, the goal is to win the two-hour time period.

As stated earlier, today original broadcast-network movies are on the decline, while original cable-network movies and miniseries are on the rise. Since 2000, the field is crowded and growing. Players include, in alphabetical order, A&E (*Shackleton* miniseries); Animal Planet (*Gentle Ben*); Comedy Central (*Porn 'n Chicken*, that network's highest-rated movie ever); Court TV (*Guilt by Association*); Disney Channel (*You Wish*); ESPN (*Season on the Brink: The Bobby Knight Story*); FX (*The Pentagon Papers*); Hallmark Channel (*Snow Queen*, while continuing to sponsor the venerable and prestigious Hallmark Hall of Fame on broadcast networks); HBO (*Live From Baghdad* and the *Band of Brothers* miniseries); Lifetime (*We Were the Mulvaneys*); MTV (*2gether*); PBS (*Copenhagen*); SciFi Channel (*Steven Spielberg Presents "Taken,"* a twenty-hour miniseries); Showtime (*Wild Iris*); TBS (*Christmas Rush*); TNT (*Nuremberg* and *The Mists of Avalon* miniseries); and VH1 (*A Diva's Christmas Carol*).

One of the advantages of a branded cable network producing original movies is to attract viewers who might otherwise not visit the channel. For example, ESPN's *Season on the Brink: The Bobby Knight Story* drew strong ratings, delivering an audience beyond the channel's hardcore sports fans.

Budgets for cable movies can vary from $3 million spent by TBS to $5 million by FX, to $11 million by TNT, to more than $40 million by Sci-Fi for the miniseries *Steven Spielberg Presents "Taken."* International cofinancing is also a way whereby a U.S. cable channel might advance part of a movie's budget to the overseas production company for exclusive rights to premiere the movie on cable in the United States.

The future of television movies will likely see more movies with subject matter that travels well, that are easily exportable to other markets in the ongoing globalization of television; international coproductions, as U.S. networks seek to reduce costs; the continuing building of film libraries; and the continuing opportunity to combine extraordinary talent with compelling stories that attract viewers around the world.

VII

MARKETING

MOTION PICTURE MARKETING

by **ROBERT G. FRIEDMAN,** vice chairman of the Motion Picture Group and COO of Paramount Pictures in Hollywood, where he is responsible for worldwide marketing and distribution of both theatrical feature films and home entertainment. Among his successes at Paramount have been *What Women Want, Mission: Impossible 2, Runaway Bride* and *Titanic,* the highest-grossing film in history. Mr. Friedman came to Paramount from Warner Bros., where he was president of worldwide advertising and publicity. He began his career in the Warner Bros. mail room and rose steadily through the ranks. Highlights of his Warner Bros. years include the marketing of Academy Award–winning motion pictures *Chariots of Fire, Driving Miss Daisy* and *Unforgiven* as well as the highly successful *Batman* and *Lethal Weapon* series of films. Mr. Friedman is a member of the Next Generation Council for the Motion Picture and Television Fund Foundation and is on the boards of directors of the Motion Picture Pioneers and the Southern California Special Olympics.

> In determining the media buys, spending levels are set based on how much the picture is expected to gross. . . . The warning becomes, Don't outspend your revenues, but don't underspend your potential.

Originally movies were driven by publicity generated on the set by studio publicity mills, created to constantly churn out provocative stories in order to keep star names and picture titles before the public. Throughout the 1960s, movies enjoyed a longevity in the marketplace, remaining in theatres for months, in contrast to the make-or-break intense competition of today. Advertising dollars were limited to newspapers and radio.

In the early 1970s the process began to change. First a company named Sunn Classics made a strong impact by distributing family-oriented films regionally, supporting them with saturation network-television advertising, the first time such an approach was methodically applied to movies. Warners refined this strategy for the national-saturation release of *Billy Jack* in 1971, spending unprecedented television advertising dollars to achieve an unusually high level of gross rating points, or GRPs. (*Gross rating points* are a measure of the level of audience tune-in to television commercials, a way of converting advertising dollars into impressions.) *Billy Jack* was highly successful, and movie marketers realized that national-television advertising was the wave of the future.

As a result, release patterns changed to make ad expenditures more efficient. The national-saturation release quickly replaced road-show exclusive runs and limited national runs as the preferred release pattern. A picture that previously opened in 500 theatres could now open in 1,000 or more and be cost-efficient, measured against the reach of network-TV buys. By the 1980s the saturation release was expanded to 2,000 or more prints, and exhibition continued building multiplexes to meet the demand. By the turn of the century, the most popular pictures were being released to over 3,000 theatres (or "engagements") with 4,000 or more prints, using multiple screens in the same complex at staggered starting times, thereby increasing seats and potential revenue.

Today competition has increased dramatically, with two or three new movies opening most weekends pushing against the second weekend of the previous openings, so that perhaps six movies are competing for the audience's awareness and choice selection. And the audience is unforgiving: There are first-choice movies, and the rest are also-rans, a list that changes every week. The work of movie marketing is a painstaking and very expensive effort to position the audience for that critical opening weekend. Our goal is to make our movie the first-choice movie for its market target; if it doesn't succeed, the picture is usually forced out by new product coming in behind it.

Advertising and publicity becomes involved once production greenlights a movie. Under the ad-pub umbrella are these disciplines: creative advertising, publicity and promotion, market research, media and international. Briefly stated, creative advertising oversees the creative strategy and execution of advertising materials, which are done in-house or through outside vendors. The publicity and promotion staff works to convey the same message in public relations, starting with unit publicists and photographers on the set, through release publicity. Market research interfaces with the creative process through surveys of advertising materials; with production in fine-tuning the film in the preview process; and with sales through marketing-opportunity studies, tracking studies and competition studies. Media is the division that controls spending, physically places the advertising through ad agencies and subcontractors, and is responsible for the strategic design and execution of the media plan. International covers these areas outside the United States and Canada. There are also administrative support groups, which assist these divisions.

The marketing of a picture is like a race, in that each discipline may start at different times, but all finish together, at the target, opening weekend. Creative advertising starts as early as publicity, in preproduction; market research begins simultaneously; media starts just prior to release, and international, which has been active throughout, really kicks in after the domestic release (except for those pictures that open overseas prior to domestic).

Let me track the involvement of these specialties through the life of a movie.

CREATIVE ADVERTISING

Early strategic thinking is the same on any picture, regardless of size. Generally during preproduction, a marketing strategy has been devised, which undergoes constant revision. As this process proceeds, we will review the screenplay and production schedule to learn if there are opportunities to shoot advertising concepts during production, since it's difficult to call everyone back for a photo session after the fact.

As marketing people we have an idea of the potential of the project at this stage, from the casting of the movie (both in front and behind the camera) and the story. During production we learn even more from the look of the picture. At that point we start thinking about which projects might have breakout success (like *Mission: Impossible* or *Tomb Raider*), although it's impossible to predict this. Also, we can sense the gemstones, the smaller movies that might break out with support from critics, from awards and ultimately from the public (such as *The Truman Show, What Women Want* and *The Talented Mr. Ripley*). This type of movie relies more on its own quality, and must be carefully handled.

Once the picture has completed principal photography, a select number of advertising and publicity people are allowed to see a rough cut in order to start working on the trailers. Occasionally we may look at dailies to get a feel of the tone and visual style of the picture. After viewing the rough cut, marketing really kicks in. The first focus is on preparing the trailer, and we take care that it reflects the important moments that the movie delivers. This becomes the backbone of all broadcast materials. Perhaps we will first create a ninety-second (:90) teaser trailer, offering just a glimpse of the movie to audiences in theatres and on our Web site as far as six months in advance of release, followed by a trailer (2:00) with actual scenes. Because the theatrical trailer is the first impression the theatre and Internet audience has, this is some of the most important, persuasive work we do.

Depending upon the long-lead interest in a movie, we would launch a Web site allowing the public to follow the progress during production all the way to the theatrical and the home video release. For *Tomb Raider,* we kept fans informed with behind-the-scenes stories during shooting; the *Mission: Impossible 2* Web site was global, in multiple languages, and featured an interactive feature whereby logging in secret code numbers would trigger privileged information. Using the Internet is a highly effective way of reaching the young moviegoer.

PROMOTION AND PUBLICITY

Once the picture is green-lighted, the publicity department meets with the filmmakers to select the unit publicist, the on-scene public relations expert during filming. The unit publicist writes the production notes, which is a history of the filming, the biographies of key personnel, and communicates to us everything that is going on during shooting, including media requests that will be fulfilled or not. Also, there is a stills photographer who chronicles production from the point of view of the motion picture camera, to supply stills of the on-camera (and off-camera) action as it proceeds. In most cases the stills photographer will shoot at the same time that the motion picture camera is capturing performance; however, some actors prefer an alternative, and stay in place after shooting a scene, posing for such stills, as if they were filming. Shooting stills during actual filming is of course preferable.

Other promotional tools, such as behind-the-scenes programs and electronic video press kits are being compiled during shooting. This is vital if certain actors will be unavailable afterward, especially for international use, since most actors can't spend the time to travel around the world for publicity. A half-hour behind-the-scenes TV program can cost from $75,000 to $350,000; a short featurette, three to seven minutes, can cost from $25,000 to $50,000. A combination can find a featurette packaged for TV stations with a series of :60 or :90 news wraps, self-contained stories that can be "wrapped around" by local newscasters, plus a selection of location footage and film excerpts that can be built into a bigger piece locally, all offered with written material about the movie. Such packages can cost from $50,000 to $100,000 to produce.

The advent of e-mail has allowed for massive electronic mailings of promotional items and/or TV commercials to those who have either logged on with a request or registered on certain Web sites, which triggers receipt of material unless the customer asks to be removed from the list. Companies such as Radical Mail can stream a :30 trailer to an e-mail client, who can see it upon logging on. In an example of pinpointed direct marketing, trailers can be targeted to potential customers via e-mail based on precise demographic categories.

Publicity is also very active in the time between the end of shooting and the release date, working at strategies to achieve placement in both print and broadcast journalism. Long-lead press such as *Vogue* and *Vanity*

Fair require exclusive photo shoots or interviews months before publication, and publicity must be prepared for this. As release approaches, a mass-audience picture may call for the creation of a press junket, where broadcast journalists from cities across the country and overseas are flown to Los Angeles to interview stars and others who made the movie. The talent sit for scores of interviews during a weekend marathon and the journalists come away with exclusive footage for their venue. Also, publicity makes sure that local print journalists receive print press kits containing still photos, production notes, biographies and suggested stories and that broadcast journalists receive electronic press kits, complete with talent interviews, sound bites from the movie and behind-the-scenes video excerpts intended for broadcast along with locally generated reviews or news about the movie. The press kits are an effort to make the journalists' job easier and, of course, to provide free advertising for the picture.

MARKET RESEARCH

In market research, advertising material is tested via intercept, where a pedestrian may be asked to respond to certain concepts, stars, images and advertising copy. Concept testing is the first measuring we do, for a sense of how the audience relates to a specific movie idea. Then we will turn to a title and star measurement (without the concept), then to the print campaign. Assume the research company has been asked by our head of market research to seek out a certain target audience, whether male or female, in a given age group, and of a certain moviegoing frequency. People who meet the criteria are recruited through intercept, usually at a shopping mall, where a booth is set up for them to watch and react to material, in exchange for a premium.

An interview is one-on-one. A subject will be shown the ads; then the interviewer will ask what the ad says; whether the ad is appealing; whether the person is interested in seeing that movie; and if so, how interested. Valuations depend on which research company is at work. A sample system might range from "definitely want to see," "probably want to see," "might," "might not," "not very interested" to "definitely not interested." These interviews are an additional series of voices that either confirm or call into question the overall approach. If a less-than-terrific response comes back, then refinement of the print campaign is necessary, by fine-tuning the image or copy. In the rare case where conceptually we are not communicating what we intend to, we may have to start from scratch.

Market research also helps us refine through testing our broadcast campaign, both trailer and television. Since the trailer is created earlier than the TV commercials, it is tested earlier. How does this testing work? Small audiences are recruited demographically, shown the trailer or TV commercials, asked questions, and the data come back to us for assessment. There are also adjective profiles, where a subject will choose from a list of adjectives to measure what the material is communicating. Separately a subject would be asked to assess the material itself. Earlier testing levels are compared with later ones, as a gauge of how well we are improving (or decreasing) interest, in addition to researching our target audiences with the intended message.

There are new market research opportunities on the Internet, with its high incidence of moviegoing among its users. We are not far from a time when instant surveys about movies or trailers can be conducted among the ever-growing Internet audience. When someone registers at a studio Web site, information is gathered that allows computers to categorize and self-select to reach any precise, defined audience segment with an e-mail message or a movie trailer, which the targeted viewer is free to open or trash. As stated about the Internet in general, e-mail is a very effective way to reach an intended audience. Market research is also involved in previewing.

PREVIEWING

Previews can be divided into two types, production or marketing, although they often overlap. A preview audience can be a recruited audience whose demographic makeup is preselected. At a production preview the production executives work closely with the filmmakers to creatively fine-tune the movie. At a marketing preview we are studying audience reaction in connection with what we've been preparing in creative advertising as to the style and message of the campaign. And just as we are constantly reassessing release strategies, we are also reviewing advertising strategies, along with expenditures commensurate with those evolving strategies.

The preview process can alter release strategies. For example, a movie that had been identified for release as a slower, single-exclusive, review-driven picture may be changed to a wide, national release, for one of two reasons: It previews either much better or much worse than expected. If it previews better, we have the chance to reach a wider audience faster. If it previews worse, it can't be released slowly, because bad word of mouth will destroy it. But if it's conceptually advertisable and might achieve grosses for perhaps the first two weekends, it could be worth releasing the picture into the market nationally to "steal a couple of weeks" before word of mouth spreads. Now consider a picture that was always planned as a national release and turns out even better than expected. This could call for an opening two weeks earlier in very few cities, to allow for strong reviews to push the word of mouth and maximize the national opening.

Sitting through a preview, one learns a lot from audience reaction and from reviewing preview cards that viewers have filled out. Preview cards are always instructive. They express not only audience likes and dislikes but also details about the demographic makeup of those who most appreciate the film. For example, if our advertising is working for younger people but the film is also playing well to older ones, that presents an opportunity to broaden the audience base. We must then go back to create advertising materials that will appeal to the older audience as well. This kind of revision can apply to male and female audience segments too. As an example at Warner Bros., *Lethal Weapon* was clearly an action picture that strongly appealed to men; but in the preview process we learned that Mel Gibson's warmth, charm and good looks overcame the genre, creating broad interest among women. With that in mind, we reviewed our material, and it became a date movie.

Are there better cities for previews than others? This depends on the movie. San Diego and Sacramento are terrific preview cities overall; Seattle is a good market to preview a sophisticated movie. Today most previewing is done in Los Angeles, where it's possible to recruit any type of audience, from sophisticated to blue collar. Consider how much activity this represents. At Paramount alone we release on average fifteen to eighteen movies a year and preview each at least twice. Most are recruited screenings, since it's best for an audience to know in advance what they are seeing. Another approach to previews is focus-group screenings, which feature a question-and-answer session with a moderator after a preview, as the filmmakers in the audience listen to the feedback.

As useful as the Internet is as a publicity tool, its power can backfire with security breaches during the preview process. Anyone can sneak into an early preview, when a movie isn't finished, and report bad news to an online chat room or Web site. This is unfortunate, because the preview process was created to allow the filmmakers to improve the product with audience feedback and complete it, then let the critics express their opinions. While a movie in progress may not be protected from a negative critique on the Internet, countermeasures can be employed in the form of planting favorable critiques as well.

At the preview stage, ad-pub meets with sales to review release strategies and screening policies, to reassess the broadcast advertising budget and to decide whether the picture will be helped or hurt by publicity. (For a sense of timing, a summer picture opening in June is previewed in March or April.) There also may be elements that one loves in the broadcast trailer or print campaign but that the test audience (recruited by market research) doesn't respond to, calling for revising the materials. What is unlikely to change from the preview is the print campaign. By that time, market research has honed in on the images that are effective and on the copy that is working to appeal to the target audience.

MEDIA

After the preview process, which helps us determine who the target audience is for the picture, we begin to devise the media strategy, around eight weeks before opening. As noted, if we learn we can broaden that audience base, we will reassess the media plan to accommodate this.

In determining the media buys, spending levels are set based on how much the picture is expected to gross: costs are driven by projected performance. The warning becomes, Don't outspend your revenues, but don't underspend your potential.

In the media buy, television is the greatest expense (broken down into network, spot and cable), followed by newspapers, magazines, radio, outdoor (billboards, subways, bus shelters, sides of buses) and Internet. There has been an explosion of movie advertising in the cable universe since cable's narrowcasting is more effective in reaching a target audience than networks' broadcasting. For some movies, cable advertising has replaced much of the network and spot advertising buying, though in overall cost network still leads the way. The levels of advertising in different media are known as *weight levels:* television weight, newspaper weight.

Let's consider television advertising. In what is known as the prebuying season (June and July for the following year), Paramount has already garnered a large number of up-front network commitments, paid for in advance. This gives us the security blanket of prebought time at fixed rates and is generally less than 50% of our total network buys, though this shifts year to year. Specific television spot advertising is committed to three to four weeks prior to opening weekend. Recognize, however, that the TV marketplace changes constantly. Buying a network spot on a Wednesday night at 9:00 for a certain program's demographics might instead deliver a substitute program or a repeat. The buyer must be aware of that and adjust accordingly. The buyer must also have enough flexibility so that if a release date shifts, entire media schedules can be changed or reassigned to other pictures.

To buy our spot and network-television advertising, we use a national agency, MediaVest, which receives a commission. They get their directions from our vice president of media, who provides an execution strategy and must approve the dollar amount to be spent. For an example of the high-end cost of network spot advertising, a recent Super Bowl :30 cost over $2 million. By comparison, a :30 for *ER* or *Friends* was in the $400,000 to $450,000 range; for *West Wing,* $300,000 to $350,000; for *Frasier,* $275,000 to $300,000. For a :30 during one of those TV series on the local level, the New York market cost $25,000 to $40,000.

In planning a media buy, formulas are used that vary from movie to movie. This is because a certain price delivers a certain size of audience, and a theoretical number of impressions upon each audience member is needed to achieve results. An equation is applied involving reach versus frequency. *Reach* is how many people see your spot; *frequency* is how many times they see it. How many impressions are required? No studies have been done relating to movies, since the product is so changeable, but in the packaged-goods world, involving soap or cars, the goal is three or more impressions.

In order to achieve the most impressions for the money, the buyer invokes reach vs. frequency in devising a spot-buying campaign. A television buy for a sample movie might find spots placed in certain important network prime-time programs, surrounded by lesser network programs, perhaps nonprime time, and placement in many more less-expensive spot market programming, perhaps in the local fringe time slots, both early (6 to 8 P.M.), late-night (after local news, or 11 P.M.) and in the narrowcast cable marketplace. Increase the efficiency of an overall buying strategy, especially the more-expensive television media, by adding a foundation of radio advertising. Another part of the buying equation is CPM or *cost-per-thousand,* a measurement of efficiency, stated on a station's rate card. With this computation the buyer learns whether too much money is being spent to reach a targeted number of people. If the same number can be reached at a lower cost per thousand, that would call for changing to a different, more cost-efficient programming mix. For example, the cost per thousand to reach females aged eighteen to thirty-four for program X may be cheaper than buying program Y to reach the same people, and therefore more economical.

A given media buy can be translated into gross-rating-points estimates for each program purchased, based on station rate cards. Gross rating points, GRPs, are a media-world measurement of the reach and frequency of a particular program. GRPs can break down into two measurements, household points and target points. *Household points,* the widely publicized TV rating figure, measures the number of American households tuning in. But each program has a specific demographic profile, and within each household there are certain target groups. *Target points* measure these groups: young adults, old adults, male, female, children and so on. Since we know through experience what levels of GRPs are required to reach the goal number and makeup of impressions at the desired efficiency, one then works backward and makes the proper buys.

The studio head of media and the people at MediaVest know all these permutations. With their budget they plan the strategy as to whom to buy, when to buy and how to buy, so that the result reaches the target audience for each movie with the greatest economy. That ties in with the earliest work on each movie, as noted, about identifying the primary and secondary audiences.

As for buying media other than TV, strategy depends on the movie, and each is an individual case. Generally, though, I use outdoor selectively, in certain cities such as Los Angeles and New York. In radio I believe that talk, all-news and easy-listening is more effective than youth radio, since adults are less-frequent station-changers. Youth radio can be effective on certain movies, such as *Save the Last Dance*. MTV is also a good vehicle to target young people, on *Total Request Live;* cable networks such as Nickelodeon and sports channels are very targetable in that they reach quite specific audiences.

HOW MUCH?

The first question in preparing the media buy is how much to spend, which depends on what the prospective gross is. That judgment can be influenced by the season, the competition, and that figure is constantly evolving. The decision is locked in from six weeks to two months before opening weekend. If magazines are included, that prolongs the lead time to three months.

The next question is what the media mix should be, utilizing that money. The average MPAA figure for advertising expenditures is at $30 million, and that includes prints.

When we prepare our advertising budgets, we include our creative costs, such as internal costs in creating the advertising campaign and the publicity campaign (much like overhead), the physical expenses of creating the various campaigns, spots and trailers, the cost of sending the filmmakers on tour, the cost of reproducing press kits and other costs. Per picture this can range from $2.5 to $8 million or more. For purposes of the following examples I'll exclude the creative costs.

Media buys differ considerably between a national release and a limited release. The following figures apply to media only, throughout their theatrical life. A low-end campaign for a national release can range from $8 to $12 million in media costs; for a bigger picture the figure can be $17 to $25 million. The first *Mission: Impossible,* released in March 1996, cost around $16 million for media; *M:I-2,* in 2000, cost around $22 million for media.

For a limited or exclusive release of a picture (in New York, Los Angeles and Toronto), in anticipation of a later wide release, media buys can range from $600,000 to $1.2 million, but this is with very little television, and most money going to newspapers and outdoors. The limited release range of media buys can vary from $500,000 or less if no further rollout is expected, to a more lavish opening, generating a national reputation, at $3 million or higher. The early, exclusive run of *A Simple Plan,* which included television, cost around $800,000 for media buys. This established a presence and generated reviews. The picture slowly widened to a national release and ultimately cost $5.5 million for media.

CLOSER TO RELEASE

As the release date approaches, the earliest concern is placement for magazine deadlines, which can be as long as four months for some, or six weeks for *Rolling Stone,* as an example. Publicity has taken the written material from the production stage, polished it and put it into the form of a print press kit. The print press kit also includes stills that have now been selected from the unit photography (eight to fifteen in black-and-white, and an equal number in color) and that capture the spirit of the movie. These print press kits are serviced to some two thousand journalists around the country, generally six to eight weeks in advance of opening. They are used to familiarize the press with the movie, or as references when they review, and to help supply feature stories for smaller papers that may not have an arts editor. A second type of press kit is the video or electronic press kit (EPK), with talent interviews and film clips. From the creative standpoint the written press kits get much more use than video press kits.

At the same time, publicity is charting artists' availabilities with an eye to setting a series of interviews with key press. This depends on how keenly an actor may want to promote the film; you can't force anyone to do an interview. Scheduling is one side of the equation; pitching stories to the media is another. All Paramount publicists are busy pitching all of our product, as coordinated by the head of publicity. For example, a publicist based in New York will try to position *Rolling Stone* for a story on, say, Leonardo DiCaprio, because his movie's demographics are similar to those of the magazine. The publicist will call the contact person, usually the arts editor or an assistant, present suggestions and determine interest. Based on that interest, conversations follow as to whether a cover is appropriate, and the kind of story content. This becomes a two-sided negotiation, between the studio publicist and the magazine, and between the publicist and the artist. Diplomacy is required, and the studio is in the middle. This process is repeated with magazines, newspapers and television stations across the country up to the first day of release, and sometimes through the second week.

Six to twelve weeks before release, on the promotion side, local market radio promotions are being discussed; local tie-ins with merchants and giveaways are going forward; and toy stores are stocking merchandising toys, such as action figures, if applicable. A newer publicity vehicle, in addition to Web sites (with keywords or Web addresses appearing in all paid advertising), is the live online chat session featuring the talent, around two weeks before release, arranged through the major portals such as AOL or Yahoo! The promotion pieces of the puzzle are all coming together much like the advertising pieces, all focused to one target, the release date.

OPENING WEEKEND

On opening weekend, sales and marketing executives stay as close as possible to theatre grosses. In addition, our market-research people are doing exit interviews, to learn how the audience is responding.

The three possibilities are that the picture opens bigger than expected, around where expected or smaller than expected. If it opens bigger, naturally support it, but that support must depend on how much bigger the numbers are than expected. This reevaluation must be based on the picture's performance, exit interviews and competition. If the picture is performing exceptionally, it may even be prudent to reduce spending and save that money for later in the run, when it will be more useful. That decision will also depend on the competitive environment and is made by the sales and marketing executives. Every picture that opens big and has the potential to run, one should chase.

If a picture opens at around expectations, the follow-through plan continues. If those expectations were low, it becomes a self-fulfilling prophecy, and nothing more than intended is spent. Such a picture may hang on for the second or third weekend, depending on what's following it into theatres, but then it may be gone. For a national release, movies have become a three-day business; if the opening grosses are not strong, the picture will not survive for an extended run.

If a picture is not performing as expected, it's virtually impossible to rescue. Once $12 to $18 million has been spent to convey a specific message to the audience, that cannot be changed. On the Friday night of the first weekend we know, by tracking grosses from exit polling, just how our picture will perform.

The foregoing were examples of national releases. A picture opens in a limited release if it is of high quality, does not possess the marquee or concept value to open wide powerfully and will probably get good reviews. If such a picture opens weakly but still gets good reviews, it might be saved, upon adjusting the message of the ad campaign. In this case there is more flexibility (although rescue depends upon the quality of the movie) because a limited amount of ad money has been spent, and the picture hasn't been exposed to a large number of people.

Exit interviews during a picture's opening will tend to coincide with our marketing previews or research screenings. This confirms that we are on target. But it becomes interesting when this is not the case, and ingenuity must be applied. *The Truman Show* is an example of a sophisticated movie with exit interviews that ran counter to market testing. It tested at roughly average levels in research screenings, largely due to the fact that this was a unique role for the well-known star, Jim Carrey. Then many critics dubbed it one of the best pictures of the year. With that stamp of approval, exit-interview ratings were close to double those of the market-research screenings. The picture opened big, we supported it and it kept growing.

Now let's take a case of a good movie with strong exit interviews and good reviews that opens at a level less than expected, perhaps due to heavy competition or other market conditions. It might be rescued with an ad campaign highlighting review excerpts, along with more spending than expected in order to support it and enhance word of mouth. *Hardball* is an example. Research screenings and reviews were strong, exits were good, but it opened below expectations. We supported it with solid review commercials and a strong second-week campaign. The second week dropoff was only 16%, indicating solid holding power, and the third week held similarly.

To sum up, if it's not a good movie, gets poor reviews and opens poorly, it can't be saved. If it's a good movie, gets good reviews and opens poorly, it might be saved. If it's not a review-driven movie, such as an action or teenage movie, and opens poorly, it probably can't be saved.

In marketing a motion picture in its theatrical release, the percentage of failure is much greater than the percentage of success, which makes it a highly expensive business. It is analogous to speeding down a mountain on a train, heading toward the release date. Nothing can push the train back up the mountain; there's no second chance, all expenditures have been made. A recent survey placed the figure of pictures not recouping prints and ad costs during domestic theatrical release at 80%.

CONSERVING COSTS

Marketing costs keep escalating. While there is no absolute solution to this, there are ways to try to conserve.

The primary expense in movie marketing is television, across network, national spot, syndication or cable. The audience base for each of these deliveries is being spread, so it takes a more varied buy to reach your target audience. This is both a blessing and a curse. For a given movie, you can be more efficient with your CPMs (costs per thousand) by laying in a base of network and then supporting it through various spot, syndication and cable strategies. Cable buys on A&E, Bravo or Lifetime, for example, can deliver older, sophisticated women more efficiently than network. But a trap to be avoided is to plan a seemingly efficient strategy with many permutations that ends up costing more than a simpler buy with fewer components.

One way to cut costs is to put more emphasis in individual markets, based on the specific movie, as a sort of brand-development index. For example, a less-sophisticated movie might call for a greater weight level in spot, reducing the network expenditure in that market, making it more efficient.

Another solution, if appropriate, is to buy networks like Fox, UPN and the WB, allowing spending to be more targeted to the youth-oriented market these networks deliver, since they are less expensive than ABC, CBS or NBC.

In general, a buying strategy to reach the target audience always comes down to an equation of reach versus frequency. When a given media buy is expensive enough to achieve a reach of 90% to 100% in the dollar mix of television, radio, Internet, newspaper and magazine, the key calculation to gauge buying efficiency becomes the frequency with which the consumer is exposed to the message. It all comes down to remaining confident and not allowing the size of the competition's dollars to influence decision-making.

In addition make sure the advertising materials are delivering on the message, since it's cheaper to improve the materials than trying to spend to achieve certain awareness and want-to-see levels with inadequate materials. This again returns to the beginning of the marketing process, when it's not enough to believe you have strong materials, either broadcast or print; that faith must be proven in market testing.

Yet another way to save money in TV is to experiment in buying strategies. For instance, use more :15 commercials, a very effective medium. If :15s can be made that deliver the same message as :30s, 50% is saved. Use them at the end of your flight, closer to the release date, once the strategic message has been delivered.

A general caution in television buying is to always reevaluate the impact of network versus spot, because costs are always changing. One season it may be more efficient to buy more network than spot, and the next season, based on shifting costs, this may be reversed.

Another area where spending is high is in newspapers. One way to save money is not buying full-page ads; three-quarters of a page commands the page. If the competition buys a full page, resist the vanity temptation to copy, even though artists may urge you to do so. The public does not evaluate whether an ad is three-quarters or a full page; they are simply responding (or not responding) to the message.

It is also useful to study historical data about cities where particular genres perform. The industry has a vast database tracking grosses on every picture's performance. This is valuable research in arriving at marketing and sales decisions. If a sophisticated picture is opening in a small town where such pictures have historically not performed, be careful. Support it, don't make it a self-fulfilling prophecy; but don't chase it.

Other ways to save money can be found in the creation of the materials. For example, create more in-house; do less; if you go outside, use a single vendor rather than two or three. *Vendors* are creative sources, outside companies or individuals who can be trailer and TV-spot makers, print and one-sheet makers. Their services are extensions of our in-house creative people. The studio head of creative advertising sets the strategy and works with an outside vendor to execute that strategy. How are vendors chosen? They are cast, much the way one casts a writer or a director of photography. Each vendor has specific strengths in his or her creative execution that lend themselves to one project over another.

INTERNATIONAL

Philosophically, the world is the same as it relates to the strategic marketing of a movie. It's not totally homogeneous, but there are reliable generalities. Some movie genres work better in certain countries than in others. Most people worldwide will like an action picture, whereas some comedies, more endemic to the United States, may not travel well. This changes where there may be peculiar nationalistic tendencies, or where the media mix is different, or where viewing habits are different.

Once that is said, there are ways, in certain territories, to sell a movie differently; but these are the exceptions, not the rule. Generally, advertising mixes differ on a country-by-country basis. In western Europe, for example, when most television was government-controlled, TV advertising was difficult to purchase; but with privatization, this has changed. In other countries it's just too expensive to buy TV in the way it is done in America, which calls for change in fulfilling marketing strategies on a local basis, as overseen by the international division.

Pictures are opening overseas earlier than previously, to take advantage of the wide reach of American publicity. Since media coverage is immediate and worldwide, the impact of an American release can generate huge revenues overseas, as with *M:I-2* and *Saving Private Ryan*. The question of when best to open abroad involves a combination of circumstances, including how long it takes for excitement to travel, local traditions and moviegoing habits.

Both domestic and international distribution are constantly reviewing their release dates and plans. In ad-pub we are preparing materials for the earliest opening, wherever that is. Of course, where a picture must be subtitled or dubbed, that creates an inherent delay in release dates for non-English-speaking countries. In Paris they insist on subtitles, but outside the city they prefer dubbing. In certain regions, such as the Far East or Latin America, it's too expensive to dub, so a picture is subtitled.

To review the divisions in relation to international, both creative and publicity work the same until a picture is completed and release schedules are being mapped out. Then international personnel take over. In each major country there are studio advertising, publicity, promotion and media-buying people, with levels of hierarchy that report back to the studio.

Here's a sampling of some major overseas markets as they relate to ad-pub issues. Japan, the second-largest-grossing country, is very expensive in terms of opening costs and television advertising; newspaper costs are small. As it relates to movies, it is a young-female-driven society, since women decide what movies to see on dates. The United Kingdom is a strong market, strategically analogous to America, as is Australia. France is unique in the world in that it is cinema-driven; movies are deeply ingrained in the culture. Although one can't buy television commercials due to government regulations, that is changing. Italy has become a stronger market since movie theatres have been upgraded. Germany continues to be a healthy market, with a growing appetite for movies. Eastern Europe represents a whole new potential revenue source. (For more details on the global market, see the article by Rob Aft, p. 458.)

Entertainment remains a key export of the United States, and advertising-publicity positions and helps generate that popularity. But what we do is movie-driven. Every movie is unique and requires different levels of expenditure, in terms of creating materials (whether they are easy to make or not), in media spending (whether it's a concept that's easy to communicate or not) or for different levels of success (whether it's working or not working). Systems can always be improved. When new media become available, they must be evaluated. If television becomes a factor in countries where it wasn't earlier, how does that change the media mix? The way to improve the business is to continue to learn, to constantly push the envelope. Don't make an average campaign, make an above-average campaign. Because the business is changing so quickly, one can't sit back. There's no time for sorrow or elation, because next week's another movie.

MARKET RESEARCH

by **KEVIN YODER,** cochief operating officer at Nielsen NRG, based in Los Angeles. A graduate of the USC Law School and a member of the California bar, he practiced law in New York and Los Angeles, specializing in mergers and acquisitions of multinational media conglomerates. Mr. Yoder helped found the Miranda Theatre Company in New York before moving to Los Angeles, where he graduated from the Peter Stark Motion Picture Producing Program at the USC School of Cinema-Television. He joined NRG as an analyst, was appointed head of the international division, later executive vice president and chief analyst of the company, and then cochief operating officer.

What research tools do studios use to launch a movie in the marketplace strategically in order to ensure that its potential is maximized? The key is in understanding the moviegoing consumer, what he or she desires at any given time, and the factors that are influencing consumer behavior.

A movie is an extremely perishable product, launched into a tough, intensely competitive marketplace, whether in the United States or overseas. In a typical year, the major studio distributors launch fifteen to twenty or more titles each, totaling close to 200 pictures. There are no longer busy seasons; there are busy seasons and busier ones. In the United States, every weekend is an opening weekend, with new pictures facing some form of competition, be it the continuing strength of last week's number-one movie or the counterprogramming appeal of a film of a different genre released on the same day.

Success depends on the product launch during the all-important opening weekend, with enormous costs at stake. These critical first days affect all other revenue streams and ancillary markets. The launch of a movie is like the end of a political campaign. If a candidate does not win on Tuesday, there is no Wednesday. In a movie campaign, if a movie does not perform strongly on opening weekend, there is no second weekend.

Most consumer products other than movies can be tested in limited strategic market launches in isolated areas. Feedback can be obtained, the product or the marketing and packaging refined and revised and tried again in a different market. Not so with movies: Once they are launched, there is no going back. One of the tools distributors and filmmakers use to inform these product launches is market research.

Research is not used to design, create or produce movies. Ideas for movies are never tested or discussed; they are some of the most closely guarded industry secrets in our economy. Instead, research addresses the market forces that the movie will face as it is offered to the public. The goal of market research is twofold: first, to provide information to help maximize the effect of advertising materials and general marketing for a movie; second, to provide filmmakers with constructive feedback, an additional tool to help them tell their story in the best way possible.

Market research must be actionable to be useful. The research should aim to simulate the actual way in which respondents experience a movie or search for information about movies. For example, as detailed below, in researching how an audience reacts to a movie, a real theatrical experience is best.

Each studio marketing division has a market research department, with senior executives responsible for understanding the factors influencing consumer decisions and advising the division on how to position or reposition media and marketing materials as a campaign "takes flight," or rolls out according to the agreed-upon plan. In addition, the market research department obtains feedback about the product itself—the movies and the degree to which they satisfy audiences interested in seeing them. This process helps filmmakers fine-tune their vision, in order to ensure that they are communicating as effectively as possible.

To conduct the nuts and bolts of the research, provide strategic marketing advice, and interpret research for optimum results for each picture, outside consultants are retained. In the entertainment industry, Nielsen NRG is the industry standard. Founded in 1978, NRG is the leading market research and consulting firm servicing the motion picture industry, covering the marketing of movies for theatrical release around the world, as well as in the home entertainment market.

NRG regularly conducts general studies of public and moviegoer attitudes and behavior, and carries out specialized research and consulting services for various clients in the motion picture industry. NRG's years of experience, and the substantial data bank gathered from its work in the theatrical field, allows it to tailor research and consulting services to specific demographic, sociographic and geographic requirements in the United States and throughout the world. *Demographics* relate to factors such as age, gender, ethnicity, economic status, location and education; *sociographics* refer to social profiles, such as whether the moviegoer is a sophisticated moviegoer or not (characterized by their taste and behavior).

In addition, NRG has developed electronic delivery systems, enhancing the accumulative value of its substantial data bank. All studies and surveys are designed to complement each other, so that the accumulated data about a motion picture, TV show or DVD title yield even more accurate and complete information than the findings of an individual study.

The entertainment industry is an industry built on relationships. NRG and its clients have forged strong working relationships at all levels, with the goal of providing the best quality data in the shortest time frame.

MARKETABILITY AND PLAYABILITY

What research tools do studios use to launch a movie in the marketplace strategically in order to ensure that its potential is maximized? The key is in understanding the moviegoing consumer, what he or she desires at any given time and the factors that are influencing consumer behavior. Who are they? What do they want? What can be done to optimize product (movie) sales (box office)? In real-world terms, how do studio distributors interpret the findings from this research to effect change? What individual or local factors come into play as a product is launched nationwide?

To answer these questions, two critical factors must be assessed for each movie: marketability and playability.

Marketability analyzes what is attracting an audience to any given movie, or what the picture has that will attract the audience. Tools assessing marketability measure the interest-generating potential of materials for the movie (such as commercials, previews in a theatre, posters or print ads), the messages about and images of the movie conveyed by these materials, and the levels of interest these materials generate. Marketability does not measure the box office potential of a movie, but it does provide a key piece of the puzzle about how the movie might fare in the marketplace.

A picture's *playability* is the way it satisfies an audience interested in seeing it. The act of purchasing the ticket is already evidence of some level of interest in seeing the movie. A key component of playability is the level of satisfaction: How satisfying is the movie? If it is highly satisfying, then most likely audience members will encourage friends to go. This spreads word of mouth about the movie, a key factor for success, and allows the movie to grow and sustain itself in the marketplace. Popular movies such as *Titanic, Forrest Gump* and *The Blair Witch Project* have high playability; they are very satisfying to a broad audience. Highly positive word of mouth helped bring in repeat viewers, allowing these pictures to become extremely profitable at the box office and beyond. Notice that playability has nothing to do with attracting the audience to the movie. Rather, it is about the outcome once the audience has purchased the ticket and attends.

To assess marketability and playability, a wide array of methodologies are available to studios and filmmakers. These tools are divided into two broad categories: qualitative and quantitative research. *Qualitative* research most often employs focus group discussions as the key methodology. *Focus groups* consist of ten to twelve individuals of narrow demographic range who meet to discuss their impressions of specific materials. Findings from focus groups or other qualitative studies do not indicate how persuasive the materials at issue might be among moviegoers or the population at large, or how interested the consumer is in buying the product; rather, they aim to provide direction and insight into the consumer and his or her attitudes. *Quantitative* research, on the other hand, can provide indicators of how persuasive the materials might be, assuming the methodologies and sampling systems are sound and eliminate bias insofar as possible. (Bias in research can never be eliminated completely.) Quantitative research can measure the effectiveness of materials, such as the intensity of interest in seeing a given movie in a theatre as produced by a thirty-second TV commercial. It can also measure the memorability of a product—how well consumers recall any given product in a crowded advertising environment. Competitive testing and tracking studies, among the most common quantitative tools used in movie marketing research, will be discussed in detail later in this article.

Now let's turn to the steps behind two of the most frequently used tools of market research: intercept studies, designed to gauge reactions to advertising materials (marketability), and recruited audience screenings, designed to elicit reactions to completed or nearly completed movies (playability).

INTERCEPT STUDIES

Let's follow the process used in a typical market research project. Assume a studio wants to test the advertising materials for an upcoming feature. Six months to a year prior to release, an executive in the studio market research department will call one of the account representatives at NRG and commission the study. They discuss the markets to be studied, the demographic composition and any other unique sociocultural or demographic attributes of the moviegoer respondents. For example, it may be decided that the study of a trailer for an upcoming slasher movie should include a sample of moviegoers who are self-identified horror fans. Or a study of the persuasiveness of marketing materials for a new movie from a popular rock star might survey fans of his or her music and compare their responses to those of the general public. These decisions are based on marketing positions established at strategic marketing meetings within the studio.

Once the study is commissioned, initial specifications, called spec letters, are drawn up and sent back to the client. Immediately, a questionnaire is developed at NRG, taking into consideration a variety of factors unique to the type of study and to the motion picture at issue. The draft questionnaire is then transmitted to the studio for review, comments and approval.

Meanwhile, the studio itself is preparing the marketing materials needed for the test. Previews are cut in rough form, commercials assembled or mock-ups of posters created. These materials are duplicated and shipped to NRG, which in turn ships them together with the appropriate survey materials to its affiliated field services (companies that organize and supervise interviewers) throughout the country.

The following morning, the fieldwork begins. Interviewers, applying rigorous research and sampling standards, begin conducting the interviews required for each study.

Once the fieldwork is completed, a courier sends the questionnaires back to NRG. All materials that were tested are also returned and destroyed, so that the confidentiality of the clients' materials is preserved. The questionnaires are then keypunched at NRG's data processing center. Results are quickly tabulated and a *topline,* or summary of key measures, is transmitted to both the market research and marketing departments of the client studio. The topline presents the results against normative bases developed over the course of NRG's accumulated years of experience in the industry. Part of what makes NRG so valuable as a consultant are these norms; no other market research provider in the entertainment industry has as extensive a basis for normative comparisons as NRG.

Simultaneously with the release of the topline information, the study is being data-processed as a whole, so that each answer from each respondent in each city is categorized and recorded. The questionnaires are returned to NRG and sent to be coded. *Coding* is the process by which the thousands of individual open-ended responses of each respondent are systematically read, categorized and tabulated for reporting. Open-ended responses (responses to questions asking for opinions or images) provide an interesting window into how respondents are thinking about a movie.

Once the data is punched, the responses coded and tallied up and the topline issued, the materials land on the desk of an analyst, where they are analyzed for impact, bearing in mind the objectives of the study and any issues that may be of special interest to the studio. Cross-tabs can be created, so that the analyst can see how many of those who say they are definitely interested in the movie, for example, also indicate that the star is their chief reason for interest.

In terms of timing of advertising material tests, most studios prefer to conduct their market research over the weekend. This is because most interviews are conducted in public places, like shopping malls or major urban centers, where a wide cross-section of people congregate, and they are likely to be more crowded over the weekend. To reduce sampling biases, an intercept technique is used. Screeners will approach individuals in a shopping mall to determine their willingness and suitability to participate in the survey. (As a rule, people around the world are more than willing to give their opinions about movies; movies provide a common cultural framework and are subjective, so it is safe to hold and express opinions about them.) A second reason for conducting fieldwork on weekends is simple: That is when people are free. Potential respondents are more likely to stop during leisure time, rather than when running errands during their lunch hour. Third, the larger pool of potential respondents available on weekends ensures that demographics can be more easily met and controlled. This helps keep costs low and the market research process more economically attractive.

To show the time frame, let's take an example. Assume that a test of three previews of coming attractions (trailers) is ordered on a Friday morning. By lunchtime, questionnaires have been developed and rushed to the studio. The key senior studio executive (the head of marketing, for example, or the head of creative advertising) has a final review of the potential trailers along with staff, and final comments, notes and edits are incorporated. The trailer is rushed to rough-form completion; final effects may not be in it, and the score and narration may be temporary. Shots used in the trailer may be taken from the assembly the director is working on, so it may contain time stamps and editing marks. Nevertheless, this trailer will be duplicated on Friday afternoon or evening and shipped to the research company.

At the same time, the questionnaire is finalized, arrangements with the fieldwork services around the country are discussed and the parameters of the study fine-tuned. There are many phone calls and e-mails back and forth, with discussion of the locations to test, approval of the demographic sample and breakdown, and comments upon and approval of the questionnaire. Friday night the questionnaires and copies of the trailer are shipped by courier from Los Angeles to testing sites nationwide.

First thing Saturday morning, the interviews begin. They are conducted all day Saturday, and the intercept department monitors the progress of each study. The intercept department has maps on the walls with indicators of where certain tests are being conducted, including our example three-trailer test. A constant influx of faxes and e-mails is reviewed over the course of the fieldwork to ensure that the studies are progressing on target. Late Saturday, at the end of the interviewing day, completed questionnaires are bundled and couriered to the data processing department. This shipment is followed on Sunday by yet another bundle, and by Sunday evening all of the questionnaires from all of the studies are either in transit back to Los Angeles or being data-processed.

Data processing continues all weekend, day and night. On Monday, a topline memorandum is issued to the studio. Questionnaires have begun to arrive in the coding department, which is hard at work in round-the-clock shifts coding answers to open-ended questions. By Tuesday or Wednesday, this work is done, the analysts have all of their data and are producing reports, conference calls are scheduled and the process is completed. In Tuesday or Wednesday marketing meetings at the studio, the results are analyzed, decisions made and the process either repeated or the trailers approved for final edit. From the initiation of the study to the delivery of the report takes less than one week. On an average weekend, tens of thousands of interviews are conducted. It is a business built on quality, speed, accuracy and actionability.

RECRUITED-AUDIENCE SCREENINGS

Commissioning recruited-audience screenings is similar to commissioning intercept studies. Calls come in to NRG about a week in advance, scheduling a given screening. The studios reserve a theatre, usually buying out a screen where one of their current releases is ending its run. Most screenings occur in the Southern California area, followed by the New York metropolitan region. Screenings in the Midwest are less frequent.

There are myriad reasons a studio might want to conduct a screening. In the best of circumstances, they may know that a film has enormous appeal to a given audience, and want to see just how broadly that appeal will extend. Thus, they may be interested in the playability of a movie as they set the target audience. In other cases, a studio may be wondering how well a movie will play, and be thinking about conducting advertised previews (sneak previews that are advertised in the newspaper) for a movie to help build word of mouth. Or a studio may simply be interested in feedback: They want to see how a picture performs as the filmmaker fine-tunes the product. The aim of the screening is always, foremost, to identify the positives about a picture. In addition, downsides are identified and their relative impact assessed.

Unlike materials testing, outlined earlier under intercept studies, which measure marketability, recruited-audience previews assess the playability of the movie—how satisfying it is to an audience interested in seeing it. And unlike intercept interviews, where the sample is strictly controlled and moviegoers nationwide are assessed, here the fieldwork is more targeted.

When a study is commissioned and the spec letter issued, the specifications include a short concept, which pitches the movie to the respondent. Field recruiters fan out into areas that feed the theater where the screening will occur and intercept individuals on the street, where they administer a short questionnaire, called a screener, that establishes the potential invitee's age, gender and, very importantly, their moviegoing behavior. The recruiter is instructed to invite only those people who are in the target of the study, who express interest in the movie based on the concept, and exhibit certain key moviegoing criteria.

If the potential invitee is within the demographic parameters of the target audience, he or she is shown the concept and asked for his or her interest based on that concept. Those who exhibit positive interest and are available on the night of the screening are presented with an invitation to attend. Audience members are strongly encouraged to call and confirm their attendance.

The screening schedule in any given week is busy and changeable. While recruiting is going on, the questionnaire for a specific screening is being developed for the studio. The market research department reviews and passes along all comments and suggests other questions or specific areas that they would like to explore. It is worth noting that while filmmakers have little involvement in the research process for marketing materials, they tend to be very involved in the recruited-audience screening process. They are, after all, among the primary end-users of the information produced.

A recruited-audience screening aims to create a typical moviegoing experience. People are not told they will be asked to complete a questionnaire. Instead, they are invited to simply sit back and enjoy the show. Concessions stands are open and audience members can come and go as they please, just as if they paid to see the movie at the theatre.

In the event some decide to leave ("walkouts"), an interviewer notes the age and gender of those who departed, the time of leaving and asks why. Most screenings have very few walkouts, just like when the audience has paid. In the event that there are significant walkouts, the exit sheets are analyzed to determine why these audience members left, such as a particularly gruesome scene in a horror movie.

Once the show is over, staff members give out questionnaires to audience members, who complete them and hand them in before leaving. Some are invited to remain and attend a short focus group discussion, an opportunity for filmmakers and studio personnel to listen to audience members' views and hear how they express their opinions about the movie they just saw.

During the focus group session, staff are hand-counting the questionnaires to provide topline information on how the movie scored in the key measures of ratings and recommendation. When the focus group is finished, usually about twenty minutes later, the big moment arrives: Studio personnel and filmmakers huddle together to review how the movie performed—what was its playability measure to this particular audience?

The questionnaire cards are then transported to the data processing center, where the data is entered overnight. Copies of the cards are made and delivered by courier to each of the key people involved in the screening (for example, the studio head, the marketing research department, the filmmakers) to arrive on their doorstep with the morning paper. Copies of the questionnaires are also delivered to the coding department, where the open-ended responses are coded and tallied.

The next day, analysts prepare a written report of the results of the screening. Usually, the studio will have scheduled an afternoon meeting with the filmmakers to discuss the findings and any thoughts about how to proceed if downsides arise from the responses. The reports never suggest changes; it is not market research's role to edit movies. Instead, they may point out areas where the response was positive and areas where the response suggests concerns. It is up to the filmmakers and the studio to decide how or whether to act upon that information.

GAUGING THE MARKETPLACE: ADVERTISING STRATEGIES, COMPETITIVE TESTS AND TRACKING

Up to this point, most of the references in this article have been specific to individual movies and issues associated with them, for a sense of what the interaction between the studio marketing research department and its primary consultant is like. The types of research studies covered have been designed to help fine-tune marketing campaigns and provide the tools to studio personnel and filmmakers to make the best possible movie they can.

Now let's focus on what happens when the movie enters the marketplace. What sorts of competitive forces will it encounter there? In a proactive sense, how can any potential obstacles be anticipated and their harmful effects eliminated? Three research tools help answer these questions: advertising strategy studies, competitive tests and tracking surveys.

Advertising Strategy Studies

Studio marketing departments sometimes discover that a picture presents unique marketing challenges that may or may not be readily apparent. For example, a new movie with an unknown cast and an unfamiliar story might not possess a clear hook to use in materials. For such a movie, advertising strategy or market positioning studies can be conducted to hone an early approach to the advertising campaign, and to illuminate and anticipate some of the issues posed by the film.

To accomplish this, telephone interviews are conducted nationwide among a cross-section of moviegoers representing the anticipated target audience for the movie. During the interviews, initial interest is elicited based on the title and stars alone. Respondents are then exposed to the movie through concept testing: A 500-word positioning description of the movie is read to gauge interest and the impact of elements contained in the description.

The resulting data obtained from the interviews of moviegoers is then analyzed according to cross-tabulations of various factors and moviegoer characteristics—such as demographics, interests and biases of the respondents, geography and moviegoing habits—against a range of questions about the movie.

An advertising strategy study such as this one will identify key target groups with interest in the movie and yield suggestions as to what might contribute to the advertising of this new movie. It will also help assess the key elements for promoting the movie and why, and any downside risks to be avoided and why. Ultimately, the conclusions suggest strategy and tactics going forward in the marketing of the new movie.

Competitive Tests

Suppose the advertising study has been completed, a presentation created, and the results discussed and reviewed in meetings with studio personnel. Marketing materials have been created and honed with reference to completed intercept testing. What happens when the movie comes into the marketplace and faces competition? How can the impact of that competition be measured to ensure the best competitive environment for the movie in question?

In such a situation, the studio may decide to assess the competitive environment by conducting a competitive test, which tests the impact of their preview of coming attractions against those of other pictures that are also opening around the same time.

There are two methodologies employed to conduct a competitive test. Both are administered via intercept interview. In the simpler version, the impact or persuasive power of the trailer for the movie in question can be assessed and measured against the persuasiveness of each of the other competitors' trailers. Each respondent is shown trailers for the other movies and asked for their order of preference in seeing each movie.

A second way to test competitiveness is to measure recall as well as persuasion. In such a method, respondents are shown the trailers in continuity (as if they were at the movies), with the trailers rotated (each trailer shown an equal number of times in the first, second and third position). Then the interviewer distracts the respondent by asking a series of unrelated questions. At the end of the interview, respondents are asked to recall the titles, top of mind (without any prompting by the interview) and what the movies were about. There are strong arguments that this methodology provides a better sense of competitive strength, since recall through clutter is the chief measure of the individual persuasive power of each preview. Both methods, however, are used, and each has its own benefits.

Tracking Surveys

As mentioned briefly earlier, one of the core tools for executives at all studios is the tracking survey. Tracking provides a snapshot of the marketplace, measuring the awareness of and interest in movies that are currently in release, about to be released or coming soon.

Tracking is a syndicated study. Unlike all of the other studies discussed in this chapter, it is not proprietary to any individual studio. Rather, tracking information is shared among all partners to the study; think of this group as a syndicate and the term "syndicated study" has a clearer resonance. All partner studios see the results for all movies in tracking studies, which helps them gauge their competitive strengths and weaknesses. Both the good and the bad are there in all their harsh numerical glory for any studio person in the syndicate to explore and meditate upon.

The study is conducted among a nationally stratified sample of moviegoers. It is not a true national sample, since moviegoing is concentrated more in some areas than in others. There are currently sixteen markets represented in tracking. Demographic controls are imposed on the study to insure that it is representative of the country at large.

The tracking study, done by telephone, is limited to a sample based on common moviegoing behavior, such as a certain level of moviegoing frequency at a theatre in a set period of time (like the past month or year). In the United States and major foreign countries, the telephone system provides the most accurate way to reach a broad cross-section of moviegoers, since there is almost total national penetration of phones. If tracking were to be conducted in a country that does not have such total use, a different methodology would have to be employed to ensure that every household has an equal chance of being represented in the study.

In the U.S., tracking is conducted several times a week. These standard days, or *waves* as they are called, can be augmented by any studio. A studio, for example, may wish to track moviegoers seven days a week as its latest action movie approaches the market, augmenting the waves daily to see how awareness is changing as the marketing campaign takes flight.

Tracking is an extremely useful tool, especially to the media divisions of marketing departments, providing a concrete gauge of how their targets are being reached. Based on this information, the media department can adjust campaign dollars away from a demographic that is being saturated and toward a target that might need bolstering. Further, marketing departments can see the impact of their hard work by looking at how strong the interest in seeing the movie is, and whether that interest is supported by good heat in terms of first choice.

Results of tracking are delivered first thing on the morning following the night the surveys were conducted. Electronic delivery puts the data on the desktop of executives when they arrive, and by the time most people are getting around to their first morning cup of coffee, the tracking data have been analyzed, digested and acted upon by studio personnel.

Overseas, tracking is conducted in key territories, most often the top four or five markets worldwide. Tracking studies are also conducted for other revenue streams, such as to track the intent to purchase DVDs both domestically and overseas, covering the top ten to fifteen markets worldwide.

Regardless of the purpose of the tracking study (theatrical release or intent to purchase DVDs) or the location (domestic or international), key data collection safeguards are built into the process. Tracking is essentially a telephone sampling of an entire marketplace, and as such biases in the data and sampling inconsistencies must be minimized. In structuring the study, key markets are chosen, representing key moviegoing cities throughout each country. The timing of calls is controlled, so that the research is conducted on a regular basis each week, which helps control biases. For example, if tracking were conducted one week at 8:00 A.M. and the next week interviews were conducted at 9:30 P.M., different types of respondents would be reached. Since the goal is to measure moviegoers' awareness and interest in certain product, calls are made when moviegoers are at home, rather than at work. Also, the days chosen reflect the timing of the marketing campaign. As the media plans roll out, and commercials and other advertising occur with more frequency, the surveys are conducted to determine the impact on the marketplace. This enables the studio to make adjustments to its plans and correct any perceived inefficiencies.

From a strict sampling perspective, tracking utilizes firm sampling guidelines. The numbers dialed are produced randomly, screening out for businesses and nonworking numbers. The sample is designed so that every household in the calling city has a statistically equal chance of being selected for the survey. Further, two-time call-back procedures are put in place; if the number is busy or there is no answer, the interviewer calls back twice, and not in succession.

At the end of each week, tracking reports are prepared that summarize how each movie is tracking. An overview of the marketplace is provided and opening prospects assessed for each title opening, pointing out key strengths among core target groups. Data are delivered to each partner studio electronically, providing even more detail by specific age, gender and other key demographic groups.

NATIONAL STUDIES AND MOVIEGOER BEHAVIOR

The one common denominator among almost all of the studies discussed so far is their focus on the performance of a specific picture. They tell the studio more about the reaction to that movie's playability and marketability than about the market in question. What about the markets themselves? How do studios keep an eye trained on the worldwide economies of widely differing cultures? How can the market research department help shed some light in that direction? To understand markets more completely, national studies are conducted of moviegoers' tastes and behaviors.

These studies occur every three to five years, roughly, and are updated periodically. For the most part, they are syndicated studies, like tracking. As discussed earlier, a syndicated study is one in which a group of companies come together to design the objectives and key lines of inquiry of a study, and share the resulting information.

A typical national study—of Spain or Germany or the United Kingdom or Japan, as examples—is designed to produce substantial information and is carried out by telephone to ensure the widest possible penetration of the market. The respondents are drawn from major cities throughout the country in question, representing a true national polling sample. When a national study is conducted, a measure of moviegoing incidence in the national population is first determined, and only those who demonstrate the requisite moviegoing threshold complete the rest of the study.

The main lines of inquiry in a national study relate to moviegoing incidence and behavior, attitudes toward films generally, attitudes toward the United States and things American, and feelings about the moviegoing experience. In addition, the moviegoing decisionmaking process is explored, as is the experience of taking children to films.

The key objectives of these studies are to determine tastes and trends in the markets regarding local product and American film product, and also to suggest ways in which to maximize the marketing of American films. Identifying characteristics of American film product generally, and identifying detrimental factors and pitfalls to be avoided, are also important aims. These studies can also provide insight into the differences that key groups in the United States demonstrate in their preferences and behaviors compared with the same groups in the overseas market studied. In the United States, national studies are not generally conducted, although moviegoing incidence is monitored constantly throughout the year.

In conclusion, one of the most difficult aspects of being in the business of producing and marketing motion pictures is anticipating what the public will want to see. Trends are hard to forecast. Given the long lead time needed to take a movie property from development through release, there is little sense in trying to capitalize on what is hot or current today, since by the time the picture is in the marketplace, tastes will surely have changed.

Once completed, the motion picture exists to be seen by audiences out there in the dark, as Norma Desmond says in Billy Wilder's classic *Sunset Boulevard.* How does the studio manage that movie and ensure the revenue streams achieve their widest potential with the consumer? Information is the key to understanding the consumer, and this is the role that market research provides to the industry: provider of information.

FILM FESTIVALS AND MARKETS

by **STEVE MONTAL,** who has served on juries and selection committees of more than forty film festivals, including Slamdance, Stockholm, Brussels, the World Festival of Animated Films in Croatia, and Festival Internacional de la Imagen in Colombia. A graduate of Yale University and the UCLA School of Theater, Film, and Television, Mr. Montal served as the founding associate dean of the North Carolina School of the Arts School of Filmmaking and as founder of the Producers Program at Chapman University. He coproduced *Viva Terra Viva,* an international concert for the environment, the first television program of its kind to be shot in the Amazon. Mr. Montal worked with the American Film Institute developing film festivals for AFI's Silver Theatre, a state-of-the-art renovation in the Washington, D.C., area. Currently he teaches, serves as a consultant to film festivals and runs business affairs and development for Caucho Technology, Inc., a software firm that he cofounded.

The easiest way to disqualify your film is to fill out the submission materials improperly.

S ince the 1990s, film festivals and markets have played an increasingly useful role in the strategic planning of finding distribution for independent films.

Let's define terms: In general, a *festival* is an established venue usually organized around screenings and prizes, dedicated to introducing movies of a certain style to a paying audience, attended by distribution executives seeking product and by opinionmakers and journalists seeking stories, as well as by a paying audience; prizewinners gain industry attention and the ability to advertise their prizes in publicity campaigns as a "stamp of approval" recognized by eclectic moviegoers. A *market* is a business venue closed to the public, either associated with a festival (as in Cannes) or not (as in AFM, the American Film Market in Santa Monica), organized to bring global buyers and sellers together in a convention atmosphere, which encourages territorial dealmaking that would otherwise require much travel and far-flung communication.

Festivals are more open to the independent film seeking distribution, with their specific calls for entries, low entry fees, rules, and publicized results intended to promote competing films, judges and winners; markets, with their high-cost day passes, are more closed to filmmakers, discourage publicity and instead are the purview of independent distributors who have already acquired certain films for their home territories and use the markets to buy or sell films territorially with other-country distributors. In light of this distinction, this article will focus on the strategies to best position an independent film seeking distribution among film festivals rather than markets.

Festivals date back to the 1930s and 1940s, when powerhouse festivals including Berlin, Cannes and Venice were launched to promote new films and talent to international filmmakers, audiences and journalists. Today the number of festivals in the United States alone has grown from a few hundred in 1990 to over a thousand.

FESTIVAL AND MARKET PROFILES

Venues have evolved into highly desirable global festivals (such as Berlin, Venice, Sundance, New York); specific film markets (AFM, MIFED); cultural festivals dedicated to specific filmmaking arts (the World Festival of Animated Films in Zagreb); and regional festivals (Kansas City Filmmakers Jubilee). The major festivals and markets are listed in this calendar, along with some regional events that are interesting and useful to filmmakers. Profiles of selected festivals and markets follow the calendar.

JANUARY
Sundance Film Festival, Park City, Utah
Slamdance Film Festival, Park City, Utah
Rotterdam Film Festival, Rotterdam, The Netherlands
Clermont-Ferrand Short Film Festival and Market, Clermont-Ferrand, France

FEBRUARY
Berlin Film Festival, Berlin, Germany
American Film Market, Santa Monica, California

MARCH
South by Southwest Film Festival, Austin, Texas
Australian International Documentary Conference (AIDC), Australia

APRIL
Kansas City Filmmakers Jubilee, Kansas City, Missouri
MIP-TV Television Market, Cannes, France

MAY
Cannes Film Festival and Market, Cannes, France
Hot Docs, Canadian International Documentary Festival, Toronto, Ontario, Canada
Seattle International Film Festival, Seattle, Washington

JUNE

Annecy Animation Festival and Market, Annecy, France
World Festival of Animated Film, Zagreb, Croatia
Sydney Film Festival, Sydney, Australia
Banff International Television Conference, Banff, Canada

JULY

Karlovy Vary International Film Festival, Karlovy Vary, Czech Republic
Melbourne International Film Festival, Melbourne, Australia
Los Angeles Latino Film Festival, Los Angeles, California

AUGUST

Deauville Festival of American Film, Deauville, France
Edinburgh International Film Festival, Edinburgh, Scotland
Venice Film Festival, Venice, Italy
Expresion en Corto Film Festival, Guanajuato, Mexico
Telluride Film Festival, Telluride, Colorado

SEPTEMBER

Toronto Film Festival, Toronto, Ontario, Canada
New York Film Festival, New York
IFP Market, New York
Sidewalk Moving Pictures Festival, Birmingham, Alabama
San Sebastian International Film Festival, San Sebastian, Spain
Rio de Janeiro International Film Festival, Rio de Janeiro, Brazil

OCTOBER

Hot Springs International Documentary Film Festival, Hot Springs,
    Arkansas
Chicago International Film Festival, Chicago, Illinois
International Film Festival of India, New Delhi, India
MIPCOM, Paris, France
Tokyo International Film Festival, Tokyo, Japan

NOVEMBER

Stockholm Film Festival, Stockholm, Sweden
International Documentary Film Festival, Amsterdam, The Nether-
    lands
Festival International du Film Indépendant, Brussels, Belgium
AFI Los Angeles International Film Festival, Los Angeles, California
Pusan International Film Festival, Pusan, Korea

DECEMBER

Havana International Latin American Film Festival, Havana, Cuba

Below are profiles of prominent premiere festivals and markets, in calendar order, intended as a guide to encourage readers to contact the specific festivals for entry requirements, travel and housing details:

1. *Sundance Film Festival* (January) in Park City, Utah. Web site: www. sundance.org. Considered the hottest venue for independent American films, this festival was developed by Robert Redford's Sundance Institute (founded in 1981) as a way to boost attention for smaller films and filmmaking talent being ignored by Hollywood. Today it bustles with distribution, acquisition and production executives as well as agents and journalists looking to find or cash in on the "next big thing." The festival receives major publicity around the world, and "Official Selection, Sundance Film Festival" on a film's poster gets the attention of discriminating moviegoers. Being picked up for distribution at Sundance is certainly a publicity bonanza, but no guarantee of commercial success. Access to the festival is via the Salt Lake City International Airport, about an hour away from Park City. Accommodations in Park City are expensive and hard to find due to the concurrent ski season, so reserve early.

2. *Slamdance Film Festival* (January) in Park City, Utah. Web site: www. slamdance.com. Slamdance has quickly grown to become a home dedicated to first-time filmmakers with projects budgeted under $500,000. In addition to its main festival, Slamdance has numerous "on the road" screenings throughout the world and has launched a European festival in Cologne, Germany. Because Slamdance runs at the same time as Sundance in Park City, accommodations are expensive and need to be reserved well in advance.

3. *Clermont-Ferrand International Short Film Festival* (January) in Clermont-Ferrand, France. Web site: www.clermont-filmfest.com. Clermont-Ferrand is regarded as the major event for short films each year. The festival includes a market and attracts buyers from as far away as Latin America and Australia. For anyone with a short film, this is the venue to attract distribution and make contacts. The festival draws 1,500 professionals to the Short Film Market, among them sixty-five TV buyers, and includes a market catalogue describing more than 2,500 new titles. Access to Clermont-Ferrand is from Paris or Nice. Accommodations tend to be moderate to expensive.

4. *Berlin International Film Festival* (February) in Berlin, Germany. Web site: www.berlinale.de. Berlin is one of the oldest (founded in 1951) and most prestigious European events, dating back to before the Berlin Wall.

The festival also includes a major film and television market, attracting buyers and sellers from every continent. The event takes place at the Potsdamer Platz, once part of East Berlin and now a showcase for the technological advancement of Germany. Access to Berlin is easy from almost every major airline. Accommodations range from luxurious hotels such as the Hilton or Westin to hostels and pensions.

5. *American Film Market* (February/March) in Santa Monica, California. Web site: www.afma.com. Founded in 1981, the American Film Market (AFM) has grown steadily to become the largest motion-picture trade event in the world. Unlike a film festival, the AFM is a marketplace where over $500 million in production and distribution deals are closed annually. Each year, more than 7,000 people convene in Santa Monica for eight days of screenings, dealmaking and hospitality. Participants come from over seventy countries and include leaders in motion-picture production, distribution and trade groups, directors, agents, writers, lawyers and bankers. The AFM is *the* annual Hollywood gathering for the global motion-picture industry. The events and receptions offer excellent ways to build contacts. Access to Los Angeles is easy from almost every major airline; accommodations range from affordable to expensive.

6. *Cannes* (May) in Cannes, France. Web site: www.festival-cannes.org. Founded in 1946 and regarded as the premier film festival in the world and a major European launching ground for Hollywood and international product. The Cannes market is expansive and features areas like the American Pavilion, which is home to U.S. entities such as the Independent Feature Project (IFP) and Kodak during the festival. Access to Cannes by airplane is usually through Nice or via Paris, then by train to Cannes. Please note: Hotels and food are unbelievably expensive.

7. *World Festival of Animated Films* (held every other June) in Zagreb, Croatia. Web site: www.animafest.hr. Zagreb, part of the former Yugoslavia, is the home to one of the most creative and vibrant animation communities in the world. The Zagreb festival was founded in 1972 and is held in accordance with the rules and protocol of ASIFA (Association Internationale du Film d'Animation). The festival continued to be held even during the Balkan war in the mid-1990s and is known worldwide as one of the friendliest places for animators. Most of the major European airlines fly to Zagreb, and Croatia Airlines has many affordable flights from hub cities such as Paris, London and Frankfurt. Accommodations in Zagreb are affordable.

8. *Karlovy Vary International Film Festival* (July) in Karlovy Vary, Czech Republic. Web site: www.iffkv.cz. The premier showcase for eastern Euro-

pean films, Karlovy Vary is a festival filled with tradition from both east and west, usually inviting many films from Sundance to have their European premiere. The event takes place in a small artists' village about two hours from Prague. Access to Karlovy Vary is easiest by flying to Prague, which is serviced by many American and European airlines. From Prague, the festival usually picks up guests at the airport, or one can take a bus or train to the festival. Accommodations range from affordable to expensive.

9. *Toronto International Film Festival* (September) in Toronto, Canada. Web site: www.bell.ca/filmfest. Launched in the mid-1970s as a modest event to bring films to Canadian film-lovers, Toronto has grown to become a major launching pad for Hollywood, international and independent films. The festival has a strong market component, filled with distributors and held at the Rodgers Industry Centre. The festival is unique in that it is easily accessible to the public and attracts a strong local audience. Toronto has one of the most pleasant festival atmospheres, as the entire city comes alive during the event. Most airlines fly to Toronto; accommodations range from affordable to expensive.

10. *New York Film Festival* (September/October) in New York City. Web site: http://www.filmlinc.com/nyff/nyff.htm. Founded in 1962 and housed at the beautiful Lincoln Center venue, the New York Film Festival has become a major showcase for American, international and independent films. The special presentations are interesting and well-prepared, often linking the New York film scene with the global market. The festival attracts a combination of Manhattan audiences, industry types and filmmakers in an exciting atmosphere. Accommodations range from affordable to expensive.

11. *International Documentary Film Festival Amsterdam* (November) in Amsterdam, The Netherlands. Web site: www.idfa.nl. Started in the late 1980s, IDFA has grown to become a hub of documentary filmmaking. The festival includes a major market, pitch forums, seminars and receptions for filmmakers to interact with industry people. IDFA is regarded as the key venue for the premiere of a documentary. Most airlines fly to Amsterdam; accommodations range from affordable to expensive.

The growth of festivals has created an independent screening circuit throughout the world to exhibit a film without a major distributor. The key challenge for filmmakers is to navigate among choices and match the right venue to their film project. One early decision is whether to approach festivals and try to get the completed film screened (in or out of competition) or to turn to film markets such as in Cannes or at the AFM (American

Film Market) in Santa Monica to try to sell it directly to a distributor. Sometimes these strategies merge, proceeding on both tracks, with the evolving results dictating future steps.

RESEARCHING FESTIVALS AND MARKETS

After consulting with hundreds of filmmakers, distributors and festival directors throughout the world, some common advice emerges to navigate through film festival calls for entries, selection committees, juries and programming.

Assume you are a producer or are in a group of filmmakers who have completed an independent film and are now seeking distribution. Take a while to research and answer the following strategic questions:

1. Will your film be suitable to submit to a major festival such as Sundance or Berlin? Will the timing work?

2. Is your film more at home in alternative festivals? If so, which ones?

3. Do you want to premiere your film in a major venue such as Berlin to compete against hundreds of filmmakers and publicists? Or do you have a local festival in your city, where you can have the advantage of premiering in your backyard?

4. Is your film designed for video and cable distribution instead of theatrical release?

5. Is your film mainstream, indie, experimental, documentary or genre-oriented? This profile could exclude certain festivals and markets that cater to other types of films.

6. Do you want to sell your film or do you want to use your film as a vehicle to promote yourself as a filmmaker? (These strategies are not mutually exclusive and are especially applicable to shorts, animation and documentaries.)

7. Do you have the funds to submit your film to festivals at an average $50 each? To travel to festivals if you get accepted? To hire a publicist if you get into a festival such as Toronto or Slamdance? To participate in a film market such as Berlin or AFM?

8. Are you willing to spend a considerable part of eighteen months away from your job and family if your film becomes a hit on the festival circuit?

9. Are you prepared to negotiate for the sale of your film with distributors? Are you familiar with what types of contracts will be needed?

10. Do you have a publicist? Agent? Attorney? Accountant?

The cycle from completion of postproduction through taking your film to festivals around the world will often take about two years. For example, one director gave up his apartment and put his life on hold to spend fourteen months on the road, promoting his film at festivals such as Karlovy Vary, Berlin and Slamdance. This becomes expensive because, even if a festival pays for hotel and travel, the filmmaker has taken time away from work developing future projects.

SUBMITTING TO FESTIVALS

A careful festival plan and budget should become part of the picture's budget, developed alongside the production planning of the film. Although this advice is ignored time and again by filmmakers, it is critical to your success. Too often, filmmakers run out of money by the end of postproduction, which is exactly the time you need to be focusing on festival submissions and expenditures. In the film's budget, create a budget line for "festivals" and include the following categories: publicist, travel, applications, shipping, telephone and promotional materials. A sample budget for an indie film with the goal of going to ten major festivals might look like this:

- Publicist—$2,000 per festival

- Travel—$750 per U.S. festival, $1,500 per international festival

- Applications—$50 average per festival

- One film print—$11,000 (at least two are recommended)

- Video transfer to Beta PAL—$200 (for festivals outside the U.S.)

- Shipping—$25 to $200, depending whether a video or film print

- Telephone—$50 per U.S. festival, $150 per international festival

- Promotional materials—$400 per festival

- FESTIVAL BUDGET: $14,475–$15,500

Add to this total a 10% contingency for unexpected costs, ranging from the fun of buying beers all night when celebrating a win to the problem of having to strike a new print in a few days because the only print was scratched at the last festival it was in.

Some filmmakers would argue that the above prices are expensive, that it can be done for less. The filmmaking group can reduce costs by doing its own publicity and by staying with family or friends when attending festivals; for example, nearby Salt Lake City often becomes a home away from home during Sundance. But festivals such as Karlovy Vary, Berlin and Venice require expensive, fixed travel and promotional costs. Assume a director of a film gets invited to Berlin and the festival picks up the airfare and hotel expenses. What if the producer or writer wants to go? What about the publicist? These extra costs would come directly out of the festival budget item. Assembling a group of key players associated with the film translates into value as everyone pitches in time and energy around the hectic day of the screening. Filmmaker Kevin DiNovis won the 1998 Slamdance Grand Jury Prize for *Surrender Dorothy* with almost no money. Kevin followed a careful plan, spending twenty hours a day promoting his film, doing all the work himself. He became friends with the festival staff and is still involved with Slamdance years later.

Ray Barry, who runs the AFI National Film Theater at the John F. Kennedy Center for the Performing Arts in Washington, D.C., has been involved with hundreds of festivals for more than three decades. According to Barry, who served on a recent jury at Slamdance, "success at festivals involves being able to develop a plan for positioning your film every step of the way. You need to find the right festivals to submit your film to, budget accordingly and promote your film every chance you get. Even though Slamdance is one of my favorite festivals, I would not recommend a Hollywood romantic comedy be submitted there. While this is an extreme example, it proves that filmmakers need to research the right venues for their film."

This underscores the common-sense rule to match your film to your targeted festivals; a common mistake finds filmmakers submitting a film that is completely inappropriate to certain festivals. Submitting a $3 million film with stars to Slamdance makes no sense for their programming sensibility, since research will find that Slamdance is dedicated to first-time filmmakers and projects under $500,000. Another mismatch would be to submit an American comedy filled with political jokes and golf terminology to an overseas festival, where subtitles might not translate the subtlety of the humor.

The next step in planning involves research. Some of the best Web sites for this include www.filmfestivals.com, www.filmthreat.com and www.ifilm.com. An extremely helpful book to consult is Chris Gore's *The*

Ultimate Film Festival Survival Guide, the most comprehensive account of festivals, including interviews with festival directors such as Sundance's Geoff Gilmore. This research will turn up festivals in every country imaginable.

Next, narrow down the list by visiting the festival Web sites and deciding if your film is a good match for the festival program. Make sure to read reviews from previous years and examine what types of films tend to be accepted and successful. If this information is not available on the Web, call the festival and have them send a catalog from the previous year.

Narrow your target list to twenty festivals, along with entry deadlines and the exact festival dates. If there is a festival that is your ideal target, such as Sundance, you may want to hold off on all entries until you know if you have been accepted there. Certain festivals such as Cannes, Venice or Karlovy Vary may request a premiere in their territory; this may affect timing and strategy. For example, if the Tokyo Film Festival requests an Asian premiere or Cannes requests a European premiere as a condition of submission, you would hold off on entries to other festivals in the region until you know if you are accepted. Other common-sense issues might involve running time; for instance, your research would show that the Berlin Film Festival places limits on the length of short films submitted to that competition.

The following preparation checklist is useful to plan submissions:

1. Festival name:

2. Dates:

3. Does the festival require a premiere?

4. Format: Will the festival screen in DVD, Beta, 16mm or 35mm?

5. Submission deadline:

6. Is your film produced within the time frame allowed by the rules (usually within twelve to twenty-four months) of the festival?

7. Personal contacts at festival:

Here's a checklist of submissions materials usually required:

1. General information and contact sheet

2. VHS screener(s) (NTSC or PAL? or DVD?)

3. Key cast and crew bios

4. B&W and color photos of a key image of your film and of the director and lead cast

5. Press kit (bios, background articles, still photos)

6. Entry fee (for international festivals, pay with a credit card, since U.S. checks are not always payable in foreign banks)

7. Release form (to insure that you own the rights to the material you are submitting)

Since festivals are overwhelmed with entries, the easiest way to disqualify your film is to fill out the submission materials improperly. In a surprising number of cases, filmmakers send films that are not eligible or do not conform to the festival's needs. Another common mistake is not filling out the contact information so even when a film has been accepted, the festival cannot find the filmmaker.

Once the submission material is ready, check that you have included everything according to the festival submission guidelines. If there are any questions, consult the festival's Web site FAQs or call the festival directly for clarification. When speaking with a festival representative, you can also make a personal contact and ask more detailed questions. Usually, people who work in festival offices are glad to speak with applicants, but not if you have waited until the last minute to submit your film. After you have double-checked your material, include a polite cover letter and mail your package.

STRATEGY AFTER ACCEPTANCE IN A FESTIVAL

After putting years into financing and producing a film, one would think that the golden parachute is acceptance in Cannes, Toronto or Sundance, which sometimes comes with free airfare and hotel, invitations to speak on panels, press interviews and, of course, admission to parties. Sounds good, doesn't it?

In reality, if you have the good fortune of being accepted to a festival, some of the hardest work is ahead.

First, there is the competition to consider. Submissions to a recent Sundance Film Festival included 390 documentaries, 854 dramatic features, 515 international films, and 2,174 short films, from which 112 feature-length films and 64 shorts were selected for both competitive and showcase screenings to an audience of more than 20,000 people. Simply put, the competition is fierce. Sundance is not only filled with filmmakers competing for the coveted awards, but also with executives, agents, publicists, press and distributors tracking every film and looking for the next *Blair Witch Project.* In addition, Slamdance takes place during the same dates as Sundance; over the years, festivals including Lapdance, Nodance and Undance have emerged as well. Success in Park City is based on preparation. Acceptances come in November, giving filmmakers about two months to prepare for some of the most intense ten days of their lives.

Next comes planning for attending the actual festival. Here is a checklist of the essentials geared to Sundance, but a variation can apply to almost any festival you choose:

1. *Publicity.* Hire a publicist familiar with Park City who is able to arrange interviews for you with press, including *Variety, Hollywood Reporter* and *IndieWire,* and to place you on discussion panels or in any other venues to publicize the film.

2. *Promotional materials.* Posters, postcards and other materials should be created in advance to promote your film in Park City. Some filmmakers give away T-shirts or baseball caps with the film's name on it to try to attract audiences to their screenings. With hundreds of films playing in less than two weeks, getting the attention of festivalgoers is not easy.

3. *Practical logistics.* Hotel rooms, phones, computer access to e-mail and setting up convenient meeting locations are all common-sense logistical basics. Finding a hotel room, for instance, sounds easy, but hotels in Park City are sometimes booked as much as a year in advance. Even if the festival provides the director with a hotel room, the publicist and additional cast or crew members will need places to stay.

4. *Print.* Obviously, the print of the film must be finished in time for the festival screening; allow enough leadtime for unanticipated delays. Consider striking a backup print in case your principal print becomes damaged during a screening.

5. *Distribution.* Arrange for the services of an entertainment lawyer in advance. This calls for the same kind of research and interviewing as with any other essential member of your team. Since the objective is to achieve a distribution deal based on your screening, be prepared and discuss the standard deal terms with your attorney in advance; know what you will and won't accept. Although it may be too expensive to have the attorney join you at the festival, he or she must be on call to negotiate with a distributor.

6. *Screenings.* The festival usually allows the filmmakers a number of screening tickets; know how many are allowed and buy more if necessary for cast, crew and friends who can attend to support the film. This also applies to parties, receptions and special events.

7. *Interviews.* Practice interview technique with the publicist or friends

who are familiar with press interviews. Sometimes the press will ask a question to throw your guard off; rehearse how to handle this or answer a different question. Most press interviews lead to valuable publicity; keep the conversation on topic, and the topic is the film. A common mistake among newcomers is to criticize companies or other films; be careful to avoid this, since it is unprofessional (even though an interviewer might encourage controversy) and takes attention away from your movie.

8. *Keep in mind.* Festivals are a frantic time; workers and guests never get enough sleep and party much too hard. Treat festival staffers and volunteers with the respect they deserve; don't become that arrogant filmmaker bossing around a festival volunteer who is working an eighteen-hour day. At Slamdance, for instance, where the motto is "for filmmakers by filmmakers," every festival participant—volunteer, filmmaker, staff member or jury member—is treated equally, creating a warm and wonderful culture over the years.

DISTRIBUTION

The theatrical distributors whose acquisition executives scour film festivals for completed movies to acquire are of two types: divisions of large studios and stand-alone companies. Miramax is owned by Disney; New Line and Fine Line are owned by Time Warner; then there are Sony Pictures Classics, Paramount Classics and Fox Searchlight. The truly independent, stand-alone distributors include Newmarket, Strand, Lions Gate (which bought Artisan), Lot 47, and IFC Films. Distributors use festivals and markets in the following ways:

1. To scout and acquire new products, mostly via negative pickup deals;

2. To announce deals and joint ventures to the press and the industry;

3. To premiere a film being distributed in the country of the festival (for example, *Hannibal* had its German premiere at the 2001 Berlin Film Festival);

4. To enter into partnerships and coproduction deals (commonplace at AFM, Berlin, Cannes and MIPCOM);

5. To host parties and receptions to publicize a film in a territory (for example, Disney held the European premiere and a major gala for the release of *Fantasia 2000* during that year's Karlovy Vary International Film Festival);

6. To announce an acquisition or the launch of a new company.

Such events have taken place for decades at festivals and become formulaic. For example, a studio has a general budget, staff and approach to bringing a major star such as Kevin Spacey to Cannes or Nicole Kidman to Venice. The biggest variable in distribution is really for the independent filmmaker, who inevitably ends up in one of two positions at a festival or market—power or need.

The ideal, most powerful position for a filmmaker is when more than one distributor is interested in the film. This, of course, improves the filmmaker's bargaining power with each, so that attention can be paid to issues like the size of the dollar advance being offered, dollar commitments to P&A (prints and advertising) and general release pattern planned, including a minimum number of screens. Other key deal terms could include a festival cash bonus and whether the distributor will support going to other festivals. For example, if the distributor is seeking worldwide rights and you have won a Sundance award, will they support a European premiere at the Berlin Film Festival? If so, will they pay airfare and hotel for key talent to attend the festival? Will they host a reception in Berlin?

Without question, the reputations of the distributors come into play. Contact other filmmakers who have experience with these distributors; ask how it was to work with them and about the type of support received in P&A, festivals, promotion and press. Most filmmakers are willing to speak candidly about their good and bad experiences. Since theatrical release drives the rest of a film's distribution, settling on the right distributor is essential. In some cases, it might be best to sign with one offering less money up front but guaranteeing opening in a certain number of theaters in the domestic market. A strong theatrical opening and favorable reviews, even in only ten cities, can make or break an independent film and help position you to secure funding for your next film.

A second-best position would find a filmmaker negotiating with only one domestic distributor. In this case, though gathering research on how the distributor handled other films is useful, one has hardly any bargaining power.

The more difficult or needy situation is when there is little or no interest from distributors during and after a festival. This says nothing about the quality of the film or its potential for success; many films have experienced strong audience response or critical acclaim at a festival but left without a distribution deal. For example, *Hype!*, a documentary chronicling the Seattle music scene, screened during Sundance 1996 to terrific responses from audiences and critics. Although there was some interest in the film and the soundtrack was being distributed by Sub Pop Records, *Hype!* left Sundance without a deal. Finally, after much persistence and hard work, producer Steve Helvey and director Doug Pray secured a distribution deal with Cinepix Film Properties ten months later. *Hype!* went on to a successful limited theatrical release and to receive distribution in cable, video and elsewhere. Another film, *You Can Count On Me,* did not achieve a distribution deal at Sundance 2000 but became a success afterwards via Paramount Classics.

Key points in a contract with a distributor include:

1. Acquisition cost

2. Advance payment

3. P&A guarantee in dollars

4. Bonuses

5. Payment/royalty schedule

6. Standard delivery items

7. Territory covered by the contract

8. Minimum number of theaters in a domestic theatrical release

The tough negotiations follow a filmmaker's return from a festival, when the attorney works with the distributor to hammer out the deal for a negative pickup agreement. This calls for the distributor to "pick up" the movie in their territory upon delivery of the negative along with standard delivery requirements, a list of numerous picture and track materials, including an interpositive print, separate music and effects soundtracks, music legal releases, the final shooting script and still photos (in black-and-white and color) of key cast and crew of the film. The process of completing delivery often takes months.

Festivals can represent the best and most stressful times in a filmmaker's career. The experience can be filled with friends, parties and sold-out screenings, but also tough critics, and perhaps a twenty-four-hour deadline to make a decision involving hundreds of peoples' lives and millions of dollars. Success at festivals is about strategy, as detailed above, but the best advice to filmmakers is . . . try to have some fun while you're at it!

VIII

THE REVENUE STREAMS

THE REVENUE STREAMS: AN OVERVIEW

by **STEVEN E. BLUME,** chief financial officer of Brillstein-Grey Entertainment in Beverly Hills, a diversified entertainment company with talent management, television and film production operations. Mr. Blume has served as chief financial officer at Solomon International Enterprises, an international television distribution and broadcasting company; as senior vice president, finance, for Largo Entertainment, a feature film company; and as chief financial officer of Hemdale Film Corporation. A graduate of California State University, Northridge, he began his career at Ernst & Young. In addition to his current duties at Brillstein-Grey, Mr. Blume is an adjunct professor at the University of Southern California School of Cinema-Television, where he teaches a graduate course, Entertainment Industry Finance and Economics.

What does it take for a film to break even, and what is meant by breakeven? It is important to understand that there are various breakeven points to a film depending on perspective.

Have you ever gone to a movie and wondered how much money was made or lost on the film? The answer is complex, depending on a labyrinth of distribution and production arrangements. To determine profit or loss in the feature film business, it is important to understand the exploitable life of a movie.

The feature film business has created clever business models that evolve over time and recognize that customers have different lifestyles and different abilities to pay. For someone who enjoys the social experience of going out to the movies, theaters offer an impressive, big-screen experience. Someone who prefers watching movies at home and controlling the experience is sure to find a home video store nearby with a variety of titles for rental or purchase. Television viewing has expanded options: Pay-television channels supply a package of programming combining recently released movies and original programming for a regular monthly price, while for those who prefer to pay only when actually viewing a film, there is the convenience of pay-per-view or video-on-demand. Vast libraries of older films can be found on basic-cable channels, sold as part of a low-cost basic-cable tier of service, often with commercials; and there is always free television, with its commercial breaks.

The major studios have grown into giant, vertically integrated conglomerates that control the revenue streams generated by their feature films throughout the world. At the same time, the biggest movies have evolved into "events" and "brands" to be further exploited through the merchandising of consumer products, novelizations, soundtracks, music publishing, comic books, theme park rides, and the gold ring of the film business, the production of evergreen sequels, remakes, spin-offs, and live-action and animated television series.

Movies are a distinct part of American culture, and one way or another, movies will find you.

WINDOWS OF EXHIBITION

The distribution life cycle of a completed film has grown over years with the advent of each new technology. This can best be expressed as staggered and timed "windows" of exhibition, triggered by the initial theatrical release of the film in each territory around the world. In all cases, deals are negotiated between the movie's owner (the financier-distributor, or studio) and a company (related or unrelated) specializing in each medium of exhibition, including timed *holdbacks,* which, for fixed time periods, contractually prevent release in subsequent media. The movie business has created these windows and holdbacks to maximize revenues with a minimum of cannibalization from one market to the next.

The following chart traces the actual life cycle of a typical film, owned worldwide by a financier-distributor studio. Assume our sample film had an exclusive six-month run in U.S. theaters, followed by a home-video release four to six months later. The pay-per-view broadcast is contractually allowed two months after the home video release, and the pay-television broadcast is prohibited until twelve months after the initial theatrical release (or six months after the initial video release). These pay-per-view and pay-television holdbacks are designed to maximize the home video potential of the film, which can represent the largest single source of worldwide revenue. Eventually, this film may be broadcast on network television, a second pay-television window, basic cable and/or syndication by independent stations across the country. Each of these broadcasters has an exclusive window to themselves, even though the film is still available in video stores. In addition, the film is released in over fifty international territories, with each one creating its own unique specific windows of exhibition. In this manner, the studio will still be generating significant revenues from this film years after its initial theatrical release. One way to remember the sequence of these windows is that they appear in the order of the most revenue generated to the movie's owner, after the time-honored theatrical run.

Medium	Window	Beginning
Theatrical	6 months	Initial theatrical release
Home video	10 years	4 to 6 months after initial theatrical release
Pay-per-view	2 months	8 months after initial theatrical release
Pay television	18 months	12 months after initial theatrical release
Network	30 months	30 months after initial theatrical release
Pay television second window	12 months	60 months after initial theatrical release
Basic cable	60 months	72 months after initial theatrical release
Syndication	60 months	132 months after initial theatrical release

While the reader will focus on specific business models for the different delivery formats in other articles later in this book, they are all covered here as an overview.

THEATRICAL DISTRIBUTION

The key to the profitability of a feature film is its theatrical run. A successful theatrical box office performance will help define and increase the value of later revenue streams such as home video and pay and free television, as well as consumer-products opportunities generated from merchandising and licensing of the characters and their likenesses.

Each territory throughout the world has its own theatrical release and its own ancillary markets. (The industry has historically used the term "ancillary," which means "subordinate," to refer to any market after theatrical. This is an antiquated notion, since most of these formats, including home video and television, have become primary sources of revenue, not secondary. For the sake of continuity, this article will continue to use the term, but I encourage industry members to redefine it to exclude home video, broadcast and pay television, which have become standard distribution outlets for most major feature films.)

Theatrical distribution of a film involves licensing and booking in movie theatres, marketing through advertising and publicity, manufacturing release prints and delivering these prints to those theaters licensed to play the movie. (Digital projection will eliminate the use and cost of prints.)

In the United States, major studios completely control the theatrical distribution arena, consistently earning more than 95% of market share. In international territories, films released by the major studios control anywhere from 45% to 90% of the box office on a country-by-country basis, with an overall average of about 65%. The studios have their own branch offices in most of the major territories, allowing them to directly distribute to theaters in those countries. In the smaller territories, the majors will distribute their films through local subdistributors. The dependent independents (those production companies that usually release through a major studio in the United States only) use local subdistributors as well, or the branch offices of major studios, to distribute their films on a territory-by-territory basis.

Significant planning goes into every aspect of theatrical release, with the distributor coordinating:

- creation of the advertising campaign, including the posters and TV spots

- the publicity effort, covering TV and magazine interviews with the stars and filmmakers

- a press junket to create important publicity

- the booking of the theaters

- the placement of the advertising in newspapers, radio and television

- the test screening of the film with audiences to determine its strengths and weaknesses

- the physical delivery of the film prints to each theater

- the expensive process of striking prints from the negative of the film

- the weekly decision to continue to support the film with additional advertising

- the coordination of commercial tie-ins with consumer products companies to copromote their products while also marketing the films.

Theatrical exhibitors (theatre owners) are involved in three separate but interrelated businesses: real estate, concession sales, and the exhibition of films. Theatre chains either own or lease the land and buildings for their theatre sites, giving rise to potentially large profits or losses tied to the value of real estate. By far, their highest-margin business segment is concession sales, typically representing 25% to 30% of a theatre's gross revenue, *none of which is shared with the studios.*

Prior to the 1950s, most of the major studios owned U.S. theatre chains. When independent theatre-owners petitioned the Justice Department to look into this as anticompetitive, a lengthy legal battle resulted. In 1948 this was resolved in the U.S. Supreme Court. In *U.S. v. Paramount, et al.,* the Court found that the theatre-owning studios had successfully conspired to restrain and monopolize interstate trade in the distribution and exploitation of films. Shortly thereafter, those studios sold off their theatre interests. Some studios have acquired partial ownership in theatres since, but this has been kept to a minimum.

The agreements between exhibitors and distributors provide that theatres must charge certain minimum prices so as not to commingle box office revenues, which are shared with the distributor, with concession revenues, which are not. The exhibitor collects the box office revenues and pays the distributor its share, called *film rental.* In general, the exhibitor retains a fixed amount per week to cover theater overhead, plus a box office percentage that generally escalates over time.

Distributors negotiate their film rental terms with exhibitors prior to the release of each film. At present, for Universal, Sony, Warner Bros., New Line, Fox and DreamWorks, these negotiated terms are firm, without the possibility of renegotiation after the run, a risky policy for theatres if the picture performs poorly. Other distributors, including Paramount, Disney and MGM, allow for a review of the terms, and a renegotiation with exhibitors at the end of the theatrical run of each film.

Typical terms of an agreement between an exhibitor and a distributor might read as follows: "A 90/10 split after deduction of the house allowance of $3,000, with a floor of 70%." This means that the film rental payable by the exhibitor to the distributor would be the greater of (a) 90% of the gross box office receipts less the negotiated house allowance of (in this case) $3,000, or (b) 70% of the gross box office receipts without regard to the house allowance. As the theatrical run progresses, the percentage of box office receipts paid to the distributor decreases. This provides incentive for the exhibitor to keep the film in the theatre for a longer period of time, thereby maximizing revenues for both the exhibitor and the distributor. On average over the life of a theatrical run, film rentals in the United

States will usually approximate 50% of the box office, give or take 5%, so a rule of thumb has developed that 100% of film rental is 50% of box office gross. On average, overseas film rental will usually approximate 40% of the overseas box office gross.

Assuming worldwide ownership of a movie, the distributor's share of proceeds from domestic theatrical goes into a *picture pot,* where it combines with later dollars in a grouping of all income and expenses, both domestic and overseas. While in reality there are often different picture pots for a given movie based on a variety of contractual requirements, we will simplify things for the moment and refer to only one picture pot, which represents the studio's pot. Later in this article, we will discuss the pots for profit participants.

No audience is too small for the movie industry, as demonstrated by the *nontheatrical market.* Licensing of nontheatrical distribution rights includes airlines, ships at sea, schools, public libraries, community groups, armed services, correctional facilities, and others. Nontheatrical revenues from a typical film might equal about 5% of the domestic theatrical film rental, and the nontheatrical window typically kicks in shortly after theatrical release.

HOME VIDEO

The invention of the VCR allowed consumers for the first time to view feature films on an individual basis directly in their homes. The growth of VCR penetration in the 1980s created an enormously lucrative new revenue stream for motion picture owners. Distributing feature films to the home video marketplace consists of the promotion and sale of videocassettes and DVDs to local, regional and national video retailers that rent or sell them to consumers for home viewing. (For more details on the home video market, see the articles by Benjamin S. Feingold, p. 408, and Paul Sweeting, p. 418.)

When video retailers began renting videos (without the obligation to share revenues with copyright holders), distributors decided to sell their titles to retailers for a high wholesale price (around $65) to compensate for their inability to share in rental revenues. As such, two pricing tiers evolved, a higher price that encouraged rental and discouraged purchase, and a lower price that encouraged purchase, known as the sell-through price (around $20). In the early days of home video, most feature films were initially priced for rental, with a re-release at sell-through pricing approximately six months to one year after the initial release. This release pattern was the norm throughout the 1980s and most of the 1990s.

The home video market continued to evolve, and in the late 1990s, re-tailers and distributors signed revenue-sharing deals. For the retailer, these revenue-sharing deals reduced their up-front cost, allowing them to order more copies of new releases, in effect guaranteeing that every customer could get any movie at any time. Under this plan the distributor was for the first time to share in rental revenues, thereby making far more profit on extremely successful titles.

The success of DVDs changed the home-viewing marketplace once again. DVDs were initially priced in the $15 to $30 range, much lower than the $65 wholesale price for videocassettes. Since the video retailers' up-front cost was much lower for DVDs than for videocassettes, retailers had no incentive to share the rental revenues with distributors, and a battle ensued. As the marketplace shifts from videocassettes to DVDs, the industry grapples with the viability of the revenue-sharing model, with retailers threatening not to renew revenue-sharing contracts with distrib-utors.

The following is a summary of the typical economics under each of the home-video pricing models (rental, sell-through and revenue-sharing):

A VHS title designated for the *rental* market might have a suggested re-tail price of around $100. Assume the video store pays a wholesale price of $65 for each unit purchased from the studio. If the video store rents the title to consumers for $3, the store would be in profits after each tape was rented twenty-two times (or twenty-two "churns" in industry parlance). The distributor receives the $65 per unit, and depending on the volume of units ordered, has probably paid about $2.50 to manufacture each unit and maybe $7.50 per unit for sales and marketing costs. As such, the dis-tributor can earn a profit of about $55 per unit without taking into ac-count the cost of tapes returned by the retail stores. A successful VHS title might sell 500,000 units priced for rental, making about $27 million of profit to be put into the studio picture pot and applied against the cost of the film.

A VHS title priced for the *sell-through* market might have a suggested retail price of $20. Assume the video store pays $13 wholesale for each unit purchased. If the store sells the title (instead of renting it) for $15, it makes a $2 profit on each unit sold. The distributor receives the $13 per unit and, depending on the volume of units ordered, has probably paid about $2.50 to manufacture each unit and perhaps $2.50 per unit for sales and market-ing costs. As such, the distributor earns a profit of about $8 per unit (with-out taking into account the cost of returns). A successful VHS title would have to sell 3,375,000 units priced for sell-through to make roughly the same $27 million profit as in the rental-market example. This amount would be placed in the studio picture pot and applied against the cost of the film.

Under the VHS *revenue-sharing* model, the retailer might pay between $6 and $10 up front for each unit to the distributor against 45% of the rental revenue collected. If a title were rented twenty times at a price of $3.50 for each rental, the gross revenue to the retailer would be $70. The distributor's 45% share of this rental revenue would be worth approximately $32 per unit. After deducting the same manufacturing and marketing costs as in rental, the distributor's net profit per unit would be $22. In this scenario, retailers would have to order 1,227,273 units for the distributor to earn the same $27 million earned under the traditional pricing model. If each unit of the same title were rented 40 times, the net receipts to the distributor would reach $65 million, a huge windfall to the studio. (40 rentals x $3.50 each = $140, x 45% is $63; minus $10 for manufacturing and marketing costs is $53; x 1,227,273 = $65,045,469.) In the real world, titles generate revenue under each pricing model, so ultimate revenues reflect such combination.

A DVD title priced for sale might have a suggested retail price of $20. Assume the video store pays $17 wholesale for each unit purchased, making a $3 profit on each unit sold. The distributor receives the $17 per unit and, depending on the volume of units ordered, has probably paid about $2.50 to manufacture each unit and perhaps $2.50 per unit for sales and marketing costs. Under this scenario, the distributor earns a profit of about $12 per unit (without taking into account the cost of returns). If, for example, a DVD title sells 5 million units, roughly $60 million of profit would be placed in the studio picture pot and applied against the cost of the film. DVD revenue-sharing and rental models are being created as of this writing.

Before we leave home video, here's an issue that will become more meaningful when we cover typical talent profit participation statements later in this article: In the early days of home video, distributors wanted to avoid having to account to profit participants for manufacturing and marketing costs, so they developed a royalty structure similar to accounting in the book industry. Under this royalty structure, the distributor considers only a contractual percentage of gross home video sales as gross receipts when reporting to profit participants.

The initial royalty rate set by the distributors for titles priced for the rental market was 20% of the gross sales, leaving the distributor with 80% of gross sales to cover their costs and earn a profit. As the distributors became more efficient and lowered their costs, their profits were increased dramatically, none of which were shared with the profit participants. In the early days, profit participants were happy to receive this 20% royalty, since it represented an entirely new and incremental revenue stream. In the sell-through market, distributors adopted a lower royalty rate, typically 10%, because the costs of releasing home video titles to the sell-through market as a percentage of the gross sales price were even higher than for titles priced to the rental market. As the major studios started or acquired their own home video distribution operations, they remained steadfast in retaining the 20%/10% royalty rates as their standard contractual rate for all profit participants. (In some selected instances, top talent can increase the royalty rate to 25%/12.5% or as high as 30%/30%.) As such, worldwide home video represents the largest difference between the studio's profit and the amount reported to the talent participants in the film.

PAY-PER-VIEW/VIDEO-ON-DEMAND

Pay-per-view (PPV) and video-on-demand (VOD) refer to home viewing through a delivery system that can be transported via satellite, cable, Internet or scrambled over-the-air. PPV or VOD is a brief window, starting eight months after theatrical and extending for two months, and has seen a lot of experimenting. Typically, pay-per-view rights would be licensed to a third party such as Viewer's Choice, which bills and collects from the customer. For example, a customer requesting a specific movie via PPV or VOD at a specific time might be charged $4, divided 10% to Viewer's Choice, 45% to the cable operator (perhaps Adelphia in Los Angeles) and 45% to the studio distributor of that movie.

PAY TELEVISION

Feature films are typically available for broadcast on premium pay-subscription television channels within one year after their initial theatrical release and six months after their initial release to the home video market. All of the studio distributors have output deals with premium pay-television broadcasters in the U.S. and other countries throughout the world. These pay-television channels may be delivered into the home via cable, satellite, or over-the-air, depending upon what's available in the consumer's neighborhood. In each case, the signals are scrambled, and a set-top box is required to unscramble the signal.

In the United States the principal premium pay-television broadcasters are Time Warner's HBO, Viacom's Showtime, and Liberty Media's Starz Encore. Under long-term output deals with studios, these companies license the pay-television broadcast rights to all of the studios' newly released theatrical films in exchange for a license fee based upon negotiated percentages of theatrical film rental, with a minimum and maximum license fee payable for each film. This can range from $2 to $3 million on the low side to $15 to $20 million on the high side. Notice that the pay-television revenue for a film is directly related to its box office performance. These pay-television licenses are usually for a period of eighteen months, beginning twelve months after the initial theatrical release, and may include a second license period of twelve months beginning after the first free-television run, which may be about five years after the initial theatrical release.

Assume a consumer pays $50 a month for combined tiers of basic cable and premium channels. That subscription revenue goes to the local cable operator, which shares it with the broadcasters (HBO, Starz, etc.) on a per-subscriber basis.

FREE TELEVISION AND BASIC CABLE

After the pay-television run, the film will be broadcast on either network television, basic-cable television, or syndicated television, in a strategic order depending upon how the copyright holder/studio negotiates with the different providers. Shortly after its theatrical release, the studio plans the film's television windows ten to fifteen years into the future. This strategy will also be influenced by the success of the film's theatrical gross.

Most theatrical films are not broadcast on the major U.S. networks. As more people are viewing feature films on videocassette, DVD, pay-television channels, and pay-per-view broadcasts in advance of their free-television availability, the average prime-time network audience for feature films has been declining. In response, U.S. networks focus on original programming, and have severely reduced time slots dedicated to feature films. In one recent thirty-five-week television broadcast season, a major network only broadcast two theatrical films. For those lucky few films that are purchased, the network pays a fixed license fee to broadcast the film for a specified number of runs over a certain number of years, perhaps in a typical range between $7 and $10 million (blockbusters would be higher), with no other pay- or free-television broadcasts during this period.

To fill this void, the basic-cable channels have stepped in, purchasing the network window debut for many theatrical feature films. In fact, TBS and TNT have recently acquired the U.S. initial network window for more than 200 films. In addition, FX, TNN, Comedy Central, A&E, and Bravo have been regularly purchasing the network window to selected features.

Shared-window deals have developed in which a broadcast network may partner with a cable channel to share the costs of the license. Permutations abound. For example, a recent successful Fox theatrical will be shown in a shared-network window on Fox's broadcast network and its FX cable network after its pay-TV run on HBO. The two Fox channels will pay around 15% of the U.S. theatrical gross to their parent company for the privilege. In another scenario, after it played on Showtime, Fox bought a modestly successful theatrical film exclusively for two runs over one year. TBS and TNT then shared multiple runs of the film over another one-year exclusive window. Then the film returned to Fox for six months, and back to TBS and TNT for their second one-year window. The film then went to Comedy Central for an eighteen-month period, completing a five-year shared basic-cable/free-television window, after which it returned to Showtime for its second premium pay-subscription television window. The license fees paid in the aggregate (excluding the Showtime windows) amounted to 15% of the domestic box office receipts. This practice of shared windows is sure to become more commonplace as other networks are owned by conglomerates that also control cable channels. Examples include Viacom's CBS, UPN, Nickelodeon and MTV; Disney's ABC, Lifetime, A&E and Disney Channel; and Time Warner's WB Network, Comedy Central, TNT and TBS.

TELEVISION SYNDICATION

The television syndication market consists of independent television stations around the country that license programming for their regional market only. A syndicator arranges for many individual regional station licenses, creating something close to a national broadcast. Each station will license a film on a cash basis, a barter basis or some combination of both.

On a cash basis, the station pays the program supplier or syndicator a flat license fee in exchange for a specified number of runs over a term of years, with no other pay- or free-television broadcasts allowed during this period. A local station operator would bid for a package of films based on the station's rate card of advertising-time value, often bidding against a rival station across town. The license fee would be paid by the station to the syndicator over the term of the license, based upon the negotiated payment terms.

On a barter basis, instead of paying a cash license fee, the station gives the syndicator a certain number of advertising spots during each broadcast. The syndicator must then arrange to sell these spots to advertisers, either through a subsidiary company or through an agent. In this manner, the station reduces its cash costs and also its inventory of advertising spots. Recently, the basic-cable channels have become aggressive buyers of motion pictures, in some cases replacing or pushing back the syndication market.

As in many other segments of the entertainment industry, there has been much consolidation in the syndication business, with many studios eliminating the middle man and becoming their own syndicators. For example, Worldvision, Spelling, Viacom and Paramount are combined under Viacom; CBS Enterprises, Group W and MaXaM are combined under a CBS brand, Eyemark; Genesis, Steven J. Cannell, and New World are now part of Fox.

INTERNATIONAL MARKETS

International markets are an increasingly important source of revenues for Hollywood feature films. In general, the overseas exhibition sector is getting stronger as theatres modernize and more multiplexes are built. More theatres translate into wider releases in many territories, timed as close to the U.S. theatrical release as possible to counteract piracy. Currently, international theatrical revenues to the major studios in the U.S. run between 85% to 105% of revenues from the domestic theatrical market. In any given year, a studio's international theatrical revenues may exceed its domestic theatrical revenues, and this trend is expected to continue since the U.S. market is considered mature.

The major overseas territories for the studios, in both theatrical and video markets, include Japan, South Korea and Australia in the Asia Pacific region, and Germany, Italy, United Kingdom, France and Spain in Europe. These territories represent between 65% and 70% of the total foreign theatrical revenues to the major studios, and between 80% and 85% of the total overseas video revenues to the major studios. Imported English-language films generally account for 60% to 90% of the box office in most territories in Europe and Latin America, with the exception of France, where their percentage can be as low as 50%. In Asia (excluding Australia), films imported from the United States account for less than 50% of the local box office receipts.

Each international territory is unique and distinct, and the entertainment business has evolved differently in each territory. For example, in Europe the sell-through video business typically generates more revenue than the video-rental business, while in Asia the video-rental business garners more revenue than sell-through. (For more on the global markets, see the article by Rob Aft, p. 458.)

CONSUMER PRODUCTS

As noted earlier, motion picture studios treat their large-scale, high-profile event movies as "brands." They seek to leverage these brands to sell other products by licensing the use of the name and likeness of the film and various characters within the film to consumer-products companies. A recent event film had more than seventy-five such licenses for a wide variety of products. The selection of a film to be branded stems from its inherent popular qualities (*Harry Potter,* for example), and planning sessions with licensees can begin more than a year before release. (For more details on consumer products, see the article by Al Ovadia, p. 446.)

Separate merchandise licenses are drawn up with companies specializing in apparel; video games and software; gifts and novelties; sporting goods; and toys and games. Because 60% to 70% of all merchandising revenues are from children or people buying for children, some of the major toy companies have formed long-term alliances with studios in order to secure licensing deals on the studio's event films. Examples have included Disney and Mattel, Fox and Galoob, and Disney with Hasbro. But the majority of merchandising deals for feature films are done on a picture-by-picture basis. Under these licensing deals, up-front advances are paid to the studio, with royalties that might range from 2% to 3% for foodstuffs, to 8% to 10% for apparel.

Retail stores typically sell about 80% of their merchandise within eight weeks of the release of the film. One way to extend this shelf life while also expanding the demographic of a property is to produce an animated television show based upon popular characters from the feature film. By keeping the characters in the public media, merchandise sales can continue for a longer period of time. Another phenomenon in the merchandising arena is the notion of "cross-licensing," whereby an entertainment property is paired with another element, such as a sport, which can bring together two fan bases, thereby attracting more clients to each. An example of this would find Warner Bros.' Looney Tunes characters partnering with an in-line skating event.

Another potent source of dollars for studios has come from promotional tie-ins with fast-food chains and companies making beverages, automobiles, telephone service, cosmetics, and credit cards. For a specific event movie, these companies can spend millions of dollars to advertise and cross-promote their products, timed with the release of the film. From the studio-distributor perspective, this type of campaign can generate $30 to $40 million of media awareness for the title, as well as in-store point-of-purchase promotion and premiums or giveaways, all of which are paid for by the consumer-products company. These expenditures represent free advertising and promotion to the distributor, and help increase the theatrical, home video and other ancillary revenue from the film. The consumer-products company typically takes a "too big to fail" mentality, expecting the association of their products with a hit film to increase sales by perhaps 10% to 20% during the course of the campaign.

For any kind of merchandising or promotional tie-in, pressure is on all parties to meet the precise release date. Toys must be on store shelves, posters on fast-food store walls, and this requires sufficient lead time, coordinated among the studio, consumer products companies and retailers.

SUBSEQUENT REVENUE

Commercially successful films can generate substantial dollars from a variety of other ancillary sources. For example, revenues from the sale of movie soundtracks can be significant, as demonstrated by *Charlie's Angels* and many other examples. In a recent year, three soundtrack albums were in the top ten for all albums sold, including the number one album of the year, which sold over nine million units. In addition, the licensing of music contained in the motion picture for sound recording, public performance and sheet music publication may generate additional royalties.

In their ever-increasing desire to leverage their brands, studios are creating theme-park rides based upon their motion pictures. While this does not directly translate into specific quantifiable revenues, it further enhances the overall assets of park-owning studios, delivering promised synergy for their wide-ranging business units.

The creation of derivative works such as remakes, sequels, animated versions, and television series based upon feature films can demonstrate huge hidden values of a film library. Examples include Universal's *The Mummy* and *Jurassic Park* franchises; Paramount's *Star Trek* franchise; New Line's *Friday the 13th* franchise; and the classic, MGM's James Bond franchise, still generating new films more than 40 years after the original. In most cases, the value of the derivative works substantially exceeds the entire revenue stream from the original.

What does the future hold? As new methods for viewing films are developed, additional revenue opportunities arise. There are exciting prospects of delivery via Internet transmission, video-on-demand services, digital distribution, wireless applications, and a host of other creative viewing choices, which will generate new business opportunities for the owners of feature film libraries. (See the article by Dan Ochiva, p. 498.) And since a substantial portion of the worldwide population has not been exposed to most U.S. motion pictures, new opportunities will be created in these emerging markets as the political, social and economic climates improve in these countries.

STUDIO FINANCIAL ANALYSIS

Now we are ready to explore how all these revenue streams come together into the various picture pots to recoup the huge investment a studio makes in a movie, and how these dollars are reported by a studio to itself and to profit participants.

What are a studio's costs and how are they recouped? What does it take for a film to break even, and what is meant by breakeven? It is important to understand that there are various breakeven points to a film depending on perspective. We are going to make some assumptions and calculations demonstrating the studio-distributor's actual revenues vs. actual costs on a typical picture comparing two different models, a breakeven model and a profit model. Then we will show how studio accounting affects three types of talent participants—the highly sought after, dollar-one gross participant; the steady prebreak gross participant and the lowly net-profit participant—each using the same performance assumptions.

Assume a hypothetical action-adventure studio movie with average worldwide costs and revenues as of this writing. A studio is the financier-distributor, owning the film in all formats in all markets around the world in perpetuity. Bear in mind that these figures are for purposes of illustration and to identify concepts. In reality, a daunting aspect of the movie business is that there is no "average"; *every picturemaking experience is a unique prototype* with expenses and revenues ebbing and flowing in each market around the world, vulnerable to an extremely wide range of performance achievement, from hit to miss.

DISTRIBUTOR'S GROSS RECEIPTS

	Breakeven model	*Profit model*
Worldwide theatrical (film rental)	$45,000,000	$80,000,000
Worldwide home video	$43,000,000	$57,000,000
Worldwide television	$27,000,000	$35,000,000
Other ancillary rights	$2,000,000	$4,000,000
Total gross receipts	$117,000,000	$176,000,000

This is a breakdown of distributor's gross receipts. Our breakeven model assumes a worldwide box office gross of $90 million, while the profit model assumes a worldwide box office gross of $160 million. Since roughly half of box office gross returns to the financing studio as film rental, the chart lists $45 million and $80 million respectively.

Worldwide home video is next. These dollar figures ($43 million in the breakeven model and $57 million in the profit model) are the amounts received by the studio through all of its home video/DVD sales activity throughout the world, including wholesale sales to retailers, revenue sharing arrangements with retailers, and other sales.

Worldwide television revenue follows, an aggregate of dollars that flow to the studio from worldwide television licensing agreements, $27 million under the breakeven model and $35 million under the profit model. Included in these worldwide TV gross receipts are payments covering licenses to pay-cable channels, basic cable channels, broadcast networks and independent TV stations globally. "Other ancillary rights" includes proceeds from nontheatrical distribution, royalties from music soundtracks, royalties from merchandise licensing, video games, book publishing and other similar exploitation. Thus we arrive at the total gross receipts of $117 million for the breakeven model and $176 million for the profit model.

Notice that the studio's accounting to itself does not deduct any of its distribution fees. These fees will take on importance when included in the prebreak gross and net-profit participants analysis later on in this article.

NEGATIVE COSTS

	Breakeven model	Profit model
Direct production costs	$55,000,000	$55,000,000
Worldwide theatrical distribution and marketing costs	$45,000,000	$45,000,000
Residuals/off-the-top deductions	$7,000,000	$9,000,000
Worldwide home video costs	$10,000,000	$13,000,000
Profit participations	$0	$0
Total costs	$117,000,000	$122,000,000

Assume our hypothetical film costs $55 million to produce and another $45 million to distribute and market around the world. Residuals are those industrywide payments a studio owes to guild members for specific posttheatrical exploitation of the picture; off-the-top deductions include taxes, insurance, MPAA dues, box office checking and collections. Worldwide home video manufacturing and marketing costs follow, higher in the profit model due to increased sales. Notice that under these two models, the studio did not pay out any profit participations. Under the breakeven model, the studio's gross receipts equal its total costs, $117 million, so the film has reached breakeven. Under the profit model, deducting total costs from gross receipts leaves a studio "cash-on-cash" profit (before deducting overhead and interest) of $54 million.

Now we will apply the same performance assumptions to a studio's accounting to three different talent profit participants, who have each negotiated cash compensation for themselves and back-end participations based on their individual bargaining power: the dollar-one gross participant, the prebreak gross participant and the net-profit participant.

Dollar-One Gross Participant's Financial Analysis

The dollar-one gross participant deal is reserved for only the top stars, directors and producers. Under this deal, the talent receives a fixed fee of cash compensation (a budget item paid during the course of production), which is considered an advance against his or her share of the adjusted gross receipts of the film, or AGR. Here are the adjusted gross receipts for the dollar-one gross participant.

ADJUSTED GROSS RECEIPTS (DOLLAR-ONE GROSS PARTICIPANT)

	Breakeven model	*Profit model*
Worldwide theatrical (film rental)	$45,000,000	$80,000,000
Worldwide home video	$10,750,000	$14,250,000
Worldwide television	$27,000,000	$35,000,000
Other ancillary rights	$2,000,000	$4,000,000
Total gross receipts	$84,750,000	$133,250,000
Less:		
Residuals/off-the-top deductions	–$7,000,000	–$9,000,000
Adjusted gross receipts	$77,750,000	$124,250,000

How do these "Total gross receipts" differ from "Distributor's gross receipts?" Worldwide home video is a percentage of what the studio actually received. Also, the studio has been able to deduct "residuals and off-the-top deductions" against all dollar-one gross participants, arriving at the term "Adjusted gross receipts."

Notice these figures are otherwise the same as for the studio's own reporting, with this *very important exception:* worldwide home video. Remember the point made earlier about how, at the bargaining table in the early days of home video, the studios achieved a favorable royalty system of reporting home video revenue to talent? Here is how that achievement pays off: To dollar-one gross participants, the studio distributor reports only a royalty—in this case, the high-end 25%—on the worldwide home video gross amounts received by its home-video affiliates. Under the breakeven case and the profit case, respectively, worldwide home video gross to the studio is $43,000,000 and $57,000,000; what is reported to this participant is 25% of that or $10,750,000 and $14,250,000, which represents both domestic and overseas home video royalties.

The dollar-one profit participant has negotiated such a favorable deal with the studio that no further deductions, except for his or her own fixed compensation, are made to calculate his or her profit percentage. Assuming this star participant receives cash compensation of $10,000,000 against 15% of the adjusted gross receipts from dollar one, his or her total compensation, both fixed and profit participation, would be $11,662,500 in the breakeven case and $18,637,500 in the profit case.

Prebreak Gross Participant's Financial Analysis

The prebreakeven gross participation is typically given to talent with a strong track record who have not yet qualified for dollar-one gross status. Assume our profit participant's back-end deal was defined as 5% of adjusted gross receipts at cash breakeven with a 10% distribution fee, with escalations keyed to the picture's performance. Notice that this participation begins after cash breakeven, and is *in addition* to the talent's fixed compensation, not against.

As with the dollar-one gross participant, the adjusted gross receipts are similar to the studio's own reporting, but instead of the rarified dollar-one gross's 25% of worldwide home video, the prebreak gross player has negotiated only 20%, based on bargaining power.

ADJUSTED GROSS RECEIPTS (PREBREAK GROSS PARTICIPANT)

	Breakeven model	Profit model
Worldwide theatrical (film rental)	$45,000,000	$80,000,000
Worldwide home video	$8,600,000	$11,400,000
Worldwide television	$27,000,000	$35,000,000
Other ancillary rights	$2,000,000	$4,000,000
Total gross receipts	$82,600,000	$130,400,000
Less:		
Residuals/off-the-top deductions	–$7,000,000	–$9,000,000
Adjusted gross receipts	$75,600,000	$121,400,000

Remember that the prebreak gross profit participant only receives his or her participation with respect to adjusted gross receipts after cash breakeven. "Cash breakeven" is defined as the point at which the studio has earned enough revenues to recoup a myriad of costs, some of which are actual out-of-pocket costs and some of which are imputed costs (to be defined in a moment).

Therefore, we have to calculate "cash breakeven" before determining whether this participant sees any back-end dollars.

ACTUAL STUDIO OUT-OF-POCKET COSTS
(PREBREAK GROSS PARTICIPANT)

	Breakeven model	*Profit model*
Direct production costs	$55,000,000	$55,000,000
Worldwide theatrical marketing	$45,000,000	$45,000,000
Worldwide home video costs	0	0
Profit participations	$0	$0
Total studio out-of-pocket costs	$100,000,000	$100,000,000

From the adjusted gross receipts the studio will deduct its actual out-of-pocket costs, except for its home video manufacturing and marketing costs. The studio absorbs these home video costs out of the 80% of home video receipts that they do not report to this participant. This represents a substantial home video profit to the studio that is not shared with the profit participant, as follows: Under the breakeven model, worldwide home video receipts were $43 million. Eighty percent of that is $34.4 million, minus the studio's worldwide home video costs of $10 million, leaving $24.4 million to the studio. Under the profit model, worldwide home video receipts were $57 million, 80% of which is $45.6 million, minus the studio's worldwide home video costs of $13 million, leaving $32.6 million to the studio. Profit participations in this case refer to any payments made to dollar-one gross participants. Assuming a dollar-one gross player's cash compensation was greater than his or her share of adjusted gross receipts, no further profit participation payment is payable. If any additional amounts had been payable to dollar-one gross participants, they would be included here.

On top of permitting the studio to deduct its actual out-of-pocket costs, the contract allows the studio to charge additional fees and expenses, or imputed costs, against certain participants. Of course the studio does not refer to these costs as imputed costs; however, it is helpful to use the term "imputed" for our purposes to identify further costs that are not out-of-pocket costs to the studio but are still charged against participants, further delaying the cash breakeven point.

IMPUTED COSTS (PREBREAK GROSS PARTICIPANT)

	Breakeven model	Profit model
Distribution fee	$8,260,000	$13,040,000
(10% of total gross receipts)		
Production overhead		
(10% of production costs)	$5,500,000	$5,500,000
Worldwide advertising charge (15%)	$4,000,000	$4,000,000
Interest	$7,000,000	$6,000,000
Total imputed costs	$24,760,000	$28,540,000

The imputed costs include the 10% distribution fee, a production overhead charge of 10%, a worldwide advertising overhead charge of 15% (assuming a $27 million worldwide advertising expenditure, part of the $45 million worldwide theatrical distribution and marketing figure found earlier) and interest at 125% of the prime rate. For simplicity, we are using a $7 million interest cost for the breakeven model and a $6 million cost for the profit model. Here is a review:

NET UNRECOUPED AMOUNT (PREBREAK GROSS PARTICIPANT)

	Breakeven model	Profit model
Adjusted gross receipts	$75,600,000	$121,400,000
Actual costs	−$100,000,000	−$100,000,000
Imputed costs	−$24,760,000	−$28,540,000
Net unrecouped amount	−$49,160,000	−$7,140,000

After deducting the studio's actual out-of-pocket costs and the additional deductions or imputed costs, at the point at which the studio breaks even, it reports a net unrecouped amount of $49 million to the prebreak gross profit participant. In the profit case, remember the studio has earned a cash-on-cash profit of $54 million for itself (explained earlier, when the studio's own accounting was described) but still reports an unrecouped amount of over $7 million to the prebreak gross profit participants. Since revenues are still insufficient to recoup costs, by definition the picture has not reached cash breakeven, and the profit participants are not entitled to any additional payments.

Notice that as the adjusted gross receipts increase, so do the distribution fees. These distribution fees continue to be computed even after cash breakeven has been achieved, creating the concept of a "rolling breakeven," whereby cash breakeven is recalculated at every accounting date so that the studio is assured of recouping all of its costs and distribution fees even if they are incurred after breakeven.

For an example of how a prebreak gross participation kicks in, assume adjusted gross receipts at cash breakeven is $130,000,000. Assume that the movie earned even more, so that total adjusted gross receipts are $135,000,000. Remember that our prebreak gross participant's deal was 5% of AGR after cash breakeven, with a 10% distribution fee. Since the additional revenue carries an additional 10% distribution fee, $555,000 of additional gross is added to the gross needed to reach cash breakeven.

Why is this figure $555,000 instead of $500,000? Here is the concept of "rolling breakeven" at work. Since each dollar of AGR carries a 10% distribution fee, an additional $50,000, or 10%, is added to the AGR, plus an additional 10% of that figure, or $5,000 for a total of $555,000. As such, the AGR after cash breakeven is equal to $4,445,000. Our participant receives 5% of that amount, or $222,250. Any further AGR dollar after cash breakeven is reached carries the 10% distribution fee (and perhaps dollar-one gross participations, if applicable), which "rolls" or pushes back the cash breakeven point, requiring more AGR to reach cash breakeven and so on and so on. . . .

Net-Profit Participant's Financial Analysis

The net-profit participation is given to the lowest level of talent participant. Assume our net-profit participant's deal called for 10% of the net profits with provisions that included a 30% distribution fee, a production overhead charge of 15%, a worldwide advertising overhead charge of 15%, interest at 125% of the prime rate, and worldwide home video included in gross receipts at a 20% royalty (the same home-video royalty as the prebreak gross participant). Both the adjusted gross receipts and the actual studio out-of-pocket costs for the prebreak gross participant would be the same for the net-profit participant. But the studio deducts additional imputed costs (including additional interest) from the net-profit participant, as follows:

IMPUTED COSTS (NET-PROFIT PARTICIPANT)

	Breakeven model	Profit model
Distribution fee		
(30% of total gross receipts)	$24,780,000	$39,120,000
Production overhead	$8,250,000	$8,250,000
(15% of production costs)		
Worldwide advertising charge (15%)	$4,000,000	$4,000,000
Interest	$9,000,000	$11,000,000
Total imputed costs	$46,030,000	$62,370,000

As with the prebreak gross participant, we deduct studio actual costs and imputed costs from the adjusted gross receipts as follows:

NET UNRECOUPED AMOUNT (NET-PROFIT PARTICIPANT)

	Breakeven model	Profit model
Adjusted gross receipts	$75,600,000	$121,400,000
Actual costs	–$100,000,000	–$100,000,000
Imputed costs	–$46,030,000	–$62,370,000
Net unrecouped amount	–$70,430,000	–$40,970,000

Clearly, the net-profit participation is specifically defined by the studio so that it rarely, if ever, pays out. So if you are a producer without the clout to negotiate a dollar-one gross participation or a favorable prebreak gross participation, how do you retain a meaningful profit participation in your film?

The Dependent Independent Producer

The most common way for a producer to improve his or her profit participation is to become a dependent independent producer, distributing a film through a major U.S. studio (hence the term "dependent") but raising additional outside financing through a variety of sources (hence the term "independent"). The most common source of financing for independent feature films is prebuys and/or equity investments from international distributors and broadcasters. Other sources include investors looking for tax shelter, various international government subsidy programs, and perhaps pure equity investors. (Please see article by Steven Gerse, p. 483.)

Under the international presale/prebuy structure, each distributor licenses the film prior to the start of principal photography, providing a minimum guarantee based on the budget of the film, while receiving the distribution rights to its own market or territory in return. The producer then uses these minimum guarantees as collateral to obtain a bank loan to finance production of the film. This territory-by-territory international distribution structure offers many advantages for the producer in comparison to the single-studio worldwide deal. Each distributor receives the distribution rights to their market or territory for a limited period of time, after which the rights revert to the producer, who can then build a library of films for future licensing and new-media opportunities. By spreading the production financing risk among several parties, the producer can exercise more control over the creative and business decisions during production, as well as control of sequels. Another advantage of this model is that it avoids the pitfall of cross-collateralization, in which profits from one territory are offset against losses in another. For example, under this independent-style structure, if a film were a hit in Germany, the German distributor would share those profits directly with the producer. If the film was a loser in France and the French distributor did not recoup its costs, those unrecouped costs would not be offset against the profits from Germany. Under cross-collateralization, they would.

Given the financial benefits, why wouldn't all producers opt for the dependent independent route? Because this method of financing and distributing films is very complex and time-consuming for the producer, who must maintain international sales and marketing executives or contract with an outside sales agent to perform these tasks for the films. Policing the multiple deals made around the world is extremely difficult, taking the producer away from the core task of making hit movies. Also, the producer must obtain enough financing to cover screenplay development costs as well as production, sales and administrative overhead for the entire operation; it's not uncommon for a producer to forgo salary to reduce operational overhead until some films are completed and some cash flow generated. Typically, most dependent independents have two principal owners, one in charge of production and the other in charge of sales and marketing.

After tracing the revenue streams that make up the exploitable life of a motion picture, we have moved on to study performance models and how differently defined profit participants are treated based on contractual definitions contained in their employment agreements with distributors. Finally, here is a review of the tables detailed in this article.

REVIEW OF TABLES

1. Studio Financial Analysis

DISTRIBUTOR'S GROSS RECEIPTS

	Breakeven model	Profit model
Worldwide theatrical (film rental)	$45,000,000	$80,000,000
Worldwide home video	$43,000,000	$57,000,000
Worldwide television	$27,000,000	$35,000,000
Other ancillary rights	$2,000,000	$4,000,000
Total gross receipts	$117,000,000	$176,000,000

NEGATIVE COSTS:

	Breakeven model	Profit model
Direct production costs	$55,000,000	$55,000,000
Worldwide theatrical distribution and marketing costs	$45,000,000	$45,000,000
Residuals/Off-the-top deductions	$7,000,000	$9,000,000
Worldwide home video costs	$10,000,000	$13,000,000
Profit participations	$0	$0
Total costs	$117,000,000	$122,000,000
Net profits (loss)	$0	$54,000,000

2. Dollar-one Gross Participant's Financial Analysis

ADJUSTED GROSS RECEIPTS

	Breakeven model	Profit model
Worldwide theatrical (film rental)	$45,000,000	$80,000,000
Worldwide home video	$10,750,000	$14,250,000
Worldwide television	$27,000,000	$35,000,000
Other ancillary rights	$2,000,000	$4,000,000
Total gross receipts	$84,750,000	$133,250,000
Less:		
Residuals/Off-the-top deductions	−$7,000,000	−$9,000,000
Adjusted gross receipts	$77,750,000	$124,250,000
Profit participant's percentage	15%	15%

Total compensation	$11,662,500	$18,637,500
Less:		
Fixed-compensation in budget	-$10,000,000	-$10,000,000
Dollar-one gross participation	$1,662,500	$8,637,500

3A. Prebreak Gross Participant's Calculation of Adjusted Gross Receipts to Reach Cash Breakeven

ADJUSTED GROSS RECEIPTS

	Breakeven model	*Profit model*
Worldwide theatrical (film rental)	$45,000,000	$80,000,000
Worldwide home video	$8,600,000	$11,400,000
Worldwide television	$27,000,000	$35,000,000
Other ancillary rights	$2,000,000	$4,000,000
Total gross receipts	$82,600,000	$130,400,000
Less:		
Residuals/Off-the-top deductions	–$7,000,000	–$9,000,000
Adjusted gross receipts	$75,600,000	$121,400,000

ACTUAL STUDIO OUT-OF-POCKET COSTS

Direct production costs	$55,000,000	$55,000,000
Worldwide theatrical marketing	$45,000,000	$45,000,000
Worldwide home video costs	0	0
Profit participations	$0	$0
Less: Total studio out-of-pocket costs	–$100,000,000	–$100,000,000

IMPUTED COSTS

Distribution fee	$8,260,000	$13,040,000
(10% of total gross receipts)		
Production overhead	$5,500,000	$5,500,000
(10% of production costs)		
Worldwide advertising charge (15%)	$4,000,000	$4,000,000
Interest	$7,000,000	$6,000,000
Less: Total imputed costs	–$24,760,000	–$28,540,000
Net unrecouped amount	–$49,160,000	–$7,140,000

3B. Pre-Break Gross Participation Calculation

For an example of how a pre-break gross participation kicks in,

Assume:

Adjusted gross receipts (AGR)	$135,000,000
AGR to reach cash breakeven	$130,555,000
AGR after cash breakeven	$4,445,000
Profit participant's percentage	5%
Pre-Break gross participation	$222,250

4. Net-Profit Participant's Financial Analysis

ADJUSTED GROSS RECEIPTS

	Breakeven model	*Profit model*
Worldwide theatrical (film rental)	$45,000,000	$80,000,000
Worldwide home video	$8,600,000	$11,400,000
Worldwide television	$27,000,000	$35,000,000
Other ancillary rights	$2,000,000	$4,000,000
Total gross receipts	$82,600,000	$130,400,000
Less:		
Residuals/Off-the-top deductions	–$7,000,000	–$9,000,000
Adjusted gross receipts	$75,600,000	$121,400,000

ACTUAL STUDIO OUT-OF-POCKET COSTS

Direct production costs	$55,000,000	$55,000,000
Worldwide theatrical marketing	$45,000,000	$45,000,000
Worldwide home video costs	0	0
Profit participations	$0	$0
Less: Total studio out-of-pocket costs	–$100,000,000	–$100,000,000

IMPUTED COSTS

Distribution fee	$24,780,000	$39,120,000
(30% of total gross receipts)		
Production overhead	$8,250,000	$8,250,000
(15% of production costs)		
Worldwide advertising charge (15%)	$4,000,000	$4,000,000

Interest	$9,000,000	$11,000,000
Less: Total imputed costs	$46,030,000	$62,370,000
Net profit (Loss)	-$70,430,000	-$40,970,000
Participant's percentage	10%	10%
Net-profit participation	0	0

IX

THEATRICAL DISTRIBUTION

THEATRICAL DISTRIBUTION

by **DANIEL R. FELLMAN,** president of Warner Bros. Pictures Domestic Distribution, based in Burbank. A distribution executive at Warner Bros. since 1978, Mr. Fellman joined the studio after serving as president of American Theatre Management Corporation. He began his career in film distribution at Paramount Pictures and has served as an executive with Loews Theatres and later Cinema National Theatres. Mr. Fellman is a past chairman and member of the board of the Foundation of the Motion Picture Pioneers; a member of the board of directors and the executive committee of the Will Rogers Memorial Fund; a past president of the Variety Club Children's Charity; and a member of the executive branch executive committee and the executive branch nominating committee of the Academy of Motion Picture Arts and Sciences.

> Our customized system can display the box office history of any actor, producer, director or film in seconds; we can analyze a marketplace, release schedule, daily grosses, reviews, demographics, trailers, TV spots, print ads, posters, Web sites and year-to-date box office performance.

Warner Bros. Pictures Domestic Distribution, a Time Warner Entertainment Company (part of the Time Warner family), is responsible for theatrical motion picture distribution in the United States and Canada, as well as for nontheatrical markets (such as airlines, cruise ships, armed forces, universities, hospitals and oil rigs). Time Warner owns two motion picture companies, Warner Bros. Pictures and New Line Cinema, which operate independent of each other.

The home office of Warner Bros. Pictures Domestic Distribution in Burbank, California, is comprised of several departments. Here is a breakdown of what executives and staffers in each department are responsible for:

- *Print:* Ordering and tracking physical film prints shipped to theatres; dealing with print labs, film depots and shipping companies that handle freight from the labs to the depots; keeping tight control over the print inventory.

- *Non-Theatrical:* Licensing films to airlines, cruise ships, the military and various other venues that are not traditional theatres.

- *Legal Affairs:* Handling all legal matters for film distribution, such as exhibitor complaints, bankruptcy proceedings, violations of our terms and conditions agreements, governmental issues and reviewing business contracts.

- *Finance:* Performing all accounting and financial reporting for corporate management.

- *Financial Administration and Operations:* Overseeing collections of receivables and monitoring the financial strength of our customers.

- *Systems and Sales Operations:* Creating and monitoring the distribution plans for our films, monitoring sales negotiations, handling billing of film rental; collecting and managing information on competitors' release schedules and box office performance; business analysis and strategic planning; developing and overseeing our computer systems and new technology.

- *Administration:* Handling all branch office and other administrative tasks, including negotiating contracts with vendors; box office checking at theatres; negotiating leases for our offices; and human resource issues.

- *Exhibitor Services:* Providing in-theatre materials and promotional information to exhibitors; making sure theatres place in their lobbies the advertising materials we create and play our trailers in front of designated films; creating various in-theatre promotions to help sell our films to the public at the grass-roots level; working closely with our promotional partners.

The Warner Bros. domestic distribution operation has dramatically changed over the years. In the 1960s, there were thirty branch offices across the United States and Canada. Today, we have major offices in New York, Los Angeles, Dallas and Toronto, with satellite offices in Montreal and Boston. Consolidation in distribution and in exhibition has allowed us to easily control our businesses from fewer locations through new technology. Each division is headed by a senior vice president, who reports to the executive vice president/general sales manager, who in turn reports directly to me.

Although we track every movie the studio has in development, our work really accelerates when a green light is given and the production process begins. Scripts are read by marketing, distribution and consumer products executives. Marketing will start conceptualizing print ads, trailers, promotions, promotional partners, publicity, online opportunities and media plans. Distribution will begin planning a release strategy, and consumer products will be evaluating prospects of additional promotional partnerships and licensing opportunities. Every campaign is molded to reach the primary and secondary audience of every film released. The marketing and releasing plans are coordinated together, and marketing executives work very closely with distribution executives in media planning, advertising and trailer placement strategies.

Once a work print is assembled, there are research screenings with recruited audiences, which will help the director fine-tune the film. (See the article by Kevin Yoder, p. 300.)

The average studio cost to produce and market a major motion picture is approximately $90 million and climbing. Warner Bros. distributes twenty-five to thirty movies a year, more than any other motion picture studio. This includes films produced by Warner Bros. Pictures as well as our family of production companies, such as Malpaso, Village Roadshow, Morgan Creek, Alcon Entertainment, Silver Pictures, Franchise Pictures, Bel-Air Entertainment, Castle Rock Pictures, Gaylord Films and Shangri-La Entertainment.

Another source of product for Warner Bros. Distribution is the acquisition of a negative pickup (when a film produced and financed outside the studio is seeking a distributor). Our senior acquisitions executive attends film festivals and is in constant contact with independent filmmakers, in pursuit of product available for domestic or international distribution.

Release plans are comprised of three basic strategies, with some variations. A *wide release* is usually the pattern for major films, opening in 700 to 3,000-plus theatres. An example is *Ocean's Eleven,* which opened in 3,075 theatres.

Next is a *limited release,* in which films open in 50 to 700 theatres, used to target a specific demographic or just test the marketplace while limiting the studio's advertising exposure. An example is the 2000 reissue of *The Exorcist,* which opened in 664 theatres.

Finally there is the *exclusive* (or *platform*) *release,* reserved for specialty films that must build an audience from reviews and word of mouth. An exclusive release might find a film opening in one or two theatres in New York, Los Angeles and Toronto, then expanding the markets slowly based on the film's initial performance. An example is *My Dog Skip.*

Sometimes it's useful to experiment on a release pattern. For example, *Best in Show* opened in a typical NY LA Toronto exclusive but played a multiple run (supported by TV) in eight theatres in the San Francisco area. This pattern proved successful and we gained the confidence to expand our media-supported multiple-release plan as we rolled out into new markets. The picture ended up grossing over $20 million.

Let's pause and define terms used to track box office grosses, such as prints, screens, theatres and locations. When we use the term *locations*—as an example, reporting to the press that a film will open in 2,000 locations—we mean theatres, not screens. Each location (or theatre) reports one gross, even if a picture is playing on four or five screens in one complex. While *Harry Potter and the Sorcerer's Stone* grossed over $90 million on its opening weekend in 3,672 locations, we had over 8,000 prints working, because many of the multiplexes ran the film on multiple screens. We monitor every print and keep track of every show on each screen.

At Warner Bros., the majority of our films open in a wide release pattern. That decision is made early, as part of the marketing-distribution strategy. The high costs of producing and marketing a film almost always require a wide release to maximize the return. Developing the release schedule is a process shared with the highest-level studio executives, in conjunction with our primary filmmakers and production partners.

Years ago, competing films would be listed on a wall chart in a conference room. Today, this information is contained in a sophisticated movie marketing system that tracks every Warner project, as well as our competitors' projects, in development, production or release. Our customized system can display the box office history of any actor, producer, director or film in seconds; we can analyze a marketplace, release schedule, daily grosses, reviews, demographics, trailers, TV spots, print ads, posters, Web sites and year-to-date box office performance. Whatever information is needed regarding talent, box office receipts or research to aid in the decisionmaking process, it's in there. It's also persuasive when talking with filmmakers and making a case for critical decisions, such as a release date.

What follows are two examples from the WB "4 Star" computer program. The first page is a chart of comparative weekend grosses for Friday, November 16 to Sunday, November 18, 2001, opening weekend for *Harry Potter and the Sorcerer's Stone*. The chart covers WB movies first, then other distributors in alphabetical order. "FSS" stands for Friday-Saturday-Sunday; "FSS WK #" refers to number of weekends in release; "FSS RUNS" refers to the number of theatres; "AVG" divides the weekend box office by the number of theatres; "CUM" means cumulative.

The second page is an excerpt from our industrywide release schedule, covering the weeks from *Harry Potter's* opening on November 16, 2001, through January 4, 2002. Notice the dense number of releases being introduced, as well as the array of target demographics. Distributors are noted with abbreviations (LIO is Lions Gate; PCL is Paramount Classics; SCL is Sony Classics).

While the summer and Christmas holidays remain the primary release

SUMMARY OF WEEKEND THEATRICAL GROSSES
WEEK # 46, 2001
FINAL

WEEKEND OF: 11/16/01 Thanksgiving - Thursday CO. PICTURE	RANK	FSS WK#	CURRENT WEEKEND					LAST WEEKEND		
			FSS RUNS	FSS BOXOFFICE	AVG	% CHG	CUM BOXOFFICE	FSS RUNS	FSS BOXOFFICE	AVG
WB Harry Potter And The Sorcerer's Stone	1	1	3,672	90,294,621	24,590	N/A	90,294,621	N/A	N/A	N/A
WB Heist	5	2	1,891	4,682,249	2,476	-40	15,004,225	1,891	7,823,521	4,137
WB Thirteen Ghosts	10	4	1,627	2,132,473	1,311	-52	37,674,219	2,351	4,445,351	1,891
WB Training Day	12	7	855	908,870	1,063	-55	74,190,371	1,407	2,023,429	1,438
AE Novocaine	18	1	105	418,098	3,982	N/A	418,098	N/A	N/A	N/A
BV Monsters, Inc.	2	3	3,461	22,716,685	6,564	-50	156,341,118	3,269	45,551,028	13,934
BV Corky Romano	23	6	258	130,813	507	-76	23,302,549	748	555,546	743
DW Last Castle, The	21	5	297	220,245	742	-72	17,924,798	924	774,145	838
FOX Shallow Hal	3	2	2,799	12,106,586	4,325	-46	40,687,100	2,770	22,518,295	8,129
FOX From Hell	17	5	605	684,192	1,131	-65	30,692,411	1,389	1,943,452	1,399
FXS Waking Life	19	5	93	235,474	2,532	-11	1,485,758	66	265,901	4,029
LIO Wash, The-LG	8	1	749	2,875,067	3,839	N/A	3,711,657	N/A	N/A	N/A
LIO Tape	24	3	29	90,967	3,137	160	181,373	7	34,981	4,997
MGM Bandits-MGM	15	6	875	768,683	878	-49	39,793,423	1,483	1,505,615	1,015
MIR Amelie	11	3	163	1,323,345	8,119	71	5,243,733	48	773,865	16,122
MIR Serendipity	14	7	964	875,313	908	-46	47,201,116	1,342	1,616,843	1,205
NL Life As A House	9	4	1,288	2,646,422	2,055	-31	8,998,627	1,288	3,818,623	2,965
NL Bones	22	4	275	189,640	690	-75	7,209,002	625	750,292	1,200
PAR Domestic Disturbance	4	3	2,881	5,377,031	1,866	-38	33,672,327	2,910	8,640,422	2,969
PCL Focus	25	5	61	73,889	1,211	-39	444,352	62	120,263	1,940
SCL Grateful Dawg	27	7	13	12,547	965	-39	203,712	20	20,562	1,028
SCL Va Savoir (Who Knows?)	26	8	21	32,390	1,542	-35	675,829	30	49,457	1,649
SON One, The-Sony	6	3	2,433	4,105,741	1,688	-55	38,274,334	2,894	9,102,733	3,145
SON Riding In Cars With Boys	16	5	962	715,256	744	-66	29,175,810	2,182	2,105,466	965
UNF Mulholland Drive	20	6	139	222,395	1,600	-42	4,691,058	199	383,075	1,925
UNI K-PAX	7	4	2,325	3,138,750	1,350	-51	45,325,425	2,581	6,387,970	2,475
USA Man Who Wasn't There, The-USA	13	3	250	893,669	3,575	-12	3,184,764	169	1,015,856	6,011
TOTALS			29,091	157,871,411	5,427	-23		30,655	122,226,691	3,987

Week #	Industry Total
45	$127,077,854
46	$160,598,935

Wknd No Of Information
Days 3 v Source
3 v

Page 1 of 1

N/A = NOT APPLICABLE, NA = NOT AVAILABLE

dates for distributors, there are many opportunities during nonholiday playtime to achieve success at the box office.

The process of licensing a film to an exhibitor has changed dramatically over the last few years. The exhibitor negotiates the terms to license a movie prior to the film's opening. In some cases, after the film has finished its run, there is a second negotiation adjusting the original contract, based

Release Schedule 2001 Thanksgiving / Christmas

46 / 16-Nov-01 / 154,685,322	47 / 23-Nov-01 / 176,503,893	48 / 30-Nov-01 / 88,566,388	49 / 7-Dec-01 / 87,452,041	50 / 14-Dec-01 / 105,627,840	51 / 21-Dec-01 / 154,339,650	52 / 28-Dec-01 / 183,284,297	1 / 4-Jan-02 / 120,774,539
Harry Potter & The Sorcerer's Stone — WB Wide	11/21/01 Out Cold — BV Wide	Affair Of The Necklace — WB Limited	Ocean's Eleven — WB Wide	Not Another Teen Movie — SON Wide	Majestic, The — WB Wide	Charlotte Gray — WB Limited	Imposter - Mir — MIR Wide
Amelie (3) — MIR Expansion	11/21/01 Black Knight — FOX Wide	Texas Rangers — MIR Wide	No Man's Land - MGM — MGM Exclusive	Vanilla Sky — PAR Wide	12/19/01 Lord Of The Rings: Fellowship Of The — NL Wide	12/25/01 Ali — SON Wide	Beautiful Mind, A (2) — UNI Wide
Novacaine — AE Limited	11/21/01 Spy Game — UNI Wide	Behind Enemy Lines — FOX Wide	Baran — MIR Exclusive	12/12/01 Behind The Sun - Mir — MIR Exclusive	Jimmy Neutron: Boy Genius — PAR Wide	12/25/01 Kate And Leopold — MIR Wide	Royal Tenenbaums (4) — BV Wide
	11/21/01 Moulin Rouge — FOX Expansion	Sidewalks Of New York (2) — PCL Expansion		12/13/01 Pinero — MIR Exclusive	How High — UNI Wide	12/25/01 In The Bedroom (2) — MIR Expansion	Gosford Park (2) — USA Expansion
	11/21/01 Sidewalks Of New York — PCL Limited			Royal Tenenbaums — BV Exclusive	Joe Somebody — FOX Wide	Royal Tenenbaums (3) — BV Expansion	01/01/02 Beauty And The Beast - IMAX — BV Limited
	11/21/01 Devil's Backbone — SCL Exclusive			Iris — MIR Exclusive	Royal Tenenbaums (2) — BV Limited	12/25/01 Shipping News — MIR Limited	
	In The Bedroom — MIR Exclusive			Lantana — LIO Exclusive	Beautiful Mind, A — UNI Exclusive	12/26/01 Gosford Park — USA Exclusive	
						12/26/01 Monster's Ball — LIO Exclusive	
						Black Hawk Down — Son Exclusive	
						I Am Sam — NL Exclusive	

Last year's Variety weekend boxoffice totals are beneath the weekend date in each column

on the movie's performance, in order to arrive at a final settlement. Movies are licensed to theatres, not sold; they are licensed to television and cable channels, not sold; however, movies *are* sold or rented to customers in the home video/DVD formats.

Warner Bros. Domestic Distribution licenses pictures on a firm-term basis. The industry is currently divided between companies that license firm and those that review terms after each engagement. Under *firm terms*, once the negotiated terms to license a film are agreed upon, that is it; the deal is firm, not subject to review. Under *review terms,* the deal can be adjusted after the grosses are reported to the distributor.

Let's pause and define the typical exhibition deal, the 90/10 deal with minimum percentage terms. An agreed-upon theatre overhead (called the *house allowance*) is deducted from the gross receipts before the box office is split 90% to the distributor and 10% to the exhibitor; this is then compared to the minimum percentage term (or *floor*). Whichever computation accrues more money to the distributor is the one that prevails for a given week. Let's say a theatre's house allowance is $5,000 and the film deal is 90/10 with a minimum floor of 70% for the first week. If the first week's gross is $24,000, deduct the house allowance, which is $5,000, and multiply the remaining $19,000 by 90%: $17,100 goes to the distributor and $6,900 stays at the theatre level. The second computation is a flat 70% minimum floor percentage of the gross, without regard to overhead: 70% of $24,000 is $16,800 (the theatre's 30% share is $7,200). Of the two computations, the first one is higher, so $17,100 is sent to the distributor for its share of that week's gross. Later in that run, assume the picture has grossed $8,000 in its fifth week (90/10 vs. 35%). After the house allowance of $5,000 is deducted, the remaining $3,000 is multiplied by 90%, which is $2,700. The second computation is a flat 35% of the $8,000 gross or $2,800. In this case, the distributor's share is $100 higher in the second computation than in the first, so $2,800 goes to the distributor and $5,200 remains at the theatre level. The longer a picture plays, the more advantageous it is to the exhibitor, due to lower minimum percentage terms.

Now let's use an example so that these concepts come to life: a license for *Harry Potter and the Sorcerer's Stone*. This *Harry Potter* license called for 90/10 against a minimum floor of 70% for the first three weeks, 60% for weeks 4 and 5, 50% for week 6, 40% for week 7 and 35% for each week thereafter.

The chart on the following page covers the performance of *Harry Potter* on a sample screen in a multiplex for the first twelve weeks of this engagement, from opening day through week 12, February 1, 2002. Column headings include "Bk Ty" referring to booking type, in this case B for booked (as opposed to tentative); the specific screens, screen count, print count, seat count, dollar gross; "HA" is the total house allowance; "Ded" refers to deductions, if any; "terms" refers to the minimum percentage terms; "90/10" represents the percentage of the gross that is yielded when applying the 90/10 method for calculating film rental; "Final F/R%" is the percentage of the gross that the distributor will invoice to the exhibitor; and "Net F/R ($)" stands for net film rental in dollars.

The first-week gross of $133,331 for this engagement includes four

Release	Bk Ty	Wk	Start Date	Days	Screen #(s)	Sc	Pr	Seats	Gross	HA	Ded	Terms (%)	90/10	Final F/R %	Net F/R ($)
Potter	B	1	11/16/01	7	9,10,11,12	4	4	1000	133,331	23,785	0	70.00%	73.94%	73.94%	98,591.40
Potter	B	2	11/23/01	7	9,10,11,12	4	4	1000	77,571	23,785	0	70.00%	62.40%	70.00%	54,299.70
Potter	B	3	11/30/01	7	9,10,11,12	4	4	1000	39,943	23,785	0	70.00%	36.41%	70.00%	27,960.10
Potter	B	4	12/07/01	7	1,11,13,17	4	4	841	22,395	20,095	0	60.00%	9.24%	60.00%	13,437.00
Potter	B	5	12/14/01	7	11,13,17	3	3	650	19,901	16,225	0	60.00%	16.62%	60.00%	11,940.60
Potter	B	6	12/21/01	7	13	1	1	216	21,539	5,835	0	50.00%	65.62%	65.62%	14,133.60
Potter	B	7	12/28/01	7	13	1	1	216	21,998	5,835	0	40.00%	66.13%	66.13%	14,546.70
Potter	B	8	01/04/02	7	13	1	1	216	9,506	5,835	0	35.00%	34.76%	35.00%	3,327.10
Potter	B	9	01/11/02	7	13	1	1	216	6,390	5,835	0	35.00%	7.82%	35.00%	2,236.50
Potter	B	10	01/18/02	7	13	1	1	216	6,262	5,835	0	35.00%	6.14%	35.00%	2,191.70
Potter	B	11	01/25/02	7	13	1	1	216	5,372	5,835	0	35.00%	0.00%	35.00%	1,880.20
Potter	B	12	02/01/02	7	13	1	1	216	3,856	5,835	0	35.00%	0.00%	35.00%	1,349.60
Adv:			Guar:					Totals:	368,064					66.81%	245,894.20

screens in this theatre. Notice that the agreed-upon house allowance for these four screens is $23,785, the figure that should be deducted from the gross in order to do the 90/10 computation. The remainder is $109,546; 90% of that is $98,591.40. The minimum floor percentage of 70% of the $133,331 gross comes to $93,331.70. Since the 90/10 computation comes out approximately $5,000 higher to the distributor than the minimum floor, that figure—$98,591.40—is the one that prevails and appears in the "Net F/R ($)" column, the net film rental in dollars.

By the second week, the 90/10 deal has yielded to the minimum percentage floor: 90/10 would accrue $48,407.40 to WB, but the 70% floor is higher, $54,299.70. For week 4, the exhibitor moves the film into smaller auditoriums; it's still playing on four screens, but the total number of seats is reduced to 841 (with the house allowance lowered to $20,095). For weeks 6 and 7, the 90/10 calculation prevails over the minimum percentage floors. By week 8, the numbers have settled comfortably into the 35% minimum percentage floor computation.

Harry Potter became a worldwide cultural phenomenon. Our studio began planning the release of *Harry Potter and the Sorcerer's Stone* with the acquisition of the property three years in advance of the release date. We chose November 16 because family films historically perform well over the holiday period. In the first three days, in the United States alone, *Harry Potter* grossed $90.2 million. Ultimately the gross was $317 million in the United States and $651 million internationally. The worldwide box office of $968 million made it the most successful film in Warner Bros. history and the second-largest worldwide gross in the history of the motion picture industry. *Titanic* is the champion at $1.8 billion worldwide ($600 million and domestically 1.2 billion internationally).

Let's follow an exhibitor-distributor negotiation on a sample picture. First, we screen our films for exhibitors in advance of release dates. Then we negotiate our film licenses with the best available theatres in each market, which in our opinion will maximize our film rental.

As an example, let's take a look at the Columbus, Ohio, market on a wide-release film. After the exhibitor trade screening, our manager who covers the Ohio territory (based in our eastern division office in New York) contacts the exhibitors that operate the theatres we want that particular film to play in to discuss and negotiate the terms of the deal. These include the film rental terms, the house allowance, the number of screens and the number of weeks the picture will play. (Since most house allowances are prenegotiated and on file, the two parties already know that figure.) After an agreement has been reached, the manager enters it into our booking system, which keeps track of all the engagements, billings and receivables.

This system also allows us to run a variety of reports to help us analyze the performance of our pictures as well as the marketplace in general.

Before 1948, many of the studios, including Warner Bros., controlled a large portion of production, distribution and exhibition. Over time, this was deemed a violation of U.S. antitrust laws by the Justice Department. As a result, those studios that owned theatres had to divest themselves of their theatre interests. Warner Bros. is a signatory of the Consent Decrees that emerged from the antitrust federal lawsuit *U.S. v. Paramount, et al.,* which was finally resolved in 1952. Since then, we license our product on a picture-by-picture, theatre-by-theatre basis.

How do distributors know whether they are getting accurate box office reporting from theatres? The studios hire checking companies, who send people to physically visit selected theatres during the run of the engagement, count the number of paid admissions, then report back to the studio for reconciliation. In some instances the checkers arrive unannounced (blind checking) and in other cases they announce themselves to the theatre manager.

Now let's turn to collections. Theatres will remit to WB our share of the week's box office receipts approximately twenty-eight days after opening day. The exhibitor submits a weekly box office statement (often in electronic format), from which we base our billing and collections. Monies are collected for the larger national circuits at the home office, and smaller circuits send payments directly to the branch offices.

We can make a very educated guess of how a picture will perform within hours of its opening, by tracking grosses from major cities on an hourly basis. We then compare these figures to the box office results of prior pictures with a similar genre, release date and print count.

Every Monday morning, studio executives meet to discuss marketing issues. We analyze the recent weekend's business and the current week's media plan. If a new film is opening, we review our tracking and make adjustments, if required.

What if a picture opens better or worse than expected? We are generally prepared either way. We thoroughly review the marketing and distribution plans for the following week, revising media or print counts as necessary.

In this very risky business, there are always pleasant surprises. One example was *Cats and Dogs,* directed by Lawrence Guterman, which exceeded our expectations by grossing $90 million in the domestic market and continued with a strong home video release. As a result, a sequel is in development.

In the distribution/marketing lexicon are the terms marketability and playability. Loosely defined, *marketability* refers to having strong materials (such as trailers and one-sheets), making the project highly advertiseable so it can be marketed effectively; *playability* refers to the audience reactions. It gets interesting when test screenings show a movie has high playability (audiences love it) but low marketability (tough to express the movie's value through advertising); this is a difficult challenge that cannot always be overcome.

Relationships with our exhibitors are better than ever before. Recently, exhibition has gone through a very difficult period, consisting of bankruptcies, theatre closings, consolidations and restructuring. Most exhibition companies have emerged from it all stronger and well positioned to prosper.

The advent of the multiplex in the last half of the twentieth century has helped exhibition (and distribution) by exhibiting the most popular films on multiple screens in the same complex, providing the public with large screens, stadium seating, digital sound, comfortable seats with cupholders and a variety of starting times. Today's generation of large multiplexes, containing up to 30 screens, are called megaplexes. These cinema destination centers usually contain food courts, gaming centers, VIP screening rooms, party rooms, even bumper cars and carousels in select locations.

While exhibitors have always worried about competition from new technology—radio, television, cable, pay cable, PPV, VHS, DVD, VOD and the Internet—the number of admissions are increasing and box office grosses are on the rise. Ticket prices are set by exhibitors, not distributors. (For annual statistics, please consult the Motion Picture Association's Web site at www.mpaa.org.)

The conversion to digital projection may only be a few years away. The industry has been waiting for 2K projector technology (referring to pixel resolution in the 2,000 range), rather than the 1K and 1.5K projectors that have been installed and tested in markets around the country since 1999. Our cinemas need to project a picture digitally that will look at least as good as 35mm film. At Warner Bros., we have committed to release our films in the digital format; in fact, all of our movies are converted to digital before release as a function of storage, DVD conversion and possible theatrical digital projection. In the near future, new digital technology will project an image that will surpass film as we know it today. In order to expedite the conversion process, the major studios have created a new company to implement standards and develop a business plan to meet the financial requirements. The studios will recoup their investment through savings in printing, shipping, storage and the reduction of piracy.

TOP FIFTY MARKETS—UNITED STATES AND CANADA
Listed in Approximate Order of Revenue Potential

1. New York Metro Area
2. Los Angeles
3. Chicago
4. Toronto
5. San Francisco
6. Philadelphia
7. Dallas
8. Washington, D.C.
9. Orange County, California
10. Atlanta
11. San Diego
12. Houston
13. Detroit
14. Phoenix
15. Montreal
16. Boston
17. San Jose, California
18. Denver
19. Seattle
20. Miami, Florida
21. Minneapolis
22. Vancouver, British Columbia
23. Baltimore
24. Sacramento
25. Orlando, Florida
26. Tampa Bay, Florida
27. Las Vegas, Nevada
28. Portland, Oregon
29. St. Louis
30. Kansas City, Missouri
31. Cleveland
32. Long Beach, California
33. San Antonio
34. Indianapolis
35. Montclair, California
36. Honolulu
37. Calgary, Alberta
38. Pittsburgh
39. Austin
40. Columbus, Ohio
41. Cincinnati
42. Milwaukee
43. Salt Lake City
44. Ventura County, California
45. Fort Lauderdale
46. Ottawa, Ontario
47. Edmonton, Alberta
48. Nashville
49. Raleigh/Durham, North Carolina
50. Memphis

INDEPENDENT DISTRIBUTION

by **BOB BERNEY,** president of Newmarket Films, the distribution arm of Newmarket Capital Group, based in New York. As former senior vice president of IFC Films, Berney oversaw the distribution of the box office phenomenon *My Big Fat Greek Wedding,* the highest-grossing independent film in U.S. history. At IFC, he also released *Y Tu Mamá También,* directed by Alfonso Cuarón. Prior to IFC Films, Berney was an independent marketing and distribution consultant responsible for the release of such films as Chris Nolan's *Memento* for Newmarket Films and Todd Solondz's *Happiness* for Good Machine International. Earlier, he served as vice president of marketing and distribution at Banner Entertainment, vice president of marketing at Orion Pictures (*Jeffrey*), vice president of marketing and distribution at Triton Films (*A Brief History of Time*), and began his marketing and distribution career at FilmDallas (*Patti Rocks*), an independent production/distribution company in partnership with New World Pictures. As a University of Texas student, Berney worked as a projectionist for AMC Theatres. After graduation, he renovated and programmed the Inwood Theatre in Dallas, which he ran as an art house venue. He and his partners later sold the theatre, now part of the Landmark Cinema chain.

> *"My Big Fat Greek Wedding* is another example of a wonderful movie financed outside the studio system that could not find a distributor."

I ndependent distribution refers to lower-budget films that are financed and distributed on a small, guerilla-style basis and not affiliated with a studio. One could argue whether Miramax is truly independent as a part of Disney, though it certainly maintains an independent sensibility. In a broader sense, independent distribution is often filmmaker-driven, using a marketing approach and release pattern that does not conform to the wide releases of the major studios. But the definition is fluid, in that studios have broadened their range of fully financed, partially financed or acquired product by establishing their own independent-style distribution labels—such as Paramount Classics, Sony Pictures Classics and Fox Searchlight—that release smaller, filmmaker-driven, movies that compete with those of stand-alone independent distributors.

The line blurs further today in exhibition, where so-called art house and mainstream exhibitors are both showing nonstudio independent movies as well as studio-distributed independent-style movies. This is a good thing; the audience is more accepting of a broader range of films, and theatres are responding by playing them. As a result, the traditional labels of "art house," "specialty" or "independent" films are no longer barriers.

Today's independent distribution era might be traced back to filmmaker John Cassavetes, whose *Faces* was self-distributed in 1968. Around that time, New York exhibitors such as Dan Talbot (New Yorker Films) and Donald Rugoff (Cinema 5) were becoming distributors because they loved movies and wanted to support independent and foreign-language films that otherwise might not get shown outside Manhattan. Earlier, American International Pictures (AIP), run by Sam Arkoff and James Nicholson, was a prolific label of teen and exploitation films, while Roger Corman's New World Pictures became known for launching young directors such as Francis Ford Coppola and Martin Scorsese and distributing films by Fellini and Truffaut. By the 1970s, Robert Shaye's New Line Cinema and Bob and Harvey Weinstein's Miramax were establishing themselves as beacons of independent-style distribution. Both of these companies were brilliant at marketing and brashly aggressive with exhibitors.

Studios woke up to the revenue potential of independent-style product, wanting to complete and build their own libraries. The first to set up an indie label was United Artists, which established UA Classics in 1980 under the guidance of Tom Bernard and Michael Barker. Their mantra was to platform-release review-driven art films, marketed slowly and carefully to control costs, creating a model that other studios followed and that still exists today. (This management team later moved to Sony Pictures Classics.)

By the 1990s, New Line had been sold to Time Warner and Miramax had been sold to Disney, and the independent world was struggling under increased marketing costs. Home video values and overseas presales shored up privately financed movies, until both avenues became less reliable, further squeezing independents. Film markets and film festivals became important venues for discovering independent product, and as they grew so did a renewed optimism. By the end of the decade, *The Blair Witch Project*, shot on digital, was picked up by independent distributor Artisan after a midnight screening at Sundance 1999 and became the most profitable film of the year.

Today, the studio-branded independent divisions are thriving. Universal offers a good example of combining highly respected independent production-distribution companies Good Machine (*Crouching Tiger, Hidden Dragon*), and USA Films, which grew out of October Films and Gramercy Films (*The Usual Suspects*), to form Focus Features. Because the studios have usurped product that, in an earlier era, would have been distributed by stand-alone independents, there are fewer indies in the field today. Among the most active are Lions Gate (including Artisan), IFC, Strand and Newmarket.

A healthy barometer for the independent world is that the audience is expanding; independent distribution is reaching a wider number of theatres than ever before. DVD has played a critical part in increasing revenue, particularly for foreign-language films and smaller independent films, and the Internet holds great promise to widen the audience further. If there is a challenge to independent revenue today, it is in television sales; not many

TV outlets are licensing independent films, aside from the Independent Film Channel and the Sundance Channel.

An important part of independent distribution is tracking projects. It's necessary to keep tabs on and attend as many film festivals as possible, since they are not only venues for discovering new movies and talent but also for marketing them. (See the article on film festivals by Steve Montal, p. 315.) Tracking involves keeping an ear to the ground, listening to stories from sets, and maintaining contacts to detect movies being put together under the radar, since early identification has its advantages. This includes learning who is investing, which talent are being combined, which territories might be sold. In a very competitive business, this kind of intelligence is key. Research provides clues to the commercial potential of a project, but there is no, absolutely no substitute for actually watching the movie, whether completed or not, to evaluate its value as early as possible.

IFC Entertainment, which started IFC Films, was part of the Bravo cable network, a division of Cablevision. When Bravo began accepting commercials, Cablevision launched the Independent Film Channel in 1994 to show movies uninterrupted. At IFC, executives Jonathan Sehring and Caroline Kaplan began investing in short films to secure product, then in feature films through IFC Productions. One highlight was *Boys Don't Cry* in 1999, which they sold to Fox Searchlight. Once a film is sold to a distributor, the branding goes to the distributor. When IFC decided to move into theatrical distribution, it was a logical next step for their business model, but also allowed them to achieve appropriate branding recognition.

When I began as a consultant for IFC in 2000, there were two separate tracks: IFC Films planned to distribute eight to ten acquired films a year, while IFC Productions continued to make films and sell them off to other distributors (such as *Monsoon Wedding* to USA Films).

Establishing a new independent distribution company calls for enough financing to acquire and properly market the proposed number of films and to pay for executive salaries, offices and overhead; good relationships with the most appropriate theatres around the country; and, perhaps most important, ancillary-rights deals for home video and television sales to protect the overall investment. Studio-based independent labels will often buy theatrical rights to English-speaking territories where the parent company has preexisting, lucrative TV output deals, giving them a leg up over true independents, who have to start from scratch. At IFC, we had the cable channel behind us, so the domestic TV component was there to help offset the acquisition investments. Parent company Cablevision also owned

Clearview Cinemas in New York and New Jersey, a strong exhibition partner.

Here are brief case studies of three better-known films:

Memento

In 2000, I was consulting with Newmarket Films, having helped Good Machine release *Happiness* after Universal, its parent company, barred Good Machine from releasing it. Will Tyrer and Chris Ball of Newmarket Films had financed *Memento* and presold overseas rights to Summit, the foreign-sales company. After screening the film alone, I was bowled over, excited about how successful the movie could be. They explained they had shopped it to all distributors and everyone turned it down. My advice was to do what Good Machine had done with *Happiness,* which was to invest their own money and allow me to release it. Newmarket agreed and put up $1.2 million for a strong marketing campaign. I met with director Chris Nolan and producers Suzanne and Jennifer Todd (Team Todd), along with Will Tyrer and Chris Ball, and convinced them to release *Memento* in an independent, nonstudio manner.

To start, Chris Nolan and his brother Jonah (writer of the original story) put up a Web site about the movie. Then, I turned to the film festival circuit, where *Memento* premiered at the Venice and Toronto festivals back-to-back, generating worldwide buzz. Next, Polaroids of lead actor Guy Pearce with the film title backwards were posted in cities, and people responded favorably to this tease on the Web site. The critical reputation was building, and by the time we went to Sundance 2001, the movie was on fire. Strategically, it was quite an effort to keep reactions just at the boiling point, without squandering momentum. Because of the growing interest, I was able to achieve proper theatres around the country to open as a platform release. (It helps if you were once a theatre owner.) At the same time, a careful series of promotions, screenings and fieldwork was put in place for all the major cities.

As with all platform releases, the rollout was dependent on prior box office performance. This underscores an important aspect of independent distribution: No one knows how the picture will perform in the marketplace, but it's vital to be ready to maximize box office potential with as powerful a campaign as available dollars allow, or to scale back if need be, should the box office not support the film. Happily, *Memento* opened in March to an amazing reception, playing into September and breaking house records. People saw it again and again because of the quality of the movie and the puzzle nature of the story, and the film became a phenomenon, grossing $24 million in some 2,000 U.S. theatres, with subsequent success on DVD.

Y Tu Mamá También

After IFC hired me to set up IFC Films, the search for product began. At Cannes 2001, I saw the film with Sara Lash, my acquisitions executive, and Jonathan Sehring, president of IFC Entertainment, in a private screening held by Good Machine (which owned some international territories in the film) and the Endeavor Agency's Sergio Aguero, the sales agent for the picture covering North America. All of the distributors were there. We loved the film, and made an aggressive push to buy it for U.S. and Canada the next day. For me, Y Tu Mamá También was a masterpiece with highly marketable elements: It was very sexy, review-driven, had a famous director, and actor Gael García Bernal, who had been in the successful Amores Perros.

In short, other distributors were thinking about it while we bought it, after making a convincing case to the sales agent and filmmakers. The case included aggressively going after the underserved Latino audience and crossing over to the art house audience. One issue was the rating, which precluded some companies from acquiring the film. It was heading for an NC-17 rating, and after Alfonso Cuarón tried to cut it for an R, we decided instead to release the film unrated, and with its original Spanish title.

The television advertising campaign for Y Tu Mamá También was a combination of cable buys for the art house audience and broadcast spot ads on national Latin networks such as Telefutura, Telemundo and Univision.

The film opened in Manhattan as a platform release in two theatres and in Los Angeles as a wide release, in 38 theatres; we spent a lot of money to reach the Latino population. In other cities with a strong Latino community, we opened in as many theatres as possible. Ultimately, the film played from March through August 2001, with upward of 400 prints, grossing about $14 million.

The deal for Y Tu Mamá También was a *standard distribution deal,* structured with an advance to the producers of under $1 million; IFC would take a 30% distribution fee, and bonuses were given to the producers at U.S. box office thresholds of $7.5 million and $10 million. Out of the film rental, IFC would take the distribution fee and recoup our marketing expenses (prints and advertising), then recoup our advance plus interest (delayed to the extent that the bonuses were being paid out). Once we recouped our costs, subsequent dollars would be shared by IFC and the producers in a sliding-scale percentage.

My Big Fat Greek Wedding

This example is more complicated. MPH Entertainment developed the project, which took off when Rita Wilson (wife of Playtone's Tom Hanks) saw Nia Vardalos's one-woman play. Eventually, HBO, Playtone and Gold Circle Films became investors, and a distribution deal set up with Lions Gate fell through.

My Big Fat Greek Wedding is another example of a wonderful movie financed outside the studio system that could not find a distributor. In retrospect this is hard to believe, but it demonstrates the difficulty of achieving distribution in general, and specifically the fallibility of judgment ingrained in the system. In the end, anyone relies on instincts and taste, and it is much easier to say no in this business than yes.

It came down to the financiers paying to distribute the movie. Paul Brooks at Gold Circle and Gary Goetzman at Playtone called, asking me to see *My Big Fat Greek Wedding.* The screening was with 600 people, a smart way of showing a comedy. The audience responded enthusiastically and I understood the commercial potential of the movie. They hired me at IFC Films to strategize the release of the film, working with Gold Circle and Playtone with the help of marketing consultant Paula Silver. There was no distributor advance payment, which was fine with IFC, since we had spent our distribution budget for the year by that point. Instead, we were looking for a service deal to bring in money.

In a "rent-a-system" *service deal,* the producers invest their own money to create awareness for ancillary-market value by hiring a distributor to do specific tasks. A deal could be structured so that the distributor only finds the theatres, only creates the marketing, or does both. This kind of deal can exist for one movie or for a series of movies, much like the relationship a successful company like Morgan Creek has with Warner Bros.

For *My Big Fat Greek Wedding,* a monthly fee was paid by the producers to IFC to release the film. The fee began as a minimum figure, but as the U.S. box office gross increased, the fee increased as well, ultimately capped at a certain level but then renegotiated as the film grew to mammoth proportions. All of the distributor's share of box office gross (100% of film rental) went to the producers. There was no distribution fee. Since IFC was looking for a no-risk deal, *My Big Fat Greek Wedding* fulfilled their objective. They had no risk and were receiving revenue from the increased monthly fees, making more money on this one movie in 2002 than any of their other projects. Their share was nowhere near what a conventional distribution deal would have garnered, but this was not the case, in light of the backstory.

The movie was released initially in eight markets. Within those markets, the idea was to open in several theatres, making it appear more like a commercial film than an art film, supported by many promotional screenings and grassroots efforts. At the grassroots level, for example, Paula Silver arranged with local Greek community groups for them to buy out complete shows of the movie on the first Friday of its opening, much like "first Friday" clubs for other urban movies. This helped the local community to feel a sense of ownership with the picture, and the word of mouth from these shows was very powerful. This was not a review-driven movie, but ultimately it didn't matter; the picture became a national obsession. The audience responded to Nia Vardalos amazingly. The marketing was driven by word of mouth, television publicity, television ads and the grassroots efforts that were so important. As an example of carefully tailored television ads, we were able to target buys to women in spot broadcast ads on programs like *The Oprah Winfrey Show, Live with Regis and Kelly* and *The View*.

My Big Fat Greek Wedding opened in April 2002 and comfortably carried into 2003, for a domestic gross of over $241 million. For me, the most important factor in distributing the movie successfully was keeping it small to make it big. It started out on 108 screens, and we resisted the temptation to expand wide and fast. Instead we held it, keeping it sold out, maintaining it as an event and tying it in people's minds to the theatre where it was playing, as we slowly expanded, topping out at 1,250 screens. At the same time, publicity was building around costars Nia Vardalos and John Corbett, who continued to travel to each market around the country, doing helpful media appearances at a pace of two cities a day.

Y Tu Mamá También is an example of a standard distribution deal and *My Big Fat Greek Wedding* an example of a service deal. A third type of independent distribution deal is the "costs off the top" deal, wherein the distributor, having advanced prints and advertising, recoups those costs from the first dollars of film rental and the remainder is split 50/50 between the distributor and the producer. There is no distribution fee in this type of deal, which is also the kind of deal being made in the college market.

When Newmarket decided to start a theatrical distribution company in 2002, I was approached to lead it. It was a good fit because we had worked together on *Memento* and they had strong connections with sales agents, financing entities and producers around the world. The first film distributed by Newmarket was *Real Women Have Curves,* in partnership with HBO Films, which had never before allowed one of its projects to open in theatres. We hit the ground running, and after two months the picture had grossed $5.8 million on only 150 screens. We continue to acquire movies at film festivals and have high hopes for these filmmaking relationships in the future.

To review, some of the touchstones of independent distribution include maintaining creative relationships with filmmakers; tracking product that is often under studio radar or rejected by the studios; grassroots marketing ingenuity, starting small and pinpointing the target audience; hand-crafted exhibitor relations; and the fact that, although this is a risky business, it can also be very rewarding. The bonus is the possibility of introducing new creative talent and work that audiences embrace, and this is an intangible benefit having nothing to do with money. When a movie excites the creative instincts with a sense of marketplace value, it comes down to bringing together experience to create luck. Much of the zeitgeist of distributing independent movies comes down to timing, taste and luck.

X

THEATRICAL EXHIBITION

THE EXHIBITION BUSINESS

by **SHARI E. REDSTONE,** president of National Amusements, Inc., the third generation of her family to lead the Dedham, Massachusetts–based company. Prior to assuming the role of president in 1999, Ms. Redstone served as National's executive vice president and vice president of corporate planning and development. She practiced corporate and criminal law before joining the company in 1994. Ms. Redstone is known for her innovative approach to the moviegoing experience and is responsible for the company's expansion in the United States, the United Kingdom, Latin America and Russia. Educated at Tufts University and Boston University Law School, Ms. Redstone is on the board of directors of Viacom; cochairman and CEO of MovieTickets.com; chairman and CEO of Rising Star Media; on the board of directors of the John Fitzgerald Kennedy Library Foundation; on the board of trustees of the Dana-Farber Cancer Institute; on the board of overseers at Brandeis University and on the board of directors and executive committee of the National Association of Theatre Owners (NATO). National Amusements is the parent company of Viacom Inc., one of the world's largest entertainment companies.

> The hallmark of the National Amusements business plan is owning the land under our theatres.

National Amusements was founded in 1936 by my grandfather, Michael Redstone. The company started as a circuit of drive-in theatres and grew into one of the largest such companies in the world. One of the first drive-in theatres National opened was on the site of a potato farm in Valley Stream, New York. This drive-in was successfully converted to the Sunrise Multiplex Cinemas in 1979. Some of our other early drive-ins were also converted to successful indoor multiplex theatres. In addition, we built the only drive-in ever permitted in any of the boroughs of New York City, the Whitestone Drive-in, which also became an indoor multiplex theatre in later years. The development of drive-in theatres, which required the acquisition of significant tracts of land, laid the foundation for the company's transition to multiple-screen theatres in subsequent years.

My father, Sumner, joined the company in the early 1960s and started building indoor multiscreen luxury theatres know as Showcase Cinemas. The first was built in Worcester, Massachusetts. Showcase Cinemas usually consisted of two to three auditoriums, featuring at least one curved, mammoth Cinerama screen, with a second large auditorium presenting both 35mm and 70mm films. Each auditorium was equipped with 900 to 1,200 rocking-chair seats. The luxurious reclining rocking-chair seat is still a trademark element within our current theatre designs. Another feature in the early days of the development of Showcase Cinemas was the advance sale of tickets and reserved seating for all performances.

By the 1980s we began exploring markets outside of the United States. Our research indicated that the United Kingdom was significantly underscreened and that British patrons were attending movies at one-fifth the frequency of Americans. In 1988, we began strategically opening theatres in the U.K., believing that patron frequency would increase with an improved moviegoing experience. We continued our overseas expansion in 1996 by building in Chile and Argentina and in 2002 by entering the Russian market. Today we have a total of 1,425 indoor screens, with state-of-the-art projection and sound. Our business plan for our overseas theatres is based on the model we have for our U.S. operation, although we take into account different trends and practices that exist in each country.

Over time, a proliferation of additional outlets for motion picture content has developed, including the saturation of U.S. households with home video and the development of pay-per-view platforms. This new distribution chain led to increased production, and by the 1990s exhibitors responded to this increase by building huge megaplexes with upwards of thirty screens. Eventually, the combination of low interest rates, aggressive developers wanting large theatres as anchor tenants and high-grossing product such as *Titanic* resulted in significant overbuilding, which could not sustain itself. By the turn of the century, many exhibitors (primarily renters, not landowners) found themselves with astronomical rent to pay in a period of unrealized box office expectations, and had to restructure under bankruptcy protection. Happily, most have emerged refreshed and stable.

Our own experience was different. Since we owned the land under the majority of our theatres, we did not carry the lease obligations that burdened many of our competitors. The real estate part of our business tended to shore up any shortfall on the exhibition side by limiting the payment of rent and maximizing our cash flow. Obviously, ownership also allowed for control and flexibility with regard to our operations and potential expansion. For example, when stadium seating was introduced, we simply made the conversion, without having to ask a landlord for permission. This practice of investing our own capital and owning the property that our theatres are built upon has been credited as one of the key factors in keeping us fiscally strong over the past decade.

The hallmark of the National Amusements business plan is owning the land under our theatres. For many of our properties we are the landlord of other businesses as well as our anchor theatre. Where there is additional space, we often add restaurants and other retail that is complementary to destination-based entertainment. On a site with significant retail development, we tend to select tenants such as Home Depot, Target, bookstores and music stores, all compatible with the operation of a cinema. We are also careful not to lease to entities that could hurt our core business or any ancillary business that we may choose to operate. The downside of such development is the substantial commitment of capital. On the upside, real-estate development creates long-term value, with assets designed to pay for themselves over time and enhance the customer experience.

At National Amusements, each decision to build a new theatre complex is based on the suitability of the real estate and location, subject to our overall objectives within a given market. Historically, the company has acquired land and built at intersections of major highways rather than in downtown areas. The site selections usually anticipate traditional growth patterns from a central city to the outlying areas, and serve to consolidate multiple population centers. We tend to prefer the operating efficiences of sixteen screens within a multiplex and believe that in most instances anything over twenty screens and/or 90,000 square feet is difficult to justify.

Since we believe the power of an exhibition circuit is determined by its presence in a given market, we tend to focus on growing in markets where we already have existing assets. This strategy conveys advantages when dealing with distributors and is also attractive to developers, who prefer to negotiate for a site with a substantial player in the market, one with the financial resources and operational expertise to bring the best exhibition experience to the patron.

What if we expand in a market where we have several locations, and the newest venue jeopardizes an existing one? Here again, the strategy of owning the land comes to the rescue. We may decide to keep the existing theatre open (since no rent is being paid) and withstand a drop in business, provided that we are still cash-flow positive. We may also decide to close the existing theatre and sell the valuable underlying real estate; ground-lease the property to one or more entities; or develop the property ourselves. Again, ownership brings flexibility. Whatever the choice, we would stipulate that no theatre be built or operated on the property.

Occasionally, we consider building a theatre in a market where we do not already have a presence. In this case, the targeted market is analyzed in terms of population size, age, income, density, education level, as well as the location, size, and quality of other theatres. Where competing theatres are present, an assessment of potential market-share capture, as well as market expansion, guides this process. If we decide that the market presents an opportunity worth pursing, members of our real estate department scour the area, analyzing opportunities and making contacts in an effort to secure an ideal site.

For exhibition companies evaluating a specific site, a key question may be whether to lease or buy. If the decision is to lease, the company may sign a build-to-suit lease wherein the developer supplies the financing and construction for the site. In most build-to-suits, a developer constructs the core auditoriums and the exhibitor pays for furniture, fixtures and equipment (FF&E), including the soundproofing, carpeting, projection-booth equipment, screens, seating and concession stands. Another option may be to enter into a ground lease, which involves a smaller annual rent but a larger capital contribution, as the exhibitor is responsible for all costs of construction. A lease can also contain elements of both. If the decision is to purchase the land and build the theatre, the exhibitor may decide to take on the additional role of landlord and bring other tenants onto the site.

At National Amusements we are very centralized, running everything from our main office in Dedham, Massachusetts. Departments include operations, film booking, finance and administration, food service and concessions, legal, real estate, marketing and advertising, construction, management information systems, international operations and international film booking. This article will concentrate on the fundamentals of theatre operations and film booking.

THEATRE OPERATIONS

For a review of operations, let's turn to the economics of a hypothetical sixteen-screen multiplex and concentrate on revenue and costs. The largest single source of revenue is ticket sales. Concessions sales represent the next-largest source of revenue. This is followed by income from in-theatre advertising (commercials or slides shown before the trailers), arcade games and the rental of theatres for business or group meetings, all of which make up miscellaneous revenue for the purpose of the table below:

Box office receipts	72.0%
Concessions sales	26.5%
Miscellaneous	1.5%
Total theatre gross	100%

The following table lists typical deductions from total theatre gross, as defined above in our hypothetical multiplex. From the total theatre gross, the largest cost to be deducted is film rental (that portion of box office receipts that is sent to the distributor). The table deducts film rental as a percentage of total theatre gross, but it should be noted that a review of financials for publicly held exhibitors measures film rental as a percentage of box office revenue only. Accordingly, the film rental percentage will be proportionally lower in our chart.

Items that are listed after film rental, in descending order, include rent (if applicable), payroll, cost of goods, utilities, taxes-licenses-insurance, repairs and maintenance, payroll taxes and benefits, supplies and services, miscellaneous (including promotional expenses and travel) and advertising. The chart deducts these separate items as percentages of "total theatre gross." "Theatre-level cash flow" is, in effect, multiplex revenue after all costs are deducted. When (corporate) overhead costs are then deducted, we achieve a "net cash flow" or profit margin of 15% (before depreciation, taxes or debt service) for our hypothetical multiplex.

From total theatre gross of deduct:	100%
Film rental	35.00%
Rent	15.00%
Payroll	12.00%
Cost of goods	4.25%
Utilities	3.00%
Taxes, licenses, insurance	2.50%
Repairs, maintenance	2.00%
Payroll taxes and benefits	2.00%
Supplies and services	2.00%
Miscellaneous	1.50%
Advertising	.75%
Theatre-level cash flow	20.00%
Less overhead	5.00%
Net cash flow	15.00%

As is evident, ours is a tough business. Industry theatre-level profit margins are generally between 15% and 45%, depending upon whether a theatre is owned or leased. At National, we strive to achieve a 35% to 45% margin.

Exhibitors have attempted to leverage theatre destination foot traffic to generate revenues through other retail applications such as arcades and the sale of merchandise. In addition, because the demographics for moviegoing overlap favorably with those for a wide range of lifestyle activities, there is demand for all forms of advertising. Recent trends include third-party corporate sponsorships for various services, as well as amenities and trademark elements within the moviegoing experience, such as sponsored popcorn or soda containers.

Food service within the theatre environment has changed considerably, growing in scope and complexity to stage a variety of offerings that cater to the moviegoing public. These offerings range from the popcorn, candy and fountain drinks associated with core concessions to branded QSR (quick-service restaurant) concepts, much as the traditional mixed-use development model places the mall food court opposite the entrance to the movie theatre. Depending upon the type of food service offered within the theatre environment, theatre-level food costs can range between 10% and 20% of concession revenue. A proper design and deployment of a food service mix is necessary to ensure labor-efficient operations that deliver both incremental sales and increased net profit. For example, we would not want to add sales of a low-margin item if it decreased sales of more profitable products.

Because hospitality is central to the moviegoing experience, we try to hire friendly people who enjoy interacting with the public. Although there is a perception that most workers at movie theatres earn minimum wage, over 90% of our employees are paid above that rate. The traditional service staff positions at the theatre level include cashiers, ushers and concession attendants. Depending upon the volume, layout and complexity of the operation, additional job categories may exist to deal with maintenance, security and cleaning. These services are often provided by external contractors. Almost every theatre in our circuit will be supervised by a management team led by a managing director, one or more house managers and any number of assistant managers.

The service staff is generally comprised of part-time hourly employees who are also attending high school or college. Hourly wage rates are usually determined by local market conditions, as various service businesses compete for the labor pool. Managers can be full-time or part-time and may be paid on a salaried or hourly basis. However, senior theatre-level managers are usually full-time, career-oriented, salaried professionals.

Standards for the coverage of regional management vary widely within the industry. The number of theatres covered by an area or district manager is driven by many variables, including the geographical dispersion, volume and screen count of the buildings. Generally, the buildings with higher volumes are grouped in smaller districts or areas, as they require more attention.

Exhibitors use various formulas to determine staffing levels, by day part, throughout the year. Annual attendance forecasts are broken down to the month, week and day part, refined and finalized as booking decisions are made for each film. For example, children's movies generate more concessions than any other category, requiring more staffing. Longer-term forecasts account for seasonal expansion and contraction with enough lead time into peak business periods for hiring and training. In the short run, business forecasts are usually done one to two weeks prior to a play-week. Attendance projections are broken down by day part, and staffing levels are usually based upon the number of staff hours necessary to service different thresholds of attendance, calculated on either an hours-per-patron or a labor-expenditure-per-patron basis.

The staffing guideline for food service provides for a range that is dependent upon anticipated revenues for the day part. We use the simple yet effective measurement of per capita (per person) sales to analyze revenues from food service. For example, if we project that 10,000 patrons are expected to visit a theatre on a given weekend and that a per capita of $3.50 is achievable, we will calculate how many staff hours are necessary to efficiently service that number of patrons and drive the expected levels of purchase. Timing between shows is also considered to maximize concession sales and minimize the time that our patrons are standing in line. By staggering the starting times of movies, management can regulate the number of guests entering and leaving the building at any one time. Accordingly, this can reduce the number of cashiers, ushers, concession attendants and security personnel required.

Business interruptions are infrequent but may consist of power outages, breaks in the film, or mechanical failure. Local management has the authority to handle these situations on the spot. There are generally no backup film prints, but since we often have a given film playing on more than one screen, if one print fails, another one can be interlocked and used in two auditoriums.

FILM BOOKING

Now that we have covered an overview of operations, we will discuss film booking. For exhibitors, the relationship with any distributor that can deliver quality product is crucial. We nurture those relationships daily. Distributors are our partners, and we need each other. It's a working relationship, and for the most part, it works well. Central to the relationship is negotiating the percentages of film rental per picture, but it goes beyond that. It includes premieres, other promotions and, most importantly, demonstrating the ability to maximize revenue for each picture.

Our company also encourages independent filmmakers. For example, we recently launched a great movie in our theatres called *Ciao America*, made by two Italian-American filmmakers unable to reach a distribution deal with any of the studios. We also created a marketing campaign for the opening of the picture in several of our markets. This is one of many examples of supporting independent filmmaking, something that gives us a great feeling of accomplishment.

On the studio side of relationships, the key is working together to maximize the value of the product. The head film buyer at National Amusements has frequent conversations with studio distribution chiefs about the nature and potential of upcoming product, the distribution calendar and strategic marketing campaigns for each title. It is important to understand as much as we can about each picture and the competitive landscape in order to determine how best to play each film (for instance, how many screens to play it on, and for how many weeks).

Because of our high number of screens in each location, we tend to book nearly every major release in most of our theatres. Years ago, exhibitors would compete with each other in certain cities to book the most desirable movies and distributors would leverage this competition to achieve the best deal and maximize the number of allocated screens for a film's release. Today, since the country is so widely screened (with approximately 35,000 screens in 2002, compared with 25,214 in 1992), every studio release is generally available in every major city. Accordingly, competition is based more on location and the quality of the moviegoing experience rather than the choice of title.

To book a film in our hypothetical sixteen-plex, the film booker, well aware of the titles being released in a particular week, will negotiate a deal with his or her counterpart at the distribution company. Negotiable points include film rental, number of screens, total seating capacity, the number of show times and the duration of the run. Depending on how complex or valuable the deal becomes, conversations can continue at the highest levels on each side. The final deal is always approved by our head film buyer and by the distributor's general sales manager. The most significant issue discussed is usually film rental, and this deserves some attention. The most common deal is the "90/10."

The key to the 90/10 calculation is the theatre's prenegotiated house allowance figure. Each exhibitor and distributor relies on a variety of facts in computing the house allowance, such as quality of the theatre, the number of screens, and the number of seats. This negotiated figure is taken into account when calculating the final payment. The house allowance is subtracted from the film's gross for the week, and the remainder is multiplied by 90% to yield the 90/10 film rental owed. If the 90/10 film rental is greater than the film rental calculated using a "floor" percentage for the same gross, then the exhibitor pays the 90/10 film rental. If the floor percentage calculation yields more film rental, then the exhibitor pays by the floor calculation method.

Examples

Assumptions

    Theatre house allowance = $10,000
    Floor percentage for week =   60%

Example A
If the film grosses $25,000 for the week:

90/10 method	Floor method
$25,000	$25,000
− 10,000	× .6
= 15,000	= $15,000 film rental
× .9	
= $13,500 film rental	

Exhibitor pays $15,000 film rental because the floor percentage rental is higher.

Example B
If the film grosses $75,000 for the week:

90/10 method	Floor method
$75,000	$75,000
− 10,000	× .6
= $65,000	= $45,000 film rental
× .9	
= $58,500 film rental	

Exhibitor pays $58,500 film rental because the 90/10 percentage rental is higher.

The 90/10 film rental calculation was created to provide the distributor with additional earning potential in the event a film was a big hit. It allows the film company to "earn" additional film rental over and above the amount they would receive based on a minimum floor percentage. Typically, the 90/10 formula applies only in the early, higher-grossing weeks of an engagement. It can, however, also figure in the later weeks of a long-running, successful film like *Titanic* or *Spider-Man*.

The recent increase in screen count has led to a significant downside for exhibitors in these film rental calculations, as the large number of screens in most cities allows for access to any film on a given weekend. Most patrons choose to see a movie on the opening weekend or the weekend that follows, and there is usually a sharp drop-off in admissions during subsequent weeks. The result is a substantial front-loading of grosses. Since exhibition's deal with distribution benefits the distributor in the early weeks (under the theory that distributors are entitled to the lion's share early to offset substantial production and marketing costs) and the balance shifts in later weeks, when the distributor receives a lower minimum percentage of the box office against the 90/10 deal, the front-loading of higher grosses harms the exhibitor. The onslaught of available product also puts pressure on a run's duration, in that today's movie runs are often abbreviated due to a surplus of product in the market. As a consequence, exhibition is often deprived of longevity of runs, and forfeits the prospect of retaining a higher percentage of the overall box office. It should be noted, however, that the increase in film production has in fact led to the release of quality product throughout the year, not just during summer and holidays. This has been a benefit for all.

In spite of the widespread use of the 90/10 deal, there is a trend toward "aggregate deals," where a certain percentage is applied to the film's entire run instead of the weekly box office. Also, some studios sell their product on a "firm term" basis, where the booker must negotiate and agree to the film rental terms in advance. Other times, the final film rental is negotiated at the end of a run.

Most movies are screened for exhibitors one to three weeks before the release date, with event pictures sometimes screened months in advance. Screenings usually take place during the day at a local theatre. Most film bookers and occasionally some people from advertising and operations will attend. Some states have anti–blind bidding laws, where movies cannot legally be booked before they are screened.

Once a movie is booked, the distributor's exhibitor relations department is in contact with our marketing and advertising department to coordinate sending the artwork (such as one-sheets, standees, elaborate banners or displays) and trailers for the film to appear at the theatre in order to guarantee prerelease awareness and excitement. The trailer can be the single most powerful marketing tool, since it is shown to a captive audience of moviegoers. Trailer content is rated by the MPAA (just as features are), and theatres are careful to place trailers with features that have compatible ratings. For example, a screen playing an R-rated film can show trailers for R-rated, PG-13, PG or G movies; a screen playing a PG movie would only show trailers with a PG or G rating.

Closer to the opening of a film, the marketing campaign appears in local newspapers. There are two kinds of ad placements. Large *display ads,* placed by the distributor, highlight a specific movie and contain a listing of all local theatres playing the film. *Directory ads* list all of our theatres and the starting times for all films. These directory ads are placed and paid for by the exhibitor. The cost of the directory ad, which comes out of our local advertising budget, is usually blocked off for the same newspaper linage every week, but it can vary if we include a big movie's promotional banner. Exhibitors also pay a portion of the cost of the display ads taken out by the studios in what is known as *co-op advertising.* As part of our financial obligations to the distributor, our co-op ad contribution (a negotiated percentage of box office gross) is deducted from the theatre's share of weekly revenue.

In general, exhibition chains contract with regional suppliers to manage the traffic of prints and trailers by third-party transportation companies. When a film arrives at the multiplex, the distributor's trailers are attached to the beginning of the print. Theatre managers usually splice other trailers, not necessarily from the same studio, in front of those trailers to reflect the upcoming slate of movies that the multiplex will be showing. Our own institutional presentation is added, along with third-party advertising, known as "rolling stock."

Rolling stock advertising is a practice that began in the mid-1990s when the industry was searching for additional revenue. While the concept is new to the United States, moviegoers in Europe have been enjoying rolling stock advertising in theatres for decades. Exhibitors try to select onscreen advertising that is tasteful, and are aware of the risk that the combination of time-consuming advertising and trailers might undermine the moviegoing experience. For this reason, most theatres show advertising (commercials or slides) as a prefeature diversion. As commercials represent a revenue stream not shared with distributors, exhibitors are careful to separate them from coming-attraction trailers selling movies, the lifeblood of our business.

Once the movie opens, grosses are transmitted to the home office electronically so that we know exactly how each screen is performing. Our company then reports the box office grosses to Nielsen EDI (a division of AC Nielsen), which releases the figures to the studios and the press.

Twice a year, exhibitors gather with distributors and vendors at industry-wide conventions: ShoWest in Las Vegas during March and

ShowEast in Orlando in the fall. At ShowEast, and occasionally ShoWest, distributors trumpet their schedule of upcoming movies, sometimes showing product reels or completed films at luncheons or dinners featuring appearances by stars, directors and producers. At both conventions, there are venues for the latest in concession foods and displays, theatre equipment, seating and any innovation that may be relevant to the operation of theatres.

Perhaps the most exciting trend in exhibition is the experimentation with luxury-style venues. A forerunner is the Gold Class Cinema that Village Roadshow opened in Australia in 2000. At National Amusements, we began to work on our own upscale moviegoing experience years ago, believing that it should be as wonderful if not more wonderful than the movie itself. Our patrons were becoming increasingly sophisticated, with higher expectations (and lower patience) than ever before. We wanted to exceed those expectations with luxury ambience and service, including reserved seating, online ticketing, a concierge desk and other amenities.

This led to our entering the Los Angeles market in 2001 with the creation of the luxury Bridge "Cinema De Lux" at the Promenade at the Howard Hughes Center next to the San Diego (405) freeway. The Bridge contains seventeen state-of-the-art auditoriums with stadium seating, digital sound, and three Director's Halls, featuring wide leather seats, reserved seating and an Elite Services Desk, which provides concierge services for our patrons. There is a small premium for seeing a movie in the Director's Hall, but all of our patrons are exposed to a very high level of service and attention for the price of a regular ticket. The theatre also features a bar and lounge selling all kinds of signature martini drinks and snacks, as well as one auditorium, "center stage," that features live entertainment before the show. There is also an IMAX theatre in the complex, with the largest commercial IMAX screen in Los Angeles. This theatre is equipped with Rear Window Captioning and Descriptive Video Service for selected films.

In 2002, we opened another Bridge Cinema De Lux in Philadelphia, with the University of Pennsylvania as our partner. The complex includes an area designed as a casual lounge, with coffee, newspapers, magazines and free Internet access for students and faculty, as well as a Media Immersion Room featuring student film and animated product. There is also a bar and a more sophisticated lounge with televisions and on occasion other forms of entertainment. This custom design fulfilled our goal of building a theatre that takes into account all of the needs and wishes of the community. We have opened another Cinema De Lux on Long Island and have several more in development.

As with many other retail operations, technology has allowed the exhibitor to bring new products and services into the theatre while streamlining operations and offsetting labor costs. Through the convenience of Internet ticketing, patrons can pay in advance with a credit card; tickets can be picked up at the theatre or even printed at home. The three major Internet ticketing companies are MovieTickets.com, Moviefone and Fandango. National Amusements is a founding partner in MovieTickets.com, along with AMC Theatres and Hollywood Media Corporation. Most multiplexes are equipped with multifunctional ATMs that provide a range of services from ticketing to the dispensing of cash. This has reduced the number of box office personnel necessary for servicing various thresholds of attendance.

One of the most talked-about innovations in exhibition is digital projection. Studios have a lot to gain with the introduction of digital projectors, as they will be able to save significantly on their print production and distribution costs. Exhibitors have been supportive, but are unwilling to pay for the digital rollout. We view the studios as the primary beneficiaries. While digital projection may afford exhibitors the flexibility of offering alternative programming to the public via satellite delivery during the day and at other times when moviegoing is traditionally low, it is still an unproven source of revenue. The studios have gotten together, however, and created a company called DCI (Digital Cinema Initiatives, LLC) to explore the development of standards for digital projection as well as to formulate a business plan. Exhibition must be careful about the transition, as many questions remain. One advantage of digital projection equipment is that it will allow for easier programming of commercials and other media, such as sporting events or concerts. On a touch-sensitive screen in the manager's office, we will be able to program certain ads or other media for specific auditoriums throughout the day, adding all sorts of flexibility for the placement of advertising and other content.

The transition to digital projection will be a slow one. Standards must be developed, and we must ensure that the technology is of such quality and durability that it will withstand later innovation. The planned obsolescence that customers find frustrating in home-computer upgrades is something we must avoid in exhibition. On the plus side, satellite distribution of digital prints around the world would reduce piracy and take advantage of the instant, global buzz on a film that the Internet and satellite television can generate. Digital projection is inevitable because it makes sense, but it must be done right.

As we look into the future of exhibition, we see wonderful opportunities. Exhibitors are faced with the challenge of distinguishing themselves from their competition, be it another exhibitor or the rising popularity of at-home entertainment. The key to success will be providing patrons with new and exciting experiences they cannot find elsewhere in an environment as compelling and entertaining as the movie itself. Our patrons deserve nothing less.

THE INDEPENDENT EXHIBITOR

by **ROBERT LAEMMLE,** owner of the Laemmle Fine Arts Theatres, a Los Angeles-area theatre chain with thirty-nine screens that specializes in exhibiting first-run foreign-language films, American independent films and quality Hollywood productions. It also provides a booking service for an additional sixteen screens in the south and southwest. He received a master of business administration from UCLA, and was honored by the French government with a Chevalier de l'Ordre des Arts et des Lettres.

Reduced zones often result in less revenue per theatre (squeezing exhibitors), even though overall city grosses would be up (pleasing distributors).

Laemmle Theatres, founded in 1938, is made up of thirty-nine screens in nine theatres in Los Angeles. In 1999 we opened the Playhouse 7 in Pasadena, and in 2001 we added the Fairfax 3 in Los Angeles and the Fallbrook 7 in West Hills, California. The organization consists of me, my son, Gregory, and my nephew Jay Reisbaum, plus nine office workers who assist with flyer program layouts, publicity and public relations, maintaining our Web site (www.laemmle.com) and other miscellaneous office work.

Our theatres are broken down as follows: The primary, first-run houses are the Sunset 5 in West Hollywood, the Royal in West Los Angeles, the Music Hall 3 in Beverly Hills, the Monica 4 in Santa Monica and the Fairfax 3. The neighborhood theatres include the Playhouse 7 in Pasadena, the Town Center 5 in Encino, and the Fallbrook 7 in West Hills and Grande fourplex in downtown Los Angeles. We primarily show foreign films and fine-arts specialty films in all our theatres, except for the Grande, which usually shows first-run Hollywood product. If there's not a "good" Hollywood film to play there, we show a foreign film. (Most distributors use the term *good* in relation to moneymaking; I use the term here in relation to quality.)

In the 1990s, several exhibition companies started building larger megaplexes, ranging from twelve to thirty screens, often near their existing, profitable theatres. But these new, successful complexes acted as vacuums, siphoning business from their older, nearby theatres and turning them unprofitable. These exhibitors, still obligated to pay long-term leases on the older theatres, found themselves in financial difficulty and sought protection under bankruptcy laws. The reorganizations that followed allowed chains to get out of their unprofitable leases and emerge stronger, at the expense of landlords left with empty theatres without operators. Two of our additions, the Fairfax 3 and the Fallbrook 7, were acquired after prior leases were vacated.

In Los Angeles there is hardly any bidding for motion pictures; most deals are the result of negotiation. Any large city is divided into *zones,* representing population centers of moviegoers. In negotiating to exhibit a film, a theatre in one zone may request clearance over those in other zones, for less competition. But with the expansion of theatre circuits and the natural shift in population densities, zone sizes are being reduced. Reduced zones often result in less revenue per theatre (squeezing exhibitors), even though overall city grosses would be up (pleasing distributors).

To review our standards of business: We don't actively compete with the big circuits. Rather, it is to our advantage to let our competition book their screens; then we negotiate for that type of product that wants to play in our theatres. Also, we have a level or standard of product that we will show. We feel that if a film is good, it will find its proper film rental, and we will assist it in making the most money possible through our promotion work. We have a very good reputation for prompt payment of film rental.

In Los Angeles, our chain is a highly desirable player of *specialty* films, a term which includes American independent, English-language (non-U.S.) independent, art-house, and foreign-language films. In the past, smaller distributors would release these films to art-house theatres. Today, with the consolidation of distribution, major studios release a range from specialty films to blockbusters. When they release a specialty film, they specifically want to play in our theatres (since they know they will get their best results) as well as in some circuit theatres that surround us. (When the Sunset 5 played *The Royal Tenenbaums,* it was the highest-grossing West Coast theatre on that film.)

Among the studio specialty labels are Fine Line, Fox Searchlight, Miramax, Paramount Classics, Sony Classics, and Universal Focus. These labels carry the clout of their parent companies, and have a lock on the most desirable specialty films. When one of them sets a national release date, often a limited release, they will negotiate to achieve the best theatres in selected cities on the specific date. Then there are smaller, independent specialized distributors, including Lions Gate (including Artisan), IFC Films, Newmarket, and Lot 47, among others, who might handle a specialty film as a platform release, starting with one or two theatres in New York and Los Angeles before expanding. Sometimes these smaller distributors must wait their turn to play in a specific specialty theatre because a studio's specialty film is already there. Sometimes a specialty film will start out as a platform release (two to fifty theatres), grow to limited release (up to 600 screens), then keep expanding wider, driven by box office success. Two films that outgrew their "specialty" label were *Shakespeare in Love* and *Crouching Tiger, Hidden Dragon*.

There are a lot of different independent distributors handling specialty films; some handle one film, some handle half a dozen. We get to know them all, and they know us. Sometimes we contact them as soon as we hear that they've acquired a certain film for domestic release; sometimes they call us and ask us to view a new film and consider playing it in one of our theatres. We also discover availability of new specialty films by reading the trades and other papers, attending several film festivals and going to private screenings, often prior to a picture's securing a distribution deal. In fact, we've been helpful in launching certain films that we've liked.

A recent foreign-film deal from a studio specialty division involved minimum terms and a minimum playing time. It called for a split of 90/10 above our house allowance, with a minimum floor for the first week at 70%, the second week at 60%, third week 50%, fourth week 40%, and subsequent weeks at 35%. These terms are for the most important specialty films.

Floors protect the distributor if the film's a disappointment; the 90/10 split also protects the distributor. For instance, let's say a theatre for one week has a $40,000 gross on a 90/10 deal with a 60% floor and a house nut of $5,000. Start with $40,000 as the gross, subtract $5,000, which is the house expense. Then split the remaining $35,000 90/10; that leaves $3,500 for the theatre and $31,500 for the distributor. How does that compare with the 60% floor figure? 60% of $40,000 is $24,000. Since a net film rental of $31,500 (the distributor's share) is about 78% of $40,000, or about 18% higher than the floor, the 90/10 split will govern, with the theatre paying a higher percentage to the distributor than the straight 60% of gross.

In the area of advertising, distributors pay the bulk of theatrical marketing costs, since a film opening theatrically increases in value in subsequent markets such as home video/DVD and television. Individual theatres contribute only a few hundred dollars each to the ad campaign in the form of "cooperative advertising."

The *nut*, or overhead, of one of our theatres includes payroll, rental on the theatre property, maintenance, insurance, utilities and standard advertising, which is a part of the usual, steady advertising each theatre bears.

Concessions are a much more significant profit center for Hollywood films than for specialty films. At multiplexes, one concession stand services multiple theatres and is constantly active. Sometimes a theatre showing a Hollywood film would even be willing to give 70% floor terms and perhaps 80% floors just to get a certain "popcorn movie"; then they make their money at the candy counter. After all, the markup on a bag of popcorn is probably around 75% (which does not, however, take into account the cost of running a concession operation). Concessions are an increasingly important source of income for our specialty theatres, since most of them are multiplexes.

Once we make a deal on a film, we put trailers on all our screens announcing the film in advance. In addition, there'll be posters at the theatres and fliers circulating with full reviews or excerpts. We also make use of our Web site to target and inform specific customers via list serves, with the help of our own webmaster, who updates the site with details of specific movies, downloadable starting times, theatre photos and information regarding jobs, newsletter subscriptions, gift certificates, and how to contact us. This represents direct customer feedback, and we appreciate every message.

In the day-to-day operation of the theatres, little emergencies arise, such as the breakdown of an air-conditioning system, plumbing problems, projection-equipment or sound problems, customer complaints, or employee problems. Otherwise the day is filled with the routine of planning advance work for future pictures.

There is one complaint that a theatre owner must voice, and that is with newspaper advertising policies. Newspapers charge higher rates for display advertising than for other forms of advertising. It's wrong that a department store can afford a half-dozen full-page ads in a city while a major film cannot because the same space just costs too much. This practice is discriminatory and should be abolished. It dates back to the days when amusement advertisers would leave town without paying their bills. Local theatres are here to stay, and they make a major contribution to the local economy; it's about time this advertising practice was corrected.

Independent exhibition exists in a more difficult climate today due to the recent expansion of circuits. In some cases independents were acquired by larger chains. In other cases expansion through new construction has resulted in overscreening certain neighborhoods, reducing revenue from individual screens and threatening local independent theatres with extinction. Independent distributors must encourage the existence of independent exhibitors because their long-run livelihoods are interconnected. Circuits will only play specialized product when it suits them; independents will always want to play these films.

Overseas, exhibition is thriving, with growth in multiplexes bringing higher revenue to both mainstream and specialty films. This is a very healthy change for the specialty film market in particular, where films can gross more outside the United States than inside. A classic example is *The Full Monty.*

Inside the United States, specialty films continue to be an important training ground for American independents, who often cross over to mainstream studio productions. Steven Soderbergh and the Coen Brothers are examples of filmmakers who have successfully crossed over to wider audiences.

No article on exhibition can be complete without reference to digital projection. In the summer of 2000, we were involved in an experiment when Miramax installed digital equipment in one theatre of the Sunset 5 for *The Ideal Husband,* which was also being shown on another screen in 35mm. It was difficult to notice any difference between the two. But digital projection will be delayed until the per-unit cost, now around $100,000, can be reduced to an economically viable figure.

Finally, let me voice concern that there are two elements of Hollywood domination overseas that are jeopardizing foreign-language films. First, in certain overseas markets (including France and Italy), attendance for American films is on the rise; for indigenous films it can be flat. This discourages local film production, and therefore there are fewer films available for import to the United States. Second, Hollywood attracts major filmmakers from all over the world who began in their native country and moved on to make Hollywood films. This is perhaps inevitable, since filmmakers are entitled to enjoy the success of their work, which usually means gaining access to a wider audience through American-financed pictures, but it can be unhappy for the local film industry that spawned them.

XI

HOME VIDEO

HOME VIDEO BUSINESS

by **BENJAMIN S. FEINGOLD,** president, business & operations, Columbia TriStar Motion Picture Group, a division of Sony Pictures Entertainment based in Culver City, California, who is responsible for the overall filmed entertainment strategy of Sony Pictures. In addition, Mr. Feingold is president and chief executive of Columbia TriStar Home Entertainment (CTHE), the worldwide home entertainment division of Sony Pictures Entertainment. Under his leadership, CTHE was at the forefront of the successful worldwide launch of the DVD format in conjunction with Sony, Toshiba and Warner Bros. Mr. Feingold is also president of Sony Pictures' Digital Studios Division, comprised of the DVD Center, the High Definition Center, the Post-Production facilities and Worldwide Product Fulfillment. Before joining Sony Pictures, he was a corporate lawyer with the New York firm Kay Scholer Fierman Hays & Handler. A magna cum laude graduate of Brandeis University, Mr. Feingold received his law degree at the Hastings College of Law, University of California, and his M.Sc. in economics from the London School of Economics.

One year later DVD was launched in Europe, and it was just a matter of time before all the studios recognized the validity of the format.

H ome video is the largest revenue stream that flows from a motion picture—larger than theatrical—although it only becomes available some four to six months after theatrical release. But when it was in its infancy, movie executives resisted a home video product that customers would own, since historically movies had always been licensed, never sold.

As a measure of studios' reluctance to embrace the new home video format as a business, some took on partners instead of plunging in alone. An example is to be found in the origins of Columbia TriStar Home Entertainment. In the mid-1980s, RCA-Columbia Home Video was formed as a joint venture between Columbia Pictures and RCA. At the time, nobody knew whether this new business of prerecorded material would be dominated by films or television programming, would be a rental market or a sale market, or if in fact there was a market at all. The idea was for RCA, owner of NBC, to supply television programming and Columbia Pictures to provide movies; since they split the overhead, if the concept failed, there would be no draconian result for either side. Earlier, TriStar Pictures had been founded in 1982 by three partners in separate revenue streams: Columbia Pictures in theatrical distribution, CBS in network television distribution and HBO in pay-television programming. TriStar Pictures contributed product to the RCA-Columbia Home Video joint venture, although some titles were initially released by CBS-Fox, a preexisting label and another example of early home video partnerships. (For more history of home video, see the article by Paul Sweeting, which follows this one.)

Today, home video is a thriving business, and distributors have moved on from joint-venture labels to their own fully owned labels.

The issue of whether this would be a rental business or sell-through (purchase) business was sorted out by the market over time. Suppliers raised the price of prerecorded home video so that a rental market began and developed; prices were raised as movies cost more to make and market. The 1980s was a period of growth, with the sell-through market developing at the end of the decade. With the exception of Disney, studio distributors were not as interested in sell-through at the time, because sell-through by definition is a volume business requiring massive distribution details of duplication, wrapping, shipping and tracking units. At the time, studios were often distributing video product through middleman companies such as Good Times, Handelman, Anderson Merchandising and Ingram. In the 1990s, the home video business grew at double-digit rates on the sell-through side, fueled initially by the powerhouse titles of Walt Disney's animated library of family films and later by the direct-to-sell-through strategies for non-kids' films led by Warners, Columbia and Fox.

Sony was looking into next-generation packaged media in their R&D center in Tokyo, and other companies that have proprietary consumer electronics businesses—such as Matsushita (Panasonic), Toshiba and Pioneer—were doing ongoing research as well. Certain executives recognized that VHS was becoming a mature business, and began to address the issue of a new format.

A group spearheaded by Warren Lieberfarb, president of Warner Home Video, and myself believed a new, digital product was needed to compete with satellite television and digitally delivered television, which were on the horizon. Warners made a number of compacts with consumer electronics companies and was working closely with Toshiba, which owned a percentage of Time Warner Entertainment at the time. Representatives from Sony, Panasonic and Toshiba came to Los Angeles in 1995 and 1996 and met with home video and motion picture executives about requirements and standards. Soon a very aggressive race was on to create the best system, since only one system would be adopted by the consumer electronics industry (thereby avoiding the VHS-Betamax rivalry of the 1970s).

In our case, we turned to Sony for their expertise in developing a new format. One of the reasons they bought Columbia Pictures was to foster synergy between the hardware of consumer electronics and the software of copyrighted content. An issue during early research into different laser and compression techniques was whether full-length movies could fit on a cost-effective format.

The model platform was derived from CD (compact disc) audio technology, with key patents controlled by Philips and Sony jointly. Sony believed strongly in lateral compatability—that is, an advanced disc format must be compatible with the existing one (in other words, a DVD machine must play CDs), forging a bond with the consumer and not forcing the older inventory into obsolescence. Because of this, DVD (digital versatile disc) was developed to be compatible with audio CD and video CD (a video format in Asia), and all would play on computers equipped with DVD drives.

Our software requirements included the idea that a two-and-a-half-hour movie had to fit on one side (thereby accommodating 99% of our films) and that parental lockout and piracy protection had to be included. There was also the expectation that DVD would allow for additional value-added behind-the-scenes features; five different audio tracks for multi-channel sound, filmmakers' commentaries, language dubbing and room for up to six subtitle streams for international markets.

In anticipation of the new format, we went through our film library, cleaned the masters and made high-definition transfers so that movies owned by Sony Pictures Entertainment would be viewed at the highest quality possible on DVD. We also built an authoring center to compress our films, which required close cooperation with Sony R&D, since no such hardware and software existed at the time.

In the end, there were two camps: Sony/Columbia-Philips and Toshiba-Matsushita-Warners. By 1996, the sides had compromised, bringing some aspects of each others' patents to the new format, which was launched the following year, in April 1997.

Retailers such as Best Buy, Circuit City, and Good Guys were bullish on DVD and eager to sell DVD players as a new revenue stream and as a cornerstone for home theatre, whereby they would sell a suite of digital products around the DVD, such as televisions, tuners, satellite receivers and speaker systems. But once the format war was settled and DVD was about to launch, another group with a conditional-play technology called DivX sold the concept to Circuit City, which wanted to sell a DivX machine (a DVD machine with a conditional access feature for limited-play DVDs). Within a year, DivX collapsed, to the tune of significant losses for Circuit City, improving the competitive position of the Best Buy chain, which had backed DVD (but not DivX) from the beginning.

As part of the DVD launch in April 1997, Columbia TriStar Home Entertainment knew it was vital to release three to four new movies to the market per month, with the strategy of including as much value-added material as possible without missing the release date. Because the format was new, it was fundamental to provide a reliable, steady stream of product to encourage customers to spring for the initial $400 to $500 cost of the DVD player.

An early indicator of success was our first preorder of 100,000 units, of *Air Force One,* in January 1998. We had never shipped more than 50,000 units on laser disc, so we knew we had, in the space of nine months, eclipsed the laser disc business, which was around eight years old; we knew we had a hit on our hands. In the first six months of DVD's rollout, Warners and Columbia were the only companies with movies in the format. One year later DVD was launched in Europe, and it was just a matter of time before all the studios recognized the validity of the format.

DVD also includes a parallel import-reducing technology called "regional coding," allowing only DVDs purchased in a specific region to be playable on machines purchased there; a DVD bought in Australia (region 2) does not work on a player bought in the United States (region 1). Regional coding was developed to protect the theatrical release and video windows internationally country-by-country as well as to impose copyright management.

Other consumer issues for DVD were release timing and price. Industry practice with VHS movies called for rental only on the *street date* (release date) of the title, with sell-through consumer repricing about six months later, after the rental dealer had recouped its investment in the rental cassette. We decided to sell DVDs at the earliest time a customer had access to VHS, when VHS was available as rental only. Another cornerstone for DVD was to encourage ownership through low pricing. The DVD price range for purchase (sell-through) was $19.95 to $24.95 retail, closer to the VHS sell-through prices for which the consumer would have to wait six months. So the customer choice became to buy the new, improved DVD format today at a low price, or rent a DVD, or rent a VHS, or wait four to six months and buy the VHS. This jump-started DVD purchases by consumers who embraced the improved picture and sound quality, low pricing and value-added features contained in DVDs.

Today DVD is a hugely successful format, the fastest-adopted consumer electronics product of all time. It's not uncommon for the first week's gross in DVD sales of a highly popular movie to exceed its first-week gross in theatres and for video/DVD net receipts to be greater than theatrical gross receipts.

To make the DVD, we convert the film (along with the value-added material) to digital linear tape in a process we call *authoring*. Along the way, *branching* is added (the navigation between chapters) and the material is put into an encoder and converted to digital tape. The digital tape is sent to a manufacturing plant that creates a glass master, used to stamp out a sample DVD sent to us for quality control approval before being returned to the plant to fill the order for hundreds of thousands (if not millions) of units.

The stamping process, known as *replication,* is similar to the making of audio CDs. In fact, as a bit of history, those studios with music divisions (Sony, Warners and Universal) had a leg up over those without in the early days of home video, since it was usually a matter of extending the music manufacturing facilities to accommodate home video. After stamping, the DVD packaging process involves a sophisticated source tag for each unit, the equivalent to a store's security tag, to discourage theft, because retail theft (or "shrinkage," in retail parlance) is so high. Then the artwork is added and the DVD units are packaged and shrink-wrapped. For certain of our accounts for which we ship directly to stores (without using a wholesaler or retail chain distribution center), units are bar-coded and price-ticketed at the manufacturing facility, so they are ready to go across the cash register; those units just need to be removed from a cardboard carton and put on the shelf. VHS units are manufactured in different plants, and that process, done in real time, takes longer than stamping DVDs.

Let's run some numbers. Assume a new-release DVD has a retail price of $19.95; the wholesale price could be around $17; the store makes $3. Of that $17 wholesale price that returns to the studio distributor, it costs around $3 to $5 to make, market and distribute the product. The balance is retained by the distributor and mingles in the "picture pot" with theatrical, TV and other revenue to help recoup the costs of the movie, including production and marketing costs as well as profit participations to talent such as actors, directors and producers.

Pricings vary depending on a title's longevity. The profit margin for retailers tends to be lower on new releases and higher on older titles. A new release, at a lower margin, will sell more units than an older title, satisfying the retailer; as the product ages, there is lower volume and a lower wholesale price but a higher profit margin for the retailer, since our manufacturing and distribution costs are lower over time. If an older movie with an $8 wholesale price sells for $9.95, that $2 profit margin to the retailer is 25% of their cost, a higher margin than $3 on $17, which is closer to 18%. The retailer's profit margin is higher on older units.

Recently a model similar to that for VHS is emerging for DVDs, involving revenue-sharing with retail stores such as Blockbuster and Hollywood. On DVD rentals, the store will pay us a minimum amount per unit plus a piece of each rental and sale transaction. Revenue-sharing grew out of consumer dissatisfaction with the copy depth at video rental stores when the most desirable VHS titles were often sold out. The traditional VHS business model charged high wholesale prices to retailers, which limited the number of units they would gamble on stocking in stores for rental. Remember, rental fees were not being shared at this time; they remained at the store level. Retailers such as Blockbuster worked with distributors on a revenue-sharing solution, pleasing both sides: With a lowered minimum initial payment, stores would be well-stocked on new titles, consumers would find their first-choice movies and distributors would share in each rental transaction based on an agreed-upon formula. At the same time we were introducing revenue sharing, in late 1997, we were also launching the DVD business, and in my view there was a balancing out.

These days, at Columbia TriStar Home Entertainment, 80% to 85% of our business is direct to retailers, with no middlemen such as wholesalers or rack-jobbers. Retailers in general fall into two categories: rental or purchase. The largest rental chains include Blockbuster, Hollywood, Movie Gallery, RogersVideo, Videotron (in Canada), rental outlets in grocery chains such as Kroger and Giant Eagle, and smaller chains such as Tower Video and Family Video. These chains may sell off their used inventory, but probably 85% of their income is from renting VHS and DVDs. The purchase business is generated by the mass-market chains such as Wal-Mart, Target, Kmart, Costco, Sam's, Shopco and Ames, consumer electronics chains such as Best Buy, Circuit City and Good Guys, and video specialty stores such as Musicland, Transworld and Virgin. Supermarkets are a hybrid; some chains only rent, some only sell, others do both.

In my capacity as president and chief executive of Columbia TriStar Home Entertainment, I track the theatrical performance of a title in the marketplace in order to prepare for its home video release, or street date, which arrives between three and six months after theatrical.

For a movie as important as *Spider-Man*, Home Entertainment had been working for a year prior to theatrical release. *Spider-Man* entailed arranging for a special crew to visit the set to capture material used in the value-added behind-the-scenes bonus chapters on the DVD; planning cross-promotions with theatrical release promotional partners such as phone companies, Cingular Wireless, food companies (Spidey has his own Kellogg's cereal) and fast-food restaurants (Hardee's in the southeast and Carl's Jr. west of the Mississippi). These deals require a long lead time to set in place, and we were on a ticking clock once we set the theatrical release date of May 3, 2002. Happily, the opening weekend of *Spider-Man* was historic, the biggest opening of all time, grossing over $123 million.

Once the home video title is released, we track transactions electronically. It's possible to track sales figures from the top eight retailers daily via EDI and the Internet. This immediacy allows us to decide whether or where to ship more units and replenish stock. Today, we "drop-ship" directly to 2,900 Wal-Mart stores, sending hundreds of thousands of units a week on trucks. As we electronically track the sales of cassettes or DVDs with links to the individual stores, we automatically manufacture and ship out new ones. It's quite a sophisticated business today.

We expect to be paid "net 30," or thirty days after sales, but we may run special programs for some retail customers asked to stock large quantities of units that allow for later payment. As indicated earlier, 80% to 85% of our home video business is billed directly to chains; the balance is billed to distributors such as Ingram and VPD, who bill their own retail customers.

The store information that flows into our computers is from mass-market retailers, the only customers set up in this way. The data is analyzed by our sales planning department—since certain titles sell better in some markets than others in the ebb and flow of consumer taste—and subsequent store orders are tweaked accordingly. This is a vivid example of supply-and-demand efficiency through the use of information systems.

At Columbia TriStar Home Entertainment, a sales force negotiates orders for new-release product with retailers. This sales force of some thirty people works in the field, visiting large and small retail customers. Also there is the sales planning department, which analyzes sales data (as mentioned earlier) as well as how the competition is doing, sales velocity at different price points and decay curves on new sell-throughs and rental stores, to decide whether to further drop the price or sell off rental inventory.

The marketing department, divided into trade marketing (which is mostly Internet-based these days) and consumer marketing, prepares the product for release. The trade marketing group advertises to store owners about our upcoming product; consumer marketing generates advertising at the customers' point-of-sale, for example corrugated displays in stores such as Wal-Mart, Best Buy and Target and on the Web at Amazon.com, as well as on broadcast and in print media. Broadcast campaigns on mega-titles such as *Spider-Man* are in the millions of dollars and include prime-time national networks and key cable networks, similar to theatrical release campaigns.

There is also a DVD creative group under marketing that acts in effect as the producers of the DVD, interfacing with the director or other creative talent involved in the value-added material. They oversee the DVD menu as well as anything on the disc other than the movie, such as commentaries, behind-the-scenes making-of, games, screenplay or other content.

The physical production group supervises the manufacturing and distribution of units, handling the details for thousands of orders serving thousands of stores, the heart of the packaged-goods business. The DVD operations group tracks the time-sensitive flow of the product, making sure it gets out the door on the right day—not too late, but not too soon either, as no retailer has extra space to store inventory.

The acquisition and production group finds nonstudio product to distribute theatrically through third parties, through our Screen Gems unit as well as on home video and on television. The result is lines of product. In addition to feature films, there are performance arts titles including the stage musical *Les Miserables, Riverdance,* Cirque du Soleil, operas including *Don Giovanni* and *Madame Butterfly,* and childrens' titles (a popular one such as *Bear in the Big Blue House: Potty Time* and *Dragon Tales* can gross $4 to $5 million).

We operate in seventy-two countries overseas and distribute product ourselves through subsidiaries in countries including Japan, Korea, Australia, New Zealand, England, Ireland, Belgium, the Netherlands, France, Germany, Italy, Spain, Brazil and Mexico; elsewhere, we distribute through licensees or joint ventures with other studios. Each subsidiary reports sales figures once a week. The English-speaking countries tend to be the strongest-performing markets in terms of per capita video/DVD consumption. Overseas is a growth part of the business, as it is in theatrical. Along with growing overseas activity comes the increased threat of piracy. Copyright-owning distributors work hard at protecting the intellectual property inherent in those copyrights wherever they are licensed or sold, but whole markets such as India and China are effectively 100% pirate markets.

In fact, offering movies over the Web has been stalled by distributors until the issue of piracy is solved via reliable encryption. Movies are available on the Web illegally, and the industry has made great strides in developing technology to discourage such piracy. Sony has joined with Warner Bros., Universal, MGM and Paramount in a venture called Movielink, offering movies on demand to customers over the Web during the pay-per-view window.

The industry in general is enjoying double-digit growth driven by consumers' love for DVD's, quality product, short windows, and value as perceived by the customers in comparison to other ways movies are consumed. For example, paying $20 to own and watch a DVD at home is a good value compared with buying two tickets to see a movie one time in a theatre, or to see a sporting event. The most active home video users are people in a specific age range (from twenty-five to forty) who do not always run to theatres on opening weekend as younger people do, so home video doesn't cannibalize theatrical. Some home-video users are functionally homebound, such as parents with young children; for them, the logistics and cost of a night at the movies is considerable. I am bullish on the growth of the prerecorded movie business worldwide.

THE VIDEO RETAILER

by **PAUL SWEETING,** reporter and columnist for *Video Business* magazine and *Variety,* who has written extensively on financial, regulatory, legal and legislative issues affecting the media. A graduate of Columbia University based in Washington, D.C., Mr. Sweeting has covered various aspects of the entertainment industry since 1984, including stints at *Billboard, New York Post* and *Music Week* (in the United Kingdom). From 1992 to 1994, he oversaw entertainment research for Chilton Research, a leading market research company.

The home video business began almost by accident.

When the first Betamax videocassette recorder (VCR) was introduced by Sony in 1976, nobody foresaw a market for prerecorded videocassettes of movies, least of all the Hollywood studios. In fact, the primary purpose of the first Betamax machines, which could only record and play back one hour of programming per tape—not nearly enough to contain a Hollywood movie—was imagined to be the recording of thirty- and sixty-minute television shows for later playback.

Two years later, as recording times increased, making it possible to record full-length movies from television, studios became terrified that the widespread home-taping of movies and other programs would destroy the movie business. In 1979, Universal Studios and the Walt Disney Company sued Sony in federal court, charging that the Betamax system contributed to copyright infringement and asking the court to ban its import and sale in the United States. The studios opened a second front in Congress, asking lawmakers to impose a special royalty levy on all VCRs and blank videotapes sold in the United States to compensate copyright owners for the imagined loss of business caused by home taping. While the legal and legislative battles over the VCR dragged on, however, some experimenting was going on in the marketplace.

Taking his cue from the adult entertainment business, which had quickly seized on the VCR's potential to create a new market for its wares, Andre Blay, the owner of a small video duplication house, approached Twentieth Century Fox about licensing their movies for distribution on videocassette. In 1977 Fox agreed to an experiment, and Blay's company, Magnetic Video, secured the rights to the first fifty studio films to be purchased by consumers for the home market. So successful was this first batch that Fox and Magnetic quickly followed with more. Other studios soon jumped in as well, either releasing movies themselves or licensing them to independent distributors, as Fox had with Magnetic Video.

Videos were now being sold in record stores, bookstores and any other place distributors could sell them, generally priced at $59.95 to $69.95. To make this new medium even more challenging for consumers, videos were being offered in two competing formats: Beta (from Sony) and VHS (from the Victor Company of Japan, or JVC). Since videocassette recorders were expensive at the time, the early audience for movies on video was relatively affluent, and happy to pay $60 or more for titles they wanted to own. The most successful pioneer purveyor of movies on video was New Yorker Arthur Morowitz, who made his fortune operating adult theaters in Times Square, and in 1978 used a portion of one of his theaters to open Video Shack, offering movies of all kinds for sale.

A NEW TWIST

By 1981, nearly all major studios were in the game (Fox eventually bought out Magnetic Video). Consumers had chosen the VHS format over the arguably superior picture quality of Beta because more titles were available on VHS, and a small but promising business was developing. Around that time, a handful of entrepreneurs brought an unexpected twist to the business. Sensing a potential market for single viewings of movies on videocassette, a few operators began experimenting with buying tapes from the studios and then *renting* them to VCR owners for $5 or $6 a night, so they could watch a movie without having to shell out $60 or $70 to own it. The most prominent of these was George Atkinson, who opened a video rental store in Los Angeles called the Video Station. Based on his early success, Atkinson opened more stores and began selling "affiliate" packages to other operators, who opened still more Video Station locations. By 1983, video rental shops were popping up all over the country, nearly all of them run by independent owner-operators, the classic "mom-and-pop" American shopkeepers.

Several factors helped fuel the early growth of video rental stores. It took relatively little capital to open a video store; a thousand square feet of retail space was enough and retail rents were relatively cheap at the time. The boom in large, enclosed shopping malls that had lured many traditional retailers away from Main Street left many strip mall developers and in-town landlords hungry for tenants. A video store could be opened and stocked for the price of a second mortgage on a middle-class home, and for thousands of Americans, this became the ticket to becoming their own bosses.

Sales of VCRs were exploding, creating huge numbers of new customers eager to rent movies. Best of all, the novelty value meant most VCR owners were happy to rent just about anything, so retailers were under no pressure to spend on new inventory. Meanwhile, the speedy growth of video stores put the new technology on a collision course with Hollywood.

Studios were aghast at the idea of people earning revenue from the rental of movies without paying royalties, and continued their efforts in the courts. Under the U.S. Copyright Act of 1976, however, the owner of a lawfully made copy of a work is entitled to do pretty much anything she wants with that copy (short of making another copy) without the consent of the copyright owner. That same principle—known as the first sale doctrine—is what allows libraries to loan books without a fee, to the dismay of publishers. The first sale doctrine entitled video stores to rent movie cassettes without paying any additional royalty to the copyright-owning studio distributors. The only revenue the studios saw came from the $30 to $35 wholesale price of each cassette.

Unhappy with that arrangement, studio representatives stormed Capitol Hill once again, seeking to repeal the first sale doctrine so that they could collect royalties from the renting of movies. At first, the studios got a sympathetic hearing from lawmakers. But video retailers began a crash program of political organizing, forming a trade association called the Video Software Dealers Association (VSDA). With support from the consumer electronics manufacturers (who wanted to make sure there were enough video shops to spur sales of VCRs) and more-established, better organized music retailers (who were also experimenting with video), the VSDA beat back the studios' best efforts at repeal, as lawmakers recognized there were video retailers in virtually every Congressional district.

By 1984, the legal side of the conflict (as opposed to the political side) was decided by the United States Supreme Court, which found in favor of Sony and against the studios in what was known as the Betamax case, *Universal v. Sony,* which in effect permitted home taping of copyrighted material with no royalty payments to the copyright-owning studios. (Sony had not yet bought a studio at this point.) This opened the floodgates for the home video business. (A vivid and detailed history of the Sony case and the early home video business is contained in James Lardner's *Fast Forward: Hollywood, the Japanese and the VCR Wars.*) Two years later, the political side of the conflict faded when Congress refused to act. In the end, studios swallowed bitterly and hit on a rough compromise. They raised the whole-sale price of cassettes from $30 or $35 each to $60 or $65, in effect charging the retailers up front for what the studios saw as their fair share of rental revenue. That expedient established the basic economics of the video business that prevailed for the next decade and a half.

THE NEW MATH

While retailers occasionally griped about the higher cost of cassettes, the higher prices did not impede the growth in numbers of video stores, which expanded rapidly from 1983 through 1987.

For the studios, the new, successful business meant deciding on one of two pricing strategies for the "street date" (release date) of a VHS title. In those days, the typical movie was priced high, $80 retail ($65 wholesale), to encourage rental; the most popular titles, with the strongest box office history, were sold lower, at a "sell-through" price of $20 to $25 ($13 to $17 wholesale), to encourage sales. For the consumer, this choice to either rent or purchase a title depended on pricing and desire, and the same factors apply to the DVD business today.

The video boom also drew other types of retailers into the market, most notably supermarkets, which found that the need to return rented cassettes drew people back into the store, providing another opportunity to sell them groceries. In the late 1980s and early 1990s, supermarket chains such as Kroger, Ralph's and Giant were among the largest video retailers in the country, taking advantage of their existing base of hundreds of storefronts to dominate their service areas. Many music chains at the time, such as the Wherehouse and Tower Records in the west, Hastings in the south and midwest and Sam Goody in the east, also established themselves as video retailers, offering the combined services of music for sale and video for rent.

But the mainstay of the business remained independently owned and operated video specialty shops. By 1987, there were probably 35,000 or so storefronts renting videos, including supermarkets, music stores, convenience stores and other nonspecialty outlets. While the higher cost of cassettes meant it took more rental turns for a retailer to earn back her investment in a title, retailers quickly became adept at managing their inventory risk.

Studios found unexpected benefits, as the new video rental business quickly developed a degree of predictability that Hollywood had not enjoyed in its other businesses. Based on the box office gross of a title, it was relatively straightforward to calculate how many videocassettes would be sold to retailers that would rent them. Even better from the studios' point of view, the money all came up front, unlike in the theatrical business, where the box office gross accumulated over time and collections from bickering theatre owners could drag out for months.

The cost of manufacturing videocassettes continued to drop as volume increased, adding to studio profits on each cassette sold. With a manufacturing cost of less than $5 per cassette and a wholesale price of $65, the video market became astoundingly profitable for Hollywood. Studios also discovered a secondary market for videocassettes, adding to the windfall. Six to nine months after a rental title was released on videocassette—long enough for rental demand to be played out—studios found they could reissue it at a much lower price for those consumers who wanted to own rather than rent it. Carrying retail prices of under $20, these reissued cassettes were eagerly snapped up by mass-market retailers like Wal-Mart, Kmart, Sears and others, who wanted to capitalize on the video boom but were not equipped to cope with the two-way traffic of the rental business. In effect, studios were able to sell such movies twice, once into the rental market and again, six months later, to the sell-through market. At the peak Christmas holiday selling season, when different kinds of retailers added video to their offerings to try to capture some of the gift-buying business, there were upwards of 120,000 storefronts in the United States offering video for sale.

NEW PLAYERS

The growth of the rental market drew a third actor into the drama: the independent wholesaler. Facing the need to buy new movies each month from each of the major studios, plus countless independent suppliers, retailers found it convenient to consolidate their buying with a single wholesaler who offered one-stop shopping. These wholesalers bought cassettes in bulk from studios and resold them in smaller batches to individual stores at a small markup. Studios found the arrangement convenient, since it was easier to do business with fifteen or eighteen wholesalers, who assumed the credit risk for their retail accounts, than with 25,000 mom-and-pop retailers. The wholesalers did most of the footwork, soliciting orders from retailers, and maintaining their own sales staff and in-house telemarketers.

Typically, retailers paid on thirty to forty-five day terms, meaning payment was due thirty to forty-five days after receiving the cassettes. That gave the retailer time to recover part of her investment before having to pay for the product. But if a retailer fell behind in payments for new inventory, or went under with bills unpaid, this became the wholesaler's problem, not the studios'.

Today, consolidation and competition among the wholesalers has whittled their number considerably, to five major operators around the country. More and more, studios are selling directly to the retailer, cutting out the middleman, and this has taken a significant toll on the independent wholesaler ranks as well.

BLOCKBUSTER

In 1987, Blockbuster video was a chain of nineteen stores based in Dallas, Texas, with revenue of about $12 million per year. It began to sell franchises to entrepreneurs as far away as Chicago, who operated under the Blockbuster name, had access to Blockbuster-developed promotional and marketing campaigns, and paid a percentage of their gross revenue to the parent company as a royalty for the use of the name. Blockbusters were bigger than most video stores (averaging about 4,500 square feet), brighter and more professionally managed.

That same year, Florida millionaire H. Wayne Huizenga (who had made his fortune building Waste Management into the nation's largest trash hauler before selling out) invested $18 million in Blockbuster and quickly assumed control. With Huizenga's drive and financial acumen, Blockbuster expanded rapidly, from nineteen stores in 1987 to more than 1,000 three years later. The company sold stock on the New York Stock Exchange to raise capital and used those funds to open new stores or acquire existing stores to convert them to the Blockbuster banner.

Under Huizenga, Blockbuster was something new in the home video universe. With its large stores and enormous financial resources, Blockbuster could stock more copies of more hit titles than competitors, easily taking business away from the mom-and-pops. Well-heeled retailers found it difficult to compete against Blockbuster, and supermarkets, for example, were forced to choose between greatly expanding their commitment to video (at the expense of their grocery business) or getting out of it altogether. Many chose to get out. By 1993, Blockbuster had over 2,500 stores and counting. Along the way it inspired many imitators, but most were unable to raise the capital to expand fast enough to compete effectively.

Today, only two other video specialty chains have anything like the national scope of Blockbuster: Hollywood Video, based in Wilsonville, Oregon, has about 1,800 stores as of this writing, while Movie Gallery, based in Dothan, Alabama, has about 1,400. Like Blockbuster, Hollywood and Movie Gallery are publicly traded companies. By the time Huizenga decided to sell out to Viacom Inc. in 1994 for some $8.2 billion, there were roughly 3,500 Blockbuster stores in the United States and another 1,000 overseas, with an annual revenue of $2.5 billion.

Along the way, Blockbuster had also become Hollywood's proverbial 800-pound gorilla. Standing astride 25% of the video rental market—accounting for more than one-third of total studio film revenue—Blockbuster was in a position to affect the profitability of any given film directly and significantly. If the chain decided not to stock a particular title in its stores, all of a studio's revenue projections for the film went out the window. If it passed on more than one film from a studio, Blockbuster could ruin the studio's fiscal quarter.

REVENUE SHARING

When Huizenga sold Blockbuster to Viacom and left the company, he took many of the retailer's senior executives with him. The new management brought in by Viacom had little experience in the video rental business, and that was quickly felt. Blockbuster's new regime moved to lessen the chain's dependence on video rentals, worried about the talk on Wall Street and elsewhere of interactive television technologies that would allow Americans to dial up any movie they wanted at any time, without having to return it to the video store. In a misbegotten attempt to compete with Wal-Mart, Blockbuster brought in T-shirts and movie-related merchandise for sale, added more video for sale and reduced the chain's breadth of rental offerings. Profits plummeted. Competitors like Hollywood Video, which had stuck to their video-rental knitting, began eating into Blockbuster's core business.

By 1997, Viacom sacked the new management and brought in a third regime, headed by former 7-11 executive John Antioco. With his background in convenience stores, where the golden rule held that you never ran out of milk, beer and cigarettes, Antioco found the video rental business's system of "managed customer dissatisfaction" hard to comprehend. Given the high wholesale cost of rental cassettes, even a chain with the financial resources of Blockbuster could not afford to stock enough units of popular movies to satisfy customer demand. On a typical Friday night, every copy of the latest hit would be checked out, leaving most customers frustrated. To Antioco, that was like a 7-11 running out of milk and cigarettes. With Americans enjoying an ever-growing array of competing entertainment options, from pay-per-view movies to a lengthening lineup of cable channels, another system had to be found. Antioco's solution was revenue sharing.

Under revenue sharing, the retailer would pay only a few dollars up front for each cassette—essentially enough to cover the studio's manufacturing costs—instead of the $65 retailers typically paid to buy cassettes wholesale. That allowed the retailer to order enough units of a title to satisfy nearly every customer who wanted to see it upon release, without facing the huge financial risk inherent to the old system. In exchange, the retailer would share with the studio a percentage of the revenue from each rental rather than keeping it all for itself. In effect, Antioco agreed to give up the very retail sovereignty that earlier video retailers had fought so hard to protect.

To the studios, what Blockbuster called revenue sharing looked more like risk sharing, and they were reluctant to go along. Under the old system, studios enjoyed sky-high profit margins, predictable revenue and faced none of the inventory risk confronting retailers. Once a cassette was sold, what happened to it was no longer the studio's problem. If it didn't rent and lost money, that was the retailer's problem. Under revenue sharing, the studios were on the hook for how well (or poorly) a title actually performed in the marketplace. If it didn't rent as well as expected, the studio felt it in its bottom line. But the studios had little choice; what Blockbuster wanted, Blockbuster got, and that set in motion the next great revolution in the home video business.

SHARE AND SHARE ALIKE?

Beginning in late 1997, Blockbuster and the studios entered into a series of agreements representing a compromise. Blockbuster would have access to the hit titles it needed on revenue-sharing terms, and in exchange it agreed to stock certain minimum quantities of every title the studio released, including titles that had performed poorly in theatres.

In most cases, Blockbuster also provided the studio with minimum revenue guarantees for each cassette it stocked. Rental revenue was typically split 60/40 in Blockbuster's favor. Blockbuster typically ended up paying $25 to $30 per cassette, once the studio's minimum revenue guarantees and its share of Blockbuster's rental revenue were factored in. While that was far less than the $60 to $65 wholesale price the studios charged independent retailers, the huge increase in the number of copies Blockbuster ordered more than made up for the lower price. Similar arrangements were achieved with other major national chains such as Hollywood Video, Movie Gallery and Hastings Books, Music and Video.

While the new system quickly revived Blockbuster and benefited the studios, its effect on independent retail operators was devastating. Armed with 100 or more copies per store of the latest hit movies, compared to the five or ten copies a well-managed independent store could afford to stock under the traditional wholesale terms, Blockbuster steamrolled the competition. As independent store operators went under, it gobbled up 40% of the video rental market. Blockbuster, Hollywood Video and Movie Gallery today account for approximately 55% of the video rental market.

Although many surviving independents clamored for access to the same revenue-sharing deals enjoyed by the major chains, most could not afford to assume the burden of stocking the minimum quantities of every title released that made the system attractive to the studios. Nor were they able to provide the detailed tracking of each rental transaction required by the studios to audit revenue-sharing payments. Instead, the studios developed a series of Rube Goldberg–like pricing plans designed to help independent retailers increase the number of copies of a title they could stock, without obligating them to sign up for every title the studios would release.

Under the independent-retailer system, a studio typically assigns to each individual retailer a base number of copies of each title to order at the traditional VHS wholesale price of $60 to $65 per unit. Retailers that meet their "goal" become eligible to order a fixed number of "bonus" units— typically 50% to 100% of the base number—at a fraction of the usual wholesale price. The aim is to reach an overall average wholesale price of roughly $25 to $40 per cassette—close to Blockbuster's price, and low enough for at least some independents to remain competitive.

DVD

Introduced in 1997, DVD is one of the most successful home entertainment formats ever developed. The DVD player, in fact, is the fastest-selling consumer electronics product in history, surpassing the VCR, the CD player and the television set.

The format's impact on the video retail business has been both dramatic and controversial. Its most important contribution has been to enhance both the rental and sale markets. Consumers who purchase DVD players tend to increase both the number of movies they buy and how frequently they rent. To some extent, that's probably due simply to the "new-toy effect." As with any new toy, people tend to use their new DVD player more than their older toys, at least until another, newer toy comes along.

DVDs are also radically changing the economics of the video business. Because studio distributors are pushing DVDs to replace VHS as quickly as the marketplace will allow, DVDs are priced lower than the same title on VHS. Most new DVD releases carry retail prices under $30 and wholesale prices of $15 to $20. The result has been to effectively eliminate the so-called rental window, during which most titles went to rental stores first and were later repriced for sale. With prices under $30—and many titles under $20—virtually all DVD releases are available for sale at Blockbuster (traditionally a rental venue) and Wal-Mart (always a purchase venue) on the same day.

On the DVD rental side, many video rental dealers initially feared widespread cannibalization of DVD rentals by purchases, but the effect has not been as severe as imagined. As noted, purchasing a DVD player seems to increase a customer's appetite for renting as well as buying. Most rental stores, in fact, have enthusiastically embraced DVDs. With their lower wholesale costs, DVDs are often more profitable for retailers to rent than VHS copies of the same movie.

Today, on the street date of a title, the customer can buy it on DVD at mass-market retailers such as Wal-Mart, Target and Kmart for $15 to $20; or buy it on DVD at consumer electronics chain stores such as Best Buy, Circuit City or Good Guys for a price in the same range; or rent it on DVD at video specialty stores such as Blockbuster, Hollywood or Movie Gallery, which are primarily rental venues, for $3.50 to $4.00; or rent it on VHS. Four to six months later, that title is available for purchase on VHS for under $20, basically the DVD price, at mass-market retailers and other venues such as supermarkets. For the rare, through-the-roof theatrical hit, the VHS might be priced on the street date at a level near the DVD price, diverting from the usual system because the studio knows that this will be a volume title for purchase.

Many video rental stores shifted their business to DVD as fast as they could persuade their customers to buy DVD players. By 2001, a handful of retailers around the country began to experiment with DVD-only stores, eliminating all VHS inventory. Soon, it's possible that revenue sharing and the complex bonus-goods buying programs developed to cope with the high cost of rental units will be a thing of the past, along with the longstanding rental window. Instead, everything will be released simultaneously for rental and sale, and rental dealers will simply purchase product outright and keep what they earn from rentals, just as they did in the days before revenue sharing. But instead of paying $60 or $70 per VHS unit, retailers will be paying $15 or $20 for DVDs. Over time, DVD sales will overtake VHS sales and the older format will slowly recede into history.

NUTS AND BOLTS

Although the home video business is an integral part of the Hollywood movie system, it operates like no other part of show business. At the nuts-

and-bolts level, it works more like the consumer packaged goods business, something relatively new to Hollywood. Unlike any other revenue stream, movies on home video involve manufacturing, warehousing and distributing physical product.

Most VHS cassettes from the major studios in North America are manufactured by Technicolor or Cinram. Each has multiple facilities. The studios deliver master tapes to the duplicating facilities, which essentially consist of a "master" VCR set on Play wired to thousands of "slave" VCRs set on Record. The process happens in real time; it takes two hours to duplicate a two-hour movie. It costs from $2 to $3 to manufacture a finished cassette, depending on volume and other factors, including the cost of the tape, the plastic shell, the packaging material and the duplicator's profit. (In industry jargon, VHS cassettes are duplicated, DVDs are replicated.)

Manufacturing DVDs is somewhat more complex, but ultimately cheaper. Once the movie has gone through a complicated digital "authoring" process (determining the aesthetics of the DVD image), a glass master disc is produced. With the master disc acting as a template, newly minted discs are simply stamped out on a high-speed press. At high volume, a finished disc costs $1.50 or less.

Depending on where the cassettes or discs are destined, bar codes and other identifying marks, along with security features, are added by the duplicator/replicator. Some studios use the same manufacturer for both VHS cassettes and DVDs. Other studios, such as Warner Bros. and Sony Pictures (Columbia), use their affiliated record companies' CD manufacturing facilities to press DVDs.

The cassettes or discs are then warehoused by the manufacturer until they are shipped to retail. The exact number produced is based on the studio's estimate of how many copies of a movie it will sell. In the case of large retail chains, such as Wal-Mart and Blockbuster, product is usually trucked directly from the manufacturer's warehouse to one or more central distribution facilities maintained by the retailer. From there, the bulk shipments are broken up into smaller lots and delivered to individual stores in a process known in the trade as "pick, pack and ship."

Since most independent video stores do not have their own distribution centers, they rely on wholesalers to perform the pick, pack and ship operation. The most sophisticated retailers have automated distribution centers, where computers and laser scanners route the bar-coded product into appropriate lots. By contrast, independent wholesalers servicing small retailers employ warehouse workers to do most of this work manually. The key for the independent is to minimize the number of shipments to each store by loading up as many of a retailer's orders from as many studios as possible into a single shipment. Most cassettes and DVDs are delivered by UPS, with the goal of reaching the store within two days of being ordered.

OVER THE COUNTER

Two types of video stores have emerged, one specializing in rental (Blockbuster and other video specialists) and one specializing in sales (Wal-Mart and other mass-market retailers). The video rental store exhibits the classic 80/20 rule of retailing: 80% of the retailer's revenue comes from 20% of the inventory. For the most part, that 20% consists of new releases, highlighted in a special section at the store entrance. After a few weeks, titles are moved from "new releases" to their appropriate genre section (action, comedy, drama), making room for even newer titles.

Both types of video retailers face similar in-store issues. Staffing requirements can be uneven, much as with movie theatres. The concentration of business on Friday and Saturday nights requires more personnel to handle weekend traffic, but fewer for the slower midweek period. Retailers are constantly looking for ways to speed up the checkout process without adding more employees. And since rented movies must also be returned, staff is required to sort and restock the returns, a time-consuming, labor-intensive process generating no revenue for the retailer.

Although most retailers have dropped membership fees, rental stores still typically maintain some sort of membership system. After all, customers are walking out the door with the retailer's property. Video stores were among the earliest retailers to maintain a membership database, with the custom later adopted by supermarkets and other stores. In many cases, registering as a member of a rental store allows the customer to set limits on how the membership will be used, such as whether children in the household are permitted to rent R-rated movies when not accompanied by the parent.

While most video retailers regard the enforcement of voluntary ratings guidelines as simply good business, the industry has come under increased scrutiny by the government for its compliance with movie and video-game rating systems. In 2001 and 2002, at the urging of Congress and the president, the Federal Trade Commission conducted a series of studies on the marketing of allegedly violent entertainment programs. As part of those studies, the agency conducted retail "sting" operations in which underage shoppers were sent into video stores (among other places) to see if they could rent and buy R-rated movies and M-rated (for Mature) video games. Nothing came of these stings, but the FTC continues to monitor this issue.

For the large rental chains such as Blockbuster and Hollywood Video, data collected at the point of sale is a valuable asset. Blockbuster boasts a database of over 65 million names, complete with detailed demographic information on the renter and a history of rental activity. The company frequently makes its database available to outside marketers, but only in general form, such as "percentage of males over 30 renting comedies." Under a law passed by Congress in the late 1980s, it is illegal for a video retailer to reveal the rental habits of a specific individual, except under court subpoena. Known as the "Bork Law," it was passed after some enterprising reporters covering the Supreme Court confirmation battle over Robert Bork tracked down the nominee's video rental records and published them.

MANY APPROACHES TO RENTING

With so many different approaches to buying and selling videos today, no two video rental stores operate in precisely the same way. Some use revenue sharing, some rely on bonus-goods programs, and some use a combination of both. No single video store, in fact, ends up paying the same price for a unit from one title to the next, or from one studio to the next. In some cases that payment is made up front, in other cases it's made over time, as the retailer shares the accumulated rental revenue with the studio. Larger retailers generally purchase titles (and share rental revenue) directly from the studio; smaller retailers still typically buy through independent wholesalers.

When a customer checks out a movie at the rental counter, the retailer's end of the transaction varies in complexity, depending on how the store's inventory is managed. If a store relies on revenue sharing, each rental of a title must be tallied so the studio's share of the proceeds can be calculated (and audited). To achieve this, the retailer requires a sophisticated point-of-sale information system. For retailers that do not rely on revenue sharing, matching the title to the studio distributor at the point of sale is not necessary, since there is no back-end split of the proceeds to worry about.

Rental retailers must keep track of when a movie is checked out, so they know if it is returned on time. Most collect the rental fee from the customer up front, then conduct a separate transaction if late fees are assessed; a few still rely on the pay-on-return system, lumping the rental fee and any late charges into a single transaction. Nearly all video rentals are cash transactions.

Used rental titles—"previously viewed" in the industry parlance—will garner from $5 to $10 for the retailer, depending on how long they have been in circulation. The sale of previously viewed titles is critical to most video rental stores, in some cases providing the retailer's entire profit from a unit. Once a title has rented often enough to earn back its cost, many retailers will try to sell the item as quickly as possible and call it a day. That's because the longer it sits on the shelf, the lower its value falls. The trick for the retailer is to sell at precisely the right time: not so soon as to be caught without inventory while rental demand for the title is still high, but not so late that the units become all but worthless. Each retailer has to decide exactly where that crossover point is, based on the movie in question, the per-unit cost, the store's particular clientele and the local competition. Sales of previously viewed units can account for 10% to 15% of the average store's total revenue, and often a higher percentage of its total profit.

Another critical, if rarely acknowledged, source of revenue for the retailer is late-return fees. Though retailers are loath to discuss it, late fees can account for 10% to 15% of a store's gross revenue, and are carefully factored into calculations when ordering new inventory.

Managed effectively, a retailer's gross profit margin from the rental business can be as high as 50% to 60%—meaning, on average, a DVD that cost the retailer $17 can generate about $25 to $27 in total revenue, including rental fees and revenue from the used market.

The terms of a movie rental have also evolved over time. In the industry's early days, video stores rented movies for one or two nights at a time, at $5 or $6 a night. Many retailers also charged a membership fee entitling customers to rent movies without leaving a deposit each time. Lifetime memberships could fetch $100 for the retailer. As competition grew, the price of overnight rentals fell, to as low as 99 cents in some markets, and membership fees disappeared.

Today, retailers are more sophisticated at pricing and packaging rentals to maximize revenue. Most rentals run for three, four or five nights, keeping more of the retailer's inventory in circulation and earning revenue over a longer period of time than under the single-night system. To the retailer, video units are like airplanes to an airline. An airplane sitting on the ground isn't generating revenue. The key to the airline's cash flow is keeping airplanes in the air—or video units in circulation. Longer rental terms also encourage consumers to rent more than one or two movies together, in the belief that they now have time to watch more. Retailers encouraged the practice by offering multititle discounts, or discounts on older titles, all of which increased their revenue per transaction—a key measure for any retailer. The average rental transaction today involves 1.8 units, ringing up $7.50 at the cash register.

SALES

Although the home video business was built on the strength of the rental market, today Americans spend nearly as much purchasing videos as they do renting them, about $8 billion annually in each sector, for a total of about $16 billion for the entire U.S. business (at a time when the U.S. theatrical box office gross is just over $8 billion).

While most traditional video rental stores also offer some titles for sale, the sale market has been built by an entirely separate class of retailer, one that sells but does not rent movies. To review, most prominent among these are the discount department store chains (mass-market retailers) such as Wal-Mart, Kmart and Target, which promote video aggressively, making them favorite outlets for the Hollywood studios. Wal-Mart is by far the largest seller of videos in the United States, accounting for roughly 25% of the sale market. Warehouse clubs, such as Wal-Mart subsidiary Sam's Club and Costco, also account for a large volume of sales. Others include the major electronics chains, such as Circuit City, Best Buy and the Wiz, supermarkets, music-based chains such as Tower and Musicland, bookstores, major toy chains such as Toys 'R' Us and any number of other types of retailer that have successfully grafted video sales onto their core business.

The video sale market comes in two distinct flavors: new releases and repriced rental product. If a movie is a big enough hit in theatres, indicating a certain degree of repeat viewing by a segment of the audience, a studio may decide to bypass the complex economics of the rental market and position the title for sale upon release by lowering the price. A sell-through title on VHS might carry a retail price of $20 and a wholesale price of $13. Although the studio's profit margin per unit is lower than if the title carried a more typical wholesale price of $30 or $35, it's hoping to make up the difference in volume. (Notice, here we use the wholesale price range of $30 to $35 as an average that results once revenue sharing and bonus-unit formulas are factored in, reducing it from the flat $65 VHS wholesale price charged when an independent retailer buys units to rent without revenue sharing or bonus programs.) At the same time, the DVD is available at a retail price between $20 and $25 with a wholesale price of $17. A major theatrical hit such as *Spider-Man,* for instance, can sell in excess of 10 million combined VHS and DVD units at a sell-through price.

The vast bulk of those sales occur through the major nonrental channels such as Wal-Mart and Costco. A retailer such as Wal-Mart, in fact, will often devote significant advertising and promotional resources to a hit sell-through title, which can have a major effect on sales, since new hit movies can draw customers into a store, where they may buy other, non-video merchandise.

Once a movie has exhausted its rental demand, the studio distributor will typically pull it from circulation and reissue it three to six months later at a greatly reduced sell-through price. The new VHS cassettes typically carry a suggested retail price of $14.95 to $19.95 and a wholesale price of $12 to $15, while the DVD price is lowered to $10 to $15 retail.

This "second bite at the apple" has been a critical piece of the business for the studios, who can expect to sell another two million to four million copies of a hit on top of what the movie has already earned from the rental market. Often a movie title will go through a series of reissues, each at a lower price, as the studio seeks to capture every last bit of demand. Although most video rental stores stock at least a limited number of repriced reissues, the vast majority of such titles are sold through the nonrental outlets such as Wal-Mart and Best Buy.

There are more than 120,000 storefronts of various types selling videos in the United States. Most video sale merchants purchase product directly from the studio distributors, although some, such as Kmart, rely partly on so-called rack-jobbers. *Rack-jobbers* are middlemen used by general merchandise retailers to manage and buy for a specific category of product, such as music or video, where the number of new product releases is high, requiring a degree of expertise to operate and stock a department effectively. In return, the rack-jobber, which typically owns the inventory, splits the revenue with the retailer in an arrangement analogous to the manufacturer-operated cosmetics counters in large department stores. The largest music and video rack-jobber in the United States is the Handleman Co., based in Troy, Michigan.

Other mass-market merchants, such as Wal-Mart, have developed sophisticated internal computer operations of their own for managing and ordering inventory, and work closely with the studio distributors to make sure they have the optimal mix of titles available in their video departments.

GOING VIRTUAL

Since 1998, online retailers have played an increasingly significant role in the video sales business. Amazon.com, which began by selling books online, is today among the largest retailers of VHS and DVDs in the U.S. Other large online video merchants include Buy.com and CDNow, a division of Bertelsmann. Because online merchants aren't paying rent on a storefront as their brick-and-mortar cousins are, they're able to maintain an extensive catalog of video titles, including many older or obscure titles that would sell too slowly to make them worth stocking at Wal-Mart.

Amazon has been able to hold its own in the hit-new-release business by offering customers the chance to "pre-order" a title for delivery immediately upon release. They typically begin soliciting preorders as soon as a studio announces the street date of a new title to the trade, generally six to eight weeks before it actually hits store shelves. Once the official street date, or release date, arrives, Amazon ships the product. Many brick-and-mortar retailers also offer preordering, but customers still have to go to the store to pick up their titles.

Online merchants have pursued two distinct approaches to operating their businesses. Some, such as Buy.com, are almost completely virtual. Buy.com maintains a limited inventory of its own, reducing the need for warehousing. Instead, it routes orders to independent wholesalers—in Buy.com's case, Nashville-based Ingram Entertainment and Chicago-based Baker & Taylor—which then ship the product from their own warehouses. By contrast, Amazon.com maintains its own massive warehousing and shipping facilities, handling most orders internally.

The advantage of the Buy.com approach is that it eliminates a retailer's need to tie up its own capital in inventory; the disadvantage is that it reduces the retailer's profit margin, since a portion of the revenue from each sale must be shared with the wholesaler who handles the shipping. The advantage of the Amazon approach is that it can increase profit margins on each sale and allows the retailer to control customer service directly, rather than relying on a third party to get the product to the customer when promised. The disadvantage is that maintaining warehouses and inventory greatly increases overhead and ties up capital, putting pressure on the retailer to maintain minimum sales volume to cover those costs.

Internet commerce is allowing retailers to develop innovative new approaches to renting. San Francisco Bay Area–based Netflix, for instance, has pioneered a subscription-based, mail-order rental plan on the Web. Netflix customers pay a flat monthly fee, starting at $19.95, entitling them to have a fixed number of DVDs checked out at any given time. The DVDs are ordered online, through Netflix's Web site, and delivered by mail along with a prepaid return envelope. Customers can create a list of titles they're interested in seeing and are notified by e-mail as the titles become available. Although there are no fixed return dates, customers cannot exceed their monthly quota of DVDs checked out at any one time. If they're at their limit, they have to return one to receive the next one they've ordered. Netflix rents only DVDs, because they're more durable than VHS cassettes and stand up better to rough treatment in the mail. For Netflix, each customer represents a predictable and guaranteed source of revenue, whether they're renting or not; for the customer, the lack of fixed return dates or late fees, as well as the elimination of trips to the video store, provide a level of flexibility and convenience not previously available.

With video stores facing increasing competition from new forms of home entertainment, and with the power and flexibility provided by the Internet, it's likely that more such innovative approaches to renting will be developed, aimed at increasing convenience and value for the customer.

MADE-FOR-VIDEO MOVIES

by **LOUIS A. FEOLA,** president, Universal Worldwide Home Entertainment, who is responsible for managing two of the studio's specialty production units, Universal Home Entertainment Productions and Universal Pictures Visual Programming, as well as Universal Cartoon Studios, based in Universal City, California. Mr. Feola joined the studio in 1978 and has held senior management positions at Universal Studios Home Video, including that of president, where he oversaw the worldwide video operation, generated record-breaking sales and launched Universal's made-for-video business. He also played an instrumental role in the introduction of the DVD format. In 1998, Mr. Feola was named president of Universal Family & Home Entertainment Productions, in charge of the development and production of made-for-video product as well as family-oriented live-action and animation television. In 2001, he was elevated to his current position.

The division functions as a studio within a studio, having produced some thirty-seven films over almost five years.

In the early 1980s, studios entered the made-for-video business primarily in the form of music videos, concerts and instructional, self-help and exercise videos. The huge sales of *Jane Fonda's Workout* tapes demonstrated the revenue potential of this new market. Around the same time, Universal produced the *Callanetics* exercise series as well as music videos such as the Doors' *Dance on Fire* and *Live at the Hollywood Bowl*. Feature-length movies distributed directly to video were also released by independents and were often tainted in retailers' and consumers' minds as poorly made films, not strong enough to achieve theatrical distribution. At the same time, the made-for-video business was being driven by the adult entertainment industry. The success of adult entertainment helped fuel the growth of videocassette recorders (VCRs) from the late 1970s forward, just as it later accelerated the growth of hotel room exhibition, pay-per-view and most recently the Internet. It was clear that if perception and product mix could be changed, made-for-video movies could become a real revenue stream for the studios.

In 1992, we presented a plan to our senior management that Universal should make six movies—three animated, three live-action—intended for distribution directly to the video market in their first windows of exhibition. The three animated films were to be sequels to *The Land Before Time*. Of the three live-action projects, two were sequels to *Darkman* and one was a sequel to *Tremors*. The three animated sequels seemed obvious, but not the three live-action movies. Why these choices? The home-video sales and TV ratings of these theatrically released films were disproportionately high based on box office performance, which indicated built-in audiences for both titles. Also, both sets of filmmakers shared our vision of trying to build something new by releasing these movies directly to the video marketplace. It would take eighteen to twenty-four months to execute our vision.

In 1994, Disney was producing a made-for-TV sequel to its animated theatrical release *Aladdin* entitled *The Return of Jafar*. Once the video executives at Disney screened footage, Disney changed its plan and released *Jafar* as a made-for-video movie that November. Coincidentally, Universal released *The Land Before Time: The Great Valley Adventure* directly to video some six weeks after Disney's *The Return of Jafar,* and no doubt we benefited from Disney's marketing muscle in the retail pipeline promoting the concept of made-for-video movies. With this one-two punch, the studio made-for-video feature-length movie model was born, with Disney and Universal at the forefront of this "new" category.

Since then, *The Land Before Time* franchise has spawned eight sequels and counting. The first eight titles in the series have sold over 51 million units worldwide, closing in on $1 billion in retail sales.

In 1998, we presented management with a strategy to set up a separate division devoted to made-for-video movies and animated TV series. Preparation for the presentation involved running financial models, addressing general administrative costs, overhead, capital needs—which included the costs to develop and produce the properties—revenue assumptions and associated distribution costs. Another important component of the business plan was our intention to maximize the value of the Universal film catalog and new brands by focusing on sequels, prequels and remakes (realizing full well that if Universal Pictures production wanted to make something, they would proceed instead of us). Management agreed, and the plan moved forward.

The original business strategy for made-for-video movies called for releasing five to seven feature-length films per year for the first five years. Year one was the ramp-up, with limited releases. Years two and three were built on prequels, sequels and remakes of Universal properties; years four and five continued our focus on catalog, but also focused on branded titles from other areas of the company or sources outside of the company. *The Hitcher* is an example of a non-Universal title targeted as a sequel based on its cult status, strong home-video sales and high TV ratings. This latter phase included other categories, such as urban movies, music-based properties and Latin-based properties, aimed at specific niche markets.

Our initial business plan was slanted toward family and animated movies, but the accelerated penetration of DVD households forced us to shift our product strategy slightly. Early DVD adapters wanted action movies, so we had to tilt the output in that direction and then reintroduce family movies into the development slate for subsequent release.

The studio's made-for-video output is housed under Universal Pictures within Universal Home Entertainment Productions, alongside Universal Cartoon Studios (animation producer of the made-for-video series *The Land Before Time, Balto,* and others, as well as the animated TV series *The New Woody Woodpecker Show* and *The Mummy*), and Universal Pictures Visual Programming. UPVP is a London-based specialty production and acquisition unit focusing on children's television programming (*Sitting Ducks, Boo!*) and long-form popular culture made-for-video projects (*Barbie in the Nutcracker, Barbie as Rapunzel, Riverdance*). Although franchise extension has been a goal of the studio for many years, the plan had never been really executed until the formation of this group.

Made-for-video films are developed and produced the same way theatrical films are, but are shot on a much shorter schedule and on smaller budgets. Our first and primary focus on any project is the writing. With excellent writing, a mysterious thing happens: the project attracts talent. We comb the marketplace for the finest writers possible. Why would established theatrical feature and television writers work on a made-for-video movie? While the money is less than they usually command, the subject matter may strike a personal chord, and our development-to-production ratio is very high, so the project is very likely to get made rather than languish in development, as is common in the feature world, where the bets are much larger.

How can our development-to-production ratio be so high? We are very selective about what is put into development, and the writers know that the decisionmaking team is small (just four or five people), so feedback is swift, much like in an independent or nonmajor studio production company.

Another great source of ideas or projects stems from a healthy exchange between the story department of the motion picture group (see article by Romy Kaufman, p. 83) and our division. We're all part of the Universal Pictures family and are encouraged to work together.

The division functions as a studio within a studio, having produced some thirty-seven films over almost five years. Within our structure, we have the following departments: acquisition team (usually for completed films or TV series as well as developed projects), business affairs, Universal Cartoon Studios, a creative team for made-for-video, a creative team for animated TV series, finance/accounting and physical production.

Our division submits our projects to a Universal Pictures green-light committee, the same people who green-light theatrical features: the chairman, the president and COO, the executive vice president and the chief financial officer. The committee reviews the project, budget and schedule, along with financial revenue forecasts from home video, television and consumer products on a worldwide basis.

Once the screenplay is locked, while fully expecting that rewriting will occur during production, we begin budgeting, hiring our production team, scheduling and boarding. (For more on production paperwork, see the article by Christina Fong, p. 250.) Preproduction can start six weeks to three months prior to shooting, depending on the film. As an example, for *Bring It On Again,* the sequel to *Bring It On,* preproduction included "cheer camp" for the actors to learn dancing and cheerleading, all built into rehearsal time.

Our live-action made-for-video movies are tightly budgeted, with a shooting schedule of approximately twenty-four to thirty days, depending on the project. Our movies are shot on 35mm film, although we are experimenting with digital production. At the lower cost of our production levels, there is no room for error.

Once we receive our green light, the division remains very hands-on through the entire production process. One of our executives is always on the set, monitoring progress and looking after the schedule. When making movies on a budget, the pressure is always on. Overhead and development are controllable, but production can be unpredictable. For example, one movie, shot outdoors on location at a time when the almanac predicted fair weather, had to withstand a weeklong rainstorm. Another film had a flying sequence scheduled to be shot on September 11, 2001; we were grounded for days. While we try to control production, we cannot always predict what will happen.

Another component of our product strategy is "opportunity financing." A project was presented to us that was put together as a French-Canadian coproduction, and Universal secured the worldwide rights (except for France and Canada, which were controlled by our partners). The director and writer were British, several key cast members were European and the film was shot in Luxembourg and France. These choices were made so the project would meet the requirements of the relevant coproduction mandates for European content. (For more on tax incentives and government subsidies, see the article by Steven Gerse, p. 483.)

An animated movie is very script-dependent as well, but the production takes eighteen months to two years to complete. Once the screenplay is approved and the green light received, the director is chosen along with the producer, artists, illustrators and other creative personnel. Character designs and modeling begin immediately. Our animation studio on the lot oversees everything through storyboards. The actual animation is done overseas—in Taiwan, Korea, Singapore, Japan or the Philippines—to keep costs down. Voice recordings, songs, and storyboards are done at Universal. Usually a foreign supervisor follows the progress of the work, divided among the teams in the foreign animation facility where the film is actually being created (usually in computers). Back at the studio, we wait for the film to be delivered to us in thirds. Watching the first third often results in calling for retakes on scenes that may be out of sync, or characters that depart from the models, or for other reasons. The process goes back and forth until it is right. This helps assure that the movie will be done properly. When producing a series of made-for-video films, it's best to make a deal with one animation house so that once the animators get past the learning curve, things run smoothly. Once the animation is completed and we are satisfied, the musical score is added (not songs, which are recorded before animation begins) and the final mix is completed.

The life cycle of our product is the same as that of theatrical features, except these projects are not released in theatres. In the United States, most of our films play out in the conventional order: airlines, home video, pay-per-view, pay TV, basic cable, then free TV. Outside the U.S., the same model is maintained whenever possible, with our movies distributed through Universal entities in major territories, or through local licensees.

We monitor a competitive calendar of all home video releases, as well as Universal Pictures releases and their corresponding home video availability dates. We do not want to compete with ourselves, but we do want to cross-promote our own projects. For example, a trailer for one of our made-for-video urban films may be attached to the home-video release of *8 Mile*.

With made-for-video movies, there is some flexibility in determining a release date. This is different than with a theatrically released film in the United States, where the home-video window is in effect a ticking clock, sandwiched between theatrical and the airing on PPV or a pay-TV channel. With our products our home video executives have more control, since a made-for-video title is being launched initially through the home video window, and a certain amount of ownership enthusiasm comes along with introducing, marketing and monitoring a brand-new movie in the home video product line. Also, our home video divisions may have a gap in their release schedule and ask our division to fill it.

In terms of sales, made-for-video product is handled just like any other home video releases. Titles are released on a designated street date, and the home video departments gear up their marketing and sales teams to make that date. Marketing dollars are budgeted separately, handled by the respective distribution entity, and expenditures are subject to our review and approval. The marketing and distribution budgets are administered as follows: domestic video, domestic television, international video and international television. To give you a sense of market size, made-for-video retail revenues, in a recent year, accounted for $2 billion of the $22 billion North American home video business. By the way, the home video business is approximately twice that of theatrical box office gross.

We also look for other opportunities. In 1998 we commissioned an original score for the 1931 *Dracula,* starring Bela Lugosi and directed by Tod Browning. The original film did not have a score, so we commissioned Philip Glass to write one. He wrote a spectacular score that was performed by the Kronos Quartet. It was so successful that Glass and Kronos took it on a live tour, performing the new score to the projected film in venues around the world, to great critical acclaim. The Philip Glass–scored *Dracula* is now available on DVD as well as VHS. This newly scored version of *Dracula* has a new copyright, separate from that of the original film.

As mentioned earlier, we also acquire finished products and invest in well-developed content. An example of acquired made-for-video product is Mattel's *Barbie in the Nutcracker* and *Barbie as Rapunzel,* both CGI (computer-generated imagery) movies. We acquired the distribution rights from Mattel for international video. An example of investing in development is *Boo!,* a television series geared to children ages six months to three years. The producer, based in England, is a company named Tell Tales. Our division prides itself on maintaining a global sensibility for our projects.

Video revenues come in first, as the video is released first, and TV revenues come in later, during their window of exhibition. Airlines are another source of revenue. While the dollar amounts can be low, they can represent a significant percentage of the made-for-video production budget, depending on the genre and timing.

Internationally, made-for-video movies follow the same pattern as features: home video, followed by the pay-TV window, then free television, depending on the market. Universal has home video operating companies in almost thirty territories. Elsewhere, the product flows as part of licensing arrangements in approximately sixty other territories. Our distribution effectively covers the world.

We are extending brands, generating revenue and income, and building a library. By introducing prequels and making sequels, we are also building upon franchises. Very often, this is best demonstrated in boxed sets. For example, we produced a made-for-video sequel to *Slap Shot.* On the twenty-fifth anniversary of the first movie, instead of marketing just the original *Slap Shot* on DVD, we were selling two movies in a boxed set.

Our products are labeled as made-for-video or direct-to-video movies, but we consider the product to be simply *movies*. The medium in which it premieres doesn't matter. Well-made, quality material will find its audience, regardless of format.

The pioneering days of made-for-video movies are behind us and the format no longer carries the stigma of its earliest years. Today it represents an established and growing revenue stream worldwide, offering opportunities to new and veteran filmmakers alike. It is a vibrant segment of our industry and will be for years to come.

XII

CONSUMER PRODUCTS

CONSUMER PRODUCTS

by **AL OVADIA,** executive vice president, Sony Pictures Consumer Products, based in Culver City, California. A veteran of the marketing, promotions and licensing industry, Mr. Ovadia began his career with NBC Television, where he held a number of senior management positions leading to vice president of Network Creative Services. From 1988 to 1995, Mr. Ovadia headed licensing and merchandising for Twentieth Century Fox, where he oversaw worldwide licensing, promotions and product placement for all of the studio's film, video and television properties, including the long-running hit series *The Simpsons*. Prior to joining Sony Pictures Consumer Products, Mr. Ovadia cofounded Mediacentrix, Inc., a Web-based syndication company, and served as its executive vice president. He previously served as executive vice president of worldwide promotions for Equity Marketing, Inc., and president of News America, the nation's largest in-grocery and direct-to-consumer marketing company. A graduate of the University of Washington in Seattle, Mr. Ovadia is a board member of the Licensing Industry Merchandisers' Association (LIMA) and the recipient of several industry awards for licensing and cross-promotion.

> We, the licensor, are paid a royalty on the wholesale selling price by the licensee that ranges from 3% to 14% depending on the item and quantities sold.

Although experiments in movie merchandising can be traced back to Charlie Chaplin's "little tramp" character being reproduced in comics and picture books, the real innovator in the field was Walt Disney, who was selling items such as Mickey Mouse watches in the 1930s and Davy Crockett caps and other toys in Disneyland in the late 1950s.

The landmark motion picture that awakened the movie industry to the huge potential of consumer products was *Star Wars* in 1977. Twentieth Century Fox was taken by surprise by the sudden success of *Star Wars,* such that the now-classic action figures were not in stores in time for Christmas; instead, customers paid for a certificate allowing them to return to the store months later, when the toys would be available. When *Star Wars*–licensed products grossed over $1 billion dollars worldwide at the retail level in the first few years, the other studios took notice and began planning productions that would lend themselves to licensing.

By 1980, the Disney organization was selling a sophisticated line of consumer products based on their own core characters, and beginning in 1987, they created a successful chain of retail stores around the world. (A similar retail-chain effort by Warner Bros. ended in 2001 after a decade.) Meanwhile, young consumers began wearing brands or movie logos on clothing as a fashion component. Columbia created a successful licensing campaign around *Ghostbusters* in 1984, and Disney enjoyed a golden age of merchandising with *The Little Mermaid* in 1989, *Beauty and the Beast* in 1991 and *The Lion King* in 1994.

But there was a learning curve along the way. When *Batman Returns* was released in 1992 and tied to a McDonald's Happy Meal, parents complained that the movie was unsuitable for the age group targeted in that program. As a result, the industry became more sensitive to selecting appropriate movies for such tie-ins.

Licensing deals for children's movies grew, reaching a peak in the mid-1990s with increasingly lucrative deals paid for by toy manufacturers and other licensees, followed by a downturn after less-than-anticipated sales of toys from movies such as *The Flintstones, Casper* and *Star Wars: Episode 1— The Phantom Menace.* Retail partners who had bought a tremendous amount of product and dedicated a significant amount of shelf space became skeptical, pulling back when those commitments did not translate into projected sales. As a result, expectations were reduced throughout the field of movie merchandising and deals were shifted downward.

Today, all studios aggressively pursue licensing deals for appropriate movies in a more settled industry. What used to be known as "licensing and merchandising" departments have given way to "consumer products" groups. The two studios that lead the way are Disney, with their unrivaled, evergreen properties like Mickey Mouse and Donald Duck, and Warner Bros., with their Looney Tunes characters such as Bugs Bunny and Daffy Duck and their DC Comics line of superheroes like Superman and Batman, which provide an ongoing revenue stream that can support a large staff. The rest of us don't have the luxury of such a stable of characters, so we work to create new licensing opportunities with carefully selected movies and television series from our development and production pipeline.

The term "franchise" has become a licensing buzzword, referring to ongoing licensing potential over a series of movies. The years 2001 and 2002 saw the launching of such franchises as Warner Bros.' Harry Potter series, New Line's *Lord of the Rings* trilogy and our first *Spider-Man* feature. The key to any franchise is its long-term merchandising potential and its appeal to more than one generation.

Let's define terms. *Merchandising* in the movie-related consumer products business refers to translating a movie's title, icon or brand to other products on an exclusive basis; merchandising also refers to raising awareness at the retail level, such as creating outposts in a store to promote these products and attract customers. This benefits the retailer on one hand and the rights-holder, or studio, on the other. *Licensing* is the contractual granting of access to the underlying rights in a particular property to a manufacturer of specific goods and/or services in exchange for a royalty and/or fee.

Consumer products licensing deals work only on appropriate pictures, often involving impulse purchases, and require a long lead time to manufacture and then distribute to the point of sale. At Sony Pictures Consumer Products, we typically do not work broadly on R-rated movies; we are careful not to market products to kids on movies they are not allowed to see.

As an example of long lead time, the first announcement to prospective licensees for *Spider-Man* was made in April 2000, two years before the movie was released. For the typical movie with licensing potential, there are two key events a year, and both take place in New York City: Toy Fair in February and the International Licensing Show in June. While there was a special-event announcement for *Spider-Man* in Los Angeles, the bulk of the work began in June at the Licensing Show, where meetings were held to pitch licensees using a sales kit containing material demonstrating Spider-Man's longevity; the character first appeared in the *Amazing Fantasy #15* comic book in 1962. In such meetings, licensees want to know the stars, the director, what kind of marketing dollars the studio will pay to support the picture and who the other promotional partners are. The idea is for the studio to offer as much information as possible, because licensees are very savvy; if they are going to risk their money and sales resources supporting *Spider-Man* instead of another movie or other licensable property, they want to know that they are making the best possible choice.

Let's turn to the types of deals that are made, in order of revenue potential. First would be the master toy license; then the video game license; then everything else. The master toy license includes action figures, twelve-inch collectible dolls, handheld video games, pull-back toys and a wide range of others. Since the master toy license typically has the most media (via television ads) and the most development dollars behind it (toys are figural, requiring manufacturing retooling), it goes first in the hierarchy of licenses. Each type of deal requires a long lead time, perhaps eighteen to twenty-four months before the movie's release. As examples, let's examine the progress of a licensed toy, then a video game, then apparel.

Toy Biz, which happens to be owned by Marvel, our venture partner on *Spider-Man,* was the master toy licensee. This was a given. Based in New York, Toy Biz had a history of creating product for Spider-Man. Since we wanted to distinguish the new Spider-Man character from what had been in the marketplace, our style guide featured costuming with textured, three-dimensional, raised webbing, inspired by swimwear worn in the Australian Olympics. The style guide, a book containing specific design requirements that must be carefully followed so that each product design is consistent, is the art bible for the character and packaging and is given to every licensee.

When production of the movie began in January 2001, we made full-body computer laser scans of the actors in costume, allowing the creation of more accurate likenesses than ever before. Let's take a six-inch posable Spider-Man action figure as an example. Toy Biz utilized these laser scans to create sculptures that were sent to our product development group for comment. Once comments were given and final approval obtained, these materials were sent to China for manufacture. The factory created molds into which plastic was injected in order to replicate the figure based on the agreed-upon specs. Every step required multiple approvals, so versions of the prototype went back and forth between Sony in Culver City, Toy Biz in New York and the Chinese factory during this process. A "first pass production sample" went to Toy Biz, which sent it to us for approval. Within Sony, the prototype had to be approved by director Sam Raimi, producer Laura Ziskin and others. Once approved, the factory went into production. Also, packaging design and copyright lines must be approved. All of this was being done a year before the picture's release date.

Now let's trace another toy, the walkie-talkie made by MGA Entertainment, which comes in a set of two, one bearing the likeness of Spider-Man, the other the Green Goblin. Not only do the toys function as walkie-talkies, but when they face each other, the two characters can carry on their own conversation; it's a very cool toy. Large retailers such as Toys R Us, KB Toys and Wal-Mart would be presented with this opportunity at their home offices by MGA and would respond with a specific order of units for their stores. When orders from all retail customers are combined, they are sent to the factory in Asia and the goods are manufactured on the appropriate scale, from thousands to perhaps millions of units. The factory makes and boxes the goods, then "drop-ships" them to locations designated by the retailers. A giant crate from Hong Kong gets off-loaded at the port of San Francisco or New York, destined to go directly to the Toys R Us distribution centers around the country. At these hubs, the goods get broken out into smaller allotments so that the proper order is sent to each Toys R Us store. All of this must be coordinated so that licensed merchandise finds its way to stores six weeks before a movie's opening. Typically, 40% of such purchases are made by consumers before the movie is released.

Assume the retail price for the walkie-talkie is $19.95. The retailer has paid a wholesale price of perhaps $12 to $14 to the manufacturer (the licensee). That wholesale price contains the cost of manufacturing and distribution as well as any royalties to be paid to the licensor; the balance would be the manufacturer's profit. Of the $19.95 paid by the consumer, $12 to $14 is retained by the retailer to recoup their wholesale cost and the balance is the retailer's profit. We, the licensor, are paid a royalty on the wholesale selling price by the licensee, that ranges from 3% to 14% depending on the item and quantities sold. Food items typically are at the lower end; soft goods and T-shirts tend to be at the high end.

If a hypothetical licensee manufacturer is targeting a 30% net margin, here's how it works: Out of one wholesale-price dollar, roughly 40 cents goes to costs of goods sold (making the toy), another eight cents to marketing; they're down to 52 cents. Let's say they have to pay us, the licensor, a royalty of 14%, or 14 cents, reducing it to 38 cents; an overhead allocation of 8 cents brings them to net 30 cents, or a 30% net margin or net profit.

These concepts vary from product to product. Fixed costs like overhead allocation don't change. But when selling a million units instead of ten, that overhead allocation is being amortized across a greater number of units, so the per-unit cost of that allocation goes down dramatically. From 8 cents in the above example, it may be lowered to a penny per unit if a million units are sold. Marketing costs and development costs can also be spread over the number of units sold; tooling and manufacturing costs per unit also drop depending on volume.

This kind of thinking sometimes lends itself to an alternative royalty approach in a "stairstep" type of deal. In most license agreements, the royalty rate remains fixed, regardless of volume. But because a lot of these costs diminish as success plays out, and the profitability of a toy company grows based on the success of the toy, we may (hypothetically) call for a 10% royalty on the first $10 million of sales, a 12% royalty on $10 to $25 million of sales and a 14% royalty on $25 to $50 million of sales, so that we share in the licensee's upside. This concept especially applies in those areas where the manufacturer puts up unusually high development costs, such as the video game business. In this case, our royalty may be 8% on the first million units sold; 9% on the next million units; 10% on the next. With higher volume, costs of stamping the units are proportionally lower, so we want to share in the success.

Let's turn to the interactive license for video games, the second-largest potential revenue stream in consumer products. This is a very time-consuming, complex process. Lead time can be even longer than with toys, eighteen months to two years, because of the complexity of the programming. Typically, we will solicit multiple partners simultaneously and receive proposals from them on which formats they want to develop against. On *Spider-Man,* Activision has the interactive license, and for the first time in video game history, a company was able to bring to market in advance of the film all five formats that they develop games for: X-Box, Playstation, Playstation 2, Game Boy Advanced and Game Cube.

First, Activision reads the script and lays out the basic design and storyline for the game. In this case, Marvel actually gave them approval to tap into other villains in the Marvel universe who do not appear in the movie in order to broaden the appeal of the video game, while the core element in the game is the battle between Spider-Man and the Green Goblin from the movie. The long period of research and development included the involvement of director Sam Raimi, a big video gamer, who added a lot creatively to the plan. The full-body scans of the actors mentioned earlier for toys were also used as a tool by Activision to replicate likenesses in the video game. Voice sessions with the real actors were done, with Tobey Maguire voicing his role as Peter Parker/Spider-Man to add to dialogue excerpts from the film, managed by Activision and our product development group. An extensive development period follows in programming out the games. Our product development group meets with the filmmakers and reports on prototype progress, gets them to sign off on it, then returns to Activision with comments, in a give-and-take similar to the toy prototype approvals described earlier. Eventually, we receive a "gold master" for sign-off, the final prototype, and once that's approved, it goes to Playstation, Nintendo and Microsoft, as examples, who analyze it, sign off on it and then manufacture it in their respective formats. From a sales standpoint, a successful video game with a retail price between $49.99 to $59.99 and a wholesale price between $30 and $38 per unit can generate $50 to $100 million in wholesale sales worldwide, a very substantial figure. With video games, it's possible to generate roughly 60% of the U.S. sales in the first six to eight weeks; on *Spider-Man,* we are projecting global sales in excess of 3 million units.

Most movie-based licenses tend to focus on boys. The target demographics for *Spider-Man* are unusually wide, with the core group aged three to eight, skewing more to boys than girls. But the video game is bought by those ranging from teens to twenties, and the age range for toys includes adults who collect *Spider-Man* figures as mementos from their youth. The key to the property is that, on some level, there are none of the usual demographic barriers. Walking around a mall one can see a forty-five-year-old man with his seven-year-old child, both wearing *Spider-Man* T-shirts.

The rest of the consumer products deals can be combined into a third type of deal, applied to items including apparel, headwear and school supplies. Publishing, bedding (sheets, pillowcases) and domestics (throw rugs, lamps, cookie jars) are in the next big category; after that, it's wide open, including backpacks, lunch kits, key rings, pen and pencil sets, binders. Worldwide, there are probably 8,000 to 10,000 separate *Spider-Man* products.

For each item, we know the best manufacturers and we pitch to all of them. We ask for proposals and set certain targets of dollar guarantees we expect to receive. As a hypothetical example in apparel, we may ask for a $250,000 guarantee in the United States against a 14% royalty. For *Stuart Little 2* and *Men in Black II*, the royalty was 10%. For *Spider-Man,* royalties were generally 14% because of our partnership with Marvel, which shared with us equally, 7% each.

For a sample T-shirt, the process is similar to the toy example given earlier. We solicit proposals, decide on a particular manufacturer and supply them with a style guide. They come back with perhaps twenty to forty designs forwarded to the studio for comments, and after some back and forth we settle on certain approved designs. The manufacturer's salespeople then present the line to their retail customers, including Wal-Mart, Kmart and Target, and orders are taken. Apparel typically is sold two seasons in advance. For *Spider-Man,* which opened in May 2002, T-shirt designs were being shown to retailers in August 2001 for placement in stores in March 2002.

As in other industries, the apparel industry runs trade shows bringing together buyers and sellers. For example, early designs can be shown at the men's apparel show MAGIC in Las Vegas in August and others at the next MAGIC, in February. Because *Spider-Man* exceeded retailers' expectations, retailers were reordering within the first two weeks of product being in their stores. For example, a strong reorder for T-shirts for a national retail chain could be 10,000 to 25,000 dozens of units.

Much of T-shirt manufacturing is done in the United States, where a company pulls from its blank inventory and prints specific designs per orders. A typical licensed T-shirt for an adult can cost in the $16 range retail ($8 wholesale); for boys, perhaps $4 retail ($2.80 to $3.20 wholesale). Naturally, lower price-point goods have a slimmer margin than higher-priced, both having the same royalty, which is a percentage of the wholesale price. On a *Spider-Man* adult T-shirt, we get paid 14% of $8, or $1.12, by the manufacturer, who uses the rest to offset costs and create a profit.

Retailers are skittish about making broad commitments to properties. Most movie licenses represent a commitment of eight to ten weeks by the retailer, with the understanding that, once the time period ends, if they escape safely without carrying inventory, they'll move on to the next property. With *Spider-Man,* not only was there tremendous pull from consumers before the movie was released, but the sell-though levels, how retailers measure success, were in the 25% to 30% range some sixteen weeks after the film opened. *Sell-through* (not to be confused with the same term used in the home video industry to define purchases rather than rentals) is a statistical definition of product flow through the store. For example, if 10% of the inventory of a given item sold in one week, you're doing well. Just prior and in the first weeks of release of *Spider-Man,* the sell-through levels were 40% to 50%, meaning 50% of the inventory of that item was moving through stores in one week. That level drove a significant amount of reorders, and what would normally be an eight-to-ten-week program quickly became one that retailers wanted to extend through the end of the year to take advantage of the video/DVD release in November and straight through the holiday season, setting up a longer-term opportunity for us.

Licensing is a risky business. Every deal with a licensee is negotiated to include a guarantee paid against a royalty percentage of the wholesale price. The typical licensing agreement, about twenty-four pages, includes four pages of specific terms; the rest is boilerplate. With a success like *Spider-Man,* all our partners are happy, from the licensees to the retailers. From each licensee, we receive a royalty statement each quarter, which we go over with a fine-tooth comb. Our contracts with licensees stipulate auditing rights, so we can go in at any time and audit their books. With an unsuccessful product, our share of royalties may not be enough to repay the guarantee, and the retailer may be stuck with items that are marked down or remaindered. In this case, the retailer might ask the licensee for mark-down money used as a credit for the retailer against future purchases. On our side, there might be a discussion with the licensee as to whether we might forgive part of the guarantee.

Another realm is the promotional area, separate from consumer products, where deals include tie-ins with quick-service restaurants or packaged-goods companies. In a *promotional tie-in,* these companies agree for a window of time to combine the focus of a movie with their services or product for mutual benefit. *Spider-Man* had a number of promotional partners in the United States, such as Cingular, the wireless phone company; Carl's Jr. and Hardee's in the quick-service restaurant category; Kellogg's; Dr Pepper; Reebok; and Hershey's, all deals done by the theatrical global promotions group to generate awareness for the movie using somebody else's media buys to supplement the studio's marketing campaign. Television advertising by these partners featured their product along with *Spider-Man* for mutual benefit.

These deals are all different, but the driving force from the studio's standpoint is media buying, not revenue; it is dollars paid in such tie-in advertising to help advertise the movie, not dollars paid to the studio. Although fees are paid for such exclusive deals, they are secondary to the level of advertising commitment, which could range from $5 to $20 million per company for TV advertising in the United States alone. For example, Kellogg's brought media to the table in exchange for the ability to feature

Spider-Man on a wide range of on-shelf exposure (cereal, Eggos, Pop-Tarts and Keebler Cookies) and they created advertising to support that; it was the advertising component that was the key for our theatrical marketing group because, in a very crowded and competitive environment, we need that extra media to lift our property above the noise and clutter. In addition, there was a separate license agreement made beyond the promotional exposure for a Kellogg's *Spider-Man* branded cereal and a *Spider-Man* branded Pop-Tart (blue and red, with webbed icing). The goal was to turn *Spider-Man* into an event. The studio spends its marketing dollars in telling a story; Kellogg's uses its marketing dollars in building awareness.

Now let's touch on the quick-service (or fast-food) restaurant tie-in, which can involve two levels. One is the kids' program, such as McDonald's Happy Meal toys or Burger King's Kid's Meals toys. Another is an adult component, typically involving a sweepstakes or a self-liquidator, whereby with the purchase of a combination food plate, a collectible item such as a watch or a glass can be bought for an additional $1.99. These programs are called self-liquidators because they pay for themselves. With *Spider-Man,* the quick-service restaurant partners were Carl's Jr. in the west and Hardee's in the east, both with the same parent company.

Promotional deals are media driven, and can typically provide up to $15 to $20 million in television advertising committed to tying the quick-service restaurant experience, for example, to building awareness for the movie. Because of the value of this kind of commitment, the quick-service restaurant is a key target partner, and any small fee they may pay becomes secondary. To repeat, this type of deal is about media exposure to help support the release of the picture, not revenue to us. Millions of impressions are also created via retail promotions with companies such as Wal-Mart, Kmart, Target and TRU. They are responsible for in-store signage, radio/TV advertising and circular expenses. In what was perhaps a first, all in-store signage for *Spider-Man* carried the May 3 release date. Because the signage was up four to six weeks prior to release, this helped build tremendous awareness. The goal is to get a huge "share of voice" (in industry jargon) from our various partners so that their tie-in advertising creates billions of impressions over a wide range of age groups. In the U.S., *Spider-Man* had around six promotional partnerships with six different companies. Around the world, quick-service restaurant deals were made with partners including KFC in the United Kingdom and South Africa, Wendy's in certain Central American countries, Bimbo in Mexico, Lomitan in Chile and Magi Noodles in Australia.

Now let's cover product placement, which is not a consumer products area but is essential to any discussion of merchandising. The classic product placement story is about M&Ms turning down an offer to be featured in *E.T. The Extra-Terrestrial* and being replaced by Reese's Pieces, which enjoyed astronomical increases in sales and popularity as a result. One recent trend is for launches of fancy cars. For example, in the 1995 James Bond movie *Goldeneye,* BMW introduced its Z3 roadster. By 2002, a prototype Lexus was featured in *Minority Report* and a new E-Class Mercedes-Benz in *Men in Black II.* The key to product placement is care, so that the effort does not backfire and detract from the movie itself. Although product placement generates nominal revenue, it has become a useful key component on the promotional side of marketing.

At Sony Pictures, the consumer products group is relatively small, about thirty-five people, compared to other studios. Executives in the domestic sales department do all the pitches to prospective licensees and make the deals with all these manufacturers. The international sales team manages thirty-plus licensing agents around the world. The business is shrinking, with a lot more licensable properties and far fewer manufacturers to take them to. Executives in product development work with the manufacturers, and with studio production and marketing executives, fielding and coordinating comments, and pushing along the approvals process explained earlier. In addition, they handle approvals on all the packaging, all the point-of-sale material, and all the TV and radio spots on a global basis. (On *Spider-Man,* they had to approve at least 10,000 pieces of information.) Finance and operations collects the money and pays the bills. The international group manages the global agents; we also have an office in Munich. The creative department includes the art director, who manages the style guide for each program and a five-person art staff. The business affairs and legal group handle contracts; marketing executives oversee all the details of advertising.

With a look to the future, one issue is that shelf space is at a premium. As the television marketplace continues to erode, there are fewer people watching more television and cable shows. Licensing competition is growing from cable networks for kids such as Nickelodeon, Cartoon Network, the WB and others, along with adult networks such as HBO, E! and the National Geographic Channel, which are creating their own entertainment properties and otherwise branding themselves. If the past reveals anything about what lies ahead, the future of licensing promises to be very exciting indeed. If we have learned one thing in this ever-growing field, it is that just when you think you have a handle on it, it changes right before your eyes. It changes because it is truly driven by the whims of consumers. What seems to be a trend can disappear as fast as it comes into vogue. Speaking for myself, that's what makes the job, and the industry, so exciting.

XIII

INTERNATIONAL

THE GLOBAL MARKETS

by **ROB AFT,** a Los Angeles–based media consultant for a variety of U.S. and international clients in the areas of film and television finance and distribution. Mr. Aft has worked as head of international sales and distribution for independent producers including the Kushner-Locke Company; Mark Damon's MDP Worldwide and Behaviour Worldwide; and Troma, Inc., under the tutelage of Lloyd Kaufman and Michael Herz. He also served as vice president of international at Trimark Pictures. Mr. Aft is a longtime board member of AFMA, the independent film distribution trade organization, where he is a member of the American Film Export Association as well as chairing the buyer accreditation committee. He holds a master's in business from Thunderbird, the American Graduate School for International Management, and is a frequent guest speaker at the USC and UCLA film schools as well as a participant on numerous industry panels.

The global independent film industry is undergoing a period of radical restructuring that is threatening the very survival of players here and abroad. Those who can adapt to the new realities will survive, the others will perish.

The film industry is a true global economy, a thriving collaboration among artists, financiers and the audience. This globalization accelerated through the 1980s and 1990s, when overseas revenues for American films grew from less than 30% of the total to well over 60%. The period also saw an unprecedented level of investment by overseas companies in the American film industry.

A global perspective is essential for decisionmakers in a world where border distinctions are increasingly blurred. A German can direct an international cast in Australia for a major studio owned by the Japanese, and it might well be considered an "American" movie. Even the term "American movie" is an artifact; today it defines a style of movie rather than its makers.

Here is a brief explanation of how the major studios and independents distribute films around the world, followed by a country-by-country analysis.

The studio side of the theatrical business is straightforward. Studios distribute their films directly through local offices in each of the major territories; these offices book the theatres and handle local marketing. For example, a Fox film opening in the United Kingdom will be managed by Fox executives based there, under the supervision of the international team at the Fox studio in Los Angeles. Disney, Warner Bros. and Sony work in the same way. However, Universal, Paramount and DreamWorks combine resources in a theatrical distribution company called UIP (United International Pictures) based in London. MGM contracts out their international distribution through Fox.

Increasingly the studios have gone to a near-simultaneous global distribution strategy, releasing in as many territories as possible within a few weeks. In this way, the studio benefits from the huge publicity generated from the U.S. release, while limiting damage from piracy. The Internet, MTV, CNN and global media assure that on Monday a global audience knows which films were in the top ten in the United States over the weekend, and those are the films they want to see.

At the same time, Americans have invested heavily in overseas and non-English language production and distribution. A vivid example is the highly successful *Crouching Tiger, Hidden Dragon,* substantially developed and funded by Miramax and Good Machine out of New York. In some cases, American companies invest overseas to combat charges of cultural imperialism; in other cases, they simply realize that local films can be extremely profitable. In a further effort to gain global market share, studios have spread their branded television outlets around the world (Fox Family, Disney Channel, Paramount/Viacom's MTV), while others have invested in theatre chains overseas.

The studios are organized in a trade organization called the MPAA (Motion Picture Association of America), and their international piracy, trade and bureaucratic activities are handled by a branch called the MPA (Motion Picture Association). Independent distributors have a similar organization called AFMA, formerly the American Film Marketing Association, now just an acronym since 40% of its members are non-U.S. companies. In addition to its other functions, AFMA organizes the American Film Market every February in Santa Monica, where producer/sellers and overseas distributors gather to make territorial licensing deals.

Financing and distribution by the independent sector is increasingly difficult due to factors including the dominance of major studios, the rise of local production overseas and the ongoing global recession. In the past, indies would develop a project and present the elements (screenplay, stars, director, budget) to overseas buyers, who would license the right to distribute the film in their territory, and those contracts would be used as collateral for a production loan to get the film made. Few of these films lived up to the sales pitch and many were costly disasters for the buyers. In response to this, some overseas distributors decided to become producers themselves and now run production-distribution companies.

Other overseas distributors have partnered with studio-level producers in "split rights" deals, whereby a studio releases a slate of films in the United States that are partly financed by a group of overseas distributors in exchange for an equity stake, some creative control and distribution rights in their respective territories. Examples of such partnerships are Mutual with Paramount and Spyglass with Disney. Mutual's partners include the BBC in England, Germany's TeleMunchen, and Toho Towa/Marubeni in Japan. Spyglass's partners include Kirch in Germany, Mediaset in Italy and Svensk Filmindustri in Scandinavia.

How do independent producers get films financed and distributed overseas? Securing the complex presales, subsidies and financing arrangements that are necessary is best left to an experienced sales company. (Most are AFMA members and can be found at www.afma.com.) These companies often function as executive producer, and their first priority is to secure a U.S. distribution deal. For all but the smallest films and art-house pictures, a U.S. deal is essential before taking the production to the major licensing markets of Cannes, MIFED in Milan and the AFM to secure international presales.

Under a *territorial presale* deal, a distributor in a particular territory agrees to pay an advance against a negotiated distribution royalty upon completion and delivery of the film (guaranteed by a completion bond; see the article by Norman G. Rudman and Lionel Ephraim, p. 207). Even though these presale contracts will probably bring less than half the financing to the film, a combination of these sales, plus private investment, subsidies and *gap financing* from a bank (the part of the production loan not covered by distribution contracts and subsidies), will complete the financing package. The gap amount is secured by the value of the territories that are not presold, in the hope that those territories will be sold upon completion of the film.

This territorial film finance business has become a game of diplomacy. As mentioned, international presales and a U.S. distribution deal are often not enough to fund a film. A producer also needs to access some of the range of subsidies that have emerged, whether they are German tax funds, U.K. sale leasebacks, or Irish or Canadian production incentives. (See article by Steven Gerse, p. 483.) And the successful independent production-distribution companies (which can be counted on two hands) are the ones who are able to navigate the global marketplace where audiences increasingly demand A-list stars, top directors and big budgets.

Before our country-by-country tour, some general observations: The global independent film industry is undergoing a period of radical restructuring that is threatening the very survival of players here and abroad. Those who can adapt to the new realities will survive, the others will perish. Despite growth in the number of multiplexes worldwide, there are actually fewer screens available for U.S. independent films due to the increased popularity of local product, combined with the ever-increasing size of studio releases. To keep up, independents have had to increase print and ad spending to secure visibility.

Theatrical ticket sales overseas have seen minimal growth despite the increase in screens. It is possible that a saturation point has been reached, but it is equally likely that this is just a symptom of global economic problems and that the numbers will start increasing once these economies rebound. Eventually growth could come from emerging markets, but that will require investment in infrastructure and changes in government policies in those countries.

Further growth could come from new technologies, which have usually favored independents. Video fueled the independent boom of the 1970s and 1980s, and cable carried independents through the 1990s. It remains to be seen whether enhanced television and the Internet will help independent films find their audiences or bring new life to old libraries. What is certain is that the studios have already made DVD dominance a global priority, and recently they have banded together to begin offering films through video-on-demand (VOD) cable, Internet and satellite systems in the United States, potentially limiting growth in these areas for independents.

Americans consider themselves technologically advanced, but the average South Korean is more likely to have a home broadband connection and many Japanese are already using their cell phones to access entertainment through the Web. The global infrastructure for exploiting these new technologies is being built, and once in place, it will deliver new revenue to independent filmmakers. Another issue is piracy. Digital formats mean perfect copies, a pirate's dream. Illegal digital copies of new releases are traded globally over the Internet with producers receiving no compensation. This issue is being addressed, with the hope that copyright legislation and enforcement will keep pace with any new technology.

The strength of the U.S. dollar against all major currencies also continues to be a problem. The dollar is now worth between 25% and 50% more than it was against major currencies at this book's last publication. A few years ago, if a French broadcaster paid 100,000 francs for a film, that equaled $20,000; today, if that broadcaster pays the same number of francs, the deal is worth only $15,000 to the American producer.

What follows is an analysis of the world's most influential markets for English-language movies. The order is based on potential revenues, which shift from year to year, but in the year 2000 it was: Japan, Germany, United Kingdom, Italy, France, Spain, Australia, Latin America, Korea, Asia (outside of Japan and Korea), Scandinavia, Benelux, Eastern Europe, and the

Middle East/Africa. These profiles represent a snapshot in time, using a template year of 2000; the reader is advised to obtain up-to-date information by reading trade publications (both domestic and overseas) and using the Internet to access Web sites that provide ongoing revised figures.

JAPAN

Japan remains the biggest overseas market for U.S. films despite a slumping economy, limited screens, a weak yen and the world's highest ticket prices (about 1,800 yen, or $15). A highly selective video market and a nearly nonexistent television market (for films that did not receive a wide theatrical release) combine to make this a very unfriendly market for most American independent films. If a film can work theatrically in Japan, the territory can easily be worth 12% to 15% of the budget; if a film is bypassed for theatrical distribution, it might not receive distribution in any other media and be worthless there.

All of the U.S. majors maintain offices in Japan, but there are also a number of very strong independent distributors, including Gaga Communications (managing the New Line product), Nippon Herald and Toho-Towa. Box office is split 50/50 with the theatres, and an average release can cost well over a million dollars. Films can be dubbed or subtitled, but most of the larger releases are subtitled.

The problem of limited screens is rapidly being addressed. In the year 2000, Japan had 2,524 screens; 740 of those are multiplex screens built over the last ten years, and building continues unabated. Japan is still drastically underscreened for a country of 130 million people. Most of the screens are controlled by three major Japanese distributors: Toei, Toho, and Shochiku. About 1,000 of the screens show exclusively Japanese-produced films. These films, mostly in the animation, horror and crime genres, account for more than 30% of tickets sold. The market for "foreign films" is dominated by American product, but art-house and European films remain extremely popular. This might be in part because young women tend to be the target audience for non-Japanese pictures, since Japanese films are almost always targeted at young men.

The video market in Japan has been in steep decline over the past several years for everything but successful theatrically released titles. This is bad news for independents, who often have to accept no advance and only a vague hope of home video revenue for their films. The total value of the video market is estimated to be $2.3 billion, by far the largest outside the United States. This trend is expected to continue, given the high (73%) penetration rate for video devices. The number of DVD titles released grew from 1,555 in 1999 to nearly 5,000 in 2000, with the number of units sold growing from 8.7 million to an astounding 30 million. If a small American picture finds home video distribution in Japan, revenues can range between $10,000 and $250,000, but the high end is rare.

The Japanese people love Japanese television. Variety shows, game shows and homegrown comedies dominate the private broadcast networks, Asahi National Broadcasting, Fuji Television Network, Nippon Television Network, Tokyo Broadcasting System, Tokyo Television Broadcasting and public broadcaster NHK, the major players in the market. It is nearly impossible for a nonblockbuster American movie to be seen in prime time, and even the biggest American series are relegated to fringe time slots on cable or satellite TV. The pay-television market has not grown as much as in other countries (with only about 30% penetration), partly because local broadcast programming is preferred over the usual pay-TV driving forces, movies and sports.

After much hype and hope, the Japanese direct-broadcast satellite market has collapsed in on itself, with the three major players, Sky TV, Perfect TV and Direct TV now one big company called SKY PerfecTV following years of mergers. There has been similar consolidation among cable providers, with Jupiter and Titus merging after Microsoft took a 60% stake in Titus in 2000. Speculation is that Japan's growing broadband market will add new life to both satellite and cable installation. Pay-TV subscribers enjoy a huge range of programming, including movie, music, sports and lifestyle channels, featuring many American standards such as Cartoon Network, Discovery Channel, Fox and Playboy. As a result, most American independent product never finds a home on Japanese television, and when it does, it is likely to be in fringe cable programming, providing very low revenue.

THE EUROPEAN UNION (EU)

Germany

Intense volatility in the German market has taken its toll. When television prices started to boom in the early 1990s, independent distribution companies were sprouting like weeds. In 1995, when Universal signed the now-legendary billion-dollar TV deal with mogul Leo Kirch's KirchMedia to supply his growing private station empire, it seemed there was no limit to what television rights could be worth. Upstart companies and many of the more traditional distributors started to pay high prices for distribution rights in all German media, with some going public on the Neuer Markt in

Frankfurt. This raised a billion dollars, split among twenty-four media companies. Soon, though, cracks started to appear. First, the traditionally strong German video market went into a steep decline for all but theatrical titles. Then video titles lost their appeal in the overstocked television marketplace, and the appetite for B and C films dried up. This intensified competition among the newly rich publicly traded companies and television conglomerates (KirchMedia and RTL) for A product.

A decisive blow came when leading indie distributor Kinowelt outbid Kirch in paying about $300 million for the television rights to a package of titles from Warner Bros., including *The Matrix*. When Kinowelt then tried to sell the same package to Kirch's TV networks, Kirch's refusal sent shockwaves through the industry. The only other company that could pay the kind of prices Kinowelt needed was RTL, and they quietly declined. Stock prices of the media companies collapsed, Kinowelt and Kirch declared bankruptcy, and movie prices plunged.

Since this upheaval, statistics have become meaningless. German companies that were gladly paying 15% to 20% of budgets for films now claim that their territory is worth half that. With a television glut at all the major German stations, the appetite is gone for anything but theatrically proven titles. As of this writing, many of the biggest of the publicly held distribution companies are struggling.

On a more hopeful note, some of the traditional German media companies like Senator have reported strong earnings and are continuing to prosper with German-language product and the occasional American independent film. Theatrical admissions continue to rise, up to 160 million admissions in 2001, up about 8% from 2000, at an average price of 11 DM or about $6. There are nearly 5,000 screens in Germany, with an increasing number in multiplexes. German films still take a relatively small percentage of box office—15% in 2000, up from 14% in 1999, but down from levels of 16% and 17% in the mid-1990s. Some films, such as 1999's *Run Lola Run,* have even had some success outside of Germany, a rare occurrence these days.

English-language films are dubbed into German for all media, with the exception of art films, which are subtitled. German distributors are active in what is known as "German-speaking Europe," which includes Switzerland, Austria and a part of Italy called Alto Adige in addition to Germany. There are distributors who function exclusively in Austria or Switzerland, but in most cases one company will acquire all German-language rights under a single agreement. All of the U.S. majors are active in Germany, and there are also a number of very strong local mainstream distribution companies, including Constantin, Senator, Splendid, Helkon, Tobis-StudioCanal, Scotia and Highlight (based in Switzerland). Arsenal, Prokino, Time, Ascot-Elite and a host of smaller independent distributors assure that good U.S. independent material will receive expert treatment in German-speaking Europe. The distributor's share of box office receipts is around 45%.

The home video market in Germany for all but A product has been steadily declining. Sell-through of DVD is increasing at an amazing rate and will soon make up 50% of video units sold; most of these are A titles. There was a 10% decline in video rental outlets recently to just over 5,000, but the number of sell-though outlets increased to more than 10,000.

On the television front, there is speculation that some of the smaller station groups, particularly ARD and ZDF, which both ended up with some of Kinowelt's Warner package, have actually been helped by the recent upheaval. They suffered greatly when prices were being bid higher, but have been the beneficiaries of attractive deals since KirchMedia and RTL have pulled back on their buying. Those two companies, through their various media holdings, account for the major channels, including Pro7, RTL and RTL Plus. Recently, German TV has been consolidating. American firms are taking part, with Time Warner joining local group Viva Media AG to run music channel Zwei, and John Malone's Liberty Media taking a major stake in Germany's cable market.

United Kingdom

Similarities between the U.S. and U.K. film industries go much deeper than language. Theatrically, the market is dominated by U.S. majors; video growth mirrored that of the U.S.; pay-TV penetration rates are similar; and local broadcast channels compete fiercely, producing much of their own product.

In theatres, U.S. production accounts for 80% of tickets sold, with another 18% going to U.K. productions. Product from the rest of Europe has never crossed the Channel well. All of the studios have offices in London, and UIP is based there. Major British independent distributors include Entertainment Film Distributors (whose releases include the New Line product), FilmFour and Pathe. There are also many active smaller independent distributors feeding niche markets.

The United Kingdom converted to multiplex theatres years ago; about half of its more than 2,800 screens are in multiscreen facilities. It is the second largest market in Europe after Germany, with about 140 million tickets sold in 2000 at an average price of about $6. The distributor-exhibitor relationship is favorable to exhibitors, who receive on average

70% of box office receipts (compared with an average of 50% in the United States).

This 30%/70% distributor/exhibitor split, coupled with an extremely high cost of prints and advertising, makes this a challenging market for smaller distributors. After a very difficult period in the 1990s following the collapse of the independent video market and the increasing size of releases from the majors, many independent distributors—including Rank, First Independent, Guild and Palace—went out of business. By the late 1990s, things turned around and smaller niche players emerged. Suddenly Helkon UK, Icon (Mel Gibson's company), Momentum, Metrodome and Optimum Releasing took their places alongside Entertainment Film Distributors, Pathe, FilmFour and Miramax as distributors to be reckoned with. These smaller players know their public, targeting them through specialized magazines, the Internet and music tie-ins to compete with the majors. Perhaps most importantly for U.S. independents, the United Kingdom is one of the few territories in the world where a film can be released on six screens in London with a limited ad expenditure and the hope to expand nationally based on the results. The New York/LA platform release is alive and well in London.

Video in the United Kingdom exploded as it did in the United States and has mirrored U.S. trends, with video sell-through and DVD sales also booming. U.K. video chains have pushed out local shops and blockbuster films have muscled independent fare off the shelves. British households receive pay TV by digital satellite rather than cable, and the penetration rate is quite high. Broadcast channels compete fiercely and produce much of their own product.

DVD represents more than 30% of home video sales and 25% of rentals. With 82% of households owning a VCR or DVD player, U.K. video penetration is by far the highest in Europe. They are supplied by not only the major British chains, HMV and Virgin, but also by America's Blockbuster brand. For films not released theatrically, however, the video market can be very difficult. Genre pictures may stand a chance of returning $30,000 to $75,000 to their producers, but most other titles have difficulty even finding video distribution.

The United Kingdom has led the world in the development of direct broadcast satellite technology. When British Satellite Broadcasting and Sky Television merged to form British Sky Broadcasting, or BSkyB, in 1991, the choices on broadcast television were limited to the two state channels (BBC1 and BBC2), Independent Television (ITV) and Channel 4, with only one broadcast station, Channel 5, added since.

The real revolution has come in pay television, found in about 40% of U.K. households, through BSkyB and their rival, ITV Digital, a joint venture of Carlton and Granada. There are literally hundreds of channels to choose from, with sports and movies driving the services. U.S. companies such as Fox, Disney, MTV and Nickelodeon are also well represented. BSkyB's philosophy has always been to offer the biggest movies available, and to this end they have established output deals with the major studios that provide for minimum license fees of a million pounds per theatrically released picture. In contrast, most independent films are licensed for between £20,000 and £50,000. License fees from broadcasters are in a similar range. Unless the film is a theatrical hit, producers can expect anywhere from £20,000 (from Channel 5) up to £100,000 (for the rare BBC sale).

One area where independent producers have managed to make money recently in the United Kingdom is in pay-per-view. Due to an excellent infrastructure, PPV has been widely embraced by the home audience, with some popular small films able to generate tens of thousands of pounds.

In September 2001, BSkyB went all digital, becoming the first DBS system to do so. The British government set a target date of 2006–2010 to convert broadcast television to an entirely digital system, an ambitious goal, but feasible considering that 8 million of the 22 million television households have already gone digital.

Italy

Italy's well-deserved reputation for quality cinema continues with such international hits as *Life Is Beautiful* and *Malena*. Italy boasts a robust and innovative production infrastructure, and in recent years this has been rewarded with a 25% share of box office for Italian pictures. Another 20% or more goes to films from other European countries, with the balance to American pictures. Thanks to improved theatres and a financial model favorable to distributors (P&A from $1 to $2 million for the average 250–300 print release, and a 50/50 split with the exhibitors), when a film is a hit in Italy producers can see millions of dollars in revenue, with some blockbusters topping $10 million at the box office.

Approximately 420 films were released on about 2,800 screens in Italy in our sample year, 2000. This is an increase in both number of films and number of screens, thanks in large part to the rapid development of multiplex theatres that stay open year-round. (Older ones would close during the summer due to lack of air-conditioning.) This has helped bring new independent distributors into a marketplace dominated by U.S. studios and three Italian majors, Medusa (the theatrical wing of Silvio Berlusconi's

Mediaset empire), RAI Cinema (theatrical arm of the state TV broadcasting giant) and Cecchi-Gori (which is experiencing financial difficulties). Eagle Pictures, Filmauro, Instituto Luce, Nexo (with the New Line product) and art-house distributors BIM and Lucky Red have all recently taken a bite out of Italian box office. However, since Italy remains a hit-driven market with dubbing expenses averaging more than $50,000 and a limited release costing more than $100,000 in P&A, smaller distributors have a hard time competing.

Italy was one of the first European countries to privatize television, in the late 1980s, when video was just developing. As a result, home video never attained the proportional level it did in the United States or United Kingdom. VCR penetration hovers around 60%, with DVD coming on strong and expected to lead. Most independent distributors (with the notable exception of Eagle) choose to focus on revenues from television, often bypassing video entirely.

Even after privatization, television continues to be dominated by state broadcaster RAI (with three channels) and private broadcasters Mediaset (which holds a 42% market share with its three channels), ORBIT and Tele Monte Carlo. Pay-TV penetration remains low, with fewer than half a million households receiving Canal Plus–owned Telepiu and News Corporation/Telecom Italia's Stream. It is expected that digital satellite television will grow quickly in Italy. TV stations seem content to buy from American majors and local producers, often limiting the market for American independent films.

France

France is rightly considered the film capital of Europe; it is where cinema was born more than 100 years ago, and its inventors, the Lumière brothers, are national heroes. French cinema is the most widely respected and globally popular non-English version of the medium, and it is a national embarrassment to the French that American films normally take more than 50% of total box office in France (62% in 2000 against only 28.5% for French films).

Because the French have positioned cinema as an art form, the government, through the Centre National Cinematographique (www.CNC.fr), administers and nurtures it in extraordinary ways. For a producer, this means that private business figures are made public, including how many prints of a film were released; the dubbing cost; the marketing expenditure; tickets sold; the split of revenues with theatres; video units sold; television deals concluded. All of this is public information reported to the

CNC. (Try getting that information from a single service anywhere else on the planet.) France is the largest European theatrical market based on number of tickets sold (155 million), but not in terms of total annual revenue, which hovers around $1 billion.

This market is comprised of a few major local players that often act as both exhibitors and distributors in partnership with local producers or with U.S. studios. Among distributors, UIP garnered 23% of market share through its combination of Universal, Paramount and MGM product; Gaumont is next with about 18%, including Disney pictures along with Gaumont-financed French movies; Warner takes another 10%, with Sony trailing at about 6%. France has a large number of very strong local distributors: BAC achieved more than 8% of market share thanks to product from Miramax; ARP totals about 5%, with several French-language productions; Metropolitan benefits from its New Line output deal and its own productions for another 5%, with the balance divided among other local independents. On average the box office gross is split 50/50 between distributors and theatres, as in the United States, with theatre ticket prices averaging around $5.60.

Unfortunately, as in the rest of the world, it is increasingly a one-week make-or-break system in France, with smaller films not getting much chance to find an audience. The French still care about directors more passionately than stars, though, and a decision to see a film will usually be made more on the director's name and review rather than cast.

The largest exhibitors are UGC, with 26% of screens, Gaumont, with 20%, and Pathe, with 19%. (Gaumont and Pathe recently joined forces to create Europalace.) The balance is made up of smaller chains and local theatres. In France, films are usually released in both dubbed and subtitled versions. The French take dubbing seriously; mainstream films are more likely to be dubbed, especially outside of Paris, while art films are almost exclusively released in their original version. The average cost of preparing a French-dubbed version of an English-language film can reach $100,000, partly due to the star salaries demanded by dubbing actors. Some of these voice specialists will dub the same star for years. In release ads, every film is designated either as V.F. (for the French version) or V.O. (for the original-language version).

Always the innovators, the French stirred exhibition controversy with the introduction of monthly chainwide passes, the Carte Illimitee from UGC and Le Passe from Gaumont. These admission cards offer customers unlimited access to these two giant chains for about $14 per month. Although successful and credited with reversing a trend in declining admissions, the concept has pressured independent exhibitors who simply cannot compete through similar promotions, though some of these smaller chains have partnered on Le Passe. The jury is still out on what this will mean to the distribution business in France, but many see it as a trend that will be adopted by chains around the world to restructure the declining revenue picture for exhibitors everywhere.

Video never really took hold in France. For a variety of reasons—including the success of pay service Canal Plus and high subscription fees at video outlets—the rental market for videocassettes accounts for only about 13% of French video revenues. The French have always preferred to own copies of films. DVD accounted for 23% of video units sold in 2000, with that percentage doubling in 2001 and continuing to accelerate. U.S. titles dominate both on videocassette (50%) and DVD (78%), with the home video distribution market dominated by U.S. studios and a few local companies such as TF1 Video and Film Office Editions, a division of publisher Filipacchi-Hachette. Unfortunately, it is estimated that 15% to 30% of all DVDs that come into France are illegally imported Region 1 discs (created for the U.S. market only), which cuts into potential revenues. As is usual in markets dominated by sell-through, the revenues for smaller films are minimal, and many films are not released due to high dubbing costs.

Television is still a major revenue source in France, with sales ranging from $25,000 for a made-for-TV film on a broadcast service to several million dollars for a first-pay run of a theatrical hit on Canal Plus. Often these deals are cut before a film has been released theatrically, with a floor amount and escalators built in for box office performance, usually expressed in terms of tickets sold. In fact, due to high dubbing and release costs, it is rare that a theatrical release will be attempted without a television deal already in place.

All of the major studios reap huge financial benefits from long-term deals with the major pay-television services in France. Canal Plus, a subsidiary of Vivendi, leads the pay-TV market and has outlets in ten other countries. In a distant second place is TPS, the newer and less-watched offshoot of broadcaster TF1. The studios also have output arrangements with national broadcast stations TF1, FR2, FR3 and M6. These deals have effectively locked many American independents out of the French television market. With a limited number of national channels compared to the U.S. (four major broadcast channels, a few regional broadcasters, and about ten cable/satellite channels), it is very difficult to find programming slots for many American films. Add to this a quota that limits the number of non-European and non-French titles and the result is a very bleak picture for American independent films on French TV. The good news, however, is the success of pay-per-view services in France, second only to the United Kingdom in EU homes wired for satellite direct-to-home viewing (five million at last count, or about 20% of French television households). As this market grows, there will be increased opportunities for what is now "niche" independent product, free of government restrictions.

The French are one of Europe's leaders in interactive television development, and this area holds much promise for satisfying Europe's most discerning film public and presenting opportunities for wider distribution of independent cinema.

Spain

Spain has emerged as one of the most dynamic film markets in Europe. It is now one of the world leaders in film production, including an increasing number of English-language films. Spain's theatrical and television markets have matured to a point where the country is well screened and well served by a large number of local theatrical distribution companies and healthy broadcast and satellite outlets. A quickly growing private regional television sector and the launch of digital terrestrial television will make Spain one of Europe's most progressive and important television markets.

The flourishing of multiplexes has given Spain more than 3,500 screens. At about $3.50 a ticket and admissions up to about 140 million in 2000, the Spanish market can represent anywhere from 4% to 6% of potential revenues. Most films are released in dubbed versions, though art films are subtitled.

Spain has a number of strong local distributors who are often also the top producers. These include Tri-Pictures, handling the New Line films and sometimes reaching 10% of tickets sold; Lola, whose sequel *Torrente 2* dominated the 2000 box office; Sogepaq, with the Miramax product; Manga; and Lauren. Together, the local distributors generate more than 25% of total box office revenues.

Spanish-produced films and coproductions have surged thanks to production tax incentives and the growth of the theatrical market. Spanish features produced in 2000 accounted for 14% of tickets sold. Many Spanish producers have started making films in English, notably Filmax and Lola. On the flip side, U.S. majors have entered the Spanish-language market, with Disney buying Lauren and Sony establishing a production subsidiary in Spain. For years, the studios were forced to make and distribute low-quality Spanish films to fulfill a quota system that was meant to help Spanish cinema. When that system ended, Spanish production ignited. Today, the majors are happily producing top-quality films and helping to develop world-class directors such as Fernando Trueba, Alejandro Amenabar and Matteo Gil.

The Spanish video market hasn't been a major revenue factor for independent films for years, but successful, theatrically released films continue to do well. DVD sales have surged at the expense of cassette sales, and the rental market for big films in both formats is stronger than ever. VCR penetration is nearly 75%, and the low adoption rate of pay television has kept rental markets healthy.

The real excitement in recent years has been in the local television market. But American independent films are tough to sell to Spanish TV due to consolidation, the high dollar and the success of locally produced programming. Add to this the aggressive deals negotiated by U.S. majors that often include vast numbers of library titles, and very little room is left for independent films. There are 12 million television households in Spain. About 2 million of those receive satellite pay television from either the Canal Plus–owned Canal Satellite or the Telefonica-owned Via Digital; there has recently been talk of the two systems merging. An additional 500,000 homes are equipped with cable. Broadcast television is led by the two channels of state-owned RTVE and two national private channels, Antena 3 and TeleCinco. Regional channels broadcast in five dialects, and there is speculation that the next advance could come in private regional channels rather than in the pay arena, which appears to have reached saturation. This effort will be helped by the rollout of digital terrestrial television.

Benelux and Scandinavia

The Benelux countries are Belgium, the Netherlands and Luxembourg, with a total population of about 27 million. Together, Benelux and Scandinavia (Sweden, Finland, Norway, Denmark and occasionally Iceland) contribute between 2% and 3% of a film's total revenue, but they can be among the most complicated to deal with.

In Belgium, the population is divided between speakers of Flemish and French, creating a problem between Benelux and French companies who each try to acquire the French rights. By law, there can only be one distributor for theatrical rights in the territory. No matter who gets the rights, fighting over release dates, cross-border flow of DVDs and TV signals, and access to language tracks will continue to plague the producer in this territory.

There are many strong local distribution companies, and one, RCV, which controls New Line's films and other major independent product, usually manages to take a substantial slice of box office revenue. It is interesting to note that Belgium, with only two-thirds the population of the Netherlands, has significantly more screens (about 500 compared to 460). The competition for screens in the Netherlands is fierce, reflected in the relatively low 40% of box office that goes to distributors; in Belgium it's closer to 50%. Belgium's screens are dominated by Kinepolis, which controls more than 50% of the exhibition business there.

Cable penetration in both countries is about 95%, and both are upgrading to digital and providing state-of-the-art broadband access. The video markets, though, have been in steep decline for all but the strongest theatrical films, and revenue sharing has been a disaster for independent distributors. Again, RCV is the dominant local player here, representing more than 10% of the market.

Most Scandinavian distributors treat Iceland separately, since their 250,000 citizens have the world's highest per-capita cinema attendance and a good film can generate tens of thousands of dollars. The total Scandinavian population is about 31 million, with Sweden representing half of that. The number of screens and attendance have held steady for years, with few new multiplexes being built compared with the rest of Europe. U.S. majors, as usual, are market leaders, with strong local players including Sandrew/Metronome, Sonet in Sweden, Finnkino in Finland, and Egmont (Nordisk). A few local films, most notably Dogma films from Lars Von Trier and his circle, will occasionally do sensational business, but for the most part the box office in Scandinavia mirrors U.S. results.

The video market for independent films has nearly ceased to exist, and the television markets, including cable, have always been uncomfortable with the level of violence in American films. In prime time, what many Americans would view as pornography is shown, but not programming involving guns. There are still potential television and video revenues in the region for independent films that can secure a theatrical release.

AUSTRALIA AND NEW ZEALAND

The Australia–New Zealand market has been going through some difficult times. Once, these markets could have meant 4% of a film's global revenue; now independent distributors feel lucky to get distribution of any kind there. How did things change? There's no easy answer, but a weak Aussie dollar, faltering economy, the introduction of a punishing 10% goods and services tax in 1999, and the domination of the Village Roadshow Group probably all played a role.

In the early 1990s, the exhibition powerhouse Village Roadshow em barked on an expansion plan, spending millions on multiplex coventures from Bangkok to Brisbane, building some of the finest theatres in the world—just before the Asian financial crisis. Village Roadshow's aggressive business plan contributed to the decline of some competing regional distributors, and it now appears that they are scaling back their regional ambitions to concentrate on their home market of Australia and New Zealand.

The real story in this market is in production. Australia–New Zealand is the second most popular location for offshore American film production after Canada, thanks to tax incentives and an impressive combination of technicians and production infrastructure. *The Matrix, The Lord of the Rings* and *Xena* all called the territory home.

Roadshow Film Distribution, a joint venture of Village Roadshow and exhibition powerhouse Greater Union, is the strongest player in theatrical distribution, owning nearly 200 of the 1,800 screens. Together, Roadshow and Hoyts control nearly 65% of the market. Roadshow distributes for Warner Bros., New Line and Franchise, as well as other U.S. independents. Buena Vista, Fox, UIP and Columbia all maintain distribution offices of their own. American pictures account for about 65% of tickets sold, with about 9% going to Australia–New Zealand films in 2000. Although these two countries are often combined as related territories, New Zealand has its own set of distributors, who have allied with Australian companies but behave very independently. On average, only about 40% of box office receipts are returned to the distributor. Australian screens went through a multiplex buildup several years ago and the number of screens is expected to hold steady at around 2,100 until the economy picks up.

Video advanced as it did in the United Kingdom and the United States, and the region boasts an impressive 87% VCR penetration rate, with 20 different video distributors. DVD saw 600% growth in 2000. Part of this incredible growth rate is because sell-through DVDs are released six months ahead of sell-through cassettes. The sell-through market is quickly overtaking revenues from rentals, and, as usual, that means that blockbusters and studio features are pushing independent films off the shelves. It is rare that an indie film not released in theatres gets any video release at all.

The television market has been rough for a number of years, with broadcast networks suffering from low advertising revenues and pay television never really achieving much success (less than 8% cable penetration rate). Broadcast is dominated by three national private networks (channels 7, 9 and 10), and public broadcasters ABC (Australian Broadcasting Corp.) and SBS. The Nine Network is the ratings leader with a 32.5% share, Seven comes in with 28.5%, and Ten is in third with about 22%.

LATIN AMERICA

Just a few years ago the Latin American market represented 5% to 6% of a film's potential revenues; Brazil alone could be half that. Today, that total number has dropped well below 3%. A combination of desperate financial conditions (recessions combined with currency devaluations), a disappearing video market and declining television revenues have wrecked the strongest of the markets: Mexico, Argentina and Brazil. Ongoing political strife has managed to hurt business in Colombia, Peru, Central America and Venezuela. But multiplex building, the development of cable and satellite delivery infrastructure and the privatization of television have set the stage for a potential comeback in these markets if the economies turn around.

These circumstances have been especially hard on local distributors. Rising costs in Argentina and falling revenues (box office was down 20% in 2001, with local distributors saying that the $6 ticket price has made cinemagoing a luxury most can't afford) are forcing many of the strongest local distributors close to bankruptcy. In Brazil, where some films are released on more than 200 screens (Brazil has nearly 2,000, and Mexico nearly 2,400), it is becoming difficult for independent distributors to compete with the American majors. Those majors continue to dominate most Latin markets, the training ground for their international executives for decades. Add to this a crippling and confusing tax situation, and what was once a thriving market has become a nightmare.

Mexico has recently stabilized, and with ticket prices relatively low for the region and attendance (and the peso) holding steady, there is hope for this market. Mexico has built up its local production business, and that has paid off with such international successes as *Amores Perros* and *Y Tu Mamá También*, both smash hits locally.

The video markets in Latin America have always been plagued by rampant piracy, but cable television has also accelerated video's decline. Following the introduction of cable in Argentina in 1992, video revenues slid 70% in a few years. Mexico and Brazil have seen less dramatic slides, but the slow, steady decline has meant that video revenues in most of the rest of the region are simply insignificant except for major pictures.

Cable has been the success story for the region, reaching a saturation point quickly in Argentina and Mexico, in about 14 million of the estimated 105 million total television homes in Latin America. However, with carrying capacity quickly being used up and a limit to what the operators can charge subscribers, many channels have had difficulty expanding, resulting in declining revenues further hurt by currency devaluations. Each of the markets is dominated by one integrated local player—Globo in Brazil, Cisneros in Argentina, Televisa in Mexico—committed to continuing to build world-class infrastructures in broadcast, satellite, cable and broadband. As anyone who watches the hugely popular Latin *telenovelas* (soap operas) can attest, you never know what tomorrow holds, and these markets will certainly swing back in the not-too-distant future.

KOREA

By the time the big financial crash came in the mid-1990s, Korea's power in the region was already waning. Part of this was due to economic problems, and part was due to the limited growth potential for broadcast television and the saturation of video. The market matured too quickly, and many local distributors were absorbed into the media divisions of *chaebols* (Korean megaconglomerates), which had unreasonable revenue growth expectations for the video and television markets. When growth slowed and the economy started to sag, these media divisions were often the first to be cut by the chaebols. Almost overnight the names of the local distributors changed from Daewoo and Samsung to unknown new companies that only wanted the top films that could be played in theatres; almost anything else was unlikely to get even video distribution. This left the U.S. studio product in control. Local product has recently come into its own, representing nearly 40% of tickets sold.

Television has long been a dead zone for American product in Korea, with about 85% of what airs being locally produced. A few years ago, Korean rights could easily bring 5% of a film's budget; today, if one is lucky enough to get a deal, it might represent 1.5%, but that still ranks Korea as the second-most lucrative market in Asia after Japan's 10%.

Korea seems to be coming out of the global recession more quickly than many of its neighbors. A weak currency and export-driven economy will help boost near-term growth. Combine that with a mature entertainment infrastructure and distributors who have learned to weather bad times, and the potential for the market is huge. Many top Korean distributors are also producers, such as Cinema Service, CJ Entertainment, Korea Pictures and CineWorld Entertainment. Recent strength of Korean films in the market will give local distributors leverage to compete against the American majors. As the market matures, it is also broadening from being a traditional action-film territory to accepting a wide range of dramas, comedies and art films. Whether these factors will improve the struggling fortunes of American independent films in Korea is yet to be seen, but there is certainly reason to hope.

ASIA (OTHER THAN JAPAN AND KOREA)

Wild fluctuations in economic fortunes have taken a toll in certain Asian markets. The region's 1998 economic collapse came at a time when many territories were maturing and beginning to provide significant revenues, largely due to the building and renovation of cinemas, the reining-in of video piracy, and the establishment of pay-television outlets and extensive cable and satellite systems.

China is a fascinating market, constantly undergoing change and development. There has been talk of the government relinquishing its monopoly on feature film distribution, but old China hands are skeptical that this will happen. As things stand, ten to twenty U.S. films are distributed annually by government-owned China Film Import under revenue-sharing deals. All of these films are from the majors, and often referred to as "quota" films. For most titles, after deductions are taken from grosses, hardly anything is left for the studio. But on the rare highly successful film, revenues can be hundreds of thousands if not more than a million dollars. China Film also releases a number of independent films, licensing these outright for between $30,000 and $100,000 for all rights. Only about twenty of these are bought each year and are subject to strict content censorship. In television, national and regional stations have provided significant revenues. The video market has developed well (for Video-CD and DVD formats only), and it is possible to receive $2,000 to $5,000 for these rights. However, most of the Chinese market is made up of pirated material, despite the government's efforts to crack down. It is easy to make grand predictions about the huge potential of this difficult market, but only time will tell.

The balance of the Asian territories have all gone into steep decline over the last few years. Each went through similar buildups—an upswing in video, cable TV looking promising, theatres being built or refurbished—but all this promise has come to nothing. The millions of dollars spent building state-of-the-art theatres in Thailand were difficult to recoup, given the devaluation of local currency. Video markets in Malaysia and the Philippines seemed to control piracy, but then cheap, easy-to-duplicate Video CDs and DVDs made those efforts futile. Myanmar, Vietnam, Cambodia and Laos showed potential for a few years, even if no sales were made. Hong Kong has become a theatrical-only territory, dominated by local films and the majors, and neither seem very happy with current box office results. Regional television networks have produced a strong cable and satellite market for independent action product. These include Hong Kong's STAR TV as well as studio-controlled HBO and AXN. Other product is very difficult to place on television.

On the theatrical side, there is high hope for video-projection theatres in many countries where the cost of building 35mm theatres and shipping prints are not supported by potential revenues, as in China and Vietnam. Tapping those markets, as well as the Indian subcontinent, has become the Holy Grail for international film distribution, and this fact has not been lost on the major studios. Now that theatre infrastructure and TV distribution are in place, as soon as the Asian economies turn around, revenues should be substantial. Local film production throughout the region is growing, and this could help fuel the comeback.

EASTERN EUROPE

The entertainment business in eastern Europe since the fall of communism is a microcosm of the history of the business. This territory is comprised of Russia (also referred to as the former Soviet Union), Poland, the Czech and Slovak republics, Hungary, the former Yugoslavia, Romania and Bulgaria. By the early 1990s each country had developed a significant theatrical business and video was beginning to escalate. A few years later, the exhibition market had become dominated by U.S. majors; video was huge; television was starting to privatize and large amounts of money were being invested in pay television. HBO was aggressively moving into the market, and many of the private webs, such as Nova Television in the Czech and Slovak republics, had American money behind them. Poland was paying more than $100,000 for the right film, and by late in the decade, license fees in Russia could top $200,000 and even a mediocre title there could bring $20,000. A producer could raise 2% of a production budget from eastern Europe.

By 2000, eastern European economies, including Russia's, were collapsing. Local currencies slid against the dollar, major studios controlled the theatrical business more than ever, and video had become a black hole as piracy and the proliferation of new television channels destroyed the business. Finally, the television markets themselves began to collapse under the weight of public and government pressures and their own profligate spending. Today, multinational media groups (including Fox, Warner Bros. and Germany's KirchMedia) have moved in to try to salvage what they can, and undoubtedly some will play important roles in the television industries in these countries. A few local theatrical distributors have managed to survive along with a handful of video distributors, but a producer who achieves 1% of a film's budget out of the entire region is fortunate. As the dust settles, it seems that prices will never get back to the lucrative "good old days" of several years ago.

OTHER SIGNIFICANT MARKETS

The Middle East, most of Africa and the Indian subcontinent have never been friendly to American independent films, but in the hands of a skilled distributor, the region can yield surprising revenue, sometimes in excess of $50,000. There are a number of seasoned distribution professionals in the region who have survived good times and bad and continue to thrive. Sales executives generally believe that prices for these markets are low, and that local distributors make a lot more money than they report. For example, the average $10,000 to $20,000 license fee for India seems ridiculous considering the population size. Archaic distribution restrictions protecting local production as well as strict censorship make this a tough market for American indies; just because India will play a film doesn't mean it will pass censorship in Egypt. Indian producers turn out hundreds of movies a year, always achieving higher box office success than American blockbusters.

Israel has been a strong market for theatrical product from the majors and for television (especially cable) from the independents. There are a number of excellent local distributors there, and prices are high relative to their population, with some films returning more than $75,000 to producers.

Turkey is more of a European territory today and had a very healthy market, especially for television, until the economy collapsed in 2000. However, it is expected to come back strongly in the next few years, especially given its aspirations to join the EU.

Usually the Middle East outside of Israel and Turkey is sold to one distribution company in a single deal that includes the Arabian countries, much of North Africa, Egypt, Iran, Iraq and Lebanon (the most profitable of the countries). India and Pakistan are sold separately. In this case, the term "sold" is used lightly, because odds of their buying anything are poor, worse that the deal will clear bureaucratic and censorship hurdles, and it's even less likely that the distributor will actually pay.

South Africa has suffered greatly in the last few years. The rand has dropped against the dollar, movie tickets are considered an expensive luxury and television money has dried up, due in part to governmental mismanagement of resources. The production business is on the rise, though, and there continue to be two excellent local distributors, Nu Metro and Ster Kinekor. Pay television has always been very successful in South Africa and continues to provide an important source of revenue. Video proceeds have fallen drastically in the last few years, but this is the only territory in the region that even has a viable video market.

The rest of Africa consists of undeveloped markets. Occasionally one of the territories (Kenya recently) will spring to life and pay a license fee for a film, but usually only pirates and a few specialized television distribution companies make any money there.

This global tour of the independent distribution business demonstrates how exciting and changeable the business is. In conclusion, on the next page is a summary chart of certain statistics in key export markets compared with the United States.

COUNTRY-BY-COUNTRY STATISTICS

TERRITORY	Percentage of Global Revenues (theatrical films)	Number of Screens	Average Ticket Price US$	Percentage Local Films	Total 2000 Admissions (millions)	Total 2000 Box Office (millions)	Average Number of Prints	Average Prints for a Top Release
USA/CANADA	37.50	39,817	5.40	92	1,529.0	8,100.0	2,000	3,000
BENELUX	1.25	977	5.50	6	21.5	213.6	100	250
FRANCE	6.00	4,762	5.60	29	165.9	828.9	250	500
GERMAN-SPEAKING	10.00	5,200	5.50	14	152.5	760.9	400	700
ITALY	6.50	2,740	5.40	24	109.8	518.1	125	250
SCANDINAVIA	1.50	2,239	7.20	10	39.1	285.0	90	250
SPAIN/PORTUGAL	4.50	3,743	3.50	14	151.0	542.1	125	300
U.K.	8.00	2,825	6.10	18	143.6	920.6	225	400
EASTERN EUROPE	1.25	5,390	1.33	5	98.8	131.0	n/a	n/a
JAPAN	10.00	2,076	14.50	32	135.4	1,586.3	150	400
SOUTH KOREA	2.00	507	5.60	35	61.7	360.0	60	125
REST OF ASIA	4.00	n/a	n/a	n/a	n/a	n/a	n/a	n/a
LATIN AMERICA	3.00	5,226	4.50	n/a	284.4	863.0	n/a	n/a
AUSTRALIA/NZ	2.50	2,134	4.20	9	96.9	449.8	150	350
ALL OTHER MARKETS	2.00	n/a	n/a	n/a	n/a	n/a	n/a	n/a

OVERSEAS TAX INCENTIVES AND GOVERNMENT SUBSIDIES

by **STEVEN GERSE,** vice president, business and legal affairs, for Walt Disney Pictures, based in Burbank, California. Mr. Gerse handles a wide range of business affairs and legal matters for Disney's motion picture division, and has a particular specialty in cofinancing arrangements and overseas production incentives. Earlier, he served as vice president, business and legal affairs, for Walt Disney Feature Animation and as senior counsel at Walt Disney Pictures. A 1983 graduate and Harno Scholar from the University of Illinois College of Law, Mr. Gerse was in private entertainment practice at Sinclair, Tenenbaum & Co. and O'Melveny & Myers, has written movie business articles and was coinstructor of a course on the international film business in the producers' program at UCLA.

It is unlikely that the producer will be able to rely solely on the tax incentives or subsidy to finance the film. The net value to the producer of such benefits can range anywhere from 2% to 20% of production costs.

B esides the traditional sources of financing available to an American motion picture producer, such as studio financing and presales, a producer of motion pictures or television programs may be able to take advantage of various financing opportunities overseas. Several countries have instituted tax incentives or subsidy programs that directly or indirectly provide funds for motion picture production in an effort to stimulate the local film industry and promote the country's culture. While such programs are not designed with American producers or American movies in mind, the U.S. producer may be able to obtain the benefits of such programs by assembling the necessary creative elements, by entering into foreign coproduction arrangements or simply by spending production or postproduction monies in a foreign country.

Along with the obvious advantage of providing precious financing, such overseas opportunities offer other attractive lures. A producer who has raised substantial financing overseas, for example, may be able to obtain more favorable overall distribution terms from not having had to presell key rights or markets in order to raise production financing. In the case of a tax-related coproduction, for example, the owner of the picture need only be concerned with covering his or her net exposure after the tax benefit rather than covering the entire investment. In addition, several countries have quotas that favor "national" films, which result in higher presale values for such films or television programming.

Although there are a variety of foreign financing opportunities that are not created by government legislation or treaty, such as below-the-line facilities, currency deals or equity investment, this chapter focuses on tax-incentive and direct-subsidy programs that either are legislated by the governments of certain countries or are private investment arrangements which take advantage of such legislation. *Tax incentives* for motion picture investment vary greatly from country to country, but each has the central feature of providing tax relief on film investments that would not otherwise be deductible or on profits that would otherwise be taxable. *Direct-subsidy* programs involve a cash investment or rebate by a government agency to finance the production of qualified films or to provide incentives for producers to film in such country. In some countries, investment from private industry has been much more significant than contribution from government in recent years, and this chapter will also note the important developments in this area.

Such tax incentive and subsidy programs often undergo a life cycle, and the appeal of a particular program may depend upon which state of the cycle the program is in. Typically, a government originates the incentive or subsidy program in order to encourage a national film industry and stimulate local employment. The tax incentives or subsidies are initially available on a rather unrestricted basis, and investors and producers from around the world are quick to capitalize, not always promoting the same goals as the country concerned. In some cases, enterprising tax promoters form limited partnerships of private investors to capitalize on tax loopholes. Then, after the program has been abused, often with much of the available funds having gone to U.S. producers to make Hollywood films, or after a large number of films have been produced solely for their benefit as tax shelters and without regard to their cultural or artistic merit, the government reacts by imposing a number of restrictions on the program. In this next stage, for example, the government may reduce the amount of the tax write-off or subsidy, or impose strict local content requirements based on the subject matter of the picture or the nationality of the artists, crew and locations, or impose distribution restrictions. Then, after filmmakers have found it difficult to produce pictures with true international appeal, a new round of political lobbying leads to the final stage, in which government policy seeks to become more practical and more benevolent to "international" pictures. The result is usually some form of formal co-production program, often consisting of specific coproduction treaties with individual countries, or modified tax write-offs with a watered-down "local content" or "local spend" test.

There are several threshold facts that a U.S. producer must realize before considering the myriad foreign financing opportunities. First, it is unlikely that the producer will be able to rely solely on the tax incentives or subsidy to finance the film. The net value to the producer of such benefits can range anywhere from 2% to 20% of production costs. Although there are some notable exceptions, the project generally must also have some compatibility with the country in which the cofinancing benefit arises, in terms of subject matter, location or nationality of the director or star, or at the very least must spend a minimum amount of funds in the applicable country. Further, the terms of the cofinancing may restrict the extent to which the American producer can fulfill the producer function and may require a foreign coproducer on board in order to obtain the benefits of that country's film program. Finally the particular financing program may impose certain distribution restrictions, such as requiring the producer to give away distribution rights for the country concerned. In addition, some of the private investment arrangements require the investor to have a "reasonable expectation of profit"; the producers therefore have to grant investors a profit participation in the film, which must be weighed against the benefit of such financing.

Although many countries have some form of production incentives, the principal sources of overseas production incentives are presently Australia, Canada, England, Ireland and Germany. The following country-by-country survey of the principal overseas tax-incentive and subsidy programs is by no means exhaustive. Although the information is current as of this writing, the benefits and requirements of the programs in this area are constantly evolving and are subject to sudden change, so the reader is encouraged to seek counsel regarding the latest details of the particular country concerned.

AUSTRALIA

Australia has been an important source of film financing over the years. While vestiges of Australia's historical incentives are still being utilized, its government has recently enacted a new rebate program designed to remove many of the uncertainties from the older systems. In fact, a review of the history of Australia's incentive programs is instructive, as it provides a good example of the "life cycle" discussed earlier.

Introduced in 1980, Division 10BA of the Australian Income Tax Assessment Act once offered significant tax concessions to investors and contributed greatly to the growth of Australia's film industry. The 10BA program originally provided the Australian taxpayer with a 150% deduction on his or her capital expenditure in a qualifying Australian picture.

Also, if the investor received profits from the film, the investor would also receive a tax exemption on such profits of up to 50% of the original investment. To be a qualifying Australian picture, the film had to generally be based on an Australian script with significant Australian "content" and use predominantly Australian actors and locations. Many of the acclaimed Australian films in the 1980s, such as *The Road Warrior, The Man From Snowy River* and *Crocodile Dundee,* were financed from 10BA-inspired funds. The 10BA provisions soon resulted in a huge tax loss to the Australian government, however, and the 150% deduction/50% exemption was reduced first to 133%/33%, then to 120%/20%, and finally to a 100% deduction in 1988. Because Australia's top marginal rates of tax were reduced from 60% to 49%, 10BA no longer was such an attractive proposition for investors. Australian film production dropped significantly in ensuing years.

The Australian government replaced some of the original 10BA benefits through the use of the Australian Film Finance Corporation (FFC) investment group, which became Australia's primary source of motion picture financing. Funded in part by the Australian government, the FFC supported certain films with equity investment, production or print and ad loans, guarantees or a combination. In return, the FFC had an equity participation in which to recoup its investment and might also require Australian distribution rights. The film had to be a "qualifying Australian film," which required considerable Australian content or creative participation, although a film could also qualify as a coproduction pursuant to Australia's extensive network of coproduction treaties. In addition to numerous Australian TV programs and local feature films, the FFC funded a number of major international movies, including *Green Card, Until the End of the World* and *Map of the Human Heart.* Government funding for the FFC, however, declined from a high of AUS$70 million in 1989 to AUS$35 million for the 1992–93 financial year.

Many non-Australian producers also began to utilize Section 51(1) of the Income Tax Assessment Act, a general investment deduction not specific to the film industry, which allowed a 100% write-off to the Australian investor over two years. The particular appeal of 51(1) to the American producer was that the film was not required to be an Australian content picture or even be shot in Australia. In some instances American producers entered into limited partnerships with Australian investors, who received a tax deduction under 51(1), to raise production financing for American projects. Recently, however, the Australian Tax Office issued a ruling that deductions for investments in motion pictures are not allowable under Section 51(1).

While 10BA still provides a 100% write-off to Australian producers of films with "significant Australian content," non-Australian producers may be able to utilize another section, Division 10B of the Income Tax Assessment Act. Division 10B provides a 100% tax deduction over two years (starting when the film is first released) to investors for films that are certified as Australian and meet certain other requirements. To qualify as "Australian," a project generally must be filmed in Australia and employ Australians. Typically, a promoter or broker will obtain investors for the film who form a company that supplies the production funds and "produces" the picture, and generates for the producer a benefit from 9% to 12% of the total production costs of the film. Among the drawbacks of the structure are that the bare copyright of the film must be owned by the Australian company (sometimes an uneasy notion for the U.S. studio) and that the investors must have a profit participation (in order to not run afoul of Australia's anti–tax avoidance measures) that is more favorable to the investor than a typical net-profit participation. Several big-budget studio productions, including *The Matrix* and *Dark City*, took advantage of 10B funds. The Australian Tax Office recently denied the tax deductions for the investors in *Moulin Rouge* and *Red Planet*, however, casting much uncertainty on whether 10B can be used for large productions.

As a response to industry lobbying and to encourage higher-budget films to continue to shoot in Australia, the government enacted Taxation Laws Amendment (Film Incentives) Act 2002. The program provides producers of motion pictures and movies made for television with a tax rebate equal to 12.5% of all funds spent in Australia. In order to qualify for this program, productions must spend at least AUS$15 million (approximately US$8.1 million) on qualified Australian expenditures and, if the film's budget is between AUS$15 million and AUS$50 million (approximately US$27 million), spend at least 70% of its total cost in Australia. The salary of one individual, such as a U.S. star or producer, can be disregarded for purposes of computing the 70%. Where qualifying Australian expenditures exceed AUS$50 million, this spend test is no longer required.

Australia also has a formal program for coproductions between Australian producers and overseas producers, although such productions became less attractive to investors as the Australian benefits were reduced. The project must have a certain percentage of Australian personnel and financial equity, and the number of Australian personnel must be at least in proportion to the Australian financial equity. The film must also be certified as a "qualifying Australian film" and thereby satisfy certain threshold requirements regarding Australian content and creative participation. The coproduction program operates strictly on a government-to-government basis, so it is restricted to countries with a national film commission, such as Canada. The United States does not qualify. An American producer may be able to utilize such a coproduction structure, however, and access 10B or FFC funds through third territories, such as the United Kingdom or Canada. The attractiveness of the Australians (as well as the British and the Canadians) as coproduction partners is that the project can be shot in English. Australia has entered into coproduction treaties with the United Kingdom, Canada and Germany, and in many cases a producer can combine benefits from more than one country.

CANADA

Like Australia, Canada's system of tax preferences for motion picture and television investment has evolved over the years, utilizing a mixture of government programs and private tax-driven investment plans, resulting ultimately in a nationwide system of labor credits that emphasize production expenditure and local employment in the country.

Wealthy Canadians face high tax rates and few write-offs, making tax-related investment incentives very attractive. Until recently, a Canadian who invested in a certified Canadian feature could write off 100% of the investment over two years against all of his or her income. A Canadian investor could receive the full write-off, even though not all of the investment was at risk. But the capital cost allowance applicable for certified productions was ultimately reduced from 100% to 30% against nonfilm income, and there are fewer and fewer productions that qualify as a result.

To qualify as a certified Canadian film, the project had to satisfy criteria based on the number of Canadians who hold key creative positions and the percentage of the costs incurred in Canada. A detailed point system was used by the Canadian Audio-Visual Certification Office (CAVCO) to measure the extent of the Canadian elements involved in the project, and the production had to amass a minimum of six points out of a possible ten in order to be certified as a Canadian film. (The point system is still used to qualify the film as having "Canadian content" for purposes of the subsidy program that will be discussed below.) A Canadian director would be worth two points, as would a Canadian writer. One point each would be awarded if the leading performer, second leading performer, production designer, director of photography, music composer or editor were Canadian. As a threshold requirement, the producer and all individuals fulfilling producer-related functions had to be Canadian, although in limited circumstances a non-Canadian could perhaps receive a courtesy credit for a producer-related function, such as "executive producer" or "executive in charge of production." Either the director or the writer had to be Canadian, and at least one of the highest-paid or second-highest-paid performers. However, CAVCO (an office of the Canadian Department of Communications) could on application recognize a production as a Canadian film if either the director and writer or both leading performers were non-Canadian, as long as all other key creative positions were filled by Canadians. In addition to satisfying the points test, at least 75% of the total remuneration paid to individuals, excluding the producer and the key creative personnel listed above, as well as payments for postproduction services, had to be paid to Canadians or for services provided by Canadians. Also, a minimum of 75% of the film processing and final postproduction costs had to be paid for services provided in Canada.

Several years ago, Canada instituted a far-reaching subsidy program of tax credits for motion picture and video productions using the same point system. Today, a film that is certified by CAVCO as a Canadian film (with at least six out of ten points, or a treaty coproduction) may qualify for the Canadian Film or Video Production Tax Credit. This provides a tax credit equal to 25% of the qualified labor expenses of the production, with labor costs limited to 48% of the film's total budget (therefore, maximum credit is 12% of the film's total cost). Since Canadians must own 100% of the copyright of the film and control worldwide distribution rights, non-Canadians generally cannot take advantage of this credit.

For non-Canadian productions, however, the Canadian federal government provides a tax credit equal to 16% of the production funds spent on Canadian labor. Known as the Film or Video Production Services Tax Credit, this program is also administered by CAVCO, but no certification as a Canadian film is necessary. In this case, a Canadian production company must either own the copyright to the production or contract with the copyright owner, and the Canadian company receives the credit after CAVCO audits the eligible costs. In addition, most of the Canadian provinces also offer additional credits based on money spent on labor from the particular province; for example, Ontario, Quebec, and British Columbia each offer a credit of 11% for amounts spent on labor from those respective provinces. The provincial credits can be combined with the federal credit for a benefit of up to 25% or so of eligible Canadian labor expenses. The provinces offer even more favorable credits for Canadian productions that also qualify for the Film or Video Production Tax Credit.

Canadian producers may also take advantage of coproduction treaties that Canada has with England, France, Germany and Israel, which allow preferential tax treatment of production expenses and access to local benefits from those countries.

UNITED KINGDOM

In terms of governmental financial assistance to motion pictures, the United Kingdom is important both as a historical reference point and as a present source of funds. Once one of the most significant government subsidy programs, England's Eady Plan provided subsidies to certain qualifying English pictures. In order to qualify, the producer had to be a British resident or the production company had to be registered in and controlled in the United Kingdom. The subsidy money was collected by the government through a levy on box office receipts from all British theatres. Unfortunately for the British film industry, the government discontinued the Eady Plan in the early 1980s.

Sale-leaseback financing has been an important source of film finance in the United Kingdom since the 1970s, and was a major factor in the growth of the U.K. film industry. Under such arrangements, an investor who purchased an unused new film negative of a qualified British motion picture could claim a capital allowance (tax deduction) of 100% of the investment in the first year. The film-leasing arrangements raised financing for a large number of British films, including *Gandhi* and some of the James Bond movies. To qualify as a British picture, the project had to be made by a British company, satisfy a labor-content test and limit its studio and postproduction work to the United Kingdom. Eventually, however, the government reduced the 100% write-off to 75%, then to 50% and beyond, so that its benefits soon were not worth the trouble.

Recently, however, U.K. tax legislation revived the tax deduction with some new qualifications. The one-year write-off is only available to investors in qualified British films with total costs of £15 million or less; for films over £15 million (approximately US$24.3 million), the write-off must be taken over three years. In order to qualify as British film it must either be made in accordance with one of the U.K.'s seven coproduction treaties or as a European Union coproduction, or must satisfy a combined UK labor/spend test (explained below). The U.K. has bilateral coproduction treaties with France, Germany, Italy, Norway, Australia, Canada and New Zealand, and is also signatory to the European Convention on Cinematographic Co-production.

Assuming it qualifies as a British film, even a U.S. studio film can access the tax benefits through a sale and leaseback structure. Basically, the master negative of the film is sold to a British entity made up of U.K. investors (the sale price is generally the cost of the film), which then leases back all distribution rights to the studio for a period of fifteen years, after which time the studio repurchases the film for a nominal amount. Essentially, the amount the studio receives from the initial sale exceeds the amount the studio puts on deposit to pay off the lease, creating the studio's benefit.

In the past, sale-leaseback deals were generally concluded with a single leasing institution, usually a division of a major British bank such as Lloyd's or Nat West, and the return to the studio was generally in the area of 9% of the film's costs (including a 15% overhead markup). Within the last several years, however, the U.K. sale-leaseback market has seen the growth of limited partnerships of individual investors (which substitutes for the individual taxpayer). Because individual tax rates are so much higher than corporate tax rates, the partnerships can offer higher returns to the studio. Competition in the marketplace has driven the return on these deals to as high as 14%. Most major films produced in the United Kingdom recently, including the *Harry Potter* films, have utilized this financing.

To satisfy the labor/spend test, (a) the company "making" the film must be registered, managed, and controlled in the United Kingdom or another country in the European Union, (b) 70% of the film's total production costs must be spent on film production activity carried out in the United Kingdom, and (c) 70% of the total labor cost of the film must be paid to residents of the United Kingdom or European Union (although the costs of up to two persons, for instance a major U.S. star, can be excluded from this, in which case the percentage requirement rises to 75%). As discussed above, a film can also qualify as a "British film" and thus qualify for the U.K. sale-leaseback if it falls within specific rules for a EU coproduction under the European Convention on Cinematographic Co-Production or within one of the coproduction treaties that the U.K. has with various other countries. For coproductions under the European Convention, the required expenditure in the U.K. is usually much lower than a straight sale-leaseback (20% rather than 70%), but the producer must satisfy a point system based on the nationality of the key creative elements (discussed more fully in the Ireland section below). Other U.K. governmental entities, such as British Screen Finance, the British Film Institute and the Film Council, provide public funding to British filmmakers.

IRELAND

The Irish film industry has grown considerably just in the last few years, due in large part to a number of tax incentives introduced by the Irish government. The most significant legislation for overseas producers has been Section 481 of the Taxes Consolidation Act of 1997 (formerly known as Section 35). Section 481 provides investors in qualified films with a tax deduction for 80% of the investment, up to a maximum collective investment of 8,250,000 Irish pounds or 55% of the film's budget (for films costing over 5 million Euros). The result is a benefit of approximately 16% of the Irish currency spent, up to a maximum of approximately US$1.7 million. (An Internet currency converter will be useful to the reader who is comparing current values.) Recent films such as *Angela's Ashes*, *The Count of Monte Cristo*, and *Reign of Fire* have been financed in this manner. In order to qualify for the Section 481 benefits, the film must be certified by the Irish Minister for Arts and Heritage. Normally this requires that at least 75% of the production work be carried out in Ireland, but the minister may at his or her discretion reduce the requirement to no less than 10%.

In fact, by structuring the production as a United Kingdom–Ireland coproduction, a producer may be able to access the U.K. sale-leaseback benefits as well as the Section 481 benefits, which can result in a combined value to the producer of up to 18% of the production costs. As mentioned above, a film can qualify as a British film for purposes of the U.K. sale lease-back by qualifying as a EU coproduction. Under the European coproduction convention, a U.K.–Ireland coproduction requires a minimum 20% spent in the United Kingdom and a minimum 20% spent in Ireland. In addition, the film must satisfy a points system that awards points when the key creative elements for the film are from the relevant EU countries. The writer, director and lead actor are each worth three points, for example, while the second lead actor is worth two points and the composer, cinematographer, art director and editor (among others) are each worth one point. In order to qualify as a coproduction, the film must achieve at least fifteen out of a possible nineteen points, but the film board of the relevant countries have discretion to qualify a film that has less than fifteen points. In Ireland, films with as few as twelve points have qualified, provided they had a strong connection to the coproduction countries, such as being filmed in Ireland with postproduction work in the U.K. The same percentage and point system rules also apply to other European coproductions under the convention.

GERMANY

Germany has been an important and much-publicized source of funds for large Hollywood productions, although the wave seems to be subsiding somewhat. It has been reported that from 1997 to 2001, over $12 billion of financing rolled into Hollywood productions from Germany. Much of this financing poured in from German investors utilizing a limited partnership structure. The most unique and remarkable aspect of this huge source of financing is that the film need not have any connection to Germany to qualify for the benefit—it could be completely filmed in the United States with all U.S. elements. For example, financing was reportedly raised in this manner for *The Grinch, Battlefield Earth,* and *The Lord of the Rings,* as well as a slew of other projects with no German elements. Several of the major studios set up huge (DM600 million) German funds for a slate of pictures. Though on the decline, German investment in Hollywood is still estimated to have been around $2 billion in 2002.

The German transaction generally takes the form of a sale-leaseback arrangement based on the U.K. model. As in the United Kingdom, German taxpayers are taxed at high rates, and the government provides a tax deduction for investment in certain motion pictures. Unlike in the United Kingdom, however, there is no requirement that the picture be certified as "German," making most pictures eligible. A German promoter or underwriter acts as general partner and recruits investors consisting either of the retail mass market or large single and institutional investors. When this model is applied to a U.S. studio picture, the studio effectively maintains business and creative control of the film, although the resulting German partnership, or KG, must exhibit certain characteristics of a "producer" of the film (for example, the underlying copyright is transferred to the KG and the KG enters into a production services agreement with the studio to produce the film). As in a sale-leaseback deal, the KG purchases the film from the studio up front, and the studio leases back the distribution rights for fifteen to eighteen years. The studio has the right to buy the film back at the end of the lease term. The return to the studio can be in the range of approximately 8.5%, and the KG can be entitled to a profit participation in the film, however remote. As with other countries, by utilizing a German coproduction the producer may be able to access the German benefits combined with the benefits from another country such as the United Kingdom or Ireland.

Due to changes in the German tax law, however, the KG and the investor must be involved in the picture at a much earlier stage, and as a result investors have been hard to come by. The German government is also threatening to eliminate or restrict the tax write-off. After all, the German tax deals do not create jobs in Germany or lead to increased local production. This uncertainty in the tax arena, along with the crash of the German stock market, has dried up many of the German deals for the time being, although a more equity-type investment arrangement seems to be gaining some momentum. Also, although profit participation is usually not a factor in these financing deals, the unexpected success of a film such as *The Fast and the Furious* has demonstrated that these deals could potentially cost more than the benefit.

OTHER COUNTRIES

Although many other countries offer tax incentives for investment in local production, for the most part they are not as accessible to the U.S. producer.

The French government provides tax incentives for individuals who invest in a qualified SOFICA, which is a company formed for the financing of audiovisual products. Individuals who have their main tax residence in France can deduct up to 25% of their cash contribution (which is subject to limits) to a SOFICA, and companies may deduct up to 50% of their investment. The individuals or companies investing in SOFICAs are not allowed to hold more than 25% of the SOFICAs, and must retain their interest for at least five years. The SOFICA program has strict French cultural content requirements, since a SOFICA can invest only in a qualified "French or European (EU country) Production" or "International Production." Belgium recently introduced a tax relief program in which an investor can write off 150% of his or her investment (up to 500,000 Euros) in a film, as long as the film spends at least that same amount in Belgium. Luxembourg provides up to 30% of funds spent in Luxembourg. New tax programs are reportedly also in the works in Austria, Italy and Spain.

A New Zealand investor can deduct 100% of his or her investment in the year the film is completed if that film is certified by the New Zealand Film Commission as a New Zealand film. In order to obtain such certification, the film must have "significant New Zealand content," for which the NZFC considers the subject of the film, the locations, nationalities and residence of the talent and crew, the owners of the production entity and the eventual copyright owners of the film. In order to bring more U.S. studio productions to New Zealand (such as the *Lord of the Rings* films, which reportedly received large tax breaks), the country is reportedly exploring a tax rebate program similar to Australia's.

U.S. RESPONSE

Not surprisingly, the lure of such overseas financing opportunities has enticed more and more productions that would otherwise be filmed in the U.S. to head for the greener pastures overseas. The increasing problem of "runaway" production (particularly to Canada) has angered U.S. labor interests, who have lost jobs to their counterparts overseas who benefit from their government's tax incentives. In 2001, a lobbying organization known as the Film and Television Action Coalition, backed by the Screen Actors Guild and other American labor unions, filed a petition asking the federal government to impose tariffs on Canadian productions. The FTAC's argument was that the Canadian government's subsidy program is illegal and warranted a countervailing tariff. The petition caused an uproar both in Canada and stateside, particularly among those U.S. interests who were lobbying the U.S. government to establish a similar subsidy program, and the petition was withdrawn (at least temporarily) in early 2002. Legislation has been introduced in Congress to provide a 25% tax credit for productions based on amounts spent on U.S. labor, and many states have introduced production incentives in an attempt to compete with other states and foreign countries for precious production activity.

XIV
THE FUTURE

ENTERTAINMENT TECHNOLOGIES: PAST, PRESENT AND FUTURE

by **DAN OCHIVA,** New York–based senior editor at *Millimeter* magazine, a leading trade publication covering the professional film and video production and postproduction industries with offices in New York and Los Angeles. A graduate of the School of the Art Institute of Chicago with an M.F.A. in film and video, Mr. Ochiva is also the technology editor for *Video Systems* magazine. Previously, he was on the staff of the American Museum of the Moving Image in Astoria, New York, and currently he serves on its acquisitions committee. In addition, Mr. Ochiva is a member of the new media committee of the New York chapter of NATAS, the National Academy of Television Arts and Sciences. This article honors Dr. Raymond Fielding for his inspiring writings on motion picture technology and history, including the authoritative *The Technique of Special Effects Cinematography.*

At some point, high-resolution video technology—whether it's called high-definition television, digital cinema or some other name—will replace film technology.

Entertainment technology has always taken a practical path. It continues to strike a balance, mixing inventive genius, entrepreneurial instincts and customer acceptance, evolving from mechanical to electronic, from analog to digital.

MOTION PICTURE PRODUCTION

Flashback: In the nineteenth century, the Industrial Revolution was a time of furious invention, transforming society and science alike. Chemical research led to the invention of photography early in the century, and breakthroughs in optical and mechanical technology led to the creation of motion pictures by the end of it. Inventors including the Lumière brothers in France, Thomas Edison in the United States, and William Friese-Greene in England are credited with advances along the way.

In May 1889, Edison ordered a Kodak still camera from the Eastman Company of Rochester, New York, which came with the first commercial, flexible roll of 35mm film. Edison and his research partner W.K.L. Dickson continued work that led to the development of the Kinetograph, one of the first motion picture cameras, in 1891, and the first commercial motion picture machine, the peep-show style Kinetoscope. Built into a wood cabinet, it was operated by a crank handle turned by the viewer, who peered into it to watch flickering images of short black-and-white films. The Lumière brothers were the first to project motion pictures, at the end of 1895.

The next year, Edison introduced the Vitascope projector at Koster & Bials' Music Hall in Manhattan's Herald Square. The basics of 35mm film technology haven't changed for over 100 years.

Many movie purists rank cinema's silent period as its greatest creative era. From the late 1890s to the late 1920s, innovators such as D. W. Griffith, Cecil B. DeMille, Abel Gance, Charlie Chaplin and Buster Keaton didn't need words, the thinking goes, to bring insight into the human condition via this new art form. But with the introduction of sound in the late 1920s, all of this was overturned. Studios went to great expense to soundproof stages and equipment. For the purists, this early preoccupation with audio inhibited creativity.

Over the years since the coming of sound, production equipment remained much the same, with periodic advances that would reduce size and weight. The studio workhorse camera was the 35mm Mitchell NC. Dangerous, fiery carbon arc lights coexisted with large tungsten bulbs as lighting technology evolved. The 1950s heralded another era of change, as the movie industry tried to compete with the pull of television by attracting people to theatres with wider screens and stereophonic sound. For example, Twentieth Century Fox acquired a widescreen system, dubbing it CinemaScope. This employed anamorphic lenses that squeezed the image taken by the camera and unsqueezed it through the theatre projection lens. The effect widened the viewing aspect ratio to 2.35:1, compared with standard 35mm aspect ration of 1.85:1.

Tech Note: Aspect Ratios

As photographers know, the *aspect ratio* refers to the width vs. height of an image. Here are the aspect ratios of some formats in this article.

Standard TV	4:3 (or 1.33:1)
Early 35mm	1.33:1
IMAX	1.43:1
HDTV	16:9 (or 1.77:1)
Later 35mm	1.85:1
Anamorphic	2.35:1
Cinerama	2.6:1
70mm	2.76:1

Studios also endorsed filming their most prestigious pictures on 70mm film (actually 65mm of image space), nearly doubling the frame size and delivering an extraordinarily vivid image to the audience, at considerably higher cost to the studio. Musicals and sweeping dramas shot in 70mm were often "roadshow" attractions, opening in a single theatre per city, with reserved seating and only two shows per day. *Lawrence of Arabia* in 1962 was among the most impressive of these films. The 70mm format went out of favor due to cost. Eventually, 70mm film stock became the basis for IMAX, covered later in this article.

Outside the studio system, independent, experimental and documentary filmmakers were also innovative. In the 1920s, 16mm cameras were developed for the amateur market and used widely by independent filmmakers. Beginning in the 1940s, film artists were using the spring-wound 16mm Bolex camera to free their work from the constraints of the tripod, along with simple editing gear and portable 16mm projectors to show their movies in apartments, churches and meeting halls. By the 1950s, television news crews used 16mm-camera systems such as the Bach Auricon to record on location. Compact 16mm cameras from companies including Éclair in France and Arri in Germany, combined with the Nagra portable sound recorder, enabled documentary filmmakers to create in a more fluid, unfettered style, dubbed *cinema verité* (cinema truth). These included the Maysles brothers, Richard Leacock and Donn Pennebaker. Albert and David Maysles, for example, created *Primary,* an intimate portrait of the presidential campaign of Senator John F. Kennedy during the hectic 1960 primaries, often shooting on foot with a handheld camera to capture casual moments with the soon-to-be president. The television fad of "reality TV," which began in the 1990s, can trace its roots to this and other pioneering cinema verité efforts. Experimental and avant-garde filmmakers such as Stan Brakhage, Maya Deren and John and James Whitney used everything from technical imperfections to unconventional camera and cutting techniques that became resources for commercials, feature films and music videos in the following decades. *The Blair Witch Project,* a runaway success in 1999, proves again that a good story, not expensive technology, remains paramount. Shot for $50,000, the filmmakers employed 16mm film as well as the consumer analog Hi-8 video format.

Production Sound

In 1926, Warner Bros.' *Don Juan* became the first feature-length film with sound recorded for musical sequences. Another Warner Bros. picture, 1927's *The Jazz Singer,* is credited as the first feature-length sound film with dialogue. The coming of sound relied on inventions such as electronic amplification, which boosted audio enough to resonate within a theatre. Audio to record and play back sound in theatres depended upon Lee DeForest's invention of the audion tube in 1906, the first device to amplify audio signals. These signals—whether dialogue, music or sound effects—could be stored on large acetate disks or in the squiggly lines of the optical soundtrack imprinted on the side of the film. By 1930, all the moviegoing public wanted to see was the latest "talkie." Silent films quickly became yesterday's technology.

The demands of sound dictated how films were shot. Noisy cameras called for the camera and camera operator to sit inside soundproof booths on the stage sets so that microphones and recorders could clearly capture voices. With these restrictions, producers favored scripts written like stage plays. The result was predictable. Many movies in the first years of the sound era were shot in static scenes using much dialogue.

In 1947, Ampex Corporation sold its first Ampex Model 200 audio tape recorders as a viable commercial product, aided by the 3M Corporation, which created the crucial magnetic tape medium for the recorders. Entertainer Bing Crosby, one of the most popular stars of the day, funded much of the initial research. In 1951, Stefan Kudelski in Switzerland built the Nagra, the first easily portable recorder that offered improved audio fidelity. A favorite of radio correspondents, Nagra was also quickly adopted by filmmakers. With these audio tape recorders, filmmakers gained portability and better audio quality in a relatively small, quiet device. Now both camera and audio crews could deliver top-notch results anywhere they might travel. In the 1970s, Dolby Laboratory's noise-reduction technology was among the techniques that further improved audio.

By the 1980s, the first digital tape recording technologies for professionals entered the market. In 1986, Sony and Philips, working with a consortium of other manufacturers, introduced DAT (digital audio tape) recording, a portable format for both professionals and consumers. However, consumer electronics firms delayed development because of copyright issues; record companies, for example, feared that the public would use the technology to make perfect copies of the recently introduced digital audio CD (compact disc). For the time being, DAT remained a high-priced professional medium. On feature locations, these first digital audio recorders didn't offer enough improvement over the workhorse Nagra analog audio machine to make a change. Many in both the film and music industries also felt the DAT's digital technology lacked the "warmth" of analog reproduction.

Microphones also improved dramatically over the decades. Designers today use software to better model the physics of sound to create smaller, sturdier, less-expensive "mics" with improved responsiveness. Meanwhile, advances in radio microphone technology allow an actor to wear a small, easily hidden mic along with a compact but powerful transmitter unit. Directors such as Robert Altman use this capability to create complex mise en scène (a French theatrical term meaning "placing on stage") with actors moving around complicated sets or locations.

Film technology has evolved as well. Improved film stocks combine finer grain with greater low-light capabilities. Lens development, aided by computer design and improved glass manufacturing techniques, offers increased resolution and better low-light potential. Meanwhile, camera systems such as Arri's Arricam now integrate digital electronics that help speed production while yielding helpful data for use in postproduction.

TELEVISION

The basic concepts of television technology existed in the late 1920s. But it wasn't until after World War II that American companies started to mass-produce TVs, marking the beginning of the television production industry. A total of about 17,000 television sets were sold in 1946, the first year they were available. By 1949, Americans were purchasing 250,000 sets every month. By 1953, two-thirds of American homes had at least one TV. Today, an estimated 98% of American households own one, with consumers spending some 40% of their free time watching television.

Broadcast stations and networks grew quickly as money poured in from advertisers seeking to reach this new, at-home audience. After years of rapid growth, by the 1970s running a broadcast network became a comfortable, steady business with station affiliates in each major U.S. market.

Not many realized it then, but an event held on September 30, 1975, marked the beginning of the end for the complacent broadcast industry. On that date, the fledgling HBO (Home Box Office) network beamed live via satellite the Muhammad Ali–Joe Frazier heavyweight fight from Manila in the Philippines to homes in the U.S. For the first time, a cable company used satellite technology to distribute live programming from half a world away. With this and other such offerings, viewers realized they could have access to unique TV programming that broadcast networks couldn't or wouldn't provide.

Cable television began simply as a way to receive an improved broadcast signal. While many people in cities could receive the broadcast over-the-air TV signal, in rural areas mountains could block it. Originally known as CATV (community antenna television), cable television debuted in the late 1940s in a mountainous region of Pennsylvania when a local TV salesman became frustrated that he couldn't sell sets because customers could not receive a signal. He placed an antenna on a tall pole situated on one of the mountain ridges and strung wire down to the TVs in the appliance store. The TV sets delivered a strong picture and customers soon began buying.

The basic concept behind satellite broadcasting traces back to a science fiction writer best known as the author of *2001: A Space Odyssey*. In 1945, long before the first satellite was launched, Arthur C. Clarke suggested that a global satellite communications system orbiting the earth 22,000 miles above the equator would enable television signals to cover the world. While the first satellite transmission to viewers took place in 1967, it wasn't until the mid-1970s that the satellite TV industry started to grow. Some of the first satellite-transmitted broadcasts came from HBO (Home Box Office), TBS (Turner Broadcasting System) and CBN (Christian Broadcasting Network, later The Family Channel).

Tech Note: Satellite Technology

The initial satellite signal format employed "C" band microwave technology, which requires a cumbersome, movable dish to receive the signal. The size and expense of these dishes led to slow adoption of the new technology. In response, "KU" band satellites were created, making satellite TV much more accessible. Launched in the early 1990s, these satellites use a stronger, higher-frequency signal that can beam to smaller eighteen-inch or thirty-six-inch dishes for home use. Satellite networks also employ compression techniques to add more channels. Today, users can choose from among 500 channels on some services. Both "C" and "KU" refer to specific frequency ranges.

High-Definition Television

Not long after World War II devastated its economy, Japan's television manufacturers began to design and market transistorized television technology so popular that it become the worldwide standard. By the 1960s, NHK (Japan Broadcast Corporation), the country's public broadcasting network, began research and development aimed at creating a new video technology that would go far beyond existing standards, and become an electronic challenger to film.

Initially known as HiVision, this high-resolution, widescreen video later acquired the acronym HDTV (high-definition television). With guidance from their government's economic planners, Japanese manufacturers worked with NHK to develop HDTV as the next generation video technology.

Tech Note: Standard TV and HDTV Resolution

The current NTSC (National Television Standards Committee) television standard, used both in the U.S. and Japan, uses 525 lines of video resolution. In Europe and many other areas of the world with either the PAL (Phase Alternating Line) or SECAM (Sequential Color and Memory) standards, televisions use a slightly higher resolution of 625 lines of video. One way to appreciate how much more resolution an HDTV signal contains is to compare the number of pixels (picture elements) per screen with those standards. The line resolution of NTSC television yields approximately 210,000 pixels per screen. HDTV, meanwhile, features twice the vertical and horizontal resolution of standard television. The full HDTV standard of 1080 (viewable) horizontal lines and 1920 vertical (or width) lines delivers about two million pixels to the screen. (Sometimes described as an 1125-line standard instead of 1080, an HDTV signal includes 45 "hidden" lines, used for closed captioning and other useful data.) For some, this improved picture resolution is so vivid that it lends a three-dimensional quality to HDTV images. Since the resolution also creates sharp graphics and readable text, HDTV is also ideal for interactive television and multimedia.

In developing the new format, NHK's in-depth research covered the range of human visual perception. The aspect ratio 16:9 was decided upon, compatible with widescreen movies shot in CinemaScope, Panavision or other anamorphic (squeezed by the camera lens, then unsqueezed by the projector lens) systems. Companies including Matsushita (Panasonic), Sony, Toshiba, and NEC worked to design the components.

In response to a request from SMPTE (the Society of Motion Picture and Television Engineers) in the United States, NHK's high-definition TV system was demonstrated at the society's 1981 conference in San Francisco. Since it was the first presentation of the system outside Japan, it attracted many professionals from TV and movie-related industries. By 1988, the Japanese Ministry of Posts and Telecommunications broadcast HiVision (an analog version of HDTV) to 205 high-resolution television sets at public sites around Japan during that year's Olympics held in Seoul, South Korea.

Many years passed until a worldwide standard for HDTV developed. Besides disagreement on a single set of technical standards, the rocky road toward HDTV included a mix of national and international politics. Meanwhile, Japanese companies spent many millions to develop production gear and TV receivers for their initial analog version of HDTV. In 1989,

NHK began a one-hour daily experimental satellite broadcasting of HDTV signals, moving to eight hours a day of test broadcasting in 1991.

In the United States the NAB (National Association of Broadcasters) became an enthusiastic supporter of HDTV. By 1993, AT&T and a group of U.S. manufacturers of satellite broadcasting receivers formed the "Grand Alliance" to help create a single U.S. HDTV standard. The group agreed on a number of technologies for that standard, including the then-emerging MPEG-2 (*MPEG* is an acronym for Moving Picture Experts Group, a standards organization) digital compression system (necessary to fit the signal into a satellite or other transmission channels); six-channel, CD-quality Dolby AC-3 audio; and a 1,920-pixel by 1,080-line interlaced picture. (Interlaced vs. progressive scanning are defined later under "DV Essentials.")

Digital HDTV transmission began in the United States in the latter half of the 1990s. By 2003, some 2,000 hours of prime-time shows, sporting events and movies were scheduled to be broadcast in HDTV, an increase of nearly 50% from the prior year.

In this same period, HDTV became part of the production and post-production workflow for studios and facilities. Although most weekly dramas and sitcoms still employed 35mm film for production, many sitcoms started to shoot in HDTV. Saving money became HDTV's strongest selling point, since the format could eliminate the cost of raw film stock, processing, and telecine transfer time. (*Telecine* machines convert film negative to a video signal, which can then be recorded to videotape or other storage media such as hard drives.) According to some producers, savings per show ran into the tens of thousands of dollars.

DV: Digital Video

At some point, high-resolution video technology—whether it's called high-definition television, digital cinema or some other name—will replace film technology. In the 1990s, another video technology, DV (digital video), began another type of revolution in media.

Tech Note: Analog and Digital

Analog and digital refer to ways of manipulating and storing information. Analog technology attempts to mimic—or create an *analogy* of—the smooth, continuous way things exist in nature. One way to visualize the difference between analog and digital is to compare types of watches. The hands of an analog watch (an old-fashioned windup type) move smoothly, continuously around the watch face. The digits of a digital watch display the same information, but that data comes in abrupt, discrete steps. Digital technology takes our analog world and *digitizes* it, breaking all of nature's smooth, continuous sights and sounds into many tiny, discrete steps, or bits, of information. Those digital bits, the binary zeroes and ones of computer data, also deliver the ability to make perfect copies. When information, music, voice and video are turned into binary digital form, they can be electronically manipulated, stored and recreated perfectly. If you make a million copies of a digital audio file, each one is exactly the same as the original.

DV (digital video) cameras, which feature much lower resolution than HDTV cameras, were originally developed for the amateur market. With the introduction of these low-cost camcorders and inexpensive yet highly capable personal-computer-based editing technology, amateur video creativity surged around the world. Suddenly, anyone with an idea, enough perseverance and access to DV technology could create and complete projects rivaling that of studios and television networks.

DV Essentials

In the 1990s, a consortium of ten leading consumer electronics companies created the international standard for DV as both a next generation consumer digital video format as well as the basis for professional-level camcorders. Originally known as DVC (digital video cassette), the DV format uses a high-density metal-evaporated tape that's a minuscule quarter-inch wide. The video is sampled at 720 pixels per scanline, similar to professional video formats. *Sampling* is a digital selection process in which data is extracted from a continuous analog signal to create a digital signal. A *scanline* is a horizontal sweep of video information across a screen. It takes 525 of these scanlines to make up a single frame of a standard U.S. TV picture.

A DV screen contains about twice the horizontal resolution produced by a standard VHS videocassette recorder. DV cameras capture 480 lines of vertical resolution in a progressive mode. VHS cameras capture 330 lines in an interlaced mode, which lowers the apparent resolution even further. HDTV cameras, in comparison, capture up to 1080 lines.

Tech Note: Progressive Scanning vs. Interlaced Scanning

Scanning displays the video signal on a TV screen. An electron beam scans line by line, from left to right, across the monitor, painting an image onto the inside of the picture tube. Standard NTSC televisions scan via interlacing: the electron beam paints the screen 60 times per second, but with only one-half of the picture information each time. Called a *field* of video, this first scan displays the odd numbered horizontal lines (1, 3, 5, 7, etc.). On the next pass of the beam, the even lines are displayed. Together, these 60 fields create 30 frames of video per second. This happens so quickly that the human eye sees the final image as one picture instead of two. DTV and some current televisions use progressive scanning, which delivers benefits over interlaced scanning. A progressively scanned TV paints *every* line on the screen 60 times per second, minimizing the flickering that some find distracting. Computer monitors use progressive scanning to make it easier to read fine details such as text.

The DV technical standard is also found in professional-level camcorders from Canon, Panasonic, Sony and others. While Sony's DVCAM products, along with Panasonic's DVCPRO products, cost many thousands of dollars more than consumer DV camcorders, the actual signal recorded onto videotape is the same. However, the professional camcorders include highly advanced electronic circuitry along with much better quality lenses, resulting in higher apparent resolution and better color quality than consumer models.

Sony also produces Digital8 camcorders, which use DV compression atop the existing Video8/Hi8 technological base. Digital8 records on Video8 or Hi8 tapes, which Sony uses in its analog camcorders. The Digital8 camcorders cost considerably less than DV camcorders, since they build on Sony's decades-long investment in analog camcorders.

Soon after the DV format was released in 1995, filmmakers found that inexpensive, compact DV camcorders, as well as the pro DVCAM and DVCPRO versions, enabled them to create more ambitious projects than just improved home movies. Transferring DV to 35mm, for example, resulted in an image that, while not matching the quality of film, still held up on large multiplex theatre screens. Some of the first dramatic feature films released using DV technology included Lars Von Trier's *Dancer in the Dark* and Thomas Vinterberg's *The Celebration*. Wim Wenders' *Buena Vista Social Club* demonstrated how compact DV camcorders could work to the director's advantage on intimate documentaries. Once again, new technology ushered in an era where filmmakers could expand their creative horizons.

Compression Enables Digital Television

Digital video signals, including HDTV, require a high bit rate, well beyond that necessary for standard NTSC video. (*Bit rate*, or data transfer rate, measures the number of *bits*—binary digits—per second that pass a point in a telecommunications network.) Current digital video bit rates range from 125 million to 270 million bits per second, with HDTV requiring considerably higher rates.

By the 1990s, advances in DSP (digital signal processing) semiconductors created a method to compress these high bit rate signals into more manageable lower bit rate ones. DSPs incorporate encoding algorithms that remove redundant information from images, thus compressing the image to achieve significant savings in transmission speed and storage. A decoding chip or circuit in the receiving device reconstructs the image before it's displayed. The term *codec*—which refers to a compression/decompression algorithm—covers both parts of the operation. (An *algorithm* is a mathematical formula.) MPEG-2 is the most widely used codec for television transmission and DVDs. For example, MPEG-2 can compress standard definition television down to bit rates between about 4–9 Mbit/s (megabits per second) and high-definition television down to 15–25 Mbit/s.

The broad term "DTV" encompasses subsets such as SDTV (digitized standard television) and HDTV. What's so important about making standard definition television digital? The benefits include the ability to clear up poor picture quality caused by "ghost" (reflected) images, or offer improved apparent resolution via line-doubling capabilities. But DTV also allows a broadcaster to transmit more than one show on a channel, called *multicasting*. A cooking show and a talk show, for example, can run at the same time because DTV technology can compress and transmit two programs over the same bandwidth. In the evening prime time period, the same broadcaster could decide to use the channel's entire bandwidth to present a single movie in HD. DTV also allows data transmission during broadcasts, for example for text messages that might include constant weather information, a city guide or other uses.

In the United States, the country's broadcasters are being mandated to be able to send both DTV and HDTV signals, according to FCC plans. But bandwidth-hogging HDTV signal costs even more to produce and broadcast than standard television, since new cameras, postproduction gear and transmitters must be bought at great expense.

HDTV Formats

In 1999, the World Broadcasting Union defined a single, worldwide digital HDTV production standard. Known as 24p (for "24 frames per second progressive"), this new international standard uses the same frame rate as that of the U.S. standard for feature films, and is compatible with traditional audio postproduction. (European countries use a slightly different standard, based on 25p.) The current specification of this standard supports a variety of display rates. These include two interlaced ones—50i and 60i—which describe today's familiar PAL and NTSC video—and the progressive-scan formats of 24p, 25p, 30p, 50p and 60p.

The two main HDTV formats in the United States are 1080i (1920 × 1080 lines interlaced) and 720p (1280 × 720 lines progressive). Both of these formats are used in HDTV production, with Sony the main manufacturer of 1080i gear, and Panasonic the leading 720p manufacturer. However, almost all HDTV viewing consists of televisions and video projectors set to display 1080i signals. Why are there two competing formats? The 720p format requires less bandwidth than a 1080i signal, even while the image quality is comparable. This allows Panasonic to record HDTV onto its DVCPRO format, a tape format half the size of Sony's HDCAM system.

The Hollywood television production community, as well as adventurous filmmakers, quickly adopted 24p HDTV production technology. Since feature film postproduction employs the same nonlinear computer-based editing and audio technology, editors and audio mixers knew how to work with the 24p format. Producers and directors embraced 24p production too, but for slightly different reasons. Video shot at 24p closely mimics film's visual aesthetic. HDTV video shot at 60i seems to convey a more "realistic," immediate feeling familiar to anyone watching the evening news. However, a 24p rate seems to create a more lyrical, "poetic" effect, similar to that of film.

Among Japanese manufacturers, Sony and Panasonic led the way in the development of 24p technology. George Lucas, creator of the famed *Star Wars* series, became the first high-profile director to use Sony's CineAlta 24p camera system for *Star Wars: Episode II—Attack of the Clones* in 2001. With that and other feature films produced on the system, HDTV finally became accepted as a tool for making motion pictures. Presently, however, the majority of directors still prefer film.

Eventually, of course, video camera technology will improve enough so that it can emulate any aspect of film. Already, newer generation image capture chips in the labs enable much higher resolution, well beyond today's best HDTV cameras, to truly rival film. But other parts of this improved video technology still lag. Current videotape recording, for example, can't record these greater amounts of data quickly enough, while compressing this video leads to lower-quality results. One recently developed HDTV camera, the Thomson Viper FilmStream, sports 9-megapixel (millions of pixels) CCDs (charged coupled devices, a silicon-based chip image technology), but must record the massive amounts of image data on a portable hard drive disk array, not videotape.

POSTPRODUCTION

What is film? Film consists of a fine powder of silver halide salts held in a gelatin emulsion, and applied to a base of a type of plastic, cellulose triacetate. Color film includes color dyes, or color couplers. When exposed to photons of light, the silver salts change chemically. For black-and-white film, the processing step creates a negative image by removing everything but the silver, held to the base by gelatin. In color film, processing washes the silver out but fixes color dyes to the film base, again with gelatin. Today's motion picture epic still relies on images held together by a purified version of gelatin, the same substance used for the very first films of over 100 years ago. Gelatin is still made today from the remains of animal hides and bones.

Film editing also remained simple over nearly a century since the first short reels were glued together. Early editing gear included a table fitted with two hand-wind cranks holding the reels of film, a bottle of glue and a steel cutting block. A small magnifying device with a built-in twelve-volt light provided a way to view the footage. As the sound era began, motorized Moviolas enabled audio editing and quickened the pace of postproduction.

Traditional film editing requires much painstaking labor. Preparing the editing material starts right after the last shot of the day. The camera assistant delivers the exposed footage to a processing laboratory. The lab develops the film overnight, creating a workprint of each reel. The next morning, an editorial assistant picks up the workprints from the lab. Made as a "one-light" transfer from the negative, the workprint can be cut up into the different shots as needed. (Less expensive one-light workprints don't use a time-consuming color correction process that's employed for the final edited material.)

Order is essential in a film editing room, so much so that an ideal editorial assistant behaves in an obsessive-compulsive manner. Cloth-lined rolling bins fill the room, each holding dozens of separate clips of film. Every clip is meticulously listed with date, shot number, take number, camera lens used, and timecode numbers. *Timecode* is a series of reference numbers on the film negative and workprint used by the negative cutter when matching the final edit of the film to the film negative before printing.

Today, however, most films edit on computers. The lab uses a telecine to transfer the developed film negative to videocassettes. The videocassettes are digitized for use in an NLE (nonlinear editing) system. If the footage needs digital manipulation, or if the film will be shown as an HDTV program, the telecine can create an HDTV signal or output higher-resolution 2K (2,000 lines of resolution) digital computer *data*—not a video signal. (In this case, a telecine works a bit like a projector, sending light through the film negative but using various electronic or special CRT—cathode ray tube—devices to create either a video or data signal.)

Video Editing

With the introduction of the first video tape recorders in the 1950s, the first video editors faced a quandary. Like film timecode, video timecode enabled editors to list the beginning and end of each edit. Unlike film, however, no images are visible on magnetic video tape. Without seeing the beginning and end of a shot, how could it be edited? An ingenious video editing tool included a special liquid that could be painted onto the iron oxide coating to make the invisible magnetic tracks visible. A razor blade, tape, and splicing block—similar to the one used in film editing—enabled the editor to carefully cut between the video frames to tape separate shots together.

In 1971, the CBS television network and videotape manufacturer Memorex combined efforts to design the CMX-600, the first digital-disk-based nonlinear editing system. The device used a disk drive the size of a refrigerator, which could hold only five minutes of low-resolution black-and-white video. While the CMX-600 foreshadowed current nonlinear editing systems, the technology was slow, cumbersome and extremely expensive.

Linear, tape-based editing continued as the standard until computer-controlled editing systems arrived. While today's nonlinear editing systems rely on hard-drive storage, linear tape editing used two or more VTR (videotape recorder) decks connected via a control panel or edit controller. This edit controller, a simple computer that sat between two (or more) VTRs, took each punched-in timecode number and moved to the correct part of the tape. To make an edit, the edit controller triggered a third VTR to record the signal as one or more VTR decks played back the sequence.

By the late 1980s, PCs (personal computers) gained enough processing power to enable them to be applied to low-cost editing systems. One leader in the development of nonlinear editing, Avid Technology, devised codecs on computer cards that enabled a Macintosh or PC to record video to hard drives. (To review, the term *codec* refers to silicon technology that can compress and decompress large signals into smaller, more manageable ones.)

The latest trend in professional postproduction blurs the boundaries between film and video origination. Called variously "digital mastering" or the "digital intermediate" process, the new model begins with the input of film digitized at the highest resolution—or HDTV—along with audio and other sound elements. The entire movie project is stored onto fast, terabyte-sized servers. Sitting at their workstations, editors, graphics artists and sound designers can access the necessary files. Subtle color, light or density changes can be made by a digital colorist. This treatment was given to the *Lord of the Rings* movies and the results are especially rich and vibrant visually. If the director wants to screen an edited sequence, an HDTV recorder on the network can output a cassette, or the files can stream directly to an attached digital cinema-type projector. After the final edit is complete, the edited digital files are sent to film recorders such as Arri's Arrilaser recorder, which translates these digital files and prints them onto film negative. If the movie goes to theatres with digital projection, DVDs, data tape files or other digital formats can be created.

Advances in CPU (central processing unit) processing power will allow editors to work more naturally, choosing their shots by talking, explaining to the computer which one they want. Phrases such as "Give me the shot where the actor reaches for the door" or "Let me hear what the actor said in the third take" will make editing into a conversation. Meanwhile, artists will create images by roughly sketching on electronic "paper" with the computer translating the results into the correct style for that particular project. To create a 3-D character, for example, the artist will don virtual reality glasses that will enable him or her to sculpt with simple hand movements.

DISTRIBUTION AND EXHIBITION

In the early silent period, the moviegoing experience was individual, with patrons visiting storefront nickelodeons and paying five cents to peer into peep-show style boxes. Theatre owners, presenting vaudeville acts, began experimenting with projecting these short filmed amusements on screens. The trend took hold. For example, at the Strand in Manhattan, by 1914 audiences attended films accompanied by music from a huge pipe organ or the occasional symphony orchestra.

By the 1920s, a number of film studios—including Paramount, Fox, MGM and Warner Bros.—each controlled production, distribution and exhibition. The golden age of cinema exhibition began, as studios attempted to outdo the other with opulent, baroque architecture, padded seating, and concession stands. Each year saw film attendance grow.

In the late 1940s, antitrust actions by the federal government stopped the studios from directly controlling film exhibition chains. This helped new, smaller chains to expand, although they could not afford to match the lavish palaces designs.

The introduction of television in the 1950s caused a more serious crisis for the Hollywood studio system. Television moved from a quirky, hard-to-view image to a slick, colorful presentation that quickly became a daily routine of American life. Studios that for years had relied on a consistent theatre audience were now threatened by free drama, sitcoms, news and sports in the home. Even the novel experience of TV advertisements seemed to capture viewers. Cinema attendance nose-dived.

Studios fought the coming of television as best they could. For example, instead of selling TV broadcasters movies from their vaults, many studios destroyed their prints rather than pay for storage. Unions at first wouldn't allow film actors to appear in TV programs. But cracks soon appeared in Hollywood's position. In 1952 Columbia Pictures formed Screen Gems, a television subsidiary designed to create TV programs. Still, studios searched for something unique. How could film compete with anything a television show could offer?

The answer was spectacle. Higher budgets enabled the production of large, lavishly staged studio productions such as *Singin' in the Rain* in 1952, *Oklahoma* in 1955, *The Ten Commandments* in 1956 and *Ben-Hur* in 1959, among many others.

Film screens themselves became larger. The debut of *This Is Cinerama* in 1952 astonished audiences with images shown on a giant, curved screen. About six times the size of a regular screen, the "Cinerama experience" also introduced multitrack sound via its seven audio channels. For the next ten years, a sprinkling of Cinerama theatres in the United States presented eight additional features that were produced with the process. For shooting, a Cinerama movie used three 35mm motion picture cameras mounted as one unit. As the cameras shared one motor, they could be kept in sync. What the middle camera captured was projected on the middle third of the huge, custom-built curved screen, with each of the other cameras projecting on either side. A small, independent company designed Cinerama, not the Hollywood studios.

To compete, studios rushed to find something similar that could be shown on conventional theatre screens. Camera and projector manufacturers created widescreen technologies with names such as VistaVision, Technirama, and Superscope. CinemaScope became the favored system. Introduced by Twentieth Century Fox in 1952, CinemaScope used specially ground anamorphic lenses first developed in Europe in the early

1900s. A version of the format is still in use today among the lens choices in Panavision's camera systems. Looking at a 35mm image shot with an anamorphic lens, people and objects appear squeezed together vertically. When projected with the correct lens, the image is unsqueezed and much wider (2.35:1) than standard (1.85:1) movies.

Another attempt at spectacle in the 1950s, 3-D movies, proved little more than a fad. Some camera systems for 3-D employed two cameras (one red filtered, one green), while others used elaborate split-screen optics. Either way, the precise camera setups required proved too complex to fit into the fast pace of standard film production. Likewise, the need for special projectors remained costly. Finally, mainstream directors considered the technique too much of a gimmick, since 3-D films often included contrived sequences that suddenly thrust people and objects toward the viewer to shock them, thereby emphasizing the effect.

Today, less than a dozen theatre chains control most film exhibition in the U.S. Their business strategy parallels that of retailers. Just as large shopping malls overwhelmed traditional, stand-alone retail businesses by offering a wider selection of stores in one place with lower prices, so have theatre chains overwhelmed stand-alone theatres by creating the multiplex (four to twenty or more screens) anchoring a mall with plenty of parking. Independent theatres still have their place, as they often offer less-publicized, independent and foreign-language movies. By the early years after the new millennium, many exhibitors were emerging from hard times and bankruptcy filings brought on by excessive theatre overbuilding, combined with ever-increasing rental splits weighing in favor of studios.

Projection technology has changed little over the years, just as film camera technology has changed little. Today's projectors are different from those used in the 1920's in three ways: Optical devices replay the film's soundtrack; lenses can project anamorphic film prints; and a system of flat platters can spool up the entire film, replacing changeovers between reels. Older projection setups needed two side-by-side 35mm projectors, each holding one twenty-minute (2,000 ft.) reel of film. An alert projectionist remained in the projection booth, as the changeover from one projector to the next required a split-second maneuver at the end of every reel: closing down one projector's shutter while opening the shutter on the second machine.

Today's automated projection systems have altered all that. Exhibitors wanted projectors that reduced or eliminated the need for highly-trained projectionists, with their union wages and work rules. Now, the many reels of film making up a feature release print are spliced together to form one continuous strand, fitting onto a massive metal platter in the projection booth. Once the projector is threaded, sophisticated computer controls allow for continuous showings as the film slowly winds its way through the projector and back onto the platter. The film will not have to be touched for the remainder of the movie's run. The projector starts, stops and rewinds the film via computer-controlled motors. The result? One projectionist can now attend to all of the screens in a multiplex, drastically lowering labor costs.

But automation can't solve every problem. Without an experienced, full-time projectionist in the booth, screenings can suffer. For example, prints can become badly scratched and even destroyed if no one notices a problem early enough. Meanwhile, the projectors' optics can lose focus and stay that way, something familiar to any sharp-eyed viewer in today's multiplexes.

A new film format debuted with IMAX, created in Canada in 1967, for giant rectangular screens up to eight stories high, using six-channel sound. The stunning IMAX image employs 70mm film, with each IMAX frame filling the equivalent of three 70mm frames, or about ten times the size (in area) of a conventional 35mm frame. The special cameras, projectors and theatres were developed from scratch by IMAX Corporation, today based in Toronto and New York City.

An IMAX camera photographs the largest frame ever used in motion pictures on horizontally moving 70mm film. Since the size and mass of the film stock make it difficult to run smoothly through the camera, a unique "rolling loop" film movement is used, advancing the film through the projector in a smooth, wavelike motion. IMAX projectors use a similar mechanism, also projecting the footage horizontally. IMAX devised a 3-D version of the format, employing LCD (liquid crystal display) glasses that deliver a virtual 3-D effect to the viewer. The bulky IMAX cameras, with their frequent magazine changes, require a large crew during production and are expensive to operate. This has limited IMAX projects to short films such as nature documentaries. Today there are some 220 IMAX-affiliated theatres in thirty countries, mostly in theme parks, museums, and science centers.

To diversify, IMAX Corporation developed a computer-intensive process that would enlarge a 35mm film negative to IMAX's format without the usual increase in film grain. The process scans a feature film's 35mm negative at a high resolution, turning each frame into digital image files. One by one, each frame can then be "printed" to IMAX film stock. *Apollo 13*, made in 1995, became the first feature film exhibited to the public in this new IMAX process in 2002.

Digital Projection

The term "digital cinema" began to be used in the 1990s, coinciding with the introduction of high-resolution digital video cameras along with a new generation of digital projectors. Most current digital projectors employ either of two standard technologies: DMD (digital micromirror device) or LCD. Texas Instruments is the sole DMD manufacturer; its DLP (digital light processing) optical semiconductor chip contains a rectangular array of up to 1.3 million hinge-mounted microscopic mirrors. Each mirror corresponds to one pixel in the projected frame. Image data from a digital video or graphic signal moves each pixel, which in turn modulates the Xenon or other powerful projection lamp and the results pass through the projection lens and onto the screen.

The other main type of projection technology, Transmitted LCD, uses a projection lamp to illuminate an LCD panel with a clear, transparent back. On the panel, the digital or graphic signal creates a display, and the lens projects the image formed by the LCD onto a theatre screen.

Introducing digital technology to the projection booth brings theatres one step closer to our growing, networked world. Now, projection manufacturers integrate Ethernet ports, touch-screen controls and sophisticated anticopying encryption to protect a movie's digital files.

Soon, studios will send their latest digital movie to the multiplex by satellite transmission or high-speed data link. Until those networks build out, however, theatres with digital projection receive movies as digital data files either on a removable hard drive or encoded onto DVDs. At the theatre, the data is loaded onto specialized hard drive storage systems that play the movie as scheduled via a control panel on the projector. The latest projection systems allow a PC to be connected to control the projection and program pre-feature advertisements and trailers.

Moving to the digital domain brings numerous advantages to the moviegoer and exhibitor alike. For the viewer, a projected digital image file never collects dust or scratches like a film print. Although the rock-steady projected image has lower resolution than a film version, it appears sharper to many moviegoers. (Even the best film projection systems eventually wear out a film print as dirt and scratches lower the film's perceived resolution.) Exhibitors gain greater control of their projection systems with digital projectors installed. Various manufacturers, including Kodak—the film industry icon—now propose elaborate networks of projectors, hard-drive storage, computers and high-speed fiber optic or satellite connections.

The multiplex of the future will run on a LAN (local area network) connecting all of the storage systems and projectors together. The exhibitor's office computers will tap into this network so that, for example, the manager could query the system to discover which movie is selling the most tickets, and instantly shift a more popular movie to a larger auditorium. No film reels would be hauled around, since the projector would simply read a different stored file to project the movie. The computer-controlled projectors wouldn't need to be checked either, as each would report any problems as they arise. During the day, a multiplex could rent out an auditorium for a business meeting, complete with large-screen data projections, or teleconferencing.

Distributors will gain more control as well. When fully implemented, digital projection will help profit margins improve with distributors saving millions, freed from the cost of striking, shipping and ultimately destroying thousands of prints of each film release. Distributors also gain better security for their movies. Encrypting the files would render movies useless if copied. For further protection, the movies could be transmitted to theatres just before showing them, with no recorded copy made at all.

The slow pace of the shift to digital reflects a mix of theatre economics, industry politics and technology. Many cinematographers, for example, consider the current resolution of digital cinema projection (2K or 2,000 pixels) inadequate when compared to that of a 35mm film frame. In response, some suggest resolutions ranging from 3K to 4K would be adequate. However, another group argues that the industry shouldn't just attempt to merely match film resolution (equal to approximately 4K) but go beyond that to 6K.

HOME VIDEO

Until 1975, most home entertainment systems consisted of a television set and perhaps a stereo receiver and LP (long playing) record turntable. That year, Sony introduced the Betamax VCR (videocassette recorder) to consumers. With the marketplace to itself, Sony sold 30,000 VCRs. By 1976, JVC launched a competing format, VHS (video home system). The VHS format could record for twice the time of Betamax on one cassette. But the Betamax format delivered a visual image superior to that of VHS. In 1977, JVC licensed four other Japanese manufacturers to begin making VHS VCRs. A price war followed. Critics contend Sony didn't seek other licensees, nor advertise enough. Consumers in the marketplace were forced to choose. A decade later, the Betamax-VHS war was effectively over, with VHS the winner, as Sony began making its own VHS machines.

Early adapters included high-income households as well as businesses and schools using the technology for training and education. One popular practice with VCRs was to *time shift* programs, recording them to watch later. Beyond that, the home consumer didn't yet have the flood of movies we enjoy today. It took ten years before VCRs reached a 50% penetration of U.S. households, so what else led to its acceptance? According to published studies, by the late 1970s the majority of videotapes sold and rented consisted of adult entertainment (also credited as a stimulus to the growth of the Internet). Today, VCRs are sold as stand-alone devices, or integrated with a TV, or combined with a second VCR (to copy tapes), or paired with DVD record/playback units.

The DVD

The acronym DVD stands for digital versatile disc. The DVD gained quick acceptance after its introduction in the 1990s (see articles by Benjamin Feingold, p. 408 and by Paul Sweeting, p. 418), perhaps because this five-inch diameter polycarbonate plastic disc encompasses home entertainment, computers and business information with a single digital format. This single format has just begun, as it's expected to eventually replace audio CDs, videotapes, laserdiscs, CD-ROMs, and video game cartridges.

But the DVD grew out of a contentious beginning. In 1994, two DVD formats were introduced: Super Disc (SD) and Multimedia CD (MMCD). Developed by two competing groups (Sony and Philips in one, the other led by Toshiba, Panasonic and Pioneer), public clashes over the formats raged throughout 1995, as neither side wanted to agree to a single standard.

Meanwhile, an informal group of major computer companies drew together. Well aware that the public's confusion during the Betamax-VHS wars slowed acceptance of a VCR format, the computer companies forced the competing camps to negotiate a single format that also provided for computer data needs.

In 1997, the DVD format was introduced and the public adopted it faster than any other consumer media technology: three times faster than CDs, and seven times faster than VCRs.

DVD terminology can be confusing. There are physical formats (such as DVD-ROM or DVD-R) and application formats (such as DVD-Video or DVD-Audio). The DVD-ROM format holds data, and usually refers to computer use. DVD-Video (often simply called DVD) defines how video programs such as movies are stored on disc and played in a DVD-Video player or a DVD computer. DVD-ROM includes recordable variations DVD-R/RW, DVD-RAM and DVD+R/RW. The application formats include DVD-Video,

DVD-Video Recording, DVD-Audio, DVD-Audio Recording, DVD Stream Recording and SACD.

The PVR: Personal Video Recorder

When Japanese manufacturers first introduced cassette-tape-based VCRs in the mid-1970s, it was assumed that viewers would use them to record and watch their favorite TV programs at a later time—in effect, time shifting. But many consumers found it too confusing to program a VCR. An inherent difficulty was the linear nature of videotape, requiring the owner's time to fast forward or rewind, searching back and forth through the length of tape to locate a particular scene.

Computer technology changed all that. In the latter half of the 1990s, the introduction of the PVR (personal video recorder), also known as the DVR (digital video recorder), brought the speed and ease of use of a PC to home video. PVRs act as computer-assisted storage dedicated to recording and storing image and sound in the MPEG-2 format.

Computers store their data on a hard drive in a series of concentric tracks; users access that information in a nonlinear way. When doing a search, there is no need to physically move through all the material on the disk drive (in contrast to the imprecise back-and-forth searches of videotape). Viewers instantly jump to any desired point in the show or movie.

Cable, satellite and other providers offer added functions when a subscriber's PVR connects to their central scheduling computer via a cable, telephone or Internet. A centralized computer offers upcoming TV schedules weeks in advance. With a click of a button, users can schedule what programs the PVR should automatically record. The computerized system also enables searches for a favorite actor, genre, or other aspect of a TV program or movie. Users can also store their preferences on the scheduling computer; it will track future program time schedules as they become available, and automatically record shows without any further input from the viewer. For those who don't subscribe to one of the scheduling services, viewers can find Web sites that offer free schedules.

The first generation of PVRs sold as separate devices by manufacturers such as TiVo and Replay. However, satellite and some cable systems have begun selling or leasing their set-top boxes with built-in PVR capabilities. Many PVRs allow users to install additional disk drive storage themselves, allowing PVRs to record many hundreds or more hours of video, and making it more useful as a media server for other tasks, such as storing family photos or music, in the expanding home entertainment center.

One prime PVR capability worries the advertising industry and networks alike. The nonlinear nature of PVRs enables viewers to instantly skip over commercials. Some PVRs even automate the task. Circuitry senses the signal change between programs and ads and stops recording until the program begins again. Some observers charge that a viewer choosing to skip over commercials is stealing. They say a viewer's decision to avoid "paying" for the program by skipping the advertising will destroy free, over-the-air television. Advertising agencies could no longer assure their clients that a requisite number of viewers were seeing their commercial, a crucial requirement of any television ad campaign. If companies then decide to pay less for advertising, the money to produce television shows would dry up, broadcasters claim.

At this early stage in the introduction of PVRs, the validity of these claims can't be judged. However, new technologies have a way of triggering changes in society. The television advertising industry, which has enjoyed decades of rapidly growing profitability, will certainly have to change.

VOD: Video-on-Demand

Since its beginnings, television worked on a "push" model: Viewers could only watch a TV show when the network scheduled it, pushing the show on them at a specific time. With the introduction of VCRs in the late 1970s, viewers could time shift shows, recording them for later viewing. Now, VOD (video-on-demand) brings even more control to the viewer, allowing them to "pull" the entertainment into their homes to watch it whenever they want.

How does it work? First, a movie studio or production company transmits the digitized program via satellite to a storage device at the network or cable system head end. (A *cable head end* includes technology such as cable routers and video servers that distribute video over the cable system.) At the head end, the server stores it in such a way as to allow multiple viewers to begin the movie whenever they choose. This is in contrast to traditional pay-per-view systems, which require the customer to tune in at a specific time.

Movies via the Internet

While cable and satellite are the traditional VOD providers, the Internet holds great promise. Movielink, an Internet-based joint venture of MGM, Paramount, Columbia, Universal and Warner Bros., began offering first-run and classic films via VOD in late 2002. The launch became Hollywood's first attempt to work with a distribution medium they had long associated with piracy. That year, the MPAA (Motion Picture Association of America) estimated that up to 350,000 movies were being illegally downloaded each day around the globe.

Movielink joined a number of other Web sites already offering video-on-demand. Some of these sites post grassroots made-for-the-Net videos, including movie parodies and celebrity sightings. Others serve up forgettable movies, B westerns, silent classics, music videos, self-help videos and more.

The Internet promises to deliver more channels and programs than even the largest 500-plus-channel satellite network can provide. As the Internet continues to move further into societies around the world, the diversity of Web-based offerings will make it a resource for a long time to come.

Programs can either stream from the Web site's server or be stored on the viewer's hard drive as one file. If only a slow Internet connection is available, however, a streaming movie will not play smoothly. Video and audio data will "drop out" randomly from the stream. Such dropout occurs due to the underlying structure of the Internet. The IP (Internet Protocol) chops data into many smaller files as it leaves the transmitting computer. These files reassemble automatically when captured by the receiving computer. But if one of the small files isn't received, the sending computer must retransmit it and the result is often reduced image quality.

What's the benefit of downloading the program and storing it for later viewing? For starters, a slow connection will not reduce quality, since the material will be played after downloading is complete. Since the program resides as a single, complete file, playback occurs in a steady, controlled fashion. This ensures a stable viewing experience, with no glitches to disturb the audio or video. Program owners fear that the downloaded entertainment could be readily copied and shared by the customer. To solve this, many such programs now include code that only allows a certain number of customer viewings, or perhaps a number of viewings within a certain time period. After that, the file becomes unusable. Other Web sites will stream a digital file that can't be captured or copied to a hard drive.

ITV: Interactive Television

Changes occurring around the world are moving television from a linear, one-way-only medium to an on-demand, participatory, nonlinear, broadband, two-way communications platform.

What is ITV? This refers to video programming that incorporates some interactivity in its design, whether it be data on video, graphics on video,

video within video, or retrieving video programming and possibly recording it on a digital hard disk drive for further use. To the viewer, "enhancements" appear as graphical and sometimes purely informational elements on the screen overlaying the program. The promise of interactive television combines the program choices of a VOD system with added services that might range from ordering take-out food and movie tickets, playing games with other viewers, and petitioning city government or even voting.

One initial experiment in ITV became a template of what was to come. In December of 1977 Qube Interactive, developed by Warner Communications, opened for business in Columbus, Ohio, as the world's first commercial interactive TV service. Qube offered an unprecedented (at that time) thirty channels of television, including ten broadcast TV channels, ten premium or pay-per-view channels, and ten channels with original interactive programming.

Qube also featured PPV (pay-per-view), gaming, a remote with buttons for interaction and community news. (Unlike VOD, where users select the start time, PPV only offers the chance to pay for an already-scheduled event, such as a concert.) Subscribers could also use Qube to do their shopping and banking, answer public opinion polls, send and receive electronic mail, and even protect their homes against burglars and fire. But the service failed. Why? The unique two-way technology designed for the service cost too much to deliver to only a small number of potential viewers. The economy of scale necessary for most new technology to succeed was simply not there.

With the lower costs of today's digital technology, however, the interest in ITV is on the rise again. Even a simple attempt at interactivity attracts TV program viewers. Game shows, for example, now allow viewers at home to play along using their PCs. As questions are posed to the contestants, viewers logged on to the game show's Web site can submit their answers. Another recent ITV demonstration enabled users to choose a different language for their TV screen and receive it through their set-top box's Internet connection.

Cable and satellite media providers/operators, also called MSOs (multiple system operators), continue to implement ITV. Some MSOs now employ software infrastructure systems from companies like Liberate Technologies, OpenTV, and Microsoft that integrate the many features needed to build an interactive network. With the more extensive control provided by these software systems, voice and high-speed data communications are integrated along with the interactive capabilities, so that users might be able to shop for groceries, order from restaurants and buy movie tickets.

THEME PARKS AND ARCADES

Games, arcades and ride simulations at theme parks, tourist centers and elsewhere continue to gain in popularity. An increasing use of film and digital video provides the basis for the next generation of amusements. Ride simulations employ the playback of high-resolution film or video with seats that are programmed to move with the action. For example, a widescreen simulation might present the point of view of a racecar driver zooming down a winding mountain road. As the film plays, a computer-controlled hydraulic system moves and lurches the audience back and forth, matching the driver's experience. The Star Tours attraction at Disneyland was an early, popular example of this technology. New simulations have included river rafting in New Zealand and intergalactic space races.

While the virtual reality world of *Star Trek's* Holodeck still lies in the future, amusement parks now present the first generations of this computer-based technology. Virtual reality games use interactive, high-speed graphics playback for a variety of effects. Players can watch screens and use a steering mechanism to drive around, or manipulate objects in a strange environment. Other current games team up players who drive virtual cars or spaceships while others search for aliens. Finally, some games create a totally immersive virtual reality world through the use of a helmet with high-resolution goggles along with a gun or sword that can be wielded in the VR realm.

Today, amusement park patrons take home photos of themselves dropped into scenes from famous movies. Until recently, this required poking one's head through a hole in a painted backdrop. Now, using blue or green screen techniques long employed in moviemaking, visitors can be composited into many more varieties of scenes. Such compositing techniques work by isolating a person or object against a green surface of a particular hue. (Green is more commonly used than blue.) When taken into a computer graphic program, the isolated image can be composited into another scene, perhaps made up entirely of computer graphic elements. The result is a video souvenir that makes any patron a star.

MUSIC VIA PERSONAL COMPUTER

Any survey of movie technology must include the early business perils of music via the personal computer, because movies are the next form of entertainment being downloaded. Since any student of the movie industry would hope to avoid the problems that the music industry has faced, this recent history is included here.

The powerful combination of the Internet and popular music took off after the introduction of the MP3 standard in the 1990s. MP3 is an audio compression technology incorporated into the MPEG-1 video standard. (MP3, a computer file format, is short for Moving Picture Experts Group, Audio Layer 3.) Besides MP3, various Internet codecs such as Windows Media, QuickTime, and RealMedia also compress audio.

By 1998, the first easy-to-use player/encoder for MP3, called Winamp, debuted online. It became an immediate hit. Until that introduction, little music was available directly over the Internet. The recording industry did little more than provide catalogs of their holdings on their Web sites. A few companies made short snippets of songs available for selection, but not whole songs. MP3 changed that. Now almost anyone could "rip" songs (extract them from a CD) to burn (record) their own personal CDs.

As MP3 gained popularity, thousands of Web sites began to post illegal collections of copyrighted music. College students created many of the sites. Students, it seems, had the time and energy to create these collections, often posting them on school servers connected by high-speed networks. Other Web sites also posted collections. The recording industry soon began a concerted legal effort to force the closure of these sites. Before long, the lawsuits prevailed. Many colleges and universities cracked down on student-run sites at the behest of the RIAA (Recording Industry Association of America). Meanwhile, legal threats forced ISPs (Internet service providers, the Web hosting companies) to close down other MP3 sharing sites proliferating on the Web.

Napster dramatically changed the situation. Created by a couple of college computer students in 1999, the Napster software program neatly sidestepped the legal problem of ISPs or other major sites posting copies of music. How? The Napster site itself didn't store any music files, only information about where those files could be found. Napster worked by collecting this data voluntarily from users, who posted on the Napster cataloging system exactly what MP3 files were stored in their computers. Other music fans could then access the Napster site and search for a particular song or artist. Those fans were then redirected to the personal computer where that material was stored.

Faced with no single entity to hold liable, the recording industry was stymied. Attempting to sue the countless number of individuals trading songs wasn't possible. Such a decentralized market wasn't something corporations and lawyers could deal with at first. Then, with a court order, the RIAA was able to insist that Napster delete access to hundreds of thousands of copyrighted song files the service listed. Within a year, Napster closed for business.

The Internet shook the entrenched business structure of the recording industry when it unleashed noncentralized file swapping, which employs peer-to-peer file transfers from computer to computer. But while the RIAA shuttered Napster, the industry still faces a new generation of other file-swapping services, such as Gnutella and KaZaA.

The issues that arose around Napster are returning to haunt efforts to launch the watching of movies over the Internet, as Hollywood moves to protect their copyrights through various types of "digital rights management software." Stay tuned.

THE COMING MEDIA MATRIX

We live in a time of radical ferment in entertainment media, both in production and consumption. As entertainment in various guises becomes an integral part of daily life, two factors lie behind its growth: digital technology and the growing networked world.

For some time, the concept of the home media center captured imaginations. In the 1950s, both families and anyone building their own bachelor pad coveted the new trend of consoles. *Consoles* usually consisted of sleek wood furniture that combined all the latest technology, including a TV set, High Fidelity or "Hi-Fi" stereo record player and radio.

Digital technology, as we've seen, changes how media is made. The move to digital devices in turn makes the coming world of networked entertainment media possible. Once it becomes digital, modern media—including movies, television and music—can be delivered in entirely new ways. While movies, for example, are still projected in movie theatres, they now also enter the home via a broadcast, cable or a satellite channel; played on a laptop computer with a DVD player; or via an Internet connection, screened on a PC. Think of our new entertainment world as the "home media matrix," an environment in which greater control brings greater rewards in an expanding media universe.

Set Top Boxes Are Just the Beginning

Until recently, cable or satellite networks provided set-top boxes solely to change channels or perhaps buy a PPV movie or concert. But now, as technology including PVRs and interactivity make their way into homes, set-top boxes become the future centerpiece of home entertainment.

One set-top box service from Microsoft, for example, creates a method for viewers to connect and integrate with the Internet, e-commerce sites, ticket agents and other services. The software giant sells its Microsoft TV family of services to cable, satellite operators, telcos and others to deliver new interactive TV products to their customers. Users can search the Internet while watching TV, build a Web page, maintain a number of private e-mail addresses, use MSN chat and messaging, search, and access information on news, money, sports, entertainment, shopping and more.

More elaborate products now combine a wider variety of media technology. Digeo, for example, created the Moxi Media Center, a device which includes a digital cable or satellite receiver, a music jukebox for MP3 files as well as music from Internet services, a PVR with 60 hours or more storage, a DVD player, a cable/DSL modem, a gateway switch to hook in the home computer and a built-in firewall to protect the computer while Web surfing.

PC manufacturers offer their own versions of a media switchboard. Microsoft helps by integrating control of home entertainment gear into its PC software, Windows XP. Windows XP Media Center Edition, an entertainment version of its Windows XP operating system, allows consumers to use a TV's remote control to catalog songs, videos and pictures, as well as check TV listings.

Both Apple Computer and Microsoft posit computers as digital media hubs, combinations of hardware and software that act like a "super switch" to connect and integrate all home-based entertainment and computer-based technologies. PC manufacturers such as HP have released computer systems that fulfill this vision. In this approach, a computer in the home entertainment center networks together televisions, DVDs, stereo systems and radios with other computers throughout the house, as well as printers and other digital devices. DV camcorders and digital still cameras could also connect to this network, enabling the downloading of files for editing.

Even standard computers can now receive and manipulate TV signals. ATI Technologies, for example, creates plug-in cards that include a TV channel selector and the other hardware necessary to decode video signals. Bundled in with the card is an internal DVD player, remote controller and access to the Gemstar/TV Guide online interactive programming guide.

But using a stand-alone PC presents a problem. Since home computers are not necessarily part of the TV viewing room, how do you connect it with the media center? Microsoft, Intel, and other manufacturers and vendors solve this by creating easy-to-install home networks. Based on the ubiquitous Ethernet standard, these networks attach one or more PCs onto a home media hub or switcher. With the rapid expansion of wireless network systems, users can even forgo the effort to wire Ethernet cable throughout the house.

What's Next?

Expect the trends affecting the world outside the home—improved networking, increased processing power, and exponential growth in storage capacity—to bring even greater changes to the home media environment. The speed of processors will finally enable consumers to interact with computers on their own terms. Using voice commands, for example, users will describe to their home computer what they want to accomplish, rather than being forced to learn how to use a computer program.

Personal computers will vie with set-top boxes to provide a wireless digital hub connecting together all the various digital media and entertainment devices in the home. PCs, for example, might become the ideal "convergence" device, selling with built-in TV tuners and wireless networking capabilities. Connected to the Internet and a cable or satellite link, PCs will make use of powerful search software to investigate new, developing entertainment and education from around the world.

The future home will be a networked home. Currently, computer manufacturers and networking companies sell inexpensive wireless network stations to connect multiple computers. Other peripherals will soon follow. Digital camcorders already sport Internet addresses, which allow them to be easily connected to the Web. This enables parents, for example, to check on the baby, while musicians can stream their band's performance to a Web-based audience. Other devices will soon join the home network, such as printers and televisions. Home servers will store the various digital media: photos, movies, audio, TV shows, and any artwork a family will come up with. With speedier computers, other new capabilities will debut. Home security using facial recognition programs, for example, will regulate who enters the house. Combined with high-speed networks, such as the next version of the Internet, known as IPv6 (or Internet 2), users will instantly access huge databases of data, images and sound.

Ultra-cheap and powerful microprocessors will continue to help make devices smaller, cheaper, faster, the mantra of our digital age. But instead of more small, stand-alone products, expect a coming wave of consumer devices to be embedded in almost everything we use.

Often described as pervasive computing, embedded chips will not only compute but create wireless networks of increasing numbers of devices working together. As these networks grow in speed and coverage, video cameras, for example, will no longer need videotape. Instead, as a scene is "taped," the signal will transfer to a home or business computing system, just as cell phones can now shoot and send images. Using a laptop computer to edit a home movie will seem old-fashioned when anyone can take a couple of flexible, roll-up color viewing screens out to the patio and describe to the computer how the movie should be edited.

When the amateur filmmaker tires of home movies, a whole new world of virtual reality beckons. Connecting to vast amounts of computer storage via high-speed links, tomorrow's home will expand to include worlds beyond anything we might imagine today.

Now that's something to look forward to.

INDEX

ABOUT THE EDITOR

JASON E. SQUIRE is a professor, writer and industry consultant on the faculty at the University of Southern California School of Cinema-Television. He helped establish "movie business" as a distinct area of academic study with his pioneering work as co-editor of *The Movie Business: American Film Industry Practice,* the first textbook in the field.

Years later, his first edition of *The Movie Business Book* was widely adopted by colleges, industry professionals and movie buffs. The second edition, translated into Japanese, German and Korean, is required reading at universities around the world. This third edition, with a substantially new roster of contributors from the top ranks of every major studio, emphasizes cutting-edge technology, the independent spirit, new revenue streams and globalization.

After a career as a movie executive, Squire joined the faculty of the USC School of Cinema-Television, where he teaches movie business, their internship program, the feature film case study class and screenwriting. In the USC Master of Professional Writing program, he teaches screenwriting. Separately, he developed and conducts career-enrichment seminars for studios such as Sony Pictures Entertainment and Warner Bros.

As a media source, Squire has written articles for *The New York Times* Sunday Money & Business section and the *Los Angeles Times* and has been a featured guest on NPR and *The CBS Evening News.*

As an industry consultant, his clients have included investors, the USA Film Festival in Dallas and Bain & Company in Chicago. He has appeared on conference panels for the AFI/Aspen Institute, Beverly Hills Bar Association, *Billboard* magazine, UCLA, and moderated a panel for the armed forces at USC's Institute for Creative Technology.

Squire began his career at age twenty-one as assistant to the vice president of production at Avco Embassy Pictures. Later, he worked at United Artists as assistant to the senior vice president of production; as the key executive in America for Italian producer Alberto Grimaldi *(The Good, the Bad and the Ugly; Last Tango in Paris)* on both coasts; and in movies for television at Twentieth Century Fox.

For Grimaldi, he worked on the development of *Red Harvest* (James Bridges, writer-director); *Gangs of New York* (Martin Scorsese, director); *The Wanderers* (Phil Kaufman, writer-director); and *Once Upon a Time in America* (Sergio Leone, director), among others. He served as Grimaldi's representative on the American post-production of Bernardo Bertolucci's epic *1900* (working with Robert DeNiro and Donald Sutherland); *Fellini's Casanova* (with Sutherland); and as production executive on *Burnt Offerings* (with Bette Davis and Karen Black).

In the recording industry, Squire was executive producer of the soundtrack albums for *Conan the Barbarian* and *Conan the Destroyer* for composer Basil Poledouris.

His dramatic writings include a screenplay adaptation of Dashiell Hammett's *Red Harvest,* made as an Italian-Spanish co-production, and a stage play, *Waiting Room.* Squire and his writing partner, Joe Singer, are developing original screenplays after their first thriller was optioned as a feature film.

As an independent producer, he worked with Nicholas Meyer (director of *Star Trek VI*), Fred Schepisi (director of *Six Degrees of Separation*), and Stan Lee (creator of Marvel Comics characters, including Spider-Man).

A native of Brooklyn, Squire graduated with honors from Syracuse University (which later featured him in their Newhouse Network alumni publication) and earned a master's degree from UCLA.

He lives in West Los Angeles, California, is active in community politics, and has served on the regional board of the Anti-Defamation League.

Related books from Open University Press
Purchase from www.openup.co.uk or order through your local bookseller

THE ANIMATION PRODUCER'S HANDBOOK

Lea Milic and Yasmin McConville

Producer at Jim Keeshen Productions in Santa Monica, California, USA and producer at Yoram Gross/EM TV in Sydney, Australia

Animation is one of the fastest-growing fields in film and television, and it is also integral to video games and web development. Drawing on their extensive experience in the field, the authors offer a systematic overview of the role of the animation producer and the production process. They explain how to develop a concept, pitch it to obtain funding, and find a market.

They offer detailed advice on recruiting a team, managing different stages of production (including overseas suppliers), quality control, budgeting and scheduling. They also outline the key aspects of 2D and 3D production. From project development, seeking investment to pre- and post-production, for film, television, and the web, *The Animation Producer's Handbook* is the 'one-stop shop' for budding animators everywhere.

Contents

Animation: A Definition and History – The Producers – The Concept and The Pitch Bible – Project Development – Setting Up The Pre-Production Process – The 2D Production Proccess: Part One – The 2D Production Process: Part Two – 2D Production – Pre-Production: 3D Animation – Production: 3D Animation – Picture Post-Production/Sound Post-Production – Producing Flash, Stop Motion & Multipath Movies – Glossary – Appendix.

224pp   0 335 220363 (EAN: 9 780335 220366) (Paperback)
         0 335 220371 (EAN: 9 780335 220373) (Hardback)

This edition is not for sale in Australia and New Zealand.

CONTEMPORARY AMERICAN CINEMA

Linda Ruth Williams and Michael Hammond (eds)
Both at University of Southampton, UK

Contemporary American Cinema is the first comprehensive introduction to post-classical American film. Covering American cinema since 1960, the book is unique in its treatment of both Hollywood and non-mainstream cinema. Critical essays from leading film scholars are supplemented by boxed profiles of key directors, producers and actors; key films and key genres; statistics from the cinema industry.

Lavishly illustrated with over fifty film stills in black and white, and colour, the book has two tables of contents allowing students to use the book chronologically, decade-by-decade, or thematically by subject. Designed especially for courses in film, cultural studies and American studies, *Contemporary American Cinema* features a glossary of key terms, fully referenced resources and suggestions for further reading, sample essay questions, suggestions for class work and a filmography.

Contents

The Sixties: 1: *Introduction: Endgames and Challenges: Key movements in American Cinema in the 1960s* – 2: *Debts, disasters and mega-musicals: The decline of the studio system* – 3: *The American New Wave, Part 1: 1967–1970* – 4. *Popular Mainstream Films,1967–1970* – 5: *Other Americas: The underground, exploitation and the avant garde* – 6: *Documentary Cinema in the 1960s* – *The Seventies:* 1: *Introduction: Key Movements in 1970s Cinema* – 2: *The American New Wave, Part 2: 1970–1975* – 3. *Popular Mainstream Films, 1970–1975* – 4: *New Hollywood and the Rise of the Blockbuster* – 5: *Blaxploitation* – *The Eighties:* 1: *Introduction: Key Movements in 1980s Cinema* – 2: *Film in the age of Reagan: action cinema and reactionary politics* – 3: *The Rise of Independent Cinema* – 4: *Disney and the Family Adventure movie since the 1970s* – 5: *Vietnam at the movies* – 6: *New Queer Cinema* – *The Nineties:* 1: *Introduction: Key Movements in 1990s Cinema* – 2: *Cameron and Co.: The Nineties Blockbuster* – 3: *New Black Cinema* – 4: *Female Directors and Women in Production* – 5: *Action Women and Muscle Men* – 6: *Home Viewing: Video and DVD* – *Suggested Further Reading* – *Essay Questions* – *Bibliography* – *Filmography* – *Index.*

Contributors include:

Michele Aaron, Jose Arroyo, Tim Bergfelder, Leslie Felperin, Lee Grieveson, Sheldon Hall, Michael Hammond, Jim Hillier, Susan Jeffords, Barbara Klinger, Peter Kramer, Richard Maltby, Jonathan Munby, Steve Neale, Stephen Prince, Eithne Quinn, Mark Shiel, Yvonne Tasker, Linda Ruth Williams, Jim Russell, Mark Jancovich, Cathy Fowler, Brian Winston, Patricia Zimmerman, Carl Plantinga, Geoff King, Jeffrey Sconce.

440pp   0 335 21831 8 (Paperback)   0 335 21832 6 (Hardback)

05265465